Taylor's Gift

Taylor's Gift

♡ Taylor's Gift

A Courageous Story *of*
Giving Life *and* Renewing Hope

Todd and Tara Storch
with Jennifer Schuchmann

R Revell

a division of Baker Publishing Group
Grand Rapids, Michigan

Published by Revell
a division of Baker Publishing Group
P.O. Box 6287, Grand Rapids, MI 49516-6287

Printed in the United States of America

ISBN 978-1-62490-333-5

Published in association with Creative Trust, Inc., Literary Division, 5141 Virginia Way, Suite 320, Brentwood TN 37027

We dedicate this book to our children Ryan and Peyton:
This is not just our story; it is your story too.
We love you deeply.

Contents

Part 3 New Beginnings

Foreword

My initial contact with Todd and Tara Storch came in the form of an email blast. A longtime friend was asking everyone to pray for a player on his volleyball team. She'd suffered a severe injury in a skiing accident. There was concern she might not survive.

And so it was that I became acquainted with the story of Taylor Storch and her family. It is a difficult one. It is a story that causes every parent to grimace, every person to wince.

It is a story that challenges the faith of the most stalwart saint. Why? Why would God give a family a child only to take her? Why so soon? Why her?

These are difficult questions. The Storch family has asked them and a thousand others. They invite you to consider their journey. They don't gloss over their pain. You won't find any pious pretentions or shallow dismissals. Instead, you will find an honest itinerary through the valley of sorrow. Sadness comingled with hope. An alchemy of doubt, determination, regret, and resolve.

Their story makes us think of a well-known Bible verse. "And we know that all things work together for good to those who love God, to those who are the called according to *His* purpose" (Rom. 8:28 NKJV).

Note the phrase "work together." Individually, the challenges of life are daunting and difficult. What good is found in the cemetery or ICU? But mixed together—by God's hands—good will happen.

The story of Taylor Storch is the story of Romans 8:28. On one hand, there is the tragic death of a delightful girl. On the other, there are the needs of ill patients, literally dying for want of a healthy organ. When the loss of Taylor met the needs of these people . . . good happened.

The prayer of this book is this: may good continue to happen. May this story bring hope to anyone who has suffered tragedy. There is life after loss. It comes after a monsoon of tears. But it comes.

May this story alert us to the potential of organ donation. Taylor's gift of life made the difference of a lifetime for the people you are about to meet. In more ways than we can imagine, she lives on.

Thank you, Storch family, for sharing your story. May God continue to bring healing until we are all finally home.

Max Lucado

Part 1

Endings

Endings

— 1 —

The Accident

MARCH 14, 2010
VAIL, COLORADO

The sun wouldn't set for another three hours, but the shadows of the snow-covered pine and spruce trees that bordered the ski run had grown longer with the afternoon. From the top of Beaver Creek Mountain, the view was exquisite. Todd Storch knew he was experiencing the trip of a lifetime, and he wanted to capture every minute of it in pictures and videos.

It was shortly after 4:00 p.m. when the three skiers pushed off from the top of Latigo, an intermediate "blue level" run. Eleven-year-old Ryan took off first. An experienced skier, he'd been on numerous father and son skiing trips with Todd, but this was the first ski trip that also included his mother and sisters. Swelling with pride, Ryan couldn't wait to show them all the things he'd learned and talked about from his past trips.

Thirteen-year-old Taylor was next. She'd graduated from ski school only minutes earlier. The instructors couldn't believe this was her first time skiing. They'd promoted her from her assigned class with her little sister, Peyton, to a much harder class with older teen boys. She handled it just fine. "She's a natural. She's been on blues and greens all day," the ski instructor had said, referring to the color codes that signified the difficulty of each run. "She's good to go."

Seconds later, Todd was the last of the three Storches to push off from the mountaintop. With poles in one hand and his Flip camera in the other, Todd took videos of the kids as he skied behind them. He couldn't have been prouder. Ryan was in the lead, showing off a bit for his older sister. Taylor skied behind her brother, her neon pink and black ski jacket and forest green helmet creating a colorful contrast to the glistening snow. A natural athlete, she looked good on skis. Todd marveled at the sight—his two kids skiing together for the first time. He reminded himself to breathe in the moment.

Back in the alpine village, his wife, Tara, and their nine-year-old daughter, Peyton, ordered hot chocolate and found a seat by the fireplace. Todd told Tara he'd meet them there with Taylor and Ryan by 4:30. The family needed to return their equipment rentals by 5:00.

Earlier in the day, Todd and Ryan had mapped out an easy route to the bottom. They had planned several pit stops along the way, which gave the three skiers a chance to reconnect so they didn't get separated on the mountain. Those stops also gave Todd the opportunity to take pictures with his phone. At the final stop, Todd dropped his backpack onto the snow, took out his good camera, and said, "Okay, guys, we're going to get a bunch of pictures here."

He snapped a few pictures, then posed his children to get the perfect mountain landscape in the background. "C'mon, Dad," Ryan said, "we're supposed to be skiing, not taking pictures."

Taylor was more tolerant of her dad's wishes. She loved having her photo taken; she'd recently opened a Facebook account and wanted to share pictures of her in the snow for all of her friends back in Texas to see.

Todd wrapped up the photo session and gave his kids their final instructions. "This is the last run, so when you finish, wait by the ski lift and then we'll go find Mom together."

Once again, Ryan pushed off first, followed by Taylor. Todd was delayed a few seconds as he put on his backpack, grabbed his poles, and once again held the Flip camera in his hand. Todd had never been so happy. It had been the perfect first day, and they still had four more vacation days to go.

The run got a little busier when their slope combined with another. Ryan, already ahead of his sister, pulled over to wait for Taylor, but when she caught up with him, instead of stopping she seemed to rapidly pick up her pace. Ryan pulled out a few feet after her, while Todd was less than a hundred feet behind them.

As the runs merged, the slopes became steeper. Though the path was extremely wide, trees now flanked both sides of the run, and the number of skiers continued to increase as they neared the bottom. Taylor was now moving too fast for the conditions. At first, she tried to snowplow—a technique used to slow a skier down—but instead, she fell backward into a squatting position, which had the effect of reducing her wind drag, and she began to increase speed at an alarming rate. Ryan and Todd watched, hopelessly unable to help, as Taylor got into trouble.

Witnesses suggested that instead of falling over to stop herself, she tried to stand and put more weight on her right side, which caused her skis to turn. As the slope steepened, she continued to pick up more speed. Like a rocket, Taylor shot toward the woods that bordered the run. Heading into the tree line, she hit a pine tree head-on, but her perilous speed made her bounce off it, and she propelled into a second tree.

Stunned at what he'd witnessed, Ryan snowplowed to a sudden stop on the trail adjacent to where Taylor lay face up, her leg unnaturally bent backward at an angle.

Seconds later, Todd skidded to a stop, overshooting the area by about five feet. He quickly kicked off his skis and ran into the woods toward his daughter. But off the main trail, the snow wasn't packed. With every step he sank into the powder, and he found it impossible to climb up the hill. After backtracking to the trail, he sidestepped up the hill until he was directly next to Taylor, then once again left the trail, tugging his boots through the deep powder until he reached his daughter.

"Is she dead?" Ryan cried out. The sickening alarm in his voice could only be heard by his dad. The other skiers on the hill didn't seem to notice what was being said—or even realize what had happened.

Todd got down on his knees, straddled Taylor, and looked into her eyes. They were dilated and watery. He leaned closer, placing his left ear against her mouth, listening for breath sounds. Then he shouted.

"Listen to me, Ryan. I need you to listen to me. She's breathing! She's just knocked out."

"Okay, okay."

"Do exactly what I tell you. Kick off your skis and put them in the snow so they form an X, and then wave your arms at the skiers as they go by. You can yell, 'Help!'"

"Okay, okay, okay," Ryan said, as he looked at his sister's limp body and the gravity of it all sank in.

"Do it now!" Todd yelled. "We have to get help. Taylor can't ski down."

Ryan immediately went to work and flagged down a skier, who used his cell phone to call the ski patrol. The time was 4:20 p.m. Within minutes, Taylor was taken off the mountain on a sled. Riding in the sled next to her were EMS officials who made sure she didn't code out on her first—and last—run down the mountain.

⚭

At 12:15 p.m. the next day, doctors at Grand Valley Junction hospital pronounced Taylor Storch dead. Her grieving parents wept by her bedside, and the doctor asked a single question that would forever change countless lives.

"Would you be willing to donate Taylor's organs?"

— 2 —

Snapshots of Taylor

Donate Taylor's organs? Her parents had obviously never discussed it. Who thinks about such things? It doesn't even cross parents' minds that their child might die in a skiing accident—let alone whether or not they should donate their child's organs. But now, in Taylor's hospital room, the unwanted question stood at attention before them. Todd and Tara didn't say anything out loud, but they both knew what the other was thinking.

What would Taylor do?

⚬

It could have happened anywhere:

In the backseat of a car.
In the lunchroom at school.
In the gymnasium after a volleyball game.
In the bathroom in front of a mirror.
Or even in her bedroom.

All it took was a couple of girls trying to snap a picture of themselves, and Taylor couldn't hold herself back. Just as the girls lined up perfectly in the viewfinder of a camera or cell phone, Taylor would sneak up behind them and position herself in the background of their photo. Sometimes, she stood there looking innocent, like she didn't even know she was in the picture. But more often, her presence was deliberate. She'd pose for the camera with a specific look—an arched eyebrow and pursed lip, a thumbs-up and a big smile, or eyes wistfully looking off into the distance while she made a heart with her thumbs and pointer fingers. No matter the occasion, Taylor had a pose. And she loved sneaking into other people's photos. Her friends thought it was hilarious because no one would know she was there until they looked at the picture.

Taylor was tall—five foot eight—and still growing. She had a lean, athletic build, perfect for a middle hitter on the volleyball team and a forward on the basketball team. She had long, straight brown hair that she wore up, down, in braids, or purposely messed up, depending on her mood and activity. But it was Taylor's eyes that were unforgettable. They were framed by long black lashes, and people compared them to the color made famous by the "little blue box" from the expensive jewelry store. Even strangers commented on the color of Taylor's eyes. Taylor had often heard her mother tell the story about the time she was two years old and an older woman in the grocery store stopped Tara.

"Excuse me, excuse me," she had said in a loud and pushy voice. "Did you put mascara on your baby?"

This was back in the days before toddler pageants made reality TV. Tara was horrified at the thought.

"No! She just has really dark lashes."

The lady turned away, obviously not believing that the little girl's eyes and lashes were natural. Over the years, others also noticed and commented. By the time she was in eighth grade, Taylor had just begun to get a glimpse of what other people saw. "My eyes are my favorite feature," she'd recently told her mother.

But when Taylor snuck into the background (or, occasionally, the foreground) of her friends' pictures, those same stunning eyes were just as often closed, crossed, or rolled upward. She was goofy and not afraid of being the punch line of her own joke—as long as it made other people laugh.

❧

Tara watched as the students of Coppell Middle School East shuffled into the welcoming gym and found seats in the bleachers. The students were happy to be out of class and were excited for the pep rally. Taylor entered with a large group of friends. The girls were easy to spot in their black and red uniforms with white trim. They found a seat on the floor with the other cheerleaders. Sitting beneath the basketball hoop, with their tricolored pom-poms on the polished wood floor in front of them, the girls laughed and talked. But Tara could see from the look on Taylor's face that she was deep in thought.

Tara knew her daughter was going through a mental checklist. Ever since Taylor had entered middle school two years earlier, she had been a list maker. It was how she kept herself organized. In her notebook she made lists of homework assignments due, and on her nightstand she always had a list of what to bring to school the next day. But Tara's favorite list was the one her daughter made during the school day—a list of things she wanted to tell her mom when she got home from school. One of the items on that list the previous day was Taylor's reluctance to perform at the pep rally. Though she was a great athlete—a starter on the school volleyball and basketball teams—Taylor was not the greatest cheerleader, and she'd confided to Tara that she was worried about the routine. She wasn't sure she could pull it off.

Principal Laura Springer took to the microphone and made some announcements to gain control of the crowd. Before becoming an administrator at East, Principal Springer had been a beloved teacher among students at the local high school. Once she arrived at the middle school, it didn't take long for their little brothers and sisters to take a liking to her as well. They called her "Springer," a name that was fine with her. Laura Springer didn't fit into the traditional models of authority anyway. She preferred jeans and T-shirts to suits and blouses, and she was just as often seen roaming the halls talking to kids as she was seen in her office talking to educators. Tara knew that the kids, Taylor included, loved her.

While Springer spoke, Tara watched Taylor retie her shoes and check to make sure the red ribbon in her hair was securely tied. When the principal stopped talking, she motioned for Taylor to come to the microphone. Taylor bounced up and strode across the floor. Then she stood at the mic to make an announcement about an upcoming event. As she finished and turned to leave, Springer stopped her.

"Taylor, stay here. I have something for you," she said.

At that moment, the volleyball coach appeared and handed Taylor a certificate.

"Congratulations! You're volleyball player of the week!"

Taylor took the certificate with all the poise of a middle schooler, and with a smile spreading across her face, she turned to rejoin her friends on the floor. Halfway there, Taylor abruptly stopped and turned around. Her smile turned to a grin as she passed Springer and the microphone on her way to the chairs where the band sat. She found her seat in the second row next to the other French horn players and checked to make sure her music was there. She was in place and ready to go as soon as the bandleader waved the baton and signaled the first notes of the East Broncos fight song.

Beginning French horn players don't make the sweetest sound by themselves, but when the middle school band played together, they actually sounded good. Taylor had never loved playing the French horn, but Todd and Tara had encouraged her to stick with it and she agreed. As the final notes of the pep song hung in the air, Tara, the other parents, and the students burst into applause. The crowd was there to celebrate all things Bronco, and the fight song was just one more element to cheer about.

As soon as the song finished, Taylor placed the French horn on her chair and scooted out of her row to find her way back to the pom-poms she'd left on the floor. She picked them up and rushed to her spot in the center of the gym to take her place in the cheerleaders' formation. Tara saw the concentration on her face as the music started and Taylor joined the other cheerleaders in a routine she hadn't quite mastered. While the other girls did standing backflips and round-offs, Taylor glanced at her mother in the crowd. "Help me!" she jokingly mouthed to Tara, acknowledging her lack of cheerleading prowess. Tara smiled, encouraging her daughter. Taylor stuck with it and struck a pose, making the best of it until the moment passed and the routine ended.

⚬⁂⚬

A few weeks later, in the lunchroom, Springer sat at a table reviewing paperwork and watching the students emerge from the cafeteria line and find seats at the crowded tables. As Taylor walked by she caught the principal's eye. Maybe it was because she didn't take herself seriously, or maybe it was because she was involved in so many activities, but Taylor seemed to get along with everyone. She was outgoing and silly one minute and warm and welcoming the next, traveling easily from group to group and from one social activity to another. Unlike some girls who felt the need to protect their status by remaining exclusive, Taylor was as comfortable hanging out with the loners and the nerds as she was the popular girls in her own crowd.

But Springer also noticed Megan, a girl who wasn't in Taylor's circle of friends; in fact, Megan wasn't in anyone's circle of friends. She was a loner and comfortable with being separated from everyone else. But others weren't as comfortable. Springer had occasionally discussed Megan's aloofness at staff meetings. She worried Megan was spending too much time alone and didn't have any friends. The staff strategized about ways to get her involved, putting her in groups for academic activities, encouraging her to get involved in school clubs and other social activities, but they soon realized that Megan didn't want anything to do with their ideas. Or with her classmates. Megan didn't want to be fixed. She appeared to be as comfortable with who she was as Taylor was. The only difference was that Taylor had tons of friends while Megan had none.

That day, as Megan sat alone at a lunch table reading a book, it was Taylor who couldn't stand it anymore. Springer watched as, without warning, Taylor got up from her table of friends, walked across the sticky cafeteria floor, and plopped her tray down next to Megan. Apparently, Taylor had decided that Megan needed a friend and that she would be that friend.

From where Springer was located she could overhear parts of the conversation.

"I've read that book," Taylor said.

"I'm only halfway through," Megan said.

Springer listened as the girls continued to talk about the book.

"Oh, that part is good. But wait until you get to the next part, it's amazing!" Taylor said.

Megan put down her book and picked up her lunch, and the two girls spent the rest of the lunch period talking about other books they'd read. When the lunch bell rang, Megan picked up her things and said goodbye to Taylor.

"Bye, Megan," Taylor said.

Taylor didn't see Springer until she dropped off her tray.

"Taylor, come here," Springer said. "I want to tell you what it means to me that you did that. For you to take your lunchtime and spend it with Megan instead of your friends tells me a lot about your character. I'm very proud of you."

Without missing a beat, Taylor said, "Springer, I didn't do it to make you proud of me." With a flip of her ponytail, she was off to class.

❧

During Taylor's first year of middle school, Todd and Tara received an unexpected call. When the phone rang, Tara was making dinner, Todd was in his home office working, and Peyton and Ryan were in their rooms. The caller ID said the call was from Coppell Middle School East. Taylor was there, at volleyball practice, so Tara immediately grabbed the phone.

It was Springer.

"I need to talk to you about Taylor," she said. "She did something I think you and Todd should know about."

From the tone of her voice, Tara knew it was something serious, so as she listened, she walked down the hall to Todd's office and motioned for him to listen in. He picked up the other receiver in time to hear Springer say, ". . . the boy had his pants down, and before I knew what was happening, Taylor jumped up and closed the door so no one would see."

"She did what?" Todd asked, unable to comprehend what he'd just heard.

Tara and Springer laughed as they realized what Todd had missed, and Springer began the story again.

"When Taylor and her friends left band a couple of weeks ago, one of the special needs boys was using the bathroom directly across the hall from the band room," Springer began.

Todd looked at Tara, confusion in his eyes, but she just smiled and motioned for him to keep listening as Springer continued.

"He had forgotten to close the door, so when Taylor and her friends left the band room, they could see the boy in the bathroom with his pants down. Some of the kids stood there and laughed at him."

"Oh, that's terrible!" Todd said.

"Well, it was. Except that Taylor sprang into action. Instead of laughing with them, she jumped up and closed the door, so the boy would have his privacy."

Todd exhaled. This was much better than what he'd thought he'd heard.

"I was coming down the hall," Springer said, "and Taylor stopped me and told me what happened. I thanked her and said, 'You were looking out for someone who really needed looking out for. Good job, Taylor.' But that wasn't good enough for her."

Springer described how Taylor peppered her with questions as the conversation continued.

"Why are all these kids down here?" Taylor asked, referring to the isolated hallway far from the rest of the school.

"Well, baby, that's just where the room—" Springer tried to answer, but Taylor interrupted.

"But why are they separated from the rest of us? They should be with us."

Springer attempted to explain. "There are a couple of kids who strip down and run around naked before we can stop them."

"Yeah, but I bet if they're in the middle of the school, they wouldn't do that," Taylor said.

"That got me thinking," Springer said to Todd and Tara, "so I decided to do something about it." Though the incident had happened a few weeks prior, Springer told them where she'd been earlier that day. "I just got back from a campus leadership team meeting where I told them about Taylor's suggestion. I got them to agree. We're moving the special ed kids to the middle of the school, thanks to Taylor."

❖

Twins Allison and Emily Sunshine were two of Taylor's best friends. Matt and Beth Sunshine, the twins' parents, had been good friends with Todd and Tara since before the girls were born. The three girls were only six weeks apart in age, and the families had only grown closer as the girls grew. Though the Sunshine family lived in Plano, about twenty minutes away from the Storch home in Coppell, the families managed to spend almost every weekend and most holidays together. On New Year's Eve they would even have T-shirts made, combining both family names into one—"The Suntorch family."

In the car with both families, on the way home from a very long Fourth of July, Tara suggested a stop at Starbucks.

"Yeah! We're going to Starbucks," Taylor said. "I'm going to get a crap-a-chino!"

"What did you say?" Tara asked. Her friends were puzzled too.

"A crap-a-chino, everybody wants to get crap-a-chinos."

"Do you mean a *Frappuccino*?"

The whole car burst into laughter, and Taylor joined them. "I always thought they were crap-a-chinos." Taylor was never one to let a good joke pass, even if it was on her. She had the self-confidence and poise to laugh at herself often.

When the families got together, Taylor, along with Allison and Emily, would lip-synch to music, write and act out skits, and make movie trailers for their favorite books, recording them on video. They called themselves AET Productions.

But even when her friends were over, Taylor always included Ryan and Peyton in what she was doing. For one video, Taylor cajoled her brother into dressing up in girls' clothes, promising that when she put it on YouTube, "No one would see it."

The video currently has more than two thousand views.

Taylor was always aware that Peyton and Ryan were watching. She took her role as a big sister seriously, and therefore picked her friends carefully. It was as if she were handpicking her girlfriends to be older sisters to her younger siblings. Taylor seemed to have a wisdom and maturity beyond her years.

Other parents noticed.

They would ask Todd and Tara how they had done it. But the Storches never had a good answer. They'd talk about how their parenting was an outpouring of their faith, or how Taylor was putting into practice the things she was learning at church and youth group. They'd tell parents how they always tried to be open with their kids and how there was a lot of laughter in their home.

But how did they tell them that their teenage daughter still wanted to snuggle with her dad while watching TV? That while other girls pulled away from their mothers, Taylor said that Tara was her best friend? Or that while most teens couldn't wait to hang out with their friends, Taylor still wanted to hang out with her brother and sister? The Storches were blessed, and they knew it.

They had a five-piece puzzle and everything fit perfectly.

◦╬◦

The Storches were looking forward to their ski trip. It would be their first family vacation without the Sunshines since anyone in the Suntorch family could remember.

On Thursday night, March 11, 2010, while Todd got the car ready and Tara finished packing, Taylor worked on the "many things" she had due before spring break. One of those things was an autobiographical website. On Monday of that week, Taylor had turned in a poem she wrote as part of that project, and now she was finishing the other pieces. The next afternoon, she turned the rest of the project into Mr. Bush, her language arts teacher, and checked it off her list.

The poem she had turned in on Monday, March 8, read:

I Am
by Taylor

> I am outgoing and friendly.
> I wonder how long is forever.
> I hear support from my family whenever I need it.
> I see myself helping people in every way I can.
> I want to be on the Ellen DeGeneres show.
>
> I am outgoing and friendly.
> I pretend I can do anything I want to.
> I feel touched by the generosity of my sister.
> I touch people's lives.
> I worry about failing.
> I cry at the thought of losing a member of my family.
>
> I am outgoing and friendly.
> I understand how to make people feel happy.
> I say with pride that I am a Christian.

I dream about becoming a teacher.
I try to make every day like my last.
I hope to become successful in life.
I am outgoing and friendly.

Later that Friday, with everything checked off her list, she got in the car with her family and they drove to Vail, Colorado.

They knew it was going to be a trip of a lifetime.

-3-

The Cowboy

JEFF KARTUS
COLORADO

Before he left the house, Jeff and his wife, Vanessa, argued, and she told him not to go. "Your blood sugar is too low; you shouldn't be driving!" she insisted. But when Jeff was in *that* mood, often caused by hypoglycemia (low blood sugar), he wouldn't listen. And that day, the consequences were extreme.

Just blocks from their house, Jeff blacked out behind the wheel of his pickup truck, had a seizure, and lost control of the vehicle. With his foot still on the gas, the truck hit the median and shot into the air. It flipped across oncoming traffic until it rolled headlong into the front yard of a house, where a tree stopped its wild rampage. Broken glass littered the street and the truck was mangled beyond recognition. Witnesses called 911.

At home, Vanessa heard the sirens and cussed. She picked up her cell phone and tried to call Jeff. "Come on, answer the phone!"

But there was no answer.

She grabbed her shoes and car keys, then tried once more.

Still no answer.

She flung open her car door, threw the phone on the front seat, and started the car. Backing out of the driveway, she headed the same direction Jeff had just minutes earlier—the same direction the sirens were coming from. Vanessa had no doubt in her mind that Jeff had been in another car accident. The only question that remained was whether this would be the one that killed him, someone else, or both.

⸙

A longtime diabetic, Jeff had a history of blacking out, often at the most inopportune times. He'd blacked out in the bathroom multiple times, resulting in several concussions. He'd blacked out in the field while supervising crews of natural gas construction workers and eventually was put on medical leave. He'd even blacked out at his insurance agent's office. A week later they'd received a letter saying their car insurance had been cancelled.

Over the years, Jeff's diabetes had gotten so bad his kidneys began to fail. His blood sugar level would drop so quickly and so far that he couldn't do anything to prevent the blackouts or the seizures that inevitably followed. Often, he'd just get "stuck" doing the last thing he was doing before his sugar dropped.

One afternoon, after running errands, Jeff backed his pickup into the garage. Unbeknownst to him, his sugar level was already dropping to a dangerously low level. After the bumper hit the rear wall of the garage, Jeff kept applying pressure to the gas pedal. With the truck bed being lighter than the cab, the truck climbed the wall a bit, and the wheels began to spin. By now, Jeff was completely out of it, his hands frozen to the wheel. Unable to comprehend why the truck wasn't working right, he pressed harder on the gas.

The engine revved and the tires began to overheat and then smoke. A neighbor noticed and called the police. Dispatchers put the call out over the emergency radio system, and a friend who worked for the local sheriff's department recognized the address and knew it was Jeff. He also knew Jeff's condition. Immediately, he called his dispatcher and requested an ambulance.

"It's a medical emergency," he told them.

By the time the emergency personnel arrived, thick black smoke was pouring out of the garage and the tires had worn down to shreds. Melted rubber oozed from underneath the truck and spread across the garage, the smell permeating the entire neighborhood. Rescue personnel pulled Jeff out from behind the wheel and dragged him outside to safety before cutting the engine. They confirmed and then treated his low blood sugar. Ambulance drivers tried to coax Jeff to go to the hospital, but he wouldn't listen. Instead, as he often did in these situations, he became combative. Friends in the sheriff's department called Vanessa at her job at the local elementary school. She came home and tried to talk to him. But it didn't matter. He refused to listen. With his lips pursed together, he became unreachable.

Since his diabetes had worsened, everyone tried to tell him what to do and how to take care of it. But Jeff was stubborn. He was a man's man, a modern cowboy who didn't want to be told what to do, even if it was in his own best interest.

Unfortunately, his deteriorating health meant Vanessa had to be with him at all times. She did her best to make him breakfast, or remind him to eat, but even with her there, if he didn't want to eat, he wouldn't. Jeff was the kind of guy who made up his own mind.

It was quickly becoming one of the few things he still had control over.

⚜

Jeff liked helping people. It made him feel good. When he was in elementary school, he thought it would be nice to help the elderly, and he started with the lady next door. As he grew, Jeff helped the neighbors by sweeping or shoveling their walks, or doing other chores around the neighborhood. No one told him he had to, and he didn't want money for his work, but he loved it when people noticed and appreciated his efforts. He was a good kid who always respected authority and never got in any trouble.

For as long as he could remember, Jeff had wanted to be a police officer. That kind of position would give him endless opportunities to help others and to gain the respect he hadn't always gotten at home. After graduating from high school, he had called the local police department to inquire about joining the force.

"Have you graduated from high school, son?" the recruiting officer had asked.

"Yes, sir. I just finished."

"Well, then come on in and fill out the paperwork."

"Yes, sir! But I want you to know I am diabetic." Jeff had integrity, and he wanted to make sure they knew about his disease. He'd been diagnosed two years earlier, even though he'd been having problems with his blood sugar for a couple of years prior to that. As soon as he had been diagnosed, they had put him on insulin, and he'd been on it since. He would be for the rest of his life.

"Aw, I'm sorry, son. You can't be a diabetic and be on the police force," the officer had said.

Crushed, Jeff had made more calls. To other police departments, to the state patrol, and to the sheriff's department. The answer was the same—they weren't hiring diabetics.

For a proud cowboy who just wanted to serve, the blow was severe and lasting. Jeff not only felt he wasn't good enough but also now felt different from everyone around him. When his mom told him the diabetes was his fault, that he hadn't gotten it from her, the cut was complete. Made to feel different and unwanted, Jeff felt as though his life was over before it started.

His dad got him a job driving cars for the executives at Excel Energy. Eventually, he moved into oil and gas construction. Because they couldn't move heavy equipment onto a homeowner's lawn, his crew was often required to dig ditches by hand. Early on, Jeff knew when his blood sugar was dropping, and he would take a break to get some food or a drink. But over the years, his blood sugar began to drop uncontrollably and without warning. Numerous times, Jeff blacked out and had seizures in the field, and his co-workers ended up having to call an ambulance. Finally, the company couldn't put up with the potential liability. Though Jeff had done his best for the company, had cracked and dry hands from the manual labor, and had deep tan lines etched in his face from more than thirty years in the sun, he no longer had a job. They placed him on disability.

To Jeff, this was just one more example of how useless and unwanted he was. Though his health was failing, the psychological toll and assault to his identity as a provider for his family were much, much worse.

⚬⚬

In 2008, Jeff's doctor told him he needed dialysis. But once the leathered cowboy heard the news he said, "No way," and turned his boots around and left. As Jeff often said, "I'll be good as long as I stay busy; it's the stopping that kills you." He knew dialysis would take away what little freedom he had left.

At home, before he could even take off his jean jacket, Vanessa announced, "You're getting dialysis."

Jeff tried to argue, but Vanessa insisted. "The doctor just called, and without dialysis, you have less than six months to live."

Reluctantly, Jeff agreed. But it was only a temporary solution. Jeff needed a transplant, and in 2009 he went on the list. Family members were tested to see if they were a match, but they weren't. A new kidney and pancreas would have to come from a stranger.

In the beginning, Jeff called the doctor's office every couple of days until someone finally explained it could take *years* before a match would come up. The waiting list was long, and he was relatively new. But it was his only hope.

⚬⚬

As Vanessa raced to follow the sirens, she prayed.

Jeff's truck had come to a stop in her co-worker's lawn. Vanessa knew it was bad. His truck had left the main street and rolled through a backyard to the front of a house located on another street, where it had hit a tree. Vanessa ran across the street, her heart pumping, to see if Jeff was still alive.

Please be breathing.

A local officer from the sheriff's department recognized her from the many calls he'd made to their house. "It's his wife," he told the officers restraining her, and they let her go. She could see that Jeff was still breathing, but paramedics didn't have much time to talk. She watched as they cautiously braced his neck. It didn't look good.

At the hospital, Jeff was put on a ventilator. He had broken both the C-6 and C-7 vertebrae, and questions arose as to whether he'd ever walk again. But once again, Jeff pulled through. This time his recovery was more difficult. He lay in the hospital for a month, and then they wanted to release him to a rehab center.

Jeff was relieved to hear that Vanessa would have none of that. She took him home and cared for him herself.

During his recovery, doctors had "frozen" his position on the organ donation list. They hadn't removed him, but he couldn't get an organ until he healed from the accident. And recovery wasn't easy. Even after months of rehab, he could barely walk. To get up the stairs, he had to sit down and go up one at a time—backward— while Vanessa helped. But they didn't give up. Together, they got him well enough to walk on his own, to have his trachea tube removed, and to get back on active status.

By now, Jeff had been on dialysis for two years, and he didn't feel well. He'd started swelling and at times he could barely bend his arm to brush his teeth. His Wrangler jeans didn't fit any longer, and the snaps on his cowboy shirts routinely popped open. His blood sugar problems were getting worse. Dialysis wasn't enough. A kidney/pancreas transplant was the only thing that could help him, but he still hadn't gotten a call. No one was sure how much longer he could physically take it.

— 4 —

The Nurse

PATRICIA WINTERS
ARIZONA

On July 4, 1976, while the rest of America watched fireworks bursting in national pride, six-year-old Patricia watched her father die. Patricia, her brother, and sister had just gotten out of their new pool and were drying off when someone noticed her father's body floating in the water.

"Reno," her mother said, calling him by his nickname, "if you're kidding, I'm going to kill you!" Patricia's mother jumped in—all 120 pounds of her—and dragged him out of the water while Patricia watched. Friends and family tried to resuscitate him, but her father died of a heart attack before the ambulance arrived. All Patricia could think was, *If he's dead, how is she going to kill him?*

Patricia's life quickly changed. After her father's death, her grandmother became her primary caretaker. Her mother became emotionally detached, went back to work, started dating, and got remarried. Within four years of her father's death, Patricia's family moved to Scottsdale, Arizona. It didn't take long for Patricia to become acutely aware that she'd *forgotten* more about her father than she remembered. The memories had faded, and that bothered her.

Now thirty-six, married, and lying on the couch too sick to get up, she watched her own two kids playing. If she died, would they remember her? Sadly, she already knew the answer. Sam was just six—the same age she was when her father died—but Jack was only four. If she died now, Sam's memory would fade over time and Jack might not remember her at all. It was a painful thought, one that devastated her already dysfunctional heart. She was dying and she knew it. Patricia closed her eyes, trying to squeeze back the tears, and offered her kids the only thing she had the strength to give them—a prayer.

Please, God, let them always know how hard I fought to be with them, how much I wanted to raise them, and how dearly I loved them.

⸎

Growing up, Patricia thought of herself as healthy. In high school, she was on the track team. She was strong and fast. She had a type A personality and was involved in a variety of activities. Before getting married, she worked full-time as a nurse, started work on her master's degree, ran marathons, and was active in her church. Heart problems weren't supposed to affect people like her. But genetics weren't in her favor. On her father's side, mortality seemed to hit by age forty-two. By that unimaginably young age, everyone had suddenly dropped dead from a heart attack. Her dad was the last to go. Patricia assumed that since she was so active, she was immune. She'd had her heart checked when she was young, she took care of herself, and everything seemed fine. What could go wrong?

⸎

During her first pregnancy, Patricia's heart rate occasionally shot into the two hundreds—much higher than it should have been—but it always came back down. As a labor and delivery nurse, she'd seen lots of women overreact to the changes in their bodies, and she didn't want to be one of them. Every pregnant woman had trouble breathing; why should she be any different? But after Sam was born, some of her symptoms persisted. And then new ones emerged.

Patricia began to have episodes where she felt as if she would pass out. Her heart rate would increase and then quickly decrease. She began experiencing tunnel vision. With her history, she knew these new symptoms could be serious. Her family doctor recommended she see a cardiologist.

Her second visit to the cardiologist resulted in a diagnosis of atrial fibrillation, or an irregular heartbeat. The doctor wanted to perform an ablation to fix it and promised she'd feel better once it was done. But Patricia was pregnant again. The procedure would have to wait.

During her second pregnancy, the symptoms worsened. At work, she would be in the delivery room, working alongside a doctor, and she'd break into a sweat. Her heart would start racing, and she'd feel as if she were going to faint. One day, when assisting her OB with a delivery, it happened again.

"Are you okay?" her doctor whispered.

"I'm fine, I just don't feel well," Patricia said.

"Has this ever happened before?"

"A few times," Patricia said. She brushed it off as she focused on the patient.

After the patient had given birth, her doctor pulled her aside and said, "We're putting you on something to keep it from happening again."

Patricia started on a low dose of medication. For a while it lowered her heart rate. She felt great, and was pleased when, in August of 2005, she gave birth to another healthy boy, whom they named Jack.

⚬⚬⚬

On the day before Thanksgiving, almost three months after giving birth to Jack, Patricia entered the hospital for the ablation. Things were going well for the young family. The boys were thriving, and her husband's mortgage business had taken off, allowing them to buy a spacious new home in an upscale neighborhood for their expanding family. Patricia worried more about thawing the turkey than the ablation.

But on Thanksgiving Day, Patricia couldn't breathe. She was constantly short of breath, and it frightened her. She called the cardiologist and he suggested she go back on her medication. She did, but it didn't help. Over the next few days, she felt so bad she couldn't even hold baby Jack.

In the emergency room, the doctors did an echocardiogram and X-rays. These were standard tests for diagnosing heart disorders, but it was the first time they'd been done on Patricia. After looking at the results, the surprised physician asked, "Why didn't you tell us you felt this bad?"

Doctors explained how the ablation had stopped her heart from racing, but the racing had actually been helping her. Now, her heart was unable to keep up with her body's needs.

"We're going to admit you," the doctor said. "You have a 10 percent ejection fraction, and we can't let you go home with that."

"What does that mean?" Joe asked after the doctor left.

"I think it has something to do with the heart pumping," Patricia said. She never liked learning about the heart because it reminded her of her family history. She called a friend, who looked it up.

"It has to do with the volume of blood flowing out of the heart. Normal is 60 percent to 70 percent," her friend said.

"Mine's 10 percent."

"Patricia! It says here that's not compatible with life!"

The cardiologist arrived. "We're sending you up to ICU, and we're starting you on meds, but we're not sure what will happen next. You need to get your things in order—right now," he said.

Patricia had worked in a hospital long enough to know that was code for, "You don't have long to live."

She was eventually diagnosed with peripartum cardiomyopathy, a serious disorder that occurs during pregnancy, which essentially meant her heart muscle wasn't contracting forcefully enough to pump blood to her vital organs. Approximately 50 percent of women with the condition spontaneously recover with medication. Another 45 percent recover, but not fully. The remainder need a pacemaker, possibly even a transplant. Patricia was in the latter category.

In January of 2006, doctors installed an ICD that would zap her heart into rhythm whenever it started to beat erratically. Though it was meant to be used only occasionally, it was soon pacing her 100 percent of the time. Still, doctors were confident that with time her functioning would increase.

⋯

In 2008, doctors at Mayo agreed that Patricia wasn't going to recover as expected. It had been more than three years since the symptoms had started, and even with the pacemaker, her heart was still operating at a mere 10 percent.

"You're going to need a transplant, but not for another five or ten years," her doctor told her.

Patricia wasn't happy with the news. If a transplant was the only thing that would cure her, she didn't want to wait ten years to get one. Constantly short of breath, she prayed, *God, how sick do I have to be before I can get better?*

But things started to deteriorate quickly. By the summer of 2008, her condition had gotten considerably worse. Her cardiologist, Dr. Copeland, decided that Patricia needed to be put on the transplant list as a status two—meaning her name was on the list but at a lower priority. Dr. Copeland expected it would still be a year before she needed a new heart, but now she was on the list in case things got worse.

And they did.

At the beginning of September, Patricia spent most of her days lying in bed or on the couch. The boys were in daycare, and it was all she could do to pick them up from school at 4:30, feed them, and watch them until bedtime at 7:30. At best, she was a mom for three hours a day. There was additional stress too. The economy was taking a toll on Joe's business, and with Patricia no longer working, the new house that had seemed like a reward now became a financial burden.

When she experienced another decrease in functioning, Dr. Copeland changed her status on the list to a B1, which meant she needed a heart sooner rather than later.

In the fall of 2008, Patricia was back in the hospital. Dr. Copeland was on vacation, and a new doctor saw her. "I don't see why you're on this list," he said. "You're on the right medications; you just need to go home and stop being so anxious." Patricia had never felt so dismissed. Not only did the doctor think she was just having anxiety, but he also took away her only hope—he removed her name from the transplant list.

Patricia fell into a dark depression. Was this somehow all in her head? Was she just an emotional woman with anxiety like the doctor said? She knew she'd been under a lot of stress, but her symptoms were very real. With no hope, what was she supposed to do?

For months, she did little more than curl up in a ball, drink, and hope to die. Friends grew worried and sent her medical records to out-of-state doctors, who confirmed her need for a transplant. But the family couldn't afford to move. Joe's business was failing, and with the housing market collapse, they were about to lose their home and their cars. Besides, Patricia was too sick to move.

In January of 2009, Patricia ended up in the hospital yet again, this time with pericarditis—an inflammation of the sac that surrounds the heart. It was more painful than childbirth, and it was the last straw in her ongoing battle to live. Though she would do anything to save her boys from experiencing what she'd experienced—the death of a parent—Patricia was ready to die.

A few days after being released from the hospital, Patricia got a call from Dr. Copeland's office. The transplant coordinator wanted to know what was going on and why she hadn't been in for her regular evaluations—a necessary condition to remain on the list.

Patricia explained how the other doctor had taken her off the list and how she'd given up hope. The coordinator was alarmed and set up an appointment for Patricia to come in immediately.

In the office, Dr. Copeland quickly put her back on the list. Because she was reinstated as a B1, he told her to expect a new heart in about three months. With renewed hope, Patricia did everything she could to fight for life. She wanted to be the best mom she could while waiting for the phone call. Patricia and Joe also promised the boys that as soon as Mommy got her new heart, they'd all go to Disneyland.

⁂

The call came at 2:00 a.m. Patricia and Joe woke up the boys and told them to get dressed. "Do you know where we're going?" Patricia asked.

"To get your new heart!" Sam said.

"Yeah, we're going to Disney!" Jack added.

After dropping the boys off at his parents' house, Joe dropped Patricia at the hospital door. But by the time he parked the car and walked up to Patricia's room, she was ready to leave. "The heart was infected. They want to wait for another one."

Sadly, they picked up the boys and went to IHOP for breakfast. Two tired and disappointed boys cried. Patricia wanted to cry too.

Getting a call means that the patient is at the top of the list, so Patricia and Joe weren't surprised when a few days later, at dinner-time, they got another call. But they hadn't even left the driveway when the doctor called them again and said, "This heart wasn't good enough. We need to wait for the perfect heart."

The boys got ice cream instead of Disney. The date was August 4, 2009.

⁂

Patricia spent most of Christmas Day 2009 in bed. It was hard to breathe and her energy was spent. She listened to the boys downstairs, playing around the Christmas tree that she'd been too tired to help decorate. It had been *four months* and there hadn't been another call. That's when Patricia decided to give up—in a totally different way.

It had taken time, but Patricia finally realized she wasn't the one in charge, and now she wanted to give control back to the One who was. *It's yours, Lord. I can't control this. It's your timing, not mine.* As she prayed, her body relaxed and she felt a burden lift from her heart.

She had always hoped that the perfect heart was out there. But now, instead of thinking about how she would receive this new heart, she started to think about the person who would be giving it. She began praying for her future donor and her donor's family. In her mind, she saw her donor as a twentysomething young woman. Maybe God needed that perfect heart to spend Christmas with *her* family. Patricia prayed the young woman didn't have children and that she was with her loved ones that Christmas Day.

She finished her prayer for the donor's family by asking for peace for them, regardless of what was happening at the moment or what was going to happen in the future.

She prayed the same prayer for her own family.

—5—

The Bike Rider

JONATHAN FINGER
COLORADO

Alone in his bed, listening to the rhythms of the hospital and the hum of the nurses' conversations outside his door, Jonathan stared death in the face and wondered if he should back down. His doctors were waiting for a decision, but it was his choice to make: dialysis or death. Jonathan had spent the last two years fighting, and he was exhausted. Hopeless, really. At twenty-two, he wondered if a lifetime of fighting was a life worth living. If he decided to forgo the dialysis, it would end. But questions remained. Was refusing dialysis taking the easy way out? Was it a sin to want to stop fighting and just give up on life? Would he be committing suicide?

He thought about the questions a lot. As a believer, he knew there was a great adventure waiting for him on the other side. It was, he believed, a place where he would receive grace, rest, and health. And it wasn't like he *wanted* to kill himself; he just wasn't sure he wanted to prolong the inevitable anymore. Jonathan didn't feel good, and he didn't feel good about himself. His failed kidney transplant, as evidenced by his high creatinine level, was the cause of his physical discomfort. The fact he hadn't taken care of the kidney he'd received less than two years earlier caused the emotional pain.

Jonathan was thoughtful, analytical, and sensitive. He didn't want to make a rash decision one way or the other without considering all the alternatives and consequences of his choice. So despite the fluid buildup in his body and his overall weakened state, he fought through the mental fog and contemplated what he should do.

A knock interrupted his thoughts. He glanced up to see a priest from his parents' church.

"Hello, Jonathan," Father Seraphim said.

Priests from his parents' church often came to visit him when he was in the hospital. They occasionally made Jonathan feel awkward as they prayed over him, read from their service books, or performed other rituals that were unfamiliar to him. Despite his uncertainty about another priest visiting, Jonathan offered him a chair.

Father Seraphim pulled it up next to Jonathan's bed, and Jonathan was quickly relieved to see he was less about the rituals and more about the conversation. The priest asked questions about Jonathan's medical condition and talked about Jonathan's family and his own. As they conversed, Jonathan became more comfortable. So when the father asked if he had any concerns, Jonathan knew it was his opportunity to talk about what was on his mind.

"I'm struggling with whether I should go on dialysis or not, and I only have until tomorrow morning to decide."

"What's the struggle?"

"I don't think I really want to, but I'm not sure it's okay to say that." The priest nodded knowingly, and Jonathan continued. "I feel guilty. I'm not sure, as a Christian, or even as a person, that it's okay for me to throw in the towel and say I'm finished. I'm only twenty-two. Can I really say I've had enough and I don't want to fight anymore? Is this even my decision to make?"

Saying aloud what so far he'd only thought frightened Jonathan, and he searched the priest's bearded face for a reaction. But Father Seraphim's knitted brow revealed only his concern.

"It is your decision to make. And it's not suicide to forsake dialysis," he said. "You're not ending your life; you're just allowing nature to take its course."

Jonathan found his response comforting.

The priest continued, "Of course, if you ask for my personal opinion, I'd hope you'd choose dialysis; you've fought valiantly to get here. But it's okay if you want to go home."

Listening to the priest's words helped Jonathan remove the guilt from his decision. That allowed him to look at both options clearly. The priest was right; Jonathan had fought hard to get to this point. Thinking of himself as a fighter helped give him a new perspective on what he wanted to do next.

⚬⁂⚬

Jonathan was in elementary school when a nasty bike wreck tossed him into the air; he hit the pavement with a sickening thud and then skidded across the rough concrete. The results were as expected—scrapes on his arms and legs and a few bruises. Everyone thought he was fine, until some unexpected symptoms emerged— the most concerning was his coffee-colored urine.

His parents took him to the doctor, and tests revealed that the discoloration was caused by blood. "Don't worry," the doctor advised. "He probably just got hit in the kidney when he fell. This happens to boxers and professional fighters all the time." But the doctor also advised Jonathan to come back if his symptoms persisted. It could be a sign of something more serious.

For the next several years, around Christmas, Jonathan seemed to come down with an upper respiratory infection and a fever. Oddly, the coffee-colored urine would also return. But the symptoms always went away. Doctors began to suspect something was wrong, and they performed some additional tests.

"We think you may have IgA nephropathy," the doctor said when the results came in. He explained how the disease impedes the kidneys' ability to filter waste, which is why it appears discolored.

For IgA patients, this frequently happens when they are fighting off an upper respiratory infection. He went on to explain that for 80 percent of patients with the disease, it wouldn't cause severe problems, but the other 20 percent would find themselves with end-stage renal failure. "The only way to know for sure is to do a biopsy."

"But he's only twelve and he feels all right. Does he really need that?" Jonathan's mother asked.

"I don't think it's necessary. His blood work is normal, and he doesn't show any loss of kidney function, so just continue what you've been doing. But you should try to stay on top of it and have his blood checked once a year."

For the first few years, Jonathan had lab work regularly. But the results showed he was fine. Over time, the lab work became less frequent. By the time Jonathan was in his late teens, a few years had gone by since he'd last had it checked.

⚬⚬

Jonathan's family owned and operated one of the premier retail piano stores in the United States. After graduating from high school, Jonathan followed in his father's footsteps and became a piano technician. By the time he was twenty, he was ready for the next step—a yearlong apprenticeship at the piano factory in Germany.

Just weeks before he was supposed to leave, someone remembered that Jonathan hadn't had a blood test in a while. To be safe, it was decided he should have a physical and blood work done before he left.

The next day his doctor called. "You need to come in immediately. Your results came back, and you have a 45 percent loss in kidney function."

Jonathan was terrified. He was supposed to leave for Germany in a week; instead, he found himself at Boulder Community Hospital, where further tests showed he had indeed lost functioning. He had the biopsy they'd discussed so many years before, and it confirmed the doctor's original diagnosis—IgA nephropathy.

Why is this happening to me? Why now? he asked himself in a fruitless search for answers. He knew the diagnosis meant he would have to go on kidney replacement therapy of some kind—either dialysis or a transplant. But for now, his doctors felt it was safe for him to go to Germany as long as he saw a doctor there. Despite the whirlwind of medical activity, he left for his year in Germany.

⊶

In Germany, the air had an odd smell to it and things tasted differently than they had back home. His food preferences began to change too. Jonathan had a sweet tooth, and he'd often crave ice cream. But in Germany his sweet tooth disappeared. Now he craved salty foods. He also noticed a taste like metal, or possibly ammonia, in his mouth. His appetite decreased, he tired easily, and he was sleeping more. Jonathan attributed these changes to his new environment.

By the time Jonathan returned from Germany in February of 2000, it was obvious his kidneys had continued to deteriorate. "You don't have another year left," his doctor said. "You're going to need a transplant before the end of the year."

Over the next few weeks, his doctor began the workup required to find a donor and to prepare Jonathan for transplant surgery. Family members were tested, and it was determined his mom was a match. Doctors told him what a privilege it was to bypass the waiting list and just move forward. The surgery was scheduled for November.

⊶

It took almost a year after the transplant before Jonathan was on a manageable dose of steroids, returned to a fit weight, and became more emotionally and physically stable. He moved to his own place and worked as a piano technician. He was also passionate about technology, and on the side, he began building websites. As things stabilized, he went back to school to become an EMT and

47

had future hopes of becoming an RN and a flight nurse. Things were finally starting to look up.

But living alone, with a busy schedule, Jonathan didn't always make the best decisions. There were days he would forget to take his medications. He felt just as good, or possibly even better, on those days, so over time he became even less consistent, then noncompliant. Soon he wondered why he was taking them at all. He stopped taking the medications entirely, and he felt great. The three months that followed were amazing. He felt better than he had since before he went to Germany. His well-being validated his belief that the drugs made him feel lousy. He was right about that—but he was wrong to think he didn't need them.

In the summer of 2002 he got really sick with a fever and other symptoms. He caught what he thought was a nasty flu. As it progressed, Jonathan's mind grew foggy, and he stopped all rational thinking. He lay in bed for weeks, unable to comprehend that he should probably see someone.

One day he woke up smacking his lips, a vague sensation of metal in his mouth. Then he realized it tasted more like ammonia. That was the wake-up call he needed. With an overwhelming sense of dread, he called his nephrologist (kidney doctor) and made an appointment for that afternoon. The tests confirmed what everyone suspected: Jonathan was rejecting his mother's kidney.

He was sent to a hospital in Denver, where they tried drastic drug therapies to stop the kidney from failing, but it was too late.

An angry doctor confronted him. "You've lost the kidney. Do you have any idea how many people are waiting to get one of those? And you just threw it away! In fact," she snapped, "your creatinine level is so high you should be comatose! You took the gift your mother gave you, and you ruined it. Start thinking about dialysis. You'll be lucky if you ever get a kidney again."

He didn't need her admonitions. Though his mind was still foggy, Jonathan understood the gravity of what had happened. But her comments made him wonder: Should he just give up?

He'd already lost hope that he'd ever feel better. Now he was just tired of fighting.

⊰⊱

As Father Seraphim got up to leave, Jonathan finally had the clarity he needed to make his decision. Dialysis or death. Jonathan looked them both square in the eye and made his choice.

He chose dialysis.

He believed what the priest had said. He *had* fought valiantly to get here, and he wasn't ready to give up yet. He also knew that going forward, his path wouldn't be easy.

For the next eight years, Jonathan underwent dialysis up to four hours a day, five days a week. He had to give up his job as a piano technician. He started working in Information Technology because he could work from home when he wasn't feeling well. Eventually, Jonathan got trained to give himself dialysis at home. It was more convenient and he felt more in control. But it still wasn't stress-free. He'd scream in pain from the leg cramps. Or a vein would explode, and he'd watch a lump as large as an orange immediately swell up under his skin. If he pulled the needle out and didn't get the gauze over his arm right away, he would spurt blood, sometimes all over the walls. There were simple frustrations too, like wanting to grab a snack, ride his bike, or travel—things he couldn't do while tied to the dialysis machine.

When his name was put back on the transplant list, Jonathan knew odds were against his finding a donor organ his body wouldn't reject. He needed the perfect kidney. Sitting in his chair, his arm hooked up to a machine that cleansed his blood, Jonathan promised himself, and God, that if he was ever given the gift of another kidney, he would treasure it.

— 6 —

The Teenager

ASHLEY ZOLLER
SOUTH DAKOTA

"Ashley, can you help with the dishes?" Dueene asked as her daughter walked from the dining room into the kitchen of JD's Pizza. It wasn't an unusual request; it was a family restaurant and everybody did what he or she could to help.

"No!" Seventeen-year-old Ashley's short, curt reply caught Dueene off guard.

Standing behind the counter, Dueene could see the dinner line was growing longer and the place was starting to fill up. She knew as soon as the pizzas were done some of the kitchen staff would have to leave their posts to make deliveries, and the restaurant would be even more shorthanded. Dueene needed help.

"Please, Ashley," Dueene begged.

A customer drummed his fingers on the countertop.

"What can I get you?" Dueene asked him.

"No!" Ashley said again, and then for emphasis, "And you can't make me!"

Dueene could hear the agitation rising in Ashley's voice, and she knew what was coming next—Ashley was about to flip out.

51

Dueene didn't have time to argue, not with customers waiting. She handed a receipt to the man on the other side of the counter and tucked a strand of blonde hair behind her ear. "Your pizza will be ready in just a minute," she promised.

Dueene was worn out.

She loved her daughter dearly and hated it when Ashley acted this way. It wasn't good for business, and it certainly wasn't good for their relationship. But Dueene also knew that Ashley was right. Though her teenager was quite capable of helping her with the dishes, if she was unwilling Dueene couldn't force her. Dueene knew from past experience that if Ashley wanted to scream and yell, there was nothing she could do to stop her.

"What can I get you?" Dueene asked the next customer.

⚜

Ashley was born frail, weighing just three pounds, fifteen ounces. For two weeks, Dueene wasn't allowed to take her beautiful baby home while she was cared for in the Neonatal Intensive Care Unit (NICU) of the Santa Barbara hospital. When she finally got Ashley home, she was so tiny that when Dueene laid a decorative pinecone next to her baby, Ashley was smaller than the pinecone. Dueene tried to coax her fragile baby girl to eat, but Ashley was difficult—she didn't want to eat.

But more was wrong than just Ashley's preemie weight. At two months old, after another stay in the hospital for pneumonia, Ashley started to cry. And she didn't stop crying for *years*.

When Dueene told people that, she knew it sounded like an exaggeration, but it was the truth: all Ashley did was cry. She cried when Dueene held her and when she put her down. She cried when she was hungry and when she was fed. She cried when she was wet and when she was dry. The crying never stopped.

And when Ashley cried, it wasn't sniveling or whimpering; she was full-blown *screaming* at the top of her lungs. She cried every day and every night—Ashley didn't sleep. No one had seen anything like it. The only relief Dueene got from what she affectionately called her "little crying machine" was the twenty-minute bursts of silence while Ashley was in the swing and it was moving. As soon as the swing stopped, the crying started again. The swing was a godsend; it was the only thing that satisfied Ashley. Dueene used it so often the metal actually bent from use.

Dueene knew something was terribly wrong. She took Ashley to the pediatrician, who recommended she see a specialist, who recommended more specialists. "It's like she's screaming bloody murder," Dueene told each of them. The doctors had lots of recommendations: gas drops, stool softeners, different brands of formula, goat's milk, and starting her on rice cereal. But they didn't have a cure for whatever caused Ashley's discomfort.

After eight months of pointless visits with no end in sight, Dueene grew frustrated. The single mom worked full-time and she wasn't getting any help from Ashley's dad. It was too much for one person. Dueene decided to move back to Rapid City, South Dakota, where she had grown up, so she could be closer to family. Ashley cried the entire flight to Rapid City and continued to wail once she was there.

❖

At age two, Ashley weighed less than twenty-five pounds and had very limited functioning. The doctor visits continued in Rapid City, where one doctor's visit led to a referral for three more. The diagnoses began to accumulate. Doctors' visits were followed by therapy visits. At three, Ashley finally learned to walk, but she didn't stop crying.

Ashley was four when a musculoskeletal specialist thought he heard a heart murmur. A team of specialists flew into Rapid City monthly, and it was recommended that Ashley see the cardiologist to have the murmur checked. Dueene set up yet another doctor's appointment, but she didn't have high expectations. However, this appointment would change their lives.

After taking one look at Ashley—her upturned nose, flattened nasal bridge, small chin, wide mouth with prominent lips, and the starburst pattern on her iris—the cardiologist said the words that unlocked the mystery that was Ashley. "She's got Williams syndrome."

Williams syndrome is a genetic mutation of the seventh chromosome that happens in one out of every seventy-five hundred newborns. Approximately twenty-five genes (out of twenty-five thousand) are deleted. Williams syndrome patients all have a consistent set of identifying traits and are vaguely elfin in appearance. The cardiologist called them "pixie people" because of their diminutive size and telltale facial characteristics. Newborns are often colicky, perhaps due to their hyperacusis (sensitive hearing). Feeding problems, low birth weight, and slow weight gain plague them from birth.

As Dueene asked more questions, she began to see how Ashley's medical history lined up with the diagnosis; though it scared her, it also gave her hope. It wasn't all bad news. Williams syndrome kids have special needs, but they also have an intriguing set of personality traits. They are highly social with remarkable verbal abilities and often have an affinity for music.

The doctor spent two hours talking to Dueene. For the first time, Dueene understood her daughter. Armed with a diagnosis, Dueene was able to more knowledgeably navigate the medical system and choose appropriate therapies for Ashley. Within weeks, Ashley stopped crying.

It had only taken four years.

⚙

Over the years, Dueene watched her daughter become more independent and discover her own interests. Ashley was crazy about monster trucks and wedding cakes; she often obsessed about them. Dueene couldn't allow Ashley to go to the fairgrounds to watch the monster trucks perform because it irritated her asthma, but she helped her daughter get a ride in one driven by a friend. It was the best day of Ashley's life. After watching shows on TV about decorative wedding cakes, Ashley decided that instead of a bride and groom on the top of her cake, she wanted his-and-her monster trucks. Her eyes lit up, her speech got faster, and she bounced in her seat as she talked about her passions.

Friendly and social, Ashley had so much about her to love, but by her teens a dark side showed up. Every morning started with a mother-daughter struggle. Ashley would get up wanting to fight. Dueene would try to get her to eat breakfast, and Ashley would respond, "I don't want to eat that. I don't like that." Further coaxing only resulted in Ashley screaming, "You can't make me!"

Ashley then refused to take her medications. After much fighting and tears on both sides, Dueene would have to physically make her.

While Ashley was in school, Dueene found a few hours of peace working at the restaurant. Then Dueene would pick her up and the fighting would start all over again. Dueene hated it. It wasn't at all what she wanted, but she also knew that sometimes Ashley couldn't control herself.

The screaming and arguing went on for years. Doctors prescribed mood stabilizers and antidepressants. They didn't seem to help. Dueene knew Ashley was having headaches and those alone made her irritable, but the irritability grew into rage.

As things worsened, Ashley began hitting Dueene, and then Dueene's boyfriend, Jeff, the only male role model in her life. The physical violence got so out of control that there were days Dueene had to physically restrain Ashley. At times, she even thought about calling the police for her own safety.

Though her crying as an infant had been frustrating and exhausting, as a teen Ashley's anger was turning into something more dangerous. Dueene wasn't sure how it would end.

♣

On a weekday in December, Dueene took eighteen-year-old Ashley to the eye doctor for a routine visit. "Have you been having headaches?" he asked.

Dueene listened as Ashley told him about the intense headaches she was experiencing almost constantly. Dueene was surprised. Though Ashley had mentioned the headaches, she hadn't complained. By this time Dueene was so used to Ashley's medical problems that she no longer got too worked up about anything. There was always something wrong with Ashley; she always had a pain somewhere. But as Dueene heard Ashley describe the severe pain knifing through the back of her eye, she thought to herself, *No wonder she's so mean.*

The eye doctor recommended they see a corneal specialist, who showed Dueene the problem: Ashley's eye was coning, an inherited condition called keratoconus. "This is likely the cause of her headaches and eye pain," he said. The doctor went on to explain that Ashley probably couldn't see well out of that eye.

While several things could be done for Ashley, her vision would continue to deteriorate. Eventually she would need a corneal transplant. "Most of my transplant patients say they wish they hadn't waited so long," the doctor said.

Dueene was shocked that her daughter needed eye surgery, but she was hopeful that the corneal transplant would help Ashley to see and feel better. Since corneas were more readily available than other kinds of donor organs, the doctor decided to go ahead and schedule Ashley for the corneal transplant while they were there.

The date was set for March 22, 2010.

Part 2

Rewriting the Stories

— 7 —

Waiting Rooms

Tara

"Would you be willing to donate Taylor's organs?" the doctor asked. I looked at Todd and I knew my answer. But I wanted to make sure we agreed. We hadn't spoken to each other about it, but we'd each had conversations with my brother Bill. As I searched Todd's eyes for his answer, the events of the past twelve hours flashed through my mind.

❖

Todd and I had ridden two and a half hours from the hospital in Vail and waited at least an hour in the St. Mary's hospital lobby before the orthopedic surgeon came out to tell us what was going on with Taylor. He was the first medical professional to talk to us since we had arrived at St. Mary's. When he sat down across from us, he introduced himself and his role.

I wanted to scream, "Just tell us how she is!" but I held my tongue.

Finally, he leaned in, rested his elbows on his knees, and told us what we'd been waiting so long to hear: "She has a fractured collarbone, and she's broken a couple of ribs. Her jaw is cracked. She's also lost some teeth, and her left leg shows a compound fracture in several places."

By now it was after midnight, and we were all very tired. I was so cold I was shaking, and I couldn't seem to wrap my mind around his words.

"Both lungs collapsed, so they put chest tubes in before she left Vail," the doctor added.

His list seemed endless. *Had they told us all this at the Vail ER?* I remembered them saying they couldn't operate on her there—that's why she had to be life-flighted to a larger hospital. Denver was out of the question because of the inclement weather, so they had sent us to St. Mary's in Grand Junction. Todd, the kids, and I had taken a hundred-and-fifty-mile shuttle ride on mountain roads while a winter storm raged around us.

"She has a pelvic fracture and she's fractured at least one clavicle," the doctor continued.

My head hurt. I tried to blink back the tears pooling in my eyes.

"We're working on her leg right now. It's pretty bad. I had to set it, and we've attached rods to hold it in place."

The tears started to flow as I thought about Taylor with rods in her legs. Volleyball was Taylor's life. Outside of school, she spent more time on the volleyball court than anywhere else. Her club team had just started playing in out-of-state tournaments. I couldn't imagine anything worse for her than missing a tournament.

"She has a tournament coming up in a few weeks. It's pretty important to her," Todd said. "Will she be able to play?"

"She's not going to make that tournament," the doctor said.

As a consultant, Todd was used to quickly assessing situations, identifying problems, and coming up with plans to fix things. But I could see he was uneasy about this.

"When we see her, I know she's going to want to know, so, how long do you think it will take her to be back on the court?" Todd asked.

"I've already done the surgery on her leg and that should heal fine," the surgeon said. "We can fix the collarbone, broken ribs, and her jaw. Under normal circumstances, if I do everything I can, it would take six months to a year, and with rehab, she would be ready to play in eighteen months, but—"

At the time, the words "normal circumstances" just whizzed right past me. "Eighteen months? That's too long!" I said, looking at Todd.

"High school . . ." he said. "She's going to be devastated!"

High school volleyball tryouts were just a few months away, and it was all Taylor and her friends talked about. Making the high school team meant everything to her.

But I couldn't think about it then; the surgeon was still talking.

". . . that's the least of your worries; broken bones aren't life-threatening. Before we can even begin to worry about that, we need to focus on her *head injuries*. Her C7 is fractured, and her brain is swelling. The neurosurgeon and her team are still in surgery trying to relieve the pressure. That's where our attention needs to be focused right now. Until we get the swelling under control, we can't worry about the rest of her injuries."

I felt my heart racing as I tried to comprehend his words. *Fractured C7? Was that the spine? Brain swelling? What did that mean?* The doctor shifted uncomfortably in his seat and then stood to leave. "The neurosurgeon will be out to talk to you as soon as she finishes. Do you have any questions?"

Todd looked at me; his eyes were red-rimmed and watery. After eighteen years of marriage, I knew he had the same question I did. His voice cracked when he asked it. "Are you saying we need to be prepared for a life or death situation?"

The doctor took a deep breath and slowly exhaled before he spoke. "You're going to need to speak to the neurosurgeon, but you need to prepare yourselves for that."

Somewhere deep inside me a scream bubbled up and exploded into the back of my throat in a burst of bile. I jumped up and ran for the restroom.

Peyton and Ryan had gone with a chaplain to get some food, so they weren't present when the doctor gave us the news. But they heard me retching when they returned. When I came out of the bathroom, I saw them searching my tearstained face for an answer, and I knew that they knew something was terribly wrong.

The kids were exhausted. We'd had two days of travel and a big day on the slopes before the accident. After the doctors at Vail had decided to life-flight Taylor, we'd rushed back to the condo and in just minutes thrown everything we'd brought with us back into our suitcases and piled it all into the Beaver Creek shuttle van that had driven us to St. Mary's. After we arrived, we'd taken up residence in the hospital lobby—our weary bodies, our suitcases, and the kind shuttle driver who just wanted to make sure we were doing okay. *How am I going to take care of these kids and be there for Taylor too? I can barely take care of myself*, I thought, looking into my children's tired and sad little faces.

The elevator door opened. The chaplain and a woman wearing black pants and a khaki overcoat walked toward us.

"They're bringing in a counselor!" I whispered to Todd as I started to panic. But the woman held out her arms to me, and I looked at her face. "Kristin!" I said, jumping off the loveseat in the lobby and running to her.

"I'm here," she said.

Kristin Balko was a sorority sister of mine from college. We'd lost touch several years earlier when she and her physician husband, Greg, had moved to Colorado. I hadn't seen her in fifteen years. "What are you doing here?" I asked.

"Greg got a call about the accident. When we heard the name we knew it was you. I figured you didn't have anybody here, so I came to get your kids."

I burst into fresh tears. I didn't know what to say. It was too much for me, watching this angel from God just swoop in and sweep up my kids. I introduced her to Ryan and Peyton, and I was even more stunned that they were willing to go with her. To me it was just proof of how badly they wanted to escape the nightmare playing out at the hospital.

As I walked the three of them to the elevator, I began crying again. The sobs took every breath I had, and suddenly I began to sway, everything went dark, and then my knees buckled and I fell to the floor.

"Oh, honey," Kristin said, rushing toward me. She put her arms around me and tried to console me.

Sobbing, I looked up at her and said what so far I'd only been thinking. "We're gonna lose her."

Todd

After the kids left, Tara and I sat together in a loveseat in the empty lobby and waited for the neurosurgeon to come speak to us. Silently, I prayed for Taylor. *C'mon, God, you've got to heal her*, I begged. Tara was freezing. The staff brought her hot blankets, but even when she was wrapped in their heat, she couldn't stop shaking. We sat there for what seemed like hours, praying and waiting for news. Finally, the surgeon came out and asked us to join her in a small conference room.

"Taylor has a severe brain injury with a lot of swelling," Dr. Pemblee* began. "We operated, trying to do everything we could, but—"

"Oh, God, have we lost our daughter?" Tara said, not wanting her to finish her sentence.

---

*Some names and identifying features of people mentioned in the book have been changed. In the case of medical professionals, some composite characters were created to simplify the story for the reader. In addition, the time frame of certain events has been adjusted for clarity.

I was on the edge of my seat. My chest burned like an invisible vise was squeezing it, preventing me from breathing.

"In the twenty-two years I've done this surgery, I've never seen anyone survive it," Dr. Pemblee said. "You need to prepare yourselves for that. That's the reality."

There was a long pause as I tried to make sense of her words. Taylor was alive? But, for how long?

Tara grabbed the edge of her seat as if to hold herself back, and then she suddenly started screaming. "Get out! Get out! I need you to leave—right now!"

"Tara, wait!" I said, grabbing her wrist.

"She's not going to die! She's not!" Tara screamed. Dr. Pemblee looked down, busying herself with the notes in her lap.

I wrapped my arms around Tara and pulled her toward me. She buried her face into my chest and sobbed.

"Can we see her?" I asked. I glanced down at Tara, "We *need* to see Taylor."

"Yes, but not yet. She's still in surgery."

Tara continued to sob into my chest. Dr. Pemblee didn't have a great bedside manner, but she was a neurosurgeon giving us neurological facts about our daughter. Facts we didn't want to believe. Tara was angry and she wanted the bearer of this unfathomably bad news gone, but I wanted to learn as much as I could. To Dr. Pemblee's credit, at least she spoke in a way we could understand. I could see compassion in her eyes even if we didn't hear it in her words. I knew that other than God Himself, she was the only one who could save our daughter.

"Once she is out of surgery, they will take her to ICU to get her stabilized. So it will be a while before you can see her. But in the meantime, I want you to be prepared for what you're going to see—"

Tara didn't want to hear any more. She pulled away from my chest and began to rock back and forth, wailing.

"She's going to have a lot of tubes connected to her. She's on a ventilator, so be aware there is a large tube in her mouth and a smaller one in her nose. She has an external fixation device—a rod, basically—on her left leg to hold it in place, and she's hooked up to several IVs. You need to know, she won't look like herself. She's got an incision on her head, and she's pretty bruised up."

It was as if my mind shut down, because I didn't hear a thing she said after that. She finished talking, and I shook her hand. As Dr. Pemblee turned to leave, Tara slipped from my grip and fell on her knees in front of me. From somewhere deep within Tara a primal wail erupted, racking her body with sobs. Once again, I wrapped my arms around her. I pulled her close and buried my face in her hair as I wept too.

"We have to plan a funeral . . . I've never planned a funeral," she said between gasps of air. I tightened my arms around my wife in an effort to comfort her, but it didn't help. She turned her crying for Taylor into crying out to the only One who could save her. "God, please, You have to do something. You have to save her!" Tara begged over and over again.

Soon, her pain turned to anger, and without realizing it she started to pound her fists into my thighs. "This is not happening; we are not losing Taylor. We're not planning a funeral!"

Tara was quickly falling apart. I grabbed her by the shoulders and gently shook her until she looked up at me. Her dark hair was matted to her tearstained face. "We can do this," I said, looking into her red, swollen eyes. "I'm here. I've got it. I'm going to be your rock."

This was the worst thing either of us had been through in our lives, and I was terrified to learn how it would turn out. I already knew I was losing my daughter. Now I feared I was also losing my wife. It broke my heart to see the woman I dearly loved in so much pain. "We're going to get through this," I repeated again and again, with as much resolve as I could. But I knew it wouldn't be okay. There was nothing I could do to fix it. *Please, God, You've got to heal Taylor*, I prayed.

After Tara quieted down, I helped her walk from the conference room back to our spot on the loveseat in the lobby. She was still shaking from the icy cold that only she could feel. After she was settled, I walked across the lobby, but I kept my eye on her while I called Matt Sunshine. Matt and Beth were our best friends. For the past thirteen years, we'd taken almost every vacation together— except this one. The Sunshines were vacationing in England and were scheduled to leave for France in a few hours. With the time difference, I knew I would wake Matt up, but I also knew he would want me to.

"We can leave and come home now," he said, after I'd told him what had happened and we'd cried together over the phone.

"There's no point. Just continue on to Paris like you planned, and when I know more, I'll let you know."

I hung up with Matt and then called Father Fred at our church in Coppell. I told him what had happened. "We've got to get some prayers going for Taylor," I said, and he agreed. We talked a few minutes longer.

I had just hung up when I saw Bill coming around the corner. Bill was Tara's oldest brother. She was the youngest, and they'd always had a special relationship. Bill was also a doctor.

"Bill's here!" I said.

Tara stood up. I grabbed her arm because I knew she was still shaky. Bill met us, and the three of us embraced.

"I'm so sorry," Bill said. "I don't understand how this could happen."

"You've got to tell us what's going on," Tara cried. "I need you to fix it, or we're going to lose her!"

I'd been texting and talking with Bill since we'd arrived at the hospital in Vail. At one point I'd even put him on speakerphone so he could hear what the ER doctors were saying. Bill heard how serious Taylor's injuries were and he wanted to be with us, but he was with his own family in Montana for their spring break. Texting back and forth, he told me there weren't any commercial flights between Montana and Grand Junction. Bill had a private pilot's license and he could fly himself, but he still needed to find a plane.

And then there was the weather. A couple of hours earlier he'd texted me and said he was on his way, but I still had no idea how he'd made it happen—I was just so thankful to see him.

"Let me fill you in," I said as we sat down.

I updated him on what the neurosurgeon had told us, and he told us how he'd gotten to Grand Junction. Through a series of connections he'd finally found a pilot with a plane, but the weather was too bad. But suddenly a two-hour window of good weather between Montana and Grand Junction had opened up. Just enough time for them to make it, if they left immediately. I knew instantly that God had done it. *Thank you.* I marveled at the miracle, but I knew we needed at least one more.

Behind me, I heard doors opening and turned to see who else was coming. A nurse had pushed open the doors that led to the Intensive Care Unit, and she was now walking toward us. "Are you Taylor's parents?" she asked.

I nodded.

"You can see her now."

–8–

Holding On to Taylor

Tara

I jumped up from the loveseat and rushed toward the open ICU doors, *desperate* to see Taylor. The nurse pointed to a room at the end of the short hallway. When I reached the door, I paused before entering. My heart was pumping madly and my stomach churned. *What will I see when I open the door?* Todd caught up with me, with Bill right behind us. I slid open the glass door and Todd entered first. As soon as Todd saw her, he burst into tears.

"Taylor, *no!*" I said as I moved past him to the far side of the bed, away from the tubes and wires that seemed to be attached to every part of her. "Baby, I'm here. Mommy is here!" I said. I climbed into bed next to her. I wanted to be as close as possible to Taylor and to feel her warm body next to mine.

"Taylor, Taylor! The doctors are wrong. Taylor, wake up! Please wake up," I pleaded. In the Vail ER, they'd told us that whenever we spoke to Taylor, her blood pressure would rise and that was a good sign. I wanted the doctors at St. Mary's to see that too, to know she was still responsive. "Taylor, please wake up. Taylor, baby, please! Mommy and Daddy are here. We're here, baby. We're here."

We didn't want much, just a flicker of an eyelid, a twitch of a finger, or even her heart rate or blood pressure to increase slightly. I rubbed her face, her chest, and I kissed her. I saw Todd rubbing her foot and heard him telling her how much we loved her. I tried to think of anything else that would prompt her to respond.

"Show us you're okay, baby, just move something!" Any positive sign would do, just something to show the doctors, and us, that she could respond, that her brain was still functioning. "Please just show the doctors that they're wrong, show them you're still here."

Nothing.

I remained on her right side, trying to avoid the rods that were elevating the sheet on her left leg. I knew I was out of control—the nurses down the hall could probably hear my wailing—but I didn't care. I looked up at my beautiful daughter's face. Even though she had a trach, stitches on her head, and blood in her hair, someone had taken the time to comb her hair and pull it back. I touched her face and saw a slight scrape on her cheek. For all the trauma she'd been through, she looked like herself, like my baby.

With my head resting on her chest, I listened to her heart beating. Bump-*bump*. Bump-*bump*. Bump-*bump*. Taylor's heart had always made a distinctive sound. It had a fast rhythm, and there was a downbeat on the second beat. I remembered how many times we'd lain like this at home, on her bed, with my head resting on her chest as she told me about her day. But, unlike then, when her heart would accelerate as she got excited about something she was telling me, there was no change in the rhythm, no slight increase in her heart rate to signal she even knew we were there.

Everything in the room seemed steady and rhythmic. The whoosh of the ventilator and the slight whirring noises of the other machines were predictable and regular. The only unpredictable sounds were ours—the sobs of a grieving family.

I don't know how long I lay there, but I know why I finally moved; another wave of nausea forced me to run for the toilet.

While I stood over the bowl on the other side of her room, I heard the nurses down the hall sobbing too.

I finished and wiped my mouth on a paper towel from the dispenser. I returned to the same side of Taylor's bed, but this time I sat on the sofa next to her. The world around me seemed to disappear, and time stopped.

I held Taylor's hand and just tried to breathe.

Todd

There is nothing more horrifying than the sound of a mother crying for her dying child—unless that mother is also your wife. It was as if my insides had been shredded and spit out; my guts spilled across the floor. The pain of that single moment in time was unbearable, indescribable. I could feel a burn spreading through my chest and a rage building in my head.

Nurses, lab technicians, and other medical professionals walked in and out of the room for the next several hours. Each time they did, Tara and I asked if they knew anything more. They didn't. Bill would inquire as to what they were doing and why. "Have you checked her oxygen?" or "Has her level gone up or down on that?" he'd want to know. Sometimes he'd suggest a new test or ask about a previous one. The staff seemed to be on top of things medically, and they were always willing to share the results with him. Several times, I heard him have conversations in the hallway, and more than once he was on the phone with the surgeons we'd talked to earlier in the night. At one point, he even went down the hall to view the CT scans with the technicians who had performed them. Each time he learned something new, he'd come back and share it with us in a way we could understand. But he didn't give us false hope.

"The doctors think that Taylor is brain-dead, but they won't know for sure until they run more tests."

Medically, the plan was to watch Taylor through the night. At 7:00 a.m., Taylor was scheduled for another CT scan to look for any signs of brain function. All of our hopes and prayers for the next five or six hours were directed at the outcome of that one test. If it showed brain function, we could continue to hope for Taylor's recovery. If it didn't, it would confirm what doctors already believed—that Taylor was brain-dead.

⚜

Being in the hospital room was like being in a casino in Las Vegas. There were no clocks on the walls, as if to deliberately keep us oblivious as to how much, or how little, time had passed. We must have been there a couple of hours when exhaustion overtook Tara and she passed out on the couch. I was thankful she would have a few minutes of peace. I sat at the end of the bed, rubbing Taylor's foot, trying to keep my anger at bay, trying to prevent the situation from overtaking me. Finally, I couldn't sit still any longer.

"I'm going to get coffee," I said to Bill. "Do you want to come with me?"

"Good idea," Bill said.

I knew we would find coffee near the nurses' station, and as we walked past them I could see their eyes were as red and puffy as ours. It wasn't looking good for Taylor. "Tell me the worst-case scenario," I said to Bill. I wanted to steel myself for whatever was going to happen, and I needed to be strong for my family. "If things don't go well tomorrow, what do I need to know?"

Bill took a deep breath and slowly stirred his coffee before answering. "If she is truly brain-dead, then they're going to ask you about taking her off the ventilator. They'll also ask if you want to donate her organs."

"How does that work?"

"If the CT scan fails to show any signs of brain activity, they will remove her from the ventilator and you can sit with her until she dies. If you choose to donate her organs, they won't remove the ventilator in your presence. Instead, you'll say goodbye, and then they'll take her to an operating room to retrieve her organs.

They'll remove her from the ventilator there. The whole process might take a little longer because there are tests they have to do before they can harvest her organs."

"I think that's what we'll do."

"Are you sure?"

"That's what Taylor would want."

"You need to discuss it with Tara," Bill advised.

"Yeah, I'll talk to her."

Back in the room, I could feel the anger building as I became lost in my own thoughts. It didn't look good for Taylor. This was all happening so fast. How would we live without her? In just a few hours, we'd gone from the best vacation ever to saying goodbye to our daughter. It didn't make any sense.

❖

I don't know how long I had been thinking about Taylor's life coming to an end—maybe an hour or more—but the weight of my thoughts eventually just snapped something inside of me. I felt loaded down with heavy burdens. Trapped. I could do nothing to stop it from happening, and I could find no way to escape. At the same time, I couldn't just sit and let this burden crush me. I had to do something. I needed an escape from the darkness and pain. I needed a way out.

Then it occurred to me: I had one.

I was scheduled to be in San Francisco next week. I started to think about the board meeting and other things that were already planned for the trip. I had a lot of work to do before I left, and more that needed to be done once I got there.

How would I get it done? What does work even look like now?

I glanced at Tara asleep on the couch. *How will I ever be able to leave my family with this going on? Could I even work again?*

My mind started spinning with the possibilities. I was supposed to leave for San Francisco the following Monday and return on Thursday. *I'll just tell Tara I won't be home until Tuesday.* She wouldn't know the difference. *And maybe I won't come back. Maybe I'll just stay on the road.* At any given time, I had about eight major projects going on. *San Francisco, New York, Denver, and then that thing in Hawaii. I could just separate myself from all of this pain.*

I shifted in the chair, and for a second, the noise of the squeaky pleather overrode the hospital sounds—the steady beeping of the machines, the hum of the heating system, and the whoosh of the ventilator. Just like the noises from the chair made the hospital sounds disappear, I wanted to do something that would make it *all* go away.

Maybe I could leave this all behind.

I could run.

With my job, I had a great excuse to be on a plane to any major city in America—I had clients in all of them. I could leave early every Sunday and come home late on Friday. Or even Saturday. In fact, I could line up so much travel that I would never have to be home. The thought was tempting.

I could go a step further. I could vanish.

I'd tell Tara and the kids I was going to work. Then I'd take a flight somewhere and disappear off the grid. There was money in the bank. With three or four days of withdrawing the maximum amount, I'd have enough money to make it to an island. I could start over doing something—anything—else. I started to think through the details of how I could make it happen.

I don't know how long I let the fantasy play out in my mind. Minutes? A half hour? More than an hour? Whatever it was, I indulged it longer than I care to admit. It seemed so attractive. If I left, I'd be free of the pain. Then Bill came in and pulled up a chair next to me, and I looked over at Tara sleeping—and I thought how hurt she would be if she knew what I was thinking.

I can't leave. I'm stuck and there's nothing I can do about it. I looked at her again. *So what? What does it matter? I'll be gone and I won't even know how they're feeling.*

I thought about family members and friends who'd chosen to run when faced with a crisis. In their wake, they'd left hurting spouses, broken kids, and troubled friends. In some cases I was the one who was hurting, broken, and troubled. I knew what that felt like, and I didn't want to do that to those I loved. I thought about Ryan and Peyton. *Right now, they're alone in a hotel room with Kristin, who is practically a stranger to them.* My heart burst for them. No matter how much I wanted to escape, I didn't want to hurt them.

But it wasn't fair. We didn't deserve this.

I didn't deserve this.

Maybe I did.

Lost in my thoughts, I started to ask, *What kind of horrible person would think about leaving their family at a time like this? Who does that?*

I did.

I realized how dark my heart could be. I was capable of further hurting those I loved most when they were already in so much pain. I started to sob at the ugliness that grew inside of me. *How had I come to this?*

I felt a hand on my shoulder and glanced up to see Bill in the chair next to me. His cheeks were tearstained and his eyes were red. I could see the empathy and love in them. *I bet he wasn't thinking about running.* I deeply respected and admired Bill. Not only were Bill and I brothers-in-law, we were also good friends. A few months earlier, we'd attended a Band of Brothers retreat together. We had spent the weekend being vulnerable about our strengths, but mostly about our weaknesses, as husbands and fathers. We'd both grown a lot spiritually that weekend. As a result, I'd learned to trust both Bill and God in new ways.

I wonder if he knows what I am thinking about right now?
Tell him.

It wasn't an audible voice; it was more like a feeling that came from somewhere inside me. Without a doubt, I knew it was the Holy Spirit prompting me to tell Bill what I was thinking. I knew I could trust Bill, but I was ashamed. Just across the room, my wife, his sister, was passed out from exhaustion and grief. My daughter was lying in the hospital bed and she was probably going to die. And I was angry at the world and trying to run away from them both. I cried harder as I realized how lost I was.

"I need your help," I said, choking on my words.

"Anything," Bill said.

"I am going to want to run from this, from my family, from the pain. I need you to help me not do that."

"Okay."

I told Bill how I had been thinking about leaving and the anger building up inside.

"I feel like an atomic bomb, Bill. I'm ready to explode. It's just so powerful. It's this scary, huge thing growing inside me, and I don't know what to do with it. I just feel so much hate and anger. It's like a violent, murderous rage. It's almost warlike. Like something a soldier feels before going into battle. I feel like I want to kill every living thing I can get my hands on."

I buried my head in my hands and sobbed. It was the first time I had really let loose since the accident. Bill put his hand on my back, and I could hear him praying for me.

When I could speak, I continued. "I know what I'm capable of. I'm going to come home from this, and either I'm going to want to save the world or destroy it. I'm not sure which one it's going to be. But I need to stay close to God, and I need your help to do it. I'm scared to death, Bill, and I need you to hold me accountable."

"I'm here for you," he said.

I looked at my hands and fingered my wedding band. "I can't handle this on my own. I can't fix this like I can fix everything else. This is too important, too big, and too horrible for me to face. I need you to hold me accountable to prayer. Help me give this pain to God. I can't do this on my own."

We talked for a while, and then Bill said, "Let's pray." He reached out and took my hand.

As Bill prayed for me, I felt the weight of my shame and guilt lift and my anger subside. I felt as though I had been to confession and now I was being cleansed, forgiven for the dark thoughts I'd been entertaining. By the time he finished praying, I knew what I was supposed to do.

"God wants me to be a husband, and He wants me to be a father. He needs me to be here for my family. I just need you to help me," I said.

"I've got your back. I'm here for you," Bill said.

And I knew he was.

I also knew God was.

The doors of hell had opened, and I had taken a good, long look. Perhaps God wanted me to get a glimpse of the evil I was capable of so I would cling to Him alone. Thankfully, graciously, mercifully, God, through the working of the Holy Spirit, had rescued me from my own thoughts and those doors had closed. I was weary from the battle, but at least my soul was comforted.

I pulled out the footrest on the chair, leaned back, and closed my eyes. My hand was on Taylor's foot, and my hope was in the Lord. I sat back to wait for the scan that would decide our future.

Tara

I opened my eyes, and it took me a minute to remember where I was. Then I saw Taylor lying next to me. Todd was sleeping in a chair, and Bill was awake in the chair next to him. It all came flooding back. I sat up and rubbed my eyes.

"What's going on?" I asked.

"Nothing has changed. We're still waiting for the CT scan at seven o'clock. Todd fell asleep a few minutes ago. You're both exhausted, you should sleep when you can," Bill said.

"I need to know what's going to happen next." The words spilled out quickly because I wasn't sure if I really wanted to know. Bill and I had been close since I was a baby. He knew what I needed to hear and how to tell me. We talked about the scan and how doctors were looking for signs of activity in Taylor's brain.

"Like blood flow?"

"Exactly."

"What happens if they don't see anything?"

"Then they're going to ask you two questions. The first will be about taking her off the ventilator." Bill explained how we could be with her as she died.

"What's the second question?"

"Would you be willing to donate her organs?"

"What would that involve?" I asked.

Bill explained how he and Todd had already had this conversation, and he didn't want to do anything to persuade me one way or the other. "You really need to talk to Todd about that," Bill advised, his voice cracking.

I nodded, and the tears began to flow again. *Bless his heart. Not only is he being a doctor for us, but he's also a brother, a brother-in-law, and a friend. And he's Taylor's uncle!* I knew he was trying to play a lot of roles to support us, but I knew he was also experiencing his own emotion.

Bill wiped his eyes with the back of his hand and then glanced at his watch.

"It's 6:48."

We had twelve minutes before Taylor was scheduled to have the CT scan. "Oh, God, please heal her. Please let there be signs of life," I prayed as I crawled into bed with her again. I slowly stroked her face. "Please, baby, you've got to show the doctors they're wrong."

—9—

Signs of Life

Tara

At 7:00 a.m., the medical technicians arrived to wheel Taylor down for her CT scan. Todd, Bill, and I prayed the entire time she was gone. At 7:30, the technicians wheeled her back in and told us we'd know the results soon.

We thought that meant 8:00.

But 9:00 came and went, and so did 10:00. By 11:00, we still hadn't heard a word. Bill walked back and forth to the nurses' station, checking to see if they'd heard anything from the doctor. Bill had the neurosurgeon's cell phone number, but he didn't want to use it—he knew she'd get back to us when she could. Todd alternated between sitting in the chair, holding Taylor's foot and talking to her, and pacing the room. I stayed as close to her as possible, lying in bed with her or just holding her hand and talking to her. I was still dealing with nausea, but there was nothing left in my stomach to throw up.

By 11:30, none of us could wait any longer. Bill picked up the phone and called Dr. Pemblee. "I hate to bug you," he said, "but the CT scan has been done, and we're all on pins and needles waiting to see what the next step is." Bill listened attentively as she spoke, and then looked at me and raised his eyebrows.

"What did she say?" I asked when he finished the call.

"She's just down the hall. I'm going to meet her so I can look at the scans."

It was such a blessing to have Bill with us. He would think of questions to ask and tests to run that we wouldn't even know about, much less consider. My heart started racing in anticipation of finally getting the news we'd been waiting so long to hear, but my stomach churned at the thought that it could be bad news.

Before he left, Bill paused in the doorway and turned to look first at me and then at Todd. "The two of you should have a conversation about organ donation, just in case."

⚛

Bill and I are extremely close and always have been. In pictures from our youth, Bill was always the one holding me. As soon as he walked back into the room after speaking with Dr. Pemblee, I knew.

"You have to tell me," I said. "You have to!" But he didn't have to. I saw his face, looked deep into his eyes, and I knew. "That's it, isn't it? There's no hope, is there?" I buried my head in my hands and began to weep. Todd was in his chair at the far end of the bed, weeping too.

Dr. Pemblee's cold exterior seemed to have melted a bit as she followed Bill into the room. With red-rimmed eyes, she simply said, "We didn't see anything to indicate brain activity."

"Are you sure? Isn't there anything you can do?" I pleaded.

She shook her head. "I'm so sorry," she said, wiping away a tear. "There's nothing more we can do."

"So, what's next?" Todd asked.

"Well, one small part of her brain looks like it still could have a small blood supply," Dr. Pemblee began. "To officially pronounce her brain-dead, we'll have to repeat the scans until that blood supply dies off."

"How many days are we talking about?" Bill asked.

"It could be one or two days, or it could be as much as a week."

"We can't do this," Bill said. "I know there has to be another way."

"Well, there is. We can take her off the ventilator and see if she breathes on her own. We could do a couple of other tests at her bedside to see if she has any involuntary response, which, from the scans, we know she won't. But we can use those tests to rule out any possibility."

"Let's do that. They don't need to sit around here waiting a week for the inevitable," said Bill.

I looked at Bill, standing next to the neurosurgeon, and pleaded with him to do something, anything.

"I'm so sorry," he said.

"There's no hope, Bill? A test? More surgery?"

He shook his head. "I looked at the scans. There's been no change between the scan they did in Vail and the one they did this morning."

Months later, when we could hear it, Bill explained that normal brain anatomy hadn't even been visible in her scans. Taylor's brain had been so badly injured it didn't even resemble a brain.

Todd sat next to me on the small sofa and wrapped his arms around me. I buried my face in his neck, where our tears merged as we wept. When we finally pulled apart, Dr. Pemblee spoke.

"I have one more question," she said. "Would you be willing to donate Taylor's organs?"

I looked at Todd to make sure we were in agreement.

"Absolutely!" he said.

"It's what Taylor would want," I agreed, and then I burst into fresh tears.

Todd

The surgical team asked us to stand outside while they removed the ventilator and performed the bedside tests. They called her death at 12:15 that afternoon, Monday, March 15, but we knew in our hearts she'd left us much earlier.

Doctors told us it would likely be the next morning before they would have everything in place to remove her organs. They said we could stay with her until then. Of course, we both wanted to.

I'd been on and off the phone since we'd left Vail, getting prayer chains started and informing friends and family what had happened. Tara's brothers were on their way to Grand Junction, along with her dad. I'd also talked to Matt Sunshine again, telling him that Taylor had died. When the nurses finished, Bill left to make a phone call. Tara and I were alone in the room with Taylor.

"What are we going to do?" Tara asked. I'd never seen her dark eyes look so sad and lonely. "How do you plan a funeral?"

I didn't have an answer. We sat in uneasy silence, and I could tell she was thinking. Finally, she said, "I'm going to call Mary Marshall." Later, we would look back on that moment and know it had been a divine revelation. Mary became one of the angels who were there for us when we needed them most.

Mary and Tara weren't the kind of friends who got together often or talked on the phone every day, but even when they hadn't seen each other in months, they could still pick up where they'd last left off. Mary had a daughter who was friends with Taylor and a son who was friends with Ryan. Tara had often talked about Mary's exquisite taste and her ability to get things done, and done right. She was the perfect person to help.

I could tell from Tara's side of the conversation that Mary already knew at least part of what was going on. Coppell is a small community. Everyone knows everyone else. As soon as one person found out about Taylor's accident, it wouldn't have taken long for word to spread.

In addition, I was a big social networking guy, both personally and professionally. I'd been tweeting and posting updates to my Facebook page since we'd left Coppell. In fact, right before the accident, I'd tweeted it was a perfect day on the slopes, it was the best family vacation we'd ever had, and that it was the trip of a lifetime.

While we were on the shuttle bus between Vail and Grand Junction, I'd used both Twitter and Facebook to ask people to pray for Taylor. Somewhere, between the mountains and the storm, I'd lost my internet connection, so I wasn't sure how much had actually gone through. But by Monday afternoon, I realized at least some of the prayer requests had. People were responding with notes of encouragement and promises of prayer.

As Tara filled Mary in on the latest details, she'd have to pause as, between sobs, the words just wouldn't come out. I knew Mary was crying with her. At one point, Tara attempted to take a deep breath, and then through her tears, she pleaded, "I just need you to do this for me because I can't."

Immediately, Mary's side of the conversation must have changed. I gathered from the answers Tara was giving that Mary must have gone into "get it done" mode.

"I don't know when her body will be back in Coppell," Tara said. "They think they'll remove her organs in the morning, so it would be sometime the next day, or the day after that at the earliest."

It was heartbreaking to listen to my wife talk about the details of our *daughter's body*. I felt a shiver down my spine. How would I ever get used to talking about her in the past tense?

Over the next hour, I had many similar conversations. While sitting at the end of Taylor's bed, and absentmindedly massaging her foot, I called Father Fred at our church, gave him an update, and let him know Mary would be calling him.

At some point, Tara said, "We should do something. People will want to help in some way; we should do something to honor Taylor's life."

After a brief discussion, we agreed we'd plant a tree at Coppell Middle School East. Taylor loved her school, and this would be a great way to memorialize her. If people wanted, they could contribute to the tree rather than sending flowers.

Tara called Laura Springer, our beloved middle school principal. She finally reached her at one of Taylor's friends' homes. Springer was with a group of middle school students who'd gathered to pray for Taylor. Tara filled her in on what had happened that morning. Together, the women cried over the phone.

"We want a way to honor her life, and we were thinking about planting a tree on the school property," Tara said.

"I'll work it out with the PTO to collect donations, and we'll get something nice," Springer promised.

Tara's brother Kary and his wife, Juli, arrived within the hour. They'd left Texas in the middle of the night and driven sixteen hours. Shortly after that, Tara's brother Chris and her dad, Bernie, made it to the hospital. Bernie had gotten on the first flight out of Abilene and flown to Dallas, where Chris had met him and joined him on the flight to Colorado. We were glad to see all of them, but each time someone new arrived, we had to repeat the whole story all over again. As soon as they hugged us, they rushed to be by Taylor's side. We could see how they loved her and how much they were hurting.

As soon as things settled down and Tara could catch her breath, someone new would show up, or she'd make a phone call, and she'd lose it again. I watched as Tara relived the trauma over and over through each of their reactions. I was worried about her. She hadn't eaten or drank anything in almost forty-eight hours. Through the night, we'd slept only fifteen minutes or so at a time. She had to be as exhausted as I was. I wasn't sure how much more she could take.

Tara

I felt as if I was losing my mind. I was having trouble thinking, and I couldn't recall things that happened only moments before. My brain was like Teflon—nothing stuck. People would ask me questions, and I would look at them blankly, not knowing what to say. Finally, Bill or Todd would answer for me.

It was late in the afternoon when the team came in. They were all wearing green scrubs with a logo stitched on the left side of their shirt, right above their hearts. I tried to read the words, but they didn't make sense. "Transplant" something. While the two men stood near the door, the woman came over to the sofa where I was sitting and knelt down in front of me

"Taylor would make a beautiful candidate for organ donation. You're willing to consider it?" she asked.

I stared at her, unable to comprehend what she was asking.

"Absolutely, absolutely!" Todd said.

When she left, things started to move quickly. Someone mentioned the need to do some tests. A male nurse came in and injected something into Taylor to prepare the organs. A sweet female nurse dressed in cheerful scrubs said, "I know you don't want those stitches showing. How does she wear her hair?"

I looked at her with a mixture of gratefulness and confusion. I wanted to open my mouth, but I couldn't. I didn't even know how to answer her. Fortunately, the nurse just figured something out.

"I think she wears her hair on the side. In a braid," she said, manipulating Taylor's long locks in her hands. While the woman braided Taylor's hair, others cleaned and washed her. I held Taylor's hand, and at one point, I thought it felt a little warm but I dismissed it. When the nurses finished, I climbed into the bed and lay next to her. I could feel Taylor's skin growing hot to the touch. Something was happening with Taylor!

"She's hot! Her body is hot!" I yelled.

A nurse came running.

"What does that mean? Is it a sign?" I asked, desperately wanting to believe they were all wrong.

The nurse tried to calm me down. "It doesn't mean anything; it's just the medications working." It happened several times, and each time the nurses would remind me this was expected and it wasn't a sign of anything.

Todd and I took turns lying with our daughter in the bed. "I'm so proud of you, Tay," he said, using her nickname. "We're both so proud of you. We love you so much. You're Daddy's girl, you know."

We stroked her face and touched her hair. We told her how beautiful she looked. We wanted to soak up every moment we could.

❖

It had to be 4:00 or 5:00 p.m. when the medical staff came in and said we needed to leave so they could do some tests on her organs. Kary and Juli were standing outside the door to Taylor's room, talking, and as Todd and I left, they stopped us.

"You guys need to talk to Ryan and Peyton."

"Are they here?" I asked. I knew they'd been to the movies and to a museum, but I'd lost track of where they'd gone next. Ryan and Peyton had been well cared for. After Kristin had picked them up, she'd taken them to a hotel associated with the hospital to sleep. When they woke up, they'd eaten and then gone with Kristin to do fun things. She texted frequently to let me know where they were, but I'd been so caught up in the fast-moving events of the afternoon I hadn't checked my phone.

"They're in the lobby," Juli said. Kristin had brought them back to the hospital, and they'd been waiting in the same lobby we'd waited in the night before. Various family members were taking turns sitting with them but, of course, they wanted to see us.

"You're right," I said. "We need to tell them." I looked at Todd for reassurance.

Todd turned toward Bill. "Where's the right place to have a meeting like this?" he asked. "Our kids are going to remember this for the rest of their lives."

"The chapel would be a good place."

We met the kids in the lobby and hugged them, and then the four of us, trailed by my family, made our way down to the chapel. My family stood outside, guarding the door so no one else would come in.

Inside the chapel, beautiful stained glass windows gave the place a peaceful feeling. Todd and I pulled four padded chairs together in a small circle. I couldn't help thinking, *There should be five of us.*

"We need to tell you something," Todd began. "This is really hard to say, but it's worse than we thought."

"Is she dead?" Ryan asked.

"She is."

"Huh," Peyton said, falling back into her chair as if she'd just lost her breath.

Todd continued, saying how this was God's plan for Taylor, but I wasn't listening anymore. My eyes were fixed on Ryan. When he heard the news, his face contorted for a second as if he couldn't understand how this had happened. Immediately, though, he seemed to refocus and accept the news.

Ryan noticed my look and mistook it for grief. "She's going to be okay. She's happy now, Mom," he said, as if he were the one telling *me* the bad news. "She's in a better place. She's with Sarge."

Sarge was our dog. He'd died five years ago.

Ryan continued to try to convince me. "We're going to be okay. It's good," he said. But in my heart, I knew he was trying to convince himself.

By now, Peyton had moved from stunned to crying. She crawled into my lap and I rocked her.

Todd

I didn't know what else to say as I watched Peyton clinging to her mother and Ryan completely cut off from any feeling of grief. *It's my fault*, I thought. I felt as though I had lied to Ryan. On the mountain while we were waiting for the ski patrol to arrive, he'd said, "She's dead!"

"No, she's not," I'd yelled. "She's breathing. She's alive, and she's going to be okay!" At the time, everything I'd said was true. I felt her pulse, and when the ski patrol arrived and put an oxygen mask on her, it even fogged up. She was breathing. It wasn't until right before they life-flighted her that they had to put her on a ventilator.

Ryan and I had skied down the mountain together. The whole way I'd talked to him. "She's okay, she's going to be fine," I'd said. I had wanted to reassure him he'd done everything right and that she would be okay.

But now she wasn't. And he wasn't either.

Sitting in the hospital chapel, watching him deny his grief, all I could think was, *He shouldn't have lost his big sister. God, he doesn't deserve to grow up this way.*

I reached out to embrace him and Tara, and we did a four-way hug and just clung together as a family. I don't know how long we stayed in the chapel, but I knew it was a long time from the looks of concern on our extended family members' faces as we emerged.

We left the chapel, and Bill offered to take the kids to get something to eat and then take them back to the little hotel for the night. Family members offered to bring food in for us and urged us to come back with them to rest. But we didn't want to. We wanted to be with Taylor.

Back upstairs in her room, I crawled into bed with her, stroked her face and hair, and held her hand. I thought about how many times I'd snuggled with her on the couch or on her bed, our foreheads pressed together as she told me her secrets. "Don't tell Mom," she'd say. "Pinky swear?"

I'd hook my pinky around hers and swear I wouldn't tell. The last time we did that she'd told me about a boy.

"He plays basketball," she'd said.

"Where does he go to church?" I asked. She told me about his church and the activities he was involved in. "What makes him special? Is he funny, or athletic?" When she couldn't stop talking about him, I asked, "Are you guys texting?"

"Well, he texted me, but I'm not sure if I want to text him back."

"Do you really like this guy?"

"He's really cute," she said, with a smile on her face as she avoided my direct question. "But don't say anything to Mom—yet."

Then she made me pinky swear I wouldn't tell anybody.

Lying next to her in her hospital bed, I remembered what it felt like to be lying beside her in her room. I thought about her lime green walls and the posters that hung on them. I remembered the T-shirt she wore and how she'd gotten into bed with those big UGG boots on. She wore those boots with everything—even shorts. It used to drive me nuts.

What I wouldn't give for her to be wearing them now.

—10—

Saying Goodbye

Tara

"Has Taylor ever used drugs?"

"No."

"Did she smoke?"

"No."

"How much alcohol did she drink?"

"She's thirteen, she doesn't drink alcohol!"

I knew the woman from Donor Alliance needed to ask these questions, but they were starting to annoy me.

We had just gotten settled back in Taylor's room when the people from Donor Alliance asked if we would mind coming to the conference room to answer a few questions and fill out some paperwork. We didn't want to leave Taylor, but the nurse in the cheerful scrubs said, "Don't worry, I'll take care of her."

The family members who hadn't returned to the hotel wanted to be there to support us. So Todd and I, along with my dad, my brothers, Chris and Kary, and Kary's wife, Juli, all squeezed into the tiny conference room. Todd and I sat in chairs at the table with Myrna, the representative from Donor Alliance, while the others sat in the background or stood along the wall.

At first, the questions were easy.

"Is she on any medication?"

"No."

"Does she have any allergies?"

"No."

"Has she ever been to Europe?"

My patience ran out, and I snapped, "She never had the chance!"

"Okay, it's okay," Myrna said.

I knew she was just doing her job, and she was doing it as compassionately as she could, but each new question was a dagger to my heart, a reminder of what we no longer had. I mourned for all I would miss with her—her first kiss, finding the boy she'd marry, having babies of her own. I folded my arms on top of the table and rested my head on them.

Todd

Something happened to us in the meeting with the Donor Alliance representative. Prior to now, Tara and I had both been moving in the same direction, but during this meeting our grieving paths diverged. Tara took the emotional route and became the center of emotive grief for our family. I took the project manager route and became the point person for all the decisions, the paperwork, and managing the information flow. Tara began to check out while I started to clock in. There was a funeral to plan and decisions to make. It gave me something to *do*.

It gave me some *control*.

"Do you just want to give permission for us to take all her organs, or do you want to choose?" Myrna asked.

"We're choosing," Tara said, her head still buried in her arms on the table.

"Yeah, we want to choose," I added. It wasn't that we wanted her to rattle off the whole list; it's just that we both needed to feel like we had a choice in something.

"Okay. I'll read the list, and then you tell me yes or no. Kidneys?"

"Yes."

"Pancreas?"

"Yes."

"Liver?"

"Yes."

"Eyes?" asked Myrna.

Though she'd been sobbing on and off through most of the interview, Tara lost it at the thought of Taylor's crystal blue eyes being taken. "No, no! Absolutely not!" Tara said, horrified.

"Now, let me explain," Myrna said calmly. "It's not her eyes; we leave her eyes. It's just the cornea. It's the clear layer on the outside. Her eyes will still look the same."

I looked at Tara, and I could see how conflicted she was. We both wanted to help others, but I could understand her reluctance. The thought of them touching Taylor's beautiful eyes was a lot to bear. This one had to be Tara's decision.

There was a pause while everyone in the room waited for her to speak.

"Okay, fine," Tara said. "It's what Taylor would want." She put her head back down in her arms and cried.

Our family was completely supportive. When we said yes, they said, "Good, good." When we said no, they said, "We understand, that's okay." When Tara started shaking because she was cold, someone grabbed a blanket for her, and when I couldn't speak, one of her brothers brought me a glass of water. Their presence made it easier for us to make some difficult decisions.

After a few more questions, Myrna was finished.

"So, what happens next?" I asked.

"I'll give you periodic updates by phone. After the initial organ placement, you'll receive some written communication, and if you want to connect with the organ recipients—"

"We're definitely going to want to connect," I said.

"So you can submit the paperwork, then it will be up to them. Let me just say, not all recipients want to connect. There are procedures that must be followed, and there are some time limits involved—"

"That's fine, but we'll want to connect," Tara said.

"Okay. We'll send you the paperwork, and you can write a letter. Just make sure there isn't a lot of personal contact information in it. All of the communication needs to go through us. And, of course, there is no guarantee that you'll receive a response."

Myrna was doing everything she could to set low expectations. She didn't want us to get our hopes up of meeting the recipients.

But our hopes were already up.

Knowing that Taylor's organs would help other people was the only thing that would allow us to make sense of Taylor's death.

⚜

By default, I was the funeral planner. I spent time on the phone with Mary Marshall and Father Fred, organizing funeral plans and making decisions. Bill was back at the hotel working on flight arrangements for the next day. He knew we wanted, *needed*, to be home as soon as this was all finished. I spoke with Matt and Beth in Paris and told them to head back to Dallas; we'd meet them there. No point in them coming to Colorado, as we would be leaving the next day.

Earlier in the day I had tweeted: "Words cannot begin 2 explain our sorrow, sadness & helplessness. God gave us Taylor for < 14 yrs. To know her, or of her, is a blessing."

People were responding to my tweet with comments, questions for more information, and most of all with prayer. Someone started a Facebook page, and by that evening, seven hundred people had joined to pray for Taylor and us. Now that we were back in Taylor's hospital room, I wrote another tweet: "Tara (Taylor's mother) and I are overwhelmed with love from near and far. Thank you."

After our family members visited with Taylor one last time, they left for the hotel. Tara and I planned to stay at the hospital with Taylor. Though we knew she was already gone, we also knew it would be the last few hours we would have with her. Later that night, a priest came in to talk and pray with us. I also spent some time reading my Bible. Romans 8:28 hit me particularly hard: "And we know that in all things God works for the good of those who love him, who have been called according to his purpose." It was fresh hope, and I clung to it with all my faith.

About that time, my client in Vail called. He was the publisher of the local Vail newspaper, and he'd been kind enough to let us stay in his corporate condo while we were on vacation.

"I'm so sorry, Todd. I just heard what happened."

We talked for a few minutes, then his tone changed a bit.

"Hey, listen. There's going to be stuff written about this. It's a huge story here, and the community is going to want to know more about what happened. As the publisher, but more importantly as your friend, I want to make sure we get the details right and we describe Taylor correctly." He paused and then said, "You don't have to tell me anything. And you don't have to give me a quote. But I want you to know there will be things written, and if there is anything you want to tell us, we'll make sure we get it out there, and we get it right."

"Oh, my gosh. I never thought of that," I said. But I should have. All of my clients were in some form of media: radio, television, or newspapers. "Of course, I want to make sure the details are correct."

He started by asking me the correct spelling of all three kids' names. He asked what school Taylor went to, how old she was, and the name of the city where we lived outside of Dallas.

I didn't give him a full-blown interview; it was difficult enough to get through answering his basic questions. The best I could do was fill in some holes, like the fact we were on our spring break vacation.

At the time, I didn't realize how that little trickle of information would turn into a raging flood of media over the next year. At the time, Tara and I didn't know or care. All we cared about was spending our last few precious hours with our daughter.

Tara

All I did was cry. The passage of time simultaneously seemed fast and slow—sometimes it stood still. The only consistent thing through the night of March 15 and into the morning of March 16 was that I never had any idea what time was actually on the clock.

"Please eat," one nurse said, handing me graham crackers and juice. I appreciated her kindness, but I couldn't drink the juice; I was shaking so badly that I nearly poured it on myself.

"Tara, you've got to eat something," Todd said, watching me. "Bill said before he left that you needed to eat." I picked up a cracker and tried to nibble on it. When Todd got busy on the phone, I set it back down.

It was hard to believe that Taylor was already gone and that in a few hours we'd say our final goodbyes and never see her again this side of heaven. *How does that make sense?* I lay still with my head on her chest and listened to her heart beating. I knew it was only pumping because of the machines, but still it was Taylor's heart, and I took consolation in knowing that even after she was gone, it would continue to beat. I thought about the person who would be receiving it and what he or she must be going through. I cried for us, for them, and for the fallen world we lived in that let things like this happen. I also prayed. *God, just help me get through these next few days.*

"I just want to meet the person who gets her heart," I said. "Even if I never get to meet any of the other recipients, I *need* to hear her heartbeat again."

I heard Todd sniffling. Though he was trying to be my rock, I knew he was grieving too.

He wrapped his arms around me. We held each other and wept.

Todd

The next morning, at exactly 6:00, the three people dressed in scrubs returned.

"Is it time?" I asked.

"Whenever you're ready," one of them said. "Whenever you're ready."

I looked at Tara quietly crying while she stroked Taylor's hair and face. *Don't they know we'd never be ready? We're letting our little girl go. How does anyone ever get ready enough to do that?*

Even after they walked out the door, I could sense them standing outside in the hallway, waiting. There was this busyness happening outside the door, and the number of people waiting seemed to continually grow. Everyone was very compassionate, but I could feel their urgency too. The longer we spent in the room, the more the tension outside the room grew.

We were crying, holding Taylor, rubbing her face and hands, kissing her, and telling her how much we loved her. "I need to hear her heart again," Tara said, leaning down to listen one more time to her daughter's heartbeat. We were trying to gather a lifetime of memories in the few minutes it took to say goodbye. I knew we weren't moving as quickly as they needed us to, but how could we?

Someone came in and gently tried to pry us away. "We're ready when you are." More medical personnel had gathered in the hallway. "The surgical team has flown in, and it looks as if she will be helping a lot of people. There's a woman in Arizona waiting for her heart, a two-year-old child will get her liver, another person will get her kidney and pancreas, and someone will get her other kidney. While nothing is confirmed until it actually happens, it looks like Taylor's gifts will help a lot of people."

There was an awkward pause, and then Tara spoke up. "We're holding up the process, aren't we?" Tears were streaming down her face. I knew she didn't want to let go. I also knew the answer to her question. Yes, we were holding them up. But what could they do? They were at our mercy, and as much as we wanted to help others, we had to let go of our daughter to do it.

"Where are you going with her?" I asked.

"We're taking her downstairs to surgery."

"We want to be with her to the very last minute, so can we—" Before I could finish my question, Tara interrupted with a statement.

"We're going with you."

Tara

We walked alongside the gurney as it moved from her room to the surgical suite, until it stopped. The next doors Taylor would go through were the operating room doors, and we couldn't go in with her. This was the end of the journey for us. Taylor would pass into the next room by herself.

We stood in the cold, sterile hallway and said our final goodbyes. We held her hand and repeatedly told her we loved her. "We're so proud of you, sweet girl. Mommy and Daddy love you so much. Ryan and Peyton love you too. They are going to be okay. We know we'll all see you again soon." It felt like a race to say everything we wanted to say before we had to leave.

Finally, we let go of her hand, kissed her, and stepped backward into the elevator—the aide had held the door open for us. While the elevator doors closed, we watched as they rolled Taylor feet first into the operating room. My last glimpse of her was the back of her braided head.

"Oh, God . . ." I said. I felt like I was going to be sick again.

As we exited the surgical elevators, we heard a commotion moving toward us. It sounded like three or four people running; I could hear the sounds of their shoes squeaking on the floor. Whoever it was, they were in a big hurry. It also sounded like they were pulling something along the tile floor.

We met them at the corner. Four men in white coats were running as fast as they could toward the surgical elevators. Each was holding a bag or pulling a cooler. Just before the doors started to close, they made it onto the elevator we'd just exited. I made eye contact with the man in the front of the elevator, and there was a sense of recognition. We both looked away before the doors slid shut.

Time had stopped for us, but the clock had just started for these men who were on a lifesaving mission. I looked at the aide who was with us, and I could see the horror on his face. I knew immediately who they were, and it was a sight we were never supposed to see.

The transplant team had come to collect Taylor's organs.

— 11 —

Homecoming

Todd

Before we left Grand Junction, Myrna, the representative from Donor Alliance, called.

We were at the hospital's small hotel, where the kids and Tara's family had spent the night. We were picking up our belongings and getting the kids packed up for a flight that afternoon Bill had arranged. Tara's dad was joining us on the flight home. Her brothers were picking up our car and driving it back to our home in Coppell. They had already left for Vail.

Tara stood in the bathroom washing her face; she still hadn't eaten or drunk anything. I wanted to get some calories in her before we left Colorado, so I'd gone to the lobby to buy her a Coke. My phone rang, and I glanced at the caller ID. When I saw it was Myrna, I sat down. I wasn't sure what to expect.

"I wanted to update you on the latest," she said. "It looks like we're going to put her organs to good use. There's a gentleman here in Colorado who will receive her pancreas and kidney. It is going to be lifesaving for him. A younger gentleman, also in Colorado, will get her other kidney. We think we've placed her heart with a woman in her late thirties in Arizona, and it looks like her liver will save the life of a young child. We also know her corneas are going to be placed, but that's all the information we have on those right now."

"Okay," I said.

I didn't know how to feel, yet somehow that news planted a seed of hope. I was grateful that something good was coming out of all of this. Mostly, I was tired and emotionally exhausted, but I wanted to soak in the information so I could tell Tara once I got back to the room.

"Thank you, Todd. And thank Tara. You have no idea what this means to the people who are receiving Taylor's organs. Thank you so very much."

⁂

We didn't talk much on the flight home. What was there to say?

My sister-in-law Wendy, Chris's wife, picked us up at the airport in Dallas. I helped Tara into the car before loading the luggage in the back, and we took off for home. We live less than five miles from the airport. It typically was about a ten-minute drive. But Wendy was driving extraordinarily slowly. It had been at least twenty minutes, and we hadn't arrived yet.

Wendy turned right onto Bethel School Road, and I could hear her on the phone, telling someone we were almost there. Just then, a small pickup truck pulled out of the parking lot in front of us. I stared in disbelief as the driver put on his flashers, driving even slower than Wendy. Unbelievably, he made a left onto the same street we were turning onto. Still on her phone, Wendy said, "We're turning onto Heartz Street now," and that's when I remembered.

Earlier that morning, I had read on a Facebook page something about picking up balloons at Tom Thumb or Kroger and meeting at a church. There was a note that alerted people we'd be home around 4:00 p.m. At the time, I wondered what they were planning and whether or not it would be appropriate. Now, it made sense. There were probably people holding balloons in our front yard.

I leaned over and whispered to Tara. "Just want to give you a heads-up. A lot of people want to welcome us home. There may be some people at the house with balloons or something, so don't be surprised when you see them."

We made the left turn onto Heartz, and as far as we could see, people were holding blue and purple balloons—Taylor's favorite colors. We were at least a half mile from our home, and people stood lined up on both sides of the street.

"Oh, wow!" Peyton said. "Look at that!"

Wide-eyed, Tara, the kids, and I stared at the crowd in disbelief as we drove down the street. Coppell is a small town, a bedroom community in the northwest corner of the Dallas/Fort Worth Metroplex. There are fewer than forty thousand residents, but it feels smaller—everyone seems to know everyone else.

When we looked at the people lining the streets, we saw friends, kids from the local elementary and junior high schools, and neighbors standing two or three people deep along the route to our house. As we crawled by in Wendy's SUV, each of them slowly released their balloon and let it float away.

Soon the Coppell sky was filled with blue and purple balloon-tears rising to heaven.

Our car was filled with tears too. Tara was bawling and calling out names of friends as soon as she made eye contact. I saw people from church, from local businesses, and kids and parents from teams I had previously coached.

The closer we got to our house, the larger the crowd grew. By the time we turned onto the street in front of our subdivision, people were standing twenty deep. News trucks lined the street, some with satellite dishes lifted into the air. Reporters with microphones roamed through the crowd, while cameramen focused their lenses toward the heavens as a thousand balloons filled the sky. Later, I learned that the mayor of Coppell had called DFW International Airport. The city is on a flight pattern, and she was worried that the balloon release would become a safety hazard for planes during takeoffs and landings.

As the pickup truck with flashing lights alerted them of our arrival, reporters and cameramen started to run toward our car, filming as they jogged through the street. The CBS, FOX, and NBC affiliates were there. I either knew people, or knew of the people, who worked at these stations. They were friends and former co-workers of mine, but I never expected them to be at my house. I never thought *we'd* be the story.

From the car window, I made eye contact with Laura Springer, standing next to a couple of Taylor's friends from middle school. Laura let go of her blue balloon the moment we passed, and I let loose the tears I'd been trying to hold back. It seemed as if the whole city had shut down and lined the streets for our sad welcome home. Family, friends, and caring people from the community—everyone we knew was there.

We turned into the driveway, and I saw our mailbox. I began to cry harder. It reminded me of a game I used to play with Taylor. When we were in the car we acted goofy, being silly and cracking each other up. One day, we came up with a game. We called it the Game of Random. I would say something like, "Adjective, adjective, noun. Noun has to be an animal."

Then she'd respond, "Okay, the *silly, magnetic hippopotamus.*" She'd laugh and then say, "Your turn!" Then I would have to come up with one.

One day, my response was "Red-painted flying monkey horse!" For months afterward, she remembered that answer, and every time she thought of the visual of a "red-painted flying monkey horse," she would burst out laughing.

Over time, the game evolved. I began giving her just one word, and she would have to make up a whole commercial about it. Last time we played, I'd said, "Mailbox."

Immediately, she'd responded with, "Is your mailbox driving you crazy? Well, don't let that happen anymore. You can have the mailbox of your dreams . . ."

At the time, the game seemed so silly.

Now it seemed like the most important thing in the world.

Tara

I had been crying off and on the whole way home, but once we turned onto Heartz Street, I lost control and just bawled the last half mile to our house. I was totally overwhelmed by the number of people who had turned out to welcome us. I knew I would never forget the pain on their faces, the love in their eyes, or the sight of nearly a thousand balloons filling the sky.

Wendy had planned ahead, and we drove straight into our garage, closed the door behind us, and left the public outside. But even the inside of our garage was packed with people. Our closest friends and relatives were waiting for us, and more poured out of the house once Wendy parked the car. When I looked up, I saw my best friend, Beth Sunshine, running toward me. Oh, how I'd missed her.

"Beth!" I sobbed, as I stepped out of the car and immediately fell into her arms.

"Matt!" She yelled for her husband's help when she couldn't support me. He came running, and the two of them carried me into the house and sat me on our family room sofa.

The house was bursting with people and activity. Someone had brought in our bags, and my friends were busy unpacking them. Others were in the kitchen organizing trays of food. Todd stood crying and confused. His dad hugged him from behind, and he bawled.

I had no idea where the kids were. I assumed friends or family were helping them get settled. I didn't have the energy to investigate.

The whole scene seemed like a montage from a movie. I heard snatches of conversations, or I'd look up and see only one person in a room of twenty people. The bits and glimpses I caught didn't add up, and nothing seemed to make sense to me. I was physically spent. I hadn't eaten in three and a half days. I'd even thrown up the graham crackers I'd nibbled on in the hospital. Todd's brother, Terry, kept offering me orange juice, but I had the shakes so badly I couldn't hold anything in my hands. "No, thanks," I said repeatedly.

Someone brought me a blanket.

I overheard someone else say, "She has to eat. She's not eating or drinking anything." I didn't realize they were talking about me until someone tried to put a Coke in my hands. I refused it.

People were coming and going. The doorbell would ring, and someone would answer it. A new person would come in to give us their condolences, drop off a casserole, or leave flowers. Todd came and sat near me. We were home, but we didn't have a plan or a purpose. We didn't know what we were supposed to do next.

My brothers Chris and Bill arrived later that evening, along with Kary and his wife, Juli. The four of them had driven our car back from Colorado.

People kept bringing me orange juice and encouraging me to take a sip. It was really starting to tick me off.

I overheard Matt saying something to Todd.

"I've tried. I can't get her to drink anything," Todd replied. This time, I knew they were talking about me.

Somehow, I found myself sitting at the table in our dining room. Bill sat across from me, and he said, "Tara, if you don't drink something right now, I am admitting you into the hospital. You can either eat or drink, or we can go to the hospital. If we go to the hospital they will give you IVs and put a feeding tube down your nose. That's the last thing your kids need to see right now."

I drank the orange juice.

ༀ

After my brothers got back to our house, Chris didn't stay long. Chris and Wendy had planned to go to Austin for spring break but had cancelled when he'd left for Colorado. Now that everyone was home, and we couldn't have a funeral for a few more days, their trip was back on. They planned to take their three boys to the hill country near Austin and go ziplining. "We'd really like to take Ryan with us, if that's okay," Chris asked. "I think it would be good for him to be away from all of this for a few days."

Chris had mentioned something about this while we were in Grand Junction, but that seemed like days ago. "What day is it?" I asked.

"Today's Tuesday, March 16."

"When will you have him back?"

"We'll have him back tomorrow, if you want him tomorrow. You let us know, and we'll bring him back," Chris said. "I just think Ryan needs to get away."

"Okay, but he'll need a bag," I said.

Allison, one of Beth's twins, spoke up. "I'll get it," she said. So she and Ryan packed a bag, and a few minutes later, he was gone.

Peyton had been distracted most of the evening with relatives who were loving her and keeping her busy. It was obvious that Todd and I were in no shape to parent.

"We'll take her home with us," Todd's dad and stepmother offered. As Peyton kissed me goodbye, she seemed relieved to go. On one hand, I hated for them to leave, but on the other, I knew it was the best thing. Neither Todd nor I could offer them the comfort they were each looking for, and they needed a way to escape the craziness.

⚙

As evening turned to night, fewer people remained in the house, and all I could think about was getting clean. I hadn't showered since Saturday night. I felt disgusting, and I wanted to wash off three days of hospital odors.

"I want to take a bath," I told Beth, sniffling. Someone filled the tub and called me when it was ready. Beth helped me up from the sofa and a few women, family and friends, followed as I shuffled into my bedroom, then the bathroom.

Bathing had always been an escape for me. For a few minutes, I could soak and relax without worrying about anyone or anything. That's all I wanted—a few moments of peace. Somehow, the thought of that simple pleasure set me off again. As soon I got into the bathroom, I fell onto the floor. I heard someone screaming Taylor's name over and over again. I didn't recognize the voice. I curled into a ball and tried to make myself as small as possible. When I buried my face in the bath mat the screams became muffled. *Am I the one screaming?*

It was like an out-of-body experience. On one hand, I could hear the most blood-chilling screams, "Tay-lorrr, Taaay-lor," coming from somewhere outside of myself. I became the observer of this woman and her pain. I'd never heard anything like it before or since.

Yet, at the same time, I was also the woman curled into a fetal position with her face buried in the bath mat, pounding her fists on the bathroom floor. I couldn't stop the screaming, and I couldn't stop hearing the screamer.

The women in the bathroom surrounded me on the floor as they tried to console me.

I have no recollection of what happened next, or of how I got undressed. The next thing I remember I was in the tub, my mom was in the bathroom with me, and Beth was leaning over the tub, shaving my legs. I was too helpless to do it myself. I was still sobbing and crying out for my daughter, but the screaming had stopped. They tried to talk to me, and it made me feel better that they tried, but I couldn't stop crying.

Someone laid out pajamas for me and pulled the covers back on the bed. When I climbed in, other women climbed in with me. Beth was on one side of me, and my friend Kathy was on the other, stroking my face. When I shivered, they got under the covers to hold me and keep me warm. Three more women sat with my mom at the end of the bed.

One was rubbing my leg, and my thoughts alternated between *stop* and *keep going*. It was frustrating and comforting at the same time. I wanted everybody to leave me alone, but I needed everybody there.

Someone had called my doctor and gotten a prescription for Xanax to help with the anxiety and Ambien to help me sleep. I finally drifted off, surrounded by these women who loved me.

I woke up five days later.

— 12 —

Honoring Taylor

Todd

When each of our three kids was born we experienced this beautiful, intimate moment where no one else seemed to exist besides Tara, our new baby, and me. But the moment was always quickly stolen when a doctor or nurse took the baby away from us for an examination. Each time someone left with our precious new baby, it bothered me. Emotionally, it made me feel helpless and insecure, as if there were things that doctor or nurse could do for our child that I couldn't. Intellectually, though, I knew it was exactly what had to happen.

Listening to Tara screaming our daughter's name from the bathroom, I felt the same way. Helpless. As if I wasn't enough. I couldn't give Tara what she needed. In that moment, as Tara's screams penetrated the walls of our house and our hearts, I could only stand by while the women in our lives tried to console her. I felt as if I'd lost her, as if she had been ripped from my arms and taken away.

It was also exactly what needed to happen. As Tara was surrounded by her sisters-in-law, her mom, and her best friends, these women were the doctors and nurses who cared for her in ways that I couldn't.

❖

We weren't expecting the local attention our story had generated. My stepbrother had to chase a cameraman from a local affiliate out of our yard after he tried to film through the windows. But apparently, it was also *regional* news. When Tara's brothers arrived that night, they showed me newspapers from Colorado, New Mexico, and Texas they'd collected on the way home; each had stories about Taylor, the accident, and, most importantly, the gift of life she'd given others through organ donation. All this attention seemed a little crazy.

A lot of people tried to reach out to us. People were calling on our cell phones and our home line. We were doing the best we could. I didn't answer my cell if I didn't recognize the number, and I asked my brother, Terry, to take care of answering the home phone. At one point, he came to me.

"We need to talk," he said. "There are a lot of people calling, and they all want the same information. We need to figure out a way to handle all of this. What if I set up a 'Remember Taylor' Facebook page?" Terry asked. My brother was a pastor for a local church and was responsible for all of their digital media, so he knew an online presence could help with some of the communications issues.

"That would be great," I said. I also asked him to contact people we wanted involved in the funeral.

I was so thankful to have someone as capable as Terry to handle things for me. By the next day, he had set up a Facebook page and uploaded pictures and videos of Taylor. For those who knew her, it became a central spot for them to share their memories. For those who didn't, it became a place they could learn more about her. The page went on to receive more than three thousand "likes."

I parked myself in the dining room, away from all the noise and chaos in the kitchen and living room. As friends and family asked questions, they came to me wanting to know everything from, "Where does Tara keep her medicine?" to "Who do you want to write the obituary?" I answered their questions, signed papers, and delegated tasks I couldn't do myself. Everybody wanted something, and sometimes they had to wait in line to get it. I was busier than my busiest day at work, except I wasn't consulting with clients; I was planning my daughter's funeral.

In the moment, I thought I was just doing what needed to be done. But occasionally, I would step back and realize that God had given me the gift of busyness. Planning the funeral and helping coordinate the household gave me purpose. As long as I was being asked to make a decision, give an opinion, or suggest a next step, I didn't have to think.

Looking back, I am so thankful to God for each one of those seemingly small tasks. They gave me something to focus on. Each one made me feel useful and needed.

⚬⚬

Early the next morning, I woke up to the sound of Tara's screams. She'd slept fitfully through the night, and then once the sun rose, she suddenly bolted upright and started screaming. Her panicked eyes were open wide and a look of alarm filled her face. I tried to comfort her, but she was unresponsive. When she finally looked at me, it was as if she didn't recognize me. My heart began pumping wildly. While she continued her bloodcurdling screams, I jumped up, got dressed, and then raced up the stairs to wake Beth. I needed help.

Matt and Beth Sunshine had basically moved in. They came straight to our house after arriving home from Paris and would spend almost two weeks living with us.

I pounded on the guest bedroom door. "Tara's screaming and I can't get her to stop! I've tried everything! I don't think she even knows I'm here," I said, crying.

Matt and Beth both jumped up. Beth ran down the stairs and I followed her, but I just couldn't go back into the bedroom. From where I stood in the hallway, Tara sounded like she was hyperventilating.

"Tara, I'm here," Beth said, holding her close. "You're gonna be all right."

Matt turned toward me. "Are you okay?"

I shook my head. I was *not* okay.

I walked into the living room, sat on the sofa, and put my face in my hands. Matt made coffee for both of us. We sat together listening to Tara dry-heaving in the bathroom, while Beth did what she could to help.

I was so grateful for Matt and Beth, but I also worried about what would happen after they left us and the kids came home. I had to get back to my job too, but how would that work out? Tara and I didn't have a plan for this new season we found ourselves in. There were no role models. And the sand was shifting under our feet.

⁂

That day, I needed to work on funeral arrangements. Mary Marshall, who so far had been handling all of the details, joined Matt and me at the funeral home to pick out a casket. I had wanted Tara to come, but she was still in bed. She was so out of it that there was no way she would be capable of making any decisions. So, once we had one picked out, I waited until Beth gave her approval before finalizing it. Over the next few days, Beth became Tara's surrogate when I needed a female opinion.

While finishing up the paperwork at the funeral home, the director asked a simple question: "Where would you like her buried?"

It hadn't occurred to me that in addition to planning Taylor's funeral, I also had to pick out a place to bury her. I knew I couldn't do it on my own, so I asked Matt to drive me.

We drove out to Restland Cemetery and spoke with a representative.

"Is there anything special you're looking for?" he asked.

I remembered something that Tara had mentioned when we were in the hospital. "Texas summers are so stinkin' hot, we'll need someplace with a tree nearby because my wife will want some shade," I told the man.

We found one spot that was perfect. There was a shady tree nearby. Matt and I both agreed it was the best spot.

"If Taylor is going to be buried here, what about you and Tara?" Matt asked. "And Ryan and Peyton?"

I kicked the dirt. "Seriously?" I said, looking at Matt. "First, I've got to pay for this and now you're telling me I have to plan my whole family's burial?" I was ticked! Not at Matt, but at the situation. I knew he was right. If I didn't buy them now, someone else would. *Oh, dear Lord, when will this end?*

I bought five plots that day.

⁂

I spent most of the day working on funeral plans. Tara spent most of the day in bed crying. Beth and the other women who surrounded her started to keep a log of everything she ate and drank. They'd update Bill or me as they saw progress.

"I got Tara to drink half a cup of orange juice."

"She just took her pill; she'll probably sleep for three hours now."

"Two bites of scrambled eggs and four sips of juice."

Her doctors prescribed anxiety medication and she was supposed to take it on a regular schedule, but she began to rebel against Beth whenever she tried to give it to her. So when someone new wanted to go in and visit Tara, Beth handed them the pill and a cup with a line on it.

"You can't come out until she's taken the pill and drank at least this much juice," Beth would tell them, pointing to the line. The medication would then knock Tara out for a few hours. She'd sleep until she woke up screaming, and then the process would start all over again.

There was always someone in bed with Tara, holding her. Whenever I went into our bedroom to check on her, the group of women tending to her would scatter like pigeons to let me through. When I left, they flocked back.

❀

At some point during the day, I got a call from Cynthia Izaguirre. Cynthia and Tara were friends, and Cynthia was also an anchor of WFAA Channel 8 News—the local ABC affiliate in Dallas. Not coincidentally, they were the only local affiliate who hadn't been in our yard when we'd arrived home.

"I know you're getting a lot of pressure from media to tell your story," Cynthia said. "But I want to do it myself. I've been friends with Tara, I know your family, and I want to make sure the story is handled right from the get-go."

"What are you planning?" I asked.

"I just want you and Tara to tell the viewers what happened, why you decided to donate Taylor's organs, and how you're doing now," Cynthia said.

As an anchor for one of the largest ABC affiliates in the country, Cynthia didn't do much reporting herself. So when she told me that *she* wanted to be the one to do the interview, I knew there would never be a better opportunity. Tara would feel safe talking to her, Cynthia would protect our family, and our story would be a way for us to honor Taylor.

Cynthia was our friend. We loved her, and I trusted her to tell the story. We agreed she could come to the house with a crew later that afternoon.

"I promise to give this story the grace it deserves," she said.

❀

When Cynthia and her crew arrived, Tara was still in bed. We went in together to get her.

"Remember that interview we talked about? The WFAA crew is here with Cynthia," I said. Tara stared at me blankly as if she had no recollection of our conversation. Her eyes were red and her face looked gaunt.

Cynthia stepped past me and gave Tara a hug.

"I look terrible," Tara said, tears lining her face.

"You just stay there. I'll take care of your hair and makeup," Cynthia said.

Beth and the other women helped Cynthia as she combed Tara's hair and powdered her face. When they finished, Tara took one look in the mirror and said, "This isn't how I look!"

She grabbed a hat and put it on to hide her hair.

We sat in the dining room and told our story. I was concerned that Tara would be out of it, but shortly before we went on camera she said, "We need to do this to honor Taylor." She took one deep breath and focused every ounce of energy she had on the conversation. Cynthia was easy to talk to, and I was proud of how well Tara did. Of course, all three of us became emotional during the interview.

After we finished, Tara went back to bed. A few hours later, she'd forgotten she'd even done the interview. Nonetheless, Cynthia managed to create a beautiful story out of it. Her piece led the ten o'clock news that night.

Between the interview and the new Facebook page, we hoped all the questions and concerns people had would be answered. Most of all, we hoped they would honor Taylor.

⚬⃝⚬

The five days after we got home seemed to follow a similar pattern. Tara would wake up screaming hysterically. Shrieks of pure terror would echo through the bedroom walls. The sounds would wake up Beth, and she'd come running. "Do you need me to help? Is there anything I can do? I can go away if you want me to." But I always wanted Beth there. She and the other women who came would take over for me. "You guys give it a try," I'd say, feeling helpless.

Eventually, Tara would calm down. Then she'd mostly be a zombie, going through the motions of living, but without any real emotion. That's when people would try to coax her to eat or drink, and she'd mostly refuse.

I'd go in to check on her and just love on her. If she was able to listen and take in information, I'd tell her the latest. "We picked out a casket." Or, "We found a plot by a tree." Often, it was just simple things. "A friend from church stopped by."

Sometimes she'd talk and tell me things that Beth or the other women had told her. Invariably, she couldn't remember half the details, so it was like playing connect the dots. She'd have a few of the details but not enough to make sense of the whole picture. Sometimes she would remember what we talked about, but most of the time she didn't. I wasn't sure if it was the medication, the lack of sustenance, or the grief.

Throughout the house, the organized chaos continued. Pockets of people mingled in the kitchen, on the back porch, in the bedroom, and in the dining room, which had now become the central planning and meeting area. Dozens of people scurried in and out of the house every day. Food and flowers filled the countertops

Beth organized the women who were all busy cleaning, packing, unpacking, and moving things. To this day, I have no idea what all they were doing. Matt and Terry were my point people and helped me do what needed to be done, especially as far as planning the funeral went. I sat at the head of mission control of funeral central, issuing orders and making decisions—thankful for something to do that made a difference.

I couldn't comfort Tara, I couldn't take care of the kids, and I couldn't make anyone's pain go away, including mine. But I *could* plan a funeral that Tara would be proud of and that would honor Taylor.

I poured everything I had into that.

—13—

A Wake

Tara

Juli, my brother Kary's wife, walked in and sat down next to me on the bed. "Tara," she said, "it's been five days. Don't you think Ryan and Peyton need to come home?"

"Five days?" I looked at her, puzzled. "How could it be five days?" It didn't seem as if they had been gone that long. "What day is it?" I asked.

"It's Sunday, March 21," Juli said.

"Sunday?" The last memory I had was of Tuesday night. *How had so much time elapsed?* "Yes, of course, they need to come home," I said.

Beth was standing near my bed, and I searched her face for answers. "Have I been that out of it?"

She nodded. "You were completely shut down. You were like a zombie. We were all here, but it's like you didn't even see us."

I considered the past few days, trying to remember. They were a blur of faces, of people trying to get me to drink or eat. But I couldn't remember any details; it was like a Sunday afternoon when you intend to sleep for just a few minutes and wake to find you've been sleeping for hours. Only in my case it was *days*, and I hadn't been sleeping. It frightened me. *Have I even talked to Peyton and Ryan in five days? Surely, I have. I've got to get a grip. I can't let this happen again.*

I had disappeared into the grief, and Juli's question about the kids helped me fight my way out of the fog. Though the pain of living in the present was intolerable, I vowed to do my best to fight through it. It was the least I could do for Ryan and Peyton.

⚭

Later that night, Todd asked me to join him, Matt, Beth, and some of the others to go through details for the next few days. Todd had arranged a funeral mass on Tuesday, March 23, at our church, St. Ann's. There would be a visitation the night before at the funeral home. "When Monsignor Duesman and Father Fred came over—"

"Wait, Monsignor Duesman and Father Fred were *here*?" I asked.

"Yes, they were here yesterday," Todd said. He looked concerned. "Don't you remember?"

I shook my head. I remembered we had spoken about including my brothers Bill and Kary, his brother, Terry, the Sunshine family, Laura Springer, and Taylor's friend Kate Dicken in the funeral mass. But I didn't realize he'd picked out the pallbearers or created a first draft of the funeral program until I saw it.

"I just want you to approve everything before I confirm it," he said, putting the document in front of me.

I was amazed at my husband. How could he manage all of this, while I still couldn't even keep food down? When I needed a shoulder to cry on, he was gentle and tender with me, but as I looked around the table, I could only marvel at his strengths—a rough draft of Taylor's obituary, photos for a slide show, and a funeral program with red ink encircling the typos. *Surely, God is protecting him*, I thought.

"What do you think of this?" he asked, sliding a piece of paper in front of me.

"It's fine," I said, barely glancing at it.

"Here are the Scriptures I picked out. Are these okay with you?" He slipped another piece of paper in front of me, and I read the first verse: "Jesus replied, 'What is impossible with men is possible with God,' Luke 18:27."

"It was on Taylor's Facebook page," he said, pointing at the verse.

Below that one was another, 2 Peter 1:17. I recognized the verse from the paraphrase that Todd said to the kids many nights when he tucked them into bed. "You're my son/daughter with whom I am well pleased. You are my delight." I started to well up, thinking how he'd never again say that to Taylor.

"You're going to be really pleased with the casket Todd picked out," Beth said, trying to change the conversation. As she and Todd went on to describe it in painstaking detail, all I could think was *I'm never going to be happy with that.* But I was thankful that someone else had taken care of it for me.

"I know you haven't had a lot of input on this," Todd said, once again referring to the funeral plans. "Is there anything you want?"

"I think someone should sing 'Finally Home,'" I said.

I remembered Taylor sitting at the bar in our kitchen, her feet swinging, as she listened to the Mercy Me song that spoke of what we'd say to God when we finally made it home.

Taylor was now home. *What was she saying to God?* I wondered.

Beth interrupted my thoughts with a question. "Do you have something you want her to wear?"

I hadn't even thought about it.

"Umm, her jeans. And her UGG boots," I said. "But I don't know what else." The tears flowed freely now, and I tried to think. I knew there were other things. *A ring she always wore, a special bracelet, and a necklace Todd's mom had given her.* But I couldn't put it all together in my mind; it was just too much. "Could the girls go shopping and maybe pick out something for her?" I asked.

"We'll take care of it," Beth said.

Emily and Allison were glad to help. Not only did Beth take them shopping for Taylor but she took care of dressing all of us.

⌘

We arrived at the funeral home for the visitation about an hour and a half before it officially began. The funeral director greeted us at the door and asked if we had any requests. "Can we turn these monitors on?" Todd said, pointing to TVs mounted in the corners of the room. "We'd like to have the slide show playing when people come in. And can you unlock the door to that room, so if we need to get away for a few minutes, we can go in?"

It was obvious Todd had been here before. His ability not only to think through the details but to think *at all* overwhelmed me. I had no idea how he did it. His strength was incredible, and as we walked toward the room where the visitation would be held, I clung to him physically and emotionally.

I could barely stand. Though nausea had made a permanent home in my stomach and I had gotten used to the feeling, my stomach now began to toss and turn violently. Peyton hung by my side, and Ryan just followed without saying a word.

As soon as we walked into the visitation area I could see Taylor's casket, and my eyes were immediately drawn to it. My heart started pounding. It became difficult to breathe. The closer I got to the coffin, the more my body shook. When I finally got a good look, I burst into tears and had to fight the urge to throw up. I stared at the young woman in the coffin with copper-colored lipstick and dark rouged cheeks, and I lost it.

"It's not her! It's not her!" I yelled. "She doesn't look like Taylor!"

Ryan and Peyton had been standing next to me, but when I started panicking, they immediately stepped back. Todd wrapped his arms around me and tried to console me. "Tara, it's her. It's Taylor," he said, holding me tight.

By now, several funeral home employees were starting to gather near us.

"It's not her! She doesn't wear lipstick. Her hair would never look that way; it doesn't look anything like her," I said, pounding my fists into Todd's chest. It didn't look like Taylor. I had a vision of what she would look like, and in my vision, I pictured Taylor looking like she was asleep. But the girl in the coffin looked like she was *dead*, and I couldn't bear that.

I turned and ran out of the visitation room, busting through the crowd of family members and intimate friends who had come to support us. Once I got to the hallway, I leaned against the wall and cried.

The makeup artist arrived with her kit. "Tell me what to change, and I'll change it," she said.

"That lipstick!" I shrieked. "She would never wear that color!"

"What color would she wear?" she asked.

I wanted to scream, "She was thirteen! She didn't even wear lipstick!" But I didn't have to answer her. Suddenly, every woman there pulled out her own tube. I looked up to see my mom, my sisters-in-law, and Beth each holding out their personal colors.

"Come with me," the makeup artist said, gently tugging my elbow.

I had a choice. I could stay in the hallway and cry about how unfair the whole situation was, or I could go with her. No matter how much I wished differently, I knew there was nothing I could do to bring Taylor back, and the visitation was going to happen with or without me. I took a deep breath and balled my hands into fists as I tried to pull myself together. *You can do this*, I told myself, digging my nails into my palms.

"Come with me," the woman said again. "We'll fix it, I promise."

I took another deep breath and forced myself back into the room. I walked toward the casket, alongside the woman holding her kit. I took another look at Taylor and fished in my purse for a Kleenex. Then I scrubbed the copper color off of Taylor's lips and applied the lipstick that Beth had given me.

"What else can I do?" the woman asked.

123

"Change that," I said, pointing at her heavily made-up cheeks. "She would never wear that much makeup." The makeup artist took some of it off, rubbed some of it in, and then asked for my approval. "How's that?"

"That's better. But see if you can fix her hair," I said, pointing to a lump. I knew I was being unpleasant, but I wanted it to look like Taylor. The woman did as I directed and turned to me once more for approval.

"Thank you," I said. "That's better."

Ryan and Peyton had remained in the room with Todd after I ran out, and they stayed away when I first returned. But slowly, they felt more comfortable, and soon Peyton was back at my side.

"Is everything okay now?" Todd asked, after I finally calmed down.

I nodded. But it felt as if I would never really be *okay* again.

Todd stood next to me, and I suddenly felt *his* body shaking. I looked over, and he was wracked with sobs. He had waited for me to be okay before he allowed himself to break down.

⁂

We were almost two hours through the visitation when Matt came up and whispered to us, "We've got to find a way to speed this up. People are standing in a line outside that wraps all the way around the building."

I knew there was a line to see us; I could see that from where we stood, but I had no idea until later that people had waited up to two and a half hours to talk to us. All I could do was concentrate on talking to the person in front of me and sucking on peppermints so I didn't lose my stomach.

Todd wanted to talk to every single person. When a flood of teenagers came in, it was as if Todd became more engaged, and his face lit up. I just wanted to retreat.

"I am so glad you came," he said, looking a young boy in the eyes and shaking his hand.

"I want you to know you are loved," he said, hugging each of Taylor's close friends.

"Thank God, you're here and that you're okay," he said to those who had traveled a distance to be with us. It was like he wanted everyone to know they were important and loved. He was energized by taking care of them. I was exhausted.

A bunch of girls from Taylor's summer camp came. They stood in a corner wailing, as their mothers tried to comfort them. *They're in shock*, I thought.

So am I.

The line continued to snake past me. Matt and others did their best to keep it moving, so we didn't talk to anyone for too long. But there were people we hadn't seen in years. One moment, I felt like I was going to fall apart, and then the next, I would see someone I hadn't seen in a long time. Their presence made me feel so loved and protected that it helped me make it through the next few minutes.

I kept my eye on Peyton and Ryan. Fortunately, some of their friends came, and they were able to escape for a few minutes to talk and play with their pals. At one point, I saw Peyton sitting alone in a chair by the casket, but before I could get to her, someone was there kneeling down talking to her and hugging her. And when that person left, there was another, and then another.

At one point, I looked to the right of me where Todd had been, and he was gone. I tried to continue talking to the person in front of me, but I could feel panic rising in my chest. I noticed Matt was nearby talking with someone else. I called his name until I got his attention and then asked, "Where's Todd?"

He could see I needed him, so he started looking for Todd. But so many people were milling about that he couldn't move and he had to strain to see the entire room. He couldn't find him either. Finally, Matt grabbed Charlie Hellmuth, a friend of ours who stands six foot three, big, and bald. Charlie looked around the room. When he located Todd, Charlie interrupted the people talking with him. "Excuse me, Todd. Tara needs you." Nobody was going to argue with Charlie. Or with a grieving wife. They let Todd go, and he rushed back to my side. I was comforted by his presence. I needed to lean into his strength.

After almost five hours, things finally wound down. By the end of the night, I was spent. But I'd done what I needed to do. I'd held myself together for Ryan and Peyton.

Lying in bed that night, waiting for sleep to kick in, I thought about Matt crying when he saw Taylor in the casket. We'd been friends for a long time; I'd never seen Matt cry before, and it touched me.

Then I worried about the kids seeing her in the casket.

When we walked out of the visitation room, I'd stopped for one last look of Taylor in the casket. The kids had too. That would be their final memory of her. Todd and I had debated letting them see her in Grand Junction, but we were afraid it would be their last image of her—bloody, bruised, and hooked up to machines. Now, I realized their last image was of their sister in a casket.

Had we done the right thing?

❖

We arrived early the next day at St. Ann's, and a church staffer shuffled us off to a holding room. Family members came in to give us a quick hug, and somebody who dropped by left a fuzzy blue elephant for Peyton, which she clung to the rest of the day.

The church was massive, with soaring ceilings, and we'd walked down that aisle countless times—practically every Sunday since we'd joined the church. But that day the aisle seemed different. Endless. The church was packed—I would later learn that more than eighteen hundred people had attended—and I felt each of their eyes on me as I followed my daughter's casket down the aisle. *Why are they staring?* The whole thing was surreal, like an out-of-body experience. It felt as if I were watching someone else in a movie. I just wanted to disappear.

Father Fred was the perfect priest to conduct Taylor's funeral. He was loved by the adults but even more by the kids, because he was appropriately light and funny when the moment called for it—like wearing tennis shoes under his sacred robes at the funeral. As the service continued, his ability to connect with humor and compassion was much appreciated.

All of our kids had been coming to church with us since they were babies, but during the funeral Ryan acted like this was the first time he'd ever been. "Why is he doing that?" Ryan asked early in the service. "What are they doing now?" he asked a few minutes later when someone got up to read Scripture. "Who is that?" he asked when someone else got up to speak. Throughout the whole service, he couldn't sit still and he couldn't stop asking questions. It was as if he had regressed from a mature twelve-year-old to an antsy six-year-old who couldn't sit still.

I tried to be patient. Sitting there with him, I realized this was the longest time the four of us had been together in one space since the accident. Maybe he was just trying to engage me in the only way he knew. Or maybe he was trying to distance himself from soaking in the emotion of the moment by asking questions rather than feeling it.

Peyton was doing something similar, in her own way. She sat quietly staring off in the distance, holding the stuffed elephant under her chin.

I understood their need to be removed from the situation. Though I was there physically, at times I felt as if I checked out emotionally, as if my body had gone into a protection mode by separating me from what was happening. Instead of being fully present, I was catching only snatches and glimpses of the funeral and then processing them in small bites. Even when Todd got up to speak, I don't remember hearing what he said.

But one moment during the funeral stood out.

On Sundays, when we recite the Lord's Prayer, the parishioners typically hold hands with the people standing next to them. So when it came to that particular moment in the funeral, I reached out to take Ryan's and Peyton's hands. Todd joined us by putting his left hand on top of ours. Since no one was sitting to his right, he had a free hand. As the prayer began and people bowed their heads and closed their eyes, I watched as Todd stretched out his arm and laid his right hand on the casket.

It was our final prayer as a family, with Taylor.

— 14 —

Finding Purpose

Todd

At almost 10:00 p.m., I thought I heard a knock on the front door. Though the house had been overflowing with people for hours after the funeral and burial at the cemetery, by now everyone except our parents and Tara's aunt had gone home. The kids were upstairs getting ready for bed. Matt and Beth, thinking things would be calm for a few hours, took the opportunity to run to their house in Plano to pick up a few things they and their girls would need for the upcoming week. When I heard a second knock, I got up, walked to the front door, and glanced out the window.

"Hey, Father Alfonse!" I said, quickly opening the door. "C'mon in!"

Like Father Fred, Father Alfonse was popular with the kids. His primary job was at the local Catholic school, but he occasionally did youth masses at St. Ann's and spoke at youth retreats. He'd been at the burial hours earlier, and we'd spoken briefly. At the time, I'd thanked him for coming and told him how much Taylor had loved his masses. "I have to leave now, but may I come by later?" he'd asked. I told him he was welcome anytime.

I showed him to the kitchen and introduced him to everyone around the table.

"Can I get you something to eat, Father?" Tara's mom said, jumping up from the table. One way Tara's mom showed her love was through serving others, especially food. She believed that when there were guests in the house you needed to feed them.

Father Alfonse took the pie she offered, sat down at the table, and asked how everyone was doing. The conversation turned to the funeral, and Father Alfonse expressed his sympathies. At some point the ski accident was brought up, and he said, "It was all part of God's plan."

Most people just nodded or sat silently contemplating his words, but Tara's dad, Bernie, couldn't let the statement go unchallenged. "Are you *kidding* me? It was an accident," Bernie said. "God didn't *plan* this."

The two men got into quite a discussion with their differing views on how a merciful God could allow pain and suffering. The sticking point seemed to be whether or not God was active and involved in every part of our lives. Tara and I stayed out of it. It didn't matter to us; whatever their conclusion was didn't change the outcome for us. Plus, we had no energy left to argue.

"I don't know how else to explain it," Father Alfonse said at last, "than to say God had a purpose in all of this and this was Taylor's purpose."

About this time, Peyton walked up to the table. She was carrying the journal someone had given her to record her thoughts and feelings about the loss of her sister. "Peyton, show Father Alfonse your journal," Tara said, to change the subject.

"You have a journal? Can I see it?" the priest asked, and then in mock seriousness he added, "Unless you wrote about your boyfriend, and you don't want me to read it."

Peyton giggled and handed it to him. "I haven't written in it yet. And I'm too young to have a boyfriend!"

Father Alfonse flipped through the blank pages. "Look at that, there's a Scripture at the bottom of every page."

"Yep," Peyton said proudly.

"Let me pick one and read it," Father Alfonse said. He randomly flipped to a page and read, "And we know that in all things God works for the good of those who love him, who have been called according to his purpose. Romans 8:28." He finished reading and then slowly looked up, glancing first at Bernie, then Tara, and then me.

As the words he read sank in, it was as if they struck a match. The Scripture was illuminating the darkness inside of me, and I wasn't sure what to do with it. I looked at Tara. From the expression on her face, I could see she felt the same way. It could have been a mere coincidence that out of all the pages in the journal, he opened to this one, but we didn't believe in coincidences. It was clear to us that God was trying to tell us something. *Could there be a purpose in this? Could Taylor's death be used for good in some way?*

Peyton interrupted my thoughts with a question for Father Alfonse, and the conversation changed direction. It grew late and Father Alfonse got up to leave. Clearly, he'd been affected by the timing of the verse he'd read too. "Can we talk another time? I'd like to check back with you and talk more about all of this," he said, as I walked him to the door.

That night, for the first time in over a week, Tara and I went to bed together at the same time. As we lay in bed, facing each other, our arms and legs intertwined, we discussed what had just happened. "Do you really think God could have a purpose for Taylor's death?" Tara asked.

"I don't know," I said. It was an honest answer. I didn't know. It was hard to understand how something so painful could ever be good, but I also knew God was God, and my ways were not His ways. I pulled Tara close and said, "If there is a purpose, or even the possibility of one, then I think it's important we try to figure out what it is."

She snuggled deep into my arms and said, "Mm-hmm," and immediately fell asleep.

❖

I woke up the next morning and stared at the ceiling. The funeral that had kept me busy for the past few days was over and our child was buried. *What am I supposed to do now?*

The calendar said I should be in New York. But how was I supposed to work? I needed to be home for my wife and kids. John and Jim, the company executives, had told me to take as much time off as I needed, but sooner or later that would end. The thought of getting on a plane and leaving my family alone without me was—well, unthinkable. They couldn't function without my help; let's face it, I could barely function myself. How was I supposed to help my clients when I couldn't help myself?

The first thing I had to do was for myself.

I had to learn to live without my daughter.

I heard Tara moan and knew screams would soon follow, but to my surprise, they didn't. Tara woke up, and for the first time since we'd been home, she didn't start screaming. Instead, she rolled out of bed and ran for the bathroom—the screams had gone, but the nausea hadn't.

"Are you okay?" I asked when she returned.

"There is a heaviness in my chest," she said, crying, "and it's making it hard to breathe."

I knew what she was feeling; I felt it too. It was like the lead bib they make you wear at the dentist's office while having an X-ray. A heavy weight wrapped around my shoulders and across my chest. It engulfed me. When I tried to breathe, the weight pressed down harder on my chest. The previous night's conversation played through my mind and I remembered something Charlie Hellmuth had told me at the visitation.

"I have never seen such an outpouring like this for a family before," he had said. "You're going to have to realize that people will want to give, but you're not going to want to receive."

What Charlie said was true. I'd much rather help someone else than have them help me.

"I know you well enough to know you're going to want to do it all yourself. And you're going to tell people 'we're fine' and 'we don't need anything,' but if you deny people the opportunity to help, you're taking away their blessing. You're taking away a gift they want to give you. So, you're going to have to figure out how to let other people help you," he said.

At the time, I hadn't been able to fully reflect on what he meant, but I was starting to get a better understanding. This wasn't going away, and there wasn't some future marker where everything would be okay. This would take time, and as much as I hated the thought of asking others for help, I would have to learn how to do just that.

Charlie went on to remind me that though I might feel abandoned, my faith would be the strength that would help me survive. "Be open to hearing, seeing, and feeling God through all of this," he said. "It's not about you, but it's about a much, much bigger picture, and there is a reason behind this that will help carry you through."

Was Charlie talking about the same thing as Father Alfonse? Could there be a purpose to Taylor's death? Could God be working even through this?

I thought about the call from Myrna I'd received back at the hotel in Grand Junction, when I'd learned that Taylor's final gift was helping so many people. In the midst of our tragic loss, knowing her organs had saved other people's lives was our only glimmer of hope.

⚜

The kids went back to school that day. Ryan was appropriately upset but did his best to make it through. Peyton was numb but she craved the distraction of normalcy that school offered. At home, the day passed with the usual visitors coming and going. Everyone except Tara had at least a few bites of the abundant food that continued to arrive in Tupperware and aluminum tins. The hours passed quickly, and soon it was night again. Everyone else was in bed but I was still restless. I sat in my office, composing an email. When I finished, I opened a browser window and googled "organ donation."

Maybe I was looking for purpose and meaning, or maybe I just wanted to know more. Regardless, I was reading everything I could find. The first link led to an article, which led to a blog, which led to an organization, and they all led to more links. It didn't take long to realize how many people were desperately waiting for organs and how few organ donors were readily available. The articles showed how hard it was to get people to register for organ donation. And without registered donors, there would always be a lack of organs for those who needed them. My inner consultant came alive, and I started asking questions. "Why is it so hard to get people to register?"

To answer that question, I did more research and quickly saw the problem seemed to stem from a lack of education. People believed the myths and didn't know the truth. They never discussed it or tried to consult anyone who had real answers. Even for those who thought it was a good idea, a conversation was never broached around the dinner table. Without good information and a clear directive from a loved one, when someone died people didn't know what to do. When they didn't know what to do, they failed to donate organs. It got me thinking. *What could I do to help educate people and lead them into conversations about organ donation?*

✧

The next day Laura Springer, the principal from Taylor's school, called to check up on us. After we returned from Grand Junction, she was one of the people who regularly called or stopped by. We'd sit out on the back porch and have a Dr Pepper, and she'd tell Tara and me stories about Taylor at school. We loved spending time with her because we treasured hearing stories about our daughter. We chatted for a few minutes, and then I asked, "How are the kids doing up there?"

"The kids aren't doing well; they're hurting. Taylor was an important part of this school. We've had counselors in, and I've asked some of the local churches to provide youth ministers to come up and hang out during lunch, in case the kids want someone to talk to."

"What can I do?"

"Would you be able to talk to them? Not only are they missing Taylor, but they're also worried about you, Tara, Ryan, and Peyton. You're all part of this community."

I didn't even have to think about it. "I'll be there tomorrow."

I had always liked Taylor's friends, but after talking with them at the visitation, I had a renewed sense of connection with them. I wanted to take care of them and let them know it was going to be okay. I wanted to be their friend and hear how they were doing.

Tara was sitting out on the back patio. When I found her, I told her about the conversation I'd had with Laura and how we'd been invited to come up to the school for lunch.

"I can't, Todd. I can't," Tara said. "You go."

I understood. It had been hard for her to see some of Taylor's closest friends at the visitation and funeral. Tara didn't receive the same kind of strength from them that I did. Though she hadn't woken up screaming for a few days, she still cried and had that same vacant look in her eyes. The nausea prevented her from eating, and now chest pains were making it hard for her to breathe. She was in no shape to leave the house.

The next day, I met Laura in the cafeteria. After all the kids got their food and sat down, she stood on the stage and said, "We've had a tough time here the past few days. We're all missing Taylor. That's why I've asked Mr. Storch to talk to you." Then she turned it over to me. I looked out across the cafeteria at the round wooden tables and watched some of Taylor's closest friends tearing up. Their heartfelt emotion touched me.

"First, I just want you to know we're surviving as a family and it's because of the love you've shown us. We're so thankful for those of you who have prayed, stopped by, sent cards, or written notes for us. Thank you for loving us."

I could hear some sniffling in the crowd. I turned in that direction and said, "It's okay to cry. We're going through all of those crazy emotions at our house too. I know this is just as tough for you as it is for the adults. But our family is going to be okay, and though it will be hard, you will be too."

Trying to lighten the mood, I talked about Taylor's sense of humor and some of the funny things she did. I told them things they might not have known about her and things they could relate to. I reminded them of how she would sneak into their photos without their knowledge. I mentioned organ donation and how it had given us great hope because even though she was not with us any longer, she was still here in some small way, by making life better for others through her gifts.

The somber mood seemed to have turned as the kids responded to the stories I told. The lunch period was almost over, so I concluded by saying, "If you see me in the grocery store, and you want to give me a hug, you can. Or if you want to come by our house, come by. We don't always know how to respond, so it's okay if you don't always know what to say. I just want you to know we're here for you if you need us."

A girl in gym shorts and a T-shirt asked, "Can I come by your house today?"

Another girl with short blonde hair asked, "I have a note I wrote to Taylor. Is there somewhere I can leave it?"

"Of course, all of you can come by anytime. You can leave the note in her bedroom, if you'd like." As I said it, I immediately realized what was happening. The kids didn't have a place to mourn or pour out their grief. They needed a place. They were too young to drive, and even if they could, they wouldn't visit the cemetery or hang out in a big church all alone. They needed somewhere to gather individually, and in small groups, to remember their friend.

Taylor's room was the place they needed.

"Pull out your cell phones," I said, "and I'll give you my number. That way you can call or text me, or you can just show up at the house. You can go upstairs to her room and just hang out for a while. Or you can write a note and leave it there, if you want. Whatever you want to do, know we love you, and we're all going to get through this together."

Afterward, I followed Laura back to her office. On the way, we talked about how the kids seemed lost. They really didn't have a place to go and needed their own space.

I sat down in her office, and I mentioned the tree account. "I know people have been making donations to the PTO account to buy a tree in honor of Taylor. Maybe we could somehow make that a spot for the kids."

"Todd, you realize that account has more than thirty thousand dollars in it, right?"

I was speechless. "Thirty thousand dollars?" It took a moment for the number to sink in, and when it did, I said, "We're not buying a thirty-thousand-dollar tree!"

Laura laughed.

"Look," I said, "I don't know how any of this stuff works, but if we've got all this money, let's use it to do something great."

She thought for a moment and then said, "The seventh grade class has the responsibility of a garden, but it has a lot of meaning to Taylor's class because they were the first ones to start it."

"Great. We'll use some of this money to spruce it up. What do you need?"

"Oh my, we need everything! It's nothing but some sad little plants, a couple of weathered picnic tables, some old bricks, and a lot of kids trying to do good work."

"Perfect. If we fix it up, maybe plant a tree or two and do a little landscaping, not only will it become a way to honor Taylor but it will also become a place for the kids to talk and grieve."

We agreed on a budget for the garden and decided the rest would be used for scholarships. Jay Praytor, who owned a local landscaping company, was also a former student of Laura's from her high school teaching days. I offered to call him and see what he could do for the budgeted amount. Laura thanked me for coming, and I thanked her for the opportunity to talk to the kids.

But I should have thanked her for giving me a purpose.

— 15 —

Opening Doors

Tara

My brother Bill knew what he was doing even if I didn't catch on right away. Somehow, he convinced me to go for a ride by telling me I needed to get out of the house. He was right. I did. So many people and so much chaos filled the house during the days immediately following the funeral that I spent most of my time either secluded in the bedroom or out on the back porch.

We'd been driving around for about ten minutes when he decided he was hungry and needed to eat. *Why didn't he just eat at the house? There is so much food available, and he could have eaten anything.* I had been trying to eat, but I just couldn't keep anything down. Bill had prescribed Phenergan Gel for my wrists. It was supposed to stop the nausea, but all it did was make me sleepy.

"Anything sound good to you?" he asked.

I shook my head.

He made a left and then a quick right onto the main road. Up ahead, I saw a Taco Bueno, and I immediately knew that's where he was headed. Bill and I were both crazy about Taco Bueno. I loved everything on their menu. If I ever had to choose a death row meal, it would be Taco Bueno.

Before he placed his order, he asked again, "Are you sure you don't want anything?"

"I'm sure."

"I'll have four bean burritos, three beef tacos, and four tostadas. And extra salsa, please."

As the cashier repeated the large order back to him, I realized he had purposely ordered all of our favorites. After paying at the window, he handed the sacks to me. "Can you hold these, please?"

Driving back to the house, I could feel the heat from the food warming my thighs through my pajamas, and it felt good. I was always cold. The aroma of the spicy food began to fill the car. Surprisingly, it didn't make me feel queasy; it made me feel hungry.

We got back to the house, and Bill asked me to join him in the kitchen while he ate. I sat down as he plated some food and purposely left it sitting in the middle of the table. It didn't take long for me to have a bite.

For days, I had only sipped protein-packed smoothies and nibbled at crackers. Finally, Bill got his way. I ate. My first real meal after Taylor's accident was a tostada from Taco Bueno.

⚬⚬

For the next eight weeks, I was never left alone. Just when things seemed to settle down, someone else would show up—friends dropping off cards, delivery services with flowers, or people bringing trays of food. Finally, someone got smart and attached a basket to the door with a note that said, "Please leave the family a note if you come by. Please don't knock at this time." That helped to calm things down a bit. Each time someone new came, they wanted to hear details about what had happened from Todd or me. They had questions, or they wanted to see how we were doing. In those rare times when I *did* want to talk, I didn't want to talk about any of *that*.

When friends came over all dressed up, wearing jewelry and makeup, it would anger me. It would tick me off that they were going on with their lives, spending time shopping and looking cute, while I was struggling just to breathe. Even smelling their perfume after they left made me mad.

But I knew the issue was me, not them. They were simply doing what they knew to do, just like all the friends who showed up to take care of us. While I didn't have the mental or emotional capacity to thank them, I couldn't have done it without them. These faithful women would come over and do laundry, make dinner, empty out cabinets, and organize the pantry. They'd make the kids' lunches, help them with their homework, and give them rides to practice or school activities, if they needed it. They cleaned, dusted, and vacuumed.

One friend even organized a meal calendar, so when anyone wanted to bring a meal, they would just call her. One day, she said to me, "I got a call from someone at your church who wanted to bring a meal to you tomorrow night, and I told them we already had it covered. They asked if there was a day next week when they could bring one, and I said we had that covered too. Then they wanted to know when the next available day was, and I laughed and told them—July 19."

It was still March.

The generosity of this community of women was surprising, and at times overwhelming, but I couldn't have made it without their help. There was a gaping hole in our lives without Taylor, but these women made sure nothing else fell through the cracks. Their presence allowed me to fully grieve.

⁂

The same afternoon that Todd visited with the kids at Coppell Middle School East, he started getting text requests to come to the house.

"Hey, Mr. Storch. It's Jordan. Is it okay if three friends and I come by at 4:15 today?"

I was in our bedroom when Todd told me he'd offered to let the kids visit Taylor's room, and now they wanted to come.

"Do you care?" he asked.

"No, I'm staying in here," I said.

But it wasn't just that day. It was *every day*. Sometimes they would text or call Todd. Sometimes they'd just show up. The doorbell would ring, and when Todd opened the door, three or four girls would be standing on the front porch. "We want to write a note to Taylor. Can we go to her room?" they'd ask.

They almost always came in groups, with the mom who drove escorting them to the door.

"Sure," Todd would say. "You know where it is; go on up."

The mom who drove would stand at the door, awkwardly trying to express her sympathies. Todd would engage her in conversation and make her feel welcome. She'd say something like, "Should I wait or come back later?"

"You can go, if you want. I'm sure they'll text you when they're done," he'd say.

Todd was a kid magnet, and he never wanted them to feel awkward. He stayed away while they were in Taylor's room and tried to make them feel comfortable when they weren't, or while they waited for their moms to pick them up. When they left, they'd hug him, and if I was there, they'd hug me too. He loved it. To me, it was just more beep, beep, beeping at the door and chaos in the house. Their cute little UGG boots, Nike shorts, and talk of volleyball tournaments were more painful reminders of what I'd lost.

❧

A few days later, Kim Dicken came to visit me. Her daughter, Kate, had been best friends with Taylor. Like she had with Emily and Allison Sunshine, Taylor had made a lot of videos with Kate and uploaded them to YouTube. They would lip-synch to their favorite songs, and when people commented about what gifted singers they were, Taylor and Kate would laugh—the truth was they couldn't sing at all.

Like so many of my other good friends, Kim had been helping out. On this particular day, only she and I were in the house. Early in the afternoon, I got up from the bedroom and walked to the kitchen to get some water. About the same time, Kim was walking down the stairs with a basket of dirty laundry. Though I hadn't been in Taylor's room since the accident, I immediately recognized the little basket she kept in her closet.

Kim had gathered up Taylor's dirty laundry—pajamas, Nike shorts, a couple of T-shirts, and volleyball socks. When I saw her come down the stairs with that basket, and I realized what was in it, I was like a two-year-old who didn't have the words to express her anger. I instinctively did the first thing that came to mind, and I slapped the basket out of her hands, knocking the laundry all over the floor. I reached down and picked up Taylor's clothes and started to bawl, and then I threw them down again.

Stunned, Kim hesitated for a second and then reached out and hugged me. She held me while I sat on the floor and cried. I was surprised at how childish I acted. I knew it was stupid, but at the time, it was just one more connection with Taylor I felt was being scrubbed away. When I finished crying and got up, Kim picked up the clothes, put them back in the basket, and went to do the laundry.

☙

My neighbor Trista was our "Grief Fairy." She had a way of sneaking into the house to do what needed to be done, then leaving again without anyone knowing she had been there. One minute I would look up and she was doing my dishes, and then I'd look again and she'd be gone. I would walk through a room, and the next time I was there things had been organized or rearranged. I'd go outside with dirty dishes standing in my sink, and when I came back in they'd be gone. Those were sure signs the Grief Fairy had been there.

One day, while Trista was sitting with me on the back porch, people kept entering and leaving the house. Each time someone went in or out, the alarm would make its annoying beeping sound.

"We've got to do something about that blasted alarm!" Todd said, as annoyed as I was.

Trista jumped up. "Where's your alarm pad?"

Todd showed her, and thirty seconds later she was back. "I fixed it so it won't beep every time you go in and out of the door," she said.

"Are you kidding me?" Todd looked at her incredulously. "Someone should have done that ten years ago!"

That was just like Trista, always there with the right thing at the right moment.

⚬╬⚬

My days were still filled with bouts of uncontrollable sobbing, nausea medication, and long periods of darkness when I disappeared into my thoughts. Days would pass and I barely realized it.

Every morning I woke up lying on my side, and the first breath I took was a good one—free, easy, and peaceful. Then, with a start, I would think, *Taylor isn't here anymore!* I'd try to remember if it was a dream or if it had really happened, and then, quickly, I'd figure it out. *Yes, this happened. Oh, God, help me! This really happened.* That's when I would awaken to the nightmare. In that horrible moment I wanted to die, but I never did. I wanted to swear, and sometimes did. I wanted to scream, and though I don't remember it, they told me I did. Though the uncontrollable screaming had stopped by now, the uncontrollable crying had not. Some days I cried until I nearly hyperventilated. Even on the days that didn't start out that bad, I dreaded everything that was yet to come.

One more day to get through.

I would roll onto my back and place my palms on my forehead. Then grief, wearing work boots, would step up onto my chest. I would be overcome by a crushing feeling. It weighed heavily on my shoulders and chest, and I could feel the weight of it spreading to my arms, legs, feet, and toes. The crushing feeling was a physical sensation I wore every moment I was awake. The weight was so heavy that I began to slouch, my chin dropping toward my chest because I could no longer hold it up. My back ached because of the hours I sat slumped over, huddled in a blanket.

The only thing that relieved the pain—both physical and emotional—was sleep. It was the only time I didn't hurt. From the time I woke up in the morning and took that second breath, I couldn't wait until it was time to take an Ambien and go back to sleep.

I missed Taylor like crazy. She had been taken from me so suddenly that I just wanted to be with her one last time. I wanted to see her, touch her, smell her, and hear her. I wanted my little girl, and I wasn't sure I wanted to live without her.

Every day I woke up, I felt disappointed she was gone and I was still here.

One afternoon, I was having a really bad day and I missed Taylor so much. In addition to the crushing weight on my chest, I felt like my heart had been shredded. The pain was so real and so unbearable that I just couldn't take it a minute longer.

"I have got to find the person who has her heart," I said to Trista, my Grief Fairy.

"Are you serious?" she asked.

"Yes. I just think it would make me feel so much better to hear her heartbeat again."

"Do you know anything about the recipient?"

"All we know is that she is a nurse from Arizona."

I told Trista about the conversation with Donor Alliance back at the hospital in Grand Junction, and how Myrna said we could write letters to the recipients but we had to wait at least six months, and then there was no guarantee they would respond.

"I have to hear her heart again, I just have to," I said. Maybe hearing *her* heart would help to heal *mine*.

— 16 —

Opposing Grief

Todd

I loved having Taylor's friends over to our house. But I also knew their presence pained Tara in ways I couldn't feel or understand. Our mourning paths had first diverged in that meeting with the Donor Alliance representatives in Grand Junction, and they'd only grown wider since.

I was looking for meaning and purpose from Taylor's death, and when I couldn't see it, I wanted to create it. But Tara's grief was unfocused, unpredictable, and uncontrollable—even to her.

Before we married, Tara and I were best friends. Afterward, we became partners in everything. Now it seemed as if I had lost my best friend and my partner. Most days, her grief confined her to the house and often to her bed. She couldn't remember simple things like what day it was or conversations we'd had only hours earlier. Her emotions ranged from anger to profound sadness. She cried uncontrollably and without provocation. People had to remind her to eat, drink, and bathe.

I began to think of her as disabled.

❖

Laura Springer and I met with Jay Praytor, and together the three of us walked the school property where the current garden sat unattended. We decided that somewhere between five and eight thousand dollars was the right amount to spend on the project.

"What can we get for that?" I asked. I hoped maybe some nice beds that would be easy for the kids to maintain, and maybe a long hose from the water source, which was located in the back of the school. That way, they wouldn't have to water the garden by carrying buckets back and forth.

"Let me see what I can work out," Jay said, promising to get back to us with a quote.

A few days later, he was back with elaborate drawings that included stonework, lighting, sidewalks, and underground sprinklers. As he talked Laura and me through the architectural designs created by a professional architect, I could see his enthusiasm building. But I cringed, knowing we didn't have the budget for all the extravagant things he wanted to do. Finally, I couldn't take it any longer.

"Jay, the budget is seven thousand dollars—eight max. We can't do all of this."

With a sparkle in his eye, Jay looked at us and said, "Every single landscaper and company I've talked to wanted to donate something. This is an eighty-thousand-dollar project, and it's basically costing us nothing!"

I was stunned.

"So, when do we get started?" Jay asked, a smile growing on his face.

We decided it would be really nice to dedicate the garden on April 19—Taylor's birthday—but that was less than a month away. "That's a pretty ambitious goal," Jay said. "If we're going to get it done in time, we need to get started immediately." He turned to Laura. "How long will it take to get permission to build and dig on city property?"

"Just get started," Laura said. "I'll ask for forgiveness later."

After that incredible meeting, anytime I drove by the school I would see backhoes chomping the dirt, stonemasons laboring, and landscaping crews sodding, planting, and trimming. They even brought in work lights, and the progress continued well into the night.

⚬

A little more than a week after I spoke to the kids at Coppell Middle School East, a dad of one of Taylor's classmates sent me a beautiful email. In his email, he told me how his daughter had been so touched by the things I'd said that day that she wanted to do something to help.

He was a big supporter of organ donation, and we immediately hit it off. I invited him over to the house, where I learned he was also a website developer. During one of our conversations, I told him how I wanted to direct people to one place on the web where they could learn more about Taylor, be educated about organ donation, and sign up to be an organ donor.

"Would you be willing to help me build a website that did all that?" I asked. He agreed. Soon I had assembled a team of people to create a new online portal. Each night, after Tara and the kids went to bed, one or more team members joined me at the kitchen table or out on the back porch. I'd tell stories about Taylor and together we would work on the design and function of the new website.

"I just want to make something good out of something so bad," I told the team. "Maybe it is just a gift we can leave, maybe it's Taylor's gift," I said, thinking out loud.

"What are we going to call this?" someone asked.

I thought for a moment and said, "What about Taylor's Gift?"

Soon, we were all referring to this thing we were building as "Taylor's Gift Foundation."

Within a few days of the funeral, I was spending hours every day working on something that had the potential to change and save lives. I would stay up until three in the morning talking with friends who agreed to partner with me. And, just like they had the school garden, the community of Coppell embraced the idea.

A law firm offered to help us file the necessary paperwork to become a 501(c)3 tax-exempt organization, so we could receive donations. Friends volunteered their time and expertise. I assembled a team of advisers. Each of these advisers introduced me to new people who wanted to help, and soon I had volunteers with marketing, publicity, legal, social media, and film backgrounds offering to help create not only a foundation and a website but also a documentary that would encourage people to donate their organs.

Taylor's Gift Foundation was a positive thing into which I could channel my energy. It gave me purpose.

⁂

In the past, when one of the kids celebrated a birthday, Tara would wake up early and decorate the kitchen. She'd arrange signs that said "Happy Birthday" and hang crepe paper streamers, banners, and balloons. She wanted to make the day extra special for the birthday boy or girl. She even did it on *my* birthday. It was an expected tradition in our family. But this year when I woke up on March 28, I knew there wouldn't be signs and streamers. No banners or balloons. I didn't want or need any of that, and Tara didn't need any pressure on her to do that sort of thing. Without traditions to navigate my choices, I spent the early morning hours thinking, *It's my birthday, what do I want?* Then the answer came. *I want to be with people.*

I called a friend who lived across the street and asked him if he would bring his fire pit into the cul-de-sac later that evening. "I want to get some people together tonight," I said.

It was a chilly day, and a bunch of friends hanging out together around a fire pit seemed like the perfect way to spend the evening. I composed a text that said, "Come to the cul-de-sac. It's my birthday," and then sent it to some of my closest friends. Immediately, people started texting back, saying they would come. The day was shaping up to be a good one.

I got busy working on things for the foundation and for the memorial garden, and the hours quickly passed. When Tara woke up, I went in and sat on the bed, and explained my plan.

"So, a few hours ago, I invited friends to come over and hang out in the cul-de-sac for my birthday. We'll have a fire pit, and we'll smoke a few cigars . . ."

A shadow crossed Tara's face as I talked.

"About forty guys have already said that they're coming," I said excitedly. "I guess the word got out."

"I cannot believe you're doing this," Tara said through clenched teeth.

"What? Inviting some guys over for my birthday?"

"It's like you think nothing's happened. And now you're throwing a party?" she said, raising her voice. I could tell she was mad.

I got up from the bed, walked to the door, and closed it. I didn't want the kids to hear us fighting. I turned back, looked her in the eyes, and said, "How *dare* you think I'm acting normal! How *dare* you think I'm not suffering! I'm trying so hard just to get through the day!" I could feel the blood pulsing in my head, and I knew my face was red with anger.

What was she thinking?

"If it hadn't been for me, the visitation, the funeral, the funeral plot, none of it would have been done! I'm the one spending hours a day trying to create a memorial garden for Taylor while you're sleeping. I'm working day and night on a website so more lives will be saved through Taylor's story. I'm the one trying to make something good come out of the pain! And yet, you have the audacity to say I'm acting like *nothing happened*?"

It wasn't like I was having a huge party with cake and balloons. It was barely a celebration. I just wanted to hang out with a few friends on my birthday. Why shouldn't I? Tara was the one lying in bed crippled by grief; should I be crippled too? *I deserved this.*

151

"Just let me have it; it's what I need," I added, and quickly left the bedroom before I could say something I'd later regret.

∞

A chill filled the night air. We all wore jackets and tried to stand as close to the fire pit as possible. All my buddies came. My dad was there, along with Tara's dad, Bernie, some of my brothers-in-law, and a number of my neighbors. When we were all assembled, I looked to my friend John Lookabaugh and said, "Would you say a prayer to bless this evening and get it started?" John and I have been friends for a long time. Not only do we share a faith in God, but we also share the same sense of humor. He prayed a beautiful prayer, and I was thankful he was there. After he finished praying, he offhandedly made a remark. I don't recall what it was, but for some reason, I found it hysterical. I doubled over in laughter.

It was the first laugh of the night, but it was also my first laugh since Taylor's accident. I wasn't sure how I felt about that. Things still weren't right between Tara and me. I tried to put it out of my mind. I just wanted to be present for the guys, but it was hard.

About midway through the evening, Ryan came running out.

"Dad, Dad!" he said, trying to get my attention. I turned to look at him. "You have to come; we've got to show you something."

I excused myself from the guys and followed Ryan into the house. Tara and Peyton were sitting on the couch in the family room and looking out the back window. The backyard looked dark. Other than the full moon, I couldn't make out much else. "Look!" Ryan said excitedly, pointing out the window. "Isn't it cool?"

"What are you looking at?"

"There's a cross around the moon!"

I looked harder and there it was—a full moon with a radiating light coming from behind it. The brilliant beams of light formed the shape of a glowing *cross*.

"Ah," I said.

"Grab a camera," Tara said.

152

The kids were excited, Tara was excited, and I was too. The cross felt like a sign. I missed my daughter, I'd fought with my wife, and it hadn't been much of a birthday. Yet, God wanted to remind me of His love for me—for all of us—and He had decorated the moon to do it.

After we took pictures, I kissed Tara and told her I was going back outside. "I hope that's okay with you," I said.

"Go," she said. I knew it wasn't what she wanted, but she was willing to let me go. Besides, neither one of us had the energy required to be upset with the other. I went back to the fire pit, and with the moon watching over all of us, I felt free to enjoy myself. I did my best to lose myself in the moment. I talked, told stories, and laughed at other people's stories. Everyone had a great time, and it was nearly 2:00 a.m. before they all went home.

I helped the neighbor pull his fire pit around back before returning home. Tara and the kids had been sleeping for hours. I climbed in bed and wrapped my arms around my sleeping wife, and fell asleep remembering how good it had felt to have fun.

⁂

Soon after my birthday, someone introduced us to Randy and Pam Cope. They'd lost their son, Jantsen, to an undiagnosed heart condition when he was fifteen. They were the first people we knew who had also lost a child. They invited us to their home, and they quickly became friends, confidantes, and a source of inspiration to us.

At that first meeting, we were sitting on their couch when Pam said, "You were handpicked—chosen—for this burden."

I could immediately see Tara didn't like that thought, but it aligned with my thinking. *Was there a purpose in Taylor's death? In our grief? Was this all, in some way, a part of God's plan?*

A few visits later, Randy and I went outside for a walk to give the women some privacy. I told him how difficult it was to watch Tara crying all the time, unable to get out of bed.

"It's okay that you don't want to see her sadness," Randy said. "And it's okay when she's sad and you're not. It's even fine to be mad at her because she's sad; just don't act on it. Don't do anything that would drive a wedge into your relationship."

Pam and Randy gave us permission to grieve separately and differently. Randy taught me how to accept Tara's sadness and her need to sleep away the days. Pam told Tara it was okay if I wanted to laugh, get lost in my work, or go outside and hang out with friends. We each needed what we needed. We didn't have to like it, but we had to respect it.

Finally, someone had given us a plan for our grief—something we could follow. It was the best advice we'd ever been given.

It saved our marriage.

— 17 —

Purpose in the Pain

Tara

I hated waking up.

It was a few weeks after Taylor's funeral, but each time I woke up, it started all over again. Every day, I relived the horror that Taylor was gone.

As soon as the kids got off to school, I'd take an antianxiety pill, and it would knock me out for four hours. If I went back to bed by eight, I wouldn't wake up until noon. Someone would force me to eat lunch, and afterward I'd go back to bed. When the kids were home from school, I'd fight through the fog and exhaustion to do my best as a parent. But it was obvious to everyone—everyone but me—I wasn't doing it well.

One day, Beth Sunshine planned to stop by for a visit. Since she lived in Plano, a thirty-minute drive from us, it was a special treat. I hadn't seen her in a while, and I was looking forward to talking with her. Beth knew me better than probably anyone except Todd, and I wanted to share a few things and get her feedback.

As soon as she walked in the door, I hugged her. "I've got so much I need to talk about."

Peyton was sitting in a chair coloring. When I led Beth past the family room, Peyton spoke up. "Mommy, come watch me color."

"Baby, I'm going to talk to Aunt Beth right now," I said.

"Please come see me color," she protested. Her coloring book was spread open on her lap and crayons littered both arms of the chair.

"Sweetie, I'm going to talk to Aunt Beth. It's been a while since I've seen her." I was already tearing up. I'd waited all day for Beth to get there, and I desperately needed her to listen while I unloaded.

I opened the back door to the patio, and Peyton said, "Mommy, you don't even see me." She didn't look up or wait for my reaction. She just kept coloring.

I took a deep breath. Peyton was right; I hadn't been there for her.

I knew the dynamics in the house had shifted. Peyton and Ryan used to get along, but I'd come to realize it was because Taylor helped keep the peace. Without Taylor to stop the bickering, their squabbles rose to new levels—both kids had been sniping at each other and picking fights. They didn't have to tell me it was because they were afraid of losing another sibling; I understood. The spats were a way to protect themselves from another potential loss.

Other changes occurred too. The first few days they were home, they slept on the floor in our room. They were now afraid to sleep upstairs in their own bedrooms. When it became obvious they weren't going to leave, someone loaned us an air mattress. Now, our bedroom had become theirs. At night, they wouldn't even go to bed unless I went with them, which meant I had to go to bed around eight o'clock. While they would quickly fall asleep, I couldn't. If I attempted to leave, they would hear me and get upset. They wanted me there beside them. So I lay on the bed, with them next to me on the floor, and prayed. Then I would text on my phone as I counted down the minutes until I could take my Ambien.

Standing behind her chair, I watched as Peyton put down one crayon and chose another. During the day, everyone who came to the house wanted a piece of me and a piece of Todd. Ryan and Peyton got pushed to the side. *I've got to be present for her*, I thought. *She's fearful of losing me too.* I glanced at Beth, and she motioned for me to go talk to Peyton. I knelt down in front of my daughter's chair, so I could look her square in the eye and really see her. "What do you want me to do, Peyton?"

"I want you to watch me color," she said. Then she quickly changed her mind. "Will you take me to the park?"

The park? I didn't feel like going to the park. The short walk would require more energy than I was capable of, but what choice did I have?

"I'll wait here," Beth said.

I grabbed a hat and Peyton's hand, and we walked to the park. It was the longest walk of my life.

She talked the entire way. I didn't say two words. She was ebullient, skipping and tugging on my arm, trying to get me to bounce along with her. All I could manage was to shuffle alongside her. I had concrete blocks for feet and a cement cape wrapped around my shoulders. Each step was slow and painful.

When we neared the park and I caught a glimpse of the distant duck pond, I knew I'd blown it. "I didn't bring any bread," I said. "I'm sorry, I forgot."

"Oh, Mommy!" Peyton said. "That's the reason we came!"

Every time we went to the park, we went to feed the ducks and we always took bread. "I'm so sorry, baby. As soon as we get there, I'll just call home and have someone bring it." I knew I couldn't make it home and back to the park again in the same day, let alone the same hour. Someone would have to help me out.

I mentally kicked myself for being so stupid. Nothing seemed right in my life. My memory was screwed up and my concept of time was completely missing. Even the simplest habits in my life— like bringing bread to the park—were messed up.

We walked up the path to the pond, and Peyton let go of my hand and skipped on ahead. I suddenly stopped short. Peyton chatted away about nothing, until she noticed that I'd stopped. She turned back to see why I'd stopped.

"What?" she asked when she saw my face.

"Look!" I said, pointing to an area just off the sidewalk.

There in the grass, someone had mowed a perfect cross, and the cross was littered with bread crumbs. They weren't mowed in and they weren't dirty; to my amazement, they had been freshly sprinkled over the grass cross. To me, it was duck manna from heaven. Tears welled in my eyes as Peyton and I picked up handfuls of the fresh crumbs. *Someone had brought bread crumbs.* That someone had left a trail of bread crumbs to the cross. It was a reminder for me that, in the midst of my mess and my pain, *Someone* saw me and loved me.

⇛

My brother Bill's wife, Sandi, was at the house one day helping me sort through a pile of cards we'd received. We were busy opening hundreds of envelopes and sorting them into piles when Sandi stopped and said, "Is this a joke?"

"What are you talking about?"

She handed me a card that didn't look anything like the muted pastel cards with flowers and flowing Scriptures that we'd been opening for the past twenty minutes. This one was square shaped and bright yellow. Dancing girls were lined up on the front. I opened the card and read, "Have you planted your tomato plant? Waiting for your call, so you can get your ten points."

I looked at Sandi. "I have no idea what this is. Who is it from? I don't get it." The envelopes had already been separated from the cards, and there was no way to match it. The next day Sandi came back and we started again. As we neared the bottom of the pile, I opened a card from Angie. It wasn't a sympathy card. It was the kind of card you send a good friend when you share an inside joke about something stupid. But Angie and I weren't that close. Her daughter had played volleyball with Taylor, so we saw each other a lot. We were friendly, but we weren't good friends.

I looked at the card in my hand. Under the preprinted message, she'd included a handwritten note: "Plant a tomato plant, call me, and you'll get ten points."

"I know who sent that card you found yesterday," I said to Sandi. "Apparently, it was the second one. Here's the first," I said, handing it to her.

Sandi looked baffled. "I still don't get it," she said after reading it.

"I think she's trying to get me to do stuff, to get over my sadness," I said. "And it kind of ticks me off. Who does she think she is?"

⋇

Randy and Pam Cope were becoming good friends. They had given us lots of solid advice, and I had great respect for Pam. Though I didn't like her saying we'd been "handpicked" for this, I liked *her*. She was the only person I knew who'd experienced what I was going through.

Pam started coming by the house, and if she thought I needed to talk, she'd ask me to take a car ride with her. Sometimes, we'd go to the park and she'd pull into a parking space. She'd turn off the car, look directly at me, and say, "Okay, talk to me." I appreciated our time together because I knew she would understand things no one else did. The next time we were alone in her car, I told her about the cards I'd gotten from Angie.

"I got another one yesterday," I said, fuming. "It said, 'Have you planted your tomato plant yet? Waiting for ten points. Your next challenge is to get a pedicure. If you do that, you'll get twenty points.'" I pounded my fists onto my pajama-clad thighs and said, "Who does she think she is? How dare she challenge me!"

Pam listened with a smirk on her face and then tried to stifle a giggle. When I exploded, she couldn't hold it back any longer, and she roared with laughter. When she got hold of herself, she simply said, "What do you know? That's really creative!"

I was dumbfounded by her response. She was supposed to know better than anyone why that was so thoughtless. "I am not planting any stupid tomatoes, Pam! I'm not. I'm constantly in my pajamas. I'm barely out of bed. I'm not doing that."

A few days later, I was sitting on the back porch when Pam walked out with a large green pot. Inside was a bag of soil, a watering can, fertilizer, and a hand tool. "C'mon," she said, handing me the trowel, "we're planting this darn tomato plant."

Later, I texted Angie and said, "Got ten points."

And that was the beginning. Over the next few months, lots of cards followed—at least one a week. Angie encouraged me to earn points for taking showers and getting a pedicure, and she even gave me a book on sex and romance, with the opportunity to earn bonus points.

Some of her challenges were easy, while others were hard and I'd have to work up to them. Her challenge for the first week of May was to go to a museum. I still wasn't showering, and I couldn't control my sobbing. How was I supposed to go to a museum? Before I could figure it out, another card arrived with a new challenge to go downtown, take a ride on the trolley, and stop at Sprinkles Cupcakes. The thought was entirely overwhelming. But it coincided with another overwhelming day.

I handed the card to Todd and said, "Here's what I want to do for Mother's Day." I knew the day would be hard, and I knew I needed to spend it with Ryan and Peyton doing something that wouldn't flood me with memories of past Mother's Days. So that's what I did on my first Mother's Day without Taylor. I visited a museum with my family, we rode a trolley, we ate Sprinkles Cupcakes, and I earned thirty more points.

I never knew what the points were for; it could have been an ice cream cone for all I knew. But the challenges got me moving again and they helped me find my smile.

◦⟊◦

I was sitting in my usual spot in my chair in the backyard, a blanket wrapped around my shoulders, staring off vacantly into the distance, when my friend Gayle walked out of the house. She handed me a box. I opened the gift, expecting it to be a blanket or maybe a book. I'd gotten a lot of those recently. But instead, there was a plate inside. On the plate was hand-painted Taylor's "I Am" poem.

I remembered Taylor writing the poem. It was due the Monday before we left on spring break. At the time, it was just another piece of homework. The assignment was to create an autobiographical website, and the poem was just one element among many. We first saw the poem shortly before the funeral, when her language arts teacher emailed us the password to Taylor's website so we could decide what to do with it.

Since then, Todd had read it at the funeral and to the kids at school during lunch. It had taken on a life of its own, spawning "I Am Taylor" videos of her friends reading it on YouTube. With tears in my eyes, I thanked Gayle for her thoughtful gift. Later, I found a special spot to display the plate in our kitchen.

⋄

"Tara, listen to this," Todd said one day. He'd been holed up in his office, and I knew he was working on something related to the website or the foundation. "I was doing some research on organ donation, and I just downloaded the annual report from Donate Life, and it says that only 37 percent of Americans are registered donors."

"That's not very high," I said.

"But listen to this: Texas is the second lowest state, with only 2 percent registered! That isn't right! We can do something about that."

"How?"

"I don't know, but I'm going to figure it out," Todd said. Though it was a huge issue, I knew Todd well enough to know that if he got his mind around it, he'd figure out a way.

A few days later, Todd came to me with a request. "Look, I know you don't like doing interviews, but WFAA has been wanting to do a follow-up piece to see how we're doing, and I've been holding them off," Todd said. "But in light of the low number of organ donors registered in Texas, I think telling our story could help more people register."

Though it had been weeks since the funeral, and the foundation was only getting started, there still seemed to be a lot of interest in Taylor's story and our desire to promote organ donation. The media continued to call, and it wasn't unusual for Todd to do a radio, newspaper, or occasional TV interview. Though he wanted me to be a part of them, I mostly stayed away. However, in light of the statistics he'd recently shown me, I now felt differently.

"I think we should do it," I agreed.

Cynthia personally picked the reporter who would interview us. His name was Gary Reaves, and we immediately liked him. We were seated in the dining room when Gary noticed the plate Gayle had made. He asked about it, and we told him the story behind the poem.

"Can you read it out loud?" he asked.

I picked up the plate without thinking and began to read it. Certain lines jumped out at me, like I was hearing them for the first time: "I wonder how long forever is . . . I want to touch people's lives. . . ." *If she only knew how many lives she's touched and is continuing to touch*, I thought. "I cry at the thought of losing a member of my family." *I wonder if she knows how many tears we've shed for her.* By the time I finished, I was crying. The only good thing to come out of Taylor's death was the lives she touched—some through inspiration, but five through direct organ donation. Though I didn't like it, I was starting to see a purpose in our pain, and it was a purpose she'd written about in her poem.

During the interview I said to Gary, "I can't wait until I can hug the person who has her heart." It was the one hope I'd clung to—the hope that I would one day hear her heartbeat again this side of heaven.

The interview ended, and as we said goodbye to Gary and the crew, I realized that if we really wanted to promote organ donation, there would be more interviews in the future just like this one.

Oh, God, if this is what You want for us, if there is some purpose in Taylor's death for us, I need a sign. And I need You; I can't do this on my own.

—18—

Looking for Confirmation

Todd

I'm a light switch guy. I'm either on, or I'm off. When I read about the low number of registered organ donors in Texas, something in me clicked on. It infuriated me and made me resolve to work harder to get Taylor's story out there. The foundation was the mechanism to make that happen, and I truly believed we could get the needle to move higher than 2 percent.

Things were already happening. The website was up and volunteers were working in several areas. A documentary producer and crew were in place, and they were beginning their initial interviews of people who would tell Taylor's story.

Not only were my days filled with the details of the upcoming garden dedication but I was also having numerous conversations regarding the foundation's evolving mission and vision, associated website photos and graphics, and the educational strategy for organ donation. While I tried to include Tara in these conversations, she couldn't participate in long drawn-out discussions; she didn't have the focus. But she helped to make simple choices, like deciding between two fonts for the website. I wanted to include her but not overwhelm her.

❖

On April 19, a month and four days after we lost Taylor, we celebrated her birthday by dedicating the newly completed garden at her school. It was unbelievable how much work Jay, his team of professionals, and the community volunteers had gotten done so quickly.

Hundreds of people turned out. It reminded me of the visitation, except this time everyone was wearing Tiffany blue (the color of Taylor's eyes) T-shirts. Taylor's friends had designed them, and everyone who came wore them—students, teachers, neighbors, volunteers, and the community at large. The crowd looked like a sea of blue, with swelling waves of purple balloons. The guests sat on the freshly mowed grass. Several people spoke, including two of Taylor's friends, Father Alfonse, and Principal Laura Springer.

I planned to speak and I looked forward to it. When I spoke in front of the kids, it energized me and fed my soul. I had no expectation that Tara or the kids would get up too; I was just pleased that Tara had come. But when I stood up, Tara, Ryan, and Peyton all stood too. They wanted to stand alongside me. As I spoke, I thanked those who had made it happen and encouraged the kids to make this garden their own. In many ways, they already had—students had painted the stones lining the garden with their original artwork. Though the space started out as a way to honor Taylor, it had truly become a community park.

The ceremony ended with tearful voices singing "Happy Birthday" to Taylor.

After the ceremony, I spoke to some parents. Out of the corner of my eye, I could see a girl waiting to talk to me. I didn't remember meeting her before, but I could tell something was troubling her; tears were streaming down her cheeks.

"Hi, I'm Mr. Storch," I said.

She started to talk, then sob. I could barely make out what she said.

"When my mom died, Taylor was the only friend who ever asked how I was."

"Oh, sweetie," I said, hugging her. I calmed her down, and she told me the whole story. Her mother had been in a car accident. People asked about the accident, and they asked about her mom, but Taylor had asked about *her*. She told me how Taylor made a point to stop every day and ask how she was. Taylor texted and sent her notes.

Through her tears, she said, "You have no idea how much that meant to me."

That young lady had no idea what her story meant to *me*. It was one of the first times since Taylor's death that I'd heard a story about my daughter that I didn't already know. Learning about this beautiful thing my child had done was amazing. If the garden never served another purpose, to me it was worth creating just to hear that one story.

⚭

It had been more than a month since Taylor's death—and since I had last been to work. I had an amazing job at the Center for Sales Strategy helping media companies develop their digital initiatives. Until we lost Taylor, I'd loved my work. But going back would be hard. If I was having a bad day, I didn't have the kind of job where I could hide in a cubicle pretending to answer email while crying inside. In my job, I had to fully engage one on one with clients, give presentations for as many as sixty people at a time, and lead team meetings. I didn't work out of an office; I worked at my clients' offices. There was no place to hide and no way to fake my emotional state.

Jim Hopes was the chief executive officer, but I reported to John Henley, the chief operating officer. Both were really great guys to work for. Though John was technically my boss, a better description would be to call him a dear friend or a brother in Christ. When we were in Grand Junction, John was one of the first people I called. We had several deep conversations as I told him what was happening with Taylor, and many times he prayed with me over the phone.

John and I hadn't yet talked about my starting back up, but I knew it probably would be soon. I wasn't sure how, or even if, I could return to work. I certainly couldn't travel. Tara was still deeply grieving. In my absence, she couldn't take care of herself, let alone the kids.

With my mind preoccupied with thoughts of the future, I needed to keep my hands busy. Tara had planted some tomato plants, and I started fertilizing them. Then I bought more dirt and planted rosemary and mint. I found some larger pots and carefully re-planted the tender tomato shoots. Each day, I'd water them and check for new growth. My time with the plants became a kind of therapy. While I was outside tending to them, I would think and pray. Sometimes I cried, and often I cried out to God.

What is it that You want me to do? What is Your plan for my life? How am I supposed to serve You in the midst of all this?

When Tara was awake, she spent a lot of time outdoors, and she would watch me work in the yard. One day, I sat down next to her and said, "I feel as if there is something more for me. I feel like I need to quit my job and be the executive director of the foundation."

Tara and I weren't talking much at this time, which, in hindsight, was a good thing. Instead of asking for her advice, I had been seeking God and praying harder than ever. While I knew my words came as a surprise, she listened as I explained my thoughts and prayers. More than anything I wanted to follow God's will. "So, I am waiting. I'm waiting to see what God is doing," I said.

⚬⃟

Grieving people are hard to be around. Grief can get ugly. It's messy. Some people don't want any part of it. Others choose to get involved. They enter your story without concern as to the sacrifices they'll have to make to love you. Father Alfonse was one of those people. He left our house late the night of the funeral, but he came back. And he came back often.

Father Alfonse was only a couple of years older than Tara and me, but he was experienced in life's mountains and valleys. He understood faith issues, not only from his priestly duties but also from walking with families through God's Word as it met up with the messiness of their lives. I didn't know why he took Tara and me on, but we were glad he did.

Since the funeral, we'd see him at least once a week, sometimes more. He'd come over to visit and hang out with Tara and me at night. Sometimes we'd call and see if he wanted to have dinner with us; other times I'd meet him for coffee. He and I would spend hours discussing suffering and grief. Occasionally, Tara would text him questions about God or just let him know how we were. He became a sounding board as we tried to figure out God's plan for our lives.

Father Alfonse encouraged me to read about Christ's suffering on the cross so I could understand my own pain. That led me to read about other people who had suffered. I began to pray and read my Bible more, something I had never done regularly. I felt the need to get up early in the morning and spend time reading and praying before I officially started my day. Often, I returned to the Scriptures late at night as I searched for purpose in my own life. Father Alfonse encouraged me, answered my questions, and comforted me as I tried to find meaning in my suffering.

I wanted to make something good come from Taylor's death. As a consultant, I often came up with solutions for my clients. That was my first instinct—to *do*. To create. To write a report. To research it to death. To fix it. But instead, a very different feeling now washed over me—God was doing something. I needed to wait on Him to see what it was.

Part of me wanted to go to work to escape my life at home. But I was also scared. I knew the statistics of how many couples got divorced after they lost a child. I'd stood by helplessly as my own parents divorced, so that also fueled my thoughts. I wanted the best for my kids, and that meant being home with them.

Then there was the foundation. We were getting ready to file paperwork for a business license and our tax-exempt status. It was time to decide whether I was all in or not. It wasn't an intellectual decision; it was a spiritual one. In the past, I wouldn't have waited for God; I would only have waited for Him to catch up with me. This time, I didn't want to get in the way of what *He* was doing. So I waited on Him.

⚬⁘⚬

Each day, I heard new stories of how our work was affecting people. Instead of stagnating, things seemed to be growing. Nearly every day, God brought a new volunteer to join me in our work. These weren't just idle people looking for something to do. These were gifted professionals with busy careers. If I had an unlimited budget, these were the people I would have gone out and hired. Instead, I randomly met them at a Starbucks, was introduced to them by a mutual friend, or they contacted me after hearing our story. Each one was a gift from God and filled a much-needed spot on my advisory team.

At times, I'd be so busy working with or talking to my advisers that I'd go a few days without talking to friends or neighbors. Inevitably, one of them would say something like, "Tell me what's happening with the foundation," or, "Catch me up since the last time we talked."

I'd honestly have to say, "I can't. I literally can't. Dude, you miss a day, you miss a year. Things are happening that fast."

I was working closely with a few key people who had volunteered their time and talents to work alongside me at a dizzying pace. Even they felt it. Pauline, one of my advisers in my innermost circle, would call in the morning and then again late in the afternoon.

"It's been six hours since we last talked. Catch me up," she'd say.

She knew from experience that even in that short time span things were popping. And some of those things were likely to be big—interview requests, offers of introductions to experts who could help, or opportunities for new fund-raisers.

Each day, amazing new opportunities presented themselves. The documentary crew was working hard and connections were opening up. The website was receiving hits from around the world.

One afternoon, I picked up the phone. It was a representative from Donate Life who'd heard about our work. "We'd love it if you would come to our banquet in June. We'd like you to present an award to the producers of *Grey's Anatomy* for a show they did about organ donation."

"I'd love to!" I said. "But I need to ask my wife."

I wasn't sure how Tara would feel about traveling. It would mean flying to California and leaving the kids at home. Taking Tara on a trip to Hollywood was unimaginable when a trip to the living room was still a big deal for her.

I waited for the right moment to talk to her. I anticipated her reply, knowing it was a lot to ask. "It's okay if you want to say no. I understand," I said. But to my surprise, she agreed.

"It would be good for the foundation and another way to honor Taylor," she said.

This was a defining moment for her, and one that only God could have orchestrated. *Thank you!* I prayed, both for the opportunity and for Tara agreeing to go.

ം⸎ം

Too many things were happening for me to ignore God's direction. Everything seemed to be pointing toward my leaving my job and working for the foundation. At the same time, I realized how dumb it sounded to give up my job. I worried that Tara would think it was a stupid idea when I told her. But I had to. I couldn't shake the feeling that this is what God wanted.

A few nights later, my opportunity arose. We were out on the back porch, sitting side by side and staring at the stars. I told her about the incredible things occurring with the foundation. In passing, I mentioned that John Henley, my friend and boss, would be in town the next week and that we needed to talk.

"I feel there is a higher purpose for me than my job. I can't imagine going back to my company and leaving y'all," I said, trying to hold back tears.

"So, what do you want to do?"

"It's been wearing on me, but I think I want to quit my job. I could work at the foundation full-time. I don't know if it is stupid or not, but I feel my attention needs to be on it and our family."

I knew this was hard for her to hear. For one thing, I couldn't answer any of her questions—like how we'd survive financially. I wiped my eyes with the back of my hands, but the tears were flowing too fast.

"I *need* to make a difference. When I see Taylor again, I want her to say, 'Good job, Daddy! You did it!'"

This was the first time I'd been so vulnerable with Tara, and I was nervous. I wasn't sure if she would cry, scream, yell, or just stare at me. But she did none of those things.

"If this is what you need to do, I'll absolutely support you," she said.

She told me she could see how much this decision had been weighing on me, and gave me a long hug.

"You've changed," she said, her warm cheek pressed against mine. "In the past, you would have made a decision and followed up on it, but now it's as if you're waiting for something," she said.

That night, we discussed all the what-ifs. I didn't have many answers except to say I was trusting God to do it. If He called me, He would equip me.

"I agree. He will take care of us," Tara said. "And you've always taken care of us. Honestly, though, it scares me a little bit."

I didn't say anything out loud, but I thought, *It scares me too.*

❖

I sought my closest friends' and foundation advisers' counsel at a breakfast meeting soon after I talked with Tara. I told them what I'd been thinking and praying about. "I give you full authority to tell me I am just a grief-stricken dad or I'm going to bankrupt my family. Tell me it's a dumb idea. Whatever you need to say, please say it."

I wanted them to talk me out of it.

In the end, nearly everyone I sought advice from thought this was something I needed to do. That God was calling me to do it. They cautioned me, they gave me advice, but they didn't say, "I don't think you should do this."

With the leading of God, the approval of my wife, and the encouragement of friends, the old Todd would have put together a financial strategy and plan for how I could quit my job and work full-time for the foundation. Numerous opportunities had presented themselves. All I needed was a strategic plan to know which ones to go after first, and then I would be off and running.

But *I* wasn't doing this. God was. So I did something completely out of character: I waited on God for a confirmation that this was what He wanted. If this was to be, I needed Him to confirm it.

—19—

Showers of Emotion

Tara

Before we lost Taylor, taking a bath or hot shower was my favorite way to relax and get away from it all. But while I was mourning, the shower wasn't a place to relax; it was a place to escape the world and to cry.

One night, after the kids had fallen asleep on the air mattress in my room, I couldn't stay in bed any longer. Sorrow overwhelmed me, and I deeply missed Taylor. I went in and turned on the shower so the water could wash away my tears and drown out the sounds of my sobs. Under the hottest water I could tolerate, I just stood and bawled. My nose was running, my head ached, and it was difficult to breathe. I couldn't breathe deeply, so I breathed faster, which caused my chest to constrict and resulted in a stabbing feeling every time I inhaled. I tried to get a grip, but sobs wracked my body. I was too overcome by grief to even wash my hair.

I can't recall ever feeling so alone.

So very alone.

It was close to bedtime, and that meant sleep. I welcomed sleep, but I couldn't stand the thought of waking up the next morning and reliving the pain all over again. I stood in the shower and silently begged, *Oh, God, please take this pain away. It feels like it will never stop. I miss Taylor so much, and I can't stand the hurt anymore. I would rather be there with You and her than down here, living with all of this pain.*

A fleeting thought raced through my mind. *What if I didn't have to wake up in the morning? I have a bottle of Ambien on the nightstand. How easy would that be? One swallow and the pain disappears.*

I suddenly understood why people chose that option. *It makes complete sense. This could be over. The pain would be completely gone, and I wouldn't have to deal with this anymore.* Instantly, I felt released from the pain. I felt happy and empowered. Just thinking about it energized me. I quickly got out of the shower, and as I dried off, I thought, *This is how it can all be over!* The weight on my chest lifted, and I felt lighter than I had since the hospital. I couldn't wait.

As I walked to my dresser and pulled out a clean pair of pajamas, my brother Bill came to mind. I remembered him sitting me down and saying, "If you ever feel like you want to take your life, and you think you might act on it, you'd better call me."

I put on my pajamas and snuggled into bed. The kids were asleep, and Todd was in his office reading or working. I picked up the Ambien bottle and looked at it, thinking. My phone was also on the nightstand, so I kept my promise and I texted Bill, "Are you there?"

I fingered the bottle while I waited for Bill to respond. But time went by and I didn't hear from him. I didn't care; I felt good knowing the pain would soon end. While I continued to wait for Bill, I texted Father Alfonse. "Are you awake?"

"Yes, what's up?"

"I need to talk to you about something, but this is between you and me."

"Of course."

Our five-piece puzzle of a family fit together perfectly as these pictures from Florida show.

We loved hanging out together . . . and when we were all together we could be really silly!

The Sunshines are like our extended family, and New Year's together as the "Suntorch" family is a tradition.

Taylor always included Peyton in her life, on big occasions and small ones.

Taylor cherished her relationship with Ryan and Peyton.

Sometimes it is the ordinary moments like this one of Taylor and Ryan that we miss the most.

Taylor challenged herself to try new things—like cheerleading—even when she felt awkward. She knew that smiling and laughing at herself always made it better!

Volleyball was a big part of Taylor's life—and became a big part of ours.

Laura Springer, Taylor's principal, with Taylor in 2009. Springer continues to look out for Ryan and Peyton.

Taylor never lost the opportunity to be a ham and make the most of a camera.

Taken on the slopes on the first day of our vacation, this photo became one of the hardest to look at in the months to come.

Bill is so important to us, and his presence in the days after the accident was a gift.

We looked out at a sea of blue, one of Taylor's favorite colors, when the memorial garden was dedicated on Taylor's fourteenth birthday. Now it serves as a beautiful gathering place for students.

It seemed whenever we didn't think we could make it one more moment, God would send an image to remind us He had not forgotten us. This image was not possible under normal circumstances at that time of day.

When we forgot bread crumbs on a walk to the park after Taylor died, God did not—even placing them within the sign of a cross.

We were nervous to meet our first recipient of Taylor's gifts, Jeff Kartus, who received Taylor's kidney and pancreas. Yet a day with Jeff, his wife Vanessa, and daughter Brooke made us realize—it was our privilege to make a decision that gave life.

Ana Lucia Cottone is a gift to us; her loving yet outspoken approach helped our family regain its footing.

A search for the perfect dress for a foundation event became one more place God confirmed His presence in our lives. This label was an answer to Tara's quick prayer.

Before receiving Taylor's kidney, Jonathan spent four hours a day on dialysis; now he lives a physically active life and has become a vital volunteer for the foundation.

When Ashley received Taylor's cornea, it not only improved her vision but also finally relieved years of intense daily pain.

One year earlier, Taylor wrote in her "I Am" poem, "*I want to be on the Ellen DeGeneres Show.*" Now she was.

Photo Credit: Michael Rozman/Warner Bros.

Patricia watched Peyton's face as she lifted the stethoscope up to her chest. As soon as Peyton heard Taylor's heartbeat, she looked up at Patricia. I was so thankful to capture the moment of their connection on my camera.

Meeting Patricia Winters—and hearing Taylor's heart—became the most significant step forward in our healing, and in our motivation to share Taylor's story.

Photo Credit: J. Ann Photography

We're so proud of Ryan and Peyton, who are now both in middle school. They were our inspiration to keep going during our darkest days. (For more photos, visit TaylorsGift.org.)

Photo Credit: Denise Stivers

I took a deep breath and then decided to go for it. "I've got a plan," I texted. "The pain is too much, and I can't do this anymore."

"Are you saying what I think you're saying?"

"I would much rather be with her than be here." While I waited for his response, I set the phone down and took the lid off the bottle so I could count the pills. His text arrived before I could finish the count.

"What makes you think if you did that, you would see her?"

I hadn't thought about that. I'd never thought about something like that before, because I'd never, ever gone down that path. *How does God feel about that? Would He turn me away?*

Before I could respond, more texts came in from him. "What makes you think that if you did it, God would welcome you with open arms?" Then, "How selfish of you to leave Ryan and Peyton like this!"

Suddenly, the idea was more complicated than it had seemed a few minutes earlier. I thought about my response and was just getting ready to text him back when he sent me a real zinger. "Do you really think Taylor would be proud of you?"

His words took my breath away. I knew for a fact she wouldn't be happy with me. *She would never be proud of me if I did that.*

It was my lowest moment ever. But through his texts, Father Alfonse helped me realize it was because I was focusing on myself—on my own pain. I'd never looked at it from Taylor's perspective. I hadn't considered her reaction at all. Neither had I thought about what it would do to Peyton and Ryan.

I certainly hadn't thought about what God would think.

I put the cap back on the bottle and set in on the nightstand. I knew then I could never do it. Ever. Father Alfonse was right. I *was* being selfish. We texted back and forth a few more times. He made me promise I wouldn't do anything.

"I promise I won't," I texted back. I meant it.

❧

My brother Kary was at the house one day, and he asked if Todd and I were seeing a counselor. We weren't. Todd had seen one a few years earlier to deal with his parents' divorce and some depression he had in the past, but I didn't believe in counseling. Counselors were for weak people with problems. That wasn't me. I was just sad, and I had every reason to feel sad.

"You might want to give this woman a try," Kary said. "Her name is Judy, and she lost her son four years ago."

I didn't want to go. I'd already lost too much control in my life. The last thing I wanted was someone else telling me what to do, how to act, and what to feel. But after much urging from friends and family, and cajoling from Todd, I finally agreed.

Our first two appointments were rough. We were supposed to go back again for a third appointment, but we couldn't find a date and time that worked for both of us to go together. Out of necessity, we went separately. And we both kept going separately. It was one of the best decisions we ever made for our marriage. Judy helped us individually understand our grief—why I wanted to sleep, and why Todd wanted to work—and how those choices played out in the context of our marriage. Like Pam and Randy Cope, she told us it was okay if our grief wasn't the same, but she also taught us how to deal with our feelings about our spouse's grief.

Counseling was hard work, but it was also very helpful. Some days I would just roll out of bed, take the kids to school, and then drive to Dallas in my pajamas for my 10:30 a.m. appointment. I would sit on her couch with my wild, uncombed hair, crying while we talked. She became a lifeline for me. Because she saw Todd and me individually, she knew what was going on with the other person and could use that knowledge effectively to help each of us. As our relationship grew, I realized that counseling wasn't for weak people—it was for strong people who wanted to get stronger. I looked forward to our visits each week. Judy and I were a lot alike, with the same sense of humor. If we had met before all of this happened, I think we would have been good friends.

❧

My new life looked drastically different from my old life. Before we lost Taylor, I was the center of the hive and life was always buzzing around me. If the kids needed rides, I picked them up or took them, or at least told Todd what time and where to go. If the kids wanted a friend over after school, they asked me. I knew what homework they had and when it was due. I was central to everything that happened in our house; the calendar of activity spun around me.

The nausea had stopped, I was sleeping less, and I was up more. But now I had zero purpose. I went from full days to having nothing on the calendar but grief. On one hand, it was good not to worry about all of those things, but it was also damaging because it left a lot of room for me to think negative thoughts. Other people had taken over my parenting duties. They were the ones picking Peyton up from school and taking Ryan to basketball. They filled the mom role because most days I couldn't physically or emotionally do it. In some ways, I felt like my only purpose was to grieve, so that's what I did all day, every day.

I didn't want something to keep my hands busy or to occupy my time; I wanted something to occupy my mind. Something like Todd had. His grief seemed to be channeled into doing something *good*. The activities of the foundation occupied his thoughts, and he had things to do all day. I wanted that too.

A few days later, Todd walked in and sat down beside me on the bed. "Why, Todd? Why us?" I asked. I struggled with that question often. It was probably a question I'd asked him before, but that day his answer was different.

"It's not even a question of why," he said. "Why not? Why not us? I can handle it." He went on to talk about how he'd seen purpose and meaning in Taylor's death.

"Great, so maybe you've found a purpose. But what about me? I used to be a mom of three; what am I now? I'm not even that. I wake up every day with this crushing feeling in my chest, wishing the morning had never come."

"I don't, Tara. I don't wake up that way at all. I wake up feeling like I can't wait for the day to get started. I hope what I said didn't hurt you. It's just the truth."

But his comments angered me. Why was God allowing him to be so strong when I felt so weak? "We are so opposite right now," I said. "How can you wake up with joy?"

"I don't know, but I do."

I wasn't angry at Todd. I was angry at God. I put my hands on my hips like a petulant two-year-old and said to God, *I'm not talking to You. You are not important to me anymore. You had control over this, and You could have made this turn out differently. I prayed and asked You to change this, and You didn't, so we're no longer talking.*

As if I needed any more proof that God and I weren't friends, I checked my Facebook later that night and saw a friend of mine, whose son had been very ill for quite some time, had posted a new status update: "Thank God! My son almost died, but God answered our prayers and healed him, and now he is completely better."

Before I could stop myself, I wrote a comment. "How lucky you are that God decided to save your child." Then I posted it and went to bed.

Lying in bed, I knew I shouldn't have written that, but it was just further proof that God answered other people's prayers but He didn't answer mine. He saved other people's sons but He didn't save my daughter. I was angry.

By the next morning my anger had faded, and I got up and deleted the comment because I regretted writing it. Unfortunately, all of our mutual friends had already seen it.

After that, it seemed like everyone's desire to fix me only increased. "Why don't you just make her get up?" they'd ask Todd.

People had expectations of grief. If I was good one day, they expected me to be better the next day. If there were faith practices that worked for them in their normal, happy lives, they thought those same faith practices would help make me normal and happy too. Pray more. Fast. Go to church. Read your Bible. Memorize Scripture. The people who made these suggestions meant well. What they didn't know was I had already tried those things and they hadn't achieved what I really wanted—my daughter back.

✧

One morning when I woke up, I had the usual question of why. *Why* swirls and never stops at an answer. Just like the mornings before it, on this day I moved past the why only to land in more dark thoughts. The cycle was starting again.

I looked above our bedroom door. We'd hung a crucifix on the wall when we moved in years earlier. Though God and I still weren't talking, I focused on the cross and tried to concentrate on my thoughts to get out of the darkness swirling around me, but my mind remained confused. I picked up a book near my bed and opened it—a devotional. I looked at the page, but the words just swam and ran together. I closed the book and looked back at the cross.

I felt so abandoned by God. I was lost and alone, and not even the God of the universe cared.

Somehow, one clear thought made its way out of my fog. *This is all for Your glory.* It was so distinct from everything else swirling in my mind that I said it out loud. "This is all for Your glory." For someone who wasn't talking to God, it was at once jarring and peaceful at the same time.

Then I said it again. "This is all for Your glory."

And again. "This is all for Your glory."

Soon, I was repeating it over and over. Even as I said it out loud I thought, *How can this ever be for Your glory?* But somewhere in the saying of it I believed it, and I started to cry. I didn't have any answers, but for some reason, I had a tiny bit of faith.

"This is all for Your glory!"

The more I opened up to the idea, the more I cried. Soon I was bawling. My faith had been—and still was—shaken, but it wasn't broken.

God and I were talking once again.

⚬⟡⚬

Before Taylor died, everything in our house ran by the clock. It had to. Three busy kids, a husband who traveled, and my volunteer work all meant that things had to happen on time and on schedule. Now, I never looked at a clock. I had no concept of time. There were days I felt too weak to shower, or even to simply stand under the hot water, and sometimes those days flowed into each other without my realizing it.

One day, Sandi came to me and said, "Tara, you have got to shower. It's been five days. People are coming over to see you, and you stink."

I had already lost fifteen pounds and I continued to lose more. I was weak and tired. Tears rolled down my cheeks because she was probably right, and I didn't have the strength to argue—but neither did I have the strength to shower.

She helped me up, and I leaned on her as we walked into the bathroom. She stripped my clothes off me, turned on the shower, and held the door while I stepped in. Once I was under the water, I didn't even have the strength to lift my hands to wash my hair. Even the water was painful as it hit my head and back. Through my tears, I could see Sandi standing on the other side of the door, watching me.

"Oh, honey," she said. I saw her take a deep breath and blow it out. "Okay, I know this is weird, but I'm doing it." Then she got in the shower with me and shut the door. "I'm going to wash you and wash your hair," she said. "I'm going to wash everything but your who-ha." She grabbed the washcloth and soap, and she kept talking as she washed my arms and legs. "Girl, I'll do everything for you, but I'm not touching that."

I couldn't take it anymore. I didn't mean to, and I certainly didn't plan to, but I smiled.

And then I chuckled, just a little.

Then I let out a big laugh.

It was my first laugh since Taylor's accident, and it had snuck up on me when I least expected it—in the shower. That moment was important. It helped me to see that there would be smiles and laughter in my future, even if I couldn't see them coming.

-20-

The Cowboy's Daughter Connects on Facebook

JEFF KARTUS
COLORADO

Nothing was ever easy for Jeff.

After two years, the cowboy finally got the kidney and pancreas he'd been waiting for. During the surgery, the doctors thought they had done a successful transplant, but somewhere a blood vessel started to leak. Because he was on blood thinners, Jeff bled out.

He actually died on the operating table.

Fortunately, doctors were able to give him a transfusion—ten pints of blood—that revived him. Because of complications, Jeff was in the hospital for nearly a month—his wife, Vanessa, and his daughter, Brooke, by his side. When he was finally released and able to go home, it was as if he had amnesia; he remembered very little about the two years he'd spent on dialysis.

But other changes were easy to see. The new pancreas cured his diabetes. No longer did he have to eat at certain times, prick his finger to test his blood sugar levels, or take insulin. The results were dramatic.

Living in Colorado, Vanessa and Brooke had seen the news reports on the local television stations about the girl who died while skiing. And while Jeff was in the hospital, one of the medical staff mentioned his donor was a young girl. Jeff had to have received her kidney and pancreas—the timing was too coincidental.

Brooke did a little bit of online detective work and came up with an email address. With Jeff and Vanessa's permission, she carefully crafted a letter telling them how much her dad's life had changed and that while they would love to make contact, she understood if it was too difficult for the family. Then she hit send.

A couple of weeks went by and she hadn't heard anything back. She wondered if she ever would.

— 21 —

Confirmation

Todd

I picked up my phone and scrolled through my list of favorites until I found John Henley, my good friend and boss at CSS. I paused for a moment, then tapped his number. It was one thing to talk to Tara and my friends about quitting my job, but quite another to tell the guy responsible for my paycheck. If he cut me off after this call, I had no backup plan. We had some money in the bank, but we weren't wealthy. It certainly wasn't enough to hold us for long.

John answered, and we made small talk. He asked how Tara and I were. I asked about business and about his wife, Cricket. I knew he could tell I was nervous, so I got right to the point.

"John, there's something I need to tell you," I started. I took a deep breath and dove in. I thanked him for being a good friend and told him how much I appreciated him as a leader. "I hope we'll still be friends, but I can no longer work for the company." I explained how Tara still wasn't well. "I can't travel like I used to, or do the job that's required, with all that's going on in my personal life."

I brought him up to speed about the foundation and all the amazing things that were happening. "John, I am so sorry, but

I need to quit so I can work full-time with the foundation. I've prayed about it, prayed with Tara about it, sought counsel from friends, and everything just seems to be leading me to this decision. I simply feel as if I'd be disobeying God if I didn't do it," I said. Then I paused to give him a chance to react.

He didn't hesitate. "I knew it before you did."

Of all the reactions I'd thought he might have, this wasn't one I'd considered.

"Not long after we heard about Taylor, Cricket said to me, 'You know, Todd's not coming back. You know there is something he has to do.' I agreed, Todd, because I knew it too. I knew."

Chills ran up my arms as he continued, "I just want you to know we're here, and we're going to support you. We'll be the first company to support your foundation. I don't know what that looks like yet, but we'll talk more next week."

John had a layover in Dallas the following week. We'd have six hours to sit down and talk face-to-face. I hung up the phone, grateful and excited. I still didn't know how it would all work out, but this was the sign from God I'd been waiting for. It was official: I would work for the foundation full-time.

⚬⁙⚬

A week later, John and I met in a Dallas restaurant. "What are your plans?" he asked. John knew me well enough to know how I operated.

"I haven't worked it all out yet," I said honestly. I didn't divulge that I was trying *not* to plan. I didn't want to get ahead of God.

"Well, Jim and I want to contribute five thousand dollars of start-up money for Taylor's Gift on behalf of CSS. If you need more, let us know. If you don't need it all, then just keep the balance as a donation."

I couldn't believe it. We'd just filed the paperwork the last few days of April. Now it was early May, and we'd already received our first major donation! It was an unexpected and generous gift. But

John wasn't done. "We'll pay you a full salary through August," he continued, "and we'll keep you on the company insurance for a year."

I'm sure my mouth was hanging open. It was beyond anything I could have hoped for or imagined. In addition to giving the first and biggest donation to Taylor's Gift, John had removed my financial worries for the next ninety days. And he'd provided insurance for my family for the next year.

"And, Todd, here's the deal: if in thirty or sixty days you think this was the stupidest decision you've ever made, you'll have a place to work. I'm not sure what your job will be, but we'll figure it out."

I couldn't wait to tell Tara. I'd asked for one more sign, and God exploded blessings like fireworks on the Fourth of July. I began to see how much better His way was than mine. If I had put together spreadsheets and business plans to make this happen, I probably would have talked myself out of leaving, because, financially, it didn't make sense. But God's math was different from mine. God had helped me stay open to what He was doing—no matter how ridiculous it sounded—and then He revealed himself to me in ways I couldn't have imagined.

I was no longer concerned about failing. With God on my side, how could I?

⁘

Now that I was actively seeking God's plan in my life, I saw Him every day. Things other businesses worked *years* to achieve, or other nonprofits one day *hoped* to have, were being handed to us. Various groups began to organize fund-raisers for us. Bracelets, hats, and T-shirts with foundation logos were being printed and sold. The media stories led to more media stories. Friends in the volleyball community offered to host a tournament with proceeds going to the foundation. The first annual 4T (Taylor's volleyball number was 4) tournament was held less than two months after Taylor's death.

The documentary on organ donation went from being a good idea one day to a fully staffed crew the next. While several documentaries had been done from the perspective of the recipients, we weren't aware of any that had been done from the perspective of the donors. By telling our story, we could encourage others to become organ donors while also honoring Taylor. It was exciting to think about the impact we could have.

Our first fund-raising dinner and kickoff event was being held in June, a week after we got back from our presentation at the Donate Life Film Festival in Hollywood.

We hoped to roll out a new version of our website, one that encompassed everything we'd become since the first website was put out. New opportunities to tell our story and encourage organ donation happened every day, and the number and quality of volunteers continued to climb.

As cofounder of the foundation, Tara needed to be brought up to speed. As my wife, her involvement and approval were important to me. But Tara wasn't ready, and even if she was, she still couldn't handle the pace. "You've got to give me only little pieces of information. I can't handle more than that right now," she said one day.

I knew she felt as if I were the strong one, but there were times I also felt weak. I missed my wife and my best friend, and I wanted her by my side while these amazing things were occurring. So, we compromised. Once a week we would sit down and I'd update her on the major highlights. It wasn't perfect, but it was the best we could do under the circumstances.

We didn't have much of a relationship at the time. She was at the lowest spot in her life, and I felt like her caretaker. She needed to grieve in her own way, so I didn't want to push her to be a mom or a wife before she was ready. And despite my outward productivity, I was still grieving too. I felt broken. And alone.

Occasionally, I still had fantasies of running away like the one I had in the hospital. *If I took money out of the bank, paid cash for an airline ticket, and flew somewhere, I could disappear off the grid for at least a month before anyone found me.* Then I'd remind myself of all of the reasons I didn't want to run.

Other days I was mad at Tara. I resented that she got taken care of, while I did all the caretaking. At times I couldn't take one more minute of hearing her cry. I would call a friend to come stay with her, and I'd leave the house.

Grief counseling with Judy was helpful, but now I was dealing with more than just the loss of my daughter. I was dealing with a wife who was incapacitated, a loss of identity because I'd quit my job, and the loss of our old lifestyle because we'd had to tighten our financial belt. In the midst of all this change, I would have to rediscover who I was.

For the most part, God kept me so busy I didn't have to think much. In addition to the foundation, my primary job was to take care of my family. While people still came to the house to help Tara out, people no longer spent the night and more of the household responsibility fell on my shoulders. I did the best I could, but sometimes things fell through the cracks.

One day Peyton came home from school and said to Tara, "Will you please start packing my lunches?"

Tara was sitting outside wrapped in a blanket as usual, with that vacant stare on her face. She could barely get out of bed to see the kids off to school; the thought of making lunches every day was beyond her. "Sweetie, Daddy is going to pack your lunch. I can't do it right now," she said.

"Please!" said Peyton. "You have to! Daddy packed it today, and all he packed was a pickle!"

A *pickle*? I *know* I packed more than a pickle.

At least I thought I did.

There was a lot going on. It was possible I had started packing her lunch but didn't finish. Tara and I knew how pathetic it must have looked to the teachers at school. They probably just shook their heads and said, "That poor family. Bless their hearts." But it was also a wake-up call for both of us. After that day, I noticed that Tara took some active steps to contain her worst grief to school hours. She also tried to be physically and emotionally present for

Ryan and Peyton when they were home. But for Peyton, the most important change was that Tara started packing lunches again.

Even so, I *know* I packed more than a pickle!

◦⚬◦

My inbox was chaos central. I was in the midst of turning over client information to my colleagues, updating past clients before I left, and trying to run the foundation. In addition, probably a hundred people were volunteering either with the foundation or at the house, and they communicated with me by email. Daily, we also received emails from strangers who'd heard our story or wanted to share theirs. We learned a lot of people were connected in ways we couldn't imagine, and it seemed they were all willing to use their connections to help us.

In the midst of all of this chaos, I received an email from a young woman named Brooke. I read her email, and everything around me came to a screeching halt. After reading Brooke's email a second time, I knew I had to share it with Tara immediately.

"Tara, this woman says she got my email from Facebook."

"So? A lot of people do that."

"I know, but listen to this," I said, reading, "'I hope I am not intruding, but I believe my dad has your daughter's kidney and pancreas, and it has saved his life.'"

"Did she say where she's from?" Tara asked, suddenly perking up.

"Colorado."

"Are you kidding? What else did she say?"

"She got our name from an article, and then went onto Facebook and got my email from there. Listen, she writes, 'I totally understand if this crosses some kind of line, or if you don't want to touch base, but we just wanted to reach out and thank you because you've touched our lives, and it's made a huge difference for my dad and for all of us.'" The email was so caring and kind that it was obvious she'd thought about it a long time before hitting send.

By now, Tara was standing behind me, reading over my shoulder. She had been working on writing our letter to Donor Alliance to pass on to the recipients, adding a paragraph here or there as she had the emotional strength and physical energy to do it.

But we'd been told we had to wait six months before we could send a letter to Donor Alliance to forward to the recipients, and it had to be sent by snail mail. So we expected the process to take months—maybe even a year. We never expected that within a few weeks of Taylor's death we'd get an email directly from a recipient, or in this case, his daughter.

Apparently, Donor Alliance didn't expect it either. We called them the next morning and said we'd heard from a Brooke Kartus who claimed her dad, Jeff, had received Taylor's kidney and pancreas. After a flurry of phone calls and some emergency meetings at their offices, Donor Alliance basically confirmed that Brooke was who she said she was. "But can you wait to contact her until we've had a chance to talk to our board? We've never had this happen before."

But there was no waiting. Tara and I had already emailed her. Why wouldn't we? We'd been told there was a chance we'd never connect with an organ recipient and now, just weeks later, we had. We'd immediately looked Brooke up on Facebook and confirmed she lived in Colorado. We couldn't wait to connect, so Tara and I had emailed her. "It was wonderful to get your email. Thank you so much for reaching out. How is your dad doing?"

We were the first donor family with Donor Alliance to connect with a recipient family through social media, and they didn't have a process for handling that yet. A couple of days later, they got back to us and said, "We can't stop you, but would you please sign this legal document releasing us from any liability before you contact her?"

By then, we'd already been chatting with Brooke on Facebook. We learned her dad lived in Colorado and had been unable to work for years because of his diabetes. Over the past few years, the diabetes had taken a toll on his health, his kidneys had failed, and he'd had to go on dialysis. After the transplant, he was able to stop both dialysis and insulin shots. His diabetes was cured! It was amazing to hear how Taylor's kidney and pancreas had made such a remarkable difference in the life of one man and his family.

People asked me how it felt to connect with someone who had received Taylor's organs. It was hard to explain. There was a sense of excitement, but "excited" wasn't really what I felt. For Tara, it was emotional. To her, it felt like a little bit of steam had been released from the pressure of her grief. She had a strong desire to connect with Jeff, to know more about him, and to help him know us and know Taylor. We made plans to visit the Kartus family in June. The kids would be out of school, and we had already planned a family trip to the beach and a weekend in California with Donate Life to present an award. The documentary crew could travel with us, and it just made sense to do it all then.

It felt important to Tara and me that Taylor's gift be acknowledged. It wasn't that we needed to be thanked or appreciated, but we wanted the person who received the gift to appreciate it. Brooke showed us that in her email. She recognized the good gift her father had received.

It was just one more confirmation that our foundation work was important. We could point to something good that had come out of Taylor's death. Jeff was a real person, a cowboy living in Colorado who had a wife, a son, a daughter, and for the first time in a long time, freedom from dialysis and daily insulin injections. Knowing Jeff was out there reminded us of how many more people just like him were out there. He was something tangible for us to cling to as we went forward with the foundation work.

That night in the kitchen, I remember sitting back and thinking, *Of course, we heard from them now. We're supposed to hear from them now.* It just fell in line with everything else God was doing. It was one more sign from God saying we were on the right course and that He would provide for us.

—22—

Of Course!

Tara

I watched the celebrities line up in front of the Donate Life signage for photos. Each one arrived with an entourage and paused to smile for the cameras before entering the ballroom. *What am I doing here?* I thought. It was hard to describe how big this moment was for me. After all, it had only been three months since the accident.

Most days I barely got dressed in clean pajamas. The farthest I got from my bedroom was the back porch. Now here I was in a cocktail dress and heels at an invitation-only, opening night, VIP cocktail reception for the Donate Life Film Festival. Looking around, I saw celebrities I recognized. Alex O'Loughlin, currently starring in *Hawaii Five-O*, stood chatting with a group of people across the room from me. Near the bar sat Olympic medalist and pro snowboarder Chris Klug. Producers and directors from shows such as *Extreme Makeover Home Edition* wandered through the crowd with network executives. Most days I could barely talk to my friends and family, and now I was standing in a group of strangers trying to make small talk. What was I doing here? My eyes were preoccupied with the room, but my mind was focused on Taylor. Losing her was the only reason we were here. I'd give anything to have her back.

"What do you do?" a pleasant woman asked. She had shoulder-length dark hair and wore a snakeskin print dress with a matching jacket.

I looked at her smiling face and tried to decide how to answer her question. "We were asked to present an award at tomorrow night's ceremony. We lost our daughter . . ." My voice trailed off, and tears started to flow. By this time, a couple of women had joined us, and someone handed me a Kleenex. I dabbed my eyes. I had on makeup for the first time in months, and I didn't want to ruin it. Through my sniffles, I continued, "Now we have a foundation to increase awareness about organ donation. We named it after our daughter. It's called Taylor's Gift. We've only started, but we believe in what we're doing."

The women in the circle became very compassionate. "Oh," and "I'm so sorry," they said. I appreciated their compassion, but I just wanted to make it through the night without more tears. I knew the best way to do it was to take the focus off me.

"Why are you here?" I asked the dark-haired woman.

"I donated a kidney to my husband."

"Oh, that's great. When?"

"About eight years ago," she said. "It really changed his life."

"That's beautiful," I said, attempting to keep the small talk going.

I introduced myself to the woman, and she said her name was Ann. She asked about my necklace—it was a tiny silver picture frame with a picture of Taylor inside—and we talked about her a little bit. Then Todd walked up with drinks for each of us. The lights dimmed, letting us know it was time for the program to start, and Ann excused herself. Once we were in our seats, someone on stage made a few announcements and then said, "Let me introduce tonight's mistress of ceremonies, Ann Lopez!"

"Todd, that's her! That's the woman I was talking to," I said, watching her walk to the mic.

Ann talked briefly about herself—it turns out she was George Lopez's wife. He was a comedian with a new show on TV that was doing very well, something he never could have done without her kidney. After a brief introduction, she went on to explain the rest of the night's lineup. Suddenly, in the middle of her remarks, she went off-script.

"You know what? Let me stop here. Tara and Todd Storch? Where are you?" Todd and I tentatively looked at each other. He nodded, and I barely raised my hand, but it was enough for her to see me in the crowd.

"They recently lost their daughter, and they donated her organs. Now, they've started a foundation called Taylor's Gift to increase awareness about organ donation." She smiled at us. "I am so impressed with you. Thank you for what you are doing. I just wanted to acknowledge that."

Everyone was looking at me, and all of a sudden the entire room burst into spontaneous applause. It was surreal. Then, as if nothing had happened, Ann gave us a huge smile and went right back to her script.

Todd called moments like these "of course" moments. Of course, God would do something to introduce us and our foundation to everyone in the room. Of course, it would be big, bold, and completely unexpected, so big that, of course, we could only give *Him* the credit. As Todd took a step of faith to quit his job and work for the foundation, this was yet another reminder of how much God cared for us and how He walked alongside us every step of the way.

Before we left that night, Ann Lopez came back over and hugged me. "You have got to keep in touch with me, you've got to!" she said.

Of course, we would.

The next night we presented an award at Donate Life's annual film festival awards ceremony. A number of people we spoke with in the entertainment industry were interested in hearing more about our documentary.

Ana Lucia Cottone was one individual who stood out. At the time, she was an executive at Lifetime Television. She looked like a California girl, young, tan, and blonde, but she was actually from Guatemala and spoke with a beautiful accent. After the presentation, she came up to Todd and me, hugged us, and said she wanted to hear our story. We liked her immediately, but our conversation was interrupted by others who came up to speak with her. She had to leave sooner than expected, but she said, "I really want to connect with you," as she left the room.

"Yeah, right," we joked to each other. "She's a network bigwig; it's not like we'll ever see her again."

She left—but she was back a few minutes later with her card. "Here's my number. I really want to stay in touch with you," she said. Then she was gone again.

The party ended, and Todd and I waited in the lobby for our Donate Life representative. Before we headed back to our hotel, we wanted to thank her again for including us. I'd been trying to hold it together all night, and I knew I wouldn't be able to do it much longer. "I'll go back inside and see if she's there," Todd said. "You can just wait here."

Todd was gone only a few seconds when Ana Lucia came back in the door, looking like she was on a mission. When she saw me she walked over and said, "I'm not done with you."

"What does that mean?" I asked.

"There's just something about you; I don't think I am done with you yet," she said.

My lip trembled, and I bit it to stop the tears that I knew were coming. Seeing my emotions surface, she said, "I know you don't know me, but I'm going to tell you a story."

I was glad; I couldn't do much talking at the time anyway.

"A very long time ago, there lived some Buddhist monks. Their village had been decimated by war and enemies were attacking their culture. To protect themselves, they had to move their village. But part of their religious tradition included this huge Buddha made of mud that they loved and worshiped. They wanted to take it with them to the new village, but they were fearful because they knew if they moved the statue, it could crack and break. Yet they couldn't move on without their Buddha."

I had no idea where the story was going, but Ana Lucia was a good storyteller, and I was hooked.

"So the whole village assembled, and the plan was to carefully work together to move this clay Buddha. But when they started to move it, the Buddha started to crack as they feared. Soon, the cracks got bigger and chunks of Buddha mud fell to the ground." Ana Lucia looked me in the eye. "But underneath the mud was gold."

She placed both her hands on my shoulders and said, "You're going to have to crack before you can find your gold."

I'm sure I said something really smart and impressive back; I think it was, "Oh, wow." But I knew then that Ana Lucia was right. She wasn't done with us yet. She offered to drive us back to our hotel so we could talk more. We've stayed in touch since then. Every time I felt as if I were going to break, or I couldn't hold it together, I'd think of her story, allow it to happen, and look for gold.

⚬⟡⚬

My extended family lived in Louisiana, so every year they went to Gulf Shores, Alabama, for a family vacation. We had never been. It was June, only three months since we had lost Taylor, but we thought that it would be good to get away and to have a strong family around us if we needed it. I knew I was a mess, but maybe being around extended family would help distract me. Distractions were good. It would get us out of the house, and we'd get to do something fun with the kids.

Once we got to Gulf Shores, we unpacked and went down to the beach. I sat near my cousins, who were there with friends. We were all talking and watching Ryan and Peyton play in the ocean. *This is going to be good,* I thought. *The kids will be distracted, they're happy, and it's all going to be fine.*

"So, you're Ray's cousin?" the guy standing next to me said.

"Yeah."

"You all just got in town?"

"Yeah, we just drove in today from Texas." My eyes were on the kids, and I wanted to make sure they didn't venture out too far. I yelled to Peyton and Ryan, "You guys need to stay close!"

"How many kids do you have?" the guy asked.

Shocked by his question, I burst into tears. I'd not been asked that since Taylor had left. *How do I answer that?*

"I have those two," I said, pointing. That was all I could say.

My cousin saw what was happening and rescued me from the conversation. I walked off down the beach so I could cry without people staring. It was the first time it happened, but it wouldn't be the last. Every time I got my nails done, chatted with a new mom at school, or met a new neighbor, that question eventually would come up. When we went into a restaurant and they said, "How many are in your party?" I'd have to stop before answering the question. Eventually, in counseling Judy helped me learn how to handle it.

"Just say you have three, and change the subject by asking them a question," she taught me.

That usually worked, but it was still a question I would never be comfortable answering again.

⋯

We made it through our first family vacation without Taylor, and we'd held it together. But on the ride home it was just the four of us, and none of us could keep up the brave front much longer. Todd asked me to drive so he could "work" on his laptop. I knew it was just a code word for his wanting to escape, but I was happy to drive. It helped to distract me too. In the back, the kids were each doing their own thing. Ryan was playing video games; Peyton was watching a movie.

About an hour into the drive, without warning, I heard sniffling from Ryan. I dabbed my eyes at the sound. Then Peyton started sniffling. Soon Ryan was bawling, Peyton was crying, and my tears were flowing. Every time Ryan cried, it just set Peyton off, and hearing them cry, well, there was no turning back the flood of grief that was drowning them. I looked over at Todd. He'd closed his laptop and was staring out the window. I knew he was trying not to cry in front of the kids, which only made me cry harder.

Our whole carload was a mess. Then I heard Todd's breathing change. He turned to look at me, and I could see anger boiling beneath the surface. By now, both kids had buried their heads in pillows and were openly sobbing. Ryan was wailing.

Under his breath Todd said, "Are you kidding me?" He raised his fist in the air and shook it at God. "This is what our family is now? This is what You want?" He was as mad as I'd ever heard him. "I can't even console my own children," he said through clenched teeth.

I couldn't look at him because a big eighteen-wheeler semi was passing to my left, and I needed to stay focused on the road. It was a plain white truck, and it pulled right in front of us. I had to hit the brakes hard. As I did, I read the only thing written on the truck—"Taylor."

"Look!" I said.

Todd looked first and then looked at me. "She's here," he said excitedly.

We told the kids to look, and through swollen eyes, they saw it too.

It didn't make our tears go away completely, and it didn't take away all our pain, but it was another "of course" moment. We were on vacation and, of course, Taylor was there too. It was as if she said, "I'm right here. I'm with you," and knowing that helped us to put the brakes on our tears.

Not long afterward, we decided to pull off the road for a stop in Alexandria, Louisiana. We realized it was probably time for a Saturday evening mass, so we looked for a church. With the emotional state we were in, we needed to hear from God.

Looking at the church, I was disappointed. It was a little country parish in a bad part of town. We considered just getting back on the road and saying some prayers out loud in the car. God would surely understand. But instead we parked and went in. When I saw the aging priest, I wondered if we had made the wrong decision. What could he have to say that would encourage us? But boy, was I wrong. During the sermon, he talked about how God had already picked out our cross, and though His path may be hard to follow, He had a divine plan for each of us. The priest said there might be hard days ahead but to keep moving in God's direction because beyond those days would shine days of glory.

To me, his words were another "of course" moment. Of course, God had a plan and, of course, we needed to be reminded that He was in charge. And, of course, He'd get that message to us just when we needed it most. I left that mass feeling that our family had been blessed by God, and we just needed to keep moving forward. To follow Him—no matter how hard it was.

⚜

We'd been back from the beach for only a few days when my neighbor Trista, the Grief Fairy, called. "I need to tell you about the email I just got. Can I come over?" she asked.

Ever since that day when I had told her I really wanted to meet the person who had Taylor's heart, she'd been searching the internet to see what she could learn. Weeks earlier, she'd read a post on Transplant Café, an online message board for transplant recipients, where someone had said they thought their sister-in-law had received Taylor's heart. Trista had investigated further, and with my permission she'd reached out to the man who'd posted the message, but it had been weeks and we hadn't heard anything.

"I've got news," Trista said. "I may have found the woman who has Taylor's heart. She's a nurse, a mother of two boys, and I'm waiting to hear if she wants to connect. If she does, is it okay if I give her your email address?"

I couldn't believe it. We'd found the woman who had Taylor's heart, and we might be able to connect! Since the day we made the decision to donate Taylor's organs, it was the one thing I wanted more than anything else. Through tear-filled eyes, I looked at Trista, who was still waiting for an answer, and said, "Of course!"

—23—

The Nurse Responds

PATRICIA WINTERS
TEMPE, ARIZONA

When the third call came, the transplant coordinator said, "We got an awesome heart; this one is really going to happen." And so it did.

As soon as Patricia woke up from the surgery, she said, "Who is she? I want to know who she is!" Somehow she sensed it was from a female donor, but the doctors couldn't tell her more.

While she was in surgery, her husband, Joe, got a call from a friend in Colorado who told him about a local skiing accident and a girl who had died, leaving her heart to a thirty-nine-year-old woman in Arizona. By the time Patricia's heart surgery was done, Joe already knew the donor, so although the doctors couldn't tell Patricia who it was, Joe could. He pulled out his laptop and showed Patricia pictures and videos of the thirteen-year-old donor.

"I can't now," Patricia said. "Please put that away." It was too soon and too much to bear, knowing that the donor was a teenage girl. As the mother of two young boys, she couldn't imagine what those parents must be going through. Though her new heart was beating strongly, it was also broken for the family who had donated their daughter's organs.

She couldn't get them out of her mind.

Over the next few months Patricia felt a pull toward the people who had given her such a precious gift. She wanted to get to know them, so while she was lying in bed with her laptop, she pulled up pictures and videos of the girl. She watched as the family started a foundation, and viewed online clips of news reports in which the mom said she wanted to reconnect with her daughter's heart. Patricia wanted that too. But as a nurse and as a mom, she respected the rules. She wouldn't contact them until the six-month waiting period was up.

But without her knowledge, one of Patricia's relatives had been posting messages on Transplant Café. Under articles about the girl's skiing accident, Patricia's relative posted a comment that said, "I know who got the girl's heart." When the girl's neighbor reached out and offered to connect the commenter to the family, the relative got scared. After a couple of weeks, he finally admitted to Patricia what had been going on and apologized for the mess he'd created.

Patricia was worried that the whole thing could be upsetting to the family. *That poor mother!* Patricia thought. She immediately emailed the neighbor: "I'm so sorry for all of this; I just found out. Of course I'd like to connect with the family."

—24—

First Meetings

Todd

After the plane landed in Denver, I turned on my phone. Tara must have forgotten to turn hers off because I heard hers ping. Then ping, ping. Then ping, ping, ping. I looked at her and said, "Wow, somebody sure wants to talk to you."

She was wrapped in a blanket and leaning against the window. I couldn't tell if she'd been crying or not, but she looked as if she could burst into tears at any moment. As the plane taxied, she reached for her phone. I got busy with mine, catching up on what I'd missed during our flight from Dallas.

Suddenly, Tara got excited. "Todd, Todd," she said, nudging me. "Trista just texted me, and she forwarded an email from Patricia Winters!" Her hand started shaking as she handed me her phone. It was an email from the heart recipient.

"Read it!" she said, obviously too nervous to do it herself.

I opened Trista's email and read the forwarded message. She said her name was Patricia Winters, that she was a nurse and a mom of two boys. She explained how a relative had left the message on Transplant Café and didn't tell her about it until recently. "Please tell the Storches they can contact me any way they want," she'd written to Trista. Then she included her contact information.

We had just arrived in Denver to meet Jeff Kartus, the pancreas/ kidney recipient, and his family. Only in God's perfect timing would we also get our first email from the heart recipient. "Well, *of course*, we'd hear from her now," I said.

The email was a big relief to me. I knew how much it meant to Tara to connect with the person who had Taylor's heart. That had been her one desire since we agreed to make the gift. "Do you want to email her back?" I asked.

"I can't. I just can't," Tara said, choking back sobs. "You do it."

I emailed Patricia and told her how happy we were to finally connect with her. "But we're at the airport. We're meeting the kidney/pancreas recipient. You can understand that Tara doesn't want to email right now, but she sends her love."

We were less than twenty-four hours from meeting the first recipient, and now I was a little conflicted. From the moment we made the decision, we both wanted to connect with the people who received Taylor's organs, but I honestly never thought we would. I didn't think we would ever know their names, let alone meet them in person. Personally, I didn't need to meet Jeff to know Taylor's gift made a difference. Nothing in my life was missing that would be made full just because I shook a recipient's hand or looked into his or her eyes.

It was different for Tara. She'd longed for a connection with the recipients since the beginning. She looked forward to meeting them and bonding with them. In some small way, I think she hoped it would connect her with Taylor.

While walking through the airport, my stomach knotted as I thought of all that could go wrong. I worried about Tara. I knew she had high expectations for the meeting. What if it didn't work out? What if the meeting didn't live up to her expectations, and she had some kind of breakdown while we were there? My most important goal for this meeting was to protect her.

But although there was a lot to consider, I still felt an incredible pull to meet them. Our goal was to encourage as many people as we possibly could to register for organ donation. Hearing an organ recipient's side of the story and sharing that in the documentary would be an emotionally powerful addition to our story. It would be hard, but I looked forward to meeting them.

⁂

"I have to get out of here," Tara said. She paced the perimeter of our hotel room. I couldn't remember the last time I'd seen her pace. I had become used to her being inactive, sitting and staring into space for hours.

"Let's take a walk," I said.

We had a couple of hours before we were to meet the documentary crew for dinner, so we decided to walk to the outdoor mall. The 16th Street Mall in Denver is a one-mile pedestrian street lined on both sides with restaurants, retailers, and street performers. As we strolled, Tara stopped occasionally to look in the shop windows.

"I need something to wear to the foundation dinner," she said.

"Maybe you should look while we're here."

We were scheduled to fly back into Dallas late Friday afternoon, and the fund-raising dinner was to be held that night at a friend's house. Though I was surprised she had the desire to shop, we both knew if she wanted to get something before the dinner, this would be her only opportunity.

"I want to find a dress. I want a sundress. And I want it to be Tiffany blue," she said.

"Good luck with that," I said, eyeing the fall collections already in the displays. I knew why she said she wanted that dress in that color. When Taylor was little, her favorite color was purple. As she grew older and became more aware of her own features, her favorite color was Tiffany blue. "Because it matches my eyes," she'd say.

Tara was still discussing the dress she wanted when she spotted one of her favorite stores. "Oh, there's an Ann Taylor; I'm going to see if they have anything."

"See the Starbucks?" I asked, pointing across the street. "I'll wait for you there. When you're finished, come and get me."

I ordered a coffee and found a seat near the window so I could people watch while I waited for my laptop to load. Through the window, I saw Tara leave Ann Taylor empty-handed and walk down the street toward another store. *Good luck finding that dress*, I thought. But I was happy she had the energy to shop. I think being away from Coppell, freed from the fear of running into people who knew her, helped.

✤

I looked up to see Tara pulling up a chair. I wasn't sure how much time had elapsed; I had become engrossed in my work. A quick glance showed she wasn't carrying any packages. She put her elbows on the table and rested her chin in her hands. She looked bummed.

"No luck?"

She shook her head. "I'm not finding anything. Everything is in fall colors."

"Maybe you're being too picky?" I asked. After all, it was a pretty tall order to find what she was looking for.

"Maybe, but it's what I want."

I looked at my watch. "You've got forty-five minutes left. Do you want to keep looking, or are you giving up?"

"I want to keep looking," she said.

I marveled at her newfound energy. Just a few weeks earlier she wouldn't have had the ability to even dress herself, let alone go shopping for a dress.

Thirty minutes later, Tara was back with a bag in her hand and a wide smile on her face. "You'll never guess what happened!" she said excitedly. "As soon as I left here, I walked outside and said, 'Taylor, you know what I'm looking for.' She's the one who always found the best clothes when we went shopping. Well, the very next store I went into had all of these dark colors, and then I saw this little piece of Tiffany blue fabric peeking from the rack. I went over and pulled out the hanger—and it was a sundress! And guess what? It was my size!"

I couldn't remember seeing Tara so excited. Even I was excited.

"But that's not all," she said, gushing. "While I was walking into the dressing room, I flipped the dress over my arm and the tag fell out. Look at this!" she urged, pulling the dress from the bag and showing me the attached tag.

I expected it to be the dress's price, and from her enthusiasm I expected it to be cheap. But instead of the price tag, she showed me a brownish-gray square tag, and written in yellow cursive at the top was a single word.

Taylor.

"Are you kidding me?" I said, picking up the tag. Finding the dress she wanted, in the way she had, was pretty unbelievable, but that tag made it seem preposterous. "It's the same font we selected for the website!"

"No way!" she said, looking closer. She hadn't noticed that.

I knew the answer to the next question before asking, but I asked it anyway, just so I could see her smile. "Did it fit?"

Like I hoped, she answered with an even bigger grin. "*Of course! It fit perfectly.*"

⁂

From everything that had happened on this trip—from the timing of Patricia's email to the "Taylor-made" dress Tara found—it was clear God was very much with us. So I'm not sure why we were so nervous on the drive to Jeff Kartus's house the next afternoon, but we were. We were both anxious, maybe even a little scared, wondering if we'd like them and if they'd like us. We had no idea what to expect. We'd never done anything like this before, nor did we know anyone who had.

As I contemplated my feelings, the best I could compare it to would be how I might have felt someday when Taylor started dating. I would want to meet the guy she was with, and I would want to connect with him. Most of all, I would want to know he would take good care of her and keep her safe. That's the same thing I wanted from Jeff.

With only a few more miles to go, we took the exit off the interstate. I silently prayed, asking God to bless our meeting. If things didn't go well, I wasn't sure how Tara or I would react.

❧

We pulled up to the Kartuses' house, and the whole family tumbled out before we even put the car in park. It was immediately obvious who Jeff was—the guy in the cowboy hat. Before I could even open my door, Tara was jumping out of the car and running toward him. I wasn't sure whether Jeff and his wife, Vanessa, were huggers or not, but they were now. I watched as Tara hugged Jeff and then said, "Where is she?"

Jeff lifted his shirt and pointed to a scar. "She's right here."

Tara ran her trembling fingers over his scar, and in his slow, methodical way, Jeff said, "I'm taking good care of her."

Thank You, God!

It could have been an awkward moment, meeting a strange woman for the first time and all she wants to do is touch your abdominal scar, but if Jeff or Vanessa were freaked out, they didn't let it show. Tara later told me, "I don't know why I did it, but it's just where my head was. I just wanted to physically touch her again somehow."

"I can't thank you enough," Jeff said, his voice faltering. "Thank you so much. I feel bad for Tara and for you. It's very unfortunate that one had to pass for one to live, but I want you to know how thankful I am that Taylor's life saved mine."

He was so appreciative; it was as if he couldn't thank us enough.

We moved to the backyard and sat on the patio. Jeff was a humble guy and down-to-earth. I watched as Tara engaged him in conversation, asking questions and answering his. Sure, a few tears emerged, but watching her converse felt like I was getting my wife back.

Jeff was open and eager to share his life with us. We learned he had been a diabetic for nearly forty years, but after Taylor's pancreas and kidney saved his life, he was completely cured of the disease.

"My sugars used to be between four and five hundred. My machine doesn't go any higher than five hundred, so who knows how high they were," Jeff said. "But now they're always between 72 and 98." With Taylor's pancreas, he no longer had to test his blood sugar or take insulin. "I gave my insulin away to a family who is struggling financially," Jeff said. "They have a daughter with diabetes and couldn't afford her medication."

Vanessa talked about how much their lives had changed. "Before the transplant, he could barely make it up and down the stairs. He slept a lot. I used to worry about him all the time." She mentioned some of his scarier experiences. "He would get so stubborn, and he refused to eat. But now it doesn't matter; he doesn't have to eat breakfast if he doesn't want to. I can go to work and not worry."

"Now, I have a normal day-to-day routine without having to worry about being tied down by my disease," Jeff said. "And Vanessa can have a normal life because she doesn't have to take care of me all the time."

It was easy to see the strain that Jeff's illness had taken on the whole family, and how different everything was now. It had been a long time since any of them had had a normal life.

Vanessa told us they noticed certain changes in Jeff right away. "He always refused dessert," she said, "but the first time they brought him a meal tray in the hospital, he went straight for the dessert. Skipped the meat and the side dish, didn't touch the fruit—he went straight for the cheesecake. He tore it up in, like, two seconds. He just downed the entire slice. It was amazing since he's never eaten sweets."

Tara burst into tears and started to sob. I tried to wipe my own tears away with the back of my hand.

Vanessa stopped talking, and I could see her looking first at Brooke and then at Jeff. Everyone was silent; she had no idea what just happened. "Are you okay?" she asked Tara tenderly.

Tara got a hold of herself, and through her tears she said, "Cheesecake was one of Taylor's favorite desserts."

Someone handed her a tissue, and I put my arm around her. I wasn't sure what would happen next, but when she looked up at me I could see her eyes glistening. This was the connection she'd been hoping for. The cheesecake made it real for her.

Though he'd had the surgery only three months earlier, and he wouldn't be able to go back to his job, Jeff was already finding volunteer work to keep himself busy and he was driving again. "You've given me a new lease on life, and my wife can now have a life without constant worry," he said.

Jeff was a man of few words, but he made them count. When he talked about the day the medical team came to pick up the dialysis equipment, he simply said, "I was glad to see it go."

It was obvious how thankful he was for the gift he'd been given and how drastically it had changed his life. "I'm not only living for me and my family, I'm living for your daughter," he said.

Tara leaned back in her chair and relaxed a bit. I knew that was exactly what she needed to hear. And I needed it too. Jeff would take care of Taylor's organs, and the gift had transformed his life. But watching Tara as she hung on his every word, I realized it was also transforming her in some way.

Tara told them about the dress she'd found the day before, and we both told stories about Taylor. As we talked, I was reminded of the first time Tara had taken her eyes off Taylor when she was only two or three. They were in a small store, so Tara knew she hadn't gone far, but the fact that Taylor wasn't in sight worried her until she found Taylor one aisle over playing with the toys. When Tara picked Taylor up, it wasn't with excitement or joy but more of a sense of relief, like, *Whew, now I can see she's okay*. That's what I saw in Tara as she spoke with Jeff. I saw a mom who knew her daughter would be okay.

Soon it was time to say goodbye. We were spent, and we knew they had to be too. We hugged and promised to stay in touch. Jeff continued to thank us, but finally I interrupted him and said, "I want to thank *you*. Thank you and your family, especially Brooke, for being willing to reach out and connect with us. You don't know how much this has helped us."

Once back in the car, we didn't even have to say anything. We knew Jeff would take care of Taylor. It was a joyous feeling to know that someone was not only living, but thriving, because of Taylor's gift.

Of course.

Taylor took care of people. That's what she did. She took care of Ryan and Peyton, she took care of her friends, and now she was caring for strangers who—through her gift—were part of our family. In the last few months, I'd heard many stories of Taylor's caretaking that I'd never heard before. Taylor wasn't the kind to come home and tell us the thoughtful things she had done, so each time someone told us a new story of her taking care of someone else—like the girl at the garden dedication whose mom had died—it was a gift to us.

Now we had gotten to hear another story, that of a man and his family, and how Taylor was caring for them from the inside out.

⚜

As our plane lifted into the skies above Denver, I noticed that Tara didn't have a blanket wrapped around her this time. Instead she sat erect, calmly reading a magazine. I reached across the armrest and took her hand.

"You know what?" I said. "We were given the *privilege* of organ donation. It wasn't just a decision, *it was a privilege*."

Her smile was all the confirmation I needed that things were going to be okay.

—25—

One Step Forward

Tara

"Todd, there must be at least a hundred people here!" I said. We had just arrived in our friend's backyard for the first official event of the Taylor's Gift Foundation, and I was awed by the turnout.

"It's happening, isn't it?" Todd asked, as he squeezed my hand.

Only hours before we had met the Kartus family in Denver, and now we were back in Dallas in the backyard of our dear friends Pete and Pauline Stein. The place was filled with friends, family, local business leaders, former co-workers, and community members who just wanted to support and encourage us. I was overwhelmed and nervous. Being around people I knew was much harder than talking to people we'd just met.

"How was the meeting with Taylor's organ recipient?" It was the first question I heard that night, and it was asked over and over again in various forms. "Did it bring you peace?" some asked. I knew what they meant. What they meant was, "Did meeting him fix you? Make you all better? Help you move on?"

The thought of having to carry on small talk, or worse yet talk about losing Taylor, with all these people made me want to ditch my shoes and run home. Instead, I prayed.

I wasn't sure how to answer their questions. It was still so new. We'd just stepped off the plane a couple of hours before, and I hadn't had enough time to process everything. Our experience with the Kartus family felt so intimate that I wasn't sure I wanted to talk about it. Even if I did, how could I explain what I was feeling?

I knew why even the best-intentioned asked me those questions. What else did I have to talk about? For the past four months all I had done was sleep and stare into space. That doesn't make for good party conversation. Fortunately, early in the night I found a topic I was happy to dwell on. Someone complimented my dress. I told them the story and then twisted my arm around to pull the tag out of the back to show them.

"Look at this tag," I'd say.

"Wow! Look at this!" they'd say, pulling another friend over. "You've got to hear the story about her dress! Tara, tell it."

For the rest of the night, I talked about finding the dress. It became my protection and insulation. It gave me something to talk about and another way to marvel at God's goodness without having to mention Taylor or the accident. Finding the dress was a blessing, and being able to talk about it at the party was a double blessing. I was grateful for both. In a way, I felt like Taylor was protecting me.

It was a full evening with dinner, an auction, and a concert. Todd made a short presentation and talked about the foundation's goals. He introduced the advisory board, thanking them for assisting in the launch of the foundation. He told them about Jeff Kartus and his family, and how dramatically different their lives were because of Taylor's gift. "Imagine how many more lives could be saved if we just got more people to register," Todd said.

He concluded by saying, "Meeting the Kartus family brought me a great deal of joy. It was a tangible example of why the work we're doing with Taylor's Gift is important and worth our sacrifices."

As people applauded, I outwardly joined in. But inside, I was thinking how different Todd and I were. While I loved meeting the Kartus family, it didn't bring me *joy*, and it didn't bring me *peace*.

Those things left my life when Taylor died. I suspected they'd never come back to me in the same way.

But meeting the Kartuses did do one thing for me—it gave me strength.

Strength to get up in the morning.

⚬⁑⚬

By late June, I found my mornings were getting a little easier. Although I didn't have to be anywhere in particular, I started setting the alarm on my phone and getting up when it went off. "When you get out of bed, make it," my counselor, Judy, said one day. "If you don't, it just calls you to get back in." She was right. So I started to make my bed. During the summer, the kids wanted to sleep in. So on a typical morning, Todd and I would have a couple hours by ourselves before they got up. He'd be out on the porch reading his Bible, and I'd just sit with him. Though we found ways to bond, we were still grieving very differently.

Todd liked to sit in Taylor's room; I didn't even want to see it. It made me anxious to even think about crossing the threshold. But I did like visiting her grave. I would go there almost every day, and sometimes I'd stay for hours. The grave had a temporary marker with only her name on it. I wouldn't even allow them to add the dates. Since the grave itself was so important to me, I wanted to be the one to pick out the headstone. But I couldn't. It wasn't that I was being stubborn; I just couldn't physically make myself describe my child in ten words or less.

It seemed so final.

Taylor's grave, like our home, had become another place for people to drop off signs of their love. People left trinkets—stuffed animals or other knickknacks. Sometimes they would decorate her grave with seasonal signs and streamers. At Easter someone left a flowered cross. My friend Beth Rathe would come out each week and exchange the old flowers for something fresh. I loved seeing flowers in red and black, the East Middle School colors, in Taylor blue and purple, or in red, white, and blue for July. It made me feel good—like people hadn't forgotten Taylor. That was important to me. One of my biggest fears was that people would forget her.

I kept a pillow and a blanket in the car, and on a typical day I would spread the blanket on the shadiest side of her grave, kick off my shoes, and lie down next to her. I'd talk to her, and I would pray.

Sometimes, I'd listen to music on my iPhone, placing one ear bud in my ear and the other on her. I almost always had a hand on her. I liked listening to Steven Curtis Chapman's *Beauty Will Rise* album. It was an album of songs dedicated to and inspired by his daughter Maria, who died in a tragic car accident. The song "SEE" was especially meaningful. It was a description of heaven as if the person were giving a tour to someone who hadn't yet been there. I would play it repeatedly and think of Taylor singing the lyrics. Another song, "Just Have to Wait," was about how I would have to wait to see her again; I cried every time I listened to that one.

One day, while sitting at her grave, I had a major pity party for myself. This wasn't how my life was supposed to turn out. I was mad and frustrated. About that time, I looked up and saw a perfect heart-shaped cloud resting in the clear, blue sky. It felt as if Taylor were reaching out to me—almost like she'd done with the blue dress. I know a lot of people believe that it isn't possible for someone on the other side to reach out, but I saw too many signs of her presence to believe that. Were the signs from her? Were they from God? It didn't really matter. They comforted me and helped me feel connected to both God and Taylor. Moments like that gave me strength to continue moving forward. Sometimes I called these signs "Taylor kisses." I would write about them in my journal, or I'd write letters in my journal to her.

Often I read while I was at her gravesite. My favorite book at that time was *Hearing Jesus Speak into Your Sorrow* by Nancy Guthrie. I would read that book only while I was with Taylor.

I tried to visit Taylor only when Peyton and Ryan weren't home. During the summer, they'd get an invitation to play at a friend's house, and I'd drop them off before heading to the cemetery. Sometimes the time to pick them up came too soon. I'd text various moms and ask if the kids could please stay and play a little longer. "I need some time," I'd text. "I'm falling apart, and I don't want them to see me like this." They always said yes.

When I got home, sometimes Todd would say, "Where have you been?"

"With Taylor," I'd answer. But I knew he already knew. I didn't want to go anywhere else. Even though he didn't feel the same way, Todd didn't tell me *not* to go. He respected my need to be there.

⁂

Todd woke up enthused about going to work. He was creating, leading, and managing a dynamic start-up. A start-up I was a part of but which overwhelmed me each time I tried to participate. In the beginning, I didn't want to hear about it. But lately, as I showed a bit of interest, Todd would see my participation as a good thing and shower me with more details than I could handle. I'd get frustrated because I couldn't take it all in. He'd get frustrated because he had to repeat himself. "We talked about this yesterday!" he said one afternoon. I believed him; I just didn't remember the conversation.

There were other times when I emerged from the fog I'd been in and really wanted to participate and know what was going on with the foundation. In those moments, I'd ask loads of questions. Sometimes, Todd misinterpreted my interest and thought I was questioning him or his abilities.

Todd was so capable and such a can-do guy that often he moved forward quickly, and it was hard for me to catch up. I never wanted him to think I was challenging him or his ideas, but neither did I want to be left out of everything.

It was complicated.

We made mistakes. Lots of them. One of us would blow up, and after we cooled off, we'd come back and say, "I'm so sorry. Let's figure out how to make this work." But it was a struggle. Everything around us had changed—our family, our marriage, and Todd's work were no longer the same. In order to keep it all together, our communication patterns had to change too.

❦

From the moment we made the decision to donate Taylor's organs, I wanted to know the person who had her heart. I wanted to connect with him or her and hug that person. But when Patricia finally reached out to me, I was suddenly hesitant about getting to know her too quickly. For the first few weeks, she emailed or texted Todd. Then as we got to know her better, I felt she needed to connect with me as much as I needed to connect with her. We began emailing and texting directly—usually late at night after our kids had gone to bed.

In the beginning I just shared generic information with her, such as, "I was born in Abilene, and I have three brothers." I learned she had been raised Catholic too. She had been single for a long time and didn't get married until she was in her thirties—at one point, she even thought she was going to be a nun. I found it was easy to connect with her because she was also a mother: she had two boys ages four and six.

One night before I fell asleep, I texted her and said, "Please tell Taylor good night."

"I always do," she texted back.

Soon we friended each other on Facebook. I was dying to see a picture of her but was disappointed when her profile picture was of her kids. Several days later, while in bed, I texted, "Okay, I'm going nuts. I need a picture of you. Can you send me one?"

"No, I'm in my pajamas," she texted back. "I look horrible. My face is swollen from steroids."

After a few more texts, we each agreed to snap a picture and send it—a sort of digital "you show me your bad photo, and I'll show you mine." So I took a picture of my face and sent it to her—no makeup and all.

Immediately she texted back, "You're way too pretty."

After a long pause and some more cajoling, she sent me a text that said, "Okay, this isn't beautiful, but here you go." It was just a quick phone shot, but it was my first glimpse of her. She was sitting on her bed wearing pink pajamas. I could see her stethoscope sitting on the table next to her bed, and my first reaction was, "Ah, there she is."

It was my first chance to see Patricia as her own person, not just an extension of Taylor. Now I had two reasons for wanting to meet Patricia in person.

⁂

I found comfort at Taylor's grave, but like Taylor's friends, Todd found comfort in her room. I rarely went upstairs, but when I did, and I saw her door open, it bothered me. I started insisting no one go in and that her door stay closed so that I wouldn't have to see inside.

One day, a dear friend confronted me about my insistence that the door stay closed. "Your children won't go in there because you want the door closed. You're making it seem as if her room is off-limits, and you're denying them the privilege of finding comfort there. You find comfort at her grave. They don't have that. Their connection is her room, and you've closed that off from them."

She was right. We opened the door to Taylor's room.

A few days later, I had to go upstairs for something. *You can do this*, I told myself, knowing the door would be wide open. I forced myself up the stairs, slowly exhaling as I took each new step. *It won't be that bad*, I promised myself. But as I reached the top step I had to catch in my breath. I couldn't believe what I saw.

"Todd! Todd! Grab a camera and get up here!" I said, moving closer to get a better view.

Todd came dashing up the stairs, with Peyton right behind him.

"Look!" I said, pointing to the carpet.

Originating from Taylor's room was a giant sunbeam. Though the sun obviously was shining on that side of the house, none of the other rooms on the same side had light spilling out into the hall. The sunbeam radiated from her room and landed on the floor outside of her door, producing a warm sunny spot on the carpet—in the shape of a cross. Todd took a couple of pictures while we marveled at the unlikely occurrence, but Peyton didn't say anything. She just lay down on top of it and pressed her nose into the carpet.

— 26 —

The Stock Market of Grief

Todd

The kids had been sleeping on the air mattress in our room for over three months. Tara wanted our bedroom back. I wanted my wife back. We also wanted to return the mattress so the family who had loaned it to us could use it for an upcoming camping trip. But Ryan and Peyton weren't ready to sleep alone in their rooms. They felt isolated and scared. We compromised by moving them both into the guest room. It was hard to get them to sleep at night at first, but eventually they did it and we were proud of them. We were all taking steps forward, but there were setbacks too.

On the Fourth of July, we went to a concert with Tara's mom and dad. About thirty seconds into the music, Ryan saw the French horns and it reminded him of Taylor. He had to get up and leave. He also didn't like going to St. Ann's. He was trying to avoid things that triggered feelings he didn't know how to deal with. Peyton had her own way of dealing with grief—she clung to Tara. Whenever Tara left, Peyton would want to know where she was going, when she would be back, and how long she would be gone.

Our house seemed like the stock market. While one person's emotional stock was rising, another's would be staying steady, while two more might be dropping. We hoped the general trend was upward, but at this point in the mourning process our emotions weren't stable enough to make any long-term projections.

By default, Tara and I were fix-it kind of people. Our first inclination was to help the kids *get past* their grief. So we went to family therapy. It didn't help. In many cases, it only made things worse for Ryan because it brought up things that were too painful for him to process. Ryan had a lot of feelings mixed up inside of him—he had seen Taylor hit the tree.

"No one knows what I've seen. You're the only one," he'd say to me on his bad days.

He was right. I did know. I had seen Taylor too, but I also knew what it had felt like to look up and see the terrified look on my son's face. More than anything, I had wanted to console him, to turn his eyes away from the scene and tell him it would be okay. But I couldn't. I was deep in the snow, straddling my injured daughter and praying she'd be okay. It had been heart-wrenching to have to choose between consoling my son and helping my daughter. It was even more painful now to look back and know I hadn't helped either one.

Thoughts of being on that mountainside, unable to help Taylor, still ripped me apart inside. After the ski patrol had loaded Taylor on the sled, Ryan and I had to ski down to the lodge.

"Can you do it," I'd asked him, "or do you need to get on my back?"

"I-I can do it," he'd stammered through tears.

"She's going to be okay!" I said, to give him strength and reassure him.

I repeated that phrase, or some version of it, all the way down the mountain. Later, we would find out she wasn't okay, and now I felt as though I had lied to him.

Ryan and I were bonded by sports and music; unfortunately, we also had another bond that no father and son should ever share: we were the ones on the mountain with Taylor. The terrible things we'd seen and the helplessness we'd felt put us in a dark and secretive society of two. We couldn't revoke our membership in this club, we couldn't escape the memories, and we couldn't talk about it.

I would have given anything to take the kids' pain away. Instead, just as Tara and I were learning to deal with each other, we had to learn to give Ryan and Peyton the grace and time to grieve in their own way.

After Ryan had a particularly bad day, I tried to find a metaphor to give him words for what he was feeling and to give him hope for the future. "Your life is like a book," I said. "When you're reading a good book, you just sail through the chapters and enjoy the ride. Then suddenly, something bad happens to the main character. Maybe there is one chapter that is really difficult, and you sort of struggle reading the book because that chapter is hard. You're not sure if you want to keep reading, or if you even want to know what happens next. But when you get to the end of the book, you love how the story turns out, and you recommend it to your friends. That's when you understand why the author put that hard chapter in there. It all makes sense once the story ends." I put my arm around him and said, "Your life is like that book, and God is writing the story. Just know that some day when He is almost finished writing, you'll be able to look back and say, 'I totally get why that chapter was there.'"

That was also my hope.

Someday, I wanted to look back and see the purpose in all of this. For now, each of us just had to keep moving through the difficult parts of the story.

❖

Since I wasn't going into an office every day, I tried to be as disciplined as possible at home. I got up at the same time every morning and went outside to sit on the back porch to read and pray. I had decisions to make for the foundation, and so many things were coming up that I had to seek direction and guidance from Scripture on a daily basis. I liked using the YouVersion app to read the Bible on my phone because I could quickly find related verses or search by topic. One day I started reading James, and for the next several days, I found myself working through his words about suffering, such as, "Consider it pure joy, my brothers, whenever you face trials of many kinds, because you know that the testing of your faith develops perseverance" (James 1:2–3). James also talked a lot about how action should come from our faith—something that resonated with me.

Tara would often join me outside. We just needed to be near each other. Over time, I noticed she was also reading. First, it was books on grief—most written by mothers who'd lost a child. Tara couldn't focus for long periods of time, and stories seemed to hold her attention the best. After a while, I noticed she had started to read devotionals. But lately, I noticed she'd also begun to pick up her Bible and read. I asked her about it one day.

"I think you reconnected with God faster than I did," she said. "You immediately saw a purpose and His divine fingerprints on things. I'm still searching."

At least she was looking in the right places.

Tara

In the hospital in Grand Junction, Todd had promised to be my rock. And he had been. I marveled at his strength. There was only one way to explain it—it was the work of the Holy Spirit.

I often imagined the Holy Spirit swirling around Todd and protecting him. How else did he have the capacity to handle the things he handled? How else could he juggle simple but overwhelming tasks, like answering the hundreds of emails that poured in? Or more complex things, like taking care of a wife who was totally incapacitated and always on the verge of losing it? Without help from God, how else could he deal with setbacks when his own loss was so fresh?

I thought about Pam Cope saying we were handpicked for this. Who were we to be chosen? But aren't we all chosen for something? We had a choice. We could follow God's leading, or we could strike out on our own. We could curl up in grief and shut everyone out, or we could stay the course, even when it got hard—even when there seemed to be no end to the pain.

"Now faith is being sure of what we hope for and certain of what we do not see" (Heb. 11:1). Faith is belief without proof. Though I didn't have evidence, I believed that one day in the future the pain would get easier. I also believed there was a place where Taylor waited for me—and I had faith that in that place all pain would be gone.

⚭

Through July and August, my relationship with Patricia, Taylor's heart recipient, continued to grow through texts and emails. We texted about our kids, our families, and her job as a nurse. Though I still wanted a bit of distance—for example, I wasn't ready to talk to her on the phone—we decided to reserve a date on the calendar for us to visit her in Phoenix. We planned a trip for Labor Day weekend and invited Gary Reaves and his crew from WFAA to come with us to do a story that would inspire organ donations. Patricia agreed, and it was all set. I was scared and excited at the same time.

As a precaution, Todd wanted to verify Patricia was who she said she was. Todd called Donor Alliance to tell them we had been corresponding, and we were planning a trip to see her in a few weeks. Once again, Donor Alliance was caught off guard. I'd only recently sent them a letter for them to send to all of the recipients, and they hadn't sent it out yet, so they hadn't received permission from the recipients to pass on contact information. After a few emergency phone calls and meetings, once again they sent us forms to sign. They also contacted Patricia to see if it was okay for them to release her name to us. Of course she agreed, and we laughed about it in our text messages.

It was real. She was real.

Patricia had Taylor's heart. She also had a stethoscope. In a few weeks, I would put that stethoscope to my ear and hear Taylor's heartbeat again.

I couldn't wait.

⚜

Overall, my days were getting better. Though I still had ups and downs—to use Todd's stock market analogy—I was trending upward. Then August hit and school started. On the first day of school, I got Ryan and Peyton off, and then I fell apart. It would have been Taylor's first day of high school.

After dropping them off, I wanted to go to bed, but I also wanted to be as close to Taylor as possible. For the first time since we'd lost her, I crawled into her bed. She was the last one to sleep in it, and the sheets had not been washed. I lay down on her pillow and inhaled the smell of her sheets.

A couple of hours later, Todd came in. "Are you okay?" he asked.

"No," I said, bursting into tears. "She'd be at high school."

"Let's go out and get lunch," he suggested. "We'll go somewhere completely out of Coppell."

And so we did. We went to a quirky little taco place that Todd had found online, and for an hour or two it distracted me. When we got back home, I went back upstairs to her room and lay there. *I have got to get up*, I told myself after I'd been there for a few minutes. *The kids will be home soon. It's their first day of school. You can't do this to them. It's already hard enough on them.* So I did. I got up, made her bed, and went downstairs.

⚜

I worried about Ryan. Not only was it his first day of middle school, but it was his first day in his sister's old school—Coppell Middle School East. I couldn't imagine how hard it would be for him. Since our life had become so public, everyone there knew what

230

had happened. In addition, now a huge memorial garden created to honor his sister stood right outside the building. I wasn't able to cope with my old life and Todd wasn't able to go back to his old job, yet we were sending our kids off to school as if nothing had happened in their lives. It was hard to contemplate.

In preparation for Ryan's first day, Laura Springer had hand-selected his classes and teachers. She'd also talked to each of them, saying, "Ryan is not Taylor's little brother. He is Ryan Storch, and he is to be treated as Ryan Storch. He is going to make it on his own. You need to let him be who he is."

Fortunately, Ryan had a great first day of school.

Unfortunately, it was his last good day for a long time.

Starting the next day, and continuing for the next several months, Ryan had one bad day after another. He would call us crying, sobbing so hard into the phone that all we could make out was, "I wanna come home, come home, come home."

Not only was the garden that contained Taylor's memorial pictures constantly in view, but various T-shirts had been made in her honor, and people were wearing them. Blue silicone bracelets bearing her name decorated the arms of both boys and girls.

One day in math class, Ryan's teacher passed out a worksheet of word problems. Problem number five said, "If you were on a mountain, and you skied down at 15 mph . . ." Ryan read the problem, got up from his desk, and left the room in tears.

"Of course you can come home," we said whenever he called. "If you're upset, we want to take care of you and help you through this."

But the truth was we were still trying to figure out our own grief, and we had very few ideas of how to handle his. There aren't 1-800 hotlines for how to handle your preteen son's sorrow. Even when experts were available, they didn't live with us and they didn't know our child like we did.

We did the best we could. But after several weeks of taking him to school only to have him call us to come back home, we had to come up with a new plan. He was missing a lot of classes and it couldn't continue. We even discussed the possibility of homeschooling him. One day, Laura Springer and the school counselors had a frank talk with us.

"He needs to stay at school," she said. "I know you want to, but you can't let him come home every time he asks. I'll be here for him if he needs me, but he has to learn to stay on his own." It was one more hard thing we were being asked to do.

The next day, Principal Springer told Ryan that if he was upset, it was fine for him to go to the counselor's office, but it was no longer fine for him to go home. As soon as the classroom got quiet, or Ryan was asked to focus independently on a task, his mind would begin to race and he couldn't handle it. There were also unforeseen triggers—like the random math question—that would set him off. If it was a little deal, he'd just go stay in the hall until he had control over his emotions. But if it was a big deal, and he was crying, he'd go to the counselor's office, or to Principal Springer's office, and beg to come home. Laura would sit with him and gently say, "I know you think I'm being unfair. But it's all out of love, Ryan. I love you so much that I have to make you do this."

When the school called, I couldn't handle hearing him in pain. I'd hand the phone to Todd because it caused me too much anxiety. Todd ended up being the contact between Laura Springer, the counselors at school, and our family. I didn't have the strength.

But Todd wasn't immune to Ryan's cries either. It got to him too. Some days, he'd hang up the phone and say, "Is it not enough that he lost his sister? Now he's got to figure out how to deal with school?"

Other days, Todd would feel sorry for himself. "We've got to take this on too? I mean, how much can we bear?" Or he'd vent his anger toward God. "My days aren't hard enough? Why does God want us to now parent a child through this?"

Peyton was having her own issues. She was clingy and whiny. It was like she had a leash and I was on the other end. She didn't want me to go anywhere without her. She seemed to regress to an earlier age. Todd knew he shouldn't take it personally. I was just her security blanket, but it was hard on him.

The emotional stocks in our family portfolio were constantly moving up and down. It was like an emotional minefield, with those who felt healthy at the moment trying not to step on those who felt weak. Just like with the real stock market, we couldn't predict what would happen to any individual stock next. We could only hope to manage it so it didn't go off the charts.

— 27 —

Her Heart Is in the Right Place

Todd

When I saw Patricia's name on my phone, I assumed she was providing more details to coordinate travel arrangements for our meeting in a couple of days. She and Tara hadn't yet spoken, so Patricia typically called me.

"I just wanted to let you know," she said, "I am in the hospital with severe abdominal pain." Her voice sounded weak, not at all like the take-charge woman I'd been dealing with.

"It's nothing to do with the heart," she quickly added. "They think it's my gallbladder, and they're going to operate."

"Oh no! Are you okay?"

"Yeah, it's not a problem. Apparently, this happens a lot during the first year following a transplant. But I just wanted you to know I'm doing everything I can to be home by the time you arrive."

"You just need to take care of yourself. We can reschedule and do this in a week, a month, or whenever," I said, as a million thoughts raced through my mind. How would I tell Tara we might have to postpone the meeting? Or worse, that Patricia had to have surgery? It was now September, and Tara had been waiting to meet her since she'd learned of her in June. She'd actually been waiting to meet Taylor's heart recipient since the day we'd left the hospital.

"No, no, I want you to come," Patricia said. "If I'm still in the hospital, you're welcome to come here. I don't care if my hair is a mess or whatever; it's not a big deal to me."

I paused to figure out how I could best respond, then decided to just say it: "Tara won't enter a hospital." I knew the smells and memories of a hospital were more than she could handle.

"Oh, yeah, of course. I'm so sorry. I didn't even think of that."

"Listen, let me figure out some things on this end. Text me your husband's number, and I'll work out the details with him. I don't want you worrying about anything. I just want you to get better."

We hung up, and I sat down. Ever since we'd been in the hospital in Grand Junction and Tara had told me how important it was for her to meet the heart recipient, I'd felt this overwhelming pressure to make it happen. And more importantly, to make it a good experience. Just when it looked like the meeting was finally happening, it appeared it could all fall apart. I started to pray.

God, what's going on here? How do I tell Tara that Patricia is in the hospital and has to have surgery?

My stomach churned. The pressure of making this trip happen weighed me down. I knew how important it was to Tara. But before I made any decisions, I needed to talk to Joe, Patricia's husband, to get more information. I hoped he'd be a less-biased source and tell us honestly whether or not Patricia was up for our visit. Once I got that taken care of, I needed to talk to Tara.

I dreaded telling her.

She had been an emotional wreck all week. I knew it was because she was thinking about the trip. I was afraid she'd be set back by the disappointment of cancelling or postponing. I couldn't fathom how Tara would react if something terrible happened to Patricia. The two women had obviously been growing close, and everything was riding on this meeting.

I got Joe on the phone. "Listen, there's no pressure from us," I said. "This does not have to happen now, but your wife thinks it still can. Can you be upfront with me and let me know if she'll be okay? Or is she just saying she's all right because she wants this meeting to happen so badly?"

Joe was in the same predicament I was. Everyone wanted it to happen, but not at the expense of anyone's health—mental or physical.

"You know, she's going to make the decision. If she feels as if she can do it, she will," he said.

Over the next twenty-four hours, Patricia talked to her doctors and the surgery was scheduled for Thursday. If all went well, she'd be released from the hospital Friday morning. We were due to return to Texas midday Saturday. It was going to be crazy, but, I hoped, worth it. Less than twenty-four hours before we left, and right before Patricia underwent surgery, Tara and Patricia spoke on the phone for the first time. Their conversation was short but cemented the bond between them. It increased their desire for a face-to-face meeting.

Please, God, I begged, *You have to protect Patricia during this surgery, and You have to allow this meeting to happen.*

∗

Our travel day was tense, until we finally received the text from Joe that Patricia was out of surgery and everything looked good. By the time we landed in Phoenix Thursday night, she was out of the recovery room and eating solid food. I breathed a huge sigh of relief and thanked God for our answered prayer. However, a lot of things still had to happen. We hoped and prayed Patricia would be released the next day and she would feel well enough to meet us. If she did, the meeting would still be on. If she didn't, I knew

Tara wouldn't go to the hospital and all our planning would have been for nothing.

Things continued to look good on Friday morning, but we knew we'd have at least six or seven hours before we would see Patricia. Tara and I hung out in downtown Phoenix, had lunch, and did some shopping. At 2:40, I got a call from one of the WFAA crew members. They had arrived and begun setting up lights, and said we should be there by 4:00. We left in plenty of time, but driving in downtown Phoenix is like driving in a lot of downtowns—not easy to get around. The one-way streets made it difficult for me to find my way back to the highway.

"Do you know where you're going?" Tara asked. She was getting anxious after the GPS seemed to be leading me in circles.

"I'm heading toward the stadium because I know I can get on the interstate near there," I said.

But somehow, I got turned around. At the next stop sign, I pulled up and paused for a second to look around and regain my bearings. "Tara, look!" I said, pointing.

"Oh my!"

Right in front of us was an Arizona State University residential building with architectural grid work on the outside. Hanging on the metal grill was a huge marble sign with white letters that read, "Taylor Place."

Tara and I stared, lost in our own thoughts. I knew we were both thinking the same thing: *Taylor is here with us.* Then a car honked, and we had to move.

"I'm calling Father Alfonse," I said. He answered the phone on the first ring. "We're on our way to meet Patricia, and you're not going to believe what just happened!" I said. "We stopped at a stop sign, and right in front of us was a big building with a sign that said Taylor Place!"

"Well, of course!" he said, laughing. "Don't you think she's there with you? Of course, she is. She's right there with you guys. But please pull over. Don't be driving and talking."

I saw a spot up ahead and eased into it while he continued to talk. As I looked around to gain my bearings, I saw a street sign, nudged Tara, and pointed.

"Father, I hate to interrupt you, but I just want you to know that I pulled over like you asked, and I'm now at the corner of Seventh and *Taylor* Streets."

He laughed again. "Of course, you are!"

Taylor Place. Taylor Street. It really felt like we were getting closer to Taylor's heart.

⁂

I wouldn't consider it hyperbole to say arriving at Patricia's home was one of the most emotional moments of our lives. Walking to the front door, Tara and I held hands. A thousand thoughts swirled through my mind. *What's this going to be like? What kind of person is she? Will I like her?* I remember having to catch my breath as we got to the door. Whatever was about to happen was going to be huge.

Tara wobbled as we made the last few steps up to the door. She had to be nervous; I was. I rang the bell and then stepped back to let Tara enter first. Joe answered the door and welcomed us in. Then Tara saw Patricia. Without saying a word, these two brave women reached out and wrapped their arms around each other. It was more than a hug; it was as if they clung to each other.

My eyes filled with tears. I knew how important this moment was for Tara, and it touched me deeply to see such a positive first impression.

The women continued their embrace—Tara's arms around Patricia's back, and Patricia's arms wrapped around Tara's neck. I tried to blink back tears as I thought about how long Tara had wanted to hug the person who had Taylor's heart. And now she was. Patricia appeared strong, though I knew how fragile she must be, just home from the hospital. I was thankful she had the strength and desire to go through with our meeting.

Almost a minute went by, and I couldn't stand it any longer. I wiped my tears away with my fingertips and joined their embrace in a three-way hug, one arm around my wife and one around the person who had my daughter's heart. The three of us stood there, just thankful to embrace each other.

The best way to explain it was that it felt like falling in love—not the romantic kind, but the kind of love you have when your first child is born. The first time you see them, you instantly love that little person, and know they belong in your family. Until you've had a child, you don't know what it feels like. But once you finally experience that kind of love, it's bigger and broader than you ever imagined. The sensation is hard to describe, but that's how I felt about Patricia. I fell in love with her as if she were the sister I never had.

But my emotions were also complicated. It was bittersweet, knowing that Taylor's heart was here only because she wasn't.

Finally we broke apart. Tara said, "I know we should probably talk or something, but I need to hear her."

Patricia took us into the kitchen and Tara sat down in a chair. Patricia grabbed her stethoscope and helped Tara insert the earpieces. Then Patricia put the head of the instrument high on her chest, just underneath the crucifix she wore around her neck. It seemed as if Patricia wanted to give this gift to Tara as much as Tara wanted to receive it. Tara looked up at me with a mixture of hope and sadness, and I reached out to hold her hand. I had no idea how Tara would react once she heard Taylor's heart, and I wanted to be with her no matter what happened next.

Patricia slowly moved the stethoscope around on her chest. "Tell me if you can hear it," she said.

Tara hesitated for a second, then looked at Patricia and closed her eyes. She nodded softly. Tara was lost in her own world, listening to the rhythmic thumping. She was very composed—peaceful and pained—all at the same time.

I felt such overwhelming relief and gratitude to God for that moment. This is the thing Tara wanted more than any other, and

I'd felt such pressure to get it for her. I'd never thought it would happen. Though I felt like we'd received so many blessings from God since Taylor's death, this was by far the biggest.

After a couple of minutes, Tara opened her eyes and said, "It's so strong."

"Oh yeah," Patricia said. "She is very strong."

Tara took off the stethoscope and handed it to me.

"I want him to hear too," she said.

I took the stethoscope and put it up to my ears.

It's hard to describe what it feels like to know that a heart beating in someone else's chest once belonged to your daughter. It was another bittersweet moment for me. I loved and hated hearing Taylor's heartbeat. I was thankful and angry. I was happy and horribly sad at the same time. There wasn't a single pure emotion; it was an awful, beautiful cocktail of contrasts.

I listened and then handed the stethoscope back to Tara. I wanted her to listen for as long as Patricia would allow.

"I'm so sorry, and I thank you at the same time," Patricia said, bursting into tears. She was a mother, and she knew what this moment meant to us—I could see it on her face. I wrapped my right arm around her, and she hugged me.

"That's all right. I'm so glad you're good," I said.

Tara listened with the stethoscope for a while, then finally took it off and set it on the table. I could see something inside her had settled. That same mixture of relief and strength I had witnessed at Jeff Kartus's house—only a million times more.

We all hugged again and then sat down. Joe had been hanging out in the corner, unsure of what his role was in all of this, but now he joined us at the table.

"How are *you* feeling?" I asked Patricia.

Joe let us know she was okay and though it had been hard, she was doing well. He was protective of her, telling her to sit down while he brought us water. They offered us chocolate Bundt cake, and we talked about our kids. We called Father Alfonse and introduced him to Patricia and Joe. We talked with him for a while, and he prayed for us over the phone. When we hung up, Patricia invited us into the living room where we would be more comfortable. Tara and Patricia sat next to each other on the couch, while Joe and I sat across the room from each other in chairs. As the four of us talked, I could see Patricia watching Tara, to make sure she was okay. And Tara was trying to mother Patricia, making sure she wasn't doing too much.

Patricia understood what it had been like for us to lose Taylor. That understanding probably came from her own near-death experiences. She told us how she had basically been in bed for eighteen hours a day and unable to do much more than lie on the couch for the remaining six. She described how hard it had been to breathe and how she had felt like such a bad mother because she couldn't take the boys to the park or to the zoo.

But Taylor's heart had changed all that.

"Do you want to listen again?" Patricia asked Tara.

"May I?" Tara asked.

"Of course!" Patricia said. "I know I would want to if our situations were reversed."

The two women sat as close as possible to each other. Soon, they were talking privately, lost in their own conversation and oblivious to the fact that Joe and I were still in the room. It was as if they were sisters, with a shared history that neither Joe nor I could relate to.

I was flooded with memories of Taylor. Of seeing Taylor smile. *Can Taylor see this?* I thought about Ryan and Peyton and wished they had come with us. But I also wondered if this was something they should see and do. Would it have been too hard for them? I was glad I didn't have to make that decision right now, and I was unsure if I ever would. What were the chances we would meet again?

Watching the women, I could see they obviously wanted this meeting to last, and Tara and I wouldn't be leaving anytime soon. "Hey, Joe, how about we go out and pick up some dinner and bring it back?" I suggested. "Maybe we can spend some time together and give them a little mom time together."

Joe agreed. As we headed out the door, I turned back to get one last glimpse of Tara. The women were so close and so comfortable with each other. They shared a space, shared their stories, and shared a stethoscope.

It took my breath away to see they also shared Taylor's heart.

—28—

Hearing Taylor's Heart

Tara

When Joe opened the door for us, and I saw Patricia for the first time, my heart began to pound. *There she is, there she is*, I thought. Patricia pulled me toward her, wrapping her arms around me. She held me as tight as she could. I did the same. There was an inexplicable bond between us, and it was created almost instantly. Seeing her, I felt a deep sense of relief. That feeling was intensified a thousand times when, a few moments later, I sat in her kitchen and heard my daughter's heart beating.

At first, all I heard was a diluted whooshing sound as Patricia searched with her stethoscope for the perfect spot on her chest. When she found it, the sounds became crystal clear.

Bump-*bump*. Bump-*bump*. Bump-*bump*. The rhythm was instantly familiar, and I recognized her heart calling out to me. It was the same distinctive sound I'd heard so many times before—lying beside her, with my head on her chest in the hospital, lying with her in her bed at home, even the very first ultrasound when she was still in my womb. A gush of warm emotion rushed over me, and I melted from the inside out. Taylor seemed to speak to me, saying

"I'm here. I'm right here." It was hard to comprehend that despite all we'd been through in the past few months, Taylor's heart had *never* stopped beating.

An overwhelming sensation of love filled me. I felt a connection with Taylor and with Patricia. I knew it wasn't physical; there was no reason for us to bond so quickly or for me to connect with Taylor's heart in the way I had. The connection was a spiritual one. The Holy Spirit is the great Comforter, and I felt as if He had embraced me and wrapped me in the comfort of knowing my daughter was safe. I finally felt the connection that I had so longed for. It was overwhelming, in such a beautiful way.

⋯

After the guys left to get food, Patricia and I sat alone in her living room, and I felt safe asking her a very intimate question.

"I'd like to hear her heartbeat like I used to—without a stethoscope. Can I put my head on your chest?"

"Of course," Patricia said, wrapping her arm around me and pulling me closer. With my eyes closed, I pressed my ear against her warm skin, marveling at the sound of my daughter's heart pumping in Patricia's chest.

Bump-*bump*. Bump-*bump*. Bump-*bump*. BOOM.

Suddenly there had been a loud kick. I waited a second, then sat up and looked at Patricia.

"Did you feel that?" she asked.

"Yes. I did."

I put my ear back to her chest—and BOOM! It happened again, like a huge kick. "What was that?" I asked.

"That was Taylor," Patricia said with a smile on her face.

"Does she do that often?"

"It's never happened before," she said. "But while you were listening, I was praying to God and asking Him to give you a sign from Taylor."

I was speechless.

"Just as soon as I finished praying, I felt it," Patricia said. "I've never felt anything like that before. But until you said something, I didn't know if you could feel it too."

By now, we were both tearing up again. The same warm feeling that washed over me in the kitchen flooded through me again. It was a precious gift from God, from Taylor, and from Patricia. I would never forget it.

⚬⟡⚬

The guys were gone a while, and as Patricia and I continued to talk, she asked me to tell her more about Taylor. I talked about how fun she was, the silly things she did with her friends, and how she always took care of the outsiders. I told her about how I would lie next to Taylor at night and we'd talk about her day. And boys.

"Right before she fell asleep, she always did the same thing," I said. "She'd tuck her Pooh bear *behind* her." I had thought that was so odd. I told Patricia how one night I asked her about it. "Why don't you snuggle with him?"

Taylor had said, "Because when I'm really tired, and I turn over, he's just there. I don't have to find him."

"I thought it was kind of silly," I told Patricia, "but once she said it, I totally understood. He was just there for her when she needed him."

"She liked Pooh?" Patricia asked, a smile forming at the corners of her mouth.

"She loved Pooh!"

"Did I tell you I have a Pooh tattoo on my right hip?"

"No way!" I said, laughing.

She showed me her Pooh tattoo and told me all about her Winnie the Pooh collection, which was now in her boys' rooms. It felt like the invisible bond we had the moment I walked in the door had only grown tighter.

When the guys returned, I told Todd about Patricia's love of all things Pooh and then about the kick in her heart after she prayed to God for a sign of Taylor. As he listened, his eyes grew wide and a smile spread across his face.

"Of course!" he said when I finished.

I witnessed a deep sense of peace settle over him.

I recognized it, because I felt it too.

Finally, at midnight, we tore ourselves away. Patricia had just gotten out of the hospital, and she needed to rest and recover.

None of us wanted our visit to end, so we decided to meet for breakfast in the morning before Todd and I headed to the airport to catch our flight. The next morning, the good feelings continued. Patricia brought her stethoscope so I could listen one more time. It was so hard to say goodbye to her. We both wanted to connect again, but we were unsure of how or when it would happen.

But we each had faith it would.

⚬⟡⚬

On the flight home, I turned to Todd and said, "This was a gift from God."

He smiled at me.

It was similar to what he'd said to me on the plane home from Denver, but now I understood it at a deeper, more profound level than I had before. Knowing that Taylor's heart had *never* stopped beating was a powerful and overwhelming thought; I was in awe. From the beginning of time, God knew that Taylor's heart needed to be with someone who wanted to connect as much as we did. And now He had made that happen. So many donor families want to meet their loved one's organ recipients but never have the opportunity. I knew God's hands were all over this—I could see His fingerprints in everything that had happened. It was only because of His grace that we had the privilege of experiencing this.

Though I didn't like it when Pam Cope first said it, by now I had come to believe we had, indeed, been handpicked for this. After meeting Patricia, I believed she had also been handpicked by God to give Taylor's heart a new home.

❧

Though the story began as a local piece about hearing Taylor's heart, our story and the foundation ended up receiving national attention when *Good Morning America* showed the piece to their audience and the hosts were clearly moved by our story. A week later, both Patricia and Joe and our family were invited to go to New York to tell our story in person on *The Today Show*.

Those who are grieving like to be distracted. Sometimes they choose inappropriate ways like alcohol or drugs, but for Todd and me, it seemed God had blessed us with some healthy distractions.

Like Ryan and Peyton.

Blue sundresses with a Taylor label.

Or friends who made me earn points by planting tomatoes.

And now this trip.

It was such a blessing to have something to look forward to. And I couldn't wait to see Patricia again.

—29—

Trust While Doing

Todd

I felt as if I had learned to trust God in new ways when I quit my job and we started Taylor's Gift. But I still struggled knowing what my roles and responsibilities were in this new partnership. I knew I was supposed to trust God to make things happen, but did that mean I should sit back and not do anything? Just wait for Him to do it all? Or was I supposed to do something—use the gifts and talents He'd blessed me with to further the mission of Taylor's Gift Foundation? And if so, how much of me and how much of Him?

Until this point, there had been very little of the old Todd *doing*. I had spent most of the previous months responding to the things God brought our way, and I had no doubt He had blessed us abundantly. However, as we prepared for the New York trip and for the *Today Show*, I wrestled with whether or not I should call some of my media connections to see if we could do more interviews while we were in NYC. Didn't it make sense to maximize our time and the foundation's exposure? On the other hand, so far I hadn't made any calls to media—they called us—so maybe I should sit back and see what else God would do.

It was a dilemma that got at the heart of who I am.

Am I a doer or a truster?

Around that time, I came across Psalm 131 in the Message version of the Bible: "God, I'm not trying to rule the roost, I don't want to be king of the mountain. I haven't meddled where I have no business or fantasized grandiose plans. I've kept my feet on the ground, I've cultivated a quiet heart" (vv. 1–2). That passage spoke to me. I hadn't fantasized grandiose plans. I had kept my feet solidly on the ground, and I didn't want to rule the roost. I just wanted to help sick people get healthy through organ donation.

I decided God would want me to use the talents and connections He'd blessed me with to further what He was already doing. I was also pretty sure those on the list waiting for organs would want the same. I was doing what I was doing not for any glory for me—I wasn't trying to be king of the mountain—I just wanted Taylor's life and death to have a purpose and meaning. So I picked up the phone and called a friend of mine in New York with lots of media connections. I told him about Taylor's Gift and how we were trying to get the message about organ donation out to as many people as possible. "We're going to be in New York in a couple of weeks to do *The Today Show*. Is there anyone else we should connect with while we're there?"

"I know a lot of people who would be interested," my friend said. "Let me make a few phone calls and get back to you."

I'd done what I could do. The rest was up to God—that's where the trust came in.

That's also where God worked.

⚬

I finally felt as if I'd found the balance between trusting and doing. As we prepared for the New York trip, I captured a couple of thoughts on my blog:

252

I am constantly drawn to two things. The first is what my grandfather instilled in me: It's not what happens to you that matters, but how you react to it that does.

The second is Taylor's favorite verse, from Luke 18:27 (NIV): What is impossible with men is possible with God.

More than anything else, these two thoughts were my vision for Taylor's Gift. Yes, we'd lost our daughter and that wasn't fair. We didn't have a choice about whether she lived or died. But faced with her loss, the question remained: How would we react to it?

The foundation was our answer.

We also knew that moving the needle on the number of organ donors wouldn't be easy. And, frankly, the kind of media attention we were getting was in the realm of the impossible. What nonprofit less than a year old could land segments on the two most-viewed morning shows? But what was impossible with men was possible with God. We were proof of that.

Whenever I dropped Taylor off at school, I would say, "Make someone's day better." I liked to think that's what we were doing with Taylor's Gift. We were working to make someone's day better through the gift of organ donation. While reflecting on the things that had happened over the past few weeks and the things scheduled for the next few days, I wrote:

> None of this would be possible without God choosing us for this journey. We are blessed. This is just a small step in the life-changing work that Taylor's Gift Foundation will make in this world. Taylor is proud of all our work, but there is so much more ahead of us.

❖

The last time I had been in New York City with my family was at the beginning of November 2006, when I'd run the New York Marathon. Tara, Taylor, and Ryan had come to cheer me on; Peyton was too young, so she had stayed at home with grandparents.

I had planned my work schedule around the event so I could be in the city with my family for a few days. I would work during the day, and when I finished I'd join Tara and the kids in exploring Manhattan. The city was special to Tara and me. It was where our relationship had moved from friendship to something more. We had taken the kids to the top of the Empire State Building and to Little Italy, where we had pointed out the restaurant Tara and I ate in when we were dating. It had been one of the best trips we'd ever been on. We had been thrilled when the kids loved it as much as we did.

As the plane descended into New York, I pointed out buildings in the skyline to Ryan and Peyton. I had an immediate sense of déjà vu. I remembered pointing out the same buildings on our last trip. It was the same son, but this time, a different daughter.

Patricia, Joe, and their boys were staying in the same hotel as we were, and they were waiting for us in the lobby. We had introductions all around, lots of hugs, and a few tears. It felt like a reunion.

After checking in, the whole crowd went out for dinner. We had a great time talking, laughing, and getting to know one another better. When we returned to the hotel room, Tara and Patricia were still texting back and forth when suddenly Tara said, "Ryan and Peyton, Mrs. Winters has her stethoscope. Would you like to hear Taylor's heart?"

Patricia was thoughtful enough to have brought her stethoscope, and she thought the kids might want to hear their sister's heartbeat again.

"I would!" Peyton said eagerly.

"I don't want to," Ryan said.

There wasn't a right or wrong answer. So Ryan and I stayed in our room while Tara and Peyton went up to Patricia's, where Peyton heard her sister's heart beating for the first time since her death.

Tara told me later that as soon as Peyton heard it, she looked up and locked eyes with Patricia, and they both smiled. Tara snapped a picture at that exact moment and showed it to me. It was incredible to see.

The next morning, I woke to the sound of rain and got up to read my Bible. In my journal I wrote:

> Sitting in the Essex House Hotel in New York City. Began the morning with the Bible. I love reading the YouVersion on the iPad. Today starts with Psalm 126, "And now, God, do it again. Bring rains to our drought-stricken lives."
>
> God is raining His blessings and glory and love on us. Yes, it is raining outside, and the rain pounds the window over our hotel room. I know You are here. I know You are with me.

Before we left the hotel, I prayed God would bless our story by using it to inspire and motivate viewers to become registered organ donors.

⁂

Being behind the scenes of *The Today Show* was an amazing experience, not only for the kids but for the adults too. Tara and I sat on the couch with Patricia between us. The three of us held hands. There was an energy among us, but no one was nervous because we had each other. Though the footage they showed made us tear up, we all stayed strong. Throughout the interview, I felt like I was at the center of God's will. I knew that sharing Taylor's story was helping to save lives—like Patricia's.

Later in the day the kids wanted to see the Empire State Building. On the way, I thought about Ryan and wondered if he remembered the last time we had visited. A feeling of nostalgia washed over me—we were doing the same things we'd done on the last family trip, only this time with Peyton. Back then, Ryan had been the younger brother—the middle child. Now he was the older brother and the oldest. Things had changed for all of us.

Being at the top of the Empire State Building is really cool. But until I'm up there, I forget that it can also be a little scary. That high up, the wind is stronger than you expect, and for some reason, looking down makes the distance to the ground seem a lot greater than when you're on the sidewalk looking up.

That night, like always, I had my camera with me. I lined up the kids and Tara so I could take their picture. Looking through the camera lens, I realized it was the same spot I'd taken a picture of Tara, Taylor, and Ryan years earlier. I was flooded with memories of Taylor and our last trip to New York, but I tried not to let my emotions show. I didn't want to ruin the experience for anyone else.

But it didn't get any easier. Ryan and Peyton chose the very same coin-activated binocular viewer that he and Taylor had argued over last time we were there. At the time, I had only one quarter, and they had to take turns. Watching Ryan go through the same motions, this time with Peyton, I thought about how much things had changed. Who was I back then? That dad would never have suspected how limited his time with his kids really was. Just like the quarter would buy only so many minutes with the binoculars, time would run out and the view would never be the same.

I was still in a nostalgic mood as we made our way back to the hotel. We passed street vendors selling jewelry, handbags, and sunglasses. A dark-haired woman had children's artwork for sale. The colors caught my eye, and I saw that they were a combination of painting and calligraphy, and each picture spelled out a child's name. When I looked up from the table, the picture on display made me stop and look again. In flowing letters and vibrant colors, it spelled: TAYLOR.

Once again, I felt as if she were with us.

I stopped to take her picture.

⚬⚬

Over the next few weeks, as the stats came in, we began to see the number of registered donors increasing nationwide. To me, it was a confirmation that we were doing exactly what we should be doing. The numbers were proof. It was very satisfying to know that our story and Taylor's Gift had played at least a small part in getting that needle to move up.

I thought back to the conversation I'd had with Tara about how one day I wanted to see Taylor and hear her say, "Good job, Daddy! You did it!"

What would she think about all of this? I closed my eyes and thought about all the people we'd met and how our world had grown. *What do you think, baby? We're not there yet, but I am giving it everything I've got.*

A vision came to mind of Taylor laughing and saying, "Let's do this, Dad. Let's get this stuff done. This is how we can save the world!"

And for a moment, all felt right.

—30—

The Bike Rider
Leaves a Message

Jonathan Finger
Colorado

For the first time since his teens, Jonathan was once again riding his mountain bike. It was an exhilarating sensation. After spending so many years on the couch, tethered to a machine, the open air felt like freedom. Though it had taken eight years, Jonathan finally had a new kidney. After his mother's donated kidney had failed, he had vowed to do everything he could to make sure the next one—if there was a next one—lasted as long as it possibly could. Now that he finally had it, he was eating right, exercising, and making sure he kept his scheduled doctor's appointments.

It was at one of those appointments that the social worker came in with a large manila envelope and said, "This is from the donor's family. Do you want to see it?"

Jonathan had wanted to connect with them from the beginning. In fact, he'd started a letter to them several times but had

259

never quite found the right words to finish it. He eagerly took the envelope, and when she left the room, he opened it.

Jonathan already knew what to expect—he'd been told the donor was a young female. Since he assumed most organ donors were much older, he thought that meant she was in her fifties or sixties. He liked to think she'd been sick for a long time and that her family was ready for her to go. But when he opened the envelope, a picture of a young girl slid out onto the floor. Jonathan was stunned. He picked up the photo and studied it, then emptied out the contents of the envelope. There were multiple pictures of the young girl and her family, accompanied by a four-page letter written by her mom.

Jonathan was immediately engrossed. The letter described who the young girl was, what she believed, and all the things she had done in her short life. It made him feel incredibly emotional. In an instant, he felt a connection to her and her family. Even without knowing them, he already thought of them as family. He remembered the letter he'd begun to write months earlier when he didn't know anything about her. Now that letter wouldn't suffice. He'd have to rewrite it before he sent it off.

But before he could, a virus set him back. Though it didn't put the kidney at risk, he was hospitalized for a while. He postponed writing the letter until he was better.

Too soon, November arrived, and the holidays were sneaking up on Jonathan. He worried that sending the letter through Donor Alliance would take too long. He wanted the family to know how thankful he was *before* Christmas. He debated about what he should do.

On November 16, while watching the local news, he saw a story about the Avalanche—the local NHL hockey team, who was playing the Dallas Stars that night. Both teams were honoring a girl who'd lived in one team's state and had died in the other's. He immediately recognized the picture of the girl they showed on the news. This was his donor!

As the story continued, Jonathan knew he couldn't wait any longer. Instead of mailing his letter, he picked up the phone and dialed the 1-800 number listed on the foundation website, and left the most awkward message of his life.

—31—

First Holidays

Tara

After returning from New York, Todd and I had to stop by Austin Elementary, where Taylor and Ryan had gone and where Peyton now attended. While we were there, a custodian stopped me and said, "Can I talk to you a minute?" She went on to tell me how her fifteen-year-old son was facing a medical issue with his heart, and it was affecting his behavior and attitude. He was leaving home and not coming back, not taking his medicine, and exhibiting other self-destructive behaviors.

"How do you cope with this?" the woman asked.

Our situations weren't the same—Taylor had died in an accident; her son was facing a long-term illness and possibly death if he didn't make some adjustments in his lifestyle. However, I understood her fear and the feeling that things were spiraling out of control. I knew how helpless she must have felt, so I said, "When I feel like you do, I pray." I then asked if I could pray for her and her son.

She nodded, trying to hold back the tears.

I knew I didn't have any concrete answers for her. Tragedy strikes different people in different ways, and the only sure thing is that

God understands our pain and will help us get through it. That was the best I could offer—a way to connect with Him. Todd was with me and joined me in praying for her. On the way home Todd said, "It really touched me when you ministered to her. Knowing how much pain you are still carrying, it was just so beautiful to see you reach out to her even in the midst of your own grief."

His words meant a lot. He was right; I dealt with a lot of pain, and I wasn't sure I could say it had lessened much. But I had come a long way from those initial days. Some days I still felt like I had a long way to go.

A few days later, I was reading Scripture when I came across 1 Peter 5:10. "The suffering won't last forever. It won't be long before this generous God who has great plans for us in Christ—eternal and glorious plans they are!—will have you put together and on your feet for good" (Message).

I already knew the good days on earth were temporary; my faith told me the bad days would soon end too. My hope was in God, not in my own ability to fix things.

♣

Among the amazing people we'd met was Ralph Strangis, the play-by-play announcer for the Dallas Stars. Ralph wanted to use his NHL connections to support Taylor's Gift, and he had worked tirelessly with the Dallas Stars to put together a fund-raiser.

The plan was to present Taylor's Gift Night at American Airlines Center, the home stadium of the Dallas Stars, on November 16, when the Stars played the Avalanche, the Colorado team. One team was from the state where Taylor had lived, and the other team was from the state where she'd died; both teams joined to support one cause.

Coaches, broadcasters, and staff from both the Stars and the Avalanche planned to wear blue Taylor's Gift ties. During warm-ups, players from each team would wrap their sticks in blue tape, and during the game, tables would be set up in the arena to give fans an opportunity to register as organ donors. They could also support the foundation through donations in the merchandise stores. In exchange, they would receive Taylor's Gift wristbands. Ralph would interview us during the first intermission, and the Stars would donate proceeds from ticket sales to the foundation.

It was an unbelievable opportunity and our whole family planned to go.

⚬⟶⟵⚬

On November 16, my parents and Todd's parents met us at the house, where we hung out until it was time to leave for the hockey game. I was always nervous before foundation events. They often required me to speak publicly, and I hated that. Even private conversations could be awkward. People wanted to hear our story, and I didn't want to tell it for fear of breaking down in public. But despite my anxieties, the awkward moments were worth it if they resulted in more people signing up to become donors.

I invited our parents into our bedroom to show them some things on the computer. "Here's what the new website looks like," I said, pulling up the latest version. I talked about how much work it took to create it and all of the volunteers and companies that were involved. "And we just got a 1-800 number," I said. "It's so cool because people can leave messages on it. When they leave a message, it transcribes it and emails it to us."

While I was showing them, an email came through with the subject "Google Voice."

"Oh, look! We just got one," I said. "Let's see what it says." I clicked it open and began to read the transcript of the call out loud.

"Hi, my name is Jonathan Finger, and I received one of your daughter's kidneys. You sent me a letter. It was blue—" I stopped reading and looked up to see four sets of wide eyes staring back at me. "Todd! Where's Todd?"

"I think he's upstairs working on the foosball table," his mother said.

I ran to the living room and yelled, "Todd! You've got to come here right now!"

Todd came right down. This time, instead of reading the transcript, I turned up the speaker and played the voice message so we could hear what he sounded like. When it finished, I played it again. And again.

We marveled at the incredible timing and the fact we all got to hear the call together.

It was such a blessing to have received Jonathan's call. It had been more than six months since I'd sent the letter to Donor Alliance, and we hadn't heard from any of the other donors. I was afraid no one else wanted to make contact. But with Jonathan's call, we had now connected with three out of the five. And in time, I believed that we would eventually connect with them all.

That night, I didn't have to be anxious at all. Just as God had given me the blue dress to talk about at that first fund-raising dinner, He gave me Jonathan to talk about at the hockey game.

"You'll never believe what happened today," I said when people wanted to chat, and then told them about the phone call.

It took us a couple of weeks to respond to Jonathan, but we finally did. Like Patricia, our early communication with Jonathan was through texts and emails. We learned that this was his second kidney transplant and he'd been on dialysis for eight years! He talked about the freedom he had now. I couldn't imagine a bigger life change.

Because of Jonathan's tech background, he and Todd also started to communicate via online chats. Soon Jonathan volunteered his talents for the new website. He became an active volunteer for the foundation.

As Todd and Jonathan worked together, they found out they shared a lot in common. Like Todd, Jonathan played several instruments, and they had a shared love of rock music. One day, while they were chatting online, they discovered they even shared the same birthday, though Jonathan was a few years younger. Just as

Patricia and I had connected so deeply, now Jonathan and Todd were doing the same thing. Once again, it was as if God had orchestrated the whole thing.

⊶

We knew our first holidays without Taylor would be hard, and we made intentional choices to minimize our pain. At Thanksgiving, for example, we didn't want to do anything we'd ever done before. We thought that meant we didn't want to be around our families and all the painful reminders of Thanksgivings past. So we rented a little cabin in Broken Bow, Oklahoma. It was far enough away from our memories and within our little budget.

We packed a ton of food and lots of games for the kids and looked forward to some great family time. Todd wanted to grill out, and I wanted to chill out. He looked forward to chopping wood, teaching the kids how to whittle, and making a fire in the fireplace. At night, he planned to take the kids outside to look up at the stars. We all wanted to make new family traditions so reminders of our old ones weren't ever-present.

Unfortunately, what we got was a lot of time alone with our thoughts. The first morning, Todd woke up and couldn't walk. He'd dislocated his back while moving the foosball table, and apparently his back had locked up on the drive to the cabin. He spent the entire trip sitting in a recliner because he was in so much pain. No fires, no grilling, no staring at the stars, no chopping wood, and no whittling. The only time he got up was to hobble to the table for meals.

I cooked every single breakfast, lunch, and dinner, and made all the snacks. I played games with the kids, drove to the local pharmacy for Todd's prescriptions, and when it wasn't raining (which was rare), took walks in the woods with the kids. There was very little chilling for me and a whole lot of doing. A few days into the trip, I began to resent Todd. I wanted him to be there for me emotionally and physically; instead, I was taking care of him.

It wasn't until later that I realized he'd probably felt the same way about me for months. How selfish of me to feel that way.

⚬⃛

Thanksgiving Day wasn't easy. I knew it wouldn't be. I woke up missing Taylor. All day long, past Thanksgiving Day memories flashed through my mind. I would briefly indulge them—Taylor's first Thanksgiving, later years of her eating her favorite casseroles, or watching the parades on TV. When the memories got too painful, I'd shove them away.

Around 11:00, I put the food in the oven and sat down with Todd while I waited for it to finish cooking. He was watching a pregame show in anticipation of an afternoon of football. Without warning, James Brown, one of the hosts of *The NFL Today* on CBS, introduced a Thanksgiving story about blessings and inspiration. I had been lost in my own thoughts, but those words caught my attention.

A video began to play, and I watched the mother of former Cincinnati Bengals receiver Chris Henry tell her story. Chris had died eleven months earlier in a tragic accident. At the time, his mother had made the difficult decision to donate his organs. As the eight-minute story unfolded, I watched as she met the four recipients—four lives that his organs had saved, four families that had been forever changed because of his gift.

I couldn't help it; I started to cry.

Each of the recipients talked about how much they wanted to thank her for their life-changing gift. One recipient's husband said, "Life isn't about the number of breaths you take; it's about the moments that take your breath away." Meeting the mother of his wife's donor was one of those moments.

I knew exactly how each of them felt.

Chris's mother explained how the recipients had become like family to her. At the end of the piece, she said, "People of faith believe that people journey into one's life for a reason. Of course my family will never be the same, but it will also never be bigger. For that, on this and every other day, I will truly, truly be forever thankful."

By this point, I was bawling. The kids, sensing the change in my mood, had wandered in to see what was going on. I tried to pull myself together and use it as a teaching moment. "Look how many people are talking about organ donation now. Did you ever think you'd see that on an NFL pregame show?"

If a national conversation about organ donation was starting, that was something to be truly thankful for. It felt great to see the exposure the issue was getting. But at the same time, I knew the only reason we even paid attention to the issue was because Taylor was gone. It was impossible not to feel sadness along with our gratefulness.

That Thanksgiving taught us a lot of lessons. We'd thought that being away from family would ease our pain, but being left to our own thoughts, without the added chaos of our family to distract us, just left us with a different kind of pain.

Most of all we learned we couldn't run from our pain—it only followed us.

⚬⚬

We made it through Thanksgiving, and our friends asked what we were doing for Christmas. My standard response was, "I just want to go to bed and wake up on the second of January." We both knew we needed to celebrate and put up decorations for the sake of Ryan and Peyton, but it was beyond our ability. Finally, friends suggested that if we got out the tree and a few boxes of decorations, they would put them up for us. So that's what we did. We left the house, and they came over and decorated the house beautifully. Nothing was in its usual place, so it was at once familiar and completely different at the same time.

It was perfect and it was a huge gift to me.

Todd

Grief was an ocean with waves continually crashing along the shoreline. Sometimes the waves were small—powerless to do much. Other days their power was enough to rock me in their wake, but if I was strong enough I'd meld and move with them so they couldn't harm me. The worst were those that pounded against me all day, threatening, like a riptide, to pull me under. Just as I'd catch my breath, an eight-footer would rise up and crash over my head, leaving me gasping for air.

Right after Taylor died, people would ask, "How are you?" As the months passed, that slowed down a bit. However, with the holidays so close, I found myself answering that question more frequently. The answer was never simple. It truly depended on the moment. For example, the fifteenth day of each month was hard because it reminded us of March 15, the day Taylor died. On those days, I often found myself supporting Tara in some way. But as Tara and the kids developed better coping skills, it was as if I could take a break from being their protector. It was then I found myself starting to slip into the abyss of grief.

That's what happened on December 15, the worst of the nine "fifteens" I'd experienced since Taylor's death.

That morning, I found myself listening to, and involved in, conversations with people planning their upcoming ski trips. Each one reminded me of my beautiful daughter. I remembered how excited she had been just nine months earlier as she got ready for our ski trip. She had been so excited to get out on the slopes and experience it all.

I'd learned enough in therapy to know that trying to run or hide from the waves of grief wouldn't help. I had learned to embrace the water. Tread. Stand. Paddle. Just let the waves rock me. It's when you fight against the waves that you lose your footing and go under. Riding them will take you back to shore. So after those morning reminders of what I'd lost, I tried to get busy. I spent most of the day in my office working on operations and accounting issues for Taylor's Gift. And the seas calmed for a bit.

But late in the afternoon the waves were back, slamming against my mind. I had gone to finish some Christmas shopping, and while I was running some errands those persistent waves seemed to find their way into my car, making it hard to think. I pulled into a parking space as my brain sloshed. It felt like seaweed: tumbling in the waves but never going anywhere.

During those moments, I tend to get very reflective and often I try to write, jotting down notes so I can think things through more thoroughly. It was my way of riding the waves until the swells stopped. But the memories kept coming—wave after wave of them. It felt like a high tide of grief, and my arms were tired; I couldn't swim anymore. I put down my pen. Nothing seemed to calm the raging waters of my grief.

By the time I got home, I was tired and sluggish. The back pain that had plagued me since Thanksgiving ached down to my toes. Maybe the grief exaggerated it that day; it was hard to tell. All I wanted was sleep. It was the only thing that would stop the emotional tides and the physical pain.

Around 8:10 p.m. we heard a knock at the door. I opened it to find the entire Coppell High School choir; they were Christmas caroling. Tara and the kids joined me at the door, and as they sang I felt the waves calm and roll back out to sea. *Thank you, God! This is exactly what I needed.*

After a couple of traditional carols, they finished with "Man in the Mirror," a song about looking at yourself and making a change. Tara and I immediately got the message, and as we did, we both teared up. Somehow, in the beauty of that moment, my pain dulled.

Before they left, the group presented us with a check for fifteen hundred dollars—money they'd raised from programs the choir had put on to support Taylor's Gift. Tara and I were touched by their selfless generosity.

As we said good night and closed the door, I knew we were blessed—genuinely blessed to be part of such a wonderful community.

That night I went to bed early. I hugged and kissed Tara and the kids, including a hug and kiss to Taylor in heaven. I said my prayers, and before I fell asleep I got out my notebook and wrote. The next day I would post it on my blog:

> I miss her so much, but know she is with me all the time. Thanks for being there with me, Christ. Thank you for allowing me to process this grief and put it to good use each and every day . . . and when I don't feel I can, continue to show me the path.
>
> Another day. Another 15th.
>
> Good night.

-32-

Change of Hearts

Tara

Christmas was miserable.

We spent it with my family in Louisiana. Like we had done with Thanksgiving, we chose to spend the day away from home so we wouldn't have to relive all the memories of Christmases past. My extended family went the extra mile to make Christmas a merry time for Ryan and Peyton. They surrounded all of us with love, laughter, and tons of Cajun food.

We were in survival mode. There's not much else to say about Thanksgiving, Christmas, and New Year's, except to thank God we made it through them. At least, I figured, the New Year meant we'd made it through our first year of holidays.

A few days later I headed to Walmart to pick up a few supplies. At the entrance, I suddenly stopped. Though it was only the first week of January, I was visually assaulted with an overwhelming abundance of pink and red. I'd been so worried about Thanksgiving and Christmas that I hadn't even considered Valentine's Day. It was one of my favorite holidays to celebrate with the kids. Every year I decorated the house and had presents for everyone at the table. I always made a pink-and-red dinner with ham, strawberries, pink mashed potatoes, and cherry 7-Up. It was my day to say, "I love you so much I'm about to burst!"

I felt as though my heart had already burst while standing in Walmart. And it only got worse as February 14 got closer. A few weeks later, when I went to buy candy for my kids, I found that the things they loved best were all packaged in threes. Three Hershey's kisses. Three SpongeBob candies. Three chocolate-covered marshmallow hearts. *I don't have three anymore.*

Valentine's Day not only snuck up on me, it sucker punched me when I wasn't watching.

One more holiday to dread.

⚬╬⚬

A few days before Valentine's Day, I heard the front door open and in walked Ana Lucia Cottone, the network executive we'd met at the Donate Life Film Festival. She was the one who'd told me the story about the clay Buddha that cracked, exposing gold underneath. We'd kept in touch and become good friends. I loved her no-nonsense style. She would say whatever was on her mind.

We'd often talked about getting together again, and knowing that pink and red were out for this Valentine's Day and "blue" was in, Todd wanted to surprise me by flying her in.

"I'm here for a week!" she announced.

I took one look at my messy house, hugged her, and burst into tears.

Ana Lucia was, in fact, the exact Valentine my heart needed. She wasn't the kind of person who let you lie around and mope. While she was extremely sympathetic, gentle, and kind, she was also willing to do whatever she could to help us get on with life. I must have looked like I really *needed* that help. By the evening of her first day, she said, "Do you ever look at yourself in the mirror and just talk to yourself?"

"No."

"You need to see yourself go through this," she said, standing me in front of a mirror. "You need to take a good look at yourself."

I looked at the face in the mirror, and it was a shock. I'd lost a lot of weight, my cheeks were gaunt, and my eyes were sunken. I looked five years older. Up to that point, I had no idea how bad I looked.

"Look at yourself and say, 'I'm going to be okay,'" she said.

Studying myself in the mirror, I resolved to do better. I had concentrated all of my available energy on taking care of Ryan and Peyton. I wasn't doing anything for myself.

But Ana Lucia wasn't just about making me better. She wanted the whole family better. When she found out we hadn't sat at the kitchen table and eaten dinner as a family since Taylor had died, she made us do it. It was hard at first, because no one knew where to sit. Were we supposed to leave Taylor's chair empty? Ana Lucia didn't care. She sat in a different chair every time, disrupting our old family traditions and helping us create new ones.

Though I was proud of the progress Ryan had made—he was adjusting well to school and had started staying through the whole mass at St. Ann's instead of leaving—it wasn't enough for Ana Lucia. She noticed that Ryan and Peyton were still sleeping in the guest room, one in the bed and the other on the floor.

"All right, this is what we're going to do," Ana Lucia said. "Ryan's room is going to be his hangout. Peyton's room will be her playroom. And we're moving both of their beds into the game room. That way, they can each sleep in their own bed but still be in the same room together."

"No, I don't really like that idea because they need to be in their own bedrooms," I said.

"But they're not in their bedrooms now, right?"

"You're right," I admitted.

So I discussed it with the kids, and we all agreed. We invited friends over to help us move the furniture. When we finished, Ryan and Peyton each slept in his or her own bed in the same room.

Ana Lucia's presence was like a fresh breeze in a stale house. She shook up our entrenched grief patterns and showed us new ways of seeing ourselves. She reminded me that it wasn't enough to just get through; I needed to learn to take care of myself again. I knew she was right. If I took care of myself, I'd also be better at taking care of my husband and kids. It was the best Valentine's Day gift I could have asked for.

Todd

March loomed large.

As January became February, March cast its shadow backward onto my heart. Not only did the upcoming March present the one-year anniversary of the skiing accident and Taylor's death, but it would also be our first spring break without Taylor. As the one-year anniversary drew closer, I couldn't stop thinking about it. Just as Tara and the kids' emotional stock seemed to be rising, mine seemed to be tanking.

In addition, I was filled with self-doubt. I was worried about how we were going to hold everything together financially. Not only did we have a lot of start-up and ongoing costs for the foundation, but the donations weren't coming in like I'd hoped. This put our foundation work and our family's financial position in jeopardy. If money didn't come into the foundation, I didn't get a salary.

After several days of being in a horrible mood and doubting everything in my life, I started asking myself some angry questions. *What the heck am I doing here? Why am I doing this? Where is God?* I didn't see God working, and I began to wonder if He'd left and I hadn't followed—or worse, that maybe He'd never been in this in the first place. I felt alone and I wanted out. I was in a bad place, a place no words could describe. I called Judy, our counselor, and asked if I could come in for an emergency appointment. She agreed.

The appointment was set for the afternoon, but before I left I had a talk with Tara. "I'm beginning to think that it's just me who wanted to do this, that it's not God's plan for us," I said, referring to my foundation work.

"What makes you say that?"

"I feel as if I am trying to control it, and I don't want to. Where is God in all of this? I need a sign from Him that this is what He wants and that He's still in charge. I'm just not seeing it."

Tara tried to comfort me, but she didn't have any answers either.

On my drive to Judy's office, Pauline Stein called. She was the friend who'd held the first Taylor's Gift fund-raiser in her backyard. She was a close adviser to the foundation and an even closer friend. As we talked, I could feel my anxiety and tension building. I was short with her, and I knew she heard it.

"You sound stressed. Are you?" she asked.

"On a scale of one to ten, I'm about an eleven hundred," I said.

"Tell me what you're stressed about."

So, I unloaded on her. I told her I had a lot of self-doubt. I was worried about the finances. Donations hadn't been coming in to the foundation like we'd hoped, and there were a lot of expenses. "I'm not even sure I'm doing what God wants anymore."

Pauline comforted me with words of affirmation and then prayed for me. Our conversation helped me be in a better place. Her call meant a lot. She reminded me I wasn't alone in this.

I arrived on time for my appointment with Judy and filled her in on my day. "But I felt a little better after talking to Pauline," I said.

"Why is that?"

"She reminded me of why I started this in the first place and that this was God's work, not mine, which He's proven so many times." Even as Pauline had said it, I knew God could prove it again.

Judy gave me some great advice about taking care of myself and being patient when I didn't see results right away. I knew she was right. I hadn't been eating or sleeping well, and I rarely exercised anymore. By the time I left her office, I felt as if there were some things I could do to help improve my mood. But I wasn't sure there was anything I could do to improve my situation. Only God could do that.

At the end of the day, I thought about stopping by a local restaurant and bar owned by friends who had done a lot to support the foundation. It was the Coppell watering hole and the center for local politics and conversation. But as I got in the car, I felt a strong compulsion to go straight home, so I did. When I arrived, Tara met me at the door with a smile on her face. "You're never going to believe what just happened."

She told me that while I was out, a boy Taylor's age had come to the door and asked for me. When she told him I wasn't home, he handed her an envelope and asked her to give it to me.

"He said it was an anonymous donation and his mom wanted him to give it to you," Tara said.

She looked for a car and didn't see one, so she asked him to write his mom's name and phone number on the envelope so we could call and thank her. And then he left.

Tara handed me the note from the envelope. It was short and basically said, "We see all the sacrifices you're making, and we appreciate all that you're doing. Keep going."

"That was nice," I said to Tara. It was so encouraging and just what I needed after the day I'd had.

With an even broader smile on her face, Tara handed me the check that accompanied the note. The first thing I noticed was that it was not a donation for the foundation; it was for us personally. I burst into tears when I read the amount.

The check was for *nine thousand dollars*.

I was stunned at the generosity and timing of the gift. It was as if God Himself had written the cashier's check and handed it to me personally. I looked at the check for more clues as to the donor and noticed it was dated *two days* earlier.

The whole time I had doubted, God already had a check prepared. Of course. *Who was I to ask God for a sign?*

How great He was to give me one anyway.

Tara

With only a few days left in February, I was dreading the month of March, but something happened to change all that. I was in the living room when I got a phone call from Eleanor, my sorority sister from college. She now lived in Pacific Palisades, and we hadn't talked in a while, so I picked up the phone eager to see how she was doing.

"I know this is a long shot," she said, "but I have tickets for *The Ellen DeGeneres Show* coming up, and I was wondering if you could come out and go with me?"

"Are you kidding?" I asked.

"No, I bid on these VIP tickets at my kid's school auction last year, and I just never had the chance to use them. I called today, and they said the only day they have VIP seating available is on March 8."

"That's, like, ten days from now . . ."

"I know it's crazy, but I'd love for you to come with me if you can."

"I would love to! Let me talk to Todd and get back to you."

I was a little concerned about whether or not I should take off and go. March 8 was exactly one week before the anniversary of Taylor's death—a day neither Todd nor I were looking forward to. In addition, we had a lot going on with the foundation and I had started to play a bigger role in things. Did it make sense for me to be gone with all of this going on?

But when I spoke to Todd, he didn't have any reservations. "You should go have a girls' trip with Eleanor. You deserve to have fun," he said.

"Are you sure?"

"Why not? You get to have a great time with your friend, and as a bonus you get to see the show too. I'll take care of the kids," he added. "Let's just figure out how to get you out there. Hopefully, we can get a cheap ticket."

I called Eleanor back and said, "It's a go! I'm just not sure how I will get there, yet. Todd is looking for a cheap ticket."

"I've already taken care of it," Eleanor said.

I was surprised, but I shouldn't have been. That was just like Eleanor.

"Wow! Thank you!" I managed to say, grateful and relieved. "I can't wait to see you again."

A couple of days later, I debated whether or not to call Ellen DeGeneres's producer; I still had her number because we'd talked to her several times in the fall. They were interested in our story but couldn't make the timing work. So if I told her I'd be in the audience, I just hoped she'd be able to give Ellen a copy of Taylor's poem. I decided to give it a try and picked up the phone.

When the producer answered, I said, "I'm not sure you'll remember me. But my name is Tara Storch, and we discussed my daughter and Taylor's Gift, the foundation we started in her honor—"

"Oh, my gosh. Yes, I remember you," she said. "How are you?"

We chatted briefly, and then I said, "I'm going to be in your audience on March 8, and I would love to meet you in person while I'm there."

"Of course! Let me give you my cell phone number. When you get here, you'll be standing in a long line. Just text me, and I'll come down and say hi to you while you're in line."

I thanked her, and we hung up. I thought about Taylor and her poem. I wished she could be there with me. *Taylor, honey, I haven't forgotten. I may not get you on the show, baby, but I'll be in the audience, and I'll do what I can to share your story.*

Later that night I texted Dina, the friend and volunteer who handled all of the media for Taylor's Gift. I told her I was going to be in the audience of Ellen's show on March 8.

Dina texted me back a single question: "When did Taylor turn in her 'I Am' poem?"

I thought about it a moment and remembered it was the Monday before we'd left on spring break. I wanted to be sure, so I checked a calendar before I texted her back.

"March 8. Of course!"

-33-

The Teenager's Mother Wants to Reach Out— but Can't

ASHLEY ZOLLER
SOUTH DAKOTA

Dueene was terrified while Ashley was in surgery. With doctors cutting her daughter's eye she feared something would go wrong. If anything happened to Ashley, she didn't know what she would do.

When Ashley woke up from surgery, Dueene was by her side. She watched Ashley look around the room, and waited to see if she noticed a difference in her vision. When Ashley finally looked at Dueene, she simply said, "I need to go to Texas."

Dueene smiled. Obviously, the anesthesia was still affecting her. Dueene brushed the hair out of her daughter's face.

"You have beautiful eyes, Mom," Ashley said.

"Thanks. Can you see them better now?"

"Yeah, you used to look like a ghost. Your face was white, and you had dark circles where your eyes should be."

Dueene smiled. She could tell the surgery had been a success.

The next morning, the doctor handed Ashley a card with varying type sizes.

"What do you see?" he asked.

"I can see the really small letters now. I couldn't see them before."

It was another indication the transplant had been a success.

Dueene knew things had really changed when, a few days later, they were both back at JD's Pizza, their family-owned restaurant. A customer asked Ashley, "What was the first thing you saw when you woke up from surgery?"

Ashley thought for a moment and said, "When I looked at my mom I thought, 'Wow, she's a cool mom.'" That was a special moment. Ashley had never said anything like that before. It was such a difference from her angry outbursts in the restaurant before her surgery. The words meant a lot to Dueene, and she treasured them.

Though the surgery was successful, the recovery was rugged. It would take eighteen months for Ashley to fully regain her stamina, and she endured a lot of pain during that time. But as the pain gradually lessened, Dueene noticed that Ashley's personality softened. She was more likely to ask for a hug than to start a fight.

Dueene noticed other differences in Ashley too. Though she was still obsessed with monster trucks, and cake, she was now also obsessed with Texas.

"When can I go to Texas?" she'd ask several times a day. "I want to go to Texas."

"You don't know anybody in Texas, I don't know anybody there, so why do you want to go to Texas?" Dueene asked her repeatedly.

But there wasn't an answer. Ashley just kept saying, "I just want to go."

Dueene found Ashley's constant talk about it amusing; it was just one more personality quirk that made her daughter unique.

❖

One day, Dueene got an envelope from Ashley's doctor. Inside was information on her daughter's cornea donor—a teenage girl named Taylor. In the letter, Taylor's mother described how her beautiful daughter had died in a tragic skiing accident. She said Taylor was a caretaker who always looked out for the special needs students at her school.

Students like Ashley, Dueene thought. Then she read that the family lived in a suburb of Dallas. *Was this why Ashley wanted to go to Texas so badly?*

It was too much to absorb. Dueene couldn't imagine life without Ashley. Now another mom was living without her daughter, and that daughter had donated her cornea so Ashley could see. It was heart-wrenching to think about what the donor family had been through.

Dueene wanted to reach out, but what would she say and how would she say it? She tried to explain it to Ashley, but Ashley couldn't grasp the concept that a girl had died, and that because of her death Ashley now had her cornea.

Dueene knew it was far too confusing for Ashley to make sense of it. It was too overwhelming for Dueene. She cried on and off for a week and then tried not to think about it.

—34—

I Am Outgoing and Friendly

Tara

When we got to the studio, I texted Kara, the producer, and told her I was outside. I held two Taylor's Gift T-shirts. I'd rolled and tied each one with a blue ribbon and attached a silicone foundation bracelet to each bundle. I'd also enclosed an envelope that contained a handwritten card, pictures of our family, and Taylor's "I Am" poem. I hoped to give them to her and Ellen.

I quickly got a reply: "I'll come find you in line."

The outside of the studio was exactly as Kara had described—a massive line with hundreds of people in it.

"Tara?"

I looked up. It was Kara. She introduced herself and gave me a quick hug. I introduced her to Eleanor, and we chatted for a few minutes. Then I said to Kara, "It's not a coincidence that I'm in the audience today. Exactly one year ago today, Taylor turned in that poem saying she wanted to be on the show."

"A year ago *today*?" Kara asked in disbelief. "Wow. That's not random."

We chatted a few more minutes before she thanked me for coming and said she had to get back to work.

"Here's a shirt for you and one for Ellen. If you have a chance, please give it to her," I said as I handed her the gifts.

"I'll give it to her after the show," Kara promised. "The show will start around four. Hopefully, I'll see you before, but if not, I'll come say hi afterward."

༄

We checked in, and a woman guided us to our seats.

"That's such a pretty turquoise sweater you're wearing, we're going to sit you right here," she said, pointing to the aisle seat in the front row. I knew the look of the audience was important for a show, but I doubted it was my sweater that nabbed us the front row. "I'll bet Kara got us these great seats," I whispered to Eleanor as she sat down beside me.

It felt surreal to be inside the studio. All I could think was how much Taylor would have loved being there with me, and I started to tear up.

Then music started playing and the lights began flashing. The energy in the room picked up as the show began taping. "I've got to stop crying," I told Eleanor. "I want Todd and the kids to see me in the audience, but they'll never show me on TV like this. There's no crying at *The Ellen DeGeneres Show*, for goodness' sake," I joked.

I knew I was at this once-in-a-lifetime event because of my daughter. I also knew Taylor would want me to enjoy the moment, so I resolved to relish the experience to its fullest. But it would be a struggle. Happiness, for me, was ever elusive.

The music swelled, and then Ellen appeared. Unbelievably, she looked directly at me, gave me a sweet smile, and pointed to her right wrist.

She's wearing the Taylor's Gift bracelet!

My hands flew to my face to cover my tears. I couldn't believe it. Kara had said she would give it to her after the show, but she was already wearing the bracelet! The music increased in volume, and Ellen started dancing in the aisles.

"Here she comes," I told Eleanor.

She danced into the audience and stopped in front of me, grabbed my shoulders, and said, "I got your note. I want to talk to you later. I read the poem and Taylor sounds like an amazing girl."

"Thank you," I said, hugging her. "Thank you for the laughter you've brought into our house."

Still dancing, she smiled at me and said, "You're doing good."

Then she danced away and continued to move through the audience.

It's hard to explain what I felt in that moment. Relief, certainly. So many things we'd done had been for the foundation, to increase organ donation registration across the United States, but this was something I'd done for *my daughter*. It had always been a dream of Taylor's to be on Ellen's show, and now she had done it. It was a personal celebration for Taylor.

We did it, baby! We did it! You're finally here!

The energy in the room was high, and with the music pumping and the lights flashing, it took me a few minutes to figure out exactly what I was feeling. But as I relaxed in my seat to enjoy the show, I recognized an old, familiar feeling I hadn't felt in a long time.

Joy.

⁂

As the show entered its final segment, Ellen sat alone on the set. After the last commercial break, she said, "I recently found out we have someone special in our audience today. Tara Storch, will you join me on stage?"

Did she just say my name? I was stunned.

I stood up and started to tremble. *This is it. This is the moment,* I thought as I steadied myself. The day had now gone from being about Taylor to being an incredible opportunity to tell people about our foundation and educate them about organ donation—and I was petrified. I hated talking to large groups, and now I would be talking to millions of viewers. I knew I'd done it on *The Today Show*, but Todd had been with me then. This time I would be all alone. One slipup and the opportunity would be gone.

Please, God, don't let me stumble as I speak.

I made it onto the stage and sat down in the chair, and Ellen clipped a microphone on me and gave me a sweet pat on my arm. I said another quick prayer and took a deep breath. When I took that breath, a sense of calm washed over me. *You can do this*, I heard inside my head. Somehow, I knew I could. I felt warm and loved, as if the Holy Spirit had enveloped me in His peace. I sat back in the chair and readied myself for whatever came next.

Ellen briefly introduced our story and talked about Taylor's poem and how much it had touched her. She then asked me about Taylor's Gift.

When I told her that Taylor had turned in the poem this very day, a year ago, Ellen got choked up. Miraculously, I held it together long enough to read the poem, and even smile at the line where Taylor said she wanted to be on *The Ellen DeGeneres Show*. As I read, I saw photos of Taylor on the monitors in front of me. When I finished, Ellen said, "What an amazing, amazing girl." Then she told the national audience she was putting the poem and the link to the foundation on her website.

In the final seconds, I had the presence of mind to say that just because someone agreed to be an organ donor on their driver's license didn't mean they were on their state's list. I reminded Ellen and the audience how important it was to double-check and that they could do it through our website.

When the show ended, Eleanor and I were able to visit with Ellen backstage. She was friendly and warm, and we didn't feel rushed. She talked with us and said she felt a special connection with Taylor's story and wanted to stay in touch. It was an unbelievable day. I'd helped make one of my daughter's dreams come true.

God had orchestrated this day in His own time. It was both a personal acknowledgment of Taylor and a public acknowledgment of our work at the foundation. But more than anything, it was a public example of Romans 8:28 and how everything works for good for those who love the Lord.

One of the lines in Taylor's poem was, "I say with pride that I'm a Christian," and now she had said it to a national audience from the set of her favorite talk show. The things she stood for, and the things she put in writing, were now made public in her death in a way they never could have been in her life.

Only God could have done it that way.

Of course.

Todd

We knew that spring break would be hard. Weeks before it happened, everyone around us was already talking about their plans and asking about ours. We couldn't afford a big trip, but we wanted to do something. We had been tiptoeing around the upcoming anniversary and trying not to talk about it, but finally Tara and I decided we needed to get it out in the open. A couple of weeks out, we took the kids for ice cream and asked them to make a list of ten places they wanted to go during their week off.

Tara and Peyton planned a couple of girls' days, while Ryan and I would do guy stuff. We all wanted to go to the zoo as a family, and we talked about going ziplining.

Though we had a plan, we weren't excited about it. Tara and I would have preferred to ignore the whole thing, but we did our best to be enthusiastic and fully present for the kids' sakes. They deserved that much and more.

On March 14, Tara and I were home alone. Both kids were at friends' houses. About 3:30, I stopped what I was doing and got up from my office to find Tara. She was already on her way down the hall to meet me.

"You know, this is about the time it happened," I said.

"I know," she said, and we hugged and cried.

But the moment didn't take us out. Taylor's life had ended, but Ryan's and Peyton's hadn't. Neither had ours—whether we liked it or not. After we cried, we pulled ourselves together, packed a few things, and when the kids got home we left for Wimberley, Texas, to go ziplining. And it was good. We had time in the car together as a family, time away from home, and the opportunity to make new memories doing something we'd never done before.

While we were in the hotel, I had a conference call with our creative agency. They wanted to unveil the new public service announcements they had just finished.

While the commercials were downloading, I asked Tara and the kids if they would rather leave or if they wanted to be a part of it. They all wanted to stay.

As the call started and the commercials played, I watched how my family engaged with the creative team. Everyone loved the work that had been done so far, and the kids were really into it. Ryan offered a couple of suggestions.

"I think you should change that," he said, pointing out one creative element he didn't like and including what he thought it should be.

The team responded enthusiastically, "That's a fantastic idea."

"I think the color isn't quite right," Peyton said.

"No, you're right, and we'll fix that," they agreed.

I marveled at how involved the kids were and how they also had something to contribute. Early on, they weren't always so supportive—it was too painful for them, while they were dealing with their own pain. Now, months later, as I watched the kids interacting with the creative team over the computer, it was especially sweet to see Peyton noticing little details and wanting to have input. The foundation had truly become a part of the family.

⚬⟡⚬

The pain was still there. The loss still hurt. But we were all steadier now. We could talk about Taylor, or the foundation, without it sweeping us out to sea emotionally. In those times when our emotions did sweep us away, we recovered and found our footing much more quickly than we had in the past. As a family, we stood together in the ocean of grief, holding on through the swells and doing our best to keep each other afloat. It wasn't always easy, but it was a beautiful thing to see.

And I thanked God for it.

Over the past year we'd suffered great loss, but we'd also gained some things. Our marriage was now stronger than it had ever been, and so was our faith. We had a deeper connection with each other and with God. While the three recipients we'd connected with certainly didn't replace Taylor, the hope for their futures replaced the despair we had in Taylor's death. Being an organ donor was Taylor's gift to them, but it was also her gift to us.

⚬⟡⚬

On the fifteenth, I wrote a note to Taylor in my notebook:

I'm not falling apart like I thought I would. A gift from you and God. One year without you. How did I ever make it?

That night as Tara and I sat together in the kitchen, I said, "If we can make it through this, we can make it through anything." But the truth was that we had done more than make it. Though it had been the hardest year of our married life, I loved Tara even more now than I did a year ago.

Tara

By June 2011, we had mostly resumed our usual activities. I know some people would call it returning to normal, or a new normal, but I didn't like those terms. In my mind, we'd never be normal again. But we were surviving. While there were still fluctuations in the stock market of our emotions, to use Todd's analogy, if we weren't trending upward, we were at least holding steady.

One day we were getting ready to leave the house as a family to head to Fossil Rim, a wildlife park. Before we left, the phone rang, and I answered it.

"My name is Dueene Zoller, and my daughter, Ashley, has Taylor's cornea," the caller said.

I took a deep breath and exhaled slowly while she continued.

"I got your letter, and I am so sorry I never wrote back," she said. "I can't imagine what you're going through."

It had been more than a year since I'd sent out the first letter, and we hadn't heard anything—I didn't think we ever would.

I went out onto the back porch so we could talk. Dueene told me she was sitting in her truck in the parking lot of JD's Pizza in Rapid City, South Dakota, where they lived. She said Ashley was a twenty-year-old special needs child.

"How's she doing?" I asked.

"Really good," Dueene said. She explained how Ashley's eye had been coning and how that had caused severe headaches. "The new cornea made the headaches go away." She told me how Ashley had woken up from her surgery and said, "I need to go to Texas!" and how odd Dueene thought that was until she received our letter. "Maybe there's a connection there?" she asked. She also told me that when she looked into Ashley's eyes, she saw Taylor.

"Thank you for calling!" I said. I could tell it was hard for Dueene to reach out. Ashley was obviously her whole world, and the thought of losing her daughter had to be hard for her to conceive. But I was thrilled to have connected with her and to hear how well Ashley was doing. I told Dueene how we'd met some of the other recipients and how we hoped one day to meet Ashley too.

The conversation was short and sweet. Now we had connected with four out of the five recipients. Wow!

After we hung up, I went into the house and told Todd and the kids about the phone call. It excited the kids, but after they heard the news, they were ready to go to Fossil Rim. In a funny kind of way, it was almost normal for them to hear about these kinds of unexpected calls, and I was pleased that they no longer triggered prolonged episodes of grief.

When we finally headed out to Fossil Rim, I stared out the car window and prayed. I thanked God for Ashley and Dueene and that they had reached out. In the hospital, we'd been told we might never connect with even one recipient, and now we'd connected with four amazing people. I couldn't wait to one day get to heaven and introduce them to Taylor.

But somehow, I felt that Taylor already knew them.

❦

I still hadn't found the peace I'd been looking for, but I resolved that I probably never would. This wasn't the way our story was supposed to be written. The natural order of things is that children are supposed to outlive their parents, grow up, get married, and have their own children. However, though we were having to rewrite our story, this wasn't the end of Taylor. Through organ donation, Taylor had already outlived herself and continued to do so each day through Jeff, Patricia, Jonathan, and now Ashley.

And with God's help, now we were learning how to live on without her.

Part 3

New Beginnings

—35—

The Cowboy

The Gift of Giving Back

JEFF KARTUS
COLORADO

The cowboy was no longer confined to the house, and because he didn't have to worry about low blood sugar, he was free to do as much physical labor as he liked. So every morning Jeff volunteered at a local stable, feeding and watering the horses and cleaning stalls. Jeff adored horses, and he didn't mind getting dirty taking care of them. But even more than caring for the horses, he enjoyed helping the people who boarded their horses there.

One of the regulars at the stable was a woman named Kim. She suffered from a chronic pain condition that affects the nervous system and can be debilitating. Kim could no longer walk and had to employ a Hoveround power wheelchair to get from her truck to the barn. But she was determined to ride her horse, Copper, no matter what. Kim had figured out a way to mount Copper by standing on the Hoveround. She'd get off by doing the same thing in reverse.

Jeff kept an eye on her during her mounts and dismounts and while she was riding. He videotaped her lessons so she could watch them later at home. And he always cleaned up after Copper. There was no way Kim could handle a shovel to clean up after him herself.

Kim told Jeff that riding Copper made her feel whole. But it was also an important part of her therapy—since a horse's gait most closely mimics a human's gait. Through riding, Kim's body built up the stamina she needed to walk short distances, which made all the difference in her quality of life.

Jeff understood. Before the transplant surgery, he'd also been confined to a wheelchair. He knew how important it was to be independent. Jeff was happy to do what he could to help Kim retain her independence.

⁂

One day, Jeff was cleaning stalls while Kim was out riding in the pasture. He heard a horse running, and looked up to see Copper running past him, his saddle askew, headed toward the stable. Jeff was confused. Did he really see what he thought he saw? Or was he losing his mind? As a result of his accidents, he'd had a lot of head trauma, and he couldn't always tell if what he saw was real or something in his head. As he tried to figure it out, he heard Kim's guide dog, Alexei.

Jeff looked out toward the fields and saw Alexei barking. Kim was lying next to her on the ground. Something had gone terribly wrong. Kim couldn't dismount without using her Hoveround to get off. Jeff knew she'd either had a seizure and fallen off or she'd been thrown. Either way, he knew she must be injured and was possibly in a lot of pain. All those car accidents flashed through his mind. His body tensed, remembering the injuries—the broken ribs, neck, and back.

Jeff knew he should call an ambulance, but when Kim had had her last seizure she'd begged him not to. He understood. He'd had enough seizures due to low blood sugar and knew what that felt like. Each time an ambulance came, they just wanted to take him to the hospital. After so many trips, he started refusing to go and begged Vanessa to take care of him at home.

But this was different; Kim had been thrown from a horse. What if she was really hurt?

Before he could make a decision, Copper circled past him again. Jeff knew he had to do something about the horse. Kim loved her horse almost as much as she loved her husband. If anything happened to Copper, it would devastate her. He took another quick look at Kim and saw she was now sitting up. That was a good sign.

He went after the horse.

Fortunately, after racing toward the stables, Copper just trotted back to his familiar pen, and Jeff was able to open the gate and let him in, securing it behind him. Kim's saddle was still askew on Copper's back, but Jeff would have to leave that for later. At least the horse was safe. He had to get to Kim.

He looked out toward the field and saw she was still sitting up. He could run out there, or he could even take a horse, but he couldn't bring her back that way. He would have to get her Hoveround and drive it out to her. He ran to where she'd parked it, but he was unfamiliar with how to operate it and couldn't get it started.

He could think of only one other option. Jeff would have to drive his truck out to the pasture. He knew this was against the rules, but he felt he didn't have any other choice. He jumped in his truck, put it in gear, and tore through the fields.

As he drove across the pasture, with his heart pounding and his mind racing, Jeff wondered if this was what Vanessa felt like every time she raced to one of his accident scenes. It was a scary feeling to know someone you cared about was injured and not know what you'd find when you arrived. As the truck bumped and bounced through the fields, tossing dirt clods into the air, he thought about Vanessa having done this very same thing so many times for him. Now he was able to do it for someone else.

Pulling up next to Kim, Jeff could see she was alert and talking.

"I'm not sure what happened," Kim said when he reached her.

Jeff checked to make sure she wasn't injured before gently lifting her into the truck.

"Is Copper okay?" she asked.

Jeff assured her that Copper was fine. He closed the door, loaded Alexei into the bed of the truck, and drove as gently as he could back to the stables. Other than a few bruises, including a bruised ego, Kim seemed fine.

"Thank you so much!" she said. "I don't know what I would have done if you hadn't been here!"

Jeff was thankful. Kim was fine, but it could have been worse. Jeff thought about all the accidents he never walked away from—the times he was put in the hospital to fight for his life.

Kim's husband later thanked Jeff for rescuing his wife. "Though riding is so good for her, it can also be dangerous. I wouldn't let her keep doing this if it weren't for you," he said.

"I'm just glad I can help," Jeff said.

✿

Eighteen months after meeting Todd and Tara, and twenty-one months after his kidney/pancreas transplant, Jeff still thought of Taylor every day. It was hard not to. His life was completely different from the one he'd lived before the transplant. Because of her gift, he was able to do what he'd always wanted to do—help others.

—36—

The Nurse

The Gift of Time

PATRICIA WINTERS
ARIZONA

Patricia beamed as she and her family walked through the gates of the Magic Kingdom and entered the happiest place on earth. After months of lying on the couch, barely having enough energy to watch her boys play by themselves on the floor, she couldn't believe she was finally here with them. Seeing the joy in her boys' eyes when they looked up and down Main Street was all the proof she needed that the park really lived up to its claims.

"Where do you want to go first?" she asked.

The boys were too overwhelmed to answer.

"Let's head over this way," she said, spotting a sign that pointed to "The Many Adventures of Winnie the Pooh."

For years, Patricia had just wished for enough energy to take the boys to the playground minutes from their house. Now, less than a year after her transplant, they were spending three days together as a family, walking, talking, riding rides, and making memories. It truly was a dream come true.

As the kids chatted about all the things they wanted to do at the park, Patricia thought of all the things she could now do that she couldn't before. The biggest one was that she could now *breathe*.

With her ever-present illness, the past few years had been especially hard. Medical bills had mounted, then Joe had lost his job, and then they'd lost their dream house. But she didn't care about that anymore. Though the house was beautiful when they moved in, she'd been sick most of the time they'd lived there and couldn't really appreciate it. Now it held only negative memories. The new house felt like a fresh start. Though their home was smaller, their fun had increased.

That wasn't the only thing that had increased. Patricia felt as if her heart was bigger. She couldn't really explain why. Could it have been all the lessons—like patience and compassion—she'd learned from being ill? It was hard for her type A personality to slow down, but she'd had to because of her illness. Now she had a greater understanding of those who moved a little slower than she did—such as the elderly and disabled. Or was it because she didn't take anything for granted anymore? Ordinary events took on greater meaning. "Each birthday and holiday is so special," she said. She believed that having a long-term illness made her a better parent because she started looking at things through the eyes of her children.

But her perspective changed in other ways too.

The illness and financial problems had been hard on her marriage and other close relationships. Patricia found herself having to forgive those closest to her for things they'd done that hurt her. In the past, Patricia would have just walked away, but now she had a new perspective about what was really important. "Knowing you were almost snuffed out can be a gift because it clarifies things for you," Patricia told her friends. "You learn that houses and things don't matter. People do."

Patricia felt as though her old heart was limited in how much it could love, but with Taylor's heart her capacity had grown. One of the easiest ways for her to see it was when she was with Tara. Patricia would say that she wasn't a huggy-touchy-feely kind of person and that she didn't express her love that way. But when she was with Tara, she did. "Every time I leave her, my heart aches," said Patricia. "I just have this sense of loss when we say goodbye. It's a new feeling for me."

Patricia has a greater sense of purpose too. She knows that life is a gift, and she doesn't want anger, lack of forgiveness, or other relationship problems to get in the way of whatever time she has left. Instead she resolves issues quickly so she can get on to what she needs to do—such as being a mother. Though being a mother to Jack and Sam is her most important job, Patricia still works as a nurse, teaching prenatal classes. In addition, she helps out with Taylor's Gift, supporting the Storches in their foundation's mission.

❖

If her boys ever look back on those dark days, Patricia hopes they will see her determination and perseverance. It would have been so much easier to give up, but she didn't. She fought hard because she loved them so much. She also knew it wasn't her fight that won the battle. There were so many times during her illness that she shouldn't have made it, and yet she did. The only explanation that made sense to her was that God had divinely intervened in her life to keep her alive until she got the perfect heart.

So through the Storches' decision, Taylor's gift, and God's grace, Patricia was able to give her boys the gift her own dad wasn't able to give her—more time.

And for that, she is eternally grateful.

—37—

The Bike Rider

The Gift of Freedom

Jonathan Finger
Colorado

The Register's Annual Great Bicycle Ride Across Iowa, better known as RAGBRAI, is the oldest and largest bicycle touring event in the world, with more than twenty thousand riders. It's like the Tour de France in Iowa, only instead of French countryside there's corn, lots of corn. But Jonathan didn't even know that much about the seven-day tour when he agreed to form a team with some of his online piano forum friends. He just thought it sounded like fun.

After researching the ride, Jonathan knew it would be a demanding physical challenge. The ride was nearly five hundred miles long, from the Missouri River to the Mississippi River, and the route wasn't flat—the first two days alone would have climbs of about four thousand feet each—and Jonathan would have to ride sixty to eighty miles a day up and down rolling hills. The ride would take place the last week of July 2011. He agreed to do it just a few months after his transplant in the fall of 2010, which didn't leave him a lot of time to recover and train.

305

In addition to having a new kidney to take care of, Jonathan had a history of heart problems that would complicate his ability to physically push himself. To participate in RAGBRAI, Jonathan would have to train hard for months, and some of that time included the Colorado winter months when he wouldn't be able to bike outdoors. Even under perfect training conditions, Jonathan knew he would be physically pushing his body further than it had ever been pushed. Even training as hard as he possibly could wouldn't guarantee that he'd have the strength and stamina required to make it to the end of the seven-day tour.

But Jonathan was determined to do it. The team would be riding for his favorite charity—Taylor's Gift Foundation.

⸎

As Jonathan trained for RAGBRAI, and began to take longer rides on his bike, he found riding gave him more opportunities to think. There was a cadence to pedaling. The sound of the sprocket teeth making their way through the bike chain had its own rhythm—calming and invigorating, peaceful and energizing, all at the same time. When he shifted gears, there was a clicking sound as the derailleur and chain shifted from one sprocket to the next. Relearning how to gear a bike and how to pedal were key parts of his training. It became the music that underscored his thoughts.

Day after day, as the wind hit his face and the sun warmed his back, he rode and he thought. He noticed how his thinking had changed. For years, he had been so busy thinking only of himself—his health, his dialysis, and his physical needs—that he hadn't been able to spend much time thinking about others. As he rode, he began to reminisce about his relationships with friends and family. It was as if he had a new freedom to think about others rather than just himself. Having that emotional freedom, alongside his new physical freedom, would take some getting used to as he began seeing and feeling the world differently.

❖

After training for months, Jonathan headed to Iowa to meet up with his online friends. The first few days of RAGBRAI went pretty much as expected. The ride was tough but manageable. Most teams rode together, one rider in front to reduce the drag for those behind, switching to a new front rider with fresh legs when the leader tired. But Team Taylor's Gift was small, and it soon became apparent that there were big differences in skill and endurance levels. Jonathan had been riding seriously for less than a year, and he hadn't been able to build up all the stamina he needed. He couldn't keep pace with the others, and they would often have to slow down to keep pace with him. Jonathan eventually told the other riders it was okay for them to go on without him. He'd just catch up to them at the final stop at the end of each day.

Alone with the cadence of his pedaling, Jonathan's thoughts turned inward. He knew he was stronger than he'd been since his teens, when the kidney disease had taken over. But how strong was he? Who was he?

For years, he'd seen himself as a vulnerable patient—someone who needed to be taken care of. When he was sick, he'd often feel weak and fearful. It was hard when he felt that way, and he knew it affected all of his relationships. But riding through Iowa on his bike, surrounded by hundreds of people yet all alone, Jonathan started to change the way he felt about himself. Each day's ride gave him new confidence and helped him know he wasn't the weak link in the chain anymore; he was the strong one, the overcomer who had survived against all odds. He began to think about what this meant for his relationships. He knew now he wouldn't have to be the focus of a relationship; for the first time, he could give and receive love equally. That one thought was exciting and free-ing. From now on, his relationships wouldn't have to be defined by who could take care of him.

❖

A few days into RAGBRAI, Jonathan stared at the approaching hill—Twister Hill—and wondered if he had enough left in him to make it to the top. The hill was already taking out more experienced riders who had dismounted to push their bikes to the top. Jonathan had already come so far physically, mentally, and emotionally that he didn't want to give up. But he was afraid he might have to. His legs were spent, and his hands and arms were numb from gripping the bike handles. He knew he could walk his bike up the hill and still be proud of the job he'd done. There would be no shame in pushing his bike to the top. It wasn't the destination, it wasn't the prize, and it wasn't even the end of the ride. This was just another obstacle in a much longer tour.

But as he approached the hill, he thought back to that dark day in the hospital when he'd wanted to die. Father Seraphim had stopped by, and Jonathan had asked him if it was okay to give up. Father Seraphim had assured him that it was his choice but reminded him of how valiantly he'd fought to make it that far. Jonathan remembered that exhaustion and how much he'd wanted to give up. Yet somehow he'd found the strength to push through, and years later he could see how that decision had paid off with a new kidney and the promise of a new life.

At the base of the hill, Jonathan's legs were screaming in pain. The sweat had soaked through the jersey on his back and mixed with the sunscreen on his face. As it dripped off his forehead, his eyes stung. But once again, Jonathan made the decision to fight. He shifted gears on his bike and pressed hard on the pedals, trying to maintain his speed as he ascended the hill. He knew that the victory was virtually meaningless. Even if he made it to the top, the ride and the mental fight continued for another twenty-five miles that day alone—and there were two more days ahead of him. But Jonathan chose to fight his way up the hill, even knowing the fight wouldn't be easy.

"We always think we're at the end of our rope, but we're not," Jonathan said. "It's such an important exercise to realize we can do much more than we think we can."

Wearing his Taylor's Gift "Be a Hero" jersey, Jonathan triumphantly made it to the top of the hill that day and rode to the finish line. It was a physical accomplishment, but it was also a mental journey—much like his life.

"I feel like I have more capacity to love now than I did. I haven't always had the energy, or the desire, or the resources to make decisions and be a proactive part of anything, and now I can," he said.

Taylor's gift has given Jonathan freedom. He has more time, greater health, the ability to play music, and the ability to push himself physically. But perhaps his greatest freedom isn't a physical one—it's an emotional one. Jonathan now has the freedom to love others fully.

—38—

The Teenager

The Gift of a Future

ASHLEY ZOLLER
SOUTH DAKOTA

"Ashley, time to get up!" Dueene said.

Ashley opened the door to her room. "Good morning, Mom."

Ashley was already dressed and ready to go; Dueene smiled at her daughter. For years, Ashley had woken up every morning ready for a fight. If it wasn't about her clothes, it was about her breakfast—usually she argued with Dueene about both. Some mornings they would fight over Ashley taking her medicine, and other days Dueene would have to force it down her. But ever since her corneal transplant eighteen months earlier, Ashley had changed. In fact, she'd become a different person.

Dueene poured herself another cup of coffee and watched Ashley hungrily wolf down her breakfast. Most mothers of twenty-year-old daughters didn't marvel at their daughters' eating habits, but Dueene did. After nearly two decades of trying to get Ashley to eat, she was finally doing it. Ashley seemed to have more of an appetite following the corneal transplant. In fact, over the past year she'd put on ten pounds and was continuing to gain weight. This was a huge accomplishment. Dueene remembered bringing her three-pound baby home from the hospital and doing everything she could to coax her to eat. Years later, she still weighed only twenty-five pounds. By the time Ashley was in high school, she seemed to have stagnated at eighty-four pounds.

But since the surgery, Ashley had blossomed to more than ninety pounds—a huge milestone. She was healthier than she'd ever been.

❈

Dueene worked seventy-five to eighty hours a week in the restaurant. When it was slow, she had time to think. In December 2011, she spent a lot of that time thinking about Ashley's future. In a few days, Ashley would turn twenty-one. That milestone birthday also meant that, as a special needs student, this would be Ashley's last year in public school. *What will she do next year?*

As Dueene stacked cups and folded pizza boxes, she knew they needed a plan for Ashley, but she wasn't sure what. On one hand, Dueene welcomed a break from parenting. Ashley had required her full-time attention, twenty-four hours a day, seven days a week, for more than twenty years. Dueene had given up a lot of her own hopes and dreams to be available for Ashley's special needs. If Ashley were able to live in some kind of group home, Dueene would experience freedom she hadn't had since Ashley was born. But Dueene also knew if Ashley were living anywhere else, she would miss her terribly.

One day, Dueene was preoccupied with thoughts of Ashley's future. "What's going on?" one of her longtime employees asked. As Dueene wiped down counters, she expressed her concerns. "I want Ashley to be independent and to have her own life. Everyone deserves to have their own life. But I'm not sure how that's going to happen yet."

"But you're doing everything you can," the employee said.

She was right. Dueene was doing whatever she could to help Ashley learn to live independently. In addition, several times a week a companion came in to teach Ashley specific skills. Together, they would go to the mall, the grocery store, or volunteer in the community. At home, the companion helped Ashley do her own laundry and learn basic household skills—such as how to clean the toilet.

"I've seen a lot of progress in her skills," the employee was quick to add.

Dueene knew she was right. "Things are getting better. I feel as if I haven't taken a deep breath in twenty years, but I'm going to start taking a lot of deep breaths soon."

ॐ

Ashley entered the restaurant immediately after school and plopped down on a bench in one of the Aztec-themed booths.

"Do you want something to drink?" Dueene asked.

"Sure."

As Dueene disappeared behind the counter and grabbed a glass, she asked Ashley about her day.

"At school, I had to wipe off all the tables. I had to work with a bully. His name is Justin. He pushes me."

"Did you push him back?"

"No."

"Good for you, Ashley." Dueene wanted to reinforce her daughter's good behavior.

In the past, when Ashley was in one of those kinds of moods, she would have decked him. One of the characteristics of Williams syndrome children is that they're fearless in the face of danger. Although Ashley was smaller, she'd take on anyone, no matter what size they were. At that time, Dueene would have been scared for the bully—Ashley's anger was that explosive. But since the transplant, her outbursts had disappeared.

"What did the teacher do?" Dueene asked, setting a drink in front of her daughter.

"He's not allowed to come near me anymore."

Dueene ran her fingers through her daughter's straight hair. Ashley had begun straightening it because she thought boys liked it that way. Dueene smiled. She knew Ashley had recently started showing more grown-up preferences. For her upcoming birthday, she wanted clothes, but not the pink and purple girly kind she had in her childhood. Instead, she wanted rocker clothes from the Hard Rock Café. Ashley also had a boyfriend—a young man with special needs whom she'd met at Walmart. The two friends socialized occasionally with a group, or they talked and texted when Dueene allowed. It was obvious that Ashley had begun to pay attention to boys—and they were paying more attention to her.

Dueene's twenty-year-old daughter was beginning to act like a teenager.

⚬

While Ashley was doing her homework, Dueene got busy in the kitchen, prepping for the busy night ahead. When the dinner rush started to build, Dueene moved to the counter to take orders and did her best to keep customers moving through the counter line. She also tried to keep her eye on Ashley in the dining room. It was an old habit.

In the past, it seemed Ashley was always agitated and angry. If the restaurant was crowded and people got in her space, it would set her off and an outburst would follow. Dueene had trained herself to look for the initial signs of Ashley's outbursts, so she could intercede and prevent a full-blown scene from taking place in front of customers.

But with a steady stream of customers and an employee out sick, Dueene was so busy she didn't have time to keep a watchful eye on Ashley. It wasn't until the end of the night, after everyone had left, that Dueene realized the place had been full all night and Ashley had not only kept out of trouble but she'd helped out too.

"How did it go?" Dueene asked as Ashley carried dirty dishes to the kitchen.

"Good. I like meeting new people here," Ashley said.

Dueene had to pause a second. *Who was this kid?* Ever since the transplant, Ashley seemed calmer. More at peace with herself. And though Dueene was always on the lookout, there hadn't been any outbursts. In fact, it had been quite the opposite—Ashley had actually been helping out at the restaurant.

Dueene's mind flipped through a few recent scenes. In June, when the Sturgis Motorcycle Rally was in town and the place was packed, Ashley had waited on several tables of bikers. And they'd left her tips. "They were cool," Ashley had said.

More recently, a sweet older couple from Alaska had come in, and Ashley had become friendly with them. She had a knack for remembering names and faces, and Dueene knew that if the couple ever came back, Ashley would remember them. As she counted the receipts, Dueene realized her daughter was growing up. She was treating people more kindly, she'd stopped having outbursts, and she'd started helping around the restaurant. Ashley seemed more capable of taking care of herself than ever before.

Until the surgery, Dueene hadn't understood how painful Ashley's headaches were or how much they had impacted her behavior. Now that they were gone, Ashley was a different person. And Dueene was just beginning to see how much she had changed.

⚘

Right after Ashley's transplant, Dueene noticed physical changes in her daughter. Though she'd had trouble sleeping since she was a baby, following the surgery she began to sleep more. Her depth perception was also better. Before the surgery, Ashley had trouble staying on the sidewalk while walking; she rarely had that problem anymore. And going up and down stairs had also gotten easier.

Ashley reported other changes to Dueene. She could see faces better, and people no longer looked like ghosts. Her grades improved, and she began doing better in school because her reading had improved—she could finally see the text.

"And I can type faster," Ashley told Dueene one day after school. "I can see the letters better on the computer."

In the future, Ashley would still be in therapy for her other Williams syndrome–related issues, but now she had the vision and clear mind to be able to work hard on those things without eye pain and headaches distracting her. For a girl whose life had always been hard, the transplant helped make it a lot easier.

∞

Dueene wanted to thank the Storches, but it took her nearly a year to finally contact them because she wasn't sure what to say. She knew her life had been tough raising Ashley, but Dueene had always adjusted. She couldn't imagine how Tara would ever adjust to losing Taylor.

The phone call was brief and not nearly as difficult as Dueene had expected. The connection between the families was made. For a few weeks after Dueene called, Ashley texted Tara occasionally, and Tara texted back. The Storches told Ashley they hoped to see her one day in Texas. Ashley wanted that too. She still couldn't understand how Taylor had died and donated her cornea so she could see again. But she could understand the pain of a mother losing her daughter.

∞

As Ashley's twenty-first birthday drew closer, Dueene knew there would be difficult decisions for her daughter in the year ahead. But now that her headaches were gone and her attitude had improved, Ashley was able to make great progress with her therapists and the other professionals who were teaching her how to live independently. In the months since the transplant, Dueene had grown more confident that one day soon Ashley would be able to lead an independent life.

Taylor's gift had given them both a future.

And that was a gift they could enjoy together.

-39-

Outlive Yourself

Todd

Currently, only four in ten adults in the United States are registered to be organ donors, yet there are more than one hundred thousand people awaiting an organ transplant. How long they will wait depends on a number of factors, including how sick they are, their blood and tissue types (rare types generally have to wait longer for matching organs to become available), and how long they've been on the list. Whether the wait is a few weeks, or as in Jonathan's case, eight years, the wait is too long. In the best-case scenarios, these patients are in medical limbo waiting for an organ so they can resume a full life. In the worst cases, they pray just to survive.

While awaiting a transplant, patients can have mounting medical bills that put pressure on their personal finances. Many have to divert their resources from other necessities such as housing, or even medications, to pay the bills they've incurred. Even with medical insurance, the lifetime maximum for many policies is a million dollars. For patients who require ongoing tests and treatments, that figure is too low. Patients can easily exceed the lifetime maximum coverage cap, and then they have to begin paying out of pocket for additional treatment. The longer a patient must wait for an organ, the greater the potential financial crisis is for them and their family.

During the wait, a patient's health only worsens. It's one thing to receive a new heart as soon as doctors recognize the need. It's another to physically waste away, hoping you will still be a viable candidate for surgery when the organ finally becomes available. Many people on the list die while waiting. Even those who live long enough to receive a needed organ often suffer additional medical complications due to the long waiting period, which makes their recovery that much more difficult.

Deteriorating health and financial situations can also lead to relationship issues. Marriages become strained as the couple deals with the emotional, financial, and physical consequences of a long-term illness. Relationships with friends and family members change as the patient requires more care. Patients move from being an equal in their relationships to being the needy one. Lives are placed on hold as patients quit jobs or school, find new childcare because they can no longer care for their children, and withdraw from public spaces and social situations where they risk contracting a virus. The longer someone waits for a transplant, the more likely the emotional and relational strain will lead to depression or a desire to just give up.

At the same time, those who have donated a loved one's organs face their own anguish, just as Tara and I did, as they try to deal with their loss. We were blessed to have a strong marriage and a community that surrounded us and loved us—even when we were hard to love. We know not everyone has this kind of support. Whom do patients turn to when they need assistance? Who lets them know it's okay for a husband and wife to grieve differently? Who reminds them there is purpose in the pain?

Whether it is a patient awaiting an organ or a grieving family who donated organs, their faith is often shaken by their circumstances. At Taylor's Gift Foundation, we want to wrap our arms around these individuals and help them through these bleak days, pointing them toward a brighter future. Though the foundation initially set out to educate youth about organ donation, we realized there were other needs—education and awareness, as well as financial and emotional support. Very quickly, we further clarified the purpose of Taylor's Gift Foundation to encompass all that we're doing.

Our mission is increasing organ donation to Regift Life, Renew Health, and Restore Families.

We've spoken to thousands of people in numerous states and helped organize grassroots events across the country. Working with our creative partner, Firehouse Agency (http://www.firehouse agency.com), we've created award-winning television commercials and billboards that have been seen by millions. We've provided scholarships to high school students and sponsored organ donor recipients to give them the opportunity to ride on the Donate Life Rose Bowl Parade float to help raise awareness about organ dona-tion. We've comforted grieving parents and helped draw attention to individuals who needed lifesaving transplants.

As I write this, we've been doing this for only about two years, yet we've already seen the needle move. In that time, more than two million new organ donors have registered in Texas, and more than thirteen million have registered across the United States. We know the work we've done has played a part in that increase.

But perhaps our biggest accomplishment is that we're starting to change the conversation about organ donation. It's not about death; it's about life.

Most Americans have a life insurance policy that, upon their death, leaves financial means to help their family continue *their lifestyle*. Organ donation is the only gift we can leave that helps people continue *their lives*.

You may not need a transplant today, and I hope you never will, but the chances are good you know someone who already has, or who one day will. The waitlist can be greatly reduced (if not eradi-cated) if enough people register. But as a small family foundation, we can't do it on our own. We need you to register—and then talk about this issue with your friends and family. Sometimes it's as simple as saying, "Do you have life insurance?" and after they respond, telling them there is another gift they can leave that may be more important. Organ donation doesn't cost anything; you can't take your organs with you, and it saves lives when you leave them here.

More importantly, a conversation about what you plan to do when you die forces you to examine how you're living. Taylor wasn't an organ donor advocate. We didn't sit around our dinner table at night and discuss this issue as a family. Since we didn't know Taylor's explicit wishes, we decided to donate because of who she was and how she lived her life. She had a kind and generous heart and always took care of outsiders. We knew without a doubt this was what she would want.

It was her life, not her death, that led us down this path.

Just like a Boy Scout who goes to a campground and leaves it in better shape than when he arrived, Taylor left the world a better place, not only for her organ recipients, but also for their friends and families.

I've had a lot of time for self-reflection over the last few years, and I've come to the conclusion that I am at my best when I am helping and serving others. My grandfather's words were true: it's not what happens to you that matters, but how you react to it that does. Life is better when we're focused on others. I am thankful that God gave me that insight very early. As a result, I have been able to fuel my grief toward something good—something that serves others.

Taylor already knew that. She lived it, and I want to be like her in that way.

I look forward to seeing her again and hearing her say, "Good job, Daddy! You did it."

—40—

The Gift of Hope

Tara

My friends Beth Rathe and Kathy Quirk were the ones who put fresh flowers on Taylor's grave weekly. They also picked up the trinkets that people left and put out seasonal displays for the holidays. One hot summer day, more than a year after Taylor's death, the three of us were talking at Taylor's gravesite when Beth said, "It's time to get it done."

"You really need to do this," Kathy added.

I knew what they were talking about. I'd made a great deal of progress during the fifteen months since Taylor had died, but there was one thing I still hadn't done—chosen a permanent headstone for Taylor's grave.

"I just can't do it," I said.

"You can, and we'll help," Beth said.

Like so many pivotal moments during my journey, I needed my friends to help me make it happen. They asked me what I wanted, and I gave them permission to work with the people who would create the designs to be etched on her headstone.

❧

A few weeks later, we all sat down in Kathy's kitchen to review their work. As soon as Beth opened the manila folder, I burst into tears. She quickly shut it.

"No," I said, grabbing a Kleenex and wiping my nose, "we have to do this. Let's just get it done."

We were all crying as we looked through the drawings for a permanent memorial for Taylor. Yet, with the Holy Spirit's comforting help, we made some decisions and sent our notes back to the designers for revisions. A few days later, they emailed me a revised drawing. I didn't like it, so I emailed them back with more detailed notes, and we repeated this process for weeks.

I wanted it to be perfect.

And I didn't want it to be final.

But by July 2011, I knew I had to force myself to make it happen. I drove to Fort Worth and sat down with the lady who was designing the layout of the stone on her computer screen. I gave her the photo of Taylor I wanted to be etched into the stone. Underneath the photo, I chose a volleyball and a heart to represent her life. On the other side, we put a cross.

I wanted her headstone to reflect her interests, her love, and her faith. Those three symbols, the volleyball, the heart, and the cross, accomplished that.

In the upper righthand corner, I had Luke 18:27 inscribed: "What is impossible with men is possible with God." Since Taylor's death, that verse had been proven true in our lives, both personally and with the foundation.

In the upper lefthand corner, I had Romans 8:28 inscribed. It was the same Scripture that Father Alfonse had come across on the night of Taylor's funeral. He had been saying that God had a purpose in all of this, and randomly opened Peyton's new journal and read: "And we know that in all things God works for the good of those who love him, who have been called according to his purpose."

❧

A few weeks later, I stood next to Taylor's grave in the swelter-ing August heat and watched the crew install her marker. Using a tape measure, they marked a space on the grass slightly larger than the headstone and then placed their shovels upright and stood on them to break through the initial layer of sod and hard earth. After the first cut, they turned over shovelfuls of brown dirt and placed them in a pile.

Watching them, I was reminded of Ana Lucia's story of the clay Buddha cracking only to reveal the gold inside. I had definitely cracked, but I had also found gold. Our marriage was stronger, we had a clear purpose in life, and though it had been shaken, my faith was now more precious to me than ever before. I had been comforted by the Holy Spirit and drawn into a more intimate relationship with God, and though I would never be thankful for Taylor's death, I was thankful for God's comfort and the spiritual growth I'd experienced.

I had feared this moment because I was afraid the tombstone was the "final nail in the coffin," and it would be an ending. But as I looked out over the emerald green cemetery grass and blue sky and saw the white clouds in the distance, I knew Taylor's death wasn't the end. Taylor also lived on in the lives and hearts of people she'd touched at school, at volleyball, and at church. Her gift became a new beginning for Jeff, Patricia, Jonathan, and Ashley. Her story inspired countless people to donate their organs, which meant that in some small way, she would live on through more recipients whom we would never meet. And she also gave us signs that she was still a part of our lives just when we needed reminders the most.

In the early days of grief, I wondered if I would ever have two good days in a row. As time passed, there were three days, then five, then there were good weeks. Back then, I was desperate to know if I would ever be happy again—it didn't feel possible. But now I know that though the pain will always be with me, it will change form and lessen over time. I'm happy again. I've found happiness in the ordinary things—watching Peyton swim, listening to Ryan chatter at the dinner table, or feeling their arms around my neck. Their humor cracks me up and I have gigantic belly laughs at their antics, something I once thought I would never have again. This new joy is more pure and precious to me than ever before.

As the workers picked up the heavy granite stone and carefully laid it on the surface they'd prepared, I saw Taylor's image, and next to it the cross. I thought about Jesus dying on the cross. The Son of God had a purpose in death. Though many thought His death was an end, on the third day they discovered that Jesus's purpose was part of something much bigger. Something eternal.

God created each of us for a purpose.

I'd always known my purpose—it was to be a mother to my three kids and a wife to Todd. But when one of those kids was taken from me, I felt like my purpose had been taken too. Some people talk about empty-nest syndrome when their kids go off to college. For a long time I felt as if my nest had been kicked and the pieces had gone flying everywhere. But once I got over the initial shock of losing one of my babies, I saw there were two more who needed me more than ever. What I came to realize over my months of searching was that my purpose hadn't changed—I was still a mom of three. But Ryan and Peyton need me in different ways now than Taylor needs me. We were a five-piece puzzle that had to be put back together with only four pieces, and we were all working hard to create a new picture of what our family would look like going forward.

Todd quickly knew his purpose was in the foundation. I rediscovered during those months of grieving that part of my purpose as his wife was to help him fulfill his God-given purpose. Now that he is working out of our home and we have the foundation, it is easier than ever for me to be a part of what he's doing.

Our purpose comes from God, who is the Author of our stories, our lives, whether we like the plot or not. He was the author while

Taylor was alive, and He was the Author of her story even in her death. But her death is not the end of her story. God is still sovereign and He is still writing. Taylor's next chapter continues—it just continues in a new setting. And mine continues as a mother of three, though I don't see one the way I used to.

I thought about Taylor, wrapped in Jesus's arms, her head on His shoulder and her ponytail tickling His neck, smiling down on us as we've muddled our way through a few dark chapters. She got to the happy part of her life's story faster than most people.

Todd and I know that each day only brings us closer to the day our stories will once again merge with hers—we have the same Author of Life.

When we die as believers, life doesn't end. It's just a new beginning of life with God.

Eternal life.

And that is the story we all look forward to living.

Todd and Tara

The title of this book is *Taylor's Gift*, but this isn't just Taylor's story, or even just our story. It's the story of a cowboy who now has the strength and ability to give back to the community, a nurse who can be an active mom and fully present for her kids, a biker who can give of himself completely, and a teenager who for the first time can see her future. It's the story of countless recipients who received organs because someone heard Taylor's story and registered to be an organ donor. It's also the story of the infinite number of gifts they will give to *their* friends and family.

Taylor's gift is a gift that keeps on giving.

To others.

To us.

But the greatest gift we've received through this journey didn't come from Taylor. It came from God.

The gift of hope.

No matter how tragic our circumstances, God was always there for us.

Whether we acknowledged Him or not, He was always there.

And whether we heard Him or not, He was always present.

He will be there for you too.

Of course He will.

You are His gift. You are His child.

Acknowledgments

After people hear our family's story, they often mention that it has inspired them. But through the good days and the bad, what has inspired us is the love and encouragement of our friends and family. We could fill another book with all of the names of those who stood by us, but we hope that in reading this book they will recognize their part in our story and our appreciation for their role in our lives.

A very special thank-you goes out to:

Bill Taylor, who was the first by our side when we needed him most. We can't fully imagine or understand how you handled everything that was thrown at you. You have been there for us in so many ways: emotionally, spiritually, silently, and physically. You have handled the roles of brother, uncle, and doctor with such grace that it amazes us. Thank you for loving us deeply and always being there.

Kary, Juli, Chris, Bernie, Kristin, and Curt, who were able to be by our side at the hospital during such a difficult time. Your presence, love, and hugs helped carry us through.

All of the friends and family who took care of us when we came home and for months afterward, especially Daniela Centeno, Pam and Randy Cope, Ana Lucia Cottone, Chris and Kim Dicken, Susie

Evans, Tresha Glowacki, Mandy Goddard, Greg Goyne, Kathy Gutierrez, Paul Haggan, Jeff Hook, Jeremy Lipsey, Lisa Marshall, Mary Marshall, Linda Medina, Jeff and Kathy Quirk, Beth Rathe, Dina Conte Schulz, Candy Sheehan, Pauline and Pete Stein, Terry Storch, Jason and Dana Thompson, Angie Thurman, Trista Wojick, Judy Ordemann, and Nancy Yingling. Your conversations, clean laundry, foundation advice, baskets of food, care of Taylor's grave, laundry soap, tomato plants, meals, cards, letters, and so much more were physical tokens of your care and concern for us. And thank you to the many more who have loved and supported our family during this time, both for things we know about and the many unseen acts you've done.

Matt, Beth, Allie, and Emily Sunshine—our Suntorch family! We have described our friendship to many as "family without the blood," and we love you deeply. So many of our special memories include you. You are forever family to us.

Laura Springer, who in our opinion is the best school principal in America and also a true friend. Your laughter, hugs, and smiles always seem available at the perfect time.

Taylor's dear friends Courtney Quirk and Kate Dicken. You opened your hearts to try to be "big sisters," and for that we will be forever grateful.

To Steve "Hutch" Hutcheson: you will always hold a special place in our family. You gave Taylor the nickname "T" and surrounded her with your beautiful faith. Thank you for your prayers and strength.

Everyone at the Center for Sales Strategy, especially John Henley, Jim Hopes, and Steve Marx. If more companies were run with the same integrity and compassion, the world would be a better place.

Father Alfonse, who helped us understand purpose in pain and showed unconditional love in the worst of times. Thank you for your advice and care. We'll never forget the day you emphatically encouraged us to write a book.

Andrea Doering at Baker Publishing, who was brave enough to reach out to grieving parents and ask if we had ever considered writing a book. Your act was a (divine?) confirmation of Father Alfonse's suggestion, and we are so thankful for you.

Jennifer Schuchmann: from the moment we talked with you, we knew you were the one to help us write this book. We know that if we had met earlier in life, we would have been the best of friends. You have a special place in our family now; you know inside jokes, what makes us tick, and how to pull us out when we turn inward. Your gift of writing is truly from God. You have handled our story with such grace and respect, and for that we are forever grateful.

Kathy Helmers at Creative Trust and the entire Baker Publishing team. Thank you for helping us through this journey. We have felt loved and protected by your experience and guidance.

Taylor's Keepers—Jeff Kartus, Patricia Winters, Jonathan Finger, Amanda Zoller, and an unnamed liver recipient—for being open to connecting with us and loving us like family. We feel a special connection to you like none other. You each have helped us have hope and strength in ways we can't truly explain.

Our extended family: thank you for all of the thoughts, prayers, laughter, notes, hugs, and encouragement. We know this has been a hard journey, and we thank you for never giving up on us.

Our parents: we know this has been tremendously difficult for you. We don't know the perspective of a grandparent, but we do know the meaning of your love for us. You have constantly surrounded us with support and prayer. Thank you for your unconditional love.

All of you have been Christ's hands and feet and have loved us when we were the hardest to love. May this book be a testimony of your love and friendship, and may it inspire others to go and do likewise.

Ryan and Peyton, who are our daily reminders that God is good. Thank you for loving us unconditionally during the worst of our grief—you've inspired us with the courage you've shown in the face of yours. Though there is a piece missing from our five-piece puzzle, the remaining pieces are tightly locked together into a new picture. Thank you for walking so bravely and faithfully through a tragedy you didn't ask for. You are our biggest blessings and our deepest love.

Finally, to God, His Son, and the Holy Spirit: thank You for Your comfort and protection during the hardest times. We marvel at how You have brought all of this together for Your good, and we hope our words honor You and give You all the glory.

Todd and Tara Storch

About the Authors

Tara Storch is wife to Todd and mom to Taylor, Ryan, and Peyton. Along with her husband she cofounded Taylor's Gift Foundation to "increase organ donation to Regift Life, Renew Health, and Restore Families." She has more than twenty years of sales and marketing experience, is an active volunteer, and is a community leader. She is a passionate speaker for their mission and helps with many aspects of the foundation including marketing, merchandise and events. She has told their story on *Good Morning America*, *The Today Show*, *The Ellen DeGeneres Show*, and other national media.

After the death of his daughter Taylor, **Todd Storch** pursued his God-given passion to promote organ donation and help others. As cofounder and president of Taylor's Gift Foundation, Todd leads an amazing core team and volunteer network. In less than two years, Todd has spoken to thousands of people across the country and, through the foundation's efforts, has helped contribute to the certification of nearly two million organ donors in Texas and over twelve million nationally. Todd has more than twenty years of experience as a senior executive in radio and digital media sales, and extensive experience helping companies build their digital and interactive divisions. Most importantly, Todd is husband to Tara and father to Taylor, Ryan, and Peyton.

Jennifer Schuchmann specializes in collaborations with celebrities and newsmakers. Among her many books, she is the coauthor with Kurt and Brenda Warner of the *New York Times* bestselling *First Things First*, with Dan Woolley of *Unshaken*, the only book written by a survivor of the Haiti earthquake, and with Jim Cymbala of *Spirit Rising*. She is also the host of "Right Now," a panel-driven television talk show that airs nationally on the NRB Network. Learn more about Jennifer at WordsToThinkAbout.com, or follow her on Twitter @Schuchmann.

g ve
LiFE

Help us help others by donating to the Taylor's Gift Foundation at TaylorsGift.org/give. Your contribution will go toward aiding families touched by organ donation.

outlive yourself

By registering to be an organ donor you have the privilege of one day saving someone's life. It's the greatest gift you could ever give. Register today at TaylorsGift.org.

♡ Taylor's Gift™

Mentoring Roxbury, Jason, John, Paul, et. al.
Table of Contents

Page:

Dedication

Dedications often recognize a parent, in this instance, Paul's mother, Anna Ploutz who was also a mentor to a small boy "Jimmy." (James Allen Proper, Superintendent and Co-author)

Mother and Roxbury graduate (1915) Anna Ploutz, believed that "if the world became a better place, however slightly, because you were in it, then your life had greater value and meaning."

Sports writer Grantland Rice, suggested that "when the one great scorer comes to   write against your name, he writes not that you won or lost, but how you played the game."

This dedication asks you to be a mentor, do random acts of kindness, better still, quietly do things for people or causes where you do not gain attention or recognition. Call mentoring by any name you like, but "helping others to succeed is likely to make you happy as well, but do it to make the world a better place..."

Anna Ploutz
1897 - 1989

Jim, the world is a better place because "you're in it". I am so very proud of you! ... thanksgiving day, Nov 25, 2004,

Printed by The Chapman Printing Company, 405 Ann Street, P.O. Box 2001, Parkersburg, WV, 26101, for the Roxbury Educational Foundation, P.O. Box 66 State Highway 30, Roxbury, N.Y., 12474.

Published by Ploutz Realty Inc. for the Roxbury Educational Foundation, P.O. Box 66, State Highway 30, Roxbury, N.Y., 12474.

Additional copies of <u>Mentoring</u> may be purchased by sending check or money order to Roxbury Educational Foundation, P.O. Box 66, State Highway 30, Roxbury, N.Y., 12474. Books are $16.99 each plus $3.00 each for tax, postage and handling. Contact REF for inquiries regarding multiple copies of <u>Mentorin</u> for schools, libraries, bookstore, etc.

The Roxbury Educational Foundation (REF) is a non-profit charitable foundati under IRS 501 (c) (3) exempt under 501 (a) tax I.D. 54-2130573 Internal Revenue Code.

Library of Congress Cataloging-in-Publication Data
Ploutz, Paul F; Proper, James A.
Mentoring: How mentoring in a small village in the Catskills of
New York affected Financier Jay Gould, Naturalist John Burroughs,
Science Educator Paul Ploutz and 1,851 others over a 100 year period.

ISBN: 0-9762897-0-9

First Edition, November 2004
Perfect Binding, text 60# opaque; 6x9, 4 color cover 100# gloss;
Type, Times New Roman 12. Approximately 81 b/w pictures on 45 pages.
Total text, pictures approximately 450.

ACKNOWLEDGEMENTS

Read "the main mentors" who chiseled Paul, (see picture inside of rear cover) from "a diamond in the rough" or merely "a blob of clay" into something apparently useful.

These mentors, thirty five in all, are listed in chronological order starting with Betty Craig, Paul's 1st teacher (he was age 5, 1936). Most are also mentioned elsewhere in the text.

Elizabeth "Betty" Craig,		Roxbury, N. Y.
Edith Ploutz,	Aunt	Roxbury, N. Y.
Etta Colby,	Elderly friend	Roxbury , N. Y.
Rudolph Gorsch, Sr.	Undertaker	Roxbury, N. Y.
Lena Lutz,	Aunt	Roxbury, N. Y.
Glen Young,	Pastor Gould Church	Roxbury, N. Y.
Catherine Fleming,	7th grade teacher	Roxbury , N. Y.
Lela Wickham,	8th grade teacher	Roxbury , N. Y.
Roland F. "Doc" Ross,	Coach	Roxbury, N. Y.
Bruce "Stub" Caswell,	Scout master	Roxbury, N. Y.
Marian Bookhout,	Theatre operator	Roxbury, N. Y.
Herman Luben,	Pastor, Gould Church	Roxbury , N. Y.
Raymond F. Cronk,	Uncle	Roxbury, N. Y.
Euclid G. Proper,	Brother in law (Jim's dad)	Grand Gorge, N. Y.
Bernard Barshearer,	Col. Nat'l Guard	Albany, N. Y.
John F. Gonsa,	Comptroller Breslaw Bros.	Schenectady, N. Y.
Robert Johnson,	SUNY professor	Oneonta, N. Y.
Emery Will,	SUNY professor	Oneonta, N. Y.
Ellis Whitaker,	SUNY professor	Oneonta, N. Y.
Lawrence B. Goodrich,	SUNY professor	Oneonta, N. Y.
Charles Helvey,	SUNY professor/NASA	Oneonta, N. Y.
Charles F. Shearer,	"G". Co. Nat'l Guard	Oneonta, N. Y.
Leta Adee,	Supervising teacher, JHS	Oneonta, N. Y.
Edna Trip,	Principal, JHS	Oneonta, N. Y.
Ron Walley,	Master teacher, JHS	Oneonta, N. Y.
Donald G. Decker,	Provost/advisor, Univ. N. Colo.	Greeley, Colorado
Harley F. Glidden,	Dept. ch. UNC	Greeley, Colorado
Jack Fisher,	Managing editor, SRA (IBM)	Chicago, Illinois
Jack Kirksey,	Livonia prin./mayor/State Rep.	Livonia, Mich.
Jerry Erspamer,	Livonia principal	Livonia, Mich.
Mary Hawkins,	THE SCIENCE TEACHER (NSTA)	Wash., D. C.
Jim Shipman,	Chair Sci. Dept, Ohio Univ.	Athens, Ohio
Roger Van Dyke,	Mgr. Diamond Stone Quarries	Albany, Ohio
Gil Crowell,	Dean, Coll. of Ed. Ohio Univ.	Athens, Ohio
Robert B. Glidden,	Pres. Ohio Univ.	Athens, Ohio

6-D

Along with mentors it seems inevitable that you may collect a few "tormentors" who simply don't care for you, like what you do, or you merely get in their way. It's normal, live with it and try not to be someone else's "tormentor."

At some bazaar level they may even help you become a better person. When you make your list its important that you have more mentors than tormentors. Make sure you do more mentoring without making life miserable for someone else. I wish you well, now go forth and prosper and may the force be with you!

Paul Ploutz
1931 - 20--

Mentoring Roxbury, *Jason,* John, *Paul, et. al.*

Preface

Jason Gould, John Burroughs, and Paul Ploutz were born and raised in Roxbury, New York. They attended a one-room schoolhouse on Hardscrabble Road. All were poor farm boys with indifferent, abusive fathers. Ploutz, born in 1931 (ten years after Burroughs died), lived on Hardscrabble Road farm at the intersection of what later became Burroughs Road near Memorial Field and John's now famous "Boyhood Rock." At one-point, Paul's uncle and aunt, Howard and Helen Ploutz, ran the Burroughs' farm until Henry Ford bought them out, returning the farm to Burroughs' control. The Burroughs' farm was about halfway between the Gould and Ploutz farms, the Gould's being in West Settlement.

These three boys of humble origins craved knowledge. The rugged Catskill Mountains of upstate New York, the village of Roxbury, and one-room schools have produced many brilliant overachievers. Poorer than Jason or John, with an abusive father, Paul admired and emulated both of them. A naturalist/professor/science educator/author/real estate developer but without Gould's millions, Paul is a genuine mix of Jay Gould and John Burroughs, thus one of our several titles **Roxbury Boys, Jason, John, Paul, et. al.**

There are numerous famous sons from Roxbury Central School to be sure, but Paul's success, from a poor farm boy with a hardscrabble lifestyle cannot be refuted. One hundred years after Gould and Burroughs, Paul is quick to acknowledge the other 1851 Roxbury school graduates. *All of them* by his insistence are included in this "One hundred-year story."

At age twelve, and many times afterward, Paul read a copy of *"The Wizard of Wall Street,"* a scathing but presumably accurate and rare book on Gould's life. Paul has done well financially but is poor compared to Gould, who at one point was believed to be the wealthiest man in the world. The Burroughs' resemblance is far more conspicuous. A nature lover even as a child, Paul's legacy is still in progress, *doing* the things about which Naturalist Burroughs wrote and complained.

What do closeknit, rural, poor villages do to help youth "beat the odds?" How do communities provide an environment that instills a child's drive for achievement?

We expect the *Roxbury Boys* story will help you discover how the thousands of small towns in America are special. This book is also a true story about *mentoring* and what you can do for your children, schools, and your community to "beat the odds."

James A Proper, Ph.D.
Superintendent of Schools
Roxbury, New York.

Thoughts on Mentoring................Robert Burr Glidden, Ph.D.

Which of us is not the beneficiary of mentors throughout our lives? The thread of mentoring runs throughout this book, a testimony to Paul Ploutz's recognition of those who mentored him, and to his pleasure and satisfaction at having been in a position to "repay" by mentoring others.

We all remember our mentors. We remember some of them very clearly, even from many years ago. We remember the people, the circumstances, the places and the way information and advice was passed on to us. We remember times when parents or teachers or clergy sat us down for formal "instruction" of one sort or another. It was their job, after all, and most of them took it very seriously. Sometimes it was gentle and kindly, sometimes it had a bit of a barb to it, but it was often a lesson given as a result of some action or experience that our mentors believed we could learn from.

Paul Ploutz was a master at that kind of mentoring because as a caring professor, it was what he *had* to do for his own satisfaction. It was not only expected of him, but it was something that satisfied him because it was an opportunity to pass on to a next generation something of himself and his experience. That is why many, probably most, college and university professors do what they do.

Some professors, of course, are better mentors than others. Mentoring is not lecturing, it is not scholarly research, it is not grading papers or writing research proposals. It is caring deeply for the pupils in your charge, It is wanting them to enjoy successes you have known in your life and profession, and it is wanting them not to make mistakes you have made. Mentoring is reflecting on one's own life experiences and then generalizing from those for the benefit of those who will come after you. It is a part of human tradition, and of course it is a human service offered by far more than teachers and professors.

Mentoring in "life" is a parental responsibility. In Paul's case, he recognizes his mother as a mentor but his father as a negative role model. In my case both parents were mentors, but they taught in different ways. They were Iowa farmers and they were full partners in the farming business. Both were very hard workers and I learned certain attitudes from their example. My father was even of temper and I cannot remember ever hearing him say an ugly word about anyone. He was proud, never wanted to be indebted to anyone, and seldom found fault with others. He was a man of few words and most of the mentoring I received from him was by example. My mother, on the other hand, was perhaps too judgmental of others; she was never shy about expressing her opinion. Both parents made whatever sacrifice was necessary for my brother's and my education, but it was my mother who, from a *very early age, made it clear that education was of paramount concern of the family and that, whatever happened, we would* leave *the farm and* go to college. She had strong views about what was worthy, and education topped the list. While my brother and I knew there were many choices in life, we knew that higher education was one that we would pursue!

The point of this personal history is that parental mentoring happens in different ways, sometimes by example, sometimes by very direct "instruction." I suppose one could say that in a sense, parenting *is* mentoring. Strong family values, when they are present, are certainly the result of parental mentoring, as usually is the case with strong spiritual values and strong educational values. In Paul's case, perhaps his mother's example was all the stronger because of the relationship between him and his father.

It occurs to me that we may gain as much by mentoring in the informal sense as in the formal. There is informal mentoring that we share with one another throughout our lives, perhaps from elementary school on through adulthood. Peer mentoring is and always has been very powerful. Sometimes it is positive and sometimes not, but we learn much about ways of doing things, ways of thinking, ways of relating with, others, ways of behaving.

It is most interesting *what we remember*...a kind word here or there that came totally unexpectedly, recognition by a colleague for something you thought had gone unnoticed, words of advice or suggestions from friends who are good enough to offer such. Often mentoring is *very* personal, dealing with issues that are too sensitive even to give as examples. In that sense, true friendship is a mentoring relationship, because mentoring is helping and that's what friends do for one another.

I remember when I was a very young teacher learning certain social graces, matters of etiquette, styles of entertaining, from a good friend who was a little older and from a more privileged background than I. And certainly I continue to learn today from colleagues whom I respect enough to call mentors. Those are all part of the informal mentoring process that is, in a sense, a continuation of learning through the oral tradition that served man for millennia before the written word.

Perhaps the main point of this book is Paul Ploutz's exploration of values acquired by growing up in a particular community, in this case, Roxbury, New York. Does the community environment itself provide a kind of mentoring? It is sometimes said, "Perhaps there's something in the water...," in reference to the influences of a given community on people who have exhibited common traits. More likely than the water is a kind of community "personality" that derives from generations of attitudes among the people. Some of that is a result of leadership but most of it is because of common interest and values that are cohesive—commonality and unity , community. Obviously, that is more likely to occur in small settings than in larger ones, or at lease it is more likely to be observed in small communities.

Paul Ploutz grew up in a small community, as did I, and as a result we have an appreciation of certain values and attitudes that pervade our lives. Perhaps good mentoring makes good mentors, and if that is the case I hope we have both passed along to our younger charges something very worthwhile.

Robert Burr Glidden, Ph.D.
President Ohio University
Athens, Ohio 45701

Beaverdam

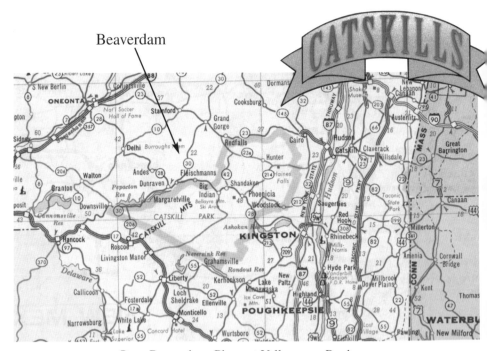

Once Beaverdam, Pleasant Valley, now Roxbury.
From 1901-2000, 1,851 boys and girls graduated from RCS.
Find Roxbury and read on...

Part I

Chapter 1:   Jason Gould   1836-1892

A Roxbury Farm Boy

Jason Gould was born May 27, 1836 on a 150-acre farm at West Settlement just over the hill from Hardscrabble Road, where his childhood neighbor, John Burroughs, lived. Jason was known as Jay. Although christened Jason he apparently didn't use Jay routinely until after 1852. Jay's grandfather, Captain Abraham Gold, settled in the Catskills in the 1780's, and by 1806 changed the family name to Gould. Jay's father was born in 1792. Jay's mother, Mary Moore, died in 1841 when he was only five. Jay was John Burr Gould's son by the first of his three wives. Jay was frail. His upbringing was largely accomplished by school along with his five older doting sisters, Betty, Sally, Annie, Nancy, and Mary who passed as "Polly." Today his sisters could be called *mentors*, as they played a very important role in his early years.

The girls loved Jay and provided him with affection, support, and to the extent possible, shielded him from the farm chores, which he detested. The Goulds kept only twenty cows. Jay's father, John Burr Gould, with all his daughters, needed brawn, not brains on the farm, and was openly disappointed with Jay's frailties. Jay was over a week old before his father named him.

The Gould family descended from confirmed Puritans. Connecticut aristocrats of Talcotts, Bradleys, and Burrs, they were quick to remind folks that they were above others. Being Puritan was all the more reason, at least in 1800, to insist on not being Jewish. More prosperous appearances were difficult to maintain. The hillside farm was indeed a "hardscrabble," but being conservative, hard-shelled, and Baptist helped to overcome the difficult environment.

Even Jay, however, went barefoot, as was the custom. It was wit and cunning that helped him elude cow flops, thistles, bullies, farm chores, even school. Jay's father openly described him as "not worth much", and locked him in the cellar one day when Jay refused to attend school. Late that evening Jay, having missed supper, the sisters became worried about his disappearance. Suddenly, his father recalled he was still in the cellar...

There are records of an earlier West Settlement log school in 1799-1800, and taught by William Sturges. David Dart, a carpenter, built the next West Settlement school around 1850. The school was a plain unpainted building between the road and West Settlement stream. During the winter, when crops were not tended, the attendance was as high as forty-five to fifty pupils crowded in, and not all were young men and women. History would later reveal that they had gained a brilliant teacher. The first teacher was a Scotchman named Mr. James Oliver. Oliver taught at the seminary several terms before going to Hobart. Oliver often stayed at the Gould farmhouse, or the Corbin home, or other homes as was the custom for teachers.

At Beechwood Seminary, Jason, like Ploutz a hundred years later, was scrawny frail, and constantly bullied. Jason, unlike Ploutz or Burroughs, was unpopular and often unwilling, but was always thirsty for knowledge, seemingly sensing that education would be his escape from ruffians, cows and the smell of manure, being barefoot, and the indifference of his father.

The Goulds and neighbor Phil Corbin built the Beechwood school between their two farms in West Settlement. John Burroughs and Jay's sisters also attended Beechwood prior to Jay and John attending the 'Ol Stone Jug school in Hardscrabble. "Beechwood" was destroyed by fire in the fall of 1924, and a new building, was erected that year.

Jason's new stepmother provided him with a younger brother, but Jay's interests were developing elsewhere. He studied logarithms and geometry as early as twelve or thirteen. Jay avoided farm work when possible. He was briefly a clerk in the "Yellow Store" (later the Corner Store) in Roxbury Village working for Edward I. Burhams, who later became a New York State senator. At age fourteen, after Beechwood Seminary, Jay enrolled himself in a school at Hobart, boarding with a blacksmith in return for keeping the books. Mr. Oliver was now teaching at Hobart.

Jason's father was completely indifferent. Jay remembers that his father believed, "I was not worth much at home and I might go ahead. Jay continues, so the next day I started off. I showed myself up at this school, and finally I found a blacksmith who consented to board me, as I wrote a pretty good hand, if I could write up his books at night. In that way I worked myself through this school."

13

The principal of the Academy at Hobart was the same Mr. James Oliver, who allowed precocious Jay to graduate his course of study in 1851. Jason was going on age fifteen. On leaving school, he became a clerk in a tin shop in Hobart, almost immediately becoming a partner and manager of the business. Never strong, or of barely "normal" health, Jay was willing, no eager, to work fifteen-hour days to gain control of his own life, earn money, and get off the damned farm.

Although christened "Jason" he apparently started using Jay routinely around 1852. December 27, 1852, Jason was already using math and surveying skills and signed a receipt "Jason" on behalf of himself and his father.

Jason's father, with daughters rather than robust sons, and steep, rocky fields, never did well on the farm.

Hardenbergh Patent and Antirent Wars

From the time of the first Dutch settlers in New York State until the American Revolution, it was the custom of the Dutch West India Company and the English Crown to grant land permits to favored individuals or groups. According to colonial law, no patent (gift) of land could contain more than two thousand acres.

The Hardenberghs, one such "favored" family, skirted the law and petitioned for land in the Catskills with an indefinite boundary. Lord Cornbury, then governor of New York and cousin to Queen Anne granted the Hardenbergh "patent" in 1708. She likely did not realize the eventual consequences of the patent.

With arguments about whether it was the east or west branch of the Delaware River described in the somewhat vague patent, it turned out to be the largest single parcel of land that royal letters ever conveyed in the history of New York State. The east branch of the Delaware starts above Roxbury nearer Grand Gorge, joining the west branch at Hancock. Originally, New York was divided into only ten counties rather than the sixty two of later years.

The Hardenberghs, as was the practice, wanted to rent, lease, or derive income from their land. It was not until 1749 that the giant task of "surveying" was attempted, taking three years to cut the giant patent into forty-two great parcels. There were major problems, not the least of which was that the Indians also had purchased the land or that it at least belonged to them.

After the 1751 survey, Johannes Hardenbergh paid the Indians 149 British pounds 19 shillings for the disputed land between the east and west branches of the Delaware.

One of the Hardenbergh family, Isaac, came to Roxbury around 1790 and became the first town supervisor. Isaac owned slaves and was required to register them. From 1799 to 1806 he registered slaves for a fee of twelve cents each. Isaac also had "a bound boy" a practice known at the time. Hiram Augustus Spooner was acquired as an "apprentice" for a period of six years.

By 1800, many of the families scattered around Delaware County and Roxbury were paying rent to the hardenberghs or to others who had purchased Hardenbergh property. Leases were in effect in West Settlement where the Goulds lived, and through most areas of Roxbury. A few folks, Erskine in Pleasant Valley (Hardscrabble), William Montgomery (1806) and Major General Otis Preston (1832), and others also had been "given" two hundred acre in land grant from the government in appreciation for their service.

Conflicting land grants, Hardenbergh Patent, Indian ownership, over 1.5 million acres of the Catskills, resulted in a legal (remember Jay's later work) mostly "unsurveying", dual grant, mess. Nevertheless the Hardenberghs continued to rent land rightly owned (likely owned).

The following lease (public record) is quoted from page 141 of Griffin's, *History of the Town of Roxbury.*

"In John F. Ballard's possession is the deed to the farm made out to Peleg Ballard December 24, 1794. This tract of 90 acres was purchased from Rachel Meier of Bergen,

N. J. ..That Rachel was possibly a Hardenbergh descendant who inherited that part of the tract as her share—and of course never saw the land."

"The price: Ten pounds of good and well-made maple sugar during the first five years. At the end of the first five years, five pounds (about $25) current and lawful money per hundred acres-- and at the end of the next five years, eight pounds of current and lawful money every year forever after." In other words, a permanent lease, an endless burden which the anti rent war was fought to eliminate.

Other leases were fixed at ten bushels of wheat for 100 acres together with four fat hens and a day's work with a team. And so it went, there were hundreds of leases both "durable" and "redemption leases." Still other leases, under certain conditions, permitted the tenant to buy the land. The durable leases were the worse, as a diligent farmer never got to own the fruits of his efforts in building a successful farm or business. There were also "one" and "three" life leases and all manner of agreements of every nature, duration, and complexity.

One durable lease stated "as long as the grass grows and the water flows," rent would need to be paid. Opposition to the leases spread from Albany (Rensselaer County) around 1838 but reached Delaware County in the early 1840's (read *Crisis in the Catskills* by Mary Bogardus). Roxbury held its first real anti rent meeting in the summer of 1844. They were called "down renters" with locals often dressed as Indians to disguise their identity. The "up-renters" were most everyone else who believed legal means would settle the lease disputes.

The Ploutz Theory on Gould's Behavior

Jay was eight years old. His father John B. Gould was a staunch *up* renter. Chauncey Burroughs was an out spoken down-renter. Jay and John Burroughs were classmates, friends, neighbors. Both farmers, Gould and Burroughs, were well-known and their alienation was seen as a serious "split," far more than a temporary spat among West Settlement neighbors. The split became so rancorous that even among the children it was considered unwise even unsafe for down or up renter children to mingle, or associate.

The prime confrontation now between people with hoes, rakes, sickles, and guns took place in "Shacksville," now known as Decker's flats, then the Bouton farm. The climax of that confrontation landed the down renters at the home of John B. Gould.

Earlier writings suggesting that Jay might have been hiding under the bed are now believed to be erroneous. It is widely believed that his father, in fact, stood his ground and "drove them off" with a gun. It was likely that Jay witnessed his father's courage and later told of his fear, thinking his father would be killed before his very eyes. Jay, now age ten, likely witnessed his father's courage in standing his ground, as reported in *(History of Delaware County)*. Children usually mirror their family's position. A sheriff (Greene More Aug 7, 1845) was shot, jails were filled, children were used as hostages, real Indians (anti renters) "disappeared."

Jay's friend John Burroughs, one year younger than Jay, recalled hiding under a neighbor's bed only to be found because he left his feet sticking out. The Beechwood Seminary was abandoned (James Oliver) when the factions finally resolved most of the differences.

Since one of the early focal point of the anti rent wars in Delaware County was in young Jay's front lawn, he had ample opportunity to see and learn the violence, financial, neighborhood disintegration, and fall out of the events beyond his comprehension, at least at the time.

Jay had to be aware that Edward O'Connor and Von Steenburgh were : 1. convicted of murder and sentenced to be hanged.

      2. that eighty-four were imprisoned or fined.

      3. that political pressure saw Governor Wright commute their sentences.

      4. that the next governor John Young acting on the petitioners 11,000 strong pardoned all the Anti-Rent convicts who then returned home.

      5. that the whole "insurrection" charged to Delaware County by the State was a staggering $63,683.20.

      6. that the money was *never* paid.

Jay had to notice that his father John Burr Gould (up) and John's father Chauncey (down) renters acknowledged each others presence again and the neighborhood kids once again spoke and played together.

Jay was a **"fast study"** and when it was all over he and his father were both alive. The entire experience served as a giant workshop of leases, land, money, social conflict and politics. His father's puritan, protect the landlords ($) up rent firmness had prevailed. Jay, at an early age enjoyed a real life prototype of the big picture, and he later surveyed the lands representing the anti rent wars in their entirety.

Jay lost his mother, and his beloved sister Polly died before her wedding date to his favorite teacher Oliver. Oliver left for Kansas. Jay hated the farm. Jay was brilliant, more to the point, the numerous conflicts, simply made him stronger even more self reliant and single- minded in purpose. People had not been all that good in solving his problems. Money, on the other hand might have saved his mother, and his sister. Oliver, avoided the anti-rent wars and removed himself from cows and manure. He was to leave town, forever and why not? Eventually Jay would do the same thing...

The neighbor boy, John Burroughs, was said to have placed a picture of their *mentor* James Oliver on his desk where it remained through much of Burroughs' life. Jay, on the other hand never looked back.

After numerous skirmishes in the antirent conflicts throughout the Catskills, Jason's father sold the farm and moved to Roxbury Village. Some reports suggest that Jay worked a tin shop with his father in Roxbury, others say Jason "hired" the same father who had earlier "sent him off" to work in the tin shop at Hobart!

By 1853, Jay's first work in surveying was Ulster County, then Albany County. About 1855, he returned to Roxbury and surveyed Delaware County making the first map in 1856. Jay, while recovering from an illness in 1856, wrote a history of Delaware County when only eighteen. *Mentor* James Oliver had taught him well as surveying requires considerable mathematical skill. Jay's next business was tanning with Zadock Pratt (Prattsville) and the first of his moral conspiracies. Several books are available, none of which are flattering. Jay is alleged to have "cooked the books" on Pratt who could neither read nor write. Pratt later committed suicide.

We have attempted to provide insight into the origin of a once simple Roxbury boy from West Settlement. West Settlement and Hardscrabble (Ploutz) are thought to be the oldest settlements outside Roxbury (Beaver Dam). John Burroughs lived between West Settlement and Hardscrabble.

The Wizard of Wall Street

Roxbury locals have assumed that the most accurate, scathing book, of many, ever written about Jay, was entitled, **The Wizard of Wall Street**; and *His Wealth, or, The Life and Deeds of Jay Gould*, published in 1892, the same year Gould died. The author, Trumbull White, described Gould as "Bribing senators, purchasing judges, organizing the greatest and most dastardly financial conspiracy the world has even seen, laying its foundation in the actual bribery of a member of the President's family."

This text has provided nearly all of the references and pictures about Gould, some not available even in book stores dealing with rare books. Only thirteen copies are known to exist. A more recent text (around 2000) entitled "Wizards of Wall Street" has caused minor confusion. It is a contemporary publication not to be confused with "*The Wizard*," a very rare book.

Local dialogue of the 1930s and 40s, repeatedly suggested that later, Gould's estate had actually "bought out the publisher," destroyed the plates, then offered a ten dollar "bounty" on any copy that could be found. Paul Ploutz's father, George, purchased a couple boxes of books, at a farm auction in the late 1930s. One yellowed copy (1892), *The Wizard of Wall Street*, was among the tattered collection. The Ploutz children were admonished not to reveal its presence, as not to incur the wrath of the Goulds.

The book was hidden in the Ploutz residence on Hardscrabble Road. Paul still has a copy now over 112 years old. Several universities have approached him asking for it to be added to their rare book collection. Information about Jason's youth is difficult to obtain and verify. As a Hardscrabble "neighbor" in the 1940s Paul had talked with elderly townsfolk who knew both Gould and Burroughs. Paul only recalls that locals "feared the Goulds but they did keep the Jews out of Roxbury." Unlike the Goulds many of the Burroughs family who lived closer were still around and no one took them seriously as they never seemed to quite make it as farmers.

Maury Klein, *The Life And Legend Of Jay Gould* (1986), John Hopkins University Press, put a kinder spin on his deeds. Klein and others, writing about Jay, apparently have access to the two copies John Hopkins University holds. In 2001, Paul offered to donate his copy of the text to the town of Roxbury where Jay, John, and Paul were born. The local Roxbury Library politely "declined" suggesting they could not guarantee its safety. Copies have been located at the following universities: California (San Diego), Johns Hopkins (2), Kentucky, Purdue, Amherst (2), Nebraska (Omaha), New Mexico, Cincinnati, Oklahoma, and Bridgewater College.

The 1972 edition of *World Book Encyclopedia* (ISBN 0 7166 0076 5), first published around 1917, with over one-hundred editions, describes Gould as "The most hated man in America."

The final sentence of Richard O'Connor's 1962 text, *Gould's Millions*, Doubleday and Company, is "His villainies emerge from the welter of old headlines only as picturesque symptoms of a time so uncomplicated that one could draw to himself a hatred now reserved for nations."

By the year 2000, it's convenient to think there were "two Goulds." The financial "lizard" of Wall Street was also a man of "family." Jay married Helen D. Miller in the winter of 1862. Helen was the idol of her children and practically unknown in society. Her home was world enough for her and it was a happy one. There are many stories of private charities of this modest woman. His home life was totally above reproach, his nature affectionate.

Jay's six children included George, Edwin, Helen, Howard, Anna, and Frank. Gould was unlike Burroughs and Ploutz, who had "affairs." Jay, even with his maids, servants, and orchid flower gardens, was impeccable in his domestic life. Jay Gould had no social ambition whatever. He was the most domestic of men and his affection and attention to his own family so deep as to leave no place for outside social influences or interest in the childhood farm, Roxbury, or Burroughs. Many accounts of Jay repeat that he "never" again visited Roxbury. Other records state that at age forty-four, (1880) he visited his birth-place and Hobart where he attended school under Mr. James Oliver. Further he "was enthusiastically received by the inhabitants at the time of his visit, as the most noted man ever born in that region."

He did have time for orchids and was very successful in growing them at his new residence at Lyndhurst. Lyndhurst was made up of well-cultivated farmlands, orchards, and dog kennels with a magnificent gray stone Elizabethan architecture presentation overlooking the Hudson.

Statues, works of art, paintings, are tastefully located throughout the mansion. Down a steep accent across his own hidden train tracks (he had his own train and cars) was the Hudson and his magnificent yacht Atlanta. The steam vessel, in spite of being 243 feet long and 15-1/2 feet deep, was essentially the fastest thing on the Hudson, and the few times it was raced set new records. When Jay was refused admittance to the New York Yacht Club (and many other clubs) he with others started their own yacht club, the American Stem Yacht Club. Jay was so wealthy with power, few things stood in his way. He could go through, over, or around any obstacle. Failing that technique he could buy, bribe, or blackmail any banker or politician.

In a nearby conservatory of four acres, Jay hired Ferdinand Mangold to grow one of the finest palm gardens in the Western Hemisphere. There were over 250 varieties of palms from maidenhair to great shadowy trees thirty feet tall with large wide leaves. They were assembled from Africa, Central and South America, Samoa, India, and wherever they could be identified. The frail farm boy who teacher James Oliver from West Settlement had *mentored* knew the names of them <u>all.</u> Jay also collected six-hundred varieties of ferns, nearly two-thousand azaleas, and eight-thousand orchid plants in over one-hundred and fifty varieties.

In another compartment, there was a "wilderness of roses, pink and white and gold and Guelder, Burgundy and Austrian in an endless tangle of color and a delirious odorous atmosphere." Jay probably never pulled another weed as he had for his mother back in Roxbury or ever again milked a cow as he had so often had to do on his father's farm. But he did own "50 cows, 25 horses, 3 bulls, 200 ducks, 500 pigeons, a thousand chickens, a half dozen deer and a span of oxen." Lyndhurst produced over two hundred and fifty tons of hay from the fields each summer. They had already filled in more than one-hundred and twenty acres of swamp to reduce the likelihood of malaria.

Jay attended the opera with his daughter-in-law as Helen's health was failing and she didn't care to go out that much anyway. She did take carriage rides with Jay as they had "fifteen or twenty carriages."

In later years, Gould sought good opinion of his fellowmen, and was more careful in his morality. A faithful husband and a kind father, he became less likely to "Plow the waters of the Hudson with the most splendid yacht ever constructed." In his later years, however, he was still a factor in elections. Political candidates sought his favors. He dictated appointments to high offices. Honorable men again sat with him on boards. His monumental wealth made him a "heavy hitter," not even presidents would cross him unnecessarily.

Now, so many years later, having absolutely escaped milking cows, sports events, cards, checkers, and physical chores, was he reconsidering values instilled as a child? Jay apparently never again spent time with John who he had wrestled with, traded marbles, knives, and pencils, with whom he had helped get into and out of scrapes.

John, on occasion, would go home with Jay. Jay apparently never went home with John, as the Goulds were cautious in dealing with people of conspicuously lesser rank. Burroughs father in earlier years had been a "bigoted, horse betting, card playing, whiskey drinking, intolerant bore" (see Ch. 2 Burroughs).

The reader will gradually discover that Gould, Burroughs, and Ploutz all had "difficult" fathers and loving mothers. Think about the significance and consequences, if any, to their careers and the concept that "dominant parents make strong children stronger and weak children weaker."

In the spring of 1850, age fourteen, while still at the local Beechwood Seminary school, Jay wrote a paper, "Honesty Is the Best Policy," extolling the virtue of self-denial, conscience, right, and honesty. During the spring term in 1855 Jay returned to teach surveying at the seminary. Jay's "honesty" paper has been frequently reprinted. The irony of his message, then his career, awaits interpretation of the psychology community. In 1866, after Jay and John had gone their separate ways, Burroughs wrote in his journal "The ambition now is to get wealth and die a Christian--- become rats if necessary to achieve these ends."

Some reports suggest that Gould fondly followed Burroughs' nature writings. Others, including John, said he never spoke to him after their school days together. The adult Gould did enjoy flower gardens and raising orchids, perhaps from earlier influences by Burrough's love of nature?

Jay died Friday morning 9:15, December 3, 1892, of tuberculosis at age fifty-six to the "much quiet rejoicing of the stock market, where railroads, in particular, rallied at hearing the good news." All of his earlier Roxbury classmates outlived him. Six rich orphans inherited, depending on which source you read, between $84 and $125 million. Numerous explanations exist to this day as to why the Gould dynasty was unable to continue like the Rockefeller's, Astors, Carnegies, DuPonts, and other robber barons. Other historians and locals suggest it has but that the Gould's never spent a dime on public relations as did other families. Jay's three sons George, Edwin, and Frank, and two daughters, Helen, Anna, even grandchildren have quietly given millions to libraries and worthy caused in the United States and Europe.

Of Jay's six children, Helen Gould Shepard's philanthropy did much to reduce the pain of Gould family history, particularly in Roxbury, New York, where Jay was born and raised. The little village of Roxbury, nestled at the headwaters of the east branch of the Delaware River, (called Pepacton by the Indians) in the Catskills is renowned for sending so many over-achieving Roxbury Boys out into the world. Helen the oldest and Frank the youngest of Jay's children financed several of the "overachievers". They provided scholarship funds for numerous Roxbury Boys and Girls who would never have otherwise attended college. More particularly they did it relatively quietly with little fan fair. Helen Gould (Mrs. Finley J. Shepard) has done more for the village of Roxbury than any individual in history. It is not a "close call."

Roxbury certainly owes many of its success to Jay's oldest daughter Helen Gould. Jay's other five children lived lavishly with little or no contact with Roxbury. Jay's youngest son, Frank Jay, provided a scholarship for Frank Booth who graduated Roxbury in 1904. Frank Gould and Frank Booth both graduated from New York University with degrees in engineering. Only Frank maintained much interest in Roxbury providing scholarships to several other worthy students.

Unlike John Burroughs' grandchildren, most of the Goulds descendents "amounted to something." But as Roxbury locals, many of whom feared the Gould influence anyway, pointed out, "Its hard to fail if you've got millions in the bank when you're born." For the next hundred years, 1901 to 2000, no Goulds graduated from Roxbury schools, whereas four Burroughs, Angie, 1931; Debora, 1979; another John 1982; and Joshua 1997, graduated.

What part of Jason's life is about the hard life in Roxbury, ridicule of his peers, or having Burroughs, as one of his only friends? Frail, sullen, intelligent, with a father he couldn't please, with little approval, but with affection largely from sisters, Jason Gould left home at fourteen. His work ethic was strong from 5:00 a.m. until whenever the job was done. Life was tough. Was that why Jason was to achieve financial success of monumental proportions?

So, as it turns out, looking back at history, General George Custer was an early American Civil War army hero. Many now see Custer as a merciless murderer slaughtering Indian squaws, papooses, and a fair number of braves as a sporting event.

The once famous Jesse James, also a Civil War veteran, was a noted bank and train robber and gunslinger. Given enough time, and fighting for the South in the Civil War, relatives are now likely proud of Jesse who was also at "the top of his game."

And so it is, in 2002, with Jay Gould, relatives and complete strangers were most likely proud. Many in Roxbury, New York are now finally, yet cautiously, proud of him. A magnificent, Jay Gould Memorial Dutch Reformed Church, of Indiana limestone with Tiffany windows certainly helped. Jay's daughter Helen, also paid for the sidewalks, and curbed the entire length of the one-mile Main Street in Roxbury. She allegedly deposited $100,000 in cash in the Roxbury bank to prevent its demise during the great depression of the 1930s. At one point, Helen even gave $100,000 to the federal government to help with the "war effort."

Helen Shepard paid the college expenses for promising Roxbury graduates, including Mildred Caswell (1919), Frederick Teichmann (22), Harry Fredenburgh (29), Herbert Lutz (32) Otis Van Aken (39) and others, attending New York University (NYU) and elsewhere. The Gould Hall building is part of the NYU Campus. This merely represented the tip of the iceberg, as to what this wonderful daughter accomplished. Jewish mothers are again proud to name sons Jay.

The Ploutz "Proclamation" and Historic Site

If anyone is ever going to "pardon" Jay, who better than another poor (local) country boy, a Hardscrabble Road Roxbury neighbor to both Burroughs and Gould? Paul attended the one-room school in Hardscrabble and his father also ridiculed him. Both Paul and Jay left home essentially penniless and started as bookeepers. Jay, of course, made far more money and never returned to Roxbury as Burroughs and Ploutz have.

Ploutz returned more frequently than Burroughs, who seldom spoke of his old friend Jay. If anyone is going to pardon Jay (at least for Delaware County) who would be more qualified to do it?

By the power vested in me, (well none really) this Roxbury Boy, Ploutz, exactly 110 years later (Jay died 1892, this sentence was written in 2002) having also been born in Roxbury, attended the one-room school as Jay, as nearby neighbor, having also escaped farm life/cows, baptized in the Jay Gould Church, having left town as Jay and his only friend Burroughs did, made a buck and now returns:

Hereby declares:

"Enough already." The Gould name, at least in Roxbury, "Shall henceforth be accepted respected, and admired." Well, daughter Helen Gould Shepard, did most of it, but Roxbury, the town, roads, schools, library, the 1,851 people who have graduated RCS this last century, even the river have profited because of Jay. It took more than a century, but "Here goes!"

"Thank you Jay, and Helen. Jay, your childhood home in West Settlement, over the Hardscrabble Road from the Burroughs and Ploutz farms, still stands; *I do declare that it should become an historic site by the state of New York.* You did a great job building railroads, your magnificent daughter Helen made Roxbury a great place to live, and you helped me a lot."

"I do therefore:

Declare that the Gould name has regained its rightful place with the Puritans and Connecticut aristocrats from whom they came to Roxbury. Go forth, prosper and May The Force Be With You,"

(signed) **Paul F. Ploutz, B.S., M.S., Ed.D., G.R.I.,**
poor farm boy, neighbor.

In Ploutz's 1999 address to RCS graduates and presentation of the plaque dedicated to John Burroughs, Ploutz also ended his commencement speech with "May the force be with you," apparently from *Star Wars* and his dedication to NASA, science education, and his beloved Roxbury.

Jason Gould, summer 1847
Jay (pictured), John and Paul milked cows the same way...

Jay's West Settlement Birth Place (picture taken 2003)
Gould's home was originally described as a "two story, box-like frame
buildingwith a coating of white paint." (Trumbull White, 1892)
The house has been remodeled several times, most recently by
neighbor Charles Faraci (RCS 1947).

25-B

Jay Gould

Jay Gould

25-C

Front View of Jay's home at Lyndhurst, N.Y.

Rear view of Jay's Lyndhurst home.

Jay's magnificant Yacht Atalanta

25-E

Jay Gould Memorial Reform Church, Roxbury, New York

Elegant Tiffany Windows Gould Church, Roxbury

25-F

Author, Ploutz, pays respect to Jay, Jay's parents and two sisters at the Gould obelisk erected in 1880. This obelisk is in the Baptist Church cemetary, approximately one mile West of Roxbury. The Burroughs family grave is a few feet away, closer to the road, leading to Stratton Falls, Roxbury, N.Y. Paul has not been able to determine if Jay actually attended this commemoration. This is the Baptist Church that both Jason (Jay) and John Burroughs attended as children.

Paul, some one hundred years later, attended the Jay Gould Memorial "Dutch" Reformed Church (1935-50) erected in Jay's honor. Paul later visited the "mother" church in Amsterdam, Holland and Holland, Michigan to discover that services (1960s) at both locations were in the native language. He recognized only the music. Paul's hardscrabble grandmother, Amelia Wiederman Ploutz was reluctant to teach her five sons and two daughters a second language.

Front view Roxbury Central School

Roxbury Central School and Library, around 1940.
Notice dedication to Helen Gould (Mrs. Finley Shepard),
Jay's daughter.

Engineering at N.Y.U.

New York University
School of Engineering and Science
University Heights
Vol. 8 No. 2 • Winter 1971-1972

Gould Hall in background
Fred Teichmann (1922) received a Gould Scholarship and spent
50 great years with N.Y.U.

Chapter 2: John Burroughs, 1837 - 1922

The "original" John Burroughs was believed to have migrated from Stratford, Connecticut, to Roxbury in 1690. His son Stephen, the eldest of ten children was born in 1695. Stephen married Patience Hinman in 1719. Their third child, Stephen Burroughs Jr. became a mathematician, astronomer, and shipbuilder, and invented the federal monetary system that Congress adopted in 1790. Stephen's younger brother, Ephraim, moved to Stamford, New York. Ephraim died in 1818 and was apparently buried in an unmarked grave between Hobart and Stamford.

One of Ephraim's seven sons, Eden Burroughs, married Rachel Avery in 1795, and moved over Stamford Mountain to the Roxbury homestead. Eden built the birch home where John grew up, cutting his own trail over Stamford Mountain, bringing Rachel by oxen, and dragging a sled. Eden and Rachel bought an adjacent house and farm in 1826. In later years, John remembered reminiscing with Julian, his only son, viewing the now rotten timbers of the original home site.

A Roxbury Farm Boy

The Kelly family, dozens of them now, in and around Roxbury, (see **Part IV**) moved from Rensselaer County to the Roxbury area around 1808. Twenty-one Kelly's graduated RCS from 1901-2000. With brown hair, and blue eyes, Amy Kelly, then eighteen, married Chauncey Burroughs on a cold February day in 1824. Their son, Hiram, was born in 1827. Olly Ann, Wilson, Curtis, Edmund, Jane, John (1837), Eden, and finally Evaline was born. Edmund died as an infant; Evaline died at age twelve. John, like Jason Gould, was one of the youngest, being seventh, in the family.

Father Chauncey told his sons that, at least in early years, he had been "A horse betting, card playing, whiskey drinking, Sabbath breaking, bigoted, intolerant bore." He later found religion, became a "severe" Baptist, and a good father, neighbor, and husband.

The Burroughs farm was located about halfway between the 150-acre Gould farm, at the head of West Settlement and the Ploutz farm, 180 acres on Hardscrabble Road. Numerous conflicting accounts of the Gould-Burroughs relationship exist.

Edward J. Renehan Jr's, well-researched book, John Burroughs, *An American Naturalist*, (ISBN 1 883789 16 8) states "The Goulds had come to Delaware County in the same migration of settlers that had brought the Burroughs family from Connecticut in the 1770's. Burroughs' great grandfather and Gould's great grandfather had been pioneers together. The families had been friends and neighbors for generations."

Local legend, at least after 1900, is less convincing. Simply put, the Goulds were still wealthy, but other than the wonderful Helen Gould Shepard and youngest brother Frank, the Goulds did not live, visit, or go to school in Roxbury. No Goulds, unlike Jay, have graduated from Roxbury Schools for one-hundred years, 1901 - 2000. They're elsewhere.

The Burroughs, since John, "Haven't gone anywhere." Were they pioneers, friends, and neighbors perhaps, a century ago? Nostalgic, but over.

Families, and family names, rise, wane, move, and even go "extinct." What happens to Roxbury, and other villages throughout the Catskills and similar towns and villages across the nation and even the world can be measured, calculated and judged.

Birth, and death certificates, as well as ten-year census reports, offers solid evidence. The number and quality of children graduating from school encompasses and reflects the entire social, political, and economic realities of life throughout the Catskills.

Education for John Burroughs, Jason Gould and Ploutz, was their ticket out of rural Roxbury. John credits his mother's genes for his being a dreamer, fisherman, and hunter. While fishing Hardscrabble Creek, his Uncle Kelly, told him horror stories that made John afraid of the dark until he was at least seventeen, a fond memory. Hard work digging in soil and removing rocks to make stonewalls on their hillside farm apparently helped to produce a thirst for knowledge. The Burroughs farm in between was over three-hundred acres. Both the Gould and Ploutz farms were economically successful, yet the Burroughs farm persistently failed, thus creating the concept that they weren't good farmers.

Unlike Jason, John actually liked cows, enjoyed giving them salt to lick, and felt that the "Quality and aroma of miles of meadow and pasture lands were defined by their presence." Once, in a moment of rapture over his love of nature at age seventeen, John said that he would "Rather be the guardian of cattle than the keeper of the great seal of the nation." Years of hard work, mowing with a scythe, hoeing, and working in the garden long hours, produced a strong boy who his stern father relied on. Loving the farm, but not the endless labor and long hours, especially in the summer, helped to increase John's interest in academic pursuits.

The Burroughs-Ploutz-Ford-Burroughs Farm

In 1919, John Burroughs deeded the homestead to his son, Julian, who did not wish to live there, or farm. In 1920, Julian and his wife, Blanche, secured Howard Ploutz and wife Helen to lease and run the farm for five years. Blanche and Helen, being sisters, wanted to keep the farm within the family. When John died in 1921, Henry Ford decided he wanted the farm. Ford then financed young Julian to break the Ploutz lease three years early. Ford had done some work plastering, and other repairs, with new rooms on the house. From 1915 until John's death in 1921, Ford had been a regular guest in Roxbury, staying at the new Roxbury Hotel, especially when accompanied by Harvey Firestone, Thomas Edison, and numerous other captains of industry.

Helen gould owned a Stanley Steamer as early as July 1902. The first Ford agency in Roxbury was in 1911 with William L. Gerowe and J. Frisbee Bouon as partners. Henry gave his friend Burroughs his first car in 1913 and kept him supplied with cars the rest of his life. John was about seventy-six and accustomed to horses, not mechanical things.

In one misadventure, John smashed the radiator of his Ford nearly driving through the barn rather than into it. John continued to drive it anyway until Ford ordered a new radiator to be installed when he discovered it on his next visit.

Burroughs, Ford, Edison, and Firestone often took trips in a car convoy. There is a picture of the four with supper over a campfire, showing an Exxon dealer in the background. It was entitled "Great Moments in American Motoring" (1971). In 2002, the Ford Motor Company once again, with a Ford at the helm, showed a nationally televised commercial of Burroughs and others in an old Model T driving off the road suggesting that the Ford Company was the first to invent the first All Purpose Vehicle (APV).

In 2001, author Ploutz (living in Ohio) suggested to Roxbury Village leaders who were interested in increasing recreational and tourism that "not enough has been made of the fact that Henry Ford spent so much time in Roxbury." At the same time the nine hole Shepard Hill golf course was up for sale for approximately five-hundred thousand dollars. Tom Hynes, town supervisor, was thought by some to be willing to "give it a try" but could not gain enough interest for the town to purchase the property.

Anna Ruteshouser (Ploutz) was Paul's mother. Anna was born 1897 in nearby Montgomery Hollow to Alexander Ruteshouser and Mary Haas Ruteshouser. The Ruteshousers came from Bavaria and Holland. The German and Dutch languages, particularly "lowland" Dutch were similar. The Haas family was primarily from Holland.

Frank Ruteshouser and Alexander owned adjoining farms on the left branch of Montgomery Hollow. An Egbert Ruteshouser from Holland came to Roxbury February 23, 1847. Ruteshouser families are no longer prominent in Roxbury, and not even the foundation of the homestead in Montgomery Hollow has been located.

Upon graduating from Roxbury Central School as valedictorian in 1915, Anna was immediately offered "a school marm's" teaching job at the same school. Anna declined. It is a family mystery to this day as to why Anna decided to work at the local Roxbury Hotel, routinely waiting on tables and changing sheets, as a housemaid. From 1915, for several years, Edison, Firestone, Ford, and others stayed at the Roxbury Hotel during their frequent excursions to see Burroughs. Anna recalled each of them. On a few occasions they would camp out, several hundred strong on the Burroughs farm or in the nearby neighbor's fields.

Perhaps the prominent Roxbury Hotel paid better than teaching. Women teachers were also expected to be single, spinsters. Her two older sisters, Ida Ruteshouser (who married Ray Cronk), and Lena Ruteshouser (who married Fred Lutz), were determined to live in Roxbury. Charles, Anna's older brother, was school custodian for many years when the consolidated Roxbury District opened in 1940. Anna, the valedictorian, according to the 1915 RCS Yearbook, was "brilliant in all her studies" and also had discovered George Ploutz living in Grand Gorge. George was tall, and handsome, with blue eyes and an eighth grade diploma, who, like Jason and John had left home at about age fourteen.

Hardscrabble Ploutz Farms

George's parents, Fritz Ploutz and Amelia Wiederman Ploutz,

were the first of the Ploutzes farming three Hardscrabble farms at one time, plus the Burroughs farm as well, before and after John Burroughs' death. Fritz and Amelia had seven children: Ernest and Edith born in Germany, then George, William, Howard, Carrie, and Floyd in Roxbury. Fritz Ploutz bought the "original" Hardscrabble Ploutz farm in 1920 from Thomas J. Riley. Riley acquired the farm from William J. Silliman in 1880, Silliman from John M. Rutherford in 1860. James M. Secord is thought to have been the "pioneer" settler at the very end of Hardscrabble Road. (see Hardscrabble map (RCS).

Hardscrabble Map

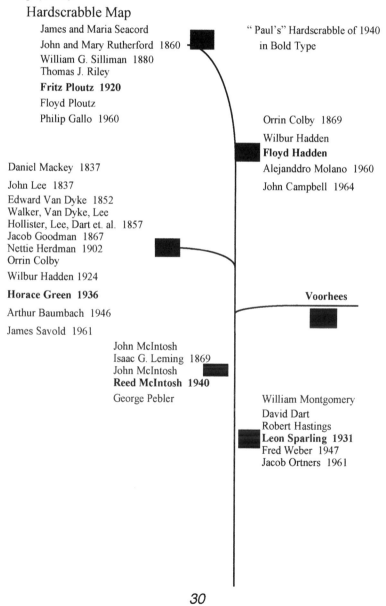

James and Maria Seacord
John and Mary Rutherford 1860
William G. Silliman 1880
Thomas J. Riley
Fritz Ploutz 1920
Floyd Ploutz
Philip Gallo 1960

Daniel Mackey 1837
John Lee 1837
Edward Van Dyke 1852
Walker, Van Dyke, Lee
Hollister, Lee, Dart et. al. 1857
Jacob Goodman 1867
Nettie Herdman 1902
Orrin Colby
Wilbur Hadden 1924
Horace Green 1936
Arthur Baumbach 1946
James Savold 1961

John McIntosh
Isaac G. Leming 1869
John McIntosh
Reed McIntosh 1940
George Pebler

" Paul's" Hardscrabble of 1940
in Bold Type

Orrin Colby 1869
Wilbur Hadden
Floyd Hadden
Alejanddro Molano 1960
John Campbell 1964

Voorhees

William Montgomery
David Dart
Robert Hastings
Leon Sparling 1931
Fred Weber 1947
Jacob Ortners 1961

30

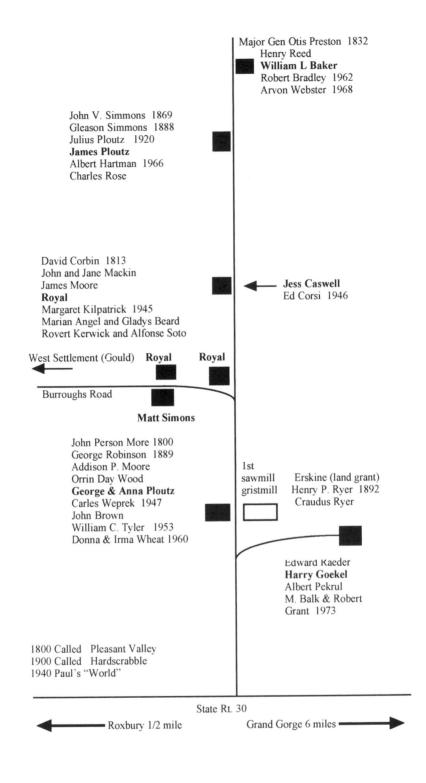

Major Gen Otis Preston 1832
Henry Reed
William L Baker
Robert Bradley 1962
Arvon Webster 1968

John V. Simmons 1869
Gleason Simmons 1888
Julius Ploutz   1920
James Ploutz
Albert Hartman 1966
Charles Rose

David Corbin 1813
John and Jane Mackin
James Moore   **Jess Caswell**
Royal   Ed Corsi 1946
Margaret Kilpatrick 1945
Marian Angel and Gladys Beard
Rovert Kerwick and Alfonse Soto

West Settlement (Gould) **Royal**   **Royal**

Burroughs Road

Matt Simons

John Person More 1800
George Robinson 1889
Addison P. Moore   1st
Orrin Day Wood   sawmill   Erskine (land grant)
George & Anna Ploutz   gristmill   Henry P. Ryer 1892
Carles Weprek 1947   Craudus Ryer
John Brown
William C. Tyler 1953
Donna & Irma Wheat 1960

Edward Raeder
Harry Goekel
Albert Pekrul
M. Balk & Robert
Grant 1973

1800 Called   Pleasant Valley
1900 Called   Hardscrabble
1940 Paul's "World"

State Rt. 30
Roxbury 1/2 mile   Grand Gorge 6 miles

31

Erma Griffin's book *History of The Town of Roxbury* (1995), second edition, included still another Ploutz farm in Batavia-Kill. A Carl Ploutz allegedly followed the Ganoung family (1796) on a farm later owned by Eber Cartwright. Local records (1900 and later) show most of the Ploutz families concentrated in Hardscrabble. In 2002, Julie Ploutz (author's daughter) identified more than 120 Ploutz families in thirty-one states, with one concentration in Kanapolos, (Kansas).

Anna was a social, outgoing, hard working Dutch girl, who for a long time was Roxbury Central School's oldest living graduate. She was also a farmer's wife, tax collector, and a restaurant owner. Anna had a daughter and three sons. She lived 'til ninety-two. Despite a hard life, surviving her husband and two sons, Anna was seemingly always happy and cheering up others.

In 1960, when son Paul married a Michigan girl whose family had attended Fordson High School, in Dearborn, Michigan, Henry Ford's home, the new wife queried "What was it like getting to know Firestone, Edison, Burroughs, and Ford? Anna replied, "Well the Burroughs were good neighbors but not especially good at farming, and in 1915 we knew that Henry sold cars, but it was no big deal." (Burroughs visited Henry in Dearborn supervising the building of a fountain made of stones from the Burroughs farm.)

Anna described Ford as most likeable of the group. He was invariably persuasive and down to earth. Unlike other great men of industry, and finance, Ford's legacy is incredibly positive, worldwide, creative, profound, and without "robber baron" association or blemish.

Ford could be tough if need be. Once in a confrontation with a labor union he retorted that "History is more or less bunk. It is tradition. We do not want tradition. We want to live in the present and the only history that is worth a tinker's damn is the history we made today. What we call evil is simply ignorance bumping its head in the dark."

Ford's legacy has survived the criticism of hindsight well beyond other great leaders, capitalists, industrialists. He spent a good bit of time in Roxbury with John Burroughs and his almost routine presence needs to be more historically acknowledged.

Burroughs, by working in Washington, D C and being in New York City, writing and being on planet earth, would have known about Gould. Burrough's writings suggest that he once saw Jay on the streets of New York, but that Jay did not see or acknowledge him. With the same Hardscrabble-West Settlement poor farm boy start, the two men could not have been more different. Gould became ever increasingly richer and financially clever, ruthless, successful, and at blazing speed. He had control of so much (not merely railroads) in the United States that when he made ovations about investments abroad it triggered a response from the Rothchilds (who "owned" Europe) that Europe "was not for sale."

Burroughs, in contrast had a lower midlevel government job. Along with new friend Walt Whitman, both donated care for Civil War causalities recovering and dying in Washington hospitals. It took John years of writing to establish himself. Being paid to write articles, especially "with a day job" John was often still poor but the Roxbury boy felt rich.

Gould's efforts were self-serving. Nothing necessarily wrong with that but really different than John who expended efforts in defending Walt Whitman from heavy criticism, or supporting John Muir and Teddy Roosevelt's efforts for Yellowstone and a national park system. Certainly overstated, but for instant clarity Gould worked for Gould, Burroughs worked for nature, the environment, and for any friend who held his philosophy.

By 1866, Gould, at thirty was already a national financier to be reckoned with. John, born a year later than Jay, now at twenty-nine was a struggling clerk, having taught a few years earlier. His friend Walt Whitman was now known to be a closeted gay. John had a "relationship" with a maid, as well as an on going relationship with Clara Barrus. His devotion to ecological causes were not yet well defined, a work in progress. When compared to any financial, moral, measure next to Jay, John was *"far back in the pack."*

Often denied, there is evidence that John cared what Jay was doing, as he wrote: "It is a curious psychological fact that the two men outside my own family of whom I have oftenest dreamed in my sleep are Emerson and Jay Gould; one to whom I owe so much, the other to whom I owe nothing; one whose name I revere, the other whose name I associate, as does the world, with the dark way of speculative finance."

Another of John's quotes, "The ambition now is to get wealth and die a Christian-- become rats if necessary to achieve these ends." Neighbor, author Ploutz asks you to read these quotes a time or two and determine for yourself Gould's effect on Burroughs. There were few men, if any, that John admired more than Emerson, yet Burroughs dreamed of both.

"Prince and pauper," phrase it anyway you like, Gould was so far ahead of Burroughs that any contest per se is silly, pointless. James Oliver, *mentor*, Roxbury, the academy contributed to two of the most colorful, creative individuals on the planet.

John's Nature Writings

John was friend to and supporter of Walt Whitman. *Notes on Walt Whitman As Poet and Person* was published in 1867 by the American News Co. of New York. Most of John's publications dealt with a reverence of nature and covered many of the topics now more often referred to as ecology. Many of his newspaper articles castigated the effects of industry yet John and Henry Ford were the best of friends. Recall that Ford "bought the farm" after John died? Many of the following books are out of print, hard to find, but most still available through Barnes and Noble and other national book stores. During John's lifetime the following books were all published by Houghton Mifflin Company.

Wake-Robin,	1871	*The Life of Audubon,*	1902
Winter Sunshine,	1875	*Far and Near,*	1904
Birds and Poets,	1877	*Ways of Nature,*	1905
Locusts and Wild Honey,	1879	*Bird and Bough,*	1906
Pepacton,	1881	*Camping and Tramping*	
Fresh Fields,	1884	*with Roosevelt,*	1907
Signs and Seasons,	1886	*Leaf and Tendril,*	1908
Indoor Studies,	1889	*Time and Change,*	1912
Riverby,	1894	*The Summit of the Years,*	1913
Whitman, A Study,	1896	*The Breath of Life,*	1915
The Light of Day,	1900	*Under the Apple Trees,*	1916
Literary Values,	1902	*Field and Study,*	1919
		Accepting the Universe,	1920

Under the Maples, 1921; *The Last Harvest*, 1922; and *My Dog Friends;* 1928 were published posthumously.

My Boyhood, with Julian, his son, was published by Doubleday, Page & Co., in 1922.

Anna Ploutz's reversal that "Time wounds all heals" seems reasonable. Not merely that she knew Burroughs and that Gould had only lived fifty-six years and John eighty-five, but that it all plays out over time. Gould's monumental contributions to the industrial well-being of America has *mellowed.* Nature, the ecology movement in America continues to grow. Ploutz, believes that *tree huggers,* rather than industrialists will gain increasing momentum in the *next* hundred years. Ever eager to .project and anticipate future events, Paul: "sees Burroughs' "nature"career continuing to escalate, Gould's "financial" career to maintain its monumental status, but more "forgiven, accepted," both giving way to the new American and world society occupied with *environmental survival.*

Either way, Roxbury was where these two farm boys started. "was there something in the water?" mused Ohio University President Robert Glidden in the introduction/mentoring of *Roxbury Boys and Girls.*

The 'Ol Stone Jug School, corner of Handscrabble and Burroughs Road. The names of many of its owners are shown on the Handscrabble map. Jay probably went to school there. Burroughs did attend this school. Paul spent lots of time there with the Royal family 1935-1942. Since the school was merely across the road from the Ploutz farm, Paul, like Jay, probably attended. By age twelve, Jay was into mathematics. By age twelve, Paul was clueless, largely into mischief, undisciplined and rebellious.

John Burroughs age Twenty (1857)

Age 25, Burroughs the school teacher, 1862

John Burroughs Homestead 1895

Burroughs Son Julian, age 7 and his dog, 1885

John and friend, Teddy, Yellowstone 1903

The Ford camping party at Horseshoe Run, near Leadmine, West Virginia, on August 10, 1918. From left to right: John Burroughs, Henry Ford, Edsel Ford, Harvey Firestone and Thomas Edison.

John convinced Teddy Roosevelt to use term "nature fakers" on those opposed to ecology.

John goes to Detroit, June 1913, to visit friend, Henry Ford.

Anna Ruteshouser (Ploutz) 1915, valedictorian and waitress for
Ford, Burroughs, Firestone, Edison, etc. at Roxbury Hotel, 1915-1920.

John Burroughs and Henry Ford at Woodchuck Lodge, Roxbury, N.Y.

One of Burroughs favorite fishing holes.
Hardscrabble creek (Ploutz farm) and popular swimming hole 1938.
Boy maybe Curtis Burroughs or Paul Ploutz.

35-G

John's Woodchuck Lodge, in Roxbury, is now a nature center.

Hardscrabble Road one mile East of Roxbury, NY on Rt. 30 (picture 2003)

Entrance to Memorial Field

Boyhood Rock at Memorial Field adjacent to John's burial site

Boyhood Rock and John's burial site

35-J

Author, Ploutz, visits the "old yellow" Baptist Church (now white) near Stratton Falls, one mile West of Roxbury Village where several of John Burroughs family is buried. Numerous writers have spelled John's father's name as Chauncey but his monument reads Chauncy.

Roxbury Superintendent of Schools and author, James Proper, pays respect to the Hinkley family. They have graduated more students (43) from RCS than any other family from 1901-2000. Jay and John are buried elsewhere, but many Hinkleys have remained in Roxbury. This monument is within a few steps of the Burroughs and Gould monuments in the Methodist Cemetery.

Paul Frederick Ploutz was born March 30, 1931. In 1931, most children were born at home, but with three older children at home, his mother decided to spend the evening with her sister and brother-in-law, Ida Ruteshouser Cronk and husband, Raymond F. Cronk, at their house in Roxbury. Paul was born at his uncle's house in town, not on the Hardscrabble farm.

After marriage, Paul's parents lived on a farm at Kortright Station up the road from East Meredith. Sister Elsie and oldest brother Milton were born at Kortright Station. Older brother Raymond was born at the Fox hospital in Oneonta. Anna had Raymond along with a huge benign cyst and stayed in the hospital several days after Raymond was released. Anna's older sister Lena Lutz took care of infant "Ray" until they could be reunited back on the farm.

Parents George and Anna sold their Kortright farm to a Mr. Larsen who was unable to maintain his payments. They regained ownership and sold again. Six months later the house burned just before Christmas, but fortunately they no longer owned it. On leaving Kortright, George and Anna moved to Hubbells Corners where George worked on the town road for two years before buying the Hardscrabble farm. Sister Elsie and oldest brother Milton attended District No. 17 school at Hubbell Corners.

George & Anna Bought The Farm

George and Anna borrowed twelve thousand dollars from Tom Riley to purchase the Hardscrabble farm and property. Even the cows were bought from Abe Soffer on credit. The initial hay to feed the cows was also financed. It was the Great Depression and they were deeply in debt. Tom Riley "bank rolled" several Roxbury village and farm families. Thanks to Helen Gould the Roxbury Bank had not gone under during the depression but was not loaning money to untried or to hopeful farmers just starting up. Riley owned the "original" Fritz Ploutz farm at the very end of Pleasant Valley (Hardscrabble) in 1920(see Hardscrabble map).

The Ploutz dairy farm on Hardscrabble Road was 180 acres, with a good amount of pasture and grassy fields to support the twenty or thirty Jersey and Guernsey cows, which George William and Anna Mae Ruteshouser Ploutz milked daily. George kept a

Holstein or two for "volume" but didn't care for the breed as the milk was "too thin."

Now with infant Paul, Raymond (2), Milton (6), and Elsie (8), George, like the Burroughs, Caswells, McInstoshs, Sparlings, Bakers, Greens, Haddens, and other "Hardscrabble" families, got up around 5:00 A.M., worked hard, and went to bed early, seven days a week. Paul's father once remarked that "you can't starve a family off a farm, and close doesn't count."

With no refrigeration, electricity, or natural gas, four children, in the depression, and making payments on the farm and house, life was tough on Hardscrabble Road, as its name implied.

Paul has little recollection of his early years, but as early as age five he went to do chores at 5:30 AM with the rest of the family, except his only sister who was relieved of farm duties. Most adults remember their childhood as fun times, only a few of Paul's recollections met those criteria. Scrawny, energetic, wiry, with long hours on the farm, his fox terrier, "Bobby," seemed his only friend. Although required to collect the eggs under the chickens after dark from the hen house some distance away, Paul was afraid of the dark. Worse still, the hens sitting on the nests, especially after dark, would usually peck his small fingers.

The Old Stone School House

At age five, Paul may have attended the Ol' Stone Jug School that Gould and Burroughs had attended earlier. The next school further up Hardscrabble road was also a one-room schoolhouse within walking distance from home. The school included grades 1-8, eight students of "assorted" grades, pot-bellied stove and an outhouse; that was it. Elsie, Milton and Ray had gone there.

Paul remembered only a few things for the entire year. The teacher was Elizabeth (Betty) Craig and Paul sat on her lap a good bit. The goldfish bowl froze nights, thawed days with the stove going; there was a flower box on the stone wall behind the school where Paul put night crawlers (fish worms). His earlier neighbors, Gould and Burroughs, had probably not gone there but as a "late developer," Paul had no clue.

By 1936, the one-room school that the *Roxbury Boys* (Jason, John, and Paul) had attended had became a residence (see Hardscrabble map). The Royal family was now Paul's closest neighbor, and black. African American now, in 1936 they were

37

"black." They also owned a small farm up the road toward West Settlement toward the Gould homestead (now Burroughs Road) and operated a summer camp for black children from "the city." The Royal family routinely fed Paul milk and cookies. Blacks were fully accepted in Roxbury and PeeWee, as Paul was now called, a name he detested, was always hungry. The Royals took him in and fed him any time he and his doggie friend, Bobby, were passing by. That would be frequently.

Years later, Paul shot his first eight point buck on the Royal farm with a Winchester lever action 30-30 caliber rifle. Brother Ray shot a four point buck (Remington 12-gauge shotgun) the same day, Thanksgiving 1947. The Royals had a son John who lived in the "city." When intoxicated John would telephone Paul's dad George late at night or any hour to see how "things were going." Matt Simon owned and operated the adjacent farm.

Matt's daughter Mary with fair complexion was thought by locals to have had an affair with John Royal. In those days women couldn't vote and they certainly couldn't have an affair, let alone with a black man. Mary M. Simon (RCS 1927) was rumored to have taken her own life, others reported that she died of Tuberculosis. Matt's health was poor, and he was forever shouting at his wife or whomever. Paul was scared of him. Even though the Ploutz and Simons' farms were adjacent, Paul never walked the property line as he did many of the other Hardscrabble farms.

"Rubbering" On the Party Line

The Ploutz's phone number in those days was 1-5, F, 1-3. It was a "party line" and one had to manually turn/ring the phone for each call. When you heard the phone ring you could tell who the call was for by the number of rings. Privacy was not available. Hearing the phone ring, then listening to other peoples calls was called "rubbering." It was largely assumed that all or most rural phone subscribers "rubbered" as how else would one keep track of what was going on? Any discussion on the phone soon became public knowledge.

Depending on what confidence was shared you might then be able to tell who was rubbering. Sometimes you could hear someone breathing, a dish rattle or even an occasional giggle. When an emergency or something important needed saying you merely asked the person who talked forever to "Get off the line" so you could use it.

Jules Bledsoe, famous for singing *"Ol'Man River"* in the film *Showboat,* was a frequent visitor of the Royal family. Paul Robeson sang "Ol' Man River" originally, but Bledsoe made it still more famous. He routinely visited the "Old Stone Jug" school years later.

Research has confirmed that (1936) Betty Craig was the 1-8 grade teacher. John Burroughs had also attended the "Ol Stone Jug" School though some ninety years or more earlier. There were several other Ploutzes and Burroughses who attended this school. The old stone house school stands to this day as a residence, at the junction of Hardscrabble and what is now called "Burroughs" Road leading to Memorial Field, Burroughs' grave. These and "Boyhood Rock," are now a recognized part of the New York State Historical Society.

PeeWee constantly roamed the 180-acre Ploutz farm, with his white dog, Bobby, a fox terrier. Finally, he roamed the neighbor's farms knowing the location of most of the large trout, fox dens, hawks nests etc. Paul may have sat on "Boyhood Rock" with his wandering dog as much as Burroughs did. Paul later admitted that at the time, he didn't even realize John was buried a few feet away in front of the rock. Certainly no disrespect was intended, and there was no inkling that in so many respects, he would emulate the cause for "nature" and work on so many of the causes about which John Burroughs had written and complained.

Jay may have attended the same schoolhouse on Hardscrabble Road. John and Jay were known to have been "classmates." John and Jay also attended another school (Beechwood Seminary) in nearby West Settlement. The Gould, Burroughs, and Ploutz farms were only a couple of miles apart. All were farmers. John was strong and helped farm the rocky slopes, though as time passed, like Jay, and later Paul, he gained some dislike for farming and seemed to realize that education was also his route to salvation.

Consolidation Creates Roxbury Central School

About 1937, the now famous "Ol' Stone Jug" school and the one further up Hardscrabble Road was closed as Roxbury started consolidation. In those days, no one flunked first grade, so Paul was routinely "promoted" and was enrolled in the second grade in the village, at the YMCA building which now houses the Roxbury Arts Group. Again, Paul has little memory of the two years spent in the second grade. He did recall that the third grade was still hard, as were the fourth and the fifth and, well, you get the idea. Paul struggled in his elementary school years. His grades were usually near the bottom of each class, each year, for several years. Other schools were closing:

District # 2 (More Settlement) school closed in 1937.

District # 3 (Hardscrabble) school closed in 1937.

Brookdale District # 4 closed in 1940, the last teacher, Mrs.Laura Van Benschoten an "effective" disciplinarian, went to the new RCS school, taught third grade and "confronted" nine-year-old Ploutz.

District 5 (West Settlement) was consolidated with Roxbury Central in 1930 but remained open until 1941. The last teacher was a Miss Nellie Enders who moved to the larger new RCS building in Roxbury Village. Miss Enders became young Paul Ploutz's fourth grade teacher (1942).

Eager, Agile, and Skinny

By the age of eight, Paul was an accomplished trout fisherman. His uncle Ray Cronk tutored him and he practiced for endless hours. Unlike city dwellers, Paul welcomed the rain. On a farm, when it rained, you could hunt or fish. The streams supplied plenty of trout for supper. The old swimming hole that Burroughs, Paul, and others used over time was on the Ploutz farm just above the old grist and saw mill. The long slender pool always had three or four feet of water, even during dry periods. With lots of surface area and woods on either side of the pool, it was partially shady. Tree roots held the bank in place and made a great place for fish (trout, chubs, suckers) to hide. (see Hardscrabble map Ch. 2) John Burroughs caught hundreds of trout there over the years.

In Burrough's day. most of the streams in Pleasant Valley, Montgomery Hollow, and elsewhere had lots of trout. With no limit of number or length, John suggested that he could "eat a hundred a day." By 1900 and after, most of the mountains around Roxbury and the Catskills had been skinned. Maples, oak, chestnut, cherry, beech, and other hardwoods had been "harvested." Without the protection of trees, Hardscrabble stream and others flooded in the spring and were nearly dry in August.

40

By the time Paul fished the 'ol swimming hole (1938 and on) the limit of trout (seldom achieved) was ten and the minimum length seven inches.

A Boy Should Have a Dog

John Burroughs had a dog. Jay Gould, at least as a wealthy adult, had kennels at Lyndhurst. Paul had "Bobby" a wire haired fox terrier. Bobbie was, his mother excluded, easily his best friend. White with black spots or was it black with large white spots, Bobby was allowed in the Hardscrabble home. Bobby was allowed in the bathroom, kitchen, front porch, and on occasion in bed next to Paul with his head on the pillow. Given his diet of woodchucks and miscellaneous varmints, his breath was so bad that even with unquestioned loyalty and compatibility he would be relegated to the floor beside Paul's bed.

Bobby had learned to surprise woodchucks, getting between them and their holes. Paul usually wore only a belt for a hunting knife and shorts with the usual junk, but also a cellophane bag for bounty.

It made little difference whether Bobby caught the woodchuck or if it found cover in a stonewall, which could be dismantled. Either way, four or five woodchuck hearts, or several nice trout were a welcome alternative to the constant supply of beef usually available to farm families. Chickens were usually raised for eggs, but when old, you just "cooked them a little longer."

One of Paul's memorable recollections of Bobby was the occasion when his father, in a rage, picked up a piece of kindling wood to beat Paul. Bobby leaped into the confrontation biting George on the wrist. George, shocked, having bought Bobby and thinking of him as "his" dog, dropped the piece of wood and walked away. My God, Bobby even saved him from his father! At age seventy-one, Paul still remember that.

Most farmers raised a pig or two. When you slaughtered a pig, the practice was to cut their throat, letting them run until "bled out." Paul recalls hiding when pigs were "harvested," as they were violent for a few minutes.

Bringing in the cows to be milked was a chore for which both Jay and John, like many farm boys, had responsibility. Paul had a special problem: "Daisy," one of the twenty-some milk cows on the farm, seemed to dislike small people, or perhaps only Paul, and would often put her head down and walk menacingly toward him. If he protested the chore, scorn, laughter, ridicule, whipping or whatever it took, was used for compliance. Such was the inevitable outcome of the slightest confrontation with his father. Young Paul "wet the bed" until he was twelve. While bed wetting in young boys is relatively common, research has shown a correlation between bed wetting and child abuse.

For young Paul, going out through the dark, often foggy, pasture at 5:30 AM, often barefooted, was a hated ritual. He would call "here Bossie" as he hunted for the herd, but what would happen if Daisy found him first! Small, skinny, but sure-footed and agile, Paul soon discovered that three or four of the cows were amenable to his jumping on their backs and riding to the barn. The cows were sure-footed even in darkness, Daisy would not bother, and you never stepped in a "pasture frisbee," barefooted or with shoes.

Gould's sisters all milked the cows and did chores while Jay usually could often "escape." It was the opposite at the Ploutz farm. Sister Elsie was spared barn chores and Paul, even at _five_, got up at _five_ to help milk and do farm chores. Surely he hated cows as much as Jay. Sadly Paul was a late bloomer though also skinny, to frail.

Paul's ability over the years to solve problems, at least his, seemed to improve with each conflict, whipping, disappointment, and hardship. His versatility in adapting to the varieties and situations encountered growing up on a farm were being developed. Like Gould, Paul was gaining resolve, but with no clue whatsoever, as to what resolve meant.

Rural Realities

You can't be starved off a farm. His father, George, like most other farmers, shot an occasional deer from the orchard to help feed the family. In the Catskills in 1935, many farmers, like the Ploutz's, would only need to prop a window open to shoot a deer. Unless you shot the deer under "the game protector's nose," the authorities wouldn't bother you taking deer to feed your family from your own land.

Eating a woodchuck sounded, well, bizarre but in addition to the family needing to eat, woodchucks eat tender blades of green grass. Chickens, which everyone seems to like, on the other hand, eat, well you know what they eat. Woodchucks also posed a significant problem. The hay wagon wheel that fell into a "chuck" hole could tip the wagon over, throwing the person as well. The Ploutz family's pet-riding horse, Prince, stepped in a chuckhole, and broke his leg at the knee. The horse had to be shot.

Today, Burroughs and "woodchuck lodge" are well known. John, and Paul later, and farm boys to this day, continue the struggle against "chucks." Ploutz, their Roxbury, neighbor, researched John Burroughs and Jay Gould, but hasn't come across evidence that they ate woodchucks. Ploutz was most likely the poorest of the three. He had little, if any, social sophistication, and readily admits eating woodchucks, especially hearts and livers as available. After being teased once at school, Paul asked his parents if other people ate woodchucks? "What difference does it make," was the simple reply.

If a dairy cow couldn't deliver, and with no veterinarian to come in time, no one could help. Shoot the cow: more beef on the table. The Ploutz's had nine cats to control rats and mice, then four litters of cats, eight each. It's more humane to smash, rather than to drown them. Chickens, well you merely chopped their heads off. By about age nine Paul had his own 410 gauge shot gun for rabbits and squirrels. Rabbits, squirrel "pie," partridge (grouse) and infrequently a pheasant, were welcome additions to the family menu.

Red fox pelts brought four or five dollars, but foxes were sly. Trapping them was difficult, but that was good money. Learning to skin animals was easy. Frequently the animal, caught by a paw, would still be alive. By nine, Paul was developing distaste over strangling or beating to death the fox, the muskrat, or mink, but was learning to do what you have to do. Dogs and cats were seldom spayed, extra calves were eaten. The cow you knew by name or had ridden from the pasture could easily end up on the dinner table.

Growing up in a rural area, often a farm, adds a survival factor, responsibility, and early insights of animal nature, relationship of man to land, and a greater dependency to family and neighbors. Food, clothing, and shelter are all reality factors. However, city children are usually not forced into the grim reality of where, or more precisely, how hamburger is produced.

In 1940, the new Roxbury Central School opened with Paul's name and all the others in a copper container within a mortar corner stone and he in the second grade (again). Records suggest that while young John Burroughs was at best a mediocre student, Ploutz struggled, often getting one of the lower grades in most subjects throughout grades three through six, excelling only in "recess." Brief, random wrestling, fistfights, aggressive activity on the swings, catwalk, teeter-totter, tag, kickball, or being called PeeWee, became routine.

A comment from his fourth grade teacher, Miss Betty Enders, in her eight-week report stated, "Paul needs a good bit of discipline." Father George, a firm advocate in "spare the rod and spoil the child," readily complied with Miss Enders philosophy and whipped him routinely. In 1940, in rural Roxbury, and many of the nation's schools, getting into trouble at school often resulted in more trouble at home. Parents coming to school to complain about the teacher were unthinkable.

The principal, William Crum, used both a paddle "board of education" and/or short garden hose to supplement those few teachers unable or unwilling to control malcontents, particularly the larger ones, RCS being a K-12 school.

Paul had heard reports that a teacher, Mr. Proskine, in "disciplining" a boy, actually broke the boy's arm, with no consequences. Paul seemed to realize that he was living on the edge. How times have changed.

USA Today February 27, 2003 page 6 A, Lawrence, Massachusetts, (a liberal state) reports that police are bringing charges against a teacher who helped tape second graders mouths shut in a game when the children requested it. Police said the game was a crime because it "scared some students." Teacher, Newman Montila age thirty-eight, is being charged with misdemeanor assault and battery. Note that police are going after the teacher rather than the school district.

Constant academic difficulty, hyperactive, impatient, frustrated, frail, but still aggressive, and conspicuously underweight, Paul, now nine or ten, relentlessly pursued attention, recognition, and approval. His thirst for attention was so strong that he often created a problem rather than go unnoticed. He was not alone of course. Mrs. Reynolds, possibly a substitute teacher, would lose all control of the third or fourth-grade class. When most or all of the children would leave their seats and run around the classroom she would actually beg them to return to their chairs offering each a lolly-pop to comply.

Life was not fun for Paul. His routine failure at school, endless criticism and discipline from his father were burdensome. His self esteem was low, his feelings of guilt high. Paul's father referred to him as "spindle shanks," painfully rejecting his frail nature. Paul was left-handed. George insisted he butter his bread, write, and do similar tasks using his right hand. If he resisted, he was either thrashed or sent to bed with an empty stomach feeling guilty because he could never gain his father's approval and disappointed him so consistently.

He disliked his father and felt guilty over that. He didn't do well at school and felt guilty over that. He couldn't do farm chores at his age like his two older brothers could and he felt guilty over that. Being left-handed meant that "he wouldn't be able to use tools effectively," and he felt guilty over that. He had been a "breach" birth child so his father would remind him that he was also going through life ass backwards. He felt guilty over that.

Over dominant parents make strong children stronger and weak children weaker is a well-known concept among psychologists. For reasons unknown his awesome perceived failure did not break him. He has, however, spent most of his life feeling guilty.

Paul, at eleven, with white-blond hair, athletic build, and fair complexion, remembers playing the role of Hansel, from the fifth-grade operetta, "Hansel and Gretel". At once, and if only for a brief period, he earned approval, recognition, and legitimate attention! In a pathetic reminder of his early childhood, interviewed at length at age seventy, Paul could remember only his "Hansel" approval experience out of the entire eight years it took him to get to the seventh grade and the classroom of Miss Catherine Fleming.

Irony, Chance, or Circumstance?

Neither Burroughs nor Jason Gould liked farming. Burroughs and Ploutz accepted it, as it was their lot. Gould, also frail, disliked farm chores, but excelled in all his book learning. Irony, random chance, or was it Roxbury's influence alone, that converted three poor farm boys into two naturalists and a financier?

Approximately one-hundred years lay between John, Jay, and Paul and the one-room schoolhouse. Hardscrabble/West Settlement, in the vernacular of the day, was, is, merely "a wide spot in the road," one small spot on a map of Roxbury, New York, in the Catskills of New York, USA, the Northern Hemisphere. In fact the map on the cover of this *Mentoring* book doesn't even bother showing Roxbury (map, courtesy State Farm Insurance Company).

What do strict fathers, loving supportive mothers, rural close-knit villages, adjacent farms/chores, one-room schools, stern religion, gifted teachers, fishing the same streams or drinking the same water, do to make some excel? Does the "success" of John, Jay, or Paul simply represent chance, the roll of the dice? As Hillary Clinton suggests, *"It takes a village."* Or is it a father never satisfied who drives them to succeed? Strong children stronger, weak children weaker? Were they born strong? Did a harsh environment make them strong while breaking the will of those less resolved?

John and Jay also realized early that education represented their escape from the farm, cows, and manure. Both had an outstanding teacher, Mr. James Oliver. Oliver arrived in Roxbury directly from the "Albany Normal School." John was twelve, extremely bashful, withdrawn, stammered, had little social aptitude, nervous, awkward, rude, naive, unsure of himself, and with long hours sweating, working with cows, most likely could have profited from more regular bathing. Precocious Jay, while often a loner, was directly opposite. How was it they were close childhood friends, seldom, if ever being in contact as adults?

Chapter 4: Gifted Teachers, Mentors

James Oliver, The Ultimate Gifted Teacher

Mr. James Oliver had a class of seven Roxbury boys aged twelve-sixteen. The West Settlement School (1849) was closer to Gould's home than the Hardscrabble site. Most of Oliver's students rose to considerable prominence. Alexander Smith, a classmate, was the eldest son of Robert and Janet Smith. A prominent West Settlement farmer, Alexander succeeded, then moved to Sully, Iowa, where two of his younger brothers were spending two terms each in the Iowa legislature.

Rice Bouton ultimately became a Methodist minister of Five Points Church in Manhattan. Five Points Church survived as the site of race riots (blacks and Irish), Civil War, and Tammany Hall political corruption protests during the most turbulent times in New York City's history. John Champlin, another Roxbury boy, became chief justice of the Kansas State Supreme Court. Burroughs and Gould, of course, became even better known. The village of Roxbury has yet to honor James Oliver. Oliver, a truly brilliant, gifted, inspiring teacher moved to Kansas, gave up teaching, and went into the mercantile business. The Boutons were a well-known Roxbury family graduating nine from RCS from 1901 - 2000. The "last" Bouton to graduate RCS was Richard (1951).

Abe Crosby, Andrew Corbin, Simon Champion, Iram More, and Peter Van Amburgh were also classmates of Jay, and likely students of James Oliver.

Gould was, by all accounts, clearly the best student in the class. Prior to Mr. Oliver, Burroughs was largely indifferent to his studies, though they were preferred to hard farm work. Roxbury schools, it seems, have had an extra measure of gifted teachers. Oliver, as was the custom in 1849, took turns boarding at the home of his students, falling in love with Jay's sister Polly, whose real name was Mary. Mary died at age 22, Oliver was despondent. It is unclear if Polly's death was the reason for Oliver leaving or giving up teaching. Many think it so. Oliver, as the years go by, is increasingly recognized as one of the greatest *mentors* that ever entered a classroom.

Mr. Oliver was the principal at the academy in Hobart in 1851. Jay, John Burroughs, Rice Bouton, and John Champlin were inspired to the "love of learning." In later years, they made it clear that Oliver was the source of their inspiration, and thirst for knowledge, not just to "shake their farm presence" but to make a difference by obtaining knowledge. Preliminary research suggests that James Oliver was one of the most skilled *mentors* of the century. In Gould's case knowledge became power and control. Algebra became fun. Surveying, buying people, and railroads could be looked at mathematically, in probabilities and dollars.

Overcoming Bacteria, Viruses, Worms

Edmund Burroughs was John Burroughs' older brother, until he died in infancy. Younger sister Evaline, born in 1840, died at twelve years, in 1852. In 1850, there were few that lived to age ninety. There was a yellow fever epidemic in 1879. Numerous other local afflictions, and newer ones, were brought from European immigrants. Jay Gould died of tuberculosis in 1892 at age fifty-six. The press speculated that Mr. Gould had a "bilious attack." A number of Gould's had died of tuberculosis in earlier days.

Life expectancy was still a "crap shoot" by today's standards. George Ploutz, PeeWee's father contracted pneumonia in 1908. He survived, but with lung problems, dying in 1956 at age sixty-two. Population densities, Burroughs friend Ford, Henry Ford's Model T, and many other influences helped circulate available diseases. Few in rural areas were dying of smog, herbicides or pesticides, as is the case today, with thousands reaching age one-hundred.

Life expectancy was steadily improving by 1900, and doctors, hospitals, and school nurses were gradually becoming available.

In 1901, Roxbury schools graduated two people, Beulah Keater Pingree and Mabel Enderlin. By 1915, RCS graduated fifteen students, including Anna Ruteshouser, Paul's mother. As valedictorian, Anna was reported to be "brilliant in all her studies." Paul, like John, credits his mother as his primary inspiration. To the best of her ability, Anna shielded the four children from her husband's tyranny, however well intended. Health was the "wild card" in the Catskills and elsewhere.

By 1943, PeeWee, now twelve, even prior to Junior high had survived intestinal worms, mumps, measles, chicken pox, whooping cough, dysentery, yellow jaundice (a form of hepatitis), scarlet fever, pink eye, croup, and pneumonia. He had also been bitten or stung by three dogs, three foxes, numerous woodchucks, weasels, gray squirrels, red squirrels, a mink, three raccoons, two muskrats, one black widow spider, several chipmunks, yellow jackets, honey bees, bumble bees, deer flies, ticks, a few rats, mice, bed bugs, and head lice. When would he ever learn?

Around 1944, the entire Roxbury School (approximately 180 students) was "yellow," with a mild form of jaundice. Kids didn't even miss school. Stories circulated that after a heavy rain, cow manure from Carl Shuster's farm in the village seeped into the village water system. Years later, Paul discovered that people who had had jaundice were never to donate blood. The disease was apparently a mild form of hepatitis and could then be passed from donor to recipient.

Later, veterans from World War II began to return to Roxbury and used the school gym and locker room. By "borrowing" apparel they circulated both athlete's foot and "crabs." Paul's clothes were very small, thus not borrowed. He escaped what was jokingly referred to as "crotch pheasants." Virtually everyone got athletes foot, then applied Asorbine Junior, which hurt so much you knew it had to be working!

Usually barefoot, Paul got roundworm eggs from the soil, which then hatched in his intestines. It was socially annoying for Paul given his insecurities. Relief was almost immediate. Going to school next day he discovered his friend and classmate Leighton Hinkley had ringworm on his temple, and his cousin, Richard Lutz, had apparently shed a tapeworm reported to be in excess of twenty-feet long.

The Ploutz family, like others, drank water that flowed through hammered lead pipes. After using asbestos potholders, leaded paint, leaded gasoline, pesticides and herbicides for the cattle, dogs, and garden, three Ploutz children, of four, Elsie, Raymond, and Paul, developed cancer. The fourth child, Milton, had committed suicide on July 4, 1943 at age twenty. While cancer could have been involved, father George's abuse seems the most plausible explanation.

Paul, with the benefit of early detection, surgery and the most modern techniques available, has survived squamous, basil cell, Bowens, skin cancer; Melanoma and Carsinoma, prostate, and colon cancer.

The humor or joke that so many *Roxbury Boys* excelled because "there may have been something in the water" probably wasn't all that funny for Paul who for the first sixteen years of his life drank water that flowed through lead pipes.

Surviving five kinds of cancer without radiation or chemotherapy is remarkable. Ploutz has participated in research at the James Cancer Institute on the campus of Ohio State University, Columbus, Ohio. They have determined that his colon cancer was not genetically induced. If his cancer was not hereditary, then of course, it was environmentally induced. Reminiscent of Rachael Carson's (1962) Silent Spring, today's children, in addition, unlike Jason, John, and Pete, need to be additionally concerned about clean air and acid rain (see PART V, Paul's ecology poems).

And so it was that rural children struggled. Many families, who by today's standards were dysfunctional, with children overworked, often underfed, and abused, with the "spare the rod and spoil the child" mentality, was simply the standard of the day.

Miss Catherine Fleming, Gifted Teacher

Miss Catherine Fleming, as was the custom, was waiting at her seventh-grade classroom door in September 1944, when Paul and other, better-behaved children, departed from the long line of yellow buses. For 180 consecutive days, excluding weekends and holidays, Miss Fleming provided approval, recognition, and the brief attention Paul had only been able to gain through fights and verbal tantrums. He "repaid" through reduction in playground altercations, detention, and disruption, as her approval was reassuring and valuable. Paul, very much like John Burroughs, was poor, awkward, very unsure, insecure, rude, naive, and with long hours sweating and working with cows, he could have also "profited from more regular bathing."

In 1844, shoes were not required in warm weather. In 1944, shoes were required to attend school. Jason and John had slates; Paul had paper for school. With two older brothers, Paul almost always had "hand-me-down" shoes, socks, underwear, shirts, and pants. They were washed, clean, but more gray than white. In later years as a "solvent" adult, Paul was often teased over his supply of socks and underwear, often numbering well over one hundred pair each. Neither Jay nor John ever "went back" to see cows. Paul remarked that "eating a hamburger" would be his closest encounter with another cow.

Later, Paul recalled a particularly painful consequence of being poor. When Phil Finch, a school bully, and the adopted son of Andrew Lutz, outgrew his clothes, his kindly parents would donate them to poor families. Paul had the misfortune of wearing one of Phil's favorites, but "donated" shirts to school. Spotting Paul at recess and recognizing his shirt, Phil pulled it from Paul's back and "reclaimed" it on the spot.

It wasn't being barebacked and scrawny that hurt, spending most of the summer with a deep tan anyway, but rather losing his shirt on the playground, with all the other boys and girls finally understanding how poor and pitiful he was.

Recalling the humiliating incident some fifty-eight-years later, Paul finally realized that it was the same fair-minded precious teacher, Catherine Fleming who acted to restore what little dignity remained for young Paul.

Some students rode the school bus an hour or more, but Paul's Hardscrabble bus loop was a mere twenty minutes from the recently constructed school (1940). Roxbury and the federal DPW program, taxpayers, and Helen Gould Shepard, Jay's daughter, provided the magnificent Roxbury Central School.

Paul was still burning from the constant well-earned sarcasm of Miss Shaylor, during the previous 180 days in the sixth grade. By age twelve Paul was likely at his worst. He hated overweight Kay Shaylor, the first teacher strong enough to control him.

He was in constant trouble exercising every test, every rule, using any technique he could in an attempt to make classmates laugh or at least draw attention to himself. The attention mechanisms produced a few favorable results, but like Burroughs he was incredibly shy around girls. When sixth grade classmates Betty Purchell and Quanita Partridge told him they were completely "available" he hid from them all day at school and fantasized about them all night at home.

The sixth grade was a very long year for Paul. From Paul's limited perspective, Shaylor had one saving grace. Most days after the noon recess was over, she would read to the entire class for fifteen or twenty minutes. Author Walter R. Brooks lived in Roxbury and wrote books entitled Freddie the Detective and similar titles about the life of a pig named Freddie. Kay was a masterful reader and could tame the entire class with her stories. During the fall reporting period, Paul entered a book-reading contest. At first he read books just to win the damn prize as he was very competitive. Then some of the books were fun. Paul read twenty-two books and legitimately won the sixth grade prize even though most everyone in class did better in school than he did.

Paul treasures his copy of *Bambi's Children* by Felix Salten (Grosset and Dunlap 1939). The written inscription inside the front cover merely says "Paul Ploutz Book Contest R. C. S. Nov. 1942." Sixty years later he still covets his first academic success and realizes that it was that "awful" Miss Shaylor who may have been the first to attempt to convert a brat into a Fulbright Scholar.

Fleming, like other gifted teachers around the world, could, as the cliché goes, "Make a silk purse from a sow's ear." She also realized, at least in Paul's case that you could catch "More flies with honey than with vinegar." Paul definitely "needed work!"

Mentors Make the Difference

Do gifted teachers seek rural environments? Do rural "down home" environments help create gifted teachers? Either way, Catherine Fleming, seventh-grade teacher and her friend, Lela Wickham, eighth-grade teacher, apparently saw young Ploutz as "a diamond in the rough" rather than the sow's ear. They clearly started Paul's transition. Truth be told, they likely had the same affect on dozens of other country ruffians and somehow taught Paul to love to read, to respect authority, and to resolve conflicts by dialogue instead of knuckles.

Paul's athletic and aggressive nature would soon put him on every sports team at Roxbury. Roland F. "Doc" Ross, was Roxbury's one-man K-12 gym teacher and coach for both boys and girls. He routinely coached basketball, baseball, soccer, cross-country running, and for any kid willing, the "lesser sports" of tennis, archery, badminton, tag, ping-pong, volleyball, touch football, balance beam, hanging rings, leather horse, and croquet. "Doc" gave encouragement and advice on swimming, diving, bowling, and other nonschool athletic activities.

Gym was a right, not taken away by attitude problems in other classes. Given what is now known about hyperactive children and their need for large muscle development, how the practice of "taking away gym," as a disciplinary measure ever began is a serious question of competence. Years later, teaching at Oneonta Junior high (1955–1958 in a very traditional setting, Paul suggested at the regular school faculty meeting, that inasmuch as Jimmy Britton had "acted up in gym" he should not be allowed to attend Miss Hope Farone's English class. Miss Edna Tripp, a stern but practical principal and other teachers, caught the tongue-in-cheek irony and terminated the practice of using gym as a carrot for proper behavior elsewhere.

Thank You R.C.S. and Mrs. Shepard.

Bless school policy: Paul couldn't participate in the extracurricular athletic program unless he was passing most, if not all subjects. There was a simple solution. His seventh and eighth-grade teachers had taught him how to address problems. Paul hunkered down, studied the minimum amount, and barely passed everything but science. Science came easily. Finally, Paul excelled in something other than being loud, disruptive, or mischievous.

In high school, William Crawford taught science with enthusiasm. An overweight bachelor with body odor, Crawford taught physics, biology, and chemistry. He did it well. After several years of teaching, the Board of Education was considering releasing him. The community became alarmed and "saved" him. It takes a village and he was a *mentor.*

The so-called "Junior High School" years, as with Jason and John and Mr. Oliver, was clearly a turning point. Rebellious Paul, long before the presence of Ritalin to drug down overactive children, came under the positive school and community influence. This phenomenon became focused in *It Takes A Village* to raise a child as expressed in 1996, by then First Lady Hillary Clinton.

Community activity, including regular participation in the Youth Fellowship Program, was conducted by Glen Young, pastor for the Jay Gould Memorial Dutch Reformed Protestant Church. In addition to occasional participation in the Sunday 10:00 A.M. regular service, the handsome, articulate, positive pastor drove miles and miles evenings to pick up Ploutz and other needy souls for evening youth services, returning them home to grateful parents.

Through the church, Jay Gould's daughter, Helen Shepard, became Roxbury's "latter-day *mentor*" for dozens of country bumpkins who never knew her name. Let us rephrase, "latter day" to "more recent," as her disdain of the Mormon religion and polygyny was profound. "Professional writers" have had a field day writing about Jay Gould. Locals enjoy talking about oldest daughter Helen who started Roxbury's first library. She helped with the Gould Church (1894) although Jay's oldest son George Jay laid the corner stone. The president of New York University Dr. Henry M. MacCracken preached the dedication ceremony. Later chapters will reveal the special relationship that Roxbury (Goulds) had with NYU.

Community influence in small towns around the USA is clearly an advantage of rural life and schools. Screw up, everybody knows, conform, lots of approval. School, teachers, and community *mentors* provide stabilizing influences on cherubs and ruffians alike.

Mentor James Oliver had a profound effect on Jay, John, and other students. Catherine Fleming was clearly responsible for the turning point in Paul's life. *"Mentoring"* is difficult perhaps impossible to measure or judge but has profound long-term effects. Many years would pass before Paul would become obsessed with *mentoring*. Future chapters will reveal how he tries to be "the village" all by himself!

Chapter 5:   Perceptions and Events

Life on a Farm

Life on the Ploutz farm, in the late 1930s and early 40s, in today's vernacular "sucked." However Paul, now past seventy, did recall several pleasant events including the annual Ploutz reunion. It was often held at the farm where he lived, with sixty to a hundred relatives showing up one Sunday each July.

The early Mores had even more highly organized reunions that thousands attended. Family reunions in rural areas are well established. More reunions dated back to Pleasant Valley prior to Roxbury or Hardscrabble names. The Ploutz clan met in Pleasant Valley, Hardscrabble, but still meets each summer in Schnevus or Oneonta, New York, or elsewhere in the Catskills.

The Ploutz family farm did have electricity prior to most neighbors with a sixty-watt battery system located in the barn. The Rural Electrical Administration (REA) ran poles/electricity the length of Hardscrabble Road. It was, in staunch Republican George's words "The only good thing Franklin Roosevelt ever did." Dan Tyler, a rich, greedy neighbor was alleged to have required a substantial sum of money to let the electric wire cross a field with a pole at the edge of Hardscrabble Road adjacent to his property. Farmers the entire length of Hardscrabble Road were furious, but finally paid what they considered extortion (see picture).

When the wires were still lying on the ground, pole to pole up the entire valley, being gradually snugged, Paul walked farm to farm to free the cable from under boulders, fences, and tree limbs. The same exact pole, in the exact location, still exists in 2002 as a reminder of Dan Tyler, and that not all country folk help each other. An irony, William C. (Bill) Tyler, Dan's son, later bought the Ploutz house with its spectacular view, remodeling the three-story wood home. One presumes Bill enjoyed the electricity.

Pinochle was a favorite card game of rural folks in the Catskills. Bridge, hearts, monopoly and similar games had not yet been invented, or at least had not become popular. Poker, billiards, pool, when available were in vogue. Pinochle (there are variations) was the game of choice, though not played on Sundays for some folk. Many farm families of Roxbury belonged to the Grange League Federation (GLF). The Grange was known to be a trusted stock company on which farmers could invest and rely. The Ploutz family and lots of other's owned stock in "The Grange." Better still there were "Grange" dances in the "Grange" hall in Roxbury. There were "Grange" pinochle contests.

On one occasion Anna Ploutz and son Paul (age twelve), after playing eight games, won the "Grange" tournament all in the same weekend evening. With forty or fifty players (four per table) Paul's self-esteem with his mother's known intelligence, carried the tournament. At age twelve the mother *mentor* was well received, acknowledged. How can a kid be all bad if his mother is Anna Ploutz?

George and Anna often visited/played pinochle with Andrew and Bertha Gray from West Settlement (near the Gould farm). Their biological son Andrew was a child. The Grays' also had an older adopted daughter. Five-year-old Paul "thinks" he recalls being undressed on the third floor attic of his Hardscrabble home. Nothing specific is recalled or implied. Children's memories are known to be unreliable, dreams, fantasy, a normal part of growing up. Paul is totally unable, in fact, to verify if the 1942 "event" ever happened. In 1936 boys attitudes might easily have been more of gratitude than remorse or emotional scars.

The Thursday, February 27, 2003, edition of *USA TODAY* (page 9 D) estimates 1,200 priests have been accused of sexual abuse of minors. Always ahead of the times, Paul, who taught child psychology for eighteen years wonders if most of the *teenage* boys were not, in fact, more grateful than abused. How many trial lawyers and attorneys have exploited this sensitive issue for their own financial gain? In many states, a minor is anyone under *eighteen* years of age. Paul, while not particularly eager to defend the Catholic Church, believes that many perfectly normal teenage boys have a need to, and are eager to search, experiment, and should not *always* and automatically be viewed as victims. Once again his disdain for lawyers surfaces. Paul seems to think that suing the church, hospital, school for damages, *in many cases* is often contrary to what is best for the child, the patient or the student, thus society at large. His CARE game (Chapter16), which was never published, attempted to help schools and youth deal with these sensitive and controversial issues.

Paul earned ten cents a quart for the blackberries that he picked and had delivered to the corner store in Roxbury, saved his earnings, and bought his first bicycle for eighteen dollars. You can do the math. In addition, Aunt Edith Ploutz, George's unmarried sister, would, on occasion, provide a quarter or two. Paul never had more than small pocket change but was learning to create "financial" opportunities. Each spring he would get seed packets, usually vegetables, walk Hardscrabble Road and hustle all the neighbors to buy seeds. Since everyone had gardens, it worked every spring for years. *GRIT* was one of the early newspapers, containing tips on gardening, wars, and politics, that country children could circulate. Paul sold the publication frequently, but did not have a conventional paper route.

It was not without consequence. One morning (see Hardscrabble map) Paul walked up Jim Ploutz's long sidewalk above Hardscrabble road toward the house. A large angry German police dog raced toward him hitting him hard and squarely in the chest putting the *GRIT* and Paul rolling. The dog then punctured the flesh on Paul's right arm a few times before Christine (Freeman) Ploutz could call the dog off. "Chrisie" bought all the papers, scolded the dog, put iodine on the wound, hugged Paul, called Anna, and sent him home.

George's response, as usual, was that it was Paul's fault, and again, "You have to know more than the dog to teach him anything."

On Sundays during the summer, the entire family, excluding sister Elsie, would drive fifteen miles to Broome Center to pick blueberries. George, with his usual efficiency had devised a belt to go around each waist with a five quart pail attached so you could pick with both hands. For several summers they seemed to be the only folks to have discovered a giant patch with hundreds of bushes nearly waist high with large berries. One Sunday, arriving about 10:00 AM for an all day pick, several cars of "city folk" were unloading. George summoned his three sons and Anna to gather in the parking lot within hearing distance of the "intruders."

As the grass was high anyway, and sometimes the land seemed like a marsh, the Ploutz family always wore high top leather boots to pick blueberries. Otherwise, George was known for hard work not humor, unless of course it had a practical side. In a loud, clear voice, he admonished each family member to be sure "Your boots are securely tied and as far up your leg as possible. Rattlesnakes cannot bite you above the leather, we don't want any more trips to the hospital. But if you do get 'hit' call me, I have a knife to bleed the bite." The "city folks" promptly left. Much later (1963) Paul used a similar ruse in Yellowstone National Park only using grizzly bears instead (Ch.13 Yellowstone National Park).

That same summer, July 1942, while picking blackberries in the woods above his house near the "Ol' Stone Jug" school, adjacent to Burroughs Road, barefoot as usual, Paul found it necessary to urinate. Setting his berry pail down, and taking a few steps forward toward a stump so as not to splash his toes, he proceeded. A boy physically relieving himself, could be a wonderful moment, unless of course, a large black bear were to stand upright, in front, not ten feet away! A new bike, a bear, and physically discovering himself, were Paul's highlights for the summer of 1942.

Edith Ploutz and Etta Colby lived next door to "Helen Anna," one of Helen Gould Shepard's two adopted daughters. Jay had made restrictions in his will of millions, with money going only to family. Regular visits to Aunt Edith's provided Paul with the drama associated over many years with her colorful lifestyle of "the rich and famous."

John and Peter Burr, sons of Olivia Shepard Burr, the other adopted daughter, often spent time in Roxbury becoming friends of Paul, brother Raymond, and other Roxbury Boys. They were very popular, unpretentious, and outgoing. Johnny (John) stayed in Roxbury one summer working as a farm hand. The Burrs have visited Roxbury over the decades. Yes, they were distantly related to Aaron Burr and of course the Gould family.

On occasion, PeeWee would get to go to Aunt Edith's house in Roxbury. The house, later the Miller Funeral Home, really belonged to housemate Miss Etta Colby. But Edith, George's older sister, ran the show. Aunt Edith liked Elsie and Paul and was the only person on earth who could manage George's "forceful" nature. In one visit when "spindle shanks" a.k.a., "PeeWee," was pushing the lawn mower around, he deliberately removed his shirt so Aunt Edith could observe the numerous raised welts on his back from his most recent whipping.

Miss Colby and Aunt Edith promptly paid Paul fifty cents, even though the job was incomplete, and took him back to Hardscrabble. With Paul quietly crouched in a nearby room listening to every word with profound satisfaction, Edith provided George with a severe tongue lashing, mainly, but not entirely, in English. The red lines showed for weeks having been imposed over a fair complexion but heavy suntan. George never once interrupted, or returned to Paul, having "squealed" on him. Paul remembers this as the major event of 1943, when both the severity and regularity of "discipline" was reduced.

Downtown Roxbury

A "hillbilly" kid in every sense of the word, Paul's trips to "downtown Roxbury" to see Aunt Edith and Miss Colby were his first contact with the "outer world." Having never seen a Jewish person, as they weren't particularly welcome in Roxbury, Gould territory, Paul was intrigued to talk to the famous Jewish author, Fannie Hurst, who stayed at the Roxbury Hotel several summers. Petite, and pale, she seemed friendly, even eager, to talk to this simple country boy. Not long after, Paul met and became friends with Irving Tyler, whom he had heard was both Catholic and a democrat. Paul's first sighting of either, "Irv" seemed like everyone else. Trips to see Aunt Edith and Etta Colby in town were always special and accounted for Paul's first movie, popcorn, olive, banana, and other strange foods never before experienced. The year 1943 was great; Roxbury was a big wonderful place.

Living next door to Helen Anna, adopted daughter of Helen Gould, the last of the Roxbury Goulds, always stretched Paul's limited imagination, as Edith and Etta kept track, then routinely shared her "outrageous" behavior. Ima Griffin, the eccentric news writer for a local weekly paper, also lived only a few houses up the street. If you are elderly you can more easily get away with being "eccentric." Ima wasn't that old, but when she walked down the sidewalk past the house "backward" to observe better whatever occurred behind her, she was known to be a nutcase.

The sidewalks that Mrs. Shepard had donated to Roxbury were by now slightly altered and tipped, with large tree roots making it uneven. Ima, often walking backward in both summer and winter, would have to turn around constantly to glance in her direction of travel to avoid tripping. Paul, often mowing the lawn, was advised not to confront her, as "You never know about people like that." Ima's brother, Walter, was seldom seen and to be avoided.

Erma Over Ima

At one visit, Miss Colby watching her neighbor walking backward down the sidewalk, remarked "there goes *Erma*." Ima had explained to her neighbors that "Erma" was more "romantic" and she would henceforth like to be called "Erma." Paul, having only recently met authors Elsa Shelly and Fannie Hurst on the same sidewalk, and being a bit strange, he (left-handed) loved the idea of a name change. He had evolved from PeeWee, Joe, Whitey, and now Pete. Erma's daring to walk backward and "be her own person" caused Paul to admire this strange person.

Some sixty-years later, upon a return visit to Roxbury, Dr. Ploutz's childhood memory was challenged: Ima or Erma Griffin? School records reveal the Miss Ima Mae Griffin graduated RCS, 1921 as valedictorian! Erma, while not a "Roxbury Boy" earned the hearts and respect of the community. Of numerous historical accomplishments perhaps one of "Erma's" best was the publishing of *The History of the Town of Roxbury*, in 1995. Erma died in 1987 and the town of Roxbury, updated and republished her earlier work. Critics, as is usually the case, have brought forward dozens of corrections, glitches, and interpretations, which differ from Erma's assessment. Ploutz (2004) smiles but truth be told, fears the same fate, the difference being a reasonable possibility he may still be alive to take the grief!

Spanning two hundred years of Roxbury history and a thousand families, Erma's book thrilled "Roxbury Boy" Paul Ploutz. Sooner or later the 1,851 graduates of RCS listed in the *"Roxbury Boys,"* who consider doing the inevitable "family tree," will need Erma's encyclopedia-like book as well as Paul's. As of 2003 her book is still available "in the town hall," Roxbury, New York 12474 (see Part II for additional information on the local legend).

As a late-blooming simple country hick, Paul Ploutz, in 1944, felt that in his heart of hearts, he could only live and be happy in Roxbury. The solution to Paul's little security and still less success, lay in the *mentoring* by teachers, a supportive and loving mother, good neighbors, and friendly townsfolk, and he seemed to realize it. It takes a village? Paul felt that he could never, never be happy elsewhere "PeeWee," had been replaced by "Joe," "Whitey," and finally "Pete" by cousin Floyd Ploutz. Paul's loyalty to Roxbury, along with his need for attention was so great that at home basketball events, with other schools, he would cheer, and jeer the opponents until hoarse.

On one occasion, at an RCS home basketball game against Margaretville, Paul's continued jeering from the bleachers so infuriated one player, Bernie Leidenheim, that he left the court, and ran into the stands to belt mouthy Paul. It made him a dubious "hero," but hero none the less. Being "hit" was a high point, how pathetic?

In later years, with four college degrees, author, having been to all fifty states, the rain forests of Costa Rica, the Amazon, Europe, North Africa, Mexico, the Caribbean and elsewhere, like Burroughs, Paul retained a profound affection for Roxbury that somehow had delivered him from poverty, hunger, worms and rebellion. By this time realizing that he could have a life, even if he wasn't in Roxbury, Paul had diluted some of his insecurities that had penetrated his very being.

Paul's only sister Elsie had graduated RCS in 1941. Anna and George had spared their only daughter from most barn chores. Unlike Gould's older sisters, Elsie was not able to buffer Paul from the realities of his existence. Paul has so little recollection of her, and most everything else of his first ten years or so, that a psychologist might conclude that much of his first ten years had simply been "blocked out."

Paul recalled that Elsie had dated Curtis Burroughs briefly in the late 1940's, probably never realizing they were distant cousins by marriage. Paul didn't like him anyway, as he was sure it was Curt who kept catching the trout out of the old swimming hole. It had taken hundreds of fat grasshoppers thrown into the water by Paul during most of the summer to fatten them up. Paul, able to count "his" trout in the clear water, looked forward to catching them himself.

But Curt got them, sometimes twice a summer! Curtis's grandfather John Burroughs often fished the same hole but that was nearly sixty years earlier. Besides the Ploutz's owned a long portion of the stream running through Hardscrabble.

At school, Paul's bag lunch usually consisted of putting a few drops of water on three or four pancakes rolled around a couple of spoons of brown sugar brought from home. An apple, if available, was included. The Roxbury School often worked out a "barter system" with local farm families, exchanging vegetables and other food for their children's lunches, with no money being involved. "Irv" and Dorothy Mead's sons Wayland and Keith N. benefited each school day from a hot cafeteria lunch. Vegetables from the Mead farm were routinely used in the school cafeteria.

Wayland Mead was one of Paul's closest friends. Paul later introduced him to the girl he was to marry and then still later Paul was best man at his wedding. Wayland, passing through the cafeteria line would sneak one or even two ice cream tubs on his tray for Paul. Wayland was otherwise, trustworthy, loyal, helpful, friendly, courteous, and kind, but only moderately thrifty, brave, clean, and reverent. Wayland was a truly solid friend, perhaps like Jason and John had been. Fifty years later, Paul and Wayland have not seen each other or talked since RCS.

Bruce "Stub" Caswell managed to get Ploutz enrolled in Troop 41, BSA. Cleaned up, Ploutz proudly wore a Boy Scout uniform. Stub, unlike Paul's father, knew you could "catch more flies with honey than vinegar." Much like Catherine Fleming and Lela Wickham, exercising positive, supportive influence, a substitute father of a sort, Scoutmaster, *mentor*, Bruce Caswell and Paul were to become life-long friends. Scouting appealed to Paul's love of nature, and in time, he became an Eagle Scout.

Caswell had built a "scout camp" on his own property and at his own expense. The troop met there weekly and held many camp outs. Stub was producing more Eagle Scouts in Roxbury than would be normal (about one scout of a hundred obtains the rank of Eagle). Later, one summer, Ploutz was assistant camp director for the Otschodela (Otsego/Schoharie/Delaware counties) scout council at Crumhorn Mountain, Oneonta, New York. Years later, Paul became council resident of the Kootaga Council (now Allohak), which included Southeastern Ohio and much of West Virginia (see picture).

Stub Caswells' *mentoring* of Paul and numerous others helped Troop 41 of Roxbury achieve area distinction. Most Eagle Scouts go on to become adult leaders. Stub's earlier relatives had also lived near the Burroughs farm. Stub's closest friends, like Burroughs, were birds, raccoons, and from time to time, people.

Roxbury schools, like most rural schools everywhere, always seemed to have budget crunches. It still managed somehow to offer both afterschool and equally important, summer activities for students. Helen Anna Shepard continued to be an influence in the community. She became Helen Anna Gaines, Helen Anna Burton, Helen Anna Koke, and finally Helen Anna Happisburg., Adopted daughter of Helen Gould, Helen Anna would allow, for a small summer fee, Roxbury folks to swim in "The Lake" for those tired of Bridal Veil and similar country streams. The benefit was that the lake had little upstream cow manure influence. The lake was an improvement from the earlier lake of Mr. Dale who had lived next door to the Burroughs farm.

Some organization, perhaps the local veterans, also offered both baseball and softball leagues, which played before dark, evening games throughout most of the summer. Ploutz, thanks to the Gould Church, some wonderful Roxbury teachers, scouts, and sports programs, in the jargon of today, was "getting a life."

The Ploutz Farm

Pleasant Valley has a better "ring" than Hardscrabble. John Persons and wife, Elizabeth Tipple, are thought to have come to "the valley" around 1800 from Albany County. The Persons built the first gristmill shortly after 1800. The mill on the Ploutz farm (see map) operated for over eighty years when during the Johnstown flood it was washed out and discontinued in May 1889. By the late 1800s most of the trees in Pleasant Valley, (Hardscrabble) Roxbury, and other parts of the Kaatskills (Catskills) had been cut. Clear cutting was routine and explains why there were floods nearly every spring after 1900. Even a hundred years later (2002) a major bridge in the rear of RCS was washed away. The Persons daughter, Deborah married Jonas More, had nine children, and rebuilt and continued the lumber operation until 1889.

During a flood, the dam at the site was washed out and the mill discontinued. Addison P. More. owned the farm at that time. The More family is often thought of as Roxbury's first family going back well before "Pleasant Valley" when Roxbury, or at least part of Roxbury, was known as "Beaver Dam." Addison More sold the farm to Orrin Day Wood, who sold it to George William Ploutz and wife Anna, successful farmers who sold it in 1947.

The mill site has disappeared. With the valleys stripped of trees, spring floods of Hardscrabble and other streams have been the norm, since before 1930. Paul "thinks" he recalls the location of the first gristmill, just above the large culvert on what is now called Pekrul Road off Hardscrabble Road.

Hardscrabble 1800 –2000

The Hardscrabble "map" is nine-year-old Paul Hardscrabble's world in 1940. Property owners of 1940 are in **bold** letters (Pg. 30).

Beaver have once again gradually reappeared in the headwaters of the Hardscrabble stream of 2000. A hundred years earlier, the stream had supplied waterpower to the factory and mills located on the Baker and Ploutz farms.

The mountains of (Beaverdam) Roxbury, are once again being covered with maple, oak, ash, and soft woods. After years of searching, American Chestnut trees, which survived the 1930 blight, have been discovered (Ferris Hill). The New York State Conservation Dept is attempting, with some success, to reintroduce the Chestnut tree by collecting and growing the few Chestnuts which seem to have survived.

Edward Corsi was the Industrial Commissioner of Labor for New York State during the period that Tom Dewey was governor. The Corsi family bought the Jess Caswell farm just up the Hardscrabble Road above the Ploutz farm. While Paul still lived on the farm, Mrs. Corsi, like the still earlier nearby Royal family, fed Paul milk and cookies when he passed through.

One day, this fine city lady told Paul she had a special surprise to show him. Eagerly walking to the barn in the rear of their home Mrs. Corsi showed Paul a newborn calf. Imagine showing a farm boy a newborn calf as a big deal surprise. He was bored, disappointed that she had earlier talked of a pending surprise for Paul. Showing a farm boy a calf, thinking it to be a pleasant surprise, how could she?

Mrs. Corsi was very disappointed that her surprise had been such a failure. In probably his very first attempt at tact, Paul asked her if they "were going to sell it or eat it?" Mrs. Corsi burst into tears. Paul and their son, Phil, older than Paul, became friends after Paul moved to Roxbury Village. Ed Corsi was prominent in the labor movement, the Dewey administration, and was recommended to serve in a federal post. Young Paul was told that W. Scott McCloud (Joe McCarthy era) called "Ed" a communist thereby effectively killing his appointment to a federal post.

Mr. Corsi was apparently not a communist. He did bring James Fusscus and other attorneys to Roxbury, some of whom stayed. Some Roxbury locals still wonder which would have been worse.

Chapter 6:   Sell the Farm, Life Begins

Like their neighbors, Burroughs and especially Gould, a hundred years later, farm work became contrary to everything they yearned to be doing. In 1944, the miracle happened. Elsie, Paul's only sister joined the Women's Army Corp (WAC) and went off to Nebraska. Milton, his twenty-year-old brother had died a few years prior. His remaining brother Raymond, George's favorite son would soon graduate RCS (1948).

Raymond preferred the marines to his father and the farm. Years earlier, when Milton was twenty, he had a passionate desire to join the service and get away from his oppressive father. George wouldn't let him join, and Milton had a "farm deferral." George did not resist Raymond's effort to join the service. A large number of Roxbury Boys became veterans and served in the military from 1901 - 1950, as recorded in **Part II** of this text.

Paul, now fifteen, was left to help on the farm, still "juicing the Jerseys" by hand.   Present-day milking machines were only gradually being utilized and were still financially prohibitive. The farm was too big and Paul was still small, but like most farm boys worked endlessly, before dawn until after dark. Father, George, had only completed the eighth grade, then nearly dying of pneumonia, married, and briefly lived in South Kortright. George and Anna had bought and paid for the Hardscrabble farm that had provided for their family. They worked without a single vacation, ever. The kids were grown, dead, or were leaving. Like Jason Gould, Paul "wasn't much" and now George's lungs, damaged from childhood pneumonia, were restricting his sixteen-hour-day. It was time to sell the farm!

Charles Weprek was among the earliest of hundreds, nay thousands, of Long Island and New York City folks "to invade the Catskills." Talk show hosts of the day referred to the Catskills as the "Jewish Alps."   Brooklyn, Bronx, Manhattan, Queens etc. gradually migrating "in." Ironically Jay, John, Paul, and other locals who made good, also frequently migrated "out." Country folk often find city dwellers loud, pushy, and aggressive. They do bring money. Roxbury, and many other villages in the Catskills and "upstate" New York, experience similar population shifts.

Charles Weprek paid forty-two thousand for the George Ploutz farm including the cattle, tractor, and all the equipment necessary to run a farm. When Henry Ford bought out Howard Ploutz's lease on the neighboring Chauncy Burrough's farm, Howard, George's brother, got to keep the cattle, tractor and farm equipment, hay wagons, chicken, pigs, refrigerator, stove. and drapes. Weprek, as the rural saying goes got the farm "lock, stock, and barrel."

Life Begins

Living across the street from the K-12, Roxbury Central School for Paul, now sixteen, was a dream come true. George and Anna having sold the historic 180-acre farm, in 1947 purchased and remodeled an older two story home on Lake Street, affectionately known to this day as "Frog Alley." There was a garage, garden, and oil heat. Paul had his own bedroom, three meals a day, no beatings, a new bicycle, time to hunt, fish, trap, wander White Man Mountain, NEW socks, underwear, shoes, shorts.

Life was good! More than that, their house was simply across the street from the school. The Ploutzes owned a vacant lot between their home and the school. The Roxbury Village library now adorns the lot that the family sold to the school for fifteen-hundred dollars.

Moving off the farm produced more time to hunt and fish. Shepard Lake above Roxbury Village was now owned by Helen Anna, Shepard, adopted daughter of Helen Gould, Jay's daughter. It was a fisherman's paradise. It was private property, patrolled, no fishing, no trespassing, no hunting, no "nothin", but stocked with large trout.

On Paul's fifth fishing trip at Shepard Lake, watchman Herman Oche apprehended him, taking his rod, reel, basket, and six beautiful fat, foot-long brook trout. Paul walked home in the rain wondering what his fate would be. Paul had visions of ending up in Siberia. He knew it was even colder in Siberia than in the Catskills. His mother, Anna, had often joked that Roxbury had two seasons, "Winter and July." No one messes with the Goulds. Perhaps Aunt Edith Ploutz who lived next door to Helen Anna could intervene?

In a rare moment of presumed support, or more likely a humbling face-off, George ordered Paul to walk to the Oche house. "Tell Oche that's my pole and basket, I want it back." Trembling to the old Dutchman's door, Paul delivered his father's dictum. By promising never to fish there again, Paul retrieved the pole, rod, basket, minus, of course, the fat trout. The feared Helen Anna withheld Paul's swimming options for the entire summer at her lake, now used for a small fee, by the entire village. Being ostracized from friends the entire summer seemed severe, but there was always Bridal Veil Falls and the old swimming hole on the farm off Hardscrabble Road. Fifty-five years later Paul visited Marshall Slauson, (Roxbury town supervisor for many years) at the Kirkside Senior Citizens Center. Marshall laughed, told Paul it was a shame he had been apprehended, as Marshall and numerous others had fished there without incident.

In the fall of 1938, having left the one-room schoolhouse, Paul started the first of his two years in the second grade in Roxbury Village. The school had been the YMCA building; today it is a cultural arts center. The Caswells lived across the street. Paul, probably seven, was eager to make friends, and getting off the school bus, saw Phil standing near a tree on a nearby lawn. Oblivious to school protocol of marching straight to class, Paul walked toward Phil, stopping close by, but without leaving the school lawn. Phil was butting his head against a tree. Paul did not know the "Billy Goat Gruff" story and was confused, yes stunned, to see another small boy, repeatedly driving his head into the trunk of a large maple tree. A teacher rounded up Paul, and the others explaining that, well, Phil was different.

Like much of his early years Paul has little recollection, so going on a bird hike eight years later when he met Phil, it seemed like he was meeting him for the first time.

The Bird Walk Awakening

The first bird walk Paul experienced occurred in Roxbury during the very first winter after leaving the farm. Stub, the famed scoutmaster of Troop 41, Roxbury, like Burroughs, often took bird walks. If wife Millie (Preston) Caswell, son Phil, or a scout or two tagged along, well all the better. Now in the scouts and recently reacquainted with Phil, it was Paul's turn to do a bird walk with Stub, the bonafide self-made naturalist.

Paul, already a nature lover, loved all birds other than crows, chickens, or turkeys. He knew, for example, that many birds "fly south in the winter" but it never had occurred to him that Roxbury was "south" for some birds in winter. So Paul, at least wanting to be macho, or worse not wanting to be thought a sissy, was going on a "bird walk," reluctantly. Further, reliable adults had cautioned him that Stub "took no prisoners," and with his smart mouth, Paul would be lucky he could stay in the scouts. In one of Paul's first scout meetings, Stub "threw" Phil Brower out of camp, out of the scout troop. So the four, Stub, Phil (later nicknamed Buzzard), Millie Caswell, and Paul walked. Keeping a list of birds as you identify them, seemed a bit silly, but reasonable. With only a dozen or so bird species on the planet, what's the point?

Within minutes "they" had identified all the birds on the planet and another dozen besides, including Burroughs, beloved vesper sparrow, which apparently John had named previously. There were chickadees, nuthatches, sparrows, woodpeckers, jays, wrens, and juncos. They seemed everywhere; this nature lover had missed the birds? Cold, calm, a bright sun on several inches of pure white snow, Phil and Stub called Paul to a pile of brush near a fence line to see something special, or at least a little out of the ordinary. Look, see, there, there gesturing into an empty pile of brush and branches, a deer?

Paul had learned to spot a deer standing motionlessly in heavy woods, or a fish's fin protruding from a rock crevice, or a path through the woods, if a single leaf had been disturbed. No hill-billy kid had spent more time than Paul sitting on the nearby Burroughs' "Boyhood Rock" or the rocks on Ploutz's farm staring at nature. Enthralled with magnificent fall colors, wondering how long a leaf thrown from a ledge could float, how fish sleep, and why bird's feet on a branch didn't come loose when the bird slept.

Was this a trick? Phil was "different," but you should be able to trust a scout master. Paul continued to stare into the brush pile as Stub, Millie, and Phil waited. Within seconds, tiny birds, several of them, were quietly jumping an inch or two, branch to branch. Paul later likened the experience to a hologram viewing one scene until finally an entirely new 3-D picture emerged.

Tiny, delicate, beautiful ruby crowned kinglets and golden crowned kinglets provided sensory overload for a thrilled boy. How could it be that he had never seen them before? In an instant, simple, yet profound awakening, the scouts were great, as they enjoyed nature without the slightest hint of embarrassment. Exciting doors were opened, and Phil, still different, was someone who could be both an inspiration and friend.

A year or two later, Paul recalls being on the school athletic field after school with a group of boys, at baseball practice. Along the nearby stream, perhaps a one-hundred-yards away, was a puzzling situation. A boy was wildly swinging a stick back and forth in the air, often above his head. To the dismay of the ball players the boy, Phil, would often run along the stream at the same time flailing away at the air. One player beckoned others to return to practice "Its only Caswell, he's finally lost it." Another quipped, "He never had it in the first place, He's always been that way. Let's play ball."

Paul, however, realized Phil had a butterfly net and was collecting "ten-spots," cordulegaster, plathemis lydia or other dragon flies, learning their Latin name, genus, and species while doing so. Some sixty-years later, Phil was surprised that Paul had in fact remembered their Latin genus and species. But no matter, "He had screwed it up" anyway, as one species emerges in the spring, the other in fall, but NOT at the same time. As teenage buddies Phil seemed delighted to explain that he was a bastard. Paul, naïve, thought that was being without a father. Phil, apparently amused, explained that his parents had only been married a few months when he was born. Phil Caswell graduated as RCS valedictorian, earned a degree in zoology from Cornell, and served a distinguished twenty plus year military career.

So Roxbury and the school with its mentors had "done it again!" Phil's desire and ability to learn was again demonstrated at age fifty, when he learned to speak both German and Russian in an intense language program designed to permit Lieutenant Colonel Caswell to recruit spies. He learned to speak two new languages in a few weeks of intensive study. Remarkable.

Making Maple Syrup

At age fifteen, Paul's first job in town was boiling sap for Carl Shuster in the spring of 1947. John Gould and George Ploutz both had skinny sons to gather sap from buckets hung on the "sugar bush" grove of hard or "sugar maples." Forty gallons of sap, or even more, has to be boiled down to at least one gallon of maple syrup, or still longer to produce candy. Shuster's stand of maples (now owned by Phil Caswell) had forty or fifty large maples each producing a rapid steady drip of sap.

Carl Shuster owned an oversized open fireplace. It had a huge tin rectangular pan positioned over the fire below. About twenty gallons of sap, several inches deep, were enough to start the boiling process. It was a great job at eighty-cents-an-hour. Paul could do this job fully as well as any rugged farm hand. Carl had numerous ten-gallon milk cans full of sap nearby. Chunks of wood could be aggressively tossed into the hearth, the sap just boiling faster. Most of the time you could just watch, making sure sparks wouldn't burn down the surrounding woods. The roaring fire up the chimney produced sparks, specks of small, still burning, little pieces of wood.

The colors of syrup you buy in the store, golden-clear, golden, amber, and dark are often a factor of how much soot falls back into the boiling pan. Paul produced only "dark" syrup. Eager to please and enjoying tending the fire, Paul was shoving as much wood in the firebox as it would take. In one batch, the flat metal, red-hot lid, covering part of the open chimney, dropped off directly into the boil pan. The lid sizzled and sank, making that batch of syrup, well, even darker!

Brother Ray's first job was making popcorn at the Roxbury Theatre. Uncle Ray Cronk had converted ad existing structure into a theatre which would seat nearly two hundred. Marion Bookhout (RCS 1929) was manager, wife Liz sold tickets, Ray sold popcorn. Popcorn sold for ten cents a box. Al the ingredients, corn, grease, and salt were supplied. Ray got two cents for each box sold. Ray thought it was the best job in town. When you weren't busy, Bookhout would let you watch the pictures, every picture, twice. Living on Lake Street (Frog Alley) you were nearby. You got to meet everyone, evenings were great to work. PeeWee (hated the name) was also hired to dust the seats periodically.

When Ray was sick, playing basketball, baseball, or whatever, Anna would fill in. As years passed, Paul gradually started "filling in". The Ploutzes did the popcorn concession for years. Marion Bookhout was still another *mentor* in rural Roxbury. With time, Marion and Paul became fishing partners. Paul had learned many of Uncle Ray Cronks fishing skills and relished the idea of coaching anyone older, especially a nice guy and employer like Marion.

In earlier years, (around 1940) the Daitch Creamery Plant had so polluted the head waters of the east branch of the Delaware River that few fish survived. By 1947, that portion of the stream above Roxbury Village was again viable, but no one thought of fishing there. Paul fished every stream, pond, and puddle, and was apparently the first to discover that the half mile portion of the stream immediately below the creamery was "back," and alive with brook trout.

The creamery had a barrier which prohibited fish from going around it and going further upstream. Given the natural tendency of fish to go upstream, the area immediately below the creamery was now the hottest fishing spot around. Paul would frequently walk back to town with his limit (ten trout) for all to see. Since he was now also in the business of selling worms and night crawlers, some bought his stuff just so they could "interview" him in a veiled attempt to discover his secret fishing spot. Farther downstream, some of the village sewers emptied directly into the stream flowing through town. It was not uncommon to see toilet paper and other objects floating along, or the paper caught on branches or twigs in the water. Lamprey eels with round sucker-shaped mouths were frequent in the stream. They were there for many years until their swimming up stream could be brought under control.

Marion Bookhout was still Paul's popcorn boss, so the secret was shared. Marion parked his truck nearby when fishing, and the secret was out. Paul had caught several hundred brook trout and a few brown trout. His reputation as a fisherman was secure.

That same summer, 1947, Paul hired himself out to William Barnecoat, a Roxbury farmer, for twenty dollars per week, Monday through Friday, mowing with a new Ford tractor. Two "city" boys were also employed. They laid down, went to the bathroom, and got a drink on a perpetual basis. They even attempted to slow Paul down, as he was making them look bad. The Gould ambition and the Burroughs integrity had finally kicked in.

Paul suggested to Mr. Barnecoat that, if he could exchange his five-foot mower for a seven foot one, he could mow more grass in less time, and "eliminate" one employee. Barnecoat was so pleased, he asked Paul to "decide" which "city" boy to keep. The end result improved, the remaining employee was assigned to Paul, with a delightful improvement in attitude. Barnecoat got more hay cut, gave Paul an additional ten dollars per week (also then saving ten). Perhaps the boy going back to New York City realized that country boy ethics is called work; well perhaps? Surviving on a farm required business savvy, awareness, and efficiency, lots of efficiency.

Paul's abusive father did a rather effective job in teaching the realities of rural life. One of Father George's philosophies was simple: 1. everyone "starts out pretty much the same (being born). 2. some fail, others succeed. 3. must be how they spend their time that makes the difference. Efficiency boy, efficiency, never walk to the barn empty-handed. Don't waste your life walking around empty-handed."

Fifty-five years later, on his twenty-acre Ohio residence site, Paul figured out how to mow grass, pick it up, and smooth the lawn towing a nine-hundred-pound roller. Doing all three tasks simultaneously was a skill his father's influence on the farm instilled in him. Efficiency still makes him happy. Paul's attempt to instill efficiency in himself and others at every opportunity, demonstrates his father's influence to this day. It can be particularly helpful or annoying.

Big Mouth, Undeveloped Brain

Gym class, which "Doc " Ross conducted, now included all of the forty-nine boys enrolled in grades nine through twelve. Only Bobby Green was shorter than Paul. The other forty-seven boys were bigger and taller, including all the bullies, acquired adversaries, and other students whose problems were probably greater than Paul's. Unlike puny Jason Gould, who would run to the schoolmaster to avoid bullies or merely to get them into trouble, Paul was verbally aggressive, and often had to rely on others to extract him from constant silly altercations.

"Doc" Ross, a superior teacher/coach, and organizer would somehow exercise the whole group, skillfully avoiding scraps, but always encouraging competition and sportsmanship. Once organized, "Doc" could conduct two or more softball games simultaneously, or two volleyball games, or shuffleboard and table tennis all at once with forty-nine boys when it was cold or raining outside. On rare occasions, with older boys who "couldn't get it behind them," he'd let them put on boxing gloves and flail away a few minutes to reduce their testosterone and adrenaline. Since he was also coach of every team, no one would want to mess up their relationship with skillful "Doc" Ross.

The smallest boy (now nicknamed Pete) and the biggest bully were always equals in the gym. In Paul's case, Raymond seventeen, the older, much larger brother also helped. Ray had pitched a "no hit, no run," 5-0, baseball game against the visiting Andes team (September 1947) and enjoyed some status. The ball is still shown in the showcase at *RCS* as of 2003. In rare cases, while clearly not a bully, cousin Floyd Ploutz Jr. who had often had the "gloves" on and prevailed, made it clear he would beat the crap out of anyone who messed with "Pete," without provocation.

Paul, by age sixteen was becoming a fast talker, learning just "when to stop" in provoking friends, adults, or teachers. Since he was still learning, cousin Floyd's services, particularly outside of school, would need to be called upon. Even cousin Floyd, however, was a *mentor*, telling Paul, to cool it and that "Paul didn't always deserve protection."

The day-by-day or hour-by-hour *mentoring* of Ploutz may be understated. It took a longer time:

1936-1937	1st grade	Elizabeth (Betty) Craig	
		Hardscrabble 1 Room School	
1937-1938	2nd grade	unknown YMCA bldg. Roxbury	
1938-1939	2nd grade	(again)	
		YMCA bldg. Roxbury Village	
1939-1940	3rd grade	Laura Van Benschoten RCS(new)	
1940-1941	4th grade	Nellie Enders	RCS
1941-1942	5th grade	unknown	RCS
1921-1943	6th grade	Kay Shaylor	RCS
1942-1944	7th grade	Catherine Fleming	RCS
1944-1945	8th grade	Lela Wickham	RCS

Mentors Everywhere, Over the Class Clown

There was Mr. Stone, social studies, homeroom teacher; Mr. Norman Collins math; Mr. William Crawford, science; Miss Sue Root, English; Miss Mary Ellen Lasher, typing; Coach Roland F. "Doc" Ross. Sure "It takes a village," but it also takes a school.

This is not to say that Paul became a model student certainly, but constant *mentoring* month by month, day by day, hour by hour, even minute by minute with generous amounts of detention in the school library with Mrs. Mildred Caswell, helped to mold Paul, much like a lump of clay. Jason Gould and John Burroughs also had a rough farm existence, "tough" fathers, loving mothers, and gifted teacher,

James Oliver. For gifted teachers, hyperactive Ploutz had Caswell, Fleming, Wickham, Stone, Collins, Root, Crawford, and Ross, all by age sixteen.

In addition to being outspoken and a weak student in most subjects, and during his high school years, Paul also managed to:

1. Deposit a small snake in a substitute teacher's desk. The snake "rose out" the very first time the draw was opened and in front of the entire class. The teacher was panic-stricken, the class roared. Paul's prank had been successful.

2. Mistakenly trap a skunk, and then enter school, in full aroma. Mr. Crum sent him home.

3. Mix iron filings and sulfuric acid together in chemistry class to produce hydrogen sulfide (smelling like rotten eggs), which he hid elsewhere in the school.

4. Gradually, but persistently, remove chalkboard erasers, one by one, from classrooms in the entire school, storing them in his hall locker. Erasers became so scarce, that teachers were storing them in their purses, removing them only long enough to erase, then back. New erasers were backordered, taking weeks to replace. When a classmate, now also inconvenienced, finally "blew the whistle," nearly fifty confiscated erasers were returned to use.

5. On the weekend hit a golf ball two-hundred yards through the second floor window of school, into the typing room. Weighing the situation carefully, Paul turned himself in Monday morning thinking, "they would likely figure it out anyway."

6. Collaborate in sneaking a condom into senior Marie Griffin's purse, which her mother later discovered. Marie was innocent but the incident produced a backlash at school. Paul's only documented lie? This may be the first time (2002) the indiscretion has ever been revealed.

7. Carry off most of the birdhouses from the Gould estate (now Kirkside Park), restore them, and mounted them in the woods above "Frog Alley," where he had also planted fifty white pines that had been legitimately donated.

8. Finger brook trout at spawning time from Shepard Lake, carrying them in successive buckets to Carl Shuster's ponds, at the base of White Man Mountain.
9. Draw Burt Hunter's name in the secret annual Christmas class exchange, only to give him a wash cloth and a bar of soap (An old gag, but truth be told Paul could likely have used it himself.)
10. Run onto Neil Ploutz's porch at Halloween, from a night function at school, and kick a lighted pumpkin to death. Problem was that Neil saw Paul do it!

By 1948, Paul was becoming more articulate, athletically successful, with minor academic potential and was learning "to work the system," talking his way out of all ten "events" listed. In one instance, he, Ray Slauson and two others, had been sent to the principal's (Mr. Crum's) office, to receive the "board of education" or hose, whichever. Even high school boys could choose between the paddle and the hose. Paul managed to "go last."

With by now, a breathless Mr. Crum, having "hosed the first three," Paul explained that he had had plenty of whippings at home, one more probably wouldn't change anything, but if only the principal "would explain why what he did was wrong, he would apologize and wouldn't do it again." Yeah right. It was a snow job, but it worked.

Detention, provided time to do homework and also provided opportunities for some attention for which he was still thirsting. Creative, mischievous, restless, and reckless, Paul managed to elude ALL corporal punishment his entire four years of high school.

There were successes. Mr. Collins, who had "written the book," taught plane geometry. Paul as usual, was acting up. Collins knowing of Paul's interest in scouting and the out doors in general convinced Paul that to be a good scout or woodsman he would need to know geometry. Using a simple "angle-side-angle" diagram, Paul could figure out the distance across a stream or river without getting his feet wet or drowning. Cool stuff! Paul passed algebra, plane geometry because of an excellent teacher who learned as much about kids as he did mathematics. Paul became so intrigued with math he scheduled "trig" with classmates Wayland Mead and Guy Numann. He lasted three or four days, his brain was ready, but not that ready.

Paul made all the teams he went out for. A "shortage" of boys improved the odds for any kid who wanted to give it a try. He was good at soccer and basketball and pitched a "2 hitter" against Fleischmans. Since he was still a bit small did better at ping-pong, bad-minton, tennis and the "lesser" sports. He rode his bicycle hundreds of hours, the seven mile trip to Grand Gorge became routine, and he did "wheelies" before it became common.

In spite of frequent visits to his Aunt Edith, who lived next door from Helen Anna, he often heard, but seldom saw Helen Anna. Helen Anna had married Gaines, shouted, and apparently boozed less frequently, had two small girls, Nancy and Ginny. A bit older, Paul didn't fish in her lake anymore, but loved to hang out on her golf course. Paul would often play all nine holes with a # 3 iron he had found. Newly acquired friend Phil Corsi and Paul frequently played golf and basketball when Phil was in Roxbury. Paul was blessed with twenty-fifteen vision and would often prowl the rough finding golf balls others had missed. After collecting a one-hundred or so, Paul would sell them back to golfers bringing him once again under Helen Anna's disapproval.

Number three hole of the course was across the upper narrow part of Helen Anna's lake. Friend and lifeguard William D. White III, would let Paul use a boat to row to the shallow end and salvage balls which had been lost. With three good balls lying in the boat, Paul heard a call from the shore. Local merchant Jim Minnerly (1930) and his guest James Fusscus summoned Paul to shore. Fusscus could see his ball in five or six feet of clear water near the shore. Before even being asked, Paul volunteered to dive in and regain it for him. While Paul was underwater, attorney Fusscus apparently removed two of the balls from the vacant boat to his pockets. Since Paul had only recently retrieved the balls, he was instantly aware they had been taken. "Where are the two balls? Who took them? James Minnerly severely chastised Paul for even suggesting such an important person would take them. "Who do you think you are? ya de ya de ya."

Some fifteen years later Minnerly approached Paul offering "an apology." Seems Mr. Fusscus, only minutes away from the boat and the third hole, revealed taking the two balls suggesting "that kid wasn't as smart as he thought he was."

So began Paul's lifelong disdain for most attorneys. Minnerly had carried his guilt on his conscience all those years, how unfortunate. Mr. Fusscus apparently stayed in Roxbury. Paul was unaware that Fusscus' son had graduated RCS (59). Paul was told that the "apple had not fallen far from the tree."

This seemingly minor golf ball experience prolonged itself and evolved into a profoundly painful experience for Paul. Janet Minnerly (1951) and her close friend Edith Mallasch (51) were popular in school, attractive, and intelligent. Paul recalled his first kiss came in 1947, age sixteen, with beautiful Edith Mallasch. Paul (49) with his childhood insecurities, wanting desperately to be accepted, was quick to notice that he soon became "dog meat" after the golf ball incident. In a further bizarre twist, Edith frequently stayed overnight at Janet's house. Apparently Janet's father also found Edith irresistible. Roxbury locals have repeated to Paul that Edith, after the affair, moved to New York City and became a "lady of the evening." Paul hasn't a clue, no information in over fifty years. And all over a couple of lousy golf balls?

Phil Caswell, Paul (eagle, Nov. 1949) and Bill White became eagle scouts about the same time. Three "eagles" from Roxbury gave Troop 41 recognition at scouting jamborees and similar events. Phil, Bill, and Paul often served as a service unit for district wide events. They were tired of sweeping pine needles for camp appearance, competing in rope tying contests etc. Phil's dad was scoutmaster, Bill's, the local Roxbury dentist. Good company to be in.

The Boy Scouts of America had an enormous impact on the aggressive, quick-tempered insecure late-blooming teenager. Paul recited the scout laws daily the way some might have prayed. Scout Master Stub was relentless in suggesting ways Paul could conform. "The way you're going you'll end up like Earl Conro."

Paul never quite knew what that meant. A year later, Paul was trying to make money by trapping below Roxbury Village. Checking his traps one cold fall morning he ran across Mr. Conro. Conro told Paul that he alone could trap there as he had "bought" the trapping rights from Hinkleys, the owners of the property. Paul left, only to discover there was no such arrangement. He now understood the scout master's admonition and appreciated the critical advise. Paul had trapped foxes, mink, and muskrats before and became adept at trapping.

Jay Gould wrote his fabled "Honesty Is the Best Policy" at a similar age (14), which Paul had recently read. Paul had also read the available copy of *The Wizard of Wall Street* containing the rest of Gould's activities. So, for the next several months Paul "pillaged" Conro's trap's of mink or muskrat. Being like Gould, especially after someone had tricked or cheated him seemed quite acceptable. Paul has remained active in the scouting movement over sixty years but no longer traps.

A year earlier (48) Paul had assembled a dozen merit badges and achieved a "Star" scout ranking. Stub Caswell received the coveted Silver Beaver Award, (Nov. 1949) the highest award available to a scout master. Numerous awards, recognition, citations, and certificates had been achieved save ONE! A big one: Lifesaving!

Why Save Douglas?

Douglas Spangenburg was nine years old and the only son of Milton Spangenburg of Roxbury. Long before Ritalin was available for hyperactive or destructive children, Doug's career as unmanageable was already secure.

Doug could not swim, but sat on the forward edge of Bridal Veil Falls anyway. A dozen older locals were swimming in the circular, deep hole immediately below the falls. Doug slid off the falls without a shriek of any sort into the deep water below. Those who saw him fall moved silently away toward shore, perhaps waiting for him to surface? He didn't.

Seconds seemed like minutes. No Doug, no bubbles, only the sense of pending disaster forming on motionless faces. More seconds. No Doug, no one seemed interested, concerned, or wanting to get involved with Doug.

Finally, Paul swam toward the center of the pool, taking a deep breath, pulled himself toward the bottom. Murky water, Doug seemingly crouched, slight kicks, arms slightly elevated all at the bottom of the pool! Paul was relatively strong. Doug was small and semi-conscience. Ignoring the techniques of the lifesaving merit badge, Paul grabbed Doug's right wrist. Kicking hard, Paul pulled him up and toward shallow water at the edge of the pool. Initially Doug was lying face down. Within a few seconds he started to sputter, cough, choke, and curse. He was saved.

The Oneonta Star daily newspaper July 1, 1948, printed, "Star Scout rescued Douglas Spangenburg 9, from certain death by drowning Tuesday afternoon at Bridal Veil Falls." Paul proudly carried the newspaper clipping to the next scout meeting expecting more attention and approval. It was not to be. Everyone thought Paul should have let him drown...

Mentors like Rudolph Gorsch make a difference in communities throughout the United States. A rotarian, volunteer firefighter, village undertaker, father, Rudy represented a pure example of why, children from rural areas have advantages over areas with higher population densities.

Rudy arranged for Paul, still a very insecure teenager, to speak about birds at a Roxbury Rotary Club meeting. He could never have known how much this single act of caring and encouragement meant. Paul was explaining something to adults of whom he had stood in awe. Wow!

Strong to dominating parents are said to make strong children stronger and weak children weaker. Perhaps rural communities serve the same ends? Deep down inside, Jason Gould, John Burroughs, and Paul Ploutz were apparently strong. Was it from growing up poor? Was it from having a stern, and in Paul's case, abusive father? Was if because of Roxbury Village's considerable influence? All three had strong-willed intelligent mothers. All three eventually had a strong desire to learn.

Anna Ploutz (1915) once told Paul, "It's a good idea to hang around people smarter than you are." In spite of his insecurities, he followed her advice, finding many willing, some eager to be *mentors*.

Rudy Gorsch and wife Frances hired Paul to baby-sit Rudy Jr. Rudy senior taught Paul how to "lose gracefully." They often played croquet at the Gorsch house, and as aggressive Paul reported, Rudy always "beat the crap out of me." Rudy Jr. (RCS 54), and Paul became good friends as adults. Frances has been an active village supporter. She was an organist for the Jay Gould Memorial Church for over thirty years.

At age ninety-two, still with a profound memory, Frances insists that she is an unofficial local historian. In developing the list of RCS graduates for Roxbury Boys, Frances and author Ploutz conferred for hours. In many instances she could recall the careers of RCS graduates from 1900 on, when school documents (yearbooks etc.) were unavailable, lost, or never existed. Paul remarked, "Here I am at 71 and the Gorschs are still helping me!"

Many people have stepped forward, volunteered to *mentor* this raw, outspoken farm boy. The reasons are unclear, but it surely does take a village to prepare "so rough a diamond" to beat the odds.

In 1949, Paul graduated from RCS, seventh in a class of twelve, with a New York State Regent's diploma, and as the cliché goes, made it "by the film on his teeth." Teacher, Sue Root, scored his French test at sixty-two percent with a circle around it. A Regents review committee removed the circle (code word for doubtful/marginal) advanced the grade to sixty-five percent, passing Paul. Pass French you pass the twelfth grade. Pass the grade you graduate. Close, very close.

George and Anna had already moved from "Frog Alley" in Roxbury and opened the Crossing Restaurant in Grand Gorge a few months before Paul graduated RCS. He drove a rusted 1935 Chevrolet truck back and forth to school daily. Only the left rear brake worked so for a sudden stop he shifted down as fast as possible. Other boys often "revved" their engines, squealed tires and "peeled" from the school parking lot. A few of the farm boys drove to school rather than ride the bus. Paul Weddleton (1943) had earlier gunned his pickup truck into the RCS parking lot and rolled it over in a cloud of dust! His reputation was seriously compromised.

Elderly Etta Colby who lived with Paul's Aunt Edith next to Helen Anna Shepard had been a *mentor*/advisor since Paul's birth but he was at last old enough to hear her advice. "Its important what people think of you. Speak to old people, drive through town carefully. Try to do that all the time, but if you can't at least wait until you're out of town."

This eighty-year old *mentor* was absolutely trustworthy. Paul was still shy, crude, or clumsy with girls under eighteen, with no interest in older women of twenty or so. Andrea Brown was a thirteen-year-old goddess. She was new in town and acquainted with Etta. Miss Colby and Paul's Aunt Edith were willing to escort them to a Saturday matinee at the new theatre in town. His heart raced with the possibilities.

His oldest brother Milton had told him exciting stories about Eleanor Sprague, a local Roxbury student. His older brother Raymond (1948) had confided about Delores Seligman (1952). Somehow Paul thought that he was finally going to get lucky! Unfortunately he had to work Saturday, he didn't have the money for admission, he had no good way to get her there, or take her home. His clothes were shabby, most of his socks had holes in the heels. Who would walk down the aisle first at the theatre? Could he work up the courage to try to hold hands? Finally the thought of rejection was so overwhelming that he backed out and was relieved to avoid the awful uncertainties and pressure. At age thirteen he and Burroughs were equally awkward. His sex life was totally fantasy, probably on target for a new teenager.

On occasion, he would see Mabel Decker who attended RCS but didn't graduate. She lived in a humble cabin in Long Woods, between Roxbury and Grand Gorge. Her father (?) Web Van Gordon and brother Walter, also lived there. Mabel was affectionally known by locals as the "swamp angel." A teenager herself, she was quickly identified as a lady of the "evening," well morning, afternoon, anytime. Mabel bragged openly that she had a regular in Roxbury at "fifteen" and another in Grand Gorge at "ten." In 1945, that was good money for the oldest profession. Paul, totally unable to express his new physical discoveries thought of Mabel but soundly rejected any possibilities, as he was developing a concern about what people thought and he was unprepared to assume any possibility of rejection. No money, no transportation, no courage to face so many unknowns. Equally intimidating was the report that when eager "guests" actually appeared at the cabin, Web would slide the muzzle of a shotgun out the narrow opening of the door and "invite" them to leave.

Ask Old People For Advice

"Ask old people for advice" resulting from Etta Colby's *mentoring* in the mid 1940s was to reappear sixty years later in Paul's commencement speech and Burroughs dedication at RCS, June 1949 (See Ch. 19 for the Ploutz advice). The rest of the quote is "They might be the last people on earth you'd approach for advice on money or sex. Most know more about these and other topics than you do. They need to give advice, you need to hear it, you'll gain respect for each other. Most advice will be clear and clean not tangled in convenience, ego. Just do it."

Etta was the only daughter of Orrin Colby who once owned the farm (Hadden) next to the Fritz Ploutz farm at the head of Hardscrabble. In rural settings, it seems everyone knows everyone. *Mentors*, perhaps unlike city living, are everywhere. You don't have to listen but they are available. Not many seventeen-year-old boys follow the advice of eighty-year-old spinsters. Paul usually followed her advice. In earlier years, Etta had recovered from tuberculosis. Her only abnormality seemed to be sensitivity to her age. The birth date on her headstone in the local (Gould) cemetery has been chipped, locals suggest she did it in an attempt to alter the evidence. She had a parrot (Polly naturally) and suggested it to be over one-hundred years old. Even clueless Paul wondered how she knew.

For the past several years Paul had taken archery seriously. Scout Master Stub Caswell had earlier given him an old Osage orange long bow. Now he bought a sixty-two-pound draw bow, 11/32, 28-inch wooden arrows, and went about it in earnest. Frances Pickett Jr. lived across the train tracks from the Grand Gorge restaurant that his parents owned. "Fran" or. "June" (for junior) was also a good fisherman but superb archer. Strong enough to routinely pull a ninety-pound bow and hold it long enough to aim, Fran was an inspiration. Both boys entered archery tournaments, frequently winning.

With a shotgun in a flurry of blasts, smoke, and powder Paul once bagged two rabbits and a partridge, all within five or six seconds, still Fran was the better hunter. He could hit rabbits, woodchucks, and deer with a rifle OR an arrow.

Having graduated the summer of 1949 this was Paul's best of times. Economic reality set in immediately. During that summer and fall, Paul lived with the Howard Slauson family in Halcottsville. Ray Slauson, a classmate and close friend, and Paul secured a job falling and clearing trees for the New York State Conservation Department. New York State was building a ski slope operation at Highmount, New York During the summer months and warm weather, working in the woods for good money and living with the Slausons seemed ideal.

Once snow was on the ground, even before Thanksgiving 1949, dropping a tree with an ax where it was supposed to go became more difficult. True, the leaves were off, and the wind had less effect, but standing on snow swinging an ax in the winter surely was not the life Paul would have envisioned.

Most of the crew of fifteen or eighteen men wielded double-bladed axes. They started at the bottom of each slope, gradually progressing upward narrowing the cleared area toward the crest of each slope. At the end of the day, each ax was sharpened then racked for use the following day. Since all the axes seemed identical, you were never quite sure if you had yours or not, though some of the true lumberjacks took there's home each day against the rules.

Paul became so proficient at dropping trees in precise spots, he had won some favor with the foreman, even though he lacked the muscle of more experienced woodsmen. Foreman Charley Bush gave Paul a yell, inquiring just where a tree about to fall would land. Eager to please the boss, who added or fired someone almost daily, Paul jumped down a mere two feet from where he was located, slipping slightly on the snow and barely touching the razor sharp ax on his left shoe.

The blood flowed quickly on the white snow making the wound of the little toe seem much worse than it was. The skin was cut, the little toe bone broken, but curiously very little pain, and the squeezed toe in an old pair of street shoes, stopped bleeding almost immediately. After a few papers were completed, Paul went back to Roxbury at the end of the day being told, they "would take care of everything," not quite knowing what that meant.
Paul was scheduled for an X-ray, which verified the bone was broken, as opposed to being cut.

It was a work-related injury, working for the great state of New York Conservation Department. Paul saw it as a temporary inconvenience. He fully expected to go back to work. His termination of employment notice was shortly received in the mail, along with an open voucher to be completed by a "hospital, surgeon, or health care professional." A termination check for one-month's work, a severance check, standard reimbursement for broken bones check, a supplemental check for pain or suffering, all if he would agree and accept being terminated, which, of course, had all ready happened.

Love The Government

The various checks totaled nearly a thousand dollars, the most money Paul had ever seen in one place. He signed and returned the forms. Thoughts of working outside in the winter at all, let alone with an ax, cow, horse, truck, or tractor, seemed now and for the first time, totally reprehensible.

Reading Gould's *Wizard of Wall Street* still another time, while "recovering," Paul recalled that Jay had gone over the mountain to Hobart with only fifty cents to his name, becoming an instant "accountant" in a tin shop when he was two-years younger than

Paul. And "I had a thousand dollars!" Still the checks continued, one canceling further employment rights, another "final" severance, and a termination of benefits agreement.

Meanwhile, Paul was hunting, shooting hoops, hanging out, with a burning desire, finally, like Jay and John, to escape by getting an education. Shirley Winne, an attractive Grand Gorge girl who had finally made a very successful attempt getting Paul over his "shyness," was off to school somewhere, it was time to move on.

Oops, what college would take him, even on probation?

Chapter 7:   Following Jay and John

By 1949, the more legitimate colleges were no longer hunting for mere bodies.   The Ivy League schools, in particular, were hunting for valedictorians and salutatorians.   Classmate Guy Numann, a whiz, went off to RPI; Wayland Mead to Cornell.   Paul was "dog meat." What to do?

Remember reading that cousins could be *mentors* too?   Dick Lutz had helped inspire the fishbait/worm business.   Gould provided the idea of cornering it.   Uncle Ray and wife Ida Ruteshouser Cronk's daughter Marian had graduated valedictorian at nearby Stanford, New York (June 1942) She had gained the second highest score ever recorded at the Stamford High School. Attractive, bright, personable, wealthy by the standards of the day, she chose Cornell University then attended Albany Business College (ABC).   Uncle Ray Cronk had also graduated ABC with high marks. Jay had started as an accountant. Paul stood in awe of his older, brighter, richer cousin Marian and she had gone to ABC.

There was a difference, however.   ABC would take anyone who could find the door, Paul could give it a try. So Paul, trying to think like Jay and John, and cousin Marian, left Roxbury and with a few bucks, enrolled at ABC, 1950, to start winter quarter. Like Gould's father, who said, "you're not much at home, you might as well go," Paul's father said. "You'll be back soon, you won't make it, you don't have what it takes." Giving Paul "one last shot," his father dropped him off at the bus stop in Herkimer, rather than taking him to 301 Hudson Avenue, Albany, New York

Paul always resented the fact that his father had "dumped" him at the bus stop. Was the "You won't make it" perversely intended to give Paul greater resolve? Well, Jay had apparently walked over Stamford Mountain to attend the Hobart School so Paul could do the same. To hell with him.

Albany Business College 1950 - 1952

Ploutz completed the entire two-year business administration, accounting and business law program with honors. He did it for himself, not to prove his father wrong, as he no longer cared what his father thought. He played "JV" basketball, became intercollegiate table tennis champion of New York State, and captain of the ABC tennis team. As president of the student government at ABC, among other duties and events, he escorted the **Albany Tulip Festival** Queen, Judy Vanderhoff, through the Annual Festival, with the Honorable Governor Thomas E. Dewey, of New York. It included dinner and hors d'oeuvres at the governor's mansion. Success, he had waited tables, worked various jobs, and like Jay and John, had done it alone. Paul's spark had been ignited.

Paul joined the Army National Guard, 27th Infantry Division Headquarters, Serial Number 21 900 201. Majoring in accounting, he was assigned to the finance section during the two weeks each summer that he was required to play "weekend warrior." Paul figured out what the troops were to be paid, rather than crawling through the sand at Camp Drum, New York Once again a *mentor*, Lieutenant Colonel Bernard Barsharer rapidly promoted him. Paul, a recruit, was promoted from private, private first class, corporal, sergeant, staff sergeant, all within a few years. An ABC classmate, Gordy Barth joined at the same time, and both spent two weeks each summer at the Camp Drum (now Fort Drum) sandtrap near Watertown, New York. Occasional "passes" to nearby Alexandria Bay did make the twoweek stint less annoying.

The local boy had shed the "highwater pants" and was learning to "schmooze" with the best of them, republicans in particular. He later supported the presidential campaigns of Republicans Thomas E. Dewey, Nelson Rockefeller, Dwight Eisenhower, Richard Nixon, two Bushes, several governors, and members of congress.

ABC Student Government

Paul's first year at Albany Business College was his first clear experience of academic success. A private, family-run college with an enrollment of a few hundred, individualized programs were encouraged. The second year, Paul was entrenched in JV basketball, serious table tennis, tennis and student government.

Rural Roxbury politics during the 1930s to 1950s were heavily republican, but New York State cities, New York City in particular, democrat. Father George was a committeeman in local republican politics, a relatively simple post. Admitted democrats in Roxbury had included only the Tylers and a few others.

Paul went to his fifth-grade class one day back in Roxbury with political buttons covering the front of his entire shirt. He had six rows of eight pins each (forty-eight states). In 1942, that would be Wendell Willkie and Charles McNary. Wearing a simple, thin, cotton pullover shirt, the sharp pins would frequently prick the skin in rows. Considering the ridiculous consequences of any sort of political response, teachers reluctantly ignored this foolish, often painful display. It did seem to serve as a primer for future political involvement.

Paul was learning rather early the grassroots, ground swell, smoke and mirrors, control, and manipulation games. Even in the 1949 RCS yearbook, a humor section suggests Paul becoming a United States senator. Well, some senator.

At ABC, the student government elected representatives from each class, accounting, law, secretarial, etc. rather casually. Class representatives then met and elected (chose) president, vice president, secretary, and treasurer. Paul went to a person in each class, suggesting they should run for representative, with suggestions on how to do it. Of course, if elected, then they would support Paul for president. Candidates often ran uncontested. The election process was rather casual, instructors suggesting, "Oh yes" we need to elect a class 'rep' today. Of course if two or three were running Paul did "as you would have done." Tell them what they need to hear to support you. In your spare time look up Jay Gould's statement "Honesty Is the Best Policy." He took care to be sure his friends, Jim Pendergast, Gordon Barth etc. were also elected. His "hand picked vice president" followed him into the presidency when Paul graduated.

Paul was elected president of the student government, Albany Business College, 1950 - 1951 by an overwhelming margin. Being student government president often put Paul in touch with the ABC owners, the Cornell family. Already friends with the family, because of his high profile as student athlete, Paul was, at last, the big "frog" he had dreamed of being.

Paul worked as a busboy and waiter at the then "upscale" Wellington Hotel. On weekends, he often did movie theatre ticket check investigations in Albany, Troy, and Schenectady, or nearby Vermont. He took a bus to a theatre in Vermont, or wherever, and tried to buy the first ticket of the performance. Later he would exit the theatre, change his shirt or jacket, and purchase a second ticket. The difference between the two numbers represented the number of paid tickets sold. Film companies are reimbursed based on the number of tickets sold. Theatre managers never expected college kids to be checkers.

Jacking Deer

One of the more interesting "jobs" Paul had landed with the help of Scout Master Stub Caswell was that of part-time game protector. Working with New York State Game Protectors Brian Burgin and Robert Van Benschoten both of Margaretville, gave his conservation credentials a great boost. A badge, brim hat and 38 revolver helped to alleviate his earlier feelings of lack of authority, power, and control.

He also got to inspect the "daily catch" of trout from Herman Osche, the old guy who had much earlier caught Paul fishing in Helen Anna's Lake. One of Herman's trout was barely the required seven inches long and Paul initially eager to "bust" him chose not to hold the grudge. The experience was likely a first for both Paul and old man Osche who had earlier "confiscated" Paul's catch.

One weekend back in Roxbury, Brian Burgin called asking Game Protector Ploutz to accompany him hunting for poachers "jacking deer." That's the shining of bright lights into a deer's eye, they stand still, you shoot them. Its usually easy and illegal. Around 2:00AM parked on a lonely country backroad flashlights could be seen with the beam playing back and forth hunting for deer. Brian and Paul quietly got out of the state vehicle and walked toward the flashlights in the field. Within a few minutes, three hunters, with high-powered rifles (30-06) with telescopic sights and flashlights attached, turned their lights on Brian Burgin and Paul Ploutz.

Obviously IF the lights were on Brian and Paul then the muzzle(s) were also pointing at them. At 6' 4" and 260 pounds Brian was an easy target. The three hunters, now together, and at approximately fifty yards distance, had their rifles trained on Brian and Paul. Deep in the woods, 2:00AM, three hunters in clear violation of law, with high-powered rifles, Brian and Paul had revolvers. It was a tense moment.

"I am Brian Burgin of the New York State Department of Conservation. Lower your lights toward the ground and continue walking toward me."

Brian took each rifle one by one, emptied the cartridges and handed the rifle and sling to Paul. Brian and Paul escorted the three back to the country road and the short distance back to the car. Brian asked them to sit in the rear of the car.

Brian summoned Paul to step outside for a brief conference as to his interpretation of events. Both agreed that though no shots were fired or deer even seen they were clearly "jacking" with no other reasonable explanation. Brian then "booked" them, keeping the rifles as evidence, and sent them on their way within walking distance back to their rented hunting lodge.

Paul and Brian were required to testify in court as all three said they were merely "Bored and out for a late evening stroll." They took their rifles along as they were after all "in the Catskills late at night" and they did live nearby. After several months, a jury trial was scheduled. All three were from Long Island (naturally) and were officers in a bank. The bank's board of directors were helpful. The three were informed that if they "won" well okay, but if they "lost" the bank could not continue to employ felons. The Long Islanders felt it too great a risk to go to trial, paid heavy fines, and the deer on Ferris Hill were once again safe.

Paul would occasionally hitch hike back to Roxbury on three-day weekends getting return rides with George Brower (1944) who was working at general electric in nearby Schenectady. Paul escorted Una Sweatman (1958) to her RCS junior prom, dated Diane Collins (salutatorian 1955), Susan Reynolds, summer guests from the Lee Croft Hotel, the summer help from Kass's Inn, Shirley Winne, and anyone else who was also home from college.

Shirley Winne's Grand Gorge high school friend Kay Pindar (local Grand Gorge prominent Chevrolet agency) and Paul did make a good couple and dated several times. Kay was bright, attractive, poised, articulate, unpretentious, wealthy, loyal, and moral. Moral, that was the problem. Kay did her best to speak *unsuccessfully* on behalf of her friend Shirley who was also a fine person by any reasonable measure. Kay married Paul's distant cousin Jack Lutz (1948) classmate to Paul's brother Raymond. Jack was also a "winner" (check the accomplishments of the Lutz family (**Part IV**). Paul never knew what happened to Shirley Winne.

Paul's sister Elsie and brother-in-law Euclid Proper, James Proper (Superintendent Schools 2000) father, owned a magnificent four-door blue Chrysler sedan and were generous in loaning it when

Paul came home for weekends. The old Royal farm on Burroughs Road had an especially private hidden driveway that was ideal for entertaining Mitzi Broome or other eager teenagers. The wealthy Broome sisters lived in one of Roxbury's finest houses where Professor Snow (Teichmann's *mentor* at NYU) had lived. Mitzi's sister hated Paul feeling that her sister "could do better."

Paul felt a bit like Robin Hood in that the more the sophisticated Judy disapproved, the greater her rogue sister's attachment was to Paul. Both girls attended RCS a few years then went to private boarding schools, as Roxbury was simply "not adequate for their proper development." Paul, the poor struggling farm boy, had been told that it was "just as easy to fall in love with a rich girl as a poor one." At the time, he still believed that it was much to early for anything else other than a summer affair. Paul and Mitzi Broome wrote to each other for a while when he was at ABC and she was at some fine academy for girls.

Paul took as many paying jobs as he could. During the intervening summer of 1950, he worked as head camp counselor at the Greer School for Boys at Hope Farm, New York Most of the boys and girls were early teenagers, usually orphans. Paul enjoyed the position of considerable responsibility and it may have set the stage for his later teaching at the junior high school level. The brief summer "guidance" position helped him realize that he could be a *mentor*! The counselor's job had been incredibly successful, rewarding, fulfilling.

An ABC classmate, and World War II purple heart recipient Richard Cronk (no relation to Paul & Roxbury Cronks) had graduated from the Greer School and lined up the job for Paul. Living several places during the two years at ABC was precarious. The address in 301 Hudson Ave. Albany and one other place burned. Cronk turned out to be a pot smoker, often drunk, who would need to wrestle Paul to the floor before eating Paul's few groceries from the refrigerator. With three living at the near campus location the rent was right.

In 1952, pot was still so difficult for Cronk to locate that Paul thought he could endure Cronk until the end of the term. Paul did smoke a cigar on occasion to celebrate a birth, wedding, or to be one of the boys, but has never inhaled. Much later in the mid 1970s when Ohio University president Harry Crewson was a guest at the Ploutz residence and "lit up," Paul walked past the other guests and asked the president to extinguish his cigar. Paul took "no prisoners" on the smoking issue.

Brad and Prentiss Cornell Jr, both professors and sons of the owner of ABC, took a liking to nonsmoking, nondrinking, eagle scout Ploutz, who would then escort their wealthy widow friends to the park, dog shows, and on occasion, college receptions, where they seemed eager to make financial contributions. Paul's tips were out of all proportion to time involved, and Paul admitted learning a great deal about "finances and accounting" hanging out with the elite. So far above his station, he found both humor and great satisfaction in the arrangement. Still an amazingly pure, naive, simple country boy at nineteen, it was years later, before he realized he could have probably solved his humble financial origins by being, well, a gigolo.

The Boyce Sisters

The elderly Boyce sisters frequented the Wellington hotel where Paul was bussing dishes. Gradually, they became acquainted. Upon learning he was also Dutch Reformed, they invited him to attend church, then dinner at their elegant Albany apartment. Peering out of his rooming house window Sunday morning at 10:00 A.M. sharp, Paul was a bit disappointed they were not there to pick him up. They knew of the Gould church back in Roxbury, and also spoke of the "mother" church both in Holland, Michigan, and Amsterdam, Holland.

All dressed up with no place to go, Paul walked down the flight of stairs out on the sidewalk. The chauffeur of the long black Cadillac, that had been sitting there all along, promptly opened the door, to admit the startled newly sophisticated country bumpkin.

Church went okay but the chauffeur seemed startled that Paul would attempt to assist the sisters, getting in and out, especially since Paul had all ready volunteered unsuccessfully to sit up front with him.

Upon arriving at the brownstone apartment house for lunch (not dinner, as it would have been called in Roxbury, supper would have been at 6:00), the doorman briefly left his post to escort folks to the elevator, activating the button to the proper floor. The maid took their wraps and Paul's well-worn jacket in to the foyer, offering unidentified hors d'oeuvres before "dinner," make that lunch.

Hungry but intimidated, seeing far too much silver surrounding the plate he thought might be his, he started to·sit. The chauffeur, having parked the limo, seemed to appear instantaneously to seat everyone carefully, then hitch all forward into proper eating position. Paul's using the butter knife to spread butter on a roll was the clue they needed. Paul's newest *mentors* then gracefully instructed him, as to which spoon, which fork, several of each, went where. So caring, gracious in manner, gentle in approach, the lump in Paul's throat real, this "random act of kindness" had a far greater impact on young Ploutz than they could have ever known.

More than seven years after Paul left the Albany area, he was in graduate school in Colorado, without money to make it home for Christmas. The Boyce sisters each sent a check for twenty-five dollars. Once again the kindness of others made Paul's life richer. In later years, often thinking of the Boyce sisters, he visited the "mother" church in Holland (Michigan) and Amsterdam. *Mentors* serve in many ways. Sometimes years pass before one realizes a *mentor* was influential in the path taken.

A few weeks prior to graduation, spring of 1951, ABC's placement service arranged for an interview in Schenectady, New York, with John F. Gonsa. Gonsa was comptroller for the Breslaw Brothers chain of twelve large department stores in the Albany area, with headquarters entitled Martin Exchange Ltd., in downtown Schenectady. Martin was the only son of the owner, Mr. Jay Breslaw. Paul took the job at forty-eight dollars per week as office manager of twenty-four female employees, working as Mr. Gonsa's assistant. Paul ran the new vintage accounting machine that was Mr. Breslaw's pride and joy, securing Paul's post in the company. All company purchases and payments of the twelve stores passed through Paul, who was quickly promoted to assistant comptroller at fifty-eight dollars per week. Jay would have been proud.

Now, like Jay Gould, finally an accountant on his own, no car, but saving a whopping fifteen dollars a week, Paul was mindful of his father's "You won't make it, You don't have what it takes." Now, he earned the right for major leaps in self-confidence.

Since Paul was also doing the payroll, he discovered that Martin Breslaw, who he had only seen twice during his eight months there, was making a whopping $11,500 per year.

Mr. Gonsa at $125 per week had to make an effort to conceal his contempt for both Jay and Martin Breslaw, saying that "Even the other Jews, call them kikes," a name of apparent disrespect, that Paul had not even heard in Roxbury.

Trustworthy, Loyal, etc.

One day at lunch, Mr. Gonsa suggested he would like to replace Paul's battered old Timex watch with something special, worthier of his loyalty and the wonderful job he was doing. He had hired Paul, who recalled, "I babysat for John Gonsa and his wife a time or two. John had approved every raise I even suggested, he was a good man, doing a good job, also looking out for me." After lunch, John escorted Paul to the jewelry counter of the main store downstairs from the office. The jewelry buyer for the firm, and Mr. Gonsa, selected a $125 elegant, Benrus three Star watch with gold band that they thought looked best on Paul, tossing his "still running" Timex into the trash.

After Paul's, "Thank you, thank you, you shouldn't have" response, out of the way, Mr. Gonsa replied, "Oh by the way, there is a minor favor you could do for me. Every so often, when you are running jewelry invoices through the accounting machine, punch furniture instead." More a prank to make the jewelry department post more profit than furniture, Paul complied with the request. It wasn't fair, but Paul knew how he had gotten the watch.

Years later, Paul realized it was perhaps only a simple prank, an indiscretion, yet wondered how he could have handled it better. Having read "The Wizard" book about Gould numerous times, Paul wondered how Gould had "cooked the books" in the Hobart tin shop, the Prattsville Tannery, and elsewhere.

At this juncture, Gould and Paul "parted company." Jay might have figured out how to own the store or at least the jewelry department! Paul loved the watch, the power, recognition, modest control, and would have probably done the same thing again. Nevertheless, even with all those wonderful *mentors*, he was still an eagle scout. It was a small test of integrity, but Paul felt that "he had flunked it."

Returning to Roxbury weekends and holidays by hitchhiking or bumming rides, Paul was able to maintain contact with school chums, even those returning home from college. After church one day, the Reverend Lubin, Gould Church pastor, inquired as to how things were going. After telling him about the watch incident, and noticing Paul's moral concern, he suggested that given the circumstance, he had handled it reasonably well. Reverend Lubin, to Paul's absolute surprise, suggested that with his "gift of gab" Paul would make "a great minister or attorney."

Attorneys and Ministers

Glen Young, Herman Lubin, and the Gould church, had played an important role with the Ploutz family. Baptized there, receiving a youth fellowship, and through church participation, young Paul sung a solo or two at the regular Sunday services.

The only attorney Paul had ever met was an elderly Ralph Ives, who, along with Uncle Ray Cronk, had taken Paul fishing several summers in the most primitive sections of Northern Quebec. The Ives had long been an admired Roxbury family, seemingly incapable of making enemies. One of the sons, Charley, "Doc" Ives had earlier set Paul's badly broken wrist after a high school soccer encounter. (see **Part II**, Ives)

Attorney Ives, an older *"mentor,"* was a friend to be trusted. Earlier, Ralph Ives the attorney had also suggested that Paul consider the "bar."

Social, and outgoing, being an accountant (even flunky comptroller) no longer seemed enough. Attorney Ives and Reverend Lubin were probably right, a successful fast talking graduate of ABC, in accounting/business law, would make a good minister. No, lawyer. Lawyer!

Returning to Breslaw Brothers the following Monday, Paul called the Albany Law School, also in Schenectady, to schedule an entrance appointment.

The dean was encouraging, but observed that Paul would have to find another year of college somewhere. They liked applicants to have a four-year college degree, but would accept three years. They could accept the two years completed at ABC, even though not fully accredited, but Paul would still need "one more year."

Ploutz homestead, Hardscrabble Road, 1935

Horses, Ned, Harry, Paul, Raymond and Anna pitching hay. Ploutz Farm approximately 1942.

Ray, Paul and mother Anna harvesting at the Ploutz Farm. No mechanical equipment working dawn to dusk.

The Still Standing "Extortion" pole 1/2 mile on left, Hardscrabble Road, Roxbury, N.Y. Picture taken September 16, 2003

George, the stern father's first new car. Hardscrabble Farm, 1940.

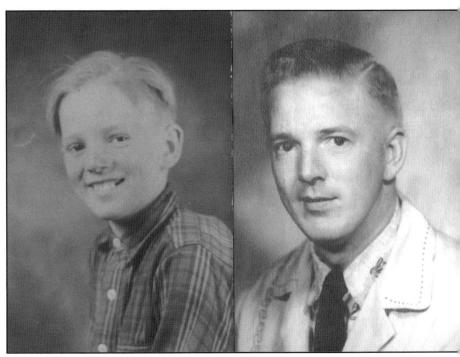

From "Pee Wee" to "Whitey"
Paul, age 14, 1945

Paul, age 20, 1951

R-L: sister Elsie, Ray Gockel, Paul, Raymond and George in rear. Sunday picnic to Locust Grove, Gilboa, 1941. They look sad because George has scolded them again.

95-E

Ploutz second home (1948) Lake Street, Roxbury Village.
Locals refer to the street as "Frog Alley"

Roxbury Central School

THIS CERTIFIES THAT

Paul Frederick Ploutz

having satisfactorily completed the four year Course of Study as prescribed by the Board of Education is hereby entitled to this

HIGH SCHOOL DIPLOMA

Given under our hands at Roxbury, New York, this twenty-seventh day of June, A. D., One thousand nine hundred forty-nine

Roderick C. Dorrance
SUPERVISING PRINCIPAL

Ernest Schumann
PRESIDENT, BOARD OF EDUCATION

1,850 other Roxbury youth have one...
(1901 - 2000)

Paul Ploutz

Baseball 1,2,3,4; Basketball 1,2,3,4; Boy Scouts 1,2,3,4; Class Officer 3,4; Intramural Winner 1,2,3,4; Magazine Campaign 1,2,3,4; Manager 1; Movie Operator 1,2,3,4; Prize Speaking 1,2,3,4; Record Board 3,4; Senior Play 4; Soccer 4; Varsity "R" Award 2,4

High School Yearbook 1949

Chapter 8:   Oneonta State Teachers College

Oneonta or "STC" for State Teachers College was the closest college around. It was just thirty-six miles from Grand Gorge, where Paul's parents, George and Anna, now lived, running a small restaurant and the other kind of "bar." Anna, at least, had agreed to help with tuition from money earned from the Crossing Restaurant. There were two train tracks there crossing New York State Route 30. Paul, for no apparent reason, dubbed the place "the Double Crossing Restaurant."

Albany Law School had required any three years of college as prerequisite to admittance.   Oneonta was a teacher's college, "a walk in the park." Paul planned to attend STC for one year, return to Albany, and attend Albany Law School. What a plan!

In the late summer of 1952, after giving a fast thirty-day resignation notice to Breslaw Brothers, Paul moved into a boarding house with a retired couple at 2 Potter Avenue, in Oneonta, New York. The eight dollars a week room rent, with Paul's persuasion, quickly converted to twelve dollars per week, room and board. In an equally fast decision, Anna helped to buy a '49 Ford four-door sedan to get around with, even though State Teachers College was walking distance. At age twenty-one, with first wheels and decent clothes, the assistant comptroller was enrolled as a freshman majoring in elementary education, or whatever. Paul needed a third year of college, anything.

A couple of years older than most freshmen, Paul was able to talk his way out of wearing a "beanie." He had only been on campus for a few days when his first guest speaker, Eleanor Roosevelt presented an evening lecture in the main college lecture hall. As an uncompromising republican, and with only a dozen or so democrats in all of Roxbury, he was reluctant to go but was encouraged to "attend" college functions.

Eleanor shrieked away for an hour or so in her usual high pitched voice. Problem was Paul, who knew she was lying, had agreed with much of what she had said. The speech was over, the mike still on, when an elderly blue-haired lady made her way up the stairs to the stage and to Eleanor.

"Oh Mrs. Roosevelt that was a wonderful speech and I want you to know that I have voted a straight democratic ticket for fifty-five years." Eleanor instantaneously replied "How courageous of you." The retort carried out across the audience of six or eight-hundred and a dozen or so older people chuckled approvingly. It was several days before Paul understood the irony of what he had heard and realized that he had a great deal to learn. Twenty-five years later (1977) he had learned alot. Tact, however, was apparently not one of the things he had learned.

Ohio University, Athens, Ohio, where Paul was "full" professor, had recently completed a magnificent seven-story library in the center of campus. It was Ohio's oldest university (1804). The trustees had decided to name it after Dr. Vernon R. Alden, the current president. At a tea reception or whatever it was, Paul chortled to Vernon that "In as much as you're still alive the trustees are taking somewhat of a chance." (Buildings are usually named after a person who is deceased) Like Eleanor Roosevelt, and without hesitation, President Alden retorted "Why thank you Paul, you're the first one to call that to my attention." Again, it was several days before Alden's appropriate comment sunk into Paul's Roxbury brain. Think about it.

In 1952, Oneonta State had a student population of about 680 students devoted entirely to elementary education. To this day, elementary education is still largely a female occupation. In 52 the enrollment was essentially six-hundred or more girls, and about eighty males, some of whom were married veterans and not in the active gene pool. Do the math; the ratio was 10:1, considering the veterans!

Paul had made the basketball team at RCS. Paul made the basketball team at little Albany Business College, but when he managed to get on the STC JV team, he spent most of the time on the bench, so he quit. Having no status himself, he had never cared about fraternities because he saw them as social crutches. He joined Sigma Tau Gamma anyway and was active for a few months. When pals Paul Longo, Peter Bielski, and others joined the "other" fraternity (Delta something) Paul dropped out. The Delts were the jocks on campus but curiously also had Don Newell, Paul's first realizations that some males were of a different persuasion.

Out of the fraternity scene, Paul became sports editor of the student newspaper and enjoyed putting his take on the college's sporting events. His spirited editorials actually increased the circulation even though he was not shy mentioning his own successes. When he won the New York State Intercollegiate Table

Tennis Championship, his trophy and extra copies of the news were everywhere. He made both the ABC and STC tennis teams (captain) but was never the tennis star that an earlier Roxbury Boy Frank Booth (1904) was. Frank toured Europe, Paul was essentially "just another player."

To gain a degree in elementary education candidates had to play the piano or at least simple one-hand notes to lead children singing. Music professor Esther Hubbard had noticed Paul's academic success. First semester, Paul received the highest grade point average of the eighty males enrolled in the program. Since he was in the National Guard, the draft exempt status wasn't in effect anyway. Miss Hubbard suggested that Paul take piano lessons for an entire year, as passing this course was required for graduation. After piano lessons for one year, Miss Hubbard said, "I have never seen anyone try so hard, yet fail so miserably."

Although a bit out of the ordinary, Miss Hubbard suggested that Paul memorize a couple of songs to play and suggest them to the examiner. Paul memorized Silent Night and Santa Lucia, in the key of C. For the "review" he placed the score on the piano and did his rendition as he had practiced dozens of times.

The examiner, generally pleased, mentioned he had passed though he had "missed a note or two." Paul felt at a loss as to how Burroughs might have handled this and he didn't have enough money for Gould's method, bribery.

Paul had always loved science, going back to science teacher "Willie" Crawford, in Roxbury. In addition to the "Mickey Mouse" education classes, numerous science courses were required. Additional science courses, of a wide variety, could also be taken as electives.

A vibrant sex life in such an environment was predictable. Paul had truly been a textbook case "late bloomer" both mentally and physically, so he had a great deal of catching up to do. The local Grants store in downtown Oneonta was one of the favorite off campus hangouts. Three girls alleged to be the most attractive in the entire city of Oneonta, Mary Dyer, Paula Spazianni, and Gretchen Billings served at the soda fountain rather than the dry goods section. In one of the more impressive highlights of his reign of exploitation Paul became "friends" with all three. By today's standards, sexual predator or male chauvinist pig would seem the more appropriate term. In the mid 1950s, however he and others of his ambition were considered "eligible bachelors."

Another great sexual/academic technique which he thought he invented was to start evenings in the college library. The professors would see him there, a positive move, and he could get his serious academic pursuits achieved. He hated the smoke from the bars anyway and you ran into "a better class of student in the library" than the bars! With the college ratio 10:1 picking up girls in the library was, not a pun more of a smile, "like shooting fish in a barrel."

Paul was sowing "wild oats" by night, and praying for crop failure days. Then at the suggestion of his newest *mentor,* Professor Dr. T. C. Helvey, Paul was persuaded to discontinue his "record keeping of co-ed conquests," then at a satisfying forty-seven. Achieving control, power, and self-esteem, through sex is historically well documented. Paul, the abused farm boy thirsted for <u>control, power and self-esteem</u>. Sisters, a mother, and daughter, five different girls in two days, he did follow Professor's Helvey's advice, he just didn't keep score anymore.

So much for law school. By carrying more than the standard fifteen credit hours each semester, and by attending summer school, Paul completed the four-year program in three years, with an extra minor in science. He got all A's, and B's, (save three courses), and graduated with highest honors. Professors of science, Emery Will, Robert Johnson, Ellis Whitaker, T.C. Helvey, and others were all *mentors.* All were gifted teachers who took an interest in Paul. Paul forgot about law school. Instead, by deciding to teach music, art, science, and literature, Paul had a totally new career goal.

Student Teaching

Part of training necessary to obtain a degree in elementary education included two classroom student teaching experiences. Mr. John Gainey, fifth-grade teacher at the Percy I. Bugbee Laboratory School, found Paul's teaching performance, while academically superior "A", was limited in classroom demeanor, "C". His final grade was "B" for the first half of the student teacher experience. One problem student named John deliberately flipped a paint dish from a girl's hand, splattering her face, clothing, desk, ceiling, and floor. Paul restrained John, backing him up against an in-class metal locker, producing a metal rattling sound echoing from other lockers. Paul was admonished for "restraining the boy," as he was only "expressing himself." When Paul explained to Mr. Gainey that he too "was expressing himself," Paul's lower grade of "B" was sealed.

Paul's next student teaching assignment was at Oneonta junior High, teaching seventh and eighth-grade math and science. Principal Miss Edna Tripp, supervising teacher Leta Adee, and the other twenty teachers "were of the old school." They may have felt that John Dewey and Dr. Spock were communists posing as educators. Desks were straight rows, screwed to the floor, students often standing to recite, in the event they were called upon.

In the new environment, the same Paul was now perceived as a bit liberal. Miss Adee, was a superior teacher, fully determined to teach Paul the "max." Students and other teachers respected her. Another *mentor*, it was a wonderful teaching and learning experience.

With *mentors* like Principal Tripp and Miss Leta Adee, Paul was gaining increased respect for teaching, and less and less for attorneys. The second student teaching assignment at seventh grade was so successful that upon graduation Paul declined an offer to teach fifth grade at Mount Kisko, New York, for $3,800 per year, in favor of teaching at Oneonta Junior High for $3,000.

Confidence, Over Confidence, and Arrogance

During 1955 through 1958, Paul became a superior teacher of math and science. He supervised student teachers and started a science club, a chess club, and a hunter safety education club (New York State Department of Conservation). He was active in Junior Chamber of Commerce; New York State Field Archery Association, Boy Scouts, merit badge attainment, taught adult education; was promoted to sergeant in the National Guard, became a part time game protector with the New York State Conservation Department (brim hat, badge, gun), and was part of the local Oneonta Education Association, NEA, and NSTA. Finally, years of perceived inadequacy were being reversed with success, attention, recognition, and self-esteem.

Paul was floating so far above the ground that Doris Moon's, Junior High School guidance counselor's assessment of Paul as "God's gift to the teaching profession," was perceived as sincere recognition of his efforts, rather than sarcasm.

Mrs. Hazel Mahon, senior teacher and matron of the Junior High School, often disagreed with Paul at weekly faculty meetings. In one emotional exchange, Mrs. Mahon staged her contempt and longevity with the usual "In *aaaalllllll* my thirty years of experience" where upon Paul calmly interrupted, and explained that she didn't have thirty years of experience! Just "One year of experience, thirty times." How endearing Paul had become.

John Delaney, STC director of student teaching, consented to write a letter of "recommendation" for Paul's employment resume. In the mid 1950s letters of recommendation were still confidential. Nonetheless, Paul learned that Delaney wrote, "Paul has an air of superiority which offends many people." Some recommendation.

An academic trick, still available, is to have your credentials mailed to a "friend" with the agreement that he or she will provide the information to you. Paul was still learning to "control" matters. It was several years before Paul discovered and removed Delaney's candid "recommendation," which Paul had always perceived as a stab in the back.

One consequence of growing up with critical, perfectionist, abusive, or even absent fathers, as was the case with Jason Gould, John Burroughs, and Paul, is that children develop low self-esteem. Then, hopefully these children develop an enormous need, a drive to succeed. Any psychology book could reveal that Gould's and Ploutz's arrogance was a cover for how insecure they really felt about themselves. Arrogance in others is incredibly annoying, Delaney was probably right. It just shouldn't have been in an agreed "recommendation."

Paul's membership in the "Albany" National Guard had been conveniently transferred to Company "C," an infantry "foot soldier" battalion in Oneonta. Paul, now a sergeant, was initially simply reporting in each Monday evening as a member of his Albany finance group, assisting the company clerk, Sergeant Charley Shearer, with records. Captain Bruce Shearer, (no relation to Charley Shearer) company commander asked/assigned Paul to assume the post of recruiting sergeant.

Sergeant Ploutz, working with company clerk Sergeant Shearer made contact with area high school students or others over eighteen years of age. They increased membership in "C" Company from 60 or so to more than 130 in a few years. Captain Shearer was so impressed with Paul, for having filled his ranks and gaining attention from the battalion commander, that the Captain convinced Paul to transfer his Albany headquarters finance status to the local Oneonta infantry company.

A Tactical Military Error

Paul became a platoon sergeant. With the ranks now having been filled with bodies, he taught others to field strip their M-1's and to perform other tasks associated with troops, who were taught and thought to be "cannon fodder" in land wars.

Working as an instructor in the Guard, with teaching experience, was laboriously simple for Paul. Captain Bruce Shearer, another local teacher, also worked a moving van operation. The captain, who was short and weighed perhaps 130 pounds, may have suffered from "small man complex" as well as being easily threatened. Shearer convinced Paul, still the fair-haired sergeant, to attend Officer's Candidate School, the OCS, where "90-day wonder school" converted heathens into officers.

On Shearer's word, and certain of acceptance to OCS, Paul enrolled at Cornell University summer session, paying the tuition and attending classes, in lieu of the typical two weeks at Camp Drum, New York It was further agreed that if for ANY reason OCS was delayed, cancelled, whatever, Paul was to be discharged, having otherwise completed his duty, with further draft immunity, both as to being a science teacher and with "sole surviving son" status.

Poor Bruce Shearer, upon opening his "military mail," discovered that as of a "particular date," no discharges, transfers, promotion of any sort were to take place, so ordered by Lieutenant Colonel William F. Sheehan, Battalion Commander. This meant that Shearer's OCS, or discharge commitment to Paul, had been effectively countermanded.

With fifteen or twenty companies under his command, who could blame Sheehan for wanting to take thousands of troops to Camp Drum for summer camp without processing dates, alterations, discharges, or other papers? He needed a precise head count.

Shearer was in a bind: bother the colonel with the "OCS" explanation or "withdraw" a commitment made to a sergeant in his own command? You guessed it! Captain Shearer sent a registered letter to Ploutz at Cornell University, ordering Paul to withdraw and report to Camp Drum. "Failure to comply will result in your arrest, incarceration and/or delivery to Camp Drum."

Paul dropped out of the two physics courses he had nearly completed which were to have helped him finish a master's degree in science. Tuition, and room expenses that had been paid in advance were forfeited.

It was an academic disaster, but the worst was yet to come. Paul left Ithaca, New York, (Cornell) drove to Camp Drum, and reported in at Shearer's Company C. At Camp Drum, Ploutz, in lieu of conventional barracks, was quartered in a small adjacent pup tent. To demonstrate what happens to soldiers who make it awkward for the captain, Paul dug latrines during the day, until blood flowed from the blisters on his palms. Inasmuch as Paul did "obey" the order, to this day, it is still unclear as to why Shearer, having broken his pledge, went to such lengths to "discipline" Ploutz.

Admittedly the worst combination of military, academic, or social injustice experienced, it lasted only two weeks. Telephone calls off base were difficult to arrange, but Ploutz managed one call, reaching his state assemblyman, Edward Mason who served Delaware and surrounding counties. Mason, sent Paul a registered letter at Camp Drum. Paul was brought to Shearer's office, and handed the letter "Official State Envelope" by First Sergeant Harry Baldo, with Captain Shearer present, inquiring of "its contents."

Ploutz, standing at attention, hands bleeding, replied, "I believe any order to open or reveal the contents of this letter, to be a violation of both federal and state law. I further request a meeting with the Judge Advocate General (JAG)". Paul did not reveal the contents of Mason's letter, but the mere presence of it, along with his brief statement did have an effect.

1. Pup tent dismantled, he returned to enlisted men's barracks, Sergeant's room.
2. No further harassment, duty, or digging.

3. Issued a "pass" to visit, party, or travel off base (used pass with first Sergeant Harry Baldo)

4. A surprise visit (chance or circumstance) to Company C from previous "boss" Lieutenant Colonel Bernard Barsherer, Division Headquarters, Finance Unit, inquiring as to how "Sergeant Ploutz was doing?" Shearer allegedly suggesting "Not so well," The Colonel remarking that Paul had always been helpful with Finance and he "would be pleased to have him back."

5. Upon returning to Oneonta and normal life, he was immediately granted an honorable discharge, after six years in the National Guard on a "sole surviving son" clause, orchestrated by the Honorable Edward Mason, Assembly State of New York The politician the moral hero, the captain morally wanting, how backward.

The wonderfully successful six years, 1952 to 1958, in Oneonta provided Paul a great environment. Aged twenty-one to twenty-six Paul had some opportunity in which to overcome the effects of leadedpaint and pipes, diseases, under nourishment, physical abuse, academic weakness, being bullied, even poverty.

Chapter 9:   A First Year Teacher

Oneonta Junior High

In the first year at Oneonta Junior High School, 1955, Paul had the conventional homeroom assignment. Teachers often moved to the students, rather than students constantly moving from class to class. Additionally, Paul was teaching five different classes, a variety of math, science, and English classes at whatever grade level was most needed. As the "last man in" Paul was assigned to whatever classes hadn't been spoken for, or demanded, by the longevity of existing teachers.

Okay at math, and a science "whiz," Paul recalled an eighth-grade student, Elaine Dommermuth, helping Paul determine the difference between verbs, adverbs, and nouns, proper or otherwise. Paul openly admitted it was not a case of the "blind leading the blind" as Elaine "knew the difference!" The two-year associate degree in accounting and law from ABC was more helpful.

Superintendent Harold Hager needed someone to teach general business at the junior high school to ninth-grade "boneheads." Principal Tripp, not wanting to "give him up" from science, reluctantly yielded Paul the interview. Miss Tripp, eager to keep Paul, coached him on how to avoid the additional assignment. Dr. Hager was a "little strange," his "Dr." was honorary from Hartwick College, which didn't even offer a doctoral program.

The secretary ushered Paul in front of the superintendent's desk. Paul stood motionless while Hager also sat motionless, perhaps sizing each other up? Having been warned about the intimidating technique, Paul waited patiently, but relaxed. Coached on not having or wanting the job anyway, he waited and, waited, finally uttering, "well?" Having learned "body language" in Psychology 101, Paul, secure with the mind-game contest, and knowing that Hager wanted him to teach general business to boneheads, Paul politely declined, knowing fullwell he'd finally end up with the job anyway.

Hager:	It would be an honor with prestige to teach the class.
Paul:	I am already teaching five classes.

Hager:	One of the other classes could be discontinued, and besides I'll add one-hundred dollars to your base salary.
Paul:	My first loyalty is to Miss Tripp, and further, since Albany Business College was not fully accredited, perhaps I couldn't be certified anyway, and one-hundred doesn't get you very far.
Hager:	Young man, I'm the superintendent of schools, I can certify a monkey to teach algebra, I will reduce your load by two classes and increase your salary three-hundred, now is there anything else?
Paul:	Thank you for this opportunity, which I accept, subject only to Miss Tripp's approval, as my principal is entitled to my time and loyalty.

Edna Tripp approved, as though she had a choice. Paul added "bone head" business to his schedule, all three came away happy.

And Still More Mentors

Six years in Oneonta, Paul, once described, was like getting "off the farm a second time." He was less naïve, eager for challenges, new experiences, and he was confident. Paul was enthusiastic to take on the world in the same way Jay went to New York City with his mousetrap, and John to Washington, D.C. Mother, Anna, had once remarked on the advantages of "Hanging out with people smarter than you are." With his high school record, graduating seventh of a class of twelve, it wasn't that hard to find smarter people!

Ron (Ronald) Walley taught at Oneonta Junior High School. Sixth graders prayed to be positioned in one of the sixth grades (of 3) that Ron taught. In addition to being a gifted teacher (*mentor*) Ron was ever eager to teach Paul teaching skills. Ron and wife Marge were avid church participants and always "shut down" on Sundays. Ron owned a small powerboat on nearby Goodyear Lake. Marge did not think it prudent to swim or water ski on Sundays. Outwardly conservative Ron was a "new-age" religious thinker. He considered his crowning achievement publishing *Eyes to See and*

Ears to Hear, The Way of Conscious Love for the Churches (Ron Walley 1979, Vantage Press. Ron was sure the book would "turn Christianity upside down." It's probably a "rare book" by now as few buyers took interest.

Ron and Paul taught hundreds of Junior High students how to water ski. Of course Paul could also use the boat by himself. Better still, Paul's cousin Richard Lutz owned a small cabin on the lake that Paul could use. Years after leaving Oneonta, Paul would visit Ron and Marge Walley's small doublewide home near Goodyear Lake.

At long last, secure enough to be "second fiddle," Paul became friends with several older overachievers, who seemed equally eager to help a young man who recognized their prominence. Ellis Whitaker was a biologist with STC. Sarcastic, Whitaker once called Paul a "sod buster" in an advanced ecology class he had managed to enroll in. Even as an undergraduate, Paul, impressed Whitaker and routinely ended up with an "A" in most of the science courses taken from him and others. Paul, having written an ecology paper on plant succession about the (swamp) river below Roxbury Village, invited the good professor to visit him. Borrowing Uncle Ray Cronk's rowboat that was tied up at the shore, Paul rowed the doubting professor out into the swamp to observe for himself the five stages (swamp to hardwood trees) of plant succession.

Paul rowed through duck weed, and algae, with water only a foot or two deep. Several huge snapping turtles paddled vigorously to gain deeper water. Paul rowing, the elderly biologist quickly stood up in the rear of the small boat, drew a revolver, and blazed away at several huge snappers. Whitaker nearly fell. The air was rancid from gunpowder.

Empty cartridges landed in the water. With reoccurring echoes from around the valley, the professor acknowledged the authenticity of Paul's ecology paper. The smoke having cleared Whitaker, only briefly embarrassed, was concerned that Paul keep the confidence that not a single turtle had been wounded!

A few weeks later, Professor Whitaker called Paul to his desk after class and invited him to fish in Catherine Creek with him. Large trout from Seneca Lake run upstream creating a fisherman's paradise. Paul caught a monster trout on a small "phoebe' metal lure with an inexpensive spinning rod.

Dr. Whitaker got "skunked" with the finest rod money could buy, but enjoyed the trip with his new Nash car produced with fold down seats for sleeping. American Motor Company, George Romney may have helped start the movement toward all-purpose vehicles (APV).

Television was relatively new. Dr. Whitaker and department chairman Dr. Emory Will had been provided the opportunity to produce a science program for WGY, Schenectady to show how television could be used for education. Paul's first ever bird identification program on TV! Using stuffed birds to show on television for identification was new, cool. Paul was wondering if idol Burroughs would come alive-he so repudiated the practice of killing, let alone *stuffing* birds.

Kenneth Lockridge, a professional photographer, was also president of the New York State Field Archer Association. In the fall of 1956, on a Friday afternoon, Ken and Paul, both avid archers, agreed to provide a 7-8-9th grade local assembly at Oneonta Junior High School where Paul was a teacher. Shooting balloons, with straw targets, amid admiring "ooh's and ah's," Mr. Lockridge announced that he and their science teacher, Ploutz, would immediately depart to go deer hunting in the Adirondacks.

A photographer has connections. Pictures and a flattering article were in the local *Oneonta Star* immediately. After providing a well-publicized assembly, and well before daylight, the following day Ken drove his station wagon, picked Paul up, and drove to Lake Meacham, in Franklin County in the Adirondacks.

On that cool, but pleasant sunny fall day, Ken gave Paul instructions as to where to walk and wait as he would walk, then circle the small loop back toward Paul. Accomplished archers, some camouflaging, they checked wind direction, locked the car, and departed. Within minutes, in heavy underbrush, two doe ran directly toward Paul, stopping barely thirty yards distance, not seeing or sensing danger.

Paul used a sixty-two pound draw "Grizzly" bow and 11/32 wooden arrows with bodkin head. The first arrow struck the deer from directly in front. The doe dropped on the spot. Only the nock was left visible, the thirty inch arrow all but disappeared. The second doe, closer and startled, also ran straight toward Paul. The second arrow barely cleared the bow before striking in the same front center location under the neck. Two deer, all in about fifteen minutes, and it was still early Saturday morning.

The "great white hunter" archery story and assembly before several hundred students was being circulating in Oneonta and surrounding counties.

Lockridge was immediately sad and glad. Shooting a deer "for" him wasn't even legal, let alone given the dilemma of his position as president of the New York State Field Archer Association! What to do? Like Professor Whitaker missing the snapping turtles, Paul promised to conceal the events. Paul and Ken returned to Oneonta, two deer on the fenders, more pictures in the papers, all within twenty-four hours of the much-publicized assembly. What a deal. Forty-six years later, Paul is now finally revealing the truth about the coup and about a great friend, archer, photographer, family man, *mentor* and community activist.

Professor T. Charles Helvey, Mentor

Professor T. Charles Helvey, was a gifted researcher. With only a two hour break between classes at STC now SUNY, (State University of New York) Helvey would find Paul, and then the two would soar the hills around Oneonta in Helvey's small private plane. "Each landing felt like a crash." Helvey *was* an inspiration, but a lousy pilot.

T. Charles Helvey bought Paul his first camera, showing him how to take pictures through a microscope. Dr. Helvey showed Paul the proper way to drink vodka, spoon of sugar, downed by a shot glass of vodka. Mrs. Helvey remarked it "was also good for colds."

Helvey showed Paul and others how to demonstrate the collision of radioactive particles in a dry-ice, super-saturated atmosphere, that in a darkened room students could actually see colliding radioactive particles. Paul reproduced the demonstration in each of his three sections of ninth-grade general science to the delight of students, principal and local newspaper. The high school science teachers, next door in the senior high school, were less impressed, not having yet mastered the relatively simple but new technique.

Mentor Helvey instructed eager Paul to build his own Geiger counter, and manage the micro-manipulator, which Helvey had also invented. Helvey's device was so delicate he could inject radioactive material into a fly's wing. He taught Paul how to pull a plane out of a spiral dive and which college courses to take, or avoid. Paul could not recall if Professor Helvey, who ended up working at the Martin Marietta Corporation and NASA research had children. Helvey treated Paul like a son.

Still Dealing with Indiscretions

Paul had made so many friends, becoming so smooth, that he was still able to survive several significant indiscretions:

1. Parking in (STC President) Royal F. Netzer's favorite, but unmarked, parking spot, then walking into the president's office, demanding the ignition keys back which he had thoughtfully left in his car.

2. Calling a Professor of English, Beryl Meek, a bitch for ridiculing him in class in front of other students. It took English department chairman, Lawrence B. Goodrich to get him out of that one. Paul had earlier driven Professor Goodrich to an education conference in New York City. Goodrich was also advisor to Sigma Tau Gamma fraternity to which Paul briefly belonged. Meek had suffered previous comments about her excessive candor.

3. Falling in love with a seventeen year-old blue-eyed blond high school cheerleader and gifted student, Mary Dyer, from Laurens, a nearby school district (he was 25). After Mary dumped him he dated Betty Nesbitt because she was wealthy, had status and besides, Mary didn't like her. Now Paul's second attempt with a "rich girl" didn't work out. Mary's quote "We have something in common, we both love Paul" was a painful and puzzling experience. He had never been truly in love before or dumped, and carried emotional scars for decades. There were several hundred available co-eds at STC at the time, go figure. Since he had been quietly two-timing Mary with locals Betty Downy and Corrine Martucci anyway, he probably deserved what he *got* not what he *wanted*.

4. Getting "worked over" by four or five high school ruffians one evening in the parking lot of an out of town nightclub, then later getting sued for $800 because the

Highway Patrol mistakenly charged the delinquents with disorderly conduct, rather than malicious mischief, an unfortunate technicality. It was in this time frame that Ploutz's lifelong distaste for attorneys was irretrievably confirmed. Thank heavens he had gone into education, instead of going to Albany Law School, Schenectady, New York.

Paul gradually gained the curios ability to associate his state of affairs with both Gould and Burroughs and how *they* would have handled difficulties. Each setback seemed to increase his resolve and commitment to doing more for nature, the environment, teaching science (Burroughs), or making money (Gould). Fortunately, he "hung out with people smarter than he was" along with willing, often eager *mentors*, who helped him teach, write or earn money.

In 1956, Paul was called from his classroom duties at Oneonta Junior High School to Grand Gorge where his father, George, was dying. George's last word was "Elsie". Reminiscent of all the perceived events of earlier years, Paul felt guilty for not feeling worse about his father's death. He felt guilty for being the lucky survivor of two brothers. He felt guilty because he couldn't cry. he felt guilty that he would have to pretend to be depressed. It would be another thirty years before Paul could even comprehend, let alone understand his mother's statement, "Your father is capable of a greater love for you than I." How pathetic. Rather than being broken his enormous drive to succeed, to be liked, to gain approval, recognition, and acceptance may have in fact resulted from George having provided none of that.

Even after numerous college courses as well as teaching child psychology for eighteen years, Paul is still unclear as to what reverence, if any, he should hold for his father. He has clearly benefited from wonderful *mentors* and father figures who sought him. Perhaps he has been a son to several great men who didn't have a son of their own. Perhaps he was merely a "late bloomer" (as is now known) with a difficult childhood and a mean father. Grow up, quit whining, get a life, go for it, work, make out, make a buck. In 1958, Paul visualized an even brighter future. Forty years later, Bill Gate's quote "life isn't fair, get used to it" became one of Paul's favorite expressions of reality.

Chapter 10:   Decker, Substitute Father and Mentor

Dr. Esther McKune had recently returned to STC Oneonta, completing her final degree in Greeley, Colorado. In early 1958, following Esther's connections with Donald G. Decker, Provost, Colorado State College, Greeley, Colorado, Paul requested a one-year leave of absence from his science teaching position at Oneonta Junior High School.

Miss Edna Tripp was now a favorite person and respected principal.   In 1958, George Peabody University and CSC at Greeley were preeminent in teacher education. Paul had already gained familiarity with the L.W. Singer science series, and knew Decker to be a senior author. Provost Decker, senior author of a prominent textbook science series, was also incoming president elect of the National Science Teachers Association.

The Power of Position

Go hitch your wagon to a star. Paul was quickly accepted into a doctoral degree program at Colorado State College, now University of Northern Colorado. Moving to Colorado was a big step, out of town, out of state. This was the same boy who, only ten years earlier, couldn't conceive how any person would or could live anywhere else than Roxbury.

His father, now deceased, could no longer resist or rant over Paul's hair brained ideas, which included a thirst for education. A liberating, joint success, Anna and Paul flew TWA's huge triple-rudder four-engine prop plane. Anna accompanied her last son to Greeley, Colorado.

The first of the Ploutz "clan" to attend college, Paul needed a map to find Colorado.   In one day he discovered both the geographical center of the United States to be Mead's Ranch in Nebraska and secondly, that he couldn't ride his bike from Colorado to the Pacific Ocean on long weekends.

Greeley was a conservative college town like STC or Hartwick College was to Oneonta, Cornell to Ithaca, and dozens of other splendid institutions across the United States where the college president has as much prestige as the city council or mayor. Greeley, of course, named after Horace Greeley was a "dry" town but larger than the college so that it could stand alone. The "sweet smell of money" drifting from the huge Monford beef processing collection point often drifted east over Greeley. Thousands of range steer provided periodic nasal reminders of Paul's farm origin.

Donald G. Decker

Decker was the ideal of a college dean. Steel rim glasses, white hair, tall, poised, slightly stiff, formal but congenial, articulately quick witted, and, as provost, the boss. In his first meeting with Decker, Paul:

1. Lined up courses to be taken for a career in science education
2. Gained formal admission to the doctoral program.
3. Discussed possible topics for the written dissertation.
4. Became house father for the on campus Sigma Chi fraternity house, which provided an in-house apartment and meals.
5. Was recommended to be faculty advisor to the College Ski Club.
6. Was provided an on campus "faculty" parking permit, sticker, and ID card.

Paul "hit the ground running," spending every moment available in pursuit of a rigorous academic load of science classes, several of which also had long hours of "lab" work. Paul took biology courses with biology majors, physics courses with physics majors, geology courses with, well you get the idea. Academic competition was keen. Much was expected and the provost's advisee ought to be able "to hold his head up" as a chemist, physicist, geneticist, astronomer, ya de ya. His chosen career, science education, presumed knowledge from astronomy to zoology (A to Z).

Paul's carefully designed program was to be broad in all the sciences, but not deep. Or as Decker politely teased, you will graduate knowing "practically nothing about practically everything." Decker also had a doctorate in science, from the University of Michigan, Ann Arbor.

Socially, 1959 was like the mountains to the west, arid. Western "hospitality" was less forthcoming, Paul as house father, then in his second year as "teaching fellow," was neither regular faculty nor student. With no parties, no sex life, no travel, no vacation, virtually all energy was devoted to academics. Near the end of the first year, Decker called Ploutz to plan his second year at Colorado State. Paul, lonesome, perhaps even homesick at twenty six, money exhausted, and his first year leave from Oneonta Junior High expiring, he explained his financial need to newest super *mentor*, Provost Decker.

Hitch Your Wagon to a Star

Donald G. Decker had one grown daughter, Judy. Paul had a deceased father he felt guilty about not even caring about. Decker, in addition to being purely academic was a bit stiff, formal. He was gradually becoming the father figure Paul never had. The perfect combination, if you please, between Paul's "idols" Burroughs and Gould.

In the late 1940's, Helen Dolman McCracken of Estes Park, Colorado joined Decker to continue the Singer Science Series. It became one of the most successfurl elementary science series in the United States. Helen had previously been married to Glen Blough (Maryland) another eminent science educator and author. Her writing skills were legendary. Years earlier Blough had apparently gone to a conference and never returned.

Decker confided to poorboy Paul that his salary as Provost, wouldn't even pay the *tax* on his royalties as author. Paul had met Professor Paul McKee, also at CSC and nationally recognized and admired for the "McKee readers."

Still another CSC prodigy, James A. Michner, was already much heralded as writing best sellers. School districts buy thousands of books at a time. Everyone seems to have heard of "Michner," but the "McKee" readers had sold millions more. As Paul looked around he saw, mingled with, and admired wealthy authors.

Most of those authors gained wealth by writing science material for children in the public schools. In 1950, it seemed to Paul that the national "author group" consisted of not more than twenty five or thirty people. THEY were deciding, "calling the shots" as to what was taught in the nation's schools! Not teachers, principals, superintendents, state or local boards of education or even the National Education Association (NEA).

Consider the numbers. In 1960, for example, there were about 17,000 second graders in the Detroit Public Schools. Elmer McDade, supervisor of science, tried to see that each child had their own book. The authors of these series were not well known outside of school environment, but became wealthy. Only the Herman and Nina Snyder, D.C. Health Series, of several, were more successful. Decker's science series gained adoptions in all fifty states.

Science teachers across the United States elected Decker as president of the National Science Teachers Association. He concurrently held the position of Provost at CSC, giving meaning to the cliche "If you want something done ask a busy person."

Three Great Changes

The theme of Decker's one-year presidency of NSTA was the K-12 curriculum. Decker's academic authority and vision in one year finally brought order to the Nation's science curriculum. In schools across America, the Kindergarten through the twelfth grade curriculum became sequential. Students no longer studied the same "bug" or health unit three years in a row!

1. Seventh, eighth, and ninth grade science classes became sequentially, life, earth, physical throughout the states.
2. Earth sciences (astronomy-geology-meteorology) were routinely offered in the high school curriculum, in addition to the previous physics, chemistry and biology.

There were other leaders to be sure, but like Burroughs who wrote quietly, modestly, Decker quietly, modestly, caused the writing of much of the nation's science curriculum. Like Gould, Decker became wealthy. In literature, as years go by, Burroughs' name is gradually joining the ranks of Whitman, Emerson, Thoreau, Muir, et. al. as our society meticulously sorts out the true naturalists, and poets from the "nature fakers" as Burroughs supplied the term for Teddy Roosevelt usage, in putting together the National Park System.

In later years, CSC, now the University of Northern Colorado, named a building after Decker. It doesn't seem like quite enough for the man who helped engineer the nations K-12 science curriculum from top to bottom.

Walt Disney, Jacque Cousteau,etc, are all giants among men, who have helped the public enjoy and appreciate nature. Textbook education writers quietly sell millions more copies. It is the Deckers of the world, who provide the public foundation of science literacy, the cornerstone of learning encouraging youth to cure our cancers, mend our hearts, or travel in time. (A quote from one of Ploutz's speeches.)

And This Man Wants to Help Me

Responding to lonesome, "financially challenged" Paul, Decker, having reviewed Paul's successful academic performance the first year, arranged to have him teach two introductory college classes. Chairman of the science division, Harley F. Glidden secured a small faculty office that Miss Edith Selberg generously shared. She was an older taskmaster and professor of biology.

A three thousand dollar stipend was included with the "understanding" that it could continue until Paul's program was complete. His student course load was reduced by only one course. A busy year finally included a few nonacademic opportunities:

1. Dating Jan Glidden, science department chairman's daughter.
2. Dating Gwen Thurmond, granddaughter of Senator Strom Thurmond, (South Carolina) who wanted Paul to take "oil and geology" courses in case he became a member of the family.
3. Skied Aspen, Vail, Copper Mt., Winter Park, Loveland Basin, etc, etc. CSC ski club was required to have a faculty advisor on all ski trips. Most faculty were too old, stiff, or didn't ski, so Paul a mere teaching fellow, was temporarily elevated to faculty status, if only to chaperone the twenty to thirty skiers. All expenses paid of course. Decker, in a rare moment of humor, remarked that having Paul chaperone the co-ed ski club to mountain ski trips, was much "like sending a rabbit to protect a head of lettuce."

4. Fishing, camping, canoeing in Yellowstone National Park, hunting deer and elk near Estes- Park, attending "Cheyenne Days" (Wyoming) rodeo.

5. Free flying lessons, with an old Civil Air Patrol cub plane flown by Lt. Col. Horace B. Monroe, WWII fighter pilot and CSC classmate. "HB's" only fear in life was getting a vulture or eagle in his prop and going down. Otherwise, sharing the cost of aviation octane, he taught Paul to land, and take off. He also taught him how to fly backwards at 10,000 feet with wind currents coming over the Rockies, carrying the tiny craft at nearly jet stream velocity, or directly into the current, looking down watching land "going the wrong way." The struggling, but happy engine, couldn't fly fast enough to maintain ground speed. Flying forward, well backward actually, created a sensation unlike anything Paul had ever experienced.

Having freshly completed a meteorology course, HB calculated the numbers, temperature, and the altitude of Denver (the mile-high city). A heavily loaded commercial plane, 5000 ft. above sea level, the ground temperature at 114 degrees, with full throttle down the runway across the entire state, was never able to lift the plane off the runway! Wow, cool stuff! H. B. Monroe went on to become president of a junior college somewhere.

A friend, not intended to be another *mentor*, per se, Paul tried to emulate HB's incredible ability to apply classroom physics, chemistry, or biology to cars or planes or any physical or mechanical everyday situation.

Sitting in the adjacent chair in Philosophical Foundations of Education, a required doctoral class taught by Leslie Day Zellany, who had written the book, Paul noticed "HB" doodling with a pencil. Paul quietly inquired, "What in the world are you doing?" Seems a local had recently jumped from one of Greeley's tallest buildings. HB was calculating "How fast he was going when he hit the sidewalk."

In another situation HB described the satisfaction involved in shooting down a "zero." He would machine gun the pilot floating down in a parachute until the body fragment slid out of the harness, reaching the ground before the chute. HB, having lost many comrades in similar fashion, Paul, thinking of his participation for six years in the Guard as a disgruntled weekend warrior, stood in awe of a survivor, now forty or older, returning to college. HB seemed relaxed, but possessed such intensity, and presence, that most professors seemed cautious with a conspicuous measure of greater respect than for other students.

Would You Drive a Sports Car?

Norm, was a house father of a large campus dormitory. Norm and Paul also became friends. Poised, conservative, even slightly dignified, Norm was frugal, a sharp dresser, so totally responsible, as to seem dull. Norm's Triumph Convertible (TR-3) was the only visible clue as to his real personality. Norm would call Paul at 10:00 PM on balmy summer evening's and roar fifty miles to Estes Park, merely for a single beer or cup of coffee to break the endless studying. The last ten miles, Canyon Road, toward Estes Park is a sports car driver's dream. Flat, blacktop, it snakes almost endlessly back and forth between high buffs and a rapid white water stream far below.

Norm had gracefully negotiated these curves dozens of times. A gentle whine with each turn and at night with no oncoming headlights, very little traffic, a balmy night, top down, the road was yours. Returning from Estes Park, and a dozen or so gentle squeals down the Canyon coming into a curve, exposed a small but loose gravel patch in both lanes. The headlights exposed the hazard in only the last second.

Triumphs sit very low. The car slid sideways on the gravel, not flipping until the outer wheels caught soil at the road edge near the stream. It happened so fast. The car, upside down, traveled three or four car lengths. Paul and Norm dazed, found themselves upside down, and trapped in the car. The smell of gasoline was strong, the whir of tires still turning. The engine stalled. The steady click, click signaled that the fuel pump was still pumping gasoline. With headlights out, it was dark, trapped upside down, beside the road.

A fire seemed inevitable. You have to be alive to worry, they were both. Wedged into the small compartment, and upside down, each acknowledging the other one to be "OK," then orientating themselves, turned the ignition key to the "off" position.

Seems the "topless" muscle car had landed on the remains of an old and now level sand pile, of years before. Remnants of the sand apparently allowed the free gasoline to quickly drain into the sand and may have cushioned the descent as the car fell to the ground.

Norm and Paul, "OK" but saturated with gasoline, scared of the car exploding, and upside down, shared the same view. There was a small moon-shaped gap between the sand and the contoured car door. Better to be used as an armrest while riding, it suggested the only possible escape from cremation. Desperate fingers gradually dug a larger and larger dip in the sand. When the hole became the same size and shape as the armrest of the car door, each escaped using the same hastily contrived technique.

The Colorado Highway Patrol was by chance, the first car to appear finding two CSC petrified graduate students, standing at the edge of the road. The patrolman, relieved, was also annoyed. "In as much as I'm NOT giving you a citation, and I am giving you a ride back to Greeley, then why not tell me where you landed, as no one could have survived in that car." They had dozens of tiny scratches from the windshield that mingled with them, a brief rash from gasoline, and ten very sore fingers from digging. Glad to be alive, Paul thought of John Burroughs' unwillingness to accept the Model T that Henry Ford was trying to give John to ride the muddy streets of Roxbury.

Not Always Serious

Tom Ryan was unlike anyone Paul had ever met. Without a lot of time to goof off, graduate student Ryan, from Chicago, in Colorado to avoid his father's scrutiny, was a lucky find. His wealthy father never visited his elegant mountain cabin in Estes Park. Ryan, thirty-ish, seemed more like Curtis Burroughs, the 1944 one from the good old Roxbury days. Seldom serious, he liked to fish, drove too fast, had a great sense of humor, and was a fun guy. Tom also gave Paul a key to the mountain pad. They double dated twice.

Ryan's first date could have passed for his mother, only some of her hair seemed missing and she was suffering a severe case of dandruff. Reluctant to double date a second time, but still eager to use the cabin on occasion, Paul inquired if "this one was drawing social security?" Ryan assured Paul "She was a knockout, barely of legal age," but he would be a little late in arriving at the cabin in Estes Park, he had to pick up some beer.

They were a little late, she was a knock out probably of legal age, but her Teddy bear did make her seem younger. Awkward in high heel shoes, she was a knock out, worthy of a Mafia chieftain's woman. Out of money, but needing beer, Tom Ryan and his lady "Tiz" fashioned two shoeboxes, cutting a coin slot in the top center. With a bright red magic marker, they wrote, "Wounded Boys from Belgium" on the boxes.

One on each side of the street in Greeley, the two walked house-to-house collecting donations for "wounded" boys from Belgium. When enough donations had been collected, they bought beer and dissolved the fund drive. After severely lecturing his host, as morally corrupt etc. etc, Paul helped to drink the beer, which did seem bitter.

Tom Ryan now a retired school teacher, aged seventy eight, lives in Englewood, Florida. After forty four years (1959–2003) on hearing of Paul's land development concepts, called to say "I always knew you would do it!"

Chapter 11: Decker Launches Paul's Career

At the suggestion of advisor Decker, Paul attended his first meeting and Annual Convention of the National Science Teachers Association in Kansas City, Kansas. In 1960 Paul's recently completed dissertation, "The Science Supervisor," landed him squarely in the post "sputnik" era. The National Defense Education Act (NDEA) financed nationwide efforts in the K-12 science program (championed by Decker et. al.) across the nation and at every grade level.

Catching up with Russians and "survival," gave a rallying cry to both science and math education. Doing the right thing for the wrong reasons, "science" became the buzzword for survival, progress, and the future.

A national emergency was on to improve the science comprehension of students, as well as the ability of our nation's schools and universities to produce scientists.

Only a handful of "science educators" held advanced degrees in 1960. Ploutz, with his 160-page dissertation on how to hire, and train science supervisors at the State Board of Education level, K-8 elementary, secondary (9-12), or K-12 district wide, was in the right spot at the right time, and almost alone.

Speaking invitations and job offers became routine. In a speech in 1961, at the Imperial College of the British Royal Academy, in London, Ploutz fanned the fire even further suggesting that "saving one's self or country, was indeed the admirable thing to do." More particularly "walk into any fourth or sixth grade classroom. Before you, are the people, who will mend your hearts or cure your cancers, do take an interest in their education."

Broadening the effort to include more than catching up with the Russians and producing bigger rockets, but in true K-12 Decker fashion, Ploutz dedicated himself to modernizing the entire science curriculum.

Paul's best paying job ever had been $3,500 year teaching grades seven through nine at Oneonta Junior High. A well-used car, two sport jackets, but no suit yet, Paul was job hunting. With his new Education Doctorate degree (Ed.D) at twenty eight, in good health, an outstanding job market, Decker's blessings, and now having spoken or traveled in forty eight states, Paul the local boy had made good.

As is often the case with young men who experience great success in a short period of time, sadly, more like Gould than Burroughs, Paul's hat fit tighter and tighter:

1. He declined a position at Harvard University working with Professor Fletcher Watson, teaching science education.
2. Declined becoming a K-8 state science supervisor for California working with the renowned Helen Heffernan, superintendent of instruction.
3. Declined becoming chairman of the Science and Math Department at Wayne State (Nebraska, not Detroit).
4. Declined a faculty appointment at Temple University, telling the Provost, he would only consider the position at the "full" professor level (instructor-assistant associate-full).
5. Declined working with the American Association for the Advancement of Science (AAAS) with Dr. Herbert A. Smith. A curious act of fate, AAAS later awarded Paul an honorary "fellow."
6. Awarded the coveted Fulbright Scholarship to teach in the schools of Diyarbakir, Turkey. His excuse, for resigning the Fulbright Grant permitting an alternate to rejoice, was money. Still "poor" he couldn't really figure out how much 17,000 Lira was. A single Turkish student on the Colorado State College campus said it was either "great or poor" depending on whether you spent it in the "black market" or in the "regular" market. That was not enough help. Numerous other social indiscretions prevailed. It seemed poor Paul could have any job available. Science was now selected as the vehicle to solve the nation's problems.

The National Science Teachers Association held regional and national meetings. J. Stanley Marshall (later president of Florida State) "Stan," Robert Binger "Bob," and a few other Florida folk, and Paul had formed a small NSTA clique. Binger, state science supervisor for Florida, located Paul still in Greeley sorting job offers. An "onsite" Florida interview would be required. A new position working with Binger, state vehicle provided, traveling Florida evaluating school science programs K-12, was available; did he want it?

Flying in and out of Stapleton Field, Denver, now routinely, Paul landed in Tallahassee, stayed with Bob and interviewed with others. Boy did this look good! Cardinals, catbirds, macaws, Paul saw birds he didn't recognize and by now "was pretty good at it." Winter temperatures in Roxbury had fallen as low as minus 35_ F. This was only his third trip to Florida, standing outside the walls of the Castillo De San Marcos in St. Augustine. The place reminded him of Ponce de Leone. Paul had, indeed, discovered the fountain of youth. He wanted in.

Waiting eagerly back in Greeley with his apartment mate David Tavel (later professor in Ohio) Paul was waiting for his Florida contract to hit the mailbox. There were still more job offers. A fat envelope with the Florida State offer was, after so many years of effort, now in hand. At exactly 2:00 PM Paul opened the envelope.

The contract offer was enclosed, even with two decals to gain entrance to restricted parking in the certain knowledge he would need them. For several minutes, the insecure boy from Hardscrabble Road fondled the various contracts like a child would sort the larger candy bars from his Halloween basket. At the precise moment Paul was to sign the contract the phone rang.

Henry: "Henry Heisner here, calling from Livonia, Michigan. We have a new K-12 position open as coordinator of science education. Would you be interested?

Paul: Thank you Henry, but I actually had a pen in my hand ready to accept a state job in Florida.

Henry: All the better. Fly here, interview, then if you take the Florida job you'll know you've made the right decision."

The Ultimate Job Interview

Advisor Decker wondered why Paul had agreed to interview in Michigan if he wanted to go to Florida. Good question, but Henry Heisner, personnel director at Livonia, a wealthy suburb outside of Detroit, was also at the "top of his game." "Enjoy a plane trip, interview, listen, leave, take another job, that's OK, I'll send you a plane ticket." Heisner was persuasive.

Our new Dr. Ploutz was provided a comfortable swivel chair in the middle of a giant perfectly shaped U. Seven principals or assistant superintendents were assembled for a lengthy interview. Advisor Decker, ever faithful, suggested that if he wasn't really interested, the least he could do was to give them a good interview. OK, Paul was going, because at the time he hadn't anything better to do than go for a plane ride before going to Florida. He would give them a good interview.

Interviewers:	"If we give you this job...?
Paul:	If I decide I want this job...!
Paul:	Who is already here, who wants this job!
Paul:	Why have you waited so long to sequence the science curriculum?
Paul:	You have a wealthy school district, but;1) no outdoor education camp; 2) no school planetarium; 3) no electronics lab in high school. Why, Why?"

During the first hour, interviewers were equally annoyed and intimidated that this upstart had the balls to challenge the leadership team of one of Michigan's finest school districts.

During the second hour, only slightly better, still not wanting the job, Paul suggested, he was in fact, glad he had come, as he had been doing "missionary work" across the states anyway. When asked a question he wasn't sure of, or thought he was going to be indecisive, he would respond "The jury is still out on that one. I'll pass for now," looking to the next question.

By the third hour, neither tired, nor intimidated, Paul interviewed them, questioning how he would be able to count on them to change or improve the science and math programs? The interviewers asked Paul if he would indeed accept the position, "Lets make it coordinator of "both" math and science. You may continue a high profile in professional organizations. We offer you $8,750 yearly salary, eleven months, mileage reimbursement for travel, eleven percent matching toward retirement, the usual benefits."

Back on campus at Greeley, Burt Thomas, professor of microbiology, had given Paul his ONLY "C" during the entire doctoral program. Thomas was an excellent teacher, older, and with several years experience. He confided to Paul that his university salary was $7,100.

Later, but not gloating, Paul explained he had accepted a position for $8,700 in the public schools. Having earlier asked Thomas to "reconsider" his "C" grade, it being the "only" one, gained two responses:

1. "You keep your 'C' grade as it will make all your A's and B's look higher."
2. "I'm truly happy for you but as far as microbiology is concerned, with your background, you know practically nothing, about practically everything."

Paul "took the road less traveled," Livonia over Florida, and it has made all the difference.

Coordinator of Science and Mathematics Education

Paul didn't know it at the time of course, but Livonia was as good as it gets. There was reportedly $80,000 in property tax evaluation behind each student. With twenty-six elementary schools, six junior highs, and two high schools, most of the principals had earned doctorates in education.

During the two-year Livonia position, the "supervisor of science" position was new, and Paul was free to do pretty much as he pleased, as long as it was about science. Since his doctoral dissertation at Greeley with Decker had been to define the role of the new "science supervisor in education," school officials assumed he must have known what he was doing. This was his first job as science supervisor since graduation. Livonia was a wealthy community and Paul, in the vernacular of today was a "happy camper."

In 1960 the National Defense Education Act (NDEA) poured vast amounts into national math and science education. Any school district could gain fifty-fifty matching funds for science and math. Ploutz saw to it that all elementary schools had lab tables, micro projectors, stereo microscopes, prisms, magnets, portable lab carts, and small motors, even war surplus parachutes. By hanging a parachute properly, and projecting light underneath, a small planetarium could replicate the night sky for children to see constellations or consider space.

The school district finally ended up with its own separate planetarium, electronic laboratories in new high schools, a sex education program, K-12 curriculum, talented/gifted science club, and experimental programs in both math and science. Paul had matched money that might have gone to athletic uniforms, musical instruments, cafeteria, band and other deserving areas. Not everyone loved his success in making Livonia's science program one of the best in the nation. Paul's efforts served to starve the art and music programs, using their dollars to match with federal funds.

National Science Supervisor's Association

By his third annual NSTA convention in 1961, having also participated in several mid-year regional conferences, Paul was entrenched. He was acquainted with most of the science textbook authors and well acquainted with most of the supervisors of science in schools and at the state level. Given this network, a new organization was about to be formed. Paul found even better jobs for a number of science teachers from Livonia. One such teacher, Mr. Elva Bailey, became director of educational programs at the Goddard Space Flight Center for NASA at Greenbelt, Maryland. Junior high science teacher, Joseph Premo, was lined up to follow Paul as Decker's newest doctoral student.

Time spent from Livonia was largely utilized for professional activities. Hunting, camping, fishing, boating, swimming, scouting, and other bachelor pursuits were on hold. Paul worked to increase his influence and ability in the belief that he could *mentor* people, and change and direct the science comprehension of every man, woman, and child on the planet!

The Viking Scientific Company

Gould's failures, much like the man, were colossal. Most successful people experience failures. Gould took the notion that multiple projects would lead to multiple successes. Many of Gould's so-called "failures" usually meant that he simply made *less* money. While cornering the gold market, manipulating a US president (Grant), creating "Black Friday," an American economic disaster, thousands financially ruined, Jay alone may have profited.

Burroughs took a try or two at farming, but was no better at vineyards and grapes than other Burroughses had been at farming. Successful men do have failures.

Ploutz, while a supervisor of science in Livonia, Michigan, and two others, incorporated the Viking Scientific Company located in Novi, Michigan. Paul was responsible for the purchase of microscopes, lab tables, chemicals, triple stained pigs, frogs for dissecting, and all science supplies for Livonia public schools. As editor for the journal of the <u>National Science Supervisors Association</u>, he was often aware of new science programs, including large purchases of science apparatus and grants for equipment.

Because of the sensitivity of conflicts of interest in the academic community, Paul agreed that Louis (Lou) Marini would be *president* of Viking. Paul, as major stock-holder had to have his name on the Michigan Articles of Incorporation. Now familiar with how Jay did business, Paul also "covered his butt" by informing the school superintendent Benton Yates of his "purchase of 1,500 shares" of The Viking Scientific Company. There were only 3,000 shares total, the other two partners owning 750 shares each.

Paul had also recently (1961) been appointed to the Science Grant Review Committee of the Michigan Department of Education. That post gave him information on *every science grant approved to every school district in the State.*

Marini had only to call on those districts that were buying equipment and had the money to spend (back to "shooting fish in the barrel)." Paul had been able to set the Novi office up with sample equipment, on loan from the Elgeet Manufacturing Company (Rochester, NY). With fast delivery assured, Viking was now in a position to sell equipment before they owned it. In some cases equipment could be shipped directly from the whole saler, Viking did the paperwork and made a profit without ever touching inventory, storing, or paying shipping expenses.

Michigan and the entire nation were in the middle of the National Defense Education Act (NDEA) trying to catch up with the Russians, who had successfully launched Sputnik. Money for science was available from local, state, and federal sources at every level, including public, and private schools, colleges and universities, and trade schools etc.

Paul could not reasonably involve himself in the day to day operation of the business, and left everything to Lou. Big mistake. In previous years, Paul had learned to play "singles" and not rely on people who would not usually be willing to work as long or hard as he would. (A lesson he had learned from Gould). The opportunity and concept of Viking *was so totally attractive, the risks so reasonable it looked and felt like something Jay would have to do.* So in his first corporate adventure Paul did not follow Jay's example.

Lou Marina took his new position as corporation president so seriously that he immediately got married (using startup money for his honeymoon). Once back in town, Lou started picking up checks for dinner, smoking cigars, and acting like the president of ENRON.

Within a few weeks Paul, was invited to attend an <u>important</u> evening meeting at the Viking office in Novi. An official from Elgeet informed the three principals that their account was *seriously* in arrears. All three would **need** to sign *affidavits of personal responsibility* beyond their corporation OR there doors would be locked, shut down, finis.

Paul, even after the encouragement of his two partners said, "NO, lock whatever you need to." The other two partners signed for personal responsibility. Paul knew that if Lou couldn't manage better, much better, there was no hope for Viking.

Viking lasted a few more weeks when partner number three's father paid for his release from his portion of debt earlier agreed to. *Viking's doors* were locked and Lou apparently moved to Rochester, New York to work off debts working for Elgeet. Within a few months, Elgeet (a relatively large company) also went "belly up." Paul was scorched, not burned like Burroughs' vineyard or Gould's Black Friday, but it was a valuable lesson in trusting the efforts of others.

Paul, while active in the American Association for the Advancement of Science (AAAS), was named a "fellow" in 1965. He was at the "top of his game" and never learned how the distinction of being named a fellow in the prestigious AAAS had occurred. He had earlier "walked" from a Fulbright Scholarship and ignored a job offer from Harvard.

Paul felt that NSTA was more in the "trenches" and more regularly put him in contact with the cutting edge "shakers and doers." Sam Schenberg of New York City, and Elmer McDaid of

Detroit, Elmer Palmer, Baltimore, for example, controlled the science programs of hundreds of thousands of students. These three, among others, were also charter members of the National Science Supervisors Association (NSSA) and helped "install" Paul as editor of their first journal. John C. Rosemergy, coordinator of science for the Ann Arbor, Michigan Public Schools, was one of Paul's three associate editors for the NSSA journal, and also director, of the Argus Planetarium, Ann Arbor. Paul could take Planetarium information to Livonia schools. Jerrold William Maben, supervisor of science from the Pontiac public schools was also an associate editor. Maben was also national membership director for NSTA. William "Bill" Forbes, Ann Arbor Public Schools, was the third associate editor of the NSSA journal.

NSTA also put Paul in contact with science textbook authors and publishers. Colleges/professors/industry have long taken an interest in how science is taught. Paul enjoyed early cordial relationships with eminent scientists who, in his words, turned out OK, and as Paul reports many of these scientists were "smaller fish like himself."

Collegiality

The principal and the administrative group of Livonia schools were the best-trained professionals Ploutz had encountered. Most principals had earned doctorates, or were working on them. New teachers were encouraged to pursue workshops and advanced degrees. Henry Heisner, director of personnel, was eager to hire the best and most experienced teachers with masters' degrees over recent graduates who cost less. Livonia paid one or two hundred more than surrounding districts and was not shy about hiring from other districts.

Principals Jerry Erspamer, Gene Erstin, Jack Kirksey, John McCann, Bill McMurtry, and others, were all good friends and avid golfers. This group of principals often "hung out" together. Paul's bowling average was only 158. Several other principals were also archers and hunters.

Principals, Jack Kirksey and Jerry Erspamer were close friends, both were married. Kirksey later to become a member of the state legislature, then mayor of Livonia, Michigan. Jack and Jerry launched creative efforts to see to it that Paul should enjoy their *marital bliss.* Wives Peg Erspamer and Pat Kirksey, also community leaders and wonderful wives, by any measure, did not retard their husbands' antics, in manipulating Paul's personal life. On occasion Paul would baby-sit for both families as well as play golf, bowl, fish, and attend constant cookouts with great friends.

Finding the Wife

Erspamer and Kirksey, working in concert with several other elementary principals, devised a clever, slightly devious plan. Combined, the dozen or so principals had a few hundred teachers in their schools. Many of these were newly hired, often recent graduates, and predominately female. Erspamer and Kirksey reasoned that Paul's efficiency could be improved if he had an available "list" of single, always attractive, young, excellent teachers. Each participating principal, now including Virginia Roberts, Wilson Elementary and other female principals, joined the eligibility lottery. This charade, in place for more than a year, seemed mutually beneficial, as Paul quietly worked the list.

There were a couple of glitches in the program. Jerry and Jack had deviously managed to add the name of a fifty year-old teacher with a face only a mother could love. As luck would have it, Paul had already met the lady in school by chance, and had discovered the bizarre plot even though the lady had no knowledge.

The lady was happily married, nearly at retirement. Obviously, Paul did not make the "blind" date. However, thinking the trick almost cruel, certainly a tad bazaar, Paul pretended that he had in fact, called the married troll, gained her agreement, and was to meet without her husband's knowledge. Then Paul phoned Erspamer "to thank him for the referral." Kirksey, willing to salvage some remnants of the foiled trick, quickly conspired with victim Paul, to now set "up" Erspamer. The incredibly ill-thought trick had gone south.

Jerry Erspamer a great father, principal, and friend, had finally been bested in harmless deceit. He came "clean" with the plot, *begging* Paul not to call the elderly married lady. The whole creative mess came quietly to rest.

Paul continued with the "real list" for more than a year. Virginia Roberts had hired several mid-year teachers and had agreed to host a meeting with all the new teachers in the district. Paul was invited along with all district administrators to meet the fifty new, mid-year teachers. Host principal Roberts took special care to introduce Dr. Ploutz, science coordinator, to new teacher Geri Pecora, a third-grade or was it fifth-grade teacher? Paul, partial to all attractive female teachers, noticed the delicate blue-eyed blonde. Principal Roberts gave enthusiastic endorsement to her teaching ability.

Later, one evening, Paul checked the principal's recommended list to discover that Miss Pecora's name was already on the list, and he had already met her! A few days later, Paul had occasion to be in the personnel office. He pulled Pecora's file and academic credentials. In two semesters, at Wayne State University (Detroit not Nebraska) she earned straight A's! This girl was a winner. Paul moved her name to the top of the list and dialed (Luzon) LU 1-0955.

Paul:	"Hello Geri, This is Paul Ploutz. I met you at Wilson School a few days ago. (January 1961)
Geri:	Who?
Paul:	Paul Ploutz, Dr. Ploutz, the science supervisor who you met at school.
Geri:	Well, yes I vaguely remember, what do you want?
Paul:	Well, er, Virginia Roberts told me what a good teacher you were, and I wondered what your social status was?
Geri:	My what?
Paul:	er, social status, are you seeing anyone?
Geri:	Oh I thought you were calling me about my science classes. I have a boy friend Carl. Why do you ask?"

Oldest of four, one time cheerleader, captain of the debate team, blue-eyed blonde, academically brilliant, and all with a fiercely Catholic mother who despised Paul. Katherine Pecora quickly sensed the growing bond between them and correctly saw Paul as a "non-Catholic from somewhere else," who might one day fast talk her equally stubborn daughter into leaving home. Katherine wanted Geri to settle down nearby, have a nice Catholic wedding with plenty of witnesses, relatives, and priests. Katherine hoped Geri might even become a hairdresser, a noble profession.

Paul's Livonia position was a ten-month contract. This allowed him to take a summer position as director of the Lake Placid Club daycare summer enrichment program for boys and girls ages eight through sixteen. The Lake Placid Club, at least in 1961, was still the ultimate location for second and third generation 1800s capitalist robber barons. Paul was provided with his own cottage at the prestigious Lake Placid which otherwise, rented for one hundred dollars a day.

The club had three dinning halls, one for "stoff" (the elite), one for "staff" (normal folks), Paul and others, and "stuff," (bottom echelon) chauffeurs, maids, and common folk.

With four college student assistants, Paul hiked, camped and swam with the financially enhanced prodigy during the day, becoming familiar with their older sisters in the evenings. "Edith," a daughter of a chief justice of the New York State Supreme Court dreaded leaving Lake Placid. She was considering postponing her pending marriage to further enjoy Paul's company. A guest, Madeline Schirvin, who ate in the elite dining hall invited Paul to eat with her. Madeline, a few years older than Paul, was also a science teacher and NSTA member from somewhere. She was also an olympic skating judge and invited Paul to "tour Europe" with her as a "companion." Paul loved to skate but gracefully declined.

Late one evening, Katie Searles, the golf pro's prolific sixteen year-old daughter, climbed the roof of Paul's cabin, forced a window open, and entered. Katie found Paul at 2:00 AM, sound asleep, so awakened him to take advantage of his purity. Are you believing any of this?

Chapter 12:   The Recent Rich

Old money seemed to have the same number of Bentleys and Rolls Royces in the parking lot as the recent rich. Either way, chauffeurs, all black hung out in the parking lot the entire day, in case "his nibs" craved a drive. Chauffeurs seemed to arrive with family. However, the club had a rent-a-maid program for the recent rich who were not yet up to speed with the social requirements of the upper class.

All in all, the children at summer camp thrived on having numerous age-level activities from a well-trained, well-paid staff. Some of the recent rich saw the summer program as a baby-sitting service. One mother with a pale, skinny seven-year-old, much like Paul, had been was totally determined to get baby-sitting services. Minimum age was eight. After mom threw a few tantrums, Paul was called "on the carpet." Paul, a bit overconfident, explained that "pushy" mothers were often the problem, and that if the president of the Lake Placid Club had a more qualified director the job was his!

Old money was usually gracious, tactful, considerate, and appreciative. New money, or the recent rich, was often arrogant, abrasive, demanding, and condescending. On at least three occasions, still single, Dr. Ploutz, now thirty with four college degrees, and totally confident, told obnoxious parents to "put it where the sun doesn't shine," smiling the entire time. Oops, one's husband was on the LPC's board of directors. At the "brief hearing" Paul explained the full circumstances and inquired as to what part of "NO" they didn't understand.

No one talked down to Jay or John by age thirty. By damn, no one was going to talk down to spindle shanks, PeeWee, Whitey, Pete, or Paul. The summer camp program was successful, with a magnificent evening campfire and program with both Algonquin and Iroquois dances and drums. Despite hugs, handshakes, gratuities, and accolades, in his heart of hearts, Paul knew he would not accept the invitation to join the esteemed Lake Placid Club, or ever work there again.

Paul was suddenly mindful of John Delaney's earlier comment about "an air of superiority, which offends many people," and later Doris Moon's "gods gift to science teaching" comment. Packing his luggage from the splendid cabin on Lake Placid, Paul realized, perhaps for the very first time, that most of the problems related to the summer experience, were because he too had often acted like the "recent rich," arrogant, abrasive, and condescending.

In a new moment of reflection, Paul accepted and realized he had flaws. Further, his father seemed less a demon now that Paul had his own flaws. Overcoming the collective experiences of childhood wasn't quite as simple as it might have been.

The ultimate realization that "mentors," be they mothers, siblings, neighbors, or teachers, make us significantly better than we would have otherwise been, is a concept that, at some point, should permeate our very being.

The Show down

Returning in September, the job in Michigan would be great. Geri Pecora, apparently defying her mother's wishes, had also written several letters during the summer. Mother Katherine now saw the relationship as a threat. Paul, the Roxbury Boy, was thought to have been twelve before he had even seen a Catholic. "Mrs. K," wanting to save her bewitched daughter from "this heathen from somewhere else" made their lives increasingly difficult.

After Paul and Geri had been dating for several months, often several times a week, Mrs. K arranged a surprise showdown to put this awful experience behind her. In the past, Paul had never made it past the front steps when picking Geri up, even after one-hundred times. This one instance, Mrs. K and perhaps a somewhat reluctant husband Stanley, invited Paul in for a "serious family discussion." Paul anticipated his indictment, lynching, confrontation, and execution.

The parents presented their case:

1. They had raised their daughter as a moral, good Catholic.
2. They believed that at least up until now, she knew right from wrong.
3. She had always respected and obeyed them.
4. Since taking up with you, she seems to have forgotten her values, and has lost respect for us, perhaps even herself.

5. Since you probably don't care about all that, and don't even know if you have any religion, you probably don't value our daughter's innocence.
6. We have let this go on for too long. Therefore, she now has the option of a clear, total break with you now, or breaking off, being disowned by her family, and moving from her home forever.

There was total silence for several seconds, which seemed far longer. Geri's sixteen-year-old brother, Ernie, stood in shock and disbelief. He was watching what to him must have seemed to be a total confrontation, like the shootout at the OK Corral. Worthy of a scene from a tense Hollywood film, Geri made her choice, walked from her parents to Paul's side of the room. Putting her hand on his shoulder, she said, "Well Paul, what shall we do?"

Previous discussions between Paul and Geri had resolved other major problems, like being Catholic. Neither, at least at the time, were considering children, but if that happened, children "were never to set foot in a Catholic church until the age of twelve." Paul remembered that Helen Gould Shepard had sent thirty-five-thousand copies of the bible to Utah to dissuade Mormons. In his own experience, Catholics referred to the rest of the world as "non-Catholic." Paul had, by now, studied many of the world's religions and felt the compromise reasonable under the circumstances. Geri agreed, and kept the twelve-year promise, only gently "testing" it a time or two over the years to see if by chance Paul might be ready to amend the agreement.

Head-on confrontations with loved ones, especially parents, are difficult. Katherine and Stanley Pecora should have known better. Geri, even as a child, was strong-willed and uncompromising, determined to make her own choices be they crayons, playdough, fingerpaint, cookies, boys, or men.

Conversely Paul, once in love, "dumped" only once, (Mary Dyer) by a seventeen-year-old cheerleader, and by now an accomplished womanizer, had never met a girl with so much strength, and intelligence. Demonstrating nerves of steel in asking Paul, "what shall we do?," Geri gave her parents her choice. Paul in a clear response replied, "Get your things, put them in my car, and then let's go."

Stanley, probably less eager for the confrontation was shocked by the choice Geri selected. Upon the immediate loss of his oldest and beloved daughter, Stanley sat in stunned disbelief. A few weeks later, Paul and Geri paid twenty-five dollars for a Livonia magistrate to complete a fifteen-minute ceremony. Roger Rood, a math teacher from Emerson Junior High, was best man and witness. There was no church, no music, no pictures, and no family.

At Stanley's request "a last meeting" was arranged before Geri and Paul were to leave for Colorado and new jobs. "Mrs. K," still livid, thought it best for Stanley to conduct, negotiate, reconcile, bless or curse the departure. Stanley's first sentence was "Well look, the damage has been done. Let's try to make the best of it." Paul's response "We do not recognize any damage done. We want to be left alone, its good we're going to Colorado. With any luck we'll never have to see you again." That was the end of the meeting.

Goodbye Michigan

Livonia schools had been a wonderful experience. The "road less traveled," the Michigan over Florida choice had been a good one. Paul had fewer *mentors* but dozens of quality friends.

Paul had received a letter from author, provost, *mentor*, Dr. Decker with the break-through Paul had fantasized about. Paul received an invitation to move to Colorado, become a junior author along with Mildred "Mim" Ballou, Ball State University, Indiana, for the new edition of the K-6 Singer Science Series. Within a few days, a second letter arrived from Jefferson County Public Schools, from Superintendent Forbes Bottomly, offering Paul the K-12 supervisor of science job at $9,700. Jefferson County had 110,000 students and eighty schools. With dual opportunities available in Colorado, Paul and Geri said goodbye to Livonia.

Livonia was to Paul as the treasury department had been to Burroughs, as surveying had been to Gould, an opportunity to grow, accept responsibility, gain the bigger picture, gain financial independence, get a wife, and get a life.

In Livonia, only (Miss) Dr. Bernice Roberts, coordinator of elementary education, spoke against Paul's innovations. Many years prior, it seems she had met Dr. Decker in the mountains of West Virginia, and the encounter had not gone well.

Using her "influence" with Dr. Leslie Bishop, coordinator of secondary education, a married man, who had become Paul's immediate superior, she gradually diluted Paul's ability to produce change and was a constant irritant. Further, in a brief two years, with all the money he needed, Paul felt the "shock" value of his tenure had been largely achieved. Mr. William Kumbier, a junior high science teacher, had also waited patiently for the job he had wanted and followed Paul as science supervisor. Paul's dual position with math was divided and provided to a prominent math teacher in the district.

Dr. Roberts, whose position was later terminated, apparently saw Paul as too influential. Working with Coordinator of Secondary Education, Leslie Bishop, worked to reduce Paul's influence. Paul's office was located between Robert's and Bishop's. Sensing a pending social awkwardness and mindful of the cliché "never get into a urination contest with a skunk," Paul knew the damage one apple could do to the bushel. Paul became aware that "Virginia and Les" had apparently become "fond" of each other. With little experience in power plays, administrative reorganizations, sexual bias, Paul's great Colorado writing opportunity was timely. Paul resigned. The principals sprung a party, and cheers, good will and fond memories prevailed.

Hello Colorado

Living in Wheatridge, then Golden, Arvada, and Lakewood, Colorado, was much the same as living in Denver. Detroit (Michigan) had been visualized as a smoky, factory city, and had turned out to be fresh air. The giant Rouge Ford plant, GM's and Chrysler's, had obtained smog control. High smoke stacks and a steady breeze from the west put much of Detroit's sludge safely over into Canada, to form acid rain.

Denver, however, the fabled mile-high city, at the eastern edge of the Rockies, had a geography, which included a gigantic dimple. The dimple, including most of downtown, allowed smog to collect. In Los Angeles, the smog couldn't be pushed over the mountains. In Denver, the adjacent high mountains protected the city from strong winds or flushing smog to Nebraska and further east. Paul discovered allergies, sinus, and hay fever, call it what you will, and was intrigued at watching skyscrapers and the dimple "fill up" with smog. Sometimes the visible layer would reach the thirtieth or fortieth floor of downtown buildings.

Paul joined the American Meteorological Society and wrote an editorial or two to the **Denver Post**. Quickly deciding that, like Burroughs, cursing progress and factories, his efforts were like sneezing in a tornado. Having occasionally smoked a pipe or cigar for status, and scholarly appearance, Paul finally decided that to be equally stupid, and he was never again to smoke anything.

Jefferson County schools formed a geographical rectangle. The district was twenty-four miles wide and approximately seventy miles long, with board offices in Denver. New wife Geri, became a 4th-5th-6th grade team teacher at Fairmont Elementary School, 1960, in nearby Wheatridge, with Miss Ilene Dean, principal.

During the two years at "Jeff" County, Paul worked long hours happily writing the earth and physical science components of the pending K-6 Singer Science Series. Paul was a workaholic author, with publisher meetings during all vacations. Three day weekends and holidays were usually held in Chicago.

Coming to Colorado, and prior to finding housing in Denver, Paul and Geri had been invited to stay with Don and Doris Decker in Greeley. Paul was now on a first name basis with newspaper editors, college presidents, numerous congressmen, Nobel scientists and other "heavy hitters."

Paul found it difficult to address eminent Dr. Decker as "Don." Hindsight is often twenty-twenty. But why had Don chosen Paul over hundreds of those available in the national author pool? Paul was still unable to fathom that now he had finally obtained the father he never had.

Too Soon Old, Too Late Smart

Paul was eagerly holding down a new job responsible for the science instruction of 110,000 students. Evenings in their apartment at 4417 Teller Street, in Wheatridge, Paul would write until 1:00 or 2:00 A.M.

Jay Gould would have done anything to succeed. Paul saw his opportunity, and was also willing to do whatever it took.

One evening a sleepy-eyed, recently married Geri, walked into the study, gently observing "You have written until two-thirty every night. I have fallen asleep alone thirty-one consecutive nights, is it time for you to take a break?"

The Singer Series had been on the market for decades starting with stories similar to the legendary McGuffee Readers. "*Sunshine and Rain*" and similar nature, science stories evolved into readers, then textbooks, one for each grade.

The series was very successful for a long time. The newest version with Paul Ploutz and Mim Ballou (Ball State) seemed to be coming along nicely. Mim (Mildred) Ballou was the other junior author. Mim was to write the biological text for the K-6 series, Paul the physical science text. The L.W. Singer Company presented Paul with an attractive option. You may start receiving an "advance" on future royalties! Draw as little or as much as you choose, they said, "Even give up your job to write full-time, take a leave of absence, whatever."

Paul discussed his extraordinary effort with Jefferson County superintendent of schools, Dr. Forbes Bottomly. Bottomly, eager for publicity of his district employees was supportive, explaining it was no big deal. Paul could leave work early, take a day or two now and then, no reason to reduce salary, "We do this all the time."

At the time, one of "Jeff County's" coaches was climbing Mount Everest on full salary, sending daily messages back to the The Denver Post, U S, and the school board, and Superintendent Bottomly thought it a smashing idea. Over time Bottomly "forgot" the early off time arrangement and once called Paul at home at 4:00PM to determine if he was playing hookie. It was an early sign of the Superintendents gradually "losing it."

Since Paul, who now had an assistant, Miss Lois Dunn, could supervise less, and write more, his advancement dilemma was dismissed. Ironically, Paul was making the wrong decision for the right reasons, backward, with mental flashbacks of his father's "left handed" response, and going through life butt first.

Chapter 13: Life In The Fast Lane

Paul continued writing night and day for several months. In perhaps the dumbest move of his entire career, Paul declined any advance royalty, remuneration, or travel reimbursement. He decided to "bust his buns," so that later there would be no deductions against his massive royalties as co-author of one of the most successful science series on the planet. Decker, while always circumspect and modest, had revealed that his substantial salary as provost wouldn't even cover the income tax on his author royalties.

This Roxbury Boy now was finally riding high, like Burroughs his nature idol, and even Gould, who he quietly admired for having so much money.

With his career in science education largely secure, the anticipated mega bucks made him the perfect blend of Burroughs and Gould. The one-room school they had all attended on Hardscrabble Road was long behind them.

Hit the Big Time

Paul was still having trouble calling the wonderful Dr. Decker "Don." It seemed like "spitting on the flag." Chicago was often the location of author-publisher meetings. It was east from Colorado and west from Syracuse for owner Frances Singer, Executive Vice President Ted Service, and Vernon Taylor, science editor. Chicago was not far for Mim Ballou from Ball State University in Muncie, Indiana.

Paul worked from 8:00 AM, took a short lunch, to 5:00 PM. Five became "Jim Beam" time for both the writing team and the publisher group. With his intelligent wife, booze, a winning publishing company, and a new super father figure, 1963 was one of the best years of Paul's new life.

Decker, new "super dad," was still mildly annoyed that Paul was too constipated to call him "Don." With evenings free, Professor Decker invited junior author Ploutz to accompany him to downtown Chicago. Like a father coaching an eligible son for his first "experience," Decker took an eager Ploutz to his first strip club.

Six or eight clubs in a row were well lit, clearly a part of the Chicago business community. Don and Paul were seated knee tight to the circular elevated stage. There were no bad seats. The minimum, two drink one dollar champagne coverage fee could be consumed, or given to the dancer, as a token of admiration, respect, appreciation, hormones, whatever. A bit smoky, with effective lighting, and accompanying music, other well-dressed businessmen seemed to be the average appreciative clientele.

The dancers, barely of legal age, eagerly drank their complimentary champagne (probably tap water) clearly enthusiastic about their role, opportunity, tips, exposure, career, stage ranking, seniority ranking, and public acceptance.

On occasion, those with IQ's above room temperature would gain the mike and breathlessly explain their need for tuition money, or to assist a dying mother. The third or fourth entertainer, or was it the fifth or sixth, squirmed, danced, and crouched ever closer to Professor Decker who sat frozen motionless. The sexy female gyrated her credentials so incredibly close, as to steam his silver-rimmed glasses. Paul, pleasantly shocked, was relieved that her knees hadn't popped his eardrums. After clearing his slightly steamed glasses, Dr. Decker remarked, "Now, can you call me Don?" It was so.

Back at the Ranch

Back at the "ranch," Jefferson County was occupied with many experimental programs including several under Paul's *mentoring:*

    a. Green, yellow, and blue, experimental versions, of high school biology.

    b. School Mathematics Study Group math program. (SMSG)

    c. The Elementary Science Study Program. (ESS)

    d. School Science Improvement Study. (SSIS)

"Jeff" County had more than five-thousand students enrolled in biology. Slightly fewer took physics, chemistry, or earth science, not including junior high school. With textbooks, microscopes, and related equipment, numerous publishers, brands, and manufacturers, teachers had lots with which to work. Strong resistance to standardization came from the teachers union. Its president, a biology teacher, would bypass his principal, the science supervisor, the director of secondary education, and deputy superintendent to appeal directly to Superintendent Bottomly. The union president would request unique equipment, but just for his own classes.

Bottomly seemed afraid of the teachers union. Of small stature, and possibly insecure, he was equally impressed by any teacher's ability to put multiple "Sir's" and "Dr's." in each sentence. His personal assistant Jim, was well over six-feet tall and "kissed up" so conspicuously that it created snickers. Careful with tax dollars, Paul called attention to the fact that standardization saved thousands of dollars. Those five-thousand biology students were using Swift and/or Bausch and Lomb microscopes. As a result of the union intervention, the district would now be purchasing an unknown bastard brand (as is the phrase). Paul, initially unaware of the personal ploy, blocked the purchase. Higher administrators supported Paul's decision. Bottomly learned that "his personal deal" has been derailed and was furious. He chastised the director of secondary education and fired the deputy superintendent, Del. G. Peterson. Ploutz was admonished for not "showing proper respect."

Only a few of the principals and administrators at "Jeff. Co" schools had doctorates. Forbes called every one by their first name, but expected everyone to call him Dr. or Sir, preferably both. The rogue biology teacher kissed up, and bought whatever he wanted.

Work for an Egotist?

Bottomly's command performance was every other Monday at the 10:00 AM meeting of the administration and staff (ad-staff). The meeting hall was shaped like the school district, rectangular and elevated at one end. The school district ran into the Rockies' high peaks, with goats, and eagles. A bit like a medieval court, Bottomly sat in an elevated throne-like chair, with successive lower levels of rank. Much like a theatre, he would enter like Johnny Carson or Dave Letterman, but without applause.

When the hall became utterly quiet, Forbes would settle into his superintendent's chair. Every soul, quietly attentive, Forbes would slowly light a new cigar in the nonsmoking hall. No one spoke without being called upon, which was seldom.

After pontification by Bottomly for up to two hours, even his loyal subjects could become drowsy, but he was the superintendent. Cliques, intimidation, fear, politics, union appeasement, ego, power, and authority all prevailed.

Paul longed for Livonia, where their ad-staff meeting also at 10:00 A.M. every Monday was held in the middle of a nearby elementary school gym. In a large circle, the assistant superintendent for instruction Paul Bennett, with Superintendent Benton Yates sitting close by, conducted the meeting with true democracy in action. Group wisdom came from reflection, dialogue, and occasional votes when consensus was not obvious. Benton Yates inspired confidence, collegiality, and teamwork.

With an eleven-month contract at Jefferson County, Paul was free to teach two graduate courses in the science curriculum at Colorado Springs. Colorado College hosted an enlarged variety of summer offerings. Wife Geri decided to enroll as a student in her husband's class. This was a new experience for both. Despite initially trying to be incognito, other students soon discovered "Geri was staying with their professor." The silly charade was quickly over, and no one was surprised that she received an "A" in the course.

Honya Holme and Nat King Cole

Long on science, scientists, and science programs, Paul and Geri eagerly developed a cordial relationship with Miss Honya Holme, the noted Broadway choreographer. Honya offered a creative dance course each summer in Colorado Springs, in an attempt to bring culture west and talent east. "My Fair Lady," "Oklahoma" and other numerous, successful Broadway plays and movies provided substantial notoriety. By living in the same dorm, sharing dorm life, occasionally lunches and dinners, Paul was to discover an entire world unknown to him, John, or Jay Gould.

In Roxbury, round and square dancing, in the Grange Hall Saturday night, with music by Mel German, was pretty much the entire program. In 1948, Paul had tried out for the high school band, but couldn't even get enough rhythm to drum. Eddie Arnold, Ernest Tubb, and Roy Acoff were the only known virtuosos.

Honya Holme had mastered a technique of setting the body's motion to a score on paper. Honya would hold out one arm and move it. Motion, not a musical note, could be recorded. Fingers, wrist, and elbow motions were all recorded with small bars, dots symbols, and signs. Now with two arms, legs, torso, and a head,

Honya could record movements or create motions right down to your kneecap. Body language was set to music.

Miss Holme often brought a small entourage from her New York studio. She could hand a protégé a dozen sheets of paper with what seemed like hieroglyphics. A quick glance at the "score" and the dancer would jump, skip, and dance the precise movements from the score. It seemed that a dozen sheets of score would be acted out in only a few seconds. Paul was thrilled, liking its visual representation equal to the Periodic Table of Elements, or even the Electro Magnetic Spectrum!

The same summer, 1961, the famous Broadmore Hotel in the Springs hosted singer Nat King Cole, already a national favorite. Paul recalled his Hardscrabble Road milk and cookies days with the Royal family and the cordial reception African Americans enjoyed in the Catskills thirty years prior. Nat's "arrangements" were with a poor black couple, across the tracks in the Spanish American and black ghetto area of Colorado Springs. The Broadmore would send their stretch limo to pick him up long enough to entertain, then return him to the ghetto.

The awful hypocrisy and injustice brought tears to Paul's eyes. Small town values did seem better. In a speech that summer, at a regional meeting of NSTA, Paul admonished a group of authors to re-examine the hundreds of picture/illustrations in elementary science textbooks. There were others who protested to be sure, but subsequent editions of science textbooks across the nation brought forth dozens of illustrations of boys and girls, some with "heavy tans." Within only a few years, other non-science books followed and some of the kids were "just plain black." Roxbury's *mentoring* and small town values prevailed throughout the publishing world. With science books first, others followed. John Burroughs complained about *the practice of killing and stuffing birds.* Paul complained about *the visual representation of children in the textbooks of America.*

In 1930 in Roxbury, it was okay to be black, but not Jewish. In Colorado in 1960, it was okay to be Spanish American, but not black. The American Indians, more abused than Jews, African Americans, Irish and others, are still relegated to scattered reservations around the country. Go figure. When will we learn? When will we ever learn?

Apparently singer and motion picture star, Harry Bellafonte, was the next African American entertainer at this prestigious resort. Bellafonte, tall, handsome, African American but with Caucasian features made it clear he would require suitable lodging, at the hotel. His "My way or the highway" attitude prevailed along with grace and talent. Jackie Robinson had been playing with the Dodgers since 1947.

Bellafonte at the time, was perhaps more accepted than superstar and "Rat Pack" Sammy Davis Jr. In later years Bellafonte became outspoken and aggressive for African American causes castigating the United States secretary of state, in 2002, and other African American in leadership positions for being Uncle Tom's.

Yellowstone National Park

Paul and Geri often visited campground I-55 at Fishing Bridge in Yellowstone National Park. Jim and Beth Carlson, originally from Minnesota were camping in nearby I-54, and were also living in Denver. Jim was also a scout, fisherman, woodsman, and outdoorsman. Beth, a registered nurse, made biscuits and oatmeal, and fried the trout that Paul and Jim caught daily, cooking like she was Martha Stewart.

During the first of several two-week campouts later, the two couples became long-term friends. In their first visit, they quickly discovered that park rangers were eager for wine, popcorn, and camp talk at 10:00 P.M. Paul often thought of John Muir, Teddy Roosevelt, Burroughs, and thousands of others who gravitated around campfires in Yellowstone and the Hetch-Hetchy Valley. Those few also enjoyed campfires at Hardscrabble in Paul's beloved Roxbury.

The Rangers, often three or four at a time, were eager for socialization with dozens of elk, grizzly, fish, fire, and tourist stories. It was a wonderful way to enjoy the fire. A large, noisy family moved in "next door." Utilizing a double site, two large tents, batteries to run TV's, loud music, and car headlights for lights, they destroyed the tranquility of a dozen campsites. Like city folks everywhere, campers laid out a perimeter, tree-to-tree with ropes defining their turf. Extra blankets hung over ropes to further define their corridor, with finally a "no trespassing," sign located in the front entrance.

This was now Paul and Geri's third or fourth visit to I-55 and the constant yelling, arguing, and music was unacceptable. But what to do? The rangers provided instructions. Like bears, we were to never, never, confront obnoxious tourists or ask them to reduce their clatter. The next day Paul and Jim each caught their limit of cutthroat trout, three each, nearly all a foot long: beautiful specimens. At the time, many of Yellowstone Lake's trout had a single inch-long worm lodged in their abdomen and flesh, which could be removed. All six were worm free!

Paul volunteered to clean the fish. The neighbors being vacant, he carefully slid fish innards under each of their two large tents. Time passed and evening came. The Rangers came, ate popcorn, enjoyed a glass of wine, and inquired as to which plan Paul had adopted.

Fish guts were easily acknowledged as the best of all possible techniques. The Ploutzes and Carlsons were careful to secure all foods in coolers, high in a tree, or in a car trunk. "Keep the fire going, and leave a candle or small light on in your tent. We'll see you tomorrow."

Around midnight, about an hour after the neighbors had finally quieted, three large black bears seeking fish guts shoved their way under the tents, growling and snorting.

Totally petrified, the neighbors struck camp in the middle of the night and left in the belief the bears had been after them. One of them had even stood on the hood of their van. They abandoned some of their rope and blankets between the trees. The rangers, happy to see tranquility returned to the forest, suggested, that "You only need a few guts under one tent!"

Chapter 14:   A Financial Disaster

In early 1963, a dispute between Francis Singer, Ted Service of Singer with Don Decker (author group) saw the termination of the renowned L.W. Singer Science Series.   Only the D.C. Heath, Herman, and Nina Schneider texts were more successful at the time. This was a major, major setback.

This decision after two years of intense effort saw thousands of dollars agonizingly down the tube. Even Paul and Geri's move to Colorado no longer made sense. Don made it clear, there would be no reconciliation. It was final, over.

Authors still owned the nearly finalized text. Paul gained Don's approval to pursue other publishers.   Ploutz, almost frantically, was conferencing with five major publishers who had "lesser" series or who were interested in commencing a new one.

Paul was flying back and forth to various corporate headquarters located in Chicago. Now traveling at his own expense and representing a series largely complete but which three others owned was a difficult dance.

Textbook companies are highly competitive. With the text nearly finished, publishers were essentially being asked to accept a "pig in a poke" With numerous contracts, which would then have to be completed, and new budget requirements to publish millions of books, most publishers seemed overwhelmed. They had no previous experience of anything of the sort.

Don Decker was unwilling to expose what the Singer problem had been or was. Paul explained that if he was able to put together a new agreement then he would want to be a "financial equal" (no more junior author).

Wheeling and dealing across the country, Paul thought of his earlier neighbor, Jay Gould going to New York City with his famous mahogany box and new mousetrap contraption.   Gould discovered that "if you build a better mouse trap" the world wouldn't necessarily come running to your door. Paul discovered much the same. Efforts to salvage the science series failed with the passing of time, complications, and confusion of focus.

Several years later, an abbreviated series, with Mim Ballou and Decker, emerged but without Paul. The series was never to regain its prominent position in the textbook world.

Forty years later (2003) Paul located Mim Ballou, who had retired in Florida. He had, after all, moved from Michigan to

Colorado with his wife to work on the Singer Series for two years and without compensation. Paul finally had the opportunity to ask Mim what had happened between Singer and Decker? Otherwise friendly, cordial, her response was that "It didn't make any difference."

Triple Salary Helps

The summer of 1963 arrived with multiple demands on Paul's eleven-month contract and four-week off period. He had now taught summer sessions at several universities. With participation in numerous experimental science curricula, Jeff. County suggested that he visit the various centers where Jeff. County teachers were writing new programs. His wife, Geri, also needed to return east to finish her master's degree program at Wayne State University in Detroit. The University of Michigan, among others, had invited Paul to teach two four-week courses. The Elementary Science Study writing team at Vassar-Harvard requested his participation, likely unaware, that the fabled Singer Series was down the drain.

Worthy of Jay Gould's financial manipulation and still Jeff County's "fair-haired boy," Paul received approval to "freelance" for four weeks on salary, teaching, and visiting writing sites as he saw fit. The Elementary Science Study, eager to add Paul's name as endorsement credibility, agreed to pay a four-week stipend for Paul to attend one week with meals and lodging in a girl's dormitory at Vassar.

The University of Michigan agreed to pay the adjunct Professor Ploutz for the four-week courses, but he taught it in three weeks. All three employers agreed to pay traveling expenses from Denver.

All plans were implemented. Geri got to Wayne State, finishing her master's degree. Paul received triple salary for four weeks, along with automatic perdiem travel allowances, which he did not have to "cook the books" to receive. Besides, they drove rather than flew. Returning to Jeff. County with their first secondhand car, a few bucks ahead, and no laborious evening writing, the playing field seemed level for a brief period. Peace and harmony were not to last.

One Larry Watts, a former Jeff. County science supervisor had returned. Superintendent Bottomly had been impressed with Larry's ability to crowd even more Dr.'s, Sir's and proper respect into whatever part of Bottomly's anatomy was presented. Watts was also of large physical frame.

Deputy Superintendent Del Peterson, an excellent administrator, was effectively "exiled." Bottomly had recruited him from the Seattle area to work as deputy superintendent. Del took the surprised demotion so hard that he was hospitalized. While hospitalized, he was removed from his position to give it to Larry Watts. Watts was the only man on earth "who for unknown reasons" disliked the eminent Don Decker and "newcomer" Paul Ploutz.

Eminent "Decker" had recently completed the "conventional" seventh-eighth-ninth grade books for Singer Company (now Random House). A decision to rearrange these three new texts was made following the K-12 format successfully introduced in 1958. The life science (biology) of all three books needed condensing for the seventh grade; the earth science portions were moved to the eighth grade; and physical science (heat-light-sound-mechanics-energy) portions of all three to the ninth grade text.

Perhaps as a consolation prize for the earlier disaster, Paul was invited to do the re-arrangement project, with his name in small print as collaborator on the newly reorganized junior high school series. Better still, original laboratory manuals for each of the three texts need to be written by Paul alone, but "yesterday!"

Here We Go Again

Once again Paul was back writing until midnight developing laboratory experiments for junior high school biology, physics, and chemistry. For the most part, the books represented true "lab" work for most schools in the United States.

Paul hastily recruited three science teachers, Paul W. Richard, life science; Clyde B. Lambert, earth science; and Bill W. Tillery, for physical science. These colleagues were to be co-authors with Paul, writing thirty bonafide laboratory experiences each. Each student was to be a full participant as opposed to the time honored students watching the teacher doing the experiment. In junior high schools across the United States, desks were often in straight rows, some screwed to the floor and even inclined. Paul's full participation manuals with every student doing labs and the teacher "watching" required new thinking. This meant new desks and new equipment for a class, as opposed to one demonstration desk, new books, smaller classes, and, equally important, the teacher abandoning lectures for supervision.

Decker, L.W. Singer Company, Ploutz, and his three co-authors, along with collaboration on the new *Basic Life, Basic Earth, Basic Physical Science* textbook, had the right product. This was a propitious moment in time. Decker's K-12 scope and sequence concept had been created during Decker's presidency of NSTA.

Paul and his co-authors were completing the manuals in late 1962. The manuals were published in 1964 and again in 1967. Decker and Paul completed the text reorganization slightly earlier. Paul was asked, no, required, to sign a statement affirming that he was "not then" or "had ever been" a member of the communist party. Senator Joseph McCarthy's influence had permeated even the textbook business.

Sir, Dr. Bottomly had always sought to have a nationally known author on staff. He had learned about Ploutz, and then hired him through Decker. Sir Bottomly approved even encouraged time off to write. Watts, now aware that the K-6 Singer program had been cancelled, was also aware that Paul was "still" often home or on an airplane somewhere, not in the office as Watts expected.

In fairness, it may be that Bottomly-Watts, in running the second largest school district in Colorado had forgotten the released-time agreement. Had they bothered to check, they would probably have been elated to learn that three additional co-authors from the district had been added to the district's accomplishments. It was not to be. Watts, clearly eager to control, reduce, or eliminate Ploutz's influence and freewheeling nature, had been keeping notes.

Forbes Bottomly perhaps like Bruce Shearer in Oneonta in the 1950s was short, perhaps physically insecure. Both his personal assistant Jim somebody, and now Larry Watts were both well over six feet tall. Bottomly called them both by their first names. They of course, called him Dr. Dr. Dr. Paul didn't see it coming, but was called to see Bottomly.

Forbes: Sorry Paul, but I find it necessary to eliminate your position.

Paul: OK.

Forbes: What?

Paul:	OK.
Forbes:	Well, you're taking it very well. Don't you even want to know why?
Paul:	I've been writing night and day. This will provide the time I need to finish the junior high school stuff I'm writing.
Forbes:	You're writing some junior high school material?
Paul:	"Yes, recall you said that I, and the coach climbing Mt. Everest, could have as much time as we needed?
Forbes:	Oh my God, yes vaguely. I must say you've taken this very well. What will you do?
Paul:	Write night and day instead of just nights. Geri is teaching at Fairmont Elementary School. Nothing much will change.
Forbes:	Er, Would you like to resign?
Paul:	Well, whatever, why resign?
Forbes:	I'd forgotten about your released time. I'm not happy firing you, so your resigning is much neater.
Paul:	Resigning would make it a little better for whoever contrived this event (referring to Watts). Having let it get this far, perhaps your opportunity to be neat has been lost.
Forbes:	Consider resigning. I will pay you a couple months extra, Announce you needed the time to write, and send a memo instructing staff to provide library related support; stuff like that.
Paul:	OK.

It was done, the only time Paul had been fired, oops, resigned.

The eleven-month contract was nearly complete anyway. With extra writing time, the junior high school writing project was swiftly concluded. Geri had finished her teaching assignment at Fairmont. Principal Ilene Dean was sorry to see her leave. Geri and Ilene remained in touch for many years.

Paul had maintained contact with the job placement offices at STC Oneonta, Colorado State College (now University of Northern Colorado), and the University of Michigan. Science teachers from beloved Livonia and Jefferson County profited from "*mentor*" Paul.

Over the years, Paul had recruited dozens of science teachers to be authors. He had helped NASA's public education programs/presenters, college teachers, scout leaders, and Audubon Society. Paul now served as *mentor* to a growing cadre of science educators. He helped candidates gain editorial positions, assisted Fulbright nominees, planetarium directors, outdoor educational specialists, and other science-related professionals. Resigning as editor for the fledgling journal of the National Science Supervisor's Association, Paul was briefly assistant national membership director, (NSTA) serving under Jerrold W. Maben. Paul's area included fifteen western states including many of his old professors, comrades, and peers.

Paul, had fed the job market over the years in science education with deserving friends. Some were now ready to provide *him* with benefits. Making lots of friends who were at or would rise to high posts would pay future dividends. John Burroughs, the naturalist, successfully cultivated Emerson, Firestone, Edison, Muir, Roosevelt, Whitman, Ford, and other prominent leaders and authors. Ploutz, the science educator cultivated many professionals. Some, like Bob Binger, would die prematurely. Friends with national or international reputations, included:

Stan Marshall, president Florida State University; Carl Sagan, Cornell; William Shockley, Nobel physicist; Al Schatz, inventor of oreomycin; Charles Helvey, Martin Marietta Corp; Werner Von Braun, Willie Ley, NASA; Bill Tillery, author; Jack Fisher, SRA; Larry Willie, IBM; Glen Blough, Univ. Md.; Sam Gates, CSC; Linus Pauling, Nobel; Walt Disney; Tom Dewey, Nelson Rockefeller, N.Y.; A. A. Allen, Cornell; Neil Armstrong, NASA; George Mallinson author, University of Michigan; Herbert A. Smith, AAAS; Fletcher Watson, Harvard; Edward Victor, author Northwestern University; Mary Hawkins, editor, NSTA; Roger Tory Peterson, author; and of course, Don Decker, *mentor*.

Placement offices enjoy folks who send people in and out. Decker had graduated from the University of Michigan. Adjunct

Professor Ploutz had taught the fast three-week summer session there, but had not been a student. It was a revelation that many placement offices will help if you never attended their institution.

Teaching at Colorado State College (CSC, Greeley) in graduate school, summer session college at Colorado College (Colorado Springs), and the University of Michigan, made Paul look pretty good on paper. He had long since "deep-sixed" Delaney's arrogant reference, packed the "five-letter credentials" with seven, carefully crafted letters, knowing their contents. Triggering all three placement offices into action, once again he gained multiple positions to sort through.

Recently, Geri's mother, now a widow, had actually spoken to Paul. Geri missed city life. Colorado locals thought anyone from east of the Mississippi was a Yankee. It would be good to return to the "east."

Paul and Geri had briefly stayed at the Deckers when moving to Colorado. Paul called Don, suggesting that it would be nice to stay "at their house a few days" on the way out of Colorado. Within a day or two, Don returned the call, instead suggesting a meeting with Superintendent Bottomly, Paul, and himself. Don was to bring Dr. Hughes, a third party observer to the meeting held at Bottomly's home.

The purpose of the meeting, apparently requested by Decker, was not clear, at least to Paul. Hughes was a psychologist. Was Decker attempting to patch things up? Was Hughes asked to determine everyone's degree of sanity? Was Bottomly, having recalled Paul's time- release agreement and Watt's purge, regretting the displeasure he had caused Paul or Decker?

Paul never learned. Nor were Paul or Geri invited to stay at the Deckers on the way east. Nor did Paul ever again see Bottomly, Watts, or Decker. Several years later Watts attempted to gain a consulting position with the Science Research Associates (SRA). Paul used his influence with IBM, SRA's parent company, to successfully block Watt's appointment. Years later, hearing of Watts's death, Paul quietly rejoiced, as those in 1892 had done for Jay.

Like Burroughs and Walt Whitman helping Civil War casualties in Washington, D.C., Paul was always interested in helping others. Like Gould, however, he seemed equally committed to shafting those who he thought had acted unfairly or against his interests. Paul seemed content with the image as the kind of guy who would do anything *for* you or *to* you, depending of course, on circumstances. He once mused that it's best to get even when the other person never realizes it. His dark side perhaps, but he would carefully use his influence resources and imagination for those who had crossed him unfairly.

Hello, Athens and Ohio University

Landing in Columbus, Ohio, on the way to an interview at Ohio University in Athens, Paul realized he had been there once before. Ohio University was creating two new universities abroad, one in Kano and a second in Abaden, Nigeria. Ohio University had been surfing the entire country for faculty. Ohio University wanted to set up dual teacher education programs, essentially in the jungle. Gilford Crowell, dean of the College of Education, had told of driving his car into his driveway one night to see a large cobra, its head inflated in his headlights, waving its head to and fro. Frightening to many, Paul, at that time still a bachelor, liked the adventure aspect well enough. But since he wasn't hunting for a jungle job, he declined.

Ohio University's enrollment in 1964 was just over eight-thousand. The city of Athens was only slightly larger. The interview went well. Paul liked the small town, and friendly atmosphere. The Appalachian hills were less rugged than the Catskills, but were hills nonetheless. Paul and Geri traded tumbleweed, flatland, and Herefords for poison ivy, hills, and dairy cattle. Since he no longer milked cattle, that seemed good. In 1962, Paul and Geri Ploutz moved from Colorado to Ohio University in Athens, Ohio.

Traveling one mile in any direction put you into hard core Appalachia, far worse than Paul had experienced elsewhere in the states. Paul was offered the position of assistant professor of (science) education by Department Chair Albert Shuster. Politely declining, Paul explained that even as associate professor, he would be experiencing a small salary cut.

Mindful of his Temple University "full professor" blunder, Paul indicated that if offered the associate post he would most likely accept. Further, he had been invited for other interviews, though "he'd be glad to hear from OU." Back at 4417 Teller St., Wheatridge, the "associate" contract arrived. With no need to bug Decker for a place to stay, Paul and Geri headed for Athens, Ohio,

45701. Paul sold both his beloved 1962 Dodge convertible and Geri's Volkswagen Bug. With smiles on their faces, they headed east in their new Olds 88 convertible!

Larry and Donna Redenbaugh, friends from an earlier Yellowstone Park fishing bridge campground named affectionately I-55, lived in Lincoln, Nebraska. Paul and Geri stopped to renew the friendship. On that Sunday afternoon, Larry and Donna had prepared a magnificent cookout. The sky was sunny, the temperature eighty degrees Fahrenheit, all wore shorts and moccasins. The friendship was warm and the beer cold. Clouds to the west suggested a brief shower. Paul cautiously put the top up on their new blue Olds 88 convertible.

Within minutes, strong wind was upon them, so hard as to tip the grill, steaks flopping to the ground. Hail stones larger than golf balls, thumped, cracked, and bounced, depending on where they landed. They cracked on the sidewalk, bounced on the hood and trunk of the Olds 88, and thumped on bare backs and heads. So many, so fast. The ground was covered, in a little over a minute or so. They had lumps on their heads and dents in the new car hood and trunk. The sun and calm returned. Walking was difficult, like walking over marbles, which rolled, rather than crushed.

One small consolation was that Paul, the science educator, who "knew practically everything (science) about practically nothing," understood exactly why it had happened and was anxious to avoid a repeat. Driving east the next day across miles of Nebraska flatland, and prairie, they noticed dozens of "dust devils," often seeing several at once. It was the tornado "season" and factors were ripe for a repeat. None of the dust devils matured into storms to roar up "tornado alley."

Welcome To Appalachia

"Hitting the ground running," Paul taught both summer sessions at OU in 1962 prior to the September opening of the fall semester. Geri had earlier applied for a teaching position in the local Athens school district. With four years of experience, having recently completed her M.S. degree and team-taught, one would think her an ideal candidate. Athens was a college town. Many professors wives were teachers. Like college towns elsewhere, there were more teachers than were needed. With schools almost ready to open, Geri read the notice of her employment in the local newspaper.

The Athens schools were a stark contrast compared to the affluent, Livonia, Michigan, district where Paul and Geri had met. "Just show up at East Elementary, and teach sixth grade," was the directive. Principal Myrna Ashworth, who lived across the street from East, would often merely walk across the street early in the morning in her housedress and slippers and "be principal."

Geri's new friend Arlene Dressel, a fifth-grade teacher, and also a professor's wife, who had arrived the previous year suggested, "The best is yet to come."

Miss Ashworth once approached Geri after a grading period, suggesting she change a boy's grade. After all, his father was an official in the National Football League, and a "poor grade wouldn't look good on the family name." Some principal.

Associate Professor Ploutz visited Geri's classroom after school one day in 1965. Paul discovered that the science texts for Geri's class of twenty-four students were published in 1931, the year he had been born. One 1931 well-used copy of Paul's beloved Singer Science Series was in the room. It did reveal that George Willard Frasier was senior author prior to Don Decker.

Later in 1968, when Martin Luther King was assassinated, Principal Ashworth refused to drop the school flag to half-mast, as instructed by the superintendent. You get the picture: Athens City was still very much in Appalachia.

Within a mile or two of Athens there were still children born without birth certificates being issued. Burying a senior citizen that had never been counted at any census or never held a social security number was not uncommon. Jokes prevailed that your "parents could get a divorce but she would still be your sister."

Ohio University existed in stark contrast to its hillbilly (now redneck) coal mining and strip mining outer environment. Established in 1804, OU had mature Ph.D. programs in the arts, sciences, and education.

OU had a "lab" school so faculty children could be schooled there, so as not to get fleas, or otherwise be contaminated at the public schools. Both of Ploutz's daughters Lori, born March 24, 1966, and Julie, born, September 2, 1972, attended the Rufus Putnam Lab School.

When Lori Lynn was born, Geri gave up teaching and became a full time mother. Nineteen Clearview Heights, Athens, Ohio, was the first home they owned. The brick home was located on three acres. Paul had a small pond dug out of southeaster Ohio's sticky red clay. The pond was often the color of tomato soup but with lilly pads, and good fishing it was an attractive addition to their "starter home." The couple swam in the pond for years prior to adding a twenty-by forty-foot in ground pool for the two girls and the neighbor's kids to enjoy. They lived in Athens for twenty-eight years prior to moving to Albany, Ohio, and setting up their private nature preserve.

During the next eighteen years at Ohio University, both the Burroughs and Gould influence became even more obvious.

Chapter 15:   Paul's Vision of Teaching Science

New Ways of Teaching Science

New ways of teaching science, with team teaching, programmed learning, ability grouping, performance advancements, and other techniques were under experimentation during 1960 through the 1980s.   Federal grants, matching funds, summer workshops, and professional training leaves permeated American education.

There were outdoor education, in-school planetariums, mixed sexes, technical and career courses, separated sexes, preschool, adult education and GEDs for earlier dropouts. Day schools, night schools, religious schools, and military schools all flourished. Art, music, and physical education programs suffered both for time in the curriculum and for money for equipment.

In all but a few school districts across the United States, muscle movement for children was deemed as absolutely necessary for healthy development.   Gym and physical education were often terminated. The idea was more subject matter and homework so our society could "catch up" with the Russians, Chinese, Germans, or to whomever we were compared unfavorably. Paul's idea was to teach elementary science totally within art, music, and gym, in school, then to ask outside of school organizations also to take responsibility.

Paul solicited 4-H Clubs, the YMCA, the YWCA, Future Farmers of America (FFA), Boy and Girl Scouts, Rainbow Girls, the Grange, and the Isaac Walton League all to sponsor educational activities, particularly in science. They worked together, in the spirit of "It takes a whole village to raise a child."

Paul thought he could coordinate/*mentor* anything. Jack Fisher, one of his NSTA friends, had taken on the role of science editor for the Science Resource Association (SRA), a subsidiary of IBM. Fisher, later, at Burgin Community College in New Jersey (and now retired) deserves the claim or shame (success or failure?) for this original approach.

Fisher arranged funding for his proposal then hired Paul Ploutz and William Shockley. Paul the educational specialist, Shockley the Nobel physicist. Shockley had invented the transistor in 1958. "Bill" was the science specialist. An example of the approach was to teach science through art, music, and gym. Water colors and paints for example, could be used for the visible spectrum teaching primary colors, transparent, translucent, and opaque. For textures, sources of color, reflection, refraction wavelengths, rainbows, the uses were endless. The piano, drum, and flute could be for sound, energy, wave length, pitch, volume, frequency modulation (FM), amplitude modulation (AM), or the speed of sound at sea level.

Science was everywhere! Physical education (PE) provided opportunities to figure air pressure in a basketball, the arc of a set shot, the friction of sneakers, and calories burned in doing pushups. Math goes well with PE too!

Paul, flying from OU (the Columbus Airport) and Bill from Stanford University, met every other weekend and occasionally holidays for several months with meals, lodging, and transportation included. Paul, with the painful two-year Singer fiasco behind him, negotiated for one-hundred dollars a day plus royalties on the innovative K-6 series. By staying at the premier Holiday Inn Hotel on the loop in downtown Chicago (555 N. Shore Dr.), eating oysters on the half shell, and gradually turning on the tower carousel high above the city, Paul felt that he was living. From Paul's point of view, this was much like Gould, roaring up and down past Manhattan Island on his magnificent yacht, Atalanta!

Thinking Like Gould

In 1964, the junior high school Singer, life-earth-physical science textbooks hit the market along with Paul's co-authored, "every student does it," lab manuals. The Singer JHS series had been well advertised, even anticipated. School districts often "recycle" science texts every three or five years.

The instant success was thus duplicated each year during the five-year period. The "every student lab" increased sales for manufacturers of science equipment, hardware, beakers, motors, microscope, etc. Texas, California, and others did "state-wide adoptions," recommending the text for use and driving text sales in other states.

Paul had been baptized at age twelve, in the Jay Gould Memorial Church. He now thought briefly, that just maybe, he would "catch up with Gould." Perhaps he would receive a royalty check, year after year, equal to his salary as professor. The textbooks and manuals went to second editions in 1967. Some years his royalty checks would equal his salary as professor, and that was great. Catching up with Gould, utter fantasy.

With his new found affluence, Paul made several investments of vacant land in Athens. Ohio University's enrollment of eight-thousand in 1964 was to nearly double during the next decade. Ohio University president Vernon Alden, a Harvard MBA grad, suggested it was "OK" with him for Paul to make some of his newly purchased land "available." The code word was subdivision. University Heights, the first of Paul's subdivisions with twenty-four half-acre lots, sold out quickly. Several of Paul's university colleagues could not fathom why or how he could dilute his teaching responsibilities. Based in part on the jealously of peers, OU conducted an investigation of Paul's activities for "conflict of interest." Paul was healthy, and never missed or cancelled a class. His evaluations by students were equal too and often better than those "investigating" him. He was also writing articles for journals and was serving on numerous college and civic committees and organizations.

Paul easily survived the first of several investigations. Other professors with high or unconventional profiles hailed his success. A few faculty members, who earlier, were merely quietly envious, would no longer speak.

The following year another subdivision "Fairway Oaks" was marketed. This time OU's director of legal affairs and planning coordinator presented themselves in Paul's off campus real estate office. They complained that the university actually owned one of the roads in Fairway Oaks and that Paul was effectively "trespassing." Neither proved accurate. Ohio University did have an easement, which allowed them to drive over the roads to reach the WOUB radio/TV tower. Ploutz, in a positive gesture, wrote a letter to university president Charles Ping. Paul explained that OU had profited and was "forever free" of maintaining the road leading to the university tower. The Athens County commissioners and township trustees were now responsible for road maintenance. Ironically, Paul had purchased the property from John Cline, one of the county commissioners. Once again Paul survived a bogus attempt by OU to eliminate or curtail his non classroom activity.

Within a few weeks, OU hired the Ellis Tower Company from Florida to replace some of the long guy wires holding their twelve-hundred-foot tower upright and straight. Some of the long wires were secured in huge concrete anchors or at the edge or within lots on the Fairway Oaks development.

Heavy construction trucks drove through residential lots cutting deep ruts into future residential lawns. One huge truck was stuck and mired to its axle. Ellis Tower employees tied a steel cable around an oak tree. The tree was judged to be over one-hundred years in age. Tying the cable around the tree, they hoped to winch the truck out of the lawn just as Paul happened by. As the steel cable tightened it turned on the tree tearing a large section of bark from the trunk.

Ohio University and its tower company were trespassing and damaging property. Realizing the university always wins and that eventually he would lose, Paul had little choice and threatened to call the sheriff. There are several large universities around the country that are located in relatively small communities. The president of Cornell, Ohio U, SUNY Potsdam, Oneonta, and others are often like the proverbial eight-hundred-pound gorilla. Their budgets and their impact on local citizens are often larger than the local mayor's. Their payroll is often largely responsible for the ultimate health of the community. Riding roughshod over the people or things that get in their way has largely become acceptable. Since their cause or final outcome is thought to be just, lesser causes or people often get stiffed. The end justifies the means. Paul seemed to have trouble remembering that the gorilla "sleeps anywhere it wants to."

Student apartments were incredibly scarce with the booming enrollment. Paul bought a dozen older homes near campus to convert to duplexes and triplexes. Remodeled houses over forty years old qualified for tax refunds. Paul assembled about forty apartments during the 1970s. Paul became a "millionaire" at approximately noon, May 15, 1979, when he bought a small house on a large lot in Athens City. The following day he hired a demolition crew who removed the entire structure within twenty-four hours.

The local bank now furious, having loaned money on the house now gone threatened to sue. Paul went to bank number two, borrowed enough money to pay off the pending "suit" and purchased still another house. A donut chain happily purchased the now vacant lot on Richland Avenue for double what it cost.

The deal closed on noon May fifteenth. Paul, now more like Gould, than Burroughs, next obtained a real estate license, and opened a Century 21 real estate franchise. It became the top office among twelve in Athens County within a few months. This was the first real estate franchise in the Athens market. Now some of the local realtors were jealous along with some of his colleagues in the School of Curriculum and Instruction.

Nearly 300 of the large bold commercial Century 21 Gold Posts with Ploutz adorned the lawns of Athens City and throughout Athens County. Ploutz was a professor of education *not* business. Some years his earnings were double that of the university's president. The number of people who were jealous and resented seeing him become wealthy seemed to multiply.

The Great Alphabets of Man

Don Decker, Paul's ultimate *mentor* had spoken often to Paul about the "Three great alphabets of man." "Any educated person should know and understand 1) the *Periodic Table of Elements*, 2) the *Geologic Time Chart*, and 3) the *Electromagnetic Spectrum*." The brash, confident young man, eager to please and impress his idol suggested he would not only devise a method to teach these three alphabets, but do it so even children could understand!

In 1970, Paul published his first educational game entitled, the "Periodic Table of Elements." He had promised Decker a game for children. Successful, other games quickly followed.

Compounds, Decimeter, 110 Animals, and later still others. Geologic Time Chart (Evolution) was a great success, and was the second of Decker's alphabets of man concept. Ploutz worked on Elements eight years, and Geological Time Chart twelve years before finally getting it field-tested and published. The third "alphabet," Electromagnetic Spectrum had yet to be presented. Jim Shipman, OU chairman of the physics department and textbook author, had made similar unsuccessful attempts. Ploutz, now the author of an even dozen classroom games, had finally found something he couldn't figure out. He reasoned that "two out of three wasn't so bad." Mental Health, Vitamins, Pirate Cache, and the Dead River games all had co-authors. "Rip Off" was about economic education and the techniques used to induce folks to buy things.

Paul had been a science supervisor in two large well-known school districts (Jefferson County, Colorado, and Livonia, Michigan), thus Lab Apparatus and 389 Science Concepts was designed to assist science teachers in setting up science programs.

For more than a decade the EDUCATIONAL GAMES company provided direction on how individual teachers and school districts could develop their own games. Mrs. Mary Hawkins and Paul held numerous meetings at annual science conferences and provided numerous workshops. Some of the meetings included more than five-hundred science teachers who had assembled at NSTA annual or regional meetings.

Mary was the associate executive secretary of the National Science Teachers Association (NSTA). Robert (Bob) Carleton, ex. sec and Mary were at the helm of NSTA for many years. Mary was editor of **The Science Teacher** with responsibility for all of NSTA's publications. A widow, she and her husband had been foreign news correspondents living in Europe prior to moving to Washington, D.C. While Paul was the originator of Educational Games he often thought of his mother's advice, "Hang out with people smarter than you are."

Mary Hawkins was smarter, much smarter. In an NSTA European trip Paul tried to order breakfast in a small French café using the two years of French obtained from Sue Root while he was still struggling academically at Roxbury Central (1948-1949). Going on and on in deliberate French, he expected a grand breakfast and ended up with only cottage cheese. Mary edited English, French, Spanish, German, well you get the idea. Paul had never thought of Mary as a *mentor* but when she finally retired from NSTA and other numerous freelance editorial positions she <u>donated</u> her entire interests in Educational Games back to Paul, insisting it all be done in writing. Mary even paid for the agreement.

In the mid 1970s The Lawhead Press of Athens, Ohio produced four of the games. More recently, the Union Printing Company, 17 West Washington, Athens, Ohio prints all of the games. Union wholesales the games to several scientific supply houses who retail them to schools across the United States Most of the games are still selling after thirty-three years (1970 - 2003) with no advertising or promotion other than being listed in supply catalogues.

Paul has finally achieved some modesty suggesting that most games are "dull" but a lightyear ahead of the alternative. At the seventh, eighth, or ninth grade level, for example, most students are asked to memorize "O" for oxygen, "C" for carbon, "H" for hydrogen etc. Simple enough, but most lesser-known elements are hard to say, or spell, and where they appear on the Periodic Table is often a mystery to beginners. Paul's game, with several simple versions and two through six players have students locate circular chips (elements) on a game board which is actually the Periodic Table. Paul jests that a few nerds love the game, and for others it's still way ahead of rote memory!

By telephone, Provost Decker, emotionally detached, but still an idol, complimented Paul on his financial and academic successes. "Good luck. If you ever finish Electromagnetic Spectrum, and if you become old and rich (like me?), you should do a game on sex education."

Paul: Why?

Decker: Because it will be the only one on the market, there is great need for it, and didn't you survive the heat over the Evolution Game pretty well?

Paul: Why will it be the only one on the market?

Decker: The others who have tried couldn't survive the inevitable criticism. If you're old and wealthy, probably you can.

Paul: Probably?

Don: You have already exceeded expectations, seem to enjoy the recognition, and if you successfully complete a sex ed. game that's the only one on the market, you'll gain all the attention you can handle.

A Mothers Admonition

That discussion Paul had with the great science educator was their last. He was unaware of Decker's retirement, health, and death. In later years, he lamented not following his idol more carefully. Don Decker had remained very poised and proper. Paul realized the role of the ultimate *mentor* is to help others and then "let go."

Paul's mother, Anna, had often told Paul that giving money anonymously was the totally unselfish form of contributing. A person's ultimate self-esteem was best served by giving without recognition, admiration, or approval from anyone. God alone would know. If you seek or need the recognition, or approval of others, that's okay, fine. When you finally learn to give without knowledge or expectation of approval of others you will finally be a fulfilled, mature, secure person. "Son, most people never reach that point, but *if the world becomes a better place, however slightly, because you were in it, that would be good."*

Welcome Julie Ann

Julie was born Labor Day, September second, 1972. The plan had been for her to be born by C section at a prearranged time in Columbus, Ohio, some seventy-five miles north of Athens. A week or so "later" was considered a safe bet. The appointment was made. The C section birth was essential, since Geri had undergone a procedure known as a Shiradca, essentially reinforcing the abdominal wall so effectively, that the so-called normal delivery, was not possible.

Apparently, Julie, now full term, was unaware of all these careful plans. Paul, Geri, and Lori, now six, spent most of "Labor Day" relaxing at 19 Clearview Hts. Geri enjoyed a short ride through the neighboring Wonder Hills residential development on the way to visit close friends, Fred and Arlene Dressel and their daughter, Lynn, a favorite playmate of Lori's. Around 4:00 P.M., Geri enjoyed a ten-minute swim in the family pool. Advanced planning had included a provision for Lori to stay with family friends when Mom and Dad would finally go to the Columbus hospital for the blessed event.

With labor pains, contractions, and water broken, Geri called her physician in Columbus, "We're on our way!" Believing that a fast trip to Columbus would solve everything, Paul, Geri, and Lori piled into their 1971 Olds 88, and headed north. Stopping briefly, they dropped Lori off at the home of her friend Susan Gaskell and parents Dr. Richard Gaskell and wife Linda, also good friends and one-time Clearview neighbors.

Irony and Hindsight

Dr. Gaskell was a pediatrician. Geri was soon in labor. Why, oh why, did they continue toward Columbus? They continued the seventy-five-mile trip toward Columbus where Dr. John

Holzaepfel was already on his way to the same hospital. Initially calm, Geri, between moans, insisted Paul should hurry.

With a straight road and his flashers on, Paul's speedometer read 120 miles per hour. Roaring up the road with flashers on did excite town marshal's, county sheriff, and the state highway patrol.

They made it fifty miles then to flashing lights, numerous cars, and wooden barricades across all lanes with the entire road sealed. A sergeant from the state police was the first to Paul's window as the hot Olds shuddered to a standstill in the middle of both lanes.

Not pausing to be interviewed, Paul hurriedly requested an escort to the Columbus Hospital, still twenty-five-miles north through other towns and villages. The experienced patrolman interjected:

Sgt.:   "No, the local Lancaster Hospital. An ambulance is on its way now, wait here.

Paul: Officer, shoot me behind the wheel if you must, but she needs to be in the hospital **now**. Lets go.

Sgt.:   Be calm, the ambulance will be here in four minutes, and if necessary we can deliver the baby ourselves. We can do that."

With Paul standing in the road, Geri is moaning in the throws of hard labor, but sewn shut, so she cannot deliver. A passionate explanation as to the ultimate consequences of uterus tearing, to a state patrolman seemed beyond his experience or comprehension.

Paul thought it likely that the child would not gain oxygen, be brain damaged, or more likely suffocate. Also, it was likely that a ruptured uterus, or torn stitches from the displaced Shirdaca, could cause Geri to bleed to death.

This was a lose-lose situation. The ambulance arrived. The hospital emergency room was only ten critical minutes away. Geri and Paul were hurried away with sirens blaring. Julie, yet unnamed, was born in the last couple of minutes in the ambulance, and on the gurney, and in the emergency entrance of the hospital. Geri was rushed to surgery with no major arteries torn or loss of blood.

Since there's still more to the story, a clipping of the events from the September 10, 1972, The Athens Messenger written by Charles W. Reamer has been provided:

"But while mother and child made it nicely, thank you - it wasn't over for the new father - not yet.

While driving him back to the place where the couple's car had been left, the accompanying officer received a call to pick up a belligerent participant in a family scrape and deliver to him to jail.

That done, the lawman had just returne to the taxi task when another radio message came in - directing him to apprehen the suspect in a combination hit-skip accident and auto theft.

The pursuit took them past the Athens couple's abandoned car - it's flasher still blinking - while the uptight father looked back wishfully - wanting deperately to quit the cops and robbers excitement and get back to his family.

Finally, when the fleeing car had been overtaken and the miscreant collared, the exhaused father begged off further involvement and walked back to his car.

This brief account can't capture the drama - the suspense -, which the couple felt that night, or can it transmit the feeling with which the father described the thrilling details of his new daughter's medical-science-defying arrival.

"This will probably be the most unusual story you've ever heard in connection with a birth announcement," said Paul Ploutz as he relived those anxious hours while giving The Messenger the other more routine details for a "New Arrivals" item.

And it was."

Chapter 16: Child Adolescent Reproductive Education

At forty-five years of age in 1976, Paul had, at least by his standards, become old and rich. Real estate, royalties, games, and rental income exceeded his salary as professor. There was Gould-like satisfaction knowing his income was more than OU's succession of presidents, Alden, Soule, or Ping, who weren't allowed to "moonlight." The poor Hardscrabble Road farm boy, now replete with a beautiful home and luxury cars had never mastered the art of humility or modesty. Paul was somehow still insecure as the skinny boy who had lost his shirt on the playground, or had to mooch lunch from classmates. Like the "recent rich," of the Lake Placid Club experience or Delaney's "air of superiority" to conceal inner feelings, Paul seemed to wear his success "on his sleeve." Few things are more annoying to others than arrogance.

Paul was outgoing, friendly, still a bit "Roxbury." Some of his pedantic colleagues found him too aggressive, bold, and confident. Numerous others were just plain jealous. Still worse in the opinion of some others, Paul always seemed to get what he wanted, including two full-year sabbatical leaves, at two-thirds salary for professional advancement, which he used to develop more games. By adding two regular faculty members as authors Dr. Charles W. Smith (math), and Dr. "Tiff" Cook (health and phys. ed.), he was also *mentoring* others to gain national prominence.

CARE stands for Child Adolescent Reproductive Education. The so-called sex ed. game suggested by Decker had been quietly underway since the last discussion with him. Having read the Kinsey Report, the Hite Report, and helping the "sex ed." program in Livonia and Jefferson County public schools, Paul concluded as had Don Decker, that a sex education game was greatly needed. NSTA, and even the National Education Association (NEA), had cautiously drawn "guidelines," generalizations, and perimeters for inclusions, without confronting the issues, anxieties, ignorance, street information, and concerns of children. Paul, at Jefferson County Schools had been available to sixth grade teachers as the "sex doctor" for class questions.   "Values" were not to be discussed.

Although the science program was sequential, sex education was seldom, if ever, a routine component of science programs across the states. In one 1961 experience, in Jefferson County

Colorado schools with the sixth grade teacher being present in the room, a sixth grader inquired "When you go down the aisle at a movie theatre, who goes first the boy or the girl?" When the teacher left the room, the question became "Can you get pregnant doing 69?" When the teacher returned: "Is it OK for a girl to ask a boy out?"

Shocked? Well, if parents don't, can't, won't help, who does? Ignorance is not really bliss, adolescents learn the "really important stuff" on the street or by participation. Teachers are too vulnerable, boards of education intimidated, parents to embarrassed to press the issue of reproductive education.

Jefferson County Schools, at any one time, had approximately fifty-five teachers teaching biology. Hardly a day went by that an angry parent, (usually a mother) didn't complain about the vocabulary, content, or teacher. The science supervisor was often used to quell parental anxiety.

Ploutz estimated that fully fifty percent of complaints were due to parental conflicts, problems, or ignorance and rarely from a lack of judgment or teacher indiscretion. Ploutz's confidence, ease, and comfort in discussing sexual topics, facilitated the retention of the "CARE" program effort.

From the mid 1960s on, Ploutz collected, recorded, and interviewed dozens of children, college students, teachers, and adults for their greatest anxieties, confusions, habits, and sexually intimidating experiences. From the womb-to-the-tomb, Paul got as much information as could be collected. In Ohio, other bible-belt states and numerous other states, laws relating to sexual dialogue with minors (children) have greatly intensified. Ministers, psychiatrists, teachers, college researchers, and even medical doctors can be at risk.

The firestorm resulting from Ploutz interviewing hundreds of children and college students was everything Decker inferred it might be. Ploutz now understands why there is not a single sex education game, unit, course, or recommended study in the United States, perhaps elsewhere on the planet. Allegations and misrepresentations by a few disgruntled students (out of thousands) led to still another investigation.

Paul, battered not broken, continues to hope that CARE and the Electromagnetic Spectrum, will one day be produced and used in the junior high schools, perhaps earlier. Author, newspaper, press, and media rights, under the first amendment, continue to be eroded. In a few instances, the reputation of physicians, parents, even day-care centers, have been compromised by normal childhood fantasies blown out of proportions by otherwise well-intended prosecutors. Paul, like others, has paid a price. Unfortunately children's limited information to this day has a street component to it.

Health and the Sunshine Boy

On the farm, usually without a shirt, little PeeWee had a dark tan on top of his otherwise blond, light complexion. Frequently peeling from excessive sunlight and with water blisters, Paul was dried by still more sunlight. So accustomed to wearing only shorts, Paul could run barefooted then slide to a dead stop in gravel, toes just fine! The effects of radiation (sunlight) are cumulative, but were not well known in the 1930s, 40s, and even later. Paul had a sixteen year experience on the farm, swimming, fishing, and camping. He was an outdoors and sun lover. In subsequent years as a lifeguard, and a convertible owner, he absorbed even more sunshine. Gardening, hiking, camping, ocean cruises, the Amazon, biking, fishing, and SCUBA diving, all exposed Paul to still more sunlight.

The hole in the ozone layer is real. More ultra violet and other rays hit the earth. With his fair complexion, the cumulative radiation caused Paul multiple skin cancers starting in the late 70s. Paul had squamous, Bowens, basil cell cancer, and precancerous growths. More than fifty biopsies, nitrogen freezes, and numerous chemical face peels eliminate his skin cancers as they appear. Ploutz, aged seventy one (2002) suggests that we all become "tree hugger" activists to reduce emissions damaging to the protective ozone layer above the earth. Paul thinks that global populations could be spared his skin cancer experiences.

Nearer the poles, Australia south, Alaska north, where the ozone even less protects earth layer than nearer the equator, skin cancer has dramatically increased. In Australia, for example, school children now cover up in eighty degree temperature to cover their skin, or skip the playground and recess altogether.

Always looking ahead, Ploutz suggests that all of those now under "sun lamps" should maintain a log of their "exposure." The time will come, when class action suits against sun parlors and similar radiation salons will inevitably arrive. People will need records "to get a fair share" of settlements. Of course victims will also need to be alive, start hugging trees now?

Paul Sells the Metric System

Most of the educational games developed in the 70s are still selling thirty years later. The Decimeter game for children ten years and older has a second version for adults, all in the same box. Presently, Union Printing Company, 17 West Washington Street, Athens, Ohio, handles the production and scientific supply companies. Paul has made no attempt to make the games available through Toys R Us or other game companies.

With increased globalization, the United States was experiencing negative economic effects from the English system of weights and measures. In one of Paul's many ventures outside of his classroom professorship, he was promoting the conversion to the metric system, or "metrification." Having already published several metric manuals for teachers and classroom use, Paul "hit the road" for metrification. With successful manuals on the market, (Charles W. Merrill Co. and Kendall-Hunt Publishing Co., 1970) Paul promoted his own manuals while promoting metrification. He routinely autographed metric manuals for many who purchased them, as is the custom.

The metric bill was stalled in Congress by public resistance not knowing how to think "metrically." Programmed learning, the newest "in" technique for teaching yourself was utilized in both of his manuals and their subsequent editions. Paul's manuals were designed to teach teachers as well as parent how to learn metrification by themselves. Happy to testify for such a worthy cause, Paul lobbied conservative Congressman Clarence Miller, who helped tip the scale for passage of the metric system for use in the United States. Metrics now would have to be used in government bidding and the automotive industry. Others followed suit. The United States was now in step with the rest of the world.

John Burroughs had earlier coined the phrase "nature fakers" to ridicule less nature-minded folks. Paul coined "tri-dozen-inch" to tease usage of the meter 0 to 100 centimeter, based on tens rather than the "36" inches, in a yardstick. There were lots of others to be sure, but Paul's tri-dozen-inch still survives for those needing to ridicule the old ways. In a similar spoof, the introduction of his

1972 (Bell & Howell) Metric Manual reads:

1. "Give them a centimeter and they'll take a kilometer."
2. "A miss is as good as a kilometer."
3. "I wouldn't touch a skunk with a 3 meter pole."
4. "He's all wool and a meter wide."
5. "There was a crooked man and he walked a crooked kilometer."
6. "A gram of prevention is worth a kilogram of cure."
7. "The Texan pulled a rabbit out of a 42 liter hat."
8. "Don't put your light under a 35 liter basket."
9. "Peter Piper picked 10 1/2 liters of pickled peppers."
10. "Oh Thumbelina, what's the difference if you're very small? When your heart is full of love you're 2.7 meters tall."

Suffering mildly from the jealously of his peers and severe criticism over the CARE game, Ploutz tried to use self-deprecating comments and humor in a gradually failing attempt to be seen merely as "one of the boys." It had worked well in Livonia but was less effective in the College of Education, at Ohio University.

Finding Humor in Science

The 1977, second edition (Charles E. Merrill) of Paul's Metric Manual dedication reads:

"This manual is fondly dedicated to former JHS students, teachers in Livonia, Michigan; Jefferson County, Colorado; and college students at Ohio University, Athens, whose writings and lesson plans have provided me with the following statements:

1. Record the odor in your observations.
2. Put a well-potted tomato in the window.
3. Concrete expands; pour the asphalt in the spaces between summer and winter.
4. Explain how a fruit fly could be confused as being three different animals.
5. The life cycle is difficult to observe because a dragonfly flies faster than you can run.

6. Keep adding baking soda, until the vinegar becomes a base.
7. Keep the jars at a temperature of about 36 degrees C. to incubate them.
8. Explain what caused the flow of water through the membranes in the experiment.
9. If you live above sea level, your measurement won't be exact.
10. You will prove that molecules of matter are in constant motion with circumstantial evidence.
11. Observe the test tube looking for suds.
12. Observe the rain gauge following precipitation.
13. What is the circumference of your waste?
14. Change the location of the drum; walk directly to the sound, beat it."

Professor, Counselor and Mentor

Paul has acknowledged that a long list of *mentors* have helped him. He fully comprehends that he might not have succeeded *at all* without them. He earnestly believes that his extensive publishing, and national and international contributions to science education would never have happened without substantial support of others. In perhaps that sole area, Paul is grateful, modest, and humble. Paul's genuine desire to be a *mentor* to college students was a reflection on all the help he had received over the years. It was "payback" time, which he eagerly accepted.

At one point, at Ohio University, Ploutz had more than one-hundred undergraduate advisees, more than thirty master's degrees, and five Ph.D. candidates. Grade inflation was rampant in the 1970s as well as now. He and co-author Charles W. Smith (math education) were nearly the only two education professors at OU who used C's, D's, and F's. Students evaluated faculty for promoting tenure. It was hard giving C grades and lower, when some faculty would give all A's, and B's.

Being a house-father for a fraternity Sigma Chi, at Colorado State College in 1959 had been an education. By 1979, the rules had changed. Now at OU, and elsewhere, there were no curfew hours. There were co-ed dorms, booze, marijuana on campus, the birth control pill. All these one-hundred plus undergraduate advisees could "talk" to Paul. If Paul realized that being a good *mentor* and being confident could also make him vulnerable, he was probably still too naive to care.

Most students saw their advisors only when they perceived a problem. Elementary Education's women's problems were primarily sex, money, grades, and parents, rather consistently, and in that order.   Perhaps because of his science education perspective, Paul felt better at counseling than many of his colleagues, who considered it a chore. Helping others through difficult times had meaning. Paul enjoyed helping struggling college students. The more severe their problems the harder he tried. One professor's concern for an advisee might be truly annoying to those with little interest in *mentoring*.

Given Paul's childhood poverty, his poor grades through high school, and his having taught every grade fifth through Ph.D., Paul was willing to help. And he did, including several instances where his advisees, both men and women would even bring their friends to his office to discuss their problems. Other faculty would, on occasion, meet at one of the students hangouts for chats over coffee or beer. Paul would only meet students on campus. Thus, the heavy traffic to his office and peculiar or unusual notes on his office door would create suspicion in those who had little or no contact with students who sought help.

Here are a few "unusual" situations, no longer confidential, in case readers think they've heard it all:.

1. Advised Mary Ann, whose father was a Mafia captain in New Jersey, as to how to become a teacher rather than join the family business.

2. The provost's daughter knew her dad was having an affair (he was).   Should she confront, transfer, etc.? The daughter was a tenant not an assigned advisee.

3. One advisee went to a phone booth, cut both wrists, changed her mind, then called Ploutz to save her.

4. Another advisee, in the office next door, was less lucky. She threw herself across the railroad tracks behind McCracken Hall, and didn't change her mind in time.

5. One advisee, realizing she was pregnant and about to be married, thought it prudent to have sex with her intended but without protection. He later informed her "not to worry." He hadn't gotten around to telling her that he was sterile, as they hadn't planned on having children anyway.

6. An advisee, admitted to "playing with a small boy," giving him a bath, when baby-sitting. Wanting to be an elementary teacher and fearing her motives, she also considered lying on the railroad tracks as a solution. She was enormously relieved to learn that, while not a recommended procedure, it was not uncommon.

There were few dull or boring times teaching. Paul's particularly wholesome attitude had been, "Wow, they pay me for this!" On the other hand, teaching magnetism (only one of many topics) hadn't changed much in eighteen years (two had been sabbaticals). Other professors seem able to teach thirty years, even more without particular change in the routine. Paul had climbed most of the mountains he had set for himself. He was getting bored.

Surviving the Vietnam Era on Campus

During the Vietnam era, the Ohio National Guard was called to duty by then Ohio governor James A. "Jim" Rhodes. Paul's later acquaintance, Dean Kaylor, was one of the five college students shot by the guard at nearby Kent State University. Dean spent the rest of his life in a wheel chair, and claimed he was only nearby "watching." He became a county commissioner in Athens County. An opportunistic "lady" married him while he was commissioner. Once voted out of office she divorced him and questioned "without his legs what good was he?"

Ohio University endured the Vietnam era better than many other campuses. At OU faculty were utilized for a midnight shift to watch that buildings were not destroyed. Paul and other male faculty were only to report efforts to burn buildings, roll automobiles, or break uptown store windows. Ohio University students, in rural South Eastern Ohio (Appalachia) were less violent than most other college campuses. The local sheriff had a large number of part-time deputies who were only too eager to crack a nightstick over any smart-ass college kid who got out of line.

Athens police chief Charles Cochran and municipal court judge Franklin Sheeter worked well together. "Cochran and Sheeter" became a community slogan dealing with hundreds of protestors.

Any demonstrator who would persist even after tear gas would almost certainly be arrested, charged, jailed, fined, and released. When necessary, ten or twenty students were "processed" at a time as the system was overloaded. At the height of problems OU faculty members were invited to stand watch. One night on Paul's watch, a junior elementary education major came near Court Street to merely watch the fracas. Students usually threw stones, started fires in garbage containers, and broke store windows.

With the stone supply exhausted a few protestors were tearing up brick sidewalks. One brick hit the future teacher with such force as to permanently dislodge one eye. University and Athens officials then requested that students no longer come to watch.

Paul taught a variety of graduate and undergraduate courses primarily related to the teaching of science in addition to child psychology/child development for eighteen years. At Oneonta in the 1950s he had earned extra dollars by teaching Adult Education and Hunter Safety instruction. During the fall hunting season, he also served as a special game protector for the New York State Conservation Department. Truth be told, he enjoyed the badge, brim hat and the .38 revolver on his hip.

At OU, Paul also gained additional income by teaching the courses required to earn an Ohio realtor's license. Teaching evening courses at OU's branch campuses also became routine for still more income.

Paul was bored. Paul had taught one science education course six times a year for eighteen years. It's now called teacher "burnout," and recognized like "compulsive behavior" as a "disorder." Paul had both. Science educator Ray Skinner, a colleague and fellow Canadian pike fisherman and friend, stopped Paul in the hallway one day to pay a compliment. Ray had also attended another long, dull, repetitive faculty meeting with which most professors can identify.

Ray: I have to hand it to you for your impartiality.
Paul: How's that?
Ray: You're just as nasty to the Dean as you are the lowest of
       students.

Skinner was right. Paul who by this time (1981) had read all of Gould, and most of Burroughs, had once dreamed of making ten-thousands dollars a year and retiring by "50."

He was now over fifty and making about twenty-thousand a month! What to do, what to do? Retire Now; No Wait, Well, okay.

Surviving Campus Politics, Gould Style

At the college, Paul's on and off again friend and associate, Dr. Lester Mills had been retired for only one year but his position had not yet been filled. Ploutz's request to retire fell on deaf ears. "You can't retire now, we don't have anybody..."

Within a few weeks, however, six or eight "coordinated" complaints about Paul's CARE project had been assembled by Ohio University's Office of Legal Affairs. Apparently unaware of CARE, or Paul's long list of successful publications, sabbaticals, or student participation, the officials apparently rushed to judgment. The University Policy of Departmental Review, college evaluations, and recommendations were all bypassed to pursue some "greater good." Perhaps it was to avoid sexual harassment issues, though no such policy or procedure had yet been established.

In a hastily scheduled meeting, legal affairs suggested to Paul that he quietly resign. Paul doesn't do anything "quietly." Ploutz employed local attorney William A. Lavelle, a former OU trustee and state chairman of the Ohio Democratic Party under Ohio governor Richard Celeste, to attend the hasty lynching. Within a few minutes, Lavelle established that no charges had in fact been made. Girls acting in concert all referred to "a game" of personal sexual questions. Paul's long track record of successful academic-type games was quickly cited to establish that the situation "wasn't going anywhere."

Legal affairs, apparently unaware that Ploutz had earlier asked to retire, now sought closure and *wanted* him to retire. Paul was offered the balance of his full year's salary as a bonus if he WOULD retire! Gould would have been proud. Paul "retired," being paid nearly twenty-thousand dollars to do something that a few weeks earlier others wouldn't let him do! Full retirement benefits included facilities use, parking, children's free tuition, etc. Many of Ploutz's friends and colleagues were left to speculate about his rapid "retirement." Paul later commented that "selling" his reputation for twenty-thousand dollars was "too Gould, not enough Burroughs."

177

The retirement incentive of nearly twenty grand seemed like a reasonable deal at the time. In (1982), OU was retrenching and eager to reduce the total number of older and higher paid professors. Paul later learned that had he waited another year to retire he might have gained two years salary. OU was "buying out" professors providing two years salary if they would retire.

Paul reported other skirmishes with the university administration. His selling real estate evenings or weekends drew an investigation for "conflict of interest" even though he was also teaching real estate courses. Teaching in two different colleges on campus usually meant parking in two different campus locations. Parking was tight and he frequently drew parking violations.

At the time, OU had a policy which allowed the faculty of each college to conduct a confidence vote of their dean. Dean Sam Goldman, in a close vote, lost. He received less than a fifty percent approval rating from the faculty in the College of Education. The School of Curriculum and Instruction (C&I) where Paul was positioned asked him to serve on the Goldman evaluation committee. Paul agreed to represent his school, thinking that Goldman leaving "was a done deal."

Goldman, however, resisted the confidence vote as well as the policy of faculty rather than the administration removing deans. Neither OU's president Charles Ping nor Provost Neil Bucklew liked the idea of faculty selecting or removing deans. The idea that a dean was the president's representative, not the faculty was gaining favor at other institutions as well. Since the provost also serves at the pleasure of the president, one could understand why they often had the same point of view. They were also related.

What to do? Faculty wants Goldman out; administration seeks to alter the procedure. Again, what to do? When Ploutz reluctantly agreed to serve on Goldman's evaluation committee he suggested at a C&I meeting that "There could be repercussions."

Within only a few days, the first of several administrative harassing were initiated. Ploutz was "investigated for conflict of interest." Investigation completed, no conflict found. Provost Bucklew, attempting to quiet the ill-will that a bogus investigation had caused, which was so obvious that it had been predicted, asked to attend the next regular C&I faculty meeting. He stated that there had been "No connection whatsoever between Paul's committee assignment and his subsequent investigation."

Curriculum and Instruction faculty members sat in stunned disbelief. No one spoke. Provost Bucklew called for any questions or comments. Seconds passed, no response or comments. He quietly left the meeting, experiencing only total silence. For a brief period, which was not to last, the entire faculty was solidified behind Paul and perceived the injustice. It was seen as a contrived and unfortunate investigation for purposes of retribution. Goldman was finally removed as dean and served as a flunky assistant to an upper-level administrator to finish his contract year.

Small world. The provost's daughter happened to be one of Paul's tenants. As an unsinkable *mentor,* Paul learned that the provost's marriage was on the rocks. Being related to the president as well, Bucklew would probably need to relocate to avoid scandal. Paul, the *mentor,* kept the secret even while he was being investigated. He was not surprised to learn that Neil Bucklew moved to West Virginia to assume the presidency at West Virginia University (WVU). Paul actually liked Bucklew, who, as provost, was cleaning up messes that others had created.

With Goldman things were less civil. The first of several investigations that Goldman inspired was about real estate. By now, Paul was also operating a very successful Century 21 real estate franchise with a dozen or more agents. Thinking himself almost immune from further real estate investigations he approached ex-dean Goldman:

"Sam you need to sell your house. Why not list it with me? There isn't anyone on the planet who wants you out of town more than I!"

Paul had been president of the student government at Albany Business College gaining political savvy in local and national elections. Campus politics was radically different. He never fully understood it. He had numerous textbooks, had conducted speaking engagements, and had a high profile in professional organizations. He also had a dozen educational games. Wasn't there someone in the administration who realized that he was helping to increase OU's prestige? Ohio University was already on the map. Former president Vernon Alden enjoyed referring to OU as "Harvard on the Hocking." Paul had declined a position at Harvard working with Fletcher Watson, a science educator. He loved OU. Paul was one of the more "published" professors in the university.

Paul could never understand why President Ping did not come to his aid. Perhaps he was busy raising money for OU and not aware of faculty problems. Perhaps he was aware, wanting Goldman to stay, Paul being against his interests? Ping was a bonafide Presbyterian minister who had served as provost in Michigan. As an admitted conservative, perhaps he was aware of the games? Mindful of Decker's caution perhaps Ping did not want a sex education game developed at OU on "his watch?"

Collegial envy and administrative harassment did not seem a fair response. Paul did love Ohio University, however, and was always good at seeing the big picture. Like people, institutions grow, trip, and stumble. The greater good of education is so much larger than the failures, indiscretions, or arrogance. *Education had, after all, been his ticket off the farm.* Paul, even having been denied the largely ceremonial emeritus designation, took it all in stride. He joined the University's Trustee Academy, committing ten-thousand dollars to university discretionary projects.

Later in 1998, Paul and Geri were guests on an Ohio University ocean cruise to the British Virgin Islands. They spent several hours with OU's new president and wife Robert and Rene' Glidden. Dancing with Rene', late evening on the upper-deck watching the evening sky, Paul's disappointments with OU were resolved. Paul, the science educator was flabbergasted that Rene' Glidden identified constellations in the Southern Hemisphere faster than he did.

Bob was not surprised; they had three daughters, one in science education with a publisher in Washington, D. C. Paul gave Rene' credit for her interest in science and thus the daughters science career. The Gliddens had three daughters, Ploutzs' two. Bob and Rene' also recalled one of Paul's earlier friends, Stan Marshall who became president of Florida State. The Gliddens were even Dutch Reformed, reminding him of his Roxbury/Gould origin. Bob then explained to Paul that large universities now have to run much more like corporations than in the past. He understood that the professor-student relationship as well as other things could suffer in a corporate structure.

Most notably, Paul felt that President Robert Glidden had two qualities beyond his predecessors:

1) Vernon Alden and Charles Ping were both superior presidents of OU and for many years. In the words of John

Delaney, from long ago in Oneonta, he said that Paul "Demonstrates an air of superiority which offends many people." Great presidents yes, but rural Appalachia is a poor setting for *any* sign of arrogance. Alden and Ping were otherwise great. Glidden never met a stranger. His unassuming enthusiastic Florida demeanor was in sharp contract to Alden's (Massachusetts) and Ping's (Michigan) reserve.

2) The big picture. Paul had demonstrated considerable versatility, taught at several universities, had been in all fifty states, along with numerous trips to Europe and third world countries. He fancied himself as seeing the "big picture" before others. Paul became convinced that Bob Glidden saw the global picture (thus for OU) more rapidly and in clearer focus than anyone he had ever met.

From Paul's point of view, the earlier flap over fire extinguishers was the most trivial and annoying of all. Paul had insisted on showing/teaching future elementary teachers how to use a fire extinguisher. Seems basic doesn't it? Buildings and Grounds, or whoever it was could never understand nor accept WHY anyone was messing with the fire extinguishers.

Ploutz could have arranged permission in advance and others might have cooperated. However, each time the issue arose and Paul "Could put out the fire" (pardon the pun) still another person would be in charge of extinguishers. Since men's dorms and other places routinely removed or discharged them, the offense was considered serious and Paul, full professor or not, was routinely maligned.

After several years of fruitless explanations, when the next telephone call arrived, Ploutz merely suggested they "Put the fire extinguishers where the sun doesn't shine." His country candor did not help.

In 1982, Paul at fifty-two had missed his goal of retiring at age fifty. Well short of Gould, but with a net worth over two million, he was retired from OU as a happy camper! Gould had died at only fifty-six. Paul reasoned that since he could still snow ski, and though he had a much smaller boat than Jay, could also water ski, and since he *was* alive, that perhaps he was much better off than Jay.

Burroughs used his various federal government jobs to expand his nature writings and to make friends in high places. Prior to retirement, Ploutz was promoted to "full" professor. He continued to teach science education and attend numerous national conferences, often "chairing" committees, panels, seminars, and workshops as time would permit.

By 1982 Ploutz had taught at five colleges/universities. Upon his retirement that year, a one-page summary of eighteen years, as follows, was prepared for him and to be used as nomination to emeritus status which was not approved:

"Dr. Paul F. Ploutz retired following eighteen years of service to Ohio University. Dr. Ploutz established himself as an aggressive, efficient professor in the college, and university, and was particularly active in the community at large.

He has designed, developed, and implemented innovative techniques for teaching science through the use of educational games, and through the use of simulation and program learning, much of which has been published.

Over a period of twenty-eight years, Paul has given an extraordinary amount of service to his profession in the College of Education as well as to the Oneonta Public Schools, the University of Northern Colorado, Greeley, Colorado, his alma mater; Colorado College, Colorado Springs, and the University of Michigan.

Dr. Ploutz is one of the more "published" professors in the College. He is the originator of the Educational Games Co., is the sole author of eight games, and co-author of five games. These games have been or are currently in use in most of the elementary and junior high schools in the United States. He is also the sole author of three metric manuals all of which have been frequently reprinted or gone to second, third editions, etc.

Paul was the co-author of three junior high school science laboratory manuals, three teachers' guides, and was collaborator with two editions of *Basic Life Science, Basic Earth Science and Basic Physical Science* with the Singer-

Random House Publishing Company. Sales of that series were several million strong, including statewide adoption in Texas, California, and throughout the United States

Ploutz had been active at both the state and national levels. Locally, Paul has been active with the United Appeal, Boy Scouts of America, the Margaret Creek Conservatory District, Chamber of Commerce, and Rotary. He is the originator and coordinator of a prostate cancer support group for the Athens, Ohio, area.

Prior to retirement in 1982, and since then, he has participated in real estate activities including, owning/managing thirty plus upscale student/faculty apartments, the development of two sub-divisions, teaching real estate courses at Ohio University and Hocking Technical College, and owning/managing a real estate franchise which became one of the dominate offices in Southeastern Ohio. He has joined the Trustees Academy at Ohio University to support the Gilford Crowell Memorial Scholarship Fund, and other endeavors."

Chapter 17:   Family and Community

Super Daughters

During the 1980s, and 1990s, Lori and Julie Ploutz, Paul and Geri's daughters, both graduated with honors from Athens High School and Ohio University. Lori completed a Ph.D. (physiology) under the guidance of noted Professor Frederick (Fritz) Hagerman, with internships at Simon Fraser University, Vancouver, Canada, and at the National Aeronautic and Space Administration (NASA) space center, Cape Canaveral, Florida. Lori, also a top athlete, swam on the OU swim team, gaining recognition at Mid-American Conference swim meets.

The first super daughter, Lori proudly gained security clearance for Paul and Geri at NASA. Even closer than the press and dignitaries, Paul stood in awe, the earth trembling, the air crackling, watching a rocket thunder off into orbit. Lori's NASA mission working with Dr. Gary Dudley was to aid the rest of the team, and to make the determination as to what was best to send into orbit. Was it to be tomato seeds, chimpanzees, microbes, jellyfish, or people?

Lori also completed a "Post-Doc" at Michigan State, with renowned researcher Ron Meyer. Lori married a Pennsylvania lad, also an OU Ph.D. Both landed at Syracuse University. Lori, at least in 2002, was a research scientist. Rob Ploutz-Snyder, was a bio-statistician for SUNY Up-State Medical College, also in Syracuse. Rob, much like the son that Paul never had, was secure enough to change his name; a decision for which Paul was grateful. Rob saw through Paul's tough exterior, suggesting his father-in-law was a "NASP" (New Age Sensitive Person (not WASP).

As older sister, Lori "cast a long shadow" for Julie, six years younger. Julie, a beautiful child, stunning blond teenager, swimmer, and a Thespian enjoyed leading roles in high school plays. Both girls followed their father's affection for science. Julie majored in zoology, thinking of physical therapy (PT). Julie, affectionately referred to by classmates as the "curve killer," discovered that physical therapists "took orders" from doctors. Admission to "PT" school was as difficult as medical school. Julie, stubborn, much like her father, was not eager to "take orders." The solution was to go to medical school. Accepted to several DO and MD schools, she decided to attend the Ohio University College of Medicine toward becoming a family physician, doctor of osteopathy (DO).

Julie, like her perfectionist mother, also excelled. She was a class officer in medical school, and did rotations at the Cleveland Clinic, the Joslin Diabetes Center, Syracuse, and other research centers. Paul and Geri now have two overachievers in the family. Julie's husband, Matt Adams, also a Pennsylvania boy, in 2002 was a computer analyst at Key Bank in Cleveland, Ohio. As of 2002, Julie Ploutz Adams was appointed an associate professor in the department of family medicine at Case Western Reserve University College of Medicine. She joined Family Medicine Specialists in Westlake, Ohio, after her residency at St. John West Shore Hospital (Cleveland area).

Unlike so many families with a collection of "A" type personalities, everyone loves everybody. The Ploutz girls both stand their ground with their hard-nosed father. Paul, surrounded by his wife, and two equally strong daughters, has finally been "liberated." A pro-choice republican and an original Burroughs treehugger, Paul is now retired with a few dollars in the bank, two wonderful son-in-laws, and a strong sense of fulfillment.

Acting Like Gould, Honestly

Retired, but not tired, Paul found it difficult to say "no." He continued to enjoy *mentoring*, donating time and often money, being a local "shaker and doer." In "retirement" (often before) Paul:

1. Served on the local Athens United Appeal Board (6 years).
2. Served as secretary for the Athens County Republican Party (6 years).
3. Worked on the campaign committees for friend and Governor Jim Rhodes of Ohio (2 terms).
4. Served as member, then chairman of the Board of Appraisal, for the Margaret Creek Conservancy District.
5. Taught the real estate courses necessary to become a licensed realtor in the state of Ohio (Ohio University and Hocking College).

6. Bought and sold beach front vacation condos in Myrtle Beach, South Carolina (retaining two for his family use).
7. Gained a license to sell all types of insurance in Ohio.
8. Gained a Series II license to sell securities and real estate investment trusts.
9. Served on the Hock-Hocking District Boy Scouts of America Committee.
10. Became council president, BSA of the Kootaga Area Council (includes Southeastern Ohio and much of West Virginia).
11. Was county chairman for the committee to re-elect the president (CREEP) for Richard Nixon. Nixon carried eighty-six of Ohio's eighty-eight counties, but not (Paul's) Athens County, a liberal college town, at least in national elections.
12. Mentored 131 individuals to gain (Century 21) real estate licenses, then sold the franchise to an agent, Mark Spezza.
13. Financed the construction or remodeling of fourteen buildings, bringing them up to code, rental condition, or sale.
14. Sold more than one-thousand homes during the "Century 21 Ploutz Realty" era, being the top office in Southeastern Ohio.
15. Moved from the original Athens home, 19 Clearview Dr. (apx.three acres) to a seventeen-acre site with a five-acre lake. He had bought the Clearview house in 1964 for $24,500. With numerous improvements, and inflation it sold in 1990, for $187,000.
16. Established Pine Lake Nature Preserve in Albany, Ohio. Stocked the lake and planted twenty-five hundred white pines, built a deck, bought a canoe, row boat, and old-folks paddle boat.
17. Established the Lee-Alexander Development Environmental Roundtable. (LEADER) Organized citizens groups in Lee and Alexander Townships to expedite airport development and other community causes. (With Fred LaSor & Rus Tippett).
18. Formed the Albany Area Chamber of Commerce, and pressed for management of the rapid growth of development, school construction, sewer lines, bicycle path etc. Members varied from a handful to over a hundred, depending on the issue. Fred La Sor, a retired U.S. diplomat, and Russell Tippett dean of Hocking College's College of Natural Resources, were the prime movers and shakers. The "round" table was Paul's

kitchen table where LEADER and many of these words were written.

Paul and Geri had visited forty-nine states but had not been to Alaska or taken an ocean cruise. Boarding a splendid Holland American cruise ship, they were quick to discover dozens, even hundred, of other nature lovers. Russ Tippett, dean of the College of Natural Resources was aboard. Russ was also an avid bird (avian) watcher, had heard of Paul, and knew about Burroughs and John Muir. They instantly became friends. Both visited the magnificent Muir Glacier. A mile long and two-hundred feet thick, it's where the Harriman expedition (1890) with Burroughs, Roosevelt, Muir, etc. had explored. By now, John's footprints had slid off in Glacier Bay, as glaciers slowly ooze along finally breaking off into enormous icebergs. Paul felt as though he was on hallowed ground, thinking more of Muir, who, like Paul, had struggled for land management.

As a child, Paul had frequently walked out on Boyhood Rock, not realizing that the closed rectangle of rocks below was John's grave. He had walked the same trails and fished the same streams as Burroughs. As an adult, in science education, he had talked the talk. Now Paul walked the walk with a lump in his throat in awe, profoundly moved. In the past twenty years he had also been sued several times, sued others a few times, acting more like Gould than Burroughs. It was better to be like Burroughs, and Paul gained new commitment.

In bright sunshine, but bitter cold, with his tears eager to freeze, Paul knew the world to be a better place because of the Burrough's, Muir's, and Decker's who made it so. It was an inspirational moment.

The Athlete (Paul Ploutz) and the Artist (Paul Grippa)

Paul's wife Geri, a city girl, was adverse to mud squeezing up between her toes. So her ocean cruises to the Caribbean, British Virgin Islands, and Alaska were, as advertised, the greatest! The rest of the family SCUBA dives Mexico, the Caymans, Antigua, and the Florida Keys. Geri usually enjoyed the pools, parrots, and occasional "jungle juice" highball. Geri had excluded herself from fishing excursions in Canada for northern pike, with tipsy boats, moose, bear, and plenty of hungry mosquitoes.

Still an avid fisherman, Paul found it difficult to find anyone his age to water ski, snow ski, or go fishing for seven or ten days in Ontario or Quebec. The fishing in Quebec had become disappointing, likely from acid rain. Sitting in a little French cafe in Paris, twenty years previously, unable to speak French, he and Geri had been treated poorly. Or more succinctly, hadn't been treated at all, being ignored more than a half-hour because they were Americans. Paul regretted that he had studied French (as a second language) one of numerous requirements to gain a Doctorate in Education (Ed.D.)

Now the "French" attitude seemed to have reached Quebec, so Ploutz and apparently thousands of other tourists came to prefer friendly Ontario. Paul would round up whomever he could for a week of Canadian fishing, some summers financing, even paying the way for some kid who couldn't otherwise go. Geri's only reason to visit Canada would be to attend Shakespeare festivals at Stratford, Ontario.

Attending Earthquakes and Volcanos

Providing group socialization with professors and their spouses on university affiliated excursions limited the amount of mud Geri would get between her toes. Trips to North Africa (sand), Paris, Amsterdam, and London (concrete) were all fine. It was South America that cooled the Ploutzes need to travel. In Mexico City, on the twenty-second floor of their hotel, daughter Lori observed the chandelier gently swinging. "Dad why is it doing that?"

Within seconds, "guttural grinds" could be detected. Mexico City was experiencing a 6.4 Richter earthquake. Tall signs and theatre marquees were the first to go. With sirens and ambulances blaring, Paul, Geri, and Lori wondered if this was their end. Like the giant Nebraska hale storm, it was over quickly. The sun was still shining but their room, including the lamps, were in disarray. The building was still standing. Everyone was scared, but alive. An adjacent building was less fortunate. At the twenty-second floor, the two buildings were a yard or so apart even though they were together at the first floor. Most folks have experienced *tremors* and even minor earthquakes. Being near the *epicenter of a 6.4 is to be avoided!*

Some improvement for Geri's city nature was noted in Costa Rica. Rocks thrown from the active volcano did not quite reach the parking lot. The red glow and bright finger flares of lava after dark could give even the heartiest a thrill. Fancy lodges in the rainforest, with your dinner choice of blackened sea bass or mahi-mahi, were memorable. With only a few bright green chameleons on your pillow, ceiling, or bathroom mirror, the accommodations seemed absolutely perfect to Paul. On occasion, a chameleon nearly a foot long would lose his grip walking across the ceiling. However, only rarely did one fall from the ceiling in the middle of night, to land on your face.

Visit the Amazon

The plane ride to Iquotis, Peru, was unremarkable. Most of the time the plane was so high you couldn't tell it was ocean below. As usual, Paul's nose was pressed to the window. Once the jet altitude was reduced, the colors seemed alive. Blue-green aqua, lots of aqua, surrounded islands large and small. The aqua color close to shore gently turned blue or green as water deepened over the white sand. Oh, to own an island down here would be so nice.

Upon their late afternoon arrival as part of small tour, Paul was delivered to one of the better hotels. This meant a shared bathroom down the hall, with no beggars allowed in the small lobby. Taxi drivers remained just outside the door, hoping to deliver tourists in their motorized, three-wheel jinricksha (cart) transportation.

A riverboat trip down the Amazon included numerous stops at jungle villages. The riverboat had fifteen small air-conditioned cabins. The craft drew only three or four feet of water. Unlike scenic cruises, the vessel was much shorter and slightly flat. Meals were delicious, served buffet style with no fancy anything. At Peru, being so far "upstream," and in the dry season, the Amazon was less than a quarter-mile wide. Even at its lowest, the river was always the color of tomato soup. Huge trees were snagged mid river and seemed to continue living.

One of the first "civilized" stops was the home of renowned painter Paul Grippa. After walking a plank, and crossing fifty feet of dry mud, several hundred wooden steps began. Zig-zagging left and right, but always sharply up, Paul started to climb the slope. Halfway up, at each corner post, the steps doubling back and forth, multi-colored parrots came to meet him. Well, macaws, actually. Grippa had fed them for generations. The parrots and people watched him paint spectacular oils on canvas of other macaws, schools of piranha, and jaguars in bright colors. He painted jungle scenes or "whatever you wanted."

Ploutz loved the four by six oil of a bluegill, so lifelike you wondered if it would swim off the canvas. Grippa, offering free tequila, daiquiris and assorted "jungle juice" beverages, caught Paul's interest. In perfect English he suggested it "was one of a pair. The other recently sold in San Francisco for nine-thousand dollars. If you want it, here now, it's yours for only four-thousand five hundred dollars."

Grippa was already a renowned painter. From time to time, he would display paintings in Paris, New York, or San Francisco. Fluent in several languages, he entertained his river guests from his elevated, relatively primitive perch, with its spectacular view of the Amazon at the junction of a much smaller river.

A favorite story of Grippas included his gallery displays in San Francisco. A bit short, paunchy, and bald, he exhibited humor and wit along with his spectacular lifelike oils of Amazonia. Art-loving widows would be absolutely taken away with his charm, not to mention the financial status of gaining several thousand dollars for every painting. Grippa, single again, had been married seven times, each wife lasting only days or weeks. Each new wife, when finally confronted with actually living in the jungle, would often "split" within days. The glamour was gone once they stepped off the boat and started the trek up the slope to a straw bed and the giant platform on the ground/trees. Always friendly Ploutz, suggested they should visit first, and then decide on possible marriage. Paul Grippa roared with laughter, explaining he had indeed tried that. They stayed even shorter periods. It was best the way he was doing it. Besides, he had lined up wife number eight who had lots of money, few expenses, and found this variety pleasing.

In France, when Paul saw the Mona Lisa at the Louvre with the bullet hole from the deranged tourist, the hole had already been patched. Burroughs, though he had an attractive mistress, would probably have liked the fish painting better. Gould would have liked the fifty percent price reduction. Paul liked Burroughs, probably Gould, and certainly the forty-five-hundred dollar fish oil painting. If you are a "married" reader, you will understand that a "fish, didn't match any of the décor at home." The Ploutzes enjoy two (Althoff) oil paintings in their residence. To this day poor Paul has gone without a fish painting, owning only a small painting by nature/whale painter "Wyland" from the United States of America, Wyland.com.

Motoring slowly down the Amazon produced hours of endless jungle scenes. They moved slowly with the current, dodging huge floating, or partially sunken trees. With seven by fifteen binoculars Paul scoured the shoreline and the skyline. This was a nature boy's dream come true. With his chair on the forward deck and his feet hung on the lower rail, the good captain would often follow close to one shoreline. The muted drone of modern twin diesels was much quieter than the "thump and smoke" of the scenes from the hit film African Queen.

Riding the river to identify birds was easier than identifying them on shore. *Birds of Costa Rica* could lie safely on a second chair, and you could flip pages back and forth in the certain knowledge you'll see another new bird. Holding both the book and the field glasses motionless in the jungle is impossible. Both temperature and humidity seemed to be in the high 90s the entire trip. Hours on the ship were special without bugs. Moving just fast enough to produce a cooling breeze, Paul could relax in sun or shade. Paul added fifty-two birds to his life list on the Amazon trip.

The boat stopped to allow jungle lovers (tourists) to visit Indian villages. Villages were located every fifty miles or so on both sides of the river. Most of the jungle seemed uninhabited but how were you to tell? Either side at any time continued to introduce new animals and trees. The scientist was a great fan of the National Geographic Society, its magazines and programs. Paul had visited poor villages in Mexico, Africa, and other third world countries. Then there was the Amazon. Tourists had been encouraged to bring thread, fishhooks, and simple games for children, and cigarette lighters for starting the twenty-four hour fire most families maintained.

The ship's guide, always present, was multilingual, had attended "a year or two of college, somewhere in Texas, once, a long time ago, can't remember when." Since he was less than thirty that seemed doubtful. His status with various tribes was clear. A few in each village and only with the permission of the chief or Shaman (religious leader) were allowed to barter, exchanging fishhooks for reed belts, hats, and fans.

In addition to a nylon fishing line and dozens of fish hooks, Paul and Geri, both educators, brought tee shirts, toys, and frisbees. As expected, the Roxbury farm boy, turned scientist, was experiencing sensory overload noticing:

1. No electricity, flashlights, candles, or matches.
2. No sick people, cemeteries, or mentally handicapped people.
3. No shoes, belts, hats, glasses, canes, tents, vehicles, or schools.
4. Most adults wore cane reeds covering their genitals.
5. Very few bracelets, rings, hair or head ornaments.
6. Little variation of custom or habit from village to village, being fifty miles apart, yet largely oblivious to one another, with distinct languages.
7. The ratio of children to adults was disproportionately high.
8. Few "old" people, most without teeth, their age difficult to establish (nor did they know).
9. Many of the village populations seemed "stabilized" from one hundred to two hundred members.
10. Children of all ages seemed to have uniform features, near perfect complexions without moles, acne, or pimples. None had split lips, protruding ears, or were knock-kneed. They were beautiful children.
11. The river fishing was still excellent, but the monkey, sloth, and wild pig populations were down. A few of the smaller children had distinct protruding bellies, a fairly reliable sign of malnutrition.
12. Cayman alligators, pythons, and jaguars were becoming uncommon. However a chief would occasionally offer an illegal jaguar pelt for US currency. Go figure?

Where Are the Cemeteries?

In one village, Paul did locate one girl, perhaps ten or twelve, blind in her right eye. With the chief's permission, using the guide as interpreter, he struck an agreement. Paul explained that the tennis-sized velcro ball and the flat frisbee "could improve her vision" (depth perception). The guide told Paul the other children would certainly take it away from her, as such toys were scarce or unknown.

The chief acknowledged "she needed to see better." Paul said he would leave it only on the condition that the game was her's alone. Of course "she could choose another person to play." The wise chief likely realized that now other children would have to accept her, so quickly approved the arrangement. Paul inquired as to how he "would make it so?" The tribal chief quickly summoned several older children, explaining the "magic vision game" only worked with the girl, giving her "exclusive powers." Well, that was close enough, though Paul still wondered where the other children were.

The guide knew each village shaman who could be persuaded to walk a jungle path, explaining which plants did what. The shaman had cures for snakebites. He would draw latex from a tree, making instant rubber bands or huff poison darts through ten foot long blowguns. Ancient remedies passed from generation to generation through the shamans. The tourists faithfully took their malaria pills. The heat was more bothersome than the mosquitoes or deer flies. Neither bothered the natives.

Termite mounds seemed to be everywhere. Villagers would break off chunks from the ground-level mounds and set them on fire. The chunks seemed to smoke indefinitely, never breaking into flame. By putting smoking termite chunks under their huts which were on stilts, they could smoke away crawling critters or flying insects, malaria mosquitoes, in particular.

To cook a monkey, the constant termite fire could ignite reeds to do so. Dozens of smoke "puffs," one per dwelling, usually smoldered twenty four hours a day, but the termites still produced mounds faster than villages burned them. Paul was thrilled to see lily pads seven feet across, to watch white, freshwater dolphins jumping in the Amazon, and to catch dinners of piranha for the "chef" to cook on the boat.

Paul thought about Burroughs' excitement as he stepped on the Alaskan glacier for the first time. The Harriman expedition named the glacier after Muir! Paul became happy by giving the little girl the frisbee game and donating fishhooks to many of the villages.

Only In Columbia

The border of Peru and Columbia on the Amazon boasts a huge open air market. A line marking the border between the two countries goes down a gradual slope to the Amazon. Peru does encourage, regulate, but does forbid practices clearly harmful to people and the environment. They seem somewhat concerned about people, animals, and the forest. Regulating, or even communicating with jungle tribes is a task, so efforts to manage anything is largely left to far more civilized, populated villages, who have electricity, and even an occasional chunk of concrete.

On the Columbia side of the line, anything goes. With no refrigeration, high humidity, and hot sun, meat spoils rapidly, and attracts so many flies one must "shoo" them away to get a good look. But, if the sloth, alligator, monkey, or pig is "almost" dead, not to worry, the meat is fresh! If the animal is already dead, well OK, is there a problem?

Customers may shop either side of the line, and there were hundreds of shoppers. A carnival atmosphere prevailed with an occasional bamboo piccolo, and straw hats available. Hungry? Run a monkey palm on a stick on one of many fires, on either side. They could fix it for you. The Colombians could eat it nearly raw, as it was fresh; the Peruvian side liked it charred to kill the fly eggs.

Living hand-to-mouth had new meaning. Paul got "the big picture," wondering if globalization would ever make it. Thousands of people were seemingly happy yet couldn't read, write, save, plan, or worry. Missionaries from hundreds of years earlier had left, died of malaria, or had given up.

But, not to worry, we're burning the rainforests to make that problem go away. We seem to be doing the same thing to South America as the Europeans did to the American Indians. We just don't shoot them. Introduce the diseases we've gotten used to, "educate" them, shoot them only if necessary, put them on reservations like the Navaho, Sioux, Apache, Ute's, Iroquois, Arapaho, Huron, Algonquin, Shawnee, and well, you get the idea.

Geri, the Shakespeare (literature), Renoir (art), Chopin (music) fan did not enjoy the heat, humidity, mosquitoes, snakes, alligators, or meat markets. Paul loved it, but agreed with Geri that their next trip "should be to Poland."

Chapter 18:   Get A Real Estate License

Entering the real estate business as a well paying hobby proved to be a wild ride for Paul. Buying a home, often the single largest investment a couple ever makes sometimes has unexpected consequences.   Realtors aren't always trusted, seems like professors usually are. Professors often covet their "turf," are jealous, envious, and take themselves very seriously, but also demonstrate conspicuous integrity. In Europe, teachers are held in particular esteem though not as high in the US, but they still enjoy modest respect.

Realtors, like every group, vary greatly. If one's entire income is based on day-to-day, or even month-to-month commissions, financial security can deteriorate quickly. A $100,000 transaction (sale) at a fairly common six percent "listing agreement" generates a $6,000 commission. Often the broker gets 50% ($3,000 in this example) and the salesman the other half, $3,000.

At one point, Paul thought it clever, for his Century 21 Franchise to have 21 agents (salespeople). A few became "million dollar agents" yet others had him investigated, even sued. Paul created the cliché "morality is often dictated by financial need." Most agents couldn't generate enough commissions to "maintain."

Paul found teachers, nurses, and secretaries with other steady incomes, who care about people and are of integrity, to be the best. Oddly, being a "salesman" per se was low on the qualification list. "Location, location, location," is a well-known real estate cliché. "Feast or famine" is equally familiar to realtors.   Listening carefully, figuring out what people want and can afford seem to be the skills necessary to succeed. Teachers, nurses, and counselors seem to excel; salesmen per se, no, no.

During a ten-day period in May 1978, Paul's real estate commissions totaled more than his university salary as a full professor for the entire year. Ohio University's administration investigated Paul for conflict of interest (or whatever it was). A few colleagues were so "green with envy" and so frustrated by the CARE fiasco that in 1982 when Paul finally retired, they quietly blocked his largely ceremonial "Emeritus status." Hurt at first, Paul recalled that the eminent reading specialist, Paul McKee and renowned author, James A. Michener, who also taught at Colorado State College, actually declined the emeritus honor, considering it frivolous.

The Ploutzes lived in Athens, Ohio, 457<u>01</u> for twenty eight years. Their mail was often sent to Georgia or West Virginia or elsewhere around the country. Sensing that Albany, Ohio, 457<u>10</u> would be a rapid growth area, they moved the nine miles west on the four-lane Appalachian Highway.

Now their mail went to New Albany, Ohio, Albany, New York, or elsewhere, there apparently being even more, or at least, better known, Albany's than Athens'!

Albany Ohios' population was barely three hundred, but did have a post office, school, and lots of trailers and doublewides mixed in with older homes.

A local "lover" with the conspicuous name of Paul <u>Platz</u> had recently moved out of Albany apparently leaving a trail of broken hearts and promises. In Paul's very first visit to the small, local post office, post-mistress Mrs. Annette Miller exclaimed "Well we finally meet, I've handled quite a lot of your mail."

Everyone seems to get "cuckoo calls," or an occasional letter, which cannot be explained. Paul received a 2:00 AM call hearing "Life is no longer meaningful without you." Geri was not amused. One call at midnight, suggested a party to be held "in a phone booth" only fifty miles away. You would need to "bring some stuff." Pot? Paul never met Mr. "Platz" or any of his admirers, and to this day he was only curious as to what Ms. Miller, post-mistress and president of Albany Village Council must wonder?

The move to Albany took Geri still farther "out in the country." Planning their new home, largely by herself, however, was a great experience. With Geri designing the house and Paul "locating" it, the couple proved to be a near perfect combination. Their Athens home was brick, approximately four thousand square feet, and on three acres.

The Albany 2,150 square feet home on seventeen acres was built at the edge of their five-acre lake. Three levels of pressure-treated deck out over the spring-fed clear water was Paul's dream realized. In complete privacy, Paul could fish, swim, boat, tinkle, feed fish and ducks, or simply enjoy the tranquility so carefully planned. The Ploutz's hosted extended family picnics, cookouts for daughter Julie's med-school buddies, Lori's faculty, and student friends, all enjoying swimming, canoeing, and the newly acquired paddleboat.

Hocking College is located at Nelsonville, Ohio, a few miles north of Athens. Vice President Roy Palmer, and Russ Tippett, dean of the College of Natural Resources, called Paul one evening. "We would like to suggest a fishing getaway meeting for visiting dignitaries." Paul replied that could be arranged, "When would you like to do this fishing get together?" Russ Tippett replied "In about an hour." Good friends since the Alaskan cruise, Paul said, sure."

The Reverend Jesse Jackson's National Rainbow Coalition group (Chicago) entourage caught their biggest bass and catfish ever! The only "complaint" was that "the beer was so cold it hurt their throats." Political candidates, proud fathers, and visiting firemen, were often welcome to the "Pine Lake Nature Preserve." Athens Rotary Club annual picnics included croquet, volleyball, horseshoes, badminton, paddleboat, and golf cart rides at Ploutz's property.

With parking for a hundred cars, catered gourmet meals, and prominent political figures, it was the way to go. Paul was trying to do *mentoring* one hundred or more at a time. The Nature Preserve quietly hosted numerous political, social, and financial groups.

Poster Boy for the Cancer Society

In 1989, Paul was diagnosed with prostate cancer. After a few tears, Paul put his "affairs in order." A high Prostate Specific Antigen (PSA) reading of 12.8 and a second opinion to confirm, he chose surgery. Dual, pea-sized cancers along with the prostate, seminal vessels were removed. Wise choice. Undergoing a radical prostate removal (prostatectomy), a three and a half-hour operation, Paul survived without radiation or chemotherapy treatments.

In an address at a local Rotary meeting, Ploutz shared his mother's advice that "its not as important what happens to you, as your reaction to it." For the next six years he organized and led an Athens-based, Rotary-sponsored, Prostate Cancer Support Group. Optimism is one thing, but the ever-positive Paul presented the "advantages" of having prostate cancer, as follows:

1. It's good for your vocabulary, as most are not familiar with impotent, incompetent, incontinent.
2. Getting your "affairs in order" (last will and testament, trust, etc.) is a good idea anyway.
3. You establish your priorities, the real ones. It happens almost over night.
4. You can no longer be sued successfully for sexual harassment or paternity suits.
5. You determine who your friends are. Usually, those "sad" are your friends, those "glad" are not.

Again, in 1998, after having colon polyps removed a second time, colon cancer was discovered. A second "get your affairs in order" was issued. Paul exclaimed very matter of fact, and without tears this time, he had "never wanted to be a perfect ass. So let's get it over with."

Now, with his fifth kind of cancer documented, the researchers at the James Cancer Hospital on the campus of Ohio State University, Columbus, Ohio, took an interest. Paul, intrigued with the procedural detail remarked that removing the donut-shaped prostate was an "in body experience." With colon cancer, the surgeon loads approximately thirty feet of tubes (intestines) in a large nearby stainless steel pan. An "out of body" experience, they then carefully examine every inch, with each end still connected to the body.

Paul participated in their genetic research project to determine, among other things, whether his cancer(s) was hereditary or environmentally induced. Environmentally produced? Remember the lead pipes, pesticides, and herbicides?

Walden Woods and Mallard Landing Subdivisions

Southeastern Ohio has fostered at least two other financial overachievers: Bob Evans, the "down on the farm sausage franchise," and Eugene Engels, owner of coal and stone quarries, as well as several hundred college apartments for Ohio University, etc. Engels' stone quarry foreman, Roger Van Dyke, became friends with Ploutz. Years before, Roger had gained approval for loaning Paul thousands of dollars on a handshake for stone for University Heights subdivision.

It took a few thousand tons of limestone to complete roads in both the University Heights and Fairway Oaks subdivisions that Paul was developing. Van Dyke retired. Engels sold the local quarries, and hundreds of acres in Albany became available by the new owners.

The retired professor received a call from the new stone quarry owners. Ploutz, who was eager to buy investment property, was a bit offended by the three new owners, "all recent rich." Despite their crude, rude, condescending manner, the sellers price seemed right. The strike busting, coal mining, gravel pit gurus offered Paul several large parcels at a reasonable price.

One parcel of 135 acres, which Paul and Geri purchased, was to become **Walden Woods**. Ponds were named Dickinson, Walden, Peterson, and <u>Burroughs</u>; the roads were named Walden Trail and Audubon Trail.

Thinking of John Muir and John Burroughs and getting the big picture, Paul realized a breathtaking opportunity was at hand! Fifty or more years earlier the 135 acres, now Walden Woods, had been raped, that is quarried. This was long before the Environmental Protection Agency (EPA) had been formed. Limestone, often twenty or thirty feet underneath had been removed, leaving rough and irregular slopes, ponds, and piles of soil. The land, now taxed at a very low rate, had gradually turned into a dumping spot for used tires, furniture, mattresses etc.

The place was "woodsy" and a mess. The land, earlier quarried, was eroded and largely abandoned. The old "haul" roads that huge trucks used to remove dynamited chunks of limestone were wide, hard, and still in place.

Largely abandoned yes, but fifty years of unrestricted flora growth was evident. The low areas had become ponds. Fertilized fish eggs, probably arriving on the feet of ducks, had "stocked" the many ponds.

Beaver, eager for hundreds of Aspen trees had moved in. In fifty years, mother nature had produced heavy undergrowth as well as flowering dogwood, honeysuckle, and wild strawberry.

Wild cherry, tulip poplar, locust, sycamore, sugar maple, and several species of willow had over taken much of the 135 acres. Birds, including wild turkey, seemed everywhere. Fox, mink, weasel, deer, skunk, beaver, and muskrat were entrenched. Paul's triple efficiency goal was to:

1. Rehabilitate "abandoned land" to the tax rolls.
2. Provide affordable home sites for nature lovers (new subdivision).
3. Create a new land management concept for plants and animals, "People being the guests."

Paul did not know if this plan, which he had committed much of his resources to, would prevail. He just felt it was the right thing to do. If only John Muir or Burroughs could be reincarnated to witness this!

Chapter 19: New Land Management Concept

It was John Muir, not John Burroughs who fought the hardest for better use of land. Muir, (Sierra Club founder 1892) more than any other single individual pioneered for Yellowstone and other national parks. It was John Muir who camped out with President Roosevelt more than others. George Perkins Marsh (Arbor Day), Henry David Thoreau *(Civil Disobedience)*, and numerous others fought in their own way to preserve nature. Burroughs was the secretary/recorder on the famous Harriman Expedition.

The glacier was named after Muir who visited Alaska seven times. Burroughs, Pinchot, Emerson, Whitman, and others have all made significant contributions. Now Rachel Carson, Ralph Nader, Al Gore, Ploutz, Tippett, Mikhail Gorbachev (Green Cross), *you,* perhaps, and tens of thousands of others will become concerned with our environment and land use.

"Barely ten years ago if someone called you a "tree hugger" it would probably not have been meant as a compliment. Now if someone calls you a tree hugger it largely means that you are perceived as a responsible person and one who cares about the enviroment." (Quote from one of Paul's presentations).

Paul's Contribution to National Land Use

In an audacious major break with convention, Ploutz's newest subdivision regulations (covenants) are about <u>wildlife</u>. <u>"people are the</u> **guests.**" The following information, now public record, has been reproduced (in part) for you consideration, to use where you live, anywhere in the United States!

Athens County Court House, instrument 9700002445, Records Volume Number 249, pages 701-705, entitled RESTRICTIONS FOR WALDEN WOODS SUBDIVISION, LEE TOWNSHIP, ATHENS COUNTY, OHIO, reads as follows:

Introduction:

Paul F. Ploutz and Geri J. Ploutz, fee owners of WALDEN WOODS, lots 1-23, according to the plat thereof on file and recorded in the public records of Athens County, herein after "Grantor," hereby make the following declarations as to the limitations, restrictions, and uses to which the lots constituting said Subdivision may be put, hereby specifying that said declarations shall constitute covenants to run with the land, as provided by law, and shall be binding on all parties, and persons claiming under them, for the benefit of, and limitations upon, all future owners in said Subdivision. This declaration of restrictions is to maintain WALDEN WOODS in its natural state and to perpetuate its diverse flora and fauna populations in a residential setting.

Walden Woods Covenant #10 Ecology:

Walden Woods is a home to preserve the natural flora and fauna. People are the guests: To Wit:

   a. LIVESTOCK:
   No domestic livestock, goats, llama, or poultry of any kind shall be kept, maintained or harbored upon said lots. Raising of wild turkeys, quail, rabbits, pigeons, pheasants, mallards, bees or other natural fauna as a hobby and on a non-commercial basis is encouraged. Houses for Bluebird, Purple Martin, Woodpeckers, Bats and other local wild species are encouraged.

   b. BIRDS:
   A bird census conducted in 1996 by Dr. Scott Moody of the Audubon Society revealed a high bird count both as to number and species. The presence of cats, or dogs, running at large, or other animals known to be destructive to birds, shall be reported to the appropriate control agency and shall be considered vermin and without protection.

   While hunting is prohibited, per se, vermin control is encouraged by all lot owners. Underbrush, and cattails, here to fore discouraged in conventional subdivisions, shall be maintained. Birds must not be bothered by cats or persons with "B B" guns. Block walls and barbed wire fences must not impede the natural movement of animals or neighbor's views. Wooden fences may be utilized for safety or aesthetic purposes. Fences without barbed wire, cages, and small sheds may be utilized for raising wildlife as described under paragraph "a" proceeding. Any permitted fencing must not be more than 48-inches high, nor of a material designed to harm fauna.

c. TREES:

While gardens, pools, tennis courts, etc. are encouraged, as lot conditions permit, "clear cutting" of large areas of flora is prohibited. Brush, branches, fallen trees, and leaves may remain natural, however owners may relocate flora to a ravine or similar area to provide alternate habitat in a more convenient or aesthetic location. Aspen suitable for beaver grow in abundance around WALDEN Pond and on adjacent lots. Beaver may cut them down, people may not. Burning is prohibited at all times, other than in controlled containers such as outside fireplaces, spits, or simple, wire or block incinerators. Sugar maple may be tapped for private consumption of syrup and syrup products. Sugar maples must have a diameter of at least 12 inches at five-feet from ground level to be tapped.

d. PONDS:

One half (50%) of the existing shoreline owned by each property owner must be allowed to remain in brush, swale, cattails or natural growth to maintain the integrity of the ponds/wildlife habitat. When ponds border two or more lots the "down stream" owner (lots 18 & 6, Emily Dickinson & Roger Tory Peterson pond) must approve of any, stocking, chemical treatment of water or significant alteration of pond habitat. Motors may not be utilized on ponds except for electrical, aesthetic aerator fountains or similar pumps used to maintain an open water area free of ice for birds in winter. Owners may install one dock of not more than 50 sq. ft. surface area, nor more than 12-feet from shore. Ponds are to keep the water on the property, to maintain wildlife/wetland habitat. Ponds are on private lot(s) and owners assume full responsibility for fishing or other recreational, aesthetic use. Lot owners who determine additional pond sites on their property may develop them using such caution as herein described. Such ponds would then comply with all existing covenants.

e. HUNTING:

Hunting and trapping are forbidden. Use of "B B", or similar pellet/air guns, sling shots, crossbows, fireworks, snare devices, poison pellets or any other device or object to kill, control or disrupt animal life is forbidden. Emergency control of mammal populations, such as deer, or raccoon may, on the advice and consent of a State or local conservation official be conducted by individual property owners. In that context lot owners may harvest/hunt deer with long bow during the regular bow hunting season on their own property.

f. PESTICIDES:

Pesticides may not be utilized for control of insects in or on, gardens, lawns, or on the exterior of premises unless so ordered by the Health Department by decree for specific emergency measures. Small amounts of "earth friendly" liquids such as emulsible oil may be used to control scales, fungus etc., on apple and other fruit trees whose main purpose is to feed deer or other animals. Pesticides within residences for control of termites, ants, roaches, etc., is permitted. Roadside spraying to control vegetation, is not permitted by Township, County or other governmental agency.

g. PETS:

Pets must not roam the property to disturb birds or other wildlife. Inside cats, if permitted outside, must wear a bell or similar device to warn birds of their intrusion. Snowmobiles, 4 X 4's, motor cycles and related all-terrain vehicles shall not be permitted to roam any lot or trail or to produce sound or disturb wildlife or the tranquility of residences, the development or nature preserve areas on adjacent lots.

h. NATURE TRAILS:

Nature trails within wooded lots, or ravines of each landowner are encouraged. Trails for bird observation, jogging, observing flora or other earth-friendly activities may be developed. Pathways may be dressed with wood chips, sawdust, sand, gravel, limestone or other naturally formed materials. Black top, concrete or similar smooth hard commercial road surfaces may not be utilized. Paths may not be wider than 6 ft, however, one place on said path, on each lot may, where space and conditions permit, be widened for a resting area, picnic table, nature oriented works of art, monuments, small amphitheater or open gazebos of not more than 225 sq. ft. floor surface, and the roof, if any, shall not be visible from Audubon or Walden Trail from May to September when foliage would conceal their presence.

Said amphitheater, if any, must to the extent possible, be made to blend with nature and be constructed without the use of concrete footers, bulldozers, vinyl or other brightly colored siding or high steeples, lights, and must be not less that 500 ft. from the prime residence nor 200 ft. from the nearest lot line of any other lot. Water and/or electricity may, as conditions permit, be introduced on trails or amphitheaters. Sinks, showers, and sewage facilities shall not be installed on any nature trail.

Copyright Exemption

In a humble effort to perpetuate "enlightened" use of land, the AUTHOR SPECIFICALLY GRANTS PERMISSION TO DUPLICATE, copy, utilize, or circulate the proceeding covenants: Introduction and ECOLOGY items a, through h. Complete covenants are available from the Recorders Office, Athens, County, Ohio 45701.

This enlightened, nature-orientated approach to land usage has received significant recognition. In May, 1997 Ohio University broadcast a presentation "Walden Woods." Other stations apparently picked up the six-minute program, repeated several times on WOUB radio, and finally, National Public Radio. The College of Education at Ohio University duplicated some hundred, six-minute cassette copies, which have been provided to the Department of Development in several states. Ploutz hopes his efforts in land management will be utilized nationally.

Paul, (Muir, Burroughs, Pinchot, Thoreau) and others would be happy to put 135 acres of previously (50 years) quarried land back on the tax values. It was a quadruple coo. Reclaim land that had been quarried, put land back on the tax rolls, provide beautiful residential lots, and provide an environment friendly to animals.

With ponds, trees, beaver, and roads all present, Walden Woods has been successful. Perhaps that's the "fifth" coo, it works, and the public is ready for it. Paul, happy to honor Burroughs, poets, and bird lovers, discovered numerous others felt the same way. As of 2002, most of these ecological lots have been sold. With several houses now built, the beavers "may cut the aspen, but the people may not."

Walden Woods was so successful that Ploutz purchased an adjacent one hundred acres and has since developed **Mallards Landing.** Unlike Paul's first two subdivisions, University Heights and Fairway Oaks, the lots in Walden Woods and Mallards Landing average four to six acres each. They were also laid out to accommodate the movement of animals. A few lots were ten acres each and others were arranged so if desired, they could be added together.

The road through Walden Woods is Walden Trail. One pond (lot #8) is **Burroughs** Pond. Another pond is named Peterson. Roger Tory Peterson had attended Burroughs funeral in Roxbury. Paul, who loves birds anyway, thought it nice that John and Roger could have "adjacent ponds." Burroughs had also accepted the appointment as the first vice president of the New York State Audubon Society in 1897. Paul having sat on Burroughs **Boy Hood Rock** as a child, not knowing John was buried only a few feet away, and contemplating his own legacy, thought the idea appropriate. He knew full well that few observers would ever grasp the significance. A second road is dutifully named Audubon Trail. The few signs in place say *nature preserve* rather than STOP. There are no guard rails. Large boulders are used instead.

One retired couple was so taken they bought six lots (25+ acres) and built a magnificent cabin in the middle. They feed wild turkeys daily, and like Paul's days on the farm naming cows, they name turkeys! They even suggest they can tell them apart. "They all look alike unless you're into nature." Ploutz thinks the Shallers are wonderful people, and, having been called a "tree hugger," wondered aloud if the term "turkey hugger" will ever come into vogue.

Mallards Landing, in the rapidly developing small town of Albany, Ohio, and across from the expanding Ohio University Airport, is becoming "the place to live." Eighteen lots, five ponds, one six-acre lake, and four beautiful homes as of 2002, Paul, was in the "right place at the right time." Now with his fourth subdivision, Paul has, as usual, suggested this **IS** his last one! History alone will *determine whether Paul's land use idea will prevail across the states.*

Surviving five kinds of cancer, as Rachel Carson, now an American hero predicted cancer for most of us (*Silent Spring* 1962), Paul "*has*" and still survives! But then again Burroughs probably never expected to be revered. Several of the Goulds died of Tuberculosis.

Going Home, the Burroughs Dedication Ceremony

Jay Gould left Roxbury, seldom if ever to return. John Burroughs left Roxbury and returned late in life. Ploutz so often "half way between Gould and Burroughs left Roxbury and returned every few years, never losing touch "with what was going on."

On most visits he stopped by the "ol" swimming hole and waterfalls on the Hardscrabble Ploutz farm. He would again sit on Boyhood Rock as he has so many times as a child on the farm sixty years prior.

In 1999, the twenty nine seniors who would graduate RCS invited Paul to deliver the commencement address for the June graduation. Paul accepted but wanted to do something special for his mother Anna (1915 valedictorian) and for Burroughs both Roxbury grads.

Roxbury Commencement June 26, 1999.
The commencement address:

Class President Walker
Principle Mulholland
Superintendent Proper
Board of Education
Faculty
Family & Friends
Class of '99

"Home at last... Fifty years ago I was here as you are now, feeling very much at home. Born here, lived here, graduated here. Most of the "Ploutz clan" from Hardscrabble Road and their families have lived nearby or in Roxbury for several generations, suspect I'm related to 20% of the 400 or so here today.

Eighty-two years ago my mother to be, Anna Ruteshouser, graduated RCS, valedictorian, 1915. Mother and today's valedictorian, Jennifer Serrie, faired much better academically. Seventh of a class of 12? Two years in the 2nd grade? The 3rd grade still tough? How comforting to learn John Burroughs wasn't much of a student, as a boy, always in the shadow of classmate Jay Gould. Today they call us late bloomers.

Since we are also honoring John Burroughs today, it would be fitting to relay a Burroughs story. In 1915, the Roxbury job market wasn't all that wonderful for the newest valedictorian. She was offered a job teaching, as was Burroughs when he graduated, or working at the Roxbury Hotel. The hotel was located at the closest thing we still have of a village square.

Why she took the job at the hotel rather than teaching remains a mystery. Sheets, pillow cases, waiting on tables, probably paid more. Maybe she was hanging around town to see my dad, I never knew.

By 1915, Burroughs was well established and had numerous guests. Anna waited on Thomas Edison, Harvey Firestone, Henry Ford, John Burroughs. Numerous others came and went, I regret not asking more questions. She did recall Burroughs and Edison as "not saying much," Firestone as "friendly," but everyone liked Mr. Ford.

When pressed for details, she recalled Ford insisting upon giving John a car, a new one, probably one of the lst in Roxbury. John was adamant in not accepting it. Roxbury streets were muddy when it rained, it back-fired, was noisy, scared the horses. John, grumpy in his later years, still wanted to get along in returning to Roxbury, declined the generous offer, but Ford prevailed, as the world in time, would discover. John kept what turned out to be the lst of other cars supplied by his good friend.

Intrigued by this story I begged mother for other anecdotes. Well son, she said, this was just four friends getting together, we knew Mr. Ford sold cars, it was no big deal in 1915. How's that for understatement? Ford helped change the world, in Roxbury around 1915, it had not yet come to pass, no big deal.

Several years later, Anna Ruteshouser married George Ploutz, bought a farm in Hardscrabble and became neighbors of the Burroughs. Sitting on "Boyhood Rock" as a child I had only vague recollections of the remaining Burroughs family. My dad didn't think they were very good farmers. Curtis, there were several, dated my sister briefly. We always blamed him for fishing the trout out of our pond every summer after we had fattened them on grasshoppers.

Before the inevitable words of wisdom offered by commencement speakers, three anecdotes, special memories of growing up in Roxbury, come to mind.

1. The perception was out that state trooper recruits on Long Island or the City who screwed up, washed patrol cars, or if they really goofed were transferred upstate to Margaretville or Horse Heads, that's up north some place. Don Weyl was justice of the peace. Carl Shuster and other farmers were routinely "busted" for crossing the road with loads of hay or farm equipment that did not have lights, directional signals, licenses etc. Don would take the heat, but dismiss the charges. We stuck together, looked out for each other, as people in small towns do, and re-elected Don when ever he ran for office.

2. Doc Ives set my broken wrist as a result of a soccer game against Fleicshman's. He was a great swimmer, 6' 6 or so, spent most of the summer up at Helen Anna Shepherd, Gaines Burton, Coke, Happisburgh's lake. A very casual guy who made house calls wearing only a nylon swimsuit and a stethoscope. Many of the proper ladies in town complained (yea right) but as the only Doctor in town "Who ya gonna call?"

3. Is Doug Spangenberg in the audience? Does any one even know him? Not here? Then I may proceed with the final anecdote. Doug was beyond "Dennis the Menace." He routinely broke glass, let air out of tires. Even at ten years, teachers quaked that he might end up in their homeroom.

The scout master of troop 41 Roxbury was Bruce (Stub) Caswell. Take note that one of today's graduates is an eagle scout. Among the many values Stub instilled over his career was to draw attention to yourself in legitimate ways. Don't even think of coming to a scout meeting with blue hair looking like a smurf. Don't pierce your tongue, nose, belly button, etc. Stub's son Phil, Bill White, and I received the coveted eagle scout award about the same time and had a quiet competition to draw attention to ourselves in legitimate, constructive ways.

Back to Doug. My opportunity to win this legitimate ego contest took place at Bridal Veil Falls, known to this day as one of the premier scenic community swimming holes. Doug who couldn't swim, was sitting fearlessly close to the edge of the falls. You guessed it, down the falls into the deep water. The fifteen or so kids and teenagers sat motionless. Doug didn't come up, still no one moved.

Bruce Caswell's training "Help other people at all times," my life saving merit badge fresh in my mind, dove into the deep pool, searching the murky water and, after several seconds, found the near motionless Doug. It took several minutes for him to recover enough to swear at us.

So, got my name, picture in the paper, "Eagle Scout earns life saving award" Big deal! Took the article to the very next scout meeting, No blue hair, hadn't punctured my navel, surely I had gained attention to myself in a legitimate way! Alas it was not to be, only a brief discussion ensued, it was generally concluded that I should have let him drown!

But on to the class of '99 and to how truly special you are. Before that would all of the parents of these special millennium miracles please stand now, and be recognized by a grateful community ....You'd heard that each snowflake is different, no two alike? Years ago, it might have been Carl Sagan, a fellow science educator from Cornell, I picked up the statement, "There are more stars in the sky, than grains of sand, on all the beaches, of all the world."

Each of you have 46 chromosomes, millions upon millions upon millions of DNA successful gene combinations that have played out over thousands of years. Like the single snow flake, or that one spec of sand in the universe, makes you incredibly special, individually unique, a mathematical and evolutionary miracle. Five billion people on earth, still you're one of a kind literally. Quite frankly you're IT. No one like you has ever lived and unless you're an identical twin, there will never be another like you! Suppose you should try, but will you ever be humble again?

Class of '99, with that under your tassel could you possibly use advice? I came 800 miles to talk to you but in all humility, with a Roxbury diploma, four college degrees, and as a professor, innumerable graduations, can't recall one single pearl of wisdom retained as a result of such a ceremony, then again, I can't remember what I had for breakfast.

Hopefully you, perhaps someone in the audience, might grab one item of advice;

Advice from Paul

1. If forced to make a choice take both.
2. Multiple projects lead to multiple successes.
3. If you can't beat them, join them, then beat them.
4. If you can't win, change the rules.
5. "No" simply means begin again at the next higher level.
6. When faced without a challenge make one.
7. Patience is a virtue, but persistence is a blessing.
   If you practice these seven things you'll be diagnosed with compulsive disorder, an Alpha or "A" type personality, something I have thoroughly enjoyed these many years.
8. Hang out with people smarter than you.
9. Don't pay retail prices. In most of the rest of the world everything is negotiable. I still pay retail for toothpaste, but that's about it.
10. Develop numerous goals, its OK to fantasize on how to achieve them.
11. Gain attention in legitimate ways. (remember no smurf/pierced body parts).
12. Ask old people for advice. They might be the last people on earth you'd approach for advice on money or sex. Most know more about these and other topics than you do. They need to give advice, you need to hear it, you'll gain respect for each other. Most advice will be clear and clean not tangled in convenience, ego. Just do it."

The following advice was mailed to me, perhaps "borrowed" from the internet. Its a little casual, but good-hearted and I hope its creator would smile knowing the advice might help the twenty-nine of you after 1999, and today:

1. Wear sunscreen. If I could offer you only one tip for the future, sunscreen would be it. The long-term benefits of sunscreen have been proved by scientists, whereas the rest of my advice has no basis more reliable than my own meandering experience. I will dispense this advice now.
2. Enjoy the power and beauty of your youth. Oh, never mind. You won't understand the power and beauty of your youth

until it's faded. But trust me, in 20 years, you'll look at photos of yourself and recall in a way you can't grasp now how much possibility lay before you, how fabulous you really looked. You are not as fat as you imagine.

3. Don't worry about the future. Or worry, but know that worrying is as effective as trying to solve an algebra equation by chewing bubble gum. The real troubles in your life are apt to be things that never crossed your worried mind, the kind that blindside you at 4:00 p.m. on some idle Tuesday.
4. Don't be reckless with other people's hearts. Don't put up with people who are reckless with yours.
5. Floss.
6. Remember the compliments you receive. Forget the insults. If you succeed in doing this, tell me how.
7. Stretch.
8. Don't feel guilty if you don't know what you want to do with your life.
9. Dance, even if you have nowhere to do it but your living room.
10. Read the directions, even if you don't follow them.
11. Accept certain inalienable truths; prices will rise. Politicians will philander. You, too, will get old. And when you do you'll fantasize that when you were young, prices were reasonable, politicians were noble and children respected their elders.
12. Don't mess too much with your hair or by the time you're 40 it will look 85.
13. Enjoy your body. Use it every way you can. Don't be afraid of it or what other people think of it. It's the greatest instrument you'll ever own.

And so family and friends, RCS faculty, Board of Education, Superintendent Proper, Principle Mulholland, Class President Walker, Valedictorian Serrie and the class of '99, you millennium miracles, make us proud, go forth from this place and prosper....

...............and may the force be with you...   (hand sign)

Back in Albany, Ohio, Paul had earlier received his annual update on Educational Games from Union Printing Company. Secondly he had been informed that, for the past several years,

Union had volunteered to provide a free 10 X 12 inch copy of Paul's much heralded poem *"What Is Home?."* Anyone who ordered one of Ploutz's dozen games would receive a free copy. Also, more than 27,000 free copies had been provided to schools across the country as of 1999.

Ploutz suggested presenting a bronze copy of his poem *What Is Home?* then dedicating it to John Burroughs. The Roxbury Board of Education and Board President Rudolph, along with Superintendent James Proper were thrilled and inquired if in fact they might get three copies (plaques). One plaque is now permanently mounted in the front entrance of the Roxbury Central School. The second plaque is currently in the BOCES office, Grand Gorge, New York. The third plaque is in the Grand Gorge Senior Citizens Center (the old school building). Paul's children's poem What Is Home? was originally written for a new science series to be published by Science Research Associates (SRA), Chicago. Paul and William Shockley (Nobel Physicist 1956-transistor) were the two consultants hired to direct the project. When IBM, SRA's parent company terminated the K-6 series, the poem still belonged to Paul. Science and Children published by NSTA agreed to publish the poem on the inside cover of the April 1970 issue.

WHAT IS HOME?

All living things, both near and far
Have reasons for being where they are.
The worm in the ground or the bird in the tree,
You in your house, or the fish in the sea.
Each seem to be suited for a certain place
Where they find food and living space.

How do you think the pig would feel
If he changed places with an eel?
Or what do you think it would be like
To live next door to a tuna or pike?
Would you expect to find tigers in trees
Or Elephants in hives like bumble bees?

And wouldn't it be a little funny
To fish in a river and catch a bunny?
Or what if the dogs and the pussycats
Moved into caves to live with the bats?
There are reasons for choosing homes, it's true,
But why do animals live in the places they do?

Paul F. Ploutz

Reproduced from SCIENCE and CHILDREN,
APRIL 1970, National Science Teachers Association,
Washington, D.C. 20036

The three bronze copies, which exist in the town of Roxbury, New York, include the Burroughs dedication and is dated June 26, 1999, the fiftieth anniversary of Ploutz's RCS graduation and his "official" return to Roxbury. Three *smaller* bronze copies as shown here are at; his current residence in Albany, Ohio, at the Walden Woods subdivision and nature preserve, Albany, and at the residence of his oldest daughter Dr. Lori Ploutz-Snyder, a research scientist at Syracuse University, Syracuse, New York.

Dr. Ploutz has released the copyright of What Is Home? As long as proper credit is cited he has agreed that it may be copied, reproduced, mounted, displayed, printed from this text *Roxbury Boys* without recourse or penalty, enjoy.

Of a dozen successful games (Educational Games Company) that he authored only one seemed to disappoint him. His game, Mental Health, barely broke even financially. With enormous energy, creativity and ambition Mental Health was created to improve the mental health of any English speaking person on earth. Most, not all of his many projects, succeeded. He discovered that it's difficult to "*mentor*" large numbers of people from a distance. Paul may have finally accepted the idea that he could not *mentor* the globe, but alas it didn't hurt to try.

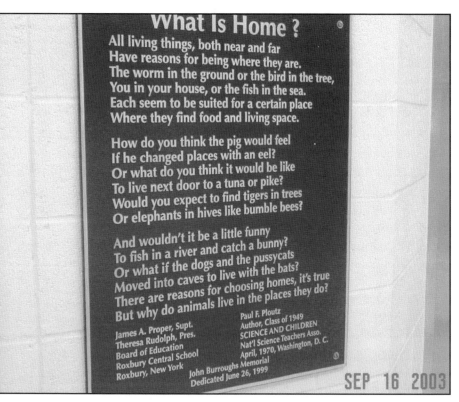

What Is Home ?

All living things, both near and far
Have reasons for being where they are.
The worm in the ground or the bird in the tree,
You in your house, or the fish in the sea.
Each seem to be suited for a certain place
Where they find food and living space.

How do you think the pig would feel
If he changed places with an eel?
Or what do you think it would be like
To live next door to a tuna or pike?
Would you expect to find tigers in trees
Or elephants in hives like bumble bees?

And wouldn't it be a little funny
To fish in a river and catch a bunny?
Or what if the dogs and the pussycats
Moved into caves to live with the bats?
There are reasons for choosing homes, it's true
But why do animals live in the places they do?

James A. Proper, Supt.
Theresa Rudolph, Pres.
Board of Education
Roxbury Central School
Roxbury, New York

Paul F. Ploutz
Author, Class of 1949
SCIENCE AND CHILDREN
Nat'l Science Teachers Asso.
April, 1970, Washington, D. C.

John Burroughs Memorial
Dedicated June 26, 1999

SEP 16 2003

Burrough's dedication/plaque/poem
June 1999, RCS

215-B

Chapter 20:   Establishing A Roxbury Foundation

Mentoring Roxbury

After delivering the graduation address at Roxbury Central School and dedicating his poem to John Burroughs on June 26, 1999, the 50th anniversary of his own Class of 1949, Paul began in earnest to recognize and appreciate how he had benefited from *mentors* during his childhood. As he recalled, and contemplated positive memories about his early teachers, church leaders, coaches, Scoutmaster, employers, relatives and neighbors, the beginning of *Mentoring* was conceived. The impact of his early initial *mentors* helped to overcome his "Pee Wee" label and the adversities of a farm life both he and Gould despised. Education has enabled Paul, Jay, John, and dozens of other Roxbury boys and girls to pursue a different and better life.

The 1999-2000 school year was also the second year as Superintendent of Schools at Roxbury Central for Dr. James Proper, Paul's nephew. Drs. Proper and Ploutz recognized how key *mentors* had helped them to believe in themselves and to take those initial, risky steps towards college. Fear and trepidation flow readily in the minds of poor, young, country lads when they ponder their uncertain futures. This dynamic motivated both Jim and Paul to envision an educational foundation which could support scholarships and related youth opportunities. They felt compelled to assist other youth to break the cycle of poverty, which traps many who never fulfill their potential.

Jim Proper's ideas for the educational foundation were launched by Paul, who suggested the possibility that the proceeds from his book might be channeled to the Foundation.

The original title, <u>*Roxbury Boy, Jason, John, Paul et. al.*</u> has been changed to include the Catskills. In fact Roxbury graduated 928 girls, only 923 boys (1851 total). Consequently   <u>Mentoring Roxbury</u> and <u>Mentoring Roxbury Boys and Girls</u> were also appropriate. The text does extol the importance of *mentoring.* Paul and Jim's original effort included forming the "Ploutz" Historical and Educational Foundation.

To better support his beloved Catskills, "girls," his admiration for the "families," and Roxbury, like Burroughs, settled for all of the things on the front cover, now including the:

Roxbury Educational Foundation

The Roxbury Educational Foundation supports the students and graduates of Roxbury Central School, such as naturalist John Burroughs, educator Paul Ploutz and financier Jay Gould, and other Roxbury Graduates by offering scholarships and guidance to those wishing to further their education.

The Foundation will also support individuals, family and community groups in their efforts to improve educational opportunities in the community.

It was important to Paul that the original board would gain a State Charter and incorporation as an educational foundation on the "first try." Further, since education had brought Jay, John, and himself some success, sought an initial board with conspicuous educational credentials to enhance approval.

As an academic "cornerstone," Paul (Ed.D), daughters Julie (D.O.), Lori, (Ph.D), son in law Robert (Ph.D) and nephew Proper (Ph.D), agreed to serve on the board. Those five board members have earned doctorate degrees. Perhaps the State Charter would have been granted in any event.

Paul's disdain for attorneys took a pause, as local attorney Herb Jordan, swiftly nursed the application through the bureaucracy. Herb did it pro bono (without pay), and did not even seek the esteem of serving on the original board.

Herb had been controversial as a result of earlier legal skirmishes with the school system. Paul believes that this timely, substantial act, adequate to heal latent concerns of teachers and others over earlier wounds. Two superintendents of school, immediately prior to Proper, had been asked to leave. Proper has been successful in getting the community to pull together once again and is equally grateful for the present community *"mentoring"* by Jordan. Life goes on for people of good will!

Don Hadden, a local community leader had been a Ploutz family friend and Hardscrabble neighbor for more than sixty years.

Superintendent Proper recruited most of the other board members with Paul's approval and recommended Mrs. Iris Mead to be board president. Iris was also president of the Roxbury Alumni Association.

The *original* charter members with addresses for the Board of Directors included:

Sandra Walcutt, PO Box 137, Roxbury, NY 12474
Beatrice Hinkley, PO BOX 158, Roxbury, NY 12474
Kellie Sullivan, 2000 County Highway 41, Roxbury NY 12474
Donald Hadden, 15 Roosevelt Avenue, Roxbury, NY 12474
Iris Mead, PO Box 1066, Margaretville, NY 12455
Julie Ploutz Adams, 615 Oakmoor Road, Bay Village, OH 44140
Lori Ploutz-Snyder, 4914 Kasson Road, Syracuse, NY 13215
Robert Ploutz-Snyder, 4914 Kasson Road, Syracuse, NY 13215
Paul F. Ploutz, Founder, 1785 Pine Lake Rd. Albany, OH 45710
James A. Proper, Supt. Roxbury Central

The First Board

On September sixteenth, 2003, the first organizational meeting of the new Roxbury Educational Foundation was held. The Affairs of the Foundation to be managed by a Board of Directors.

Bylaws were approved and the National Bank of Stamford was identified as the Foundation's depository. The foundation will use 53729 State Highway 30, Roxbury, NY 12474 as its first official original address. Frank Spinelli of Roxbury resigned and two new board members, Mabel Faoro of Grand Gorge and Joan Dugan Pebler, RCS, President Class of 1957, were welcomed.

The "multi *Mentoring*" book nears final editing, the Roxbury Educational Foundation is a reality. Paul states neither would have happened without the foresight and vision of Superintendent James "Jim" Proper. The popular superintendent will soon retire. Paul's daughters Julie, Lori, and son-in-law Rob are poised to "resign" once the board has taken root and is strong. As is common, it is presumed that Founder Ploutz who also funded the corporation, will continue for life as a board member, advisor and *mentor* has he had been for so many.

Paul has again demonstrated his affection for Roxbury and his *mentoring* skills for those he cares for, John Burroughs, Jay Gould, the people of Roxbury, and you.

James Allen Proper, founder Paul F. Ploutz (1949), and Robert B. Glidden, President of Ohio University, and others acknowledge the affect of rural schooling on Burroughs, Gould's early days at Beechwood Seminary and Ploutz's career as a result of Roxbury teachers, *mentors*. Reference is also made to the concept of *"It Takes A Village"* by Hillary Rodman Clinton, as to the unique impact of rural education.

Part II includes brief information on many, and the names of **all** the graduates from Roxbury schools during the last one hundred years.

Proper and Ploutz have written this material in their private capacity. Glidden, the small Iowa townboy, who became president of a major university, is known for *mentoring* high school graduates from across the United States and around the globe.

Mentoring, Dreams and Aspirations

Delighted to *mentor* Roxbury with "his" new foundation Ploutz never seems to be content with the present.

His heros' are those who anticipate, even see the future. Those individuals with the unique ability to "see the big picture," thus make future innovative plans. Paul sees being "before his time" a blessing, others at times, see futuristic thinking a curse. Ploutz, even before the present Foundation had been solidified, envisioned what REF could do for Roxbury.

Here is some of that vision:

This FOUNDATION should be involved in various education-related activities to benefit young people, the Roxbury community or surrounding area. Initially, fundraising might provide scholarships, books, computers or travel. In the long term future the Foundation could involve nationwide, corporate funding to build, staff and maintain a "Ploutz Sports Center" Roxbury with meeting rooms, and auditorium, conference center, swimming pool, climbing walls, gymnasium, locker rooms, food court, hiking trails, etc. Efforts of the next one-hundred years, 2001-2100, must obviously be developed by the board.

Recognition of graduates after 1950 and newer families must become an integral part of the FOUNDATION in future years with greater participation from "newer" folk. Paul discerns some xenophobic response from his own Roxbury generation, but also believes that Roxbury's future is pretty much what folks are willing to make of it. The Catskills (Roxbury) are a "natural" for tourism, ecology, and recreation. Fear of outside influences, protecting the status quo, resisting change is a formula for extinction.

The obvious phrase was coined by Howard Cosell is that "Roxbury's future is in front of it." It has not been established that Ploutz like Burroughs will be buried in Roxbury. Paul hopes that the REF can make *dreams and aspirations* come true!

A Future Mission Statement

A. The purposes of this corporation should include historical, charitable and educational, namely to benefit the past, present and future, of Roxbury, including the Central School District, and the other members of the communities located in the said district, and to encourage, solicit, seek and accept contributions of money and property of all kinds for use in providing such benefits to the community.

Immediate goals could include:

A. Focusing on education, economics through historical, ecological, and educational based business including tourism.
  1. Village sports arena
  2. Major library expansion
  3. Village computerization
  4. Bike, nature paths
  5. School advanced placement; college credit courses at RCS; branch campus status with SUNY, Hartwick, etc.
  6. Radio station
  7. Chamber of Commerce, tourism bureau

B. Recognize, promote, celebrate, one-hundred years of Roxbury Boys graduating from Roxbury 1901-2000; 923 males, 928 females, total 1,851 graduate from the century.

C. Identify and perpetuate the historical significance, implications and careers of three Roxbury Graduates:

1. Jason Gould	Beechwood Seminary	1849-50
2. John Burroughs	Beechwood Seminary	1849-50
	(Society in existence)	
3. Paul Ploutz	Roxbury Central School	1949-50

The first of the two new societies to include:

1. The Gould Family

   Particularly honoring the historical and educational contributions of Helen Gould Shepard (Jay Gould's daughter) in Roxbury. No Gould (family name) graduated from Roxbury schools from 1901-2000, however the Gould contributions to Roxbury's history and education likely surpass those of any other person or family.

Henceforth The FOUNDATION honors Jason Gould, his home site in West Settlement, and his studies at Beechwood Seminary, one of Roxbury's first schools. *Mentor* of one of Roxbury's first and inspirational teachers, a Mr. James Oliver should somehow be included. The FOUNDATION, fully acknowledges Gould's legendary financial excesses and those of other robber-barons, now make a long overdue *distinction*. Other "barons" did little, if anything, for Roxbury. Gould's life, through his daughter, has greatly enhanced the village of Roxbury.

"Time heals all wounds," Anna Ploutz, 1915 RCS valedictorian and mother of Paul Ploutz, creator of the FOUNDATION, observed that "time wounds all heals," as well. Gould died December 2, 1892. One hundred and ten years of Gould bashing is excessive. The FOUNDATION is perfectly positioned both to apologize to remaining Goulds and from this day forward, to honor the Roxbury boy from West Settlement.

2. The Ploutz Family

   Anna Ploutz was valedictorian in RCS class of 1915. Her yearbook included "brilliant in all her studies," Three of her four children also graduated from RCS. Among them Dr. Paul F. Ploutz, class of 1949 went on to become a nationally known science educator, editor, author, Fulbright recipient, professor,

and real estate developer. Ploutz gave the RCS commencement address (June 1999) fifty years after his graduation and donated three bronze plaques entitled "What Is Home" at RCS, NCOC and the Grand Gorge Civic Center.

Gould, John Burroughs, and Ploutz, one-hundred years later, are thought to have attended the Ol' Stone Jug School house, adjacent to the Ploutz farm on Hardscrabble Road. Ploutz occupied three farms on Hardscrabble Road and for a brief period, Howard Ploutz (an uncle) ran the fourth and then Burroughs farm as well, before Henry Ford "bought them out."

Neighbor to the Burroughs family, bonafide nature lover, ecologist, Paul like Burroughs, was a poor to mediocre student, spending two years in the second grade. A poor skinny farm boy, also ridiculed by his father, possesses elements of both Burroughs and Gould. A dairy farm, rural, poor, and skinny, with geographical identify, and school, form convincing identity and credibility.

Creation of the FOUNDATION along with his desire to recognize others (1,851 RCS graduates), represent a community sentiment and loyalty beyond that noticed in *either* Burroughs or Gould.

The *individual or group historical markers should be located in Roxbury village,* school property, birth site, parks or such other locations either prominent or semiprivate (trails-homes, etc.) as to be available to community, tourists and historical facilities.

a. Recognition to include, permanent bronze, brass, marble:

1. Roadside historical land marks.
2. Free standing plaques, markers, monuments and statues.
3. To further enhance educational and historical records, future museums, cultural centers, tourist centers, etc. Continue to reflect Roxbury's family history.
4. Efforts in renaming streets, roads, streams, trails, present or future buildings, are to be encouraged. Goals designed to enhance the heritage, image, quality of life, of the school and community, are goals of the FOUNDATION.

D. New societies (in addition to Gould & Ploutz) are recommended for the ten most numerous families. These <u>ten</u> families graduated 244, thirteen percent, of all 1901-2000 graduates! *These ten families have been a stabilizing, social, moral, historical and academic influence on Roxbury* and must be recognized. New societies for the next most numerous families are suggested if interest is presented.

1. The FOUNDATION will provide a meeting place and organizational criteria and assistance to these societies and any other of the 669 Roxbury Families with RCS graduates 1901-2000 who demonstrate adequate interest, support, organization.
2. Societies formed, while otherwise independent, are bonafide members of the FOUNDATION society. The President of such a society may serve on the FOUNDATION Board. In this fashion those families who have moved to Roxbury-Grand Gorge since 1950 and who are dedicated and committed to the community may participate and support the Town of Roxbury (Grand Gorge), and RCS through the FOUNDATION and its board, committees and activities.

The FOUNDATION office shall attempt to provide assistance to family societies by address, telephone, computer. To the extent possible "family" genealogy available on computer programs should be used to enhance national searches for Hinkley, Morse, Ballard, Finch, Schultis, Lutz, Kelly, Mead, Slauson, German etc.

Identification and recognition of 20 of Roxbury's "Original" Families.

Family Ranking by number: Number of family graduating
From 1901-2000

1. Hinkley	(43)
2. Morse	(29)
3. Ballard	(26)
4. Finch	(26)
5. Schultis	(24)
6. Lutz	(23)
7. Kelly	(21)
8. Mead	(20)
9. Slauson	(17)
10. German	(15)
11. Davis	(14)

County Commissioner campaign yard sign. L-R: Paul, Julie, Lori and wife Geri.
He lost. 1972

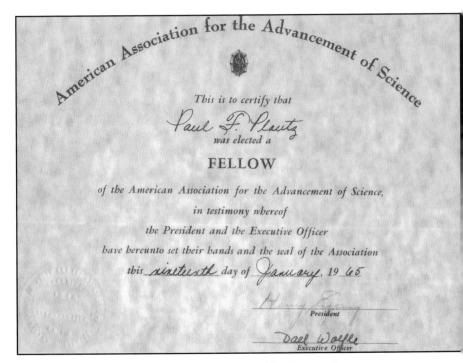

American Association for the Advancement of Science

This is to certify that

Paul F. Plautz

was elected a

FELLOW

of the American Association for the Advancement of Science,

in testimony whereof

the President and the Executive Officer

have hereunto set their hands and the seal of the Association

this _nineteenth_ day of _January_, 19 _65_

Henry Eyring
President

Dael Wolfle
Executive Officer

Recognition by the Scientific Community

> "Yes, creating
> educational games
> can make you a
> good living, but
> more importantly,
> it can make for
> someone else —
> a difference."
>
> Dr. Paul F. Ploutz
> Educational Games Company

Games With An Education in Mind

"Elements" was the first of a dozen games.

Mr. Ploutz urges those who have an interest in developing their own educational ideas, concepts and aspirations, to come to the Inventors Network Program meeting on June 11. Not only will he share with you his own personal bumps and bruises; and be handing out bandages, but he will also give us a look at what kind of games Santa will have in his grab bag this year.

Paul F. Ploutz holds four degrees including a Doctorate in Science Education; has taught in New York, Michigan, Colorado, and at the Ohio University in Athens; and is the author of numerous textbooks, manuals and more than a dozen educational games. Ploutz has also been active in numerous local, state and national organizations. Dr. Ploutz and his wife, Geri, have 2 daughters and reside at 19 Clearview Heights in Athens, Ohio 45701.

Newpaper cartoon making fun of Ploutz Educational Games. (source unknown)

L-R: President Kootaga Area Council B.S.A. (Ohio & West Virginia), a new eagle scout and Governor Arch Moore, West Virginia

Governor Arch Moore, West Virgina, congratulating Ploutz for 50 years of support to scouting.

Tenth District U. S.
Representative Clarence E.
Miller, named an Ohio
University Honorary Alumnus
in October, 1973, and Dr. Pau
Ploutz tested the metric scales
they are holding. Miller (l.)
weighs in at 81 kilograms and
Ploutz (r.) made it to 89.
Miller agrees with Ploutz'
claim that metric conversion is
inevitable and supports a
carefully planned change-over.

he Coming of the Kilogram

Ploutz lobbies Congress to pass the U.S. switch to the
metric system of weights and measurements.

Cleveland Mayor, Governor of Ohio and U.S. Senator
George Voinovich asks Paul, a republican, for support.

Paul, Century 21 Real Estate Broker
Athens County, Ohio (1980)
During his tenure as broker, he licensed 131 real estate salesmen.

Dr. Julie and Dr. Paul
March 1987

Two doc's: Lori L. Ploutz Ph.D (left) and Julie A. Ploutz D.O.
Ohio University Campus
Lori places the ceremonial hood on her sister at the formal graduation ceremony.
223-G

Meet the Doctor
Julie Adams, DO

A recent addition to University Hospitals Health System Primary Care Physician Practices, Dr. Julie Adams has joined the practice Family Medicine Specialists, with Richard Below, DO, David Brill, DO, John Thomas, MD and John Victor Wirtz, MD. Dr. Adams will have admitting privileges at University Hospitals, St. John West Shore Hospital and Fairview Hospital.

Training & Education — Dr. Adams received her medical degree from Ohio University College of Osteopathic Medicine and served her Family Practice residency at St. John West Shore Hospital in Westlake.

Special Interests — Dr. Adams has special interests in preventive medicine in adolescents and children as well as women's health.

Personal — Dr. Adams enjoys swimming, traveling, reading and knitting. She resides in Bay Village with her husband.

Julie's first real job!

Ploutz Nature Preserve, Albany, Ohio
Paul feeding Mallards & Canadian Geese from rear deck of residence, 2001.

-R: Iris Mead, Donald Hadden, Founders Paul Ploutz & Jim Proper; Kelli Sullivan,
Beatrice Hinkley, Sandra Walcott
First board meeting of the Roxbury Educational Foundation

11. Davis	(14)
12. Van Valkenburg	(13)
13. Purchell	(12)
14. Schuman	(12)
15. Cartwright	(11)
16. Van Aken	(11)
17. Reed	(11)
18. Roberts	(11)
19. Sherwood	(11)
20. Smith	(11)

E. Identification/recognition of (1901-1950) RCS graduates;
    1. Major national achievements with universities, industry (17)
    2. Profound and unique service to RCS and community   (6)
    3. Military, homeland defense   (11)

Thirty-four have, with information from Marion Cronk Gile, Marshall Slauson (1932), Elsie Ploutz Proper (41), Eva Teichmann (42), Alvin Van Aken (1944), Ester Finch Snyder (1946), Richard "Dick" Bouton (1947), Ronald Ballard (1948), Frances Gorsch, et. al. over a three year period, founder Ploutz hereby confirms the selection for individual and group recognition. A future second edition can be considered to make corrections, omissions. People *who purchase Roxbury Boys/Girls are invited to write corrections*, additions and mail them to the Foundation Office currently at Roxbury Central. Since the author(s) did not know most of those identified, the broad input of community members and information from the Roxbury village library, is acknowledged, with gratitude.

F. Significant National Educational, Industrial Achievements:

1903	Claude Thomas	Civil Engineer
1904	Frank Booth	Manufacturing, RCS College Scholarships
1905	Andrew Hamilton	Engineer
	George Hubbell	Mechanical Engineer
1907	Harry M. Clark	Author, engineer
1915	Grant Morse	Author, professor
1918	Cecil M. Shultis	Engineer
1919	Preston W. Edsall	Professor

1922	Frederick L. Teichmann	Professor, author, Engineer
1926	Rudolph Blythe	Pharmaceutical Researcher
1931	George Brandow	Professor
1934	J. Frances Allen	Professor
	Lochie J. Allen	Professor
	Walter F. Meade	Naturalist, author, Photographer
1939	Otis Van Aken	Engineer, Boeing
1940	Marvin Russell Blythe	Author, Mathematics
1949	Guy Numann	CEO manufacturing Corporation

G. Profound and unique service to RCS and the community:

1909	Zena R. Travis	Superintendent Schools
1921	Ima Mae Griffin	Author, Roxbury Historian
1924	Bruce Caswell	Naturalist, Scout Master
1928	Charles K. Ives	M.D, Roxbury, N. Y.
1934	Olive MacLaury	Professor, local ornithologist
1945	Richard Lutz	Carpenter, contractor, Feed stores

H. Military hero's and homeland defense:

1927	John Harold Kelly	Lt. Col. Army
1929	David Pitkethly	Lt. Col. Army
1932	Douglas White	W.W.11 Pilot
1934	Robert Brandow	Lt. Col. Army
1935	James Bouton	Lt. Col. Intelligence
1938	James Cantwell	POW, Bataan Death march
1938	Marshall Stoutenburgh	POW, Bataan Death
1941	Julian Wiederman	German POW WWII Army
1946	Vincent Long	WW11 Air Force Engineer
1946	Kenneth Underwood	WW11 Pilot; TWA@JFK
1950	Philip Caswell	Lt.Col. Army Intelligence

I. On going Historical Perspective

Once achieved, or largely underway, the next one-hundred year primary goals, are to further mobilize community energy, resources.

J. Ecological endeavors; identify and mobilize support for individual school and community earth friendly activities.

1. Identify community as a "bird sanctuary."
2. Explore raising wild turkeys, ginseng, fish hatchery, tree seedlings, organic foods.
3. Create, protect, beaver expansion and resultant habitat (Roxbury once named Beaverdam).
4. Create, explore sun, wind to create electricity.

K. Fund Raising

Fund raising will need to be broad based, nationwide, state, and local. Historical and/or educational projects shall be an important on going component individually, or in partnership, with other organizations, schools, colleges, state recreational, historic and tourism efforts. Not *nearly enough has been made* of Gould and Burroughs Roxbury origin.

The full story of Ford, Firestone, Edison, et. al. presence, has yet to be presented effectively. Fritz Teichmann ('22, see **Part II**), is the ideal model of a Roxbury boy, leaving the farm for education, and making his country a better place. His story, equal to Burroughs, certainly Gould or Ploutz, et. al. craves recognition.

Assets of the foundation are NOT to be utilized for "normal" budget deficits, failures, replacement, or bail out contingencies. Projects must have broad appeal, utilization for major patrons of the town and schools.

Schools: Public or private schools, Roxbury-Grand Gorge, Rotary, VFW, Senior Citizens, and other groups, are encouraged to provide volunteer use of "start-up" assistance, meeting places, of family societies as assistance described in "D" and on going support of the Foundation.

Further individual recognition, to be determined by the FOUNDATION board. While *all* are RCS graduates most, if not all, are represented in *Roxbury Boys/Girls* in the period 1901-1950. Since honoring all 1851 RCS graduates of the Century is the founders original goal, the task of developing specific criteria for additional "appointments" from 1950 on will need be developed by the FOUNDATION.

Local Attorney Herb Jordan *mentored* Jim and Paul through the legal requirements of a foundation and *tax exemption status.*

A few locals observed that neither Gould or Burroughs, in fact, had graduated from RCS! As both founder and project financier Paul "ruled" that they graduated from "Roxbury." They *did* attend the Hardscrabble School (Pleasant Valley) and Beechwood Seminary in West Settlement. There *was* no Central High even in existence prior to the 1930s and the idea that he and 1851 others were claiming to be Roxbury grads, with "Jason and John" left out, was unthinkable! They graduated with what Roxbury had at the time.

On the additional advise of Robert J. Miller and Associates, local grant writer Peg Ellsworth, Iris Mead et. al., the foundation was made emphasizing education and family recognition. According to Fed tax exemption under section 501 (c) (3) the foundation must be established primarily for educational purposes. Miller and Associate of Tonawanda, NewYork, professional Grant Development and Fund Raising Counsel, gave several practical suggestions. Some of the new board members "to be" were largely interested in scholarships for graduating seniors *now.* Miller suggested "there are mechanisms to preserve the family name and the descriptive name without confusing the donors." Paul's desire to *mentor* the community, not merely yearly graduates, was preserved in the final mission statement, and like Jason and John, "got his way."

" The Journey has been wonderful, I've mentored a "ga-zillion" people, became a bonafide tree hugger and I came from Roxbury. Perhaps as my mother (Anna) had hoped, the world is slightly better because I was here."

Paul F. Ploutz

#

PART II

Unique Achievements

Womens Suffrage at RCS

The original title *Roxbury Boys* seemed sexist, even offensive to some, so we changed it. Regrettably, however, that was the way it was for at least the first part of the nineteenth century. The 1914 RCS Yearbook (second oldest yearbook printed), devotes an entire page to a suffrage debate "held at High School," as follows:

The Debating Teams

The Phi Sigma Debate

December 5, 1913   Held at High School

Resolved: Women should be granted the right of suffrage on equal terms with men.

AFFIRMATIVE.	NEGATIVE.
M. Leland Lewis (1914)	Ralph H. Beaumont (did not graduate)
James T. Cronk (1913)	Grant D. Morse (1915)
Roy Van Ake (1915)	George Muller (1916)
Cecil Mackey	W. Francis Minnerly (1915)

Decided in favor of the Negative

Unique Achievements: Roxbury Boys and Girls

The author has added the date of graduation. **Part III** provides additional information on most graduates. Pictures of the RHS debaters were included in the yearbook along with a picture of Florence L. Enderlin who did not get an opportunity to debate. Is there any justice? In 1913, Florence Enderlin was salutatorian; 1914, Edna Morse was valedictorian; 1915 Anna Ruteshouser (author Ploutz's mother) was valedictorian! To further belabor the point, review the classes **(Part III)** and discover how frequently women were valedictorian, salutatorian, or <u>both</u>.

The old yearbook does not reveal how the negative vote was obtained. It was probably not the teachers voting as most teachers, at least then, were female.

Since then, society has moved through the "glass ceiling" concept and women have become CEO's of large corporations. Women college presidents hold positions of power and prestige. Congress gave women the right to vote in 1915. Rather than make a feint attempt to rewrite history, the author confesses that Roxbury was *like everywhere else*, at least in that respect.

Of the RCS graduates selected here for significant, profound, or unique recognition from the first fifty years of the century, a few were women. Dozens of other RCS graduates served in other ways, probably in ways even beyond those recognized here. William Dudley (1913), was valedictorian, went to WWI and was Roxbury's first pilot. Second Lt. George Griffin was a German POW who earned an Air Medal and two Oak Leaf Clusters. James Cantwell, and Marshall Stoutenburgh (1938 classmates), for example, were POW's, and survived the catastrophic Bataan Death March in WWII. Julian Wiederman,(1941), Paul's cousin, was a POW in Nazi Germany. There were others.

Seven Roxbury boys became Lieutenant Colonel after 1900; John Kelly (27), David Pitkethly (29), Robert Brandow (34), James F. Bouton (35), and Philip Caswell (1950). Later, Wayne Brainerd (76), and Anthony P. German (77), gained the rank of Lt. Col. Frederick Teichmann, (22) while essentially a civilian, was ranked Colonel to assist in aeronautical and engineering research in Europe during WWI.

WWII pilots included Douglas White (1932), and Kenneth Underwood (46). Vincent Long (46), became an Air Force Engineer.

More than seventy men from the Town of Roxbury served in the Civil War. Several served in the brief war of 1912. George S. Cartwright (1880), and hundreds of others have served in the military. Major General Otis Preston, the highest ranking officer in the area Militia, built the first factory on the Baker farm in Hardscrabble (see map). A complete listing of the men and women who have served in the military would require more pages than are available in this text.

Part III & IV identifies veterans from 1901-2000. The American Legion office, Main Street, Roxbury, New York and Erma Griffin's book *History of the Town of Roxbury*, have records and antidotes from *all* of our nation's wars. Roxbury boys have served in substantial numbers in our nation's wars. We have listed only Roxbury veterans from 1901–2000, who graduated RCS, but there were others, hundreds of others. In subsequent editions of *Mentoring Roxbury et. al.* we hope to add the numerous omissions of RCS graduates from 1950-2000 who served, or who are now serving their country.

You may review the chronological list of RCS graduates and identify graduates who were officers, pilots and foot soldiers. Veterans, rotarians, eagle scouts, valedictorians, salutatorians, class presidents, and those who attended college, and became teachers are listed. Additions (and corrections) particularly for omissions of those graduating after 1950, could be entered directly in your copy of this book, or wait for a revision or future author.

Twenty-six "Overachievers"

have been identified from1901-1950. Since NONE have been left out we have dared to identify some very deserving people heretofore not thoroughly recognized. Moreover, at this point we have been able to include detailed information on only part of the twenty six selected. We expect that future authors or revisions would expand the present information. Our own impression is that the list is wonderfully academic hopefully indicative that RCS schools and the community have done a splendid job of *mentoring!*

YEAR	GRADUATE	COMMENT
1903	Claude Thomas	Civil Engineer
1904	Frank Booth	Provided College Scholarships:
1905	Andrew Hamilton	Engineer
1905	George Hubbell	Mechanical Engineer
1907	Harry M. Clark	Author; Engineer
1908	Tallman C. Bookhout	C Pres; Salutatorian, RCS Prin.
1909	Zena R. Travis	Superintendent of Schools
1915	Grant Morse	Author; Professor
1918	Cecil M. Shultis	Engineer
1919	Preston W. Edsall	Professor
1921	Irma May Griffin	Author; Local Historian

1922	Frederick L. Teichmann	Author; Professor; Engineer
1924	Bruce Caswell	Naturalist; Scout Master Troop41
1926	Rudolph Blythe	Pharmaceutical Researcher
1928	Charles K. Ives	Roxbury's Physician
1931	George Brandow	Professor
1934	J. Frances Allen	Professor
1934	Lochie J. Allen	Professor
1934	Walter F. Mead	Author, Photographer, Naturalist
1934	Olive MacLaury	Professor; Local Ornithology
1936	Bruce S. Mead	Valedictorian; College;WWII; Airline Pilot;
1939	Otis Van Aken	Boeing Aviation; Engineer
1940	Marvin Russell Blythe	Author; Mathematician
1945	Richard Lutz	Carpenter, Contractor, Feed Stores
1946	Robert Preston	Class President; WWII, SUNY Cortland; Teacher; Principal
1949	Guy Numann	CEO; Manufacturing Corporation

1903

Claude Thomas, Civil Engineer
(information in the next edition)

1904

Frank Booth, Civil Engineer

Frank's parents ran a dry goods store in Grand Gorge, but he attended school in Roxbury. He and Harold Humphrey were the only two grads in 1904. Frank's love of Roxbury/Grand Gorge and country was evident at an early age. Shortly after graduation, Frank was selected to deliver a speech at the Fourth of July celebration in Grand Gorge. Harold became manager of an inn. Frank wanted more, bright and ambitious he had planned on attending college. As a Roxbury Boy Frank, like Burroughs, enjoyed hiking. He could recognize songbirds by their voices and was an avid trout fisherman.

In 1904, becoming an attorney was still considered to be an honorable goal and profession. That's what Frank wanted to do. In addition to the store, his father had worked for the government.

The Booths' had neglected to carry insurance on their Grand Gorge store. When it burned, Frank's goals of attending college were dashed, and he had to settle on attending Oneonta Normal School. One could gain teaching credentials by attending for only two years.

Frank Gould, youngest of Jay's children provided Frank Booth with a scholarship in engineering at New York University. Frank Gould, prior to his death in 1965, donated $2.5 million to NYU. Older sister Anna was also generous with NYU (Gould Memorial Library) and numerous other gifts and donations. Frank Gould played a dominant role in Booth's life. Both graduated from NYU with degrees in engineering. Frank Gould spent much of his time and a great deal of money in France. Three wives, booze, and for many years a European playboy, Gould was seldom in Roxbury. On occasion, demonstrating his athletic nature he played golf with Finley J. and sister Helen (Gould) Shepard at the Roxbury Golf Course, which Helen and Finley had carved out of the mountain near the earlier Gould and Burroughs farms.

Frank Booth was also athletic, social, and outgoing. He was a Roxbury Boy who seemed to profit from Gould's mentoring by developing leadership qualities. At NYU, Frank was class vice president two years and class president for two years. He was invited to join Psi Upsilon fraternity, and later Delta Iota Delta, a prominent service organization.

Frank played both varsity football and varsity baseball while attending engineering classes. Upon graduation, his first job break was a position in Mexico (1912-1914). His tasks included designing machinery to test the quality of ore being mined, as well as managing the operations of a plant that processed more than a thousand tons of ore per day!

Mexican turmoil in 1915 included constant fighting between federal soldiers and rebels. The safety of Americans working in Mexico could not be assured. President Wilson finally sent the US Marines into Vera Cruz to rescue Americans. Frank was rescued, but escaped under the British flag.

In need of a job, he fell back on his Oneonta Normal training, taking a teaching position in New Jersey. Lawrenceville, a private school, needed someone to teach mechanical drawing and art. With a degree in civil engineering the mechanical drawing part was, in today's vernacular, a "cake walk."

The art part, well Roxbury folk believe that small

towns/schools produce graduates who have to be versatile, and creative. Frank enrolled in an art course in a nearby town staying one day ahead of the class he was teaching. He would then repeat what he had learned the previous day. The year 1917 was a big one for Frank. He married Edith Weck a Brooklyn city girl. It may have been the *mentoring* received under Frank Gould's influence, but Booth managed to marry a girl with a wealthy father, Edward. Edward was the owner and manufacturer of cutlery, surgical instruments and hospital supplies.

Frank also joined the army in 1917 and was sent to Texas to be on border patrol. Relations with Mexico weren't all that good. With teaching credentials and an engineering degree, World War I saw him quickly promoted to second lieutenant and on his way to Europe. He was part of the first American Expeditionary Force. One of many assignments was to guard the president on one of Wilson's first European trips. After serving in the army, Frank enrolled in the AEF University College of Business in Paris. Once again, his athletic versatility surfaced. His tennis was so outstanding that he toured Europe playing tennis for the college.

Upon returning to the states, Frank worked briefly in Chicago for General Electric, then returned to Brooklyn for the birth of his first daughter Helen in 1920. Frank became factory manager in Brooklyn in 1923, later vice president. When Maria Weck retired in 1944, son-in-law Frank became president. Edward Weck and Company prospered.

The patriotism that Frank had demonstrated in 1904 now presented itself. Shortly after Pearl Harbor (Dec 7, 1941) Frank exhorted Weck employees to increase productivity as their patriotic duty. It became clear that his motive was patriotism, not profit in exciting workers to produce medical supplies. During WWI his company hired many women, and went to a fifty-four-hour work week, greatly increasing the production of surgical instruments for both the army and navy. Frank's company was honored because of loyalty to his factory employees, now mainly women, and increasing the production of needed surgical supplies. In 1943, Weck & Company received the Army-Navy Award for excellence in war production.

Frank had been a member of the Gould Church in Roxbury. Adults had noticed his faith, sense of fair play, and simple integrity in dealing with others. Roxbury Rotary now (again) has a sign marking the headwaters of the east branch of the Delaware River placed near Grand Gorge. It falls down periodically, then is resurrected every twenty years or so.

Frank had huge vegetable and flower gardens in Roxbury, and even while living and raising his three daughters (Mary, Frances, Noel) in Larchmont, often returned to Roxbury. In 1945, he wrote to a friend "Although I have left the mountains they have never left me. They still influence me and they are drawing me back." In Larchmont, Frank was president of the Men's Club, member of the Orienta Beach Club, Larchmont Yacht Club, elder, and Sunday school teacher.

Frank was often described as "larger than life," heroic, immense integrity with a gracious manner and genuine gift for bringing out the best in others. Booth had also been a *mentor*, quietly paying the college expenses of Roxbury Boys with little or no notice or recognition. As a Roxbury Boy, his love of nature reminds some of the Burroughs influence.

By the year 2000, the careers of many CEO's, attorneys, Wall Street financiers, professional athletes, even priests, seem in disarray. "Honesty Is the Best Policy" written by Roxbury Boy Jay Gould at age fourteen is a haunting reminder that "It Takes a Village." Roxbury was that village.

Frank Booth wrote, "Search out the good that you find in everyone. Accept people the way you find them. Do not try to change the things you find in your friends that you do not like. The influence of your example is far more powerful than anything you can say to them. Whenever you are deeply disturbed have a silent hour with God. Do not pour out your troubles to Him but listen for what he will say to you."

Acknowledgement of information on Frank Booth: granddaughter, Barbara Johnson, Halcottsville, New York; Roxbury Yearbook 1904; Roxbury Village Library.

#

1905

Andrew Hamilton, Engineer

(information to be added in next edition)

\#

1905

George Hubbell, Mechanical Engineer

(Information to be added in next edition)

\#

1907

Harry M. Clark, Author, Engineer

(Information to be added in next edition)

\#

1908

Tallman C. Bookhout, Class President, Salutatorian,
Principal, Preacher

(Information to be added in next edition)

\#

Zena R. Travis, Superintendent of Schools

Miss Zena R. Travis was born November 3, 1890, in the same house in Meeker Hollow, Roxbury, in which she died on Friday June 23, 1967, at the age of seventy-six. She was the youngest daughter of Elmer and Nora Todd Travis. She was descended from the early pioneers of Roxbury, on both sides of the family, and spent most of her life in the Roxbury area, though she was widely known throughout New York State as an educator of youth.

She graduated from Roxbury High School in the class of 1909 as salutatorian. Fred W. Enderlin, the only male in the class of five students was valedictorian. The other four all went to college and became teachers. Zena graduated Oneonta Normal school in 1911. She taught in California for a time, as well as in Delaware County. In 1921, Zena succeeded Fayette W. Whitney as superintendent of the supervisory district that then included Roxbury, Andes, Margaretville, Fleischmanns, and Grand Gorge. At that time, she was the youngest district superintendent in the state, and upon her retirement in 1958, after a career of thirty-seven years, she had the most years as superintendent of anyone in the state.

When she became superintendent in 1921, the countryside was dotted with one-room schoolhouses. She would occasionally visit these rural schools, and it was always an exciting event for those students when she came! Roxbury was centralized in 1930, and she presided when the new Roxbury Central School was built in 1939 and during the construction of other new school buildings in the district. She also supervised the formation of the Board of Cooperative Services for third supervisory district in 1957. In 1965, the Grand Gorge Central School honored Miss Travis by naming its honor society chapter in her name.

She was a member of the Jay Gould Memorial Reformed Church, the Coeur de Lion chapter, Order of the Eastern Star and the Wawaka Grange of Halcottsville. Surviving are a brother, Harvey J. Travis of Middletown, and adopted daughter, Marie Travis Green (RCS 1945), a granddaughter, Barbara Green. She and her late sister Arna Travis brought up two nieces and four nephews, the children of another sister who's now deceased.

Acknowledgement of information: Roxbury Yearbook 1909; Esther Finch Snyder (1946); **Catskill Mountain News**; Roxbury Village Library.

#

1915

Grant Morse, Author; Professor

Chauncy F. and Annie Dent Morse brought their son Grant into the world (Vega) November 11, 1897. It was a historical event for Chauncy as Grant D. was the first of seven children, as well as the beginning of the third generation of Grants from their Vega farm. Grant was the oldest then Edith, Mary, Grace, Ruth, Harrison, and Lindon B., was the youngest.

Father Chauncy ran the farm, but was also a teacher, having graduated from the Stamford Seminary. Grant attended the Vega School, which was only a short walk or horse and wagon ride from the Morse farm. His younger brother described him as a "very serious person and inclined to teach us all." Even his sense of humor had an academic side.

"Going back home from school each day Grant would "school them" in the short trip. Coming from school, if they knew their lesson, he would stop at a certain rock along the mountain road where he had previously placed some candy. If they knew their lesson they would be "compensated" with candy. If not—no candy. That particular rock with a hole in it, is still on the road over Vega Mountain to the homestead (Lindon Morse 2003)." While he did farm chores before and after school, like the earlier Jay Gould, his younger sisters and brothers described Grant as "too studious." This author has been unable to determine where Grant received his master's and doctoral degrees.

While this writing is about Grant's life it must include the profound effect and contributions of the Morse family. From 1901 until 2000, thirty Morses' have graduated from RCS.

Two valedictorians, four teachers, a ship's captain, nurse, four veterans, a merchant marine official, a superintendent of schools, scout master, author, eagle scout, and several successful business men, often insurance (see **Part IV** alphabet). That is <u>not</u> counting fifteen others, this being a "first edition," the other careers have yet to be added.

Grant graduated in 1915 with a class of fourteen other over achievers. Anna Ruteshouser (author's mother) was valedictorian; Roy Van Aken, salutatorian; Francis Minnerly, class president and future dentist. Six of the class became teachers. With four males and ten females, the abundant talent of the class of 1915 became legend.

In the much heralded local suffrage debate of "equal terms with men" held December fifth, 1913 at the high school, alas, Grant, along with classmate W. Francis Minnerly, represented the negative, which prevailed! (even great men make mistakes).

Grant married Marjorie Saxe of Saugerties, December 27, 1925, more than ten years after he graduated. Marjorie was a Methodist minister's daughter. Grant and Marjorie had two sons Roger A. (Ithaca) and Stanley C. (Millbrook). Two daughters Jean Kallop (Vorheesville) Shirley died at age two in August 1934.

After one year in a prep school, Grant entered New York University graduating in 1920. He taught for a few years in area schools and eventually worked in the New York State public school system for forty years.

He was principal of Saugerties High in 1924 and superintendent only two years later. While superintendent, he received his doctorate degree. He then served as superintendent of Saugerties School District for thirty-seven years. One of his hobbies was bees. He maintained several hives, from which he extracted his own honey.

In 1964, the Saugerties school board renamed the former Blue Mountain School the Grant D. Morse Elementary School in recognition and remembrance of his time and devotion to the education of children.

He became principal of Tioga Central School and the Washington Academy in Salem. He was also an assistant professor at the State Teachers College at Cortland. (STC, then SUNY). He became president of the New York State Teachers Association and the School Master's Club of the Mid Hudson Valley. He was a member of the Saugerties Methodist Church.

Grant was equally active in civic affairs as a member of the

American Legion Post 72, the Saugerties Rotary Club, and the Men's Garden Club of Stuart, Florida, while serving as editor of The Green Thumb, its publication. Grant wrote four books and numerous magazine articles on entomology.

Acknowledgement for information provided by: Lindon B. Morse (brother 1933), RCS Yearbook 1915; recollections of 1915 classmate Anna Ruteshouser (Ploutz) as told to author.

#

1918

Cecil M. Shultis, Engineer

(Information to be added in next edition)

#

1919

Preston W. Edsall, Professor

(Information to be added in next edition)

#

1921

Irma May Griffin, Author, Local Historian

Irma Mae Griffin (born Ima May Griffin) was a noted writer and historian. She was born on May 22, 1903, the daughter of James and Matilda (Morse) Griffin. She had a younger sister, Mary (Griffin) Eignor and a brother, Morse Griffin. She was devoted to her family and spent much of her adult life caring for her father and brother.

Irma was educated in the Roxbury schools, and from an early age showed a strong interest in reading and writing. She consistently earned high marks in English and was valedictorian of the Roxbury high school, class of 1921. According to the Saturday, July 2, 1921, edition of the Roxbury Times "The touching valedictory address by Miss Ima Griffin is considered as good as the best valedictory ever given in Roxbury." There were eight graduates that year, all earning New York State regents diplomas. The State Normal and Training School in Oneonta awarded her a diploma in 1923, which gave her a state teaching license for life.

After a brief teaching career, she returned to Roxbury to work for the Golden Seal Insurance Company. She continued working there until 1929 when the company was forced to close due to the Great Depression. Later, she became a real estate agent for the Raymond Korzendorfer Agency, a career that spanned more than thirty years. In this capacity, she made use of her extensive knowledge of the town.

Irma's writing career began in 1932 when she was asked to write local news for the *Oneonta Star*. She also wrote extensively for the Catskill Mountain News, the Stamford Mirror-Recorder and the Walton Reporter. In 1939, as part of a national competition held by the National Editorial Association, she was named "Best Country Correspondent" for her columns in the Oneonta Star.

Collecting information about Roxbury and its people was a life long passion. Irma compiled numerous scrapbooks full of information, which the Roxbury Public Library in the Irma Mae Griffin History Room now holds. This knowledge prompted local leaders to encourage her to write a history of the town of Roxbury. This led to the publication in 1953 by Irma Mae Griffin and Carolyn Evelyn More of the 281 page, History of the Town of

Roxbury. In 1976, a revised edition was published, updating the original and in her words correcting "the many defects and inaccuracies of the first history." (Still available from the Roxbury Town Library.)

In acknowledgement of her role as chronicler and keeper of local history, she was named Roxbury School historian, Roxbury Alumni historian, and served many years as the official historian of the town of Roxbury.

Irma Griffin not only wrote about the history of Roxbury, but also was an active participant in town life. She belonged to the Eastern Star, the United Methodist Church, the Roxbury Library, the RCS Alumni Association, and the National Grange. Her inquisitiveness about activities in the town, and about the lives of its people was an invaluable asset in her role of writer and historian.

Irma was honored on May 1, 1981, with an Irma Mae Griffin Night and again on August 23, 1987, on Irma Mae Griffin Day. On these occasions, local citizens expressed their appreciation and gratitude for her contributions to the town of Roxbury. On October 26, 1987, Irma passed away in the house where she grew up in her beloved Roxbury.

Twelve-year-old author Ploutz met "Ima" on the streets of Roxbury. Several other references to this colorful individual appear in Chapter 5. With instantaneous quick wit, a unique off-center sense of humor, and an outgoing friendly nature, *everyone* knew Ima. Erma, as she choose to be called, was eccentric, really eccentric. Early in his career Jay Gould surveyed Delaware County. Erma Griffin "surveyed" the entire Roxbury Village and its families, becoming a legend in her day.

There was more information available about "Irma" than any of the RCS graduates from 1901 to 2000. Many Roxbury town folk remember her, but in particular, help was supplied by Frances Gorsch, Ester Finch Snyder, James G. and Ann Eignor, (pictures); The Roxbury Times (long gone) the 1921 RCS *Yearbook*, and of course her own book.

#

Frederick Kurt Teichmann, Author, Professor, Engineer

Frederick was born in Germany May twenty-sixth, 1905. His parents Albin and Lilli Moehle Teichmann, both professional chefs, arrived in New York City in 1906. Albin and Lilli moved to Roxbury in 1909 to operate a summer boarding house and farm. "Fritz" started school at the age of five in Montgomery Hollow. Neither of his parents or Fritz spoke English, only German. Albin's brother Emil also came to Roxbury, working as a gardener for Mrs. Shepard.

Earlier maps identify the mountain as Schultheis Mountain. Mr. Schultheis built and operated a private club, which in 1909, became the Teichmanns' boarding house. The property was called Ironwood Post. The Schumann family originally owned the Schulthesis property. The Schumanns operated a stone quarry and owned to the top of the mountain. The Schumann family also owned the farm halfway up the mountain, which Fritz later bought in 1933. It was where he spent his summers until 1997.

Teichmanns' closest neighbors were the Schumanns, who also spoke German and served as their interpreters. The Schumanns son Elmer was Fritz's age and was his interpreter. Fritz ended up teaching his parents English, even using his schoolbooks. Those who lived on the mountain developed sturdy legs, and the children walked to school. During winter, Fritz and Elmer often rode their sleds to the foot of the mountain and walked from there to Montgomery Hollow. Fritz's father would pick up the sleds loading them onto his horse-drawn sleigh after he took milk to the creamery at the foot of the hill. It was dark by the time the Teichmann children walked home from school, and Lilli would take a lantern outside and yodel to the children to guide them home in the dark.

Fritz held at least one job in town while still in high school, working for Andrew Lutz, a prominent merchant. When Fritz graduated from high school (1922), Albin and Lilli invited his entire class of seven and the three teachers for dinner. The splendid meal was in the boarding house dining room with its spectacular view of Roxbury Village. Fritz told about how one of his 1922 classmates at a Roxbury reunion only a few years ago recalled the dinner. "It was a multi course affair with much specialized silverware, a shellfish course, a soup course, culminating in baked Alaska. Hand churned ice cream was served on a hot summer's day and the meringue baked in a wood stove, all at a time when they had only an ice box and no electricity. Everyone looked to Fritz to see what utensils to use, but Fritz had no idea."

Their farm was near the top of Teichmann mountain. The dirt road up the mountain was straight. Straight up, often fifteen degrees with a few trees and a stone wall on either side. In winter, it was often impossible to get their milk to the creamery. Getting out was not the greatest problem, getting back in could be difficult or impossible. The location provided a spectacular view to the west in any season. The steep road in was half a mile long. A stone wall and a row of maples, aspen, and oak clearly lined each edge of the road. In the winter, the road would drift full, several feet deep making the road disappear. In the early 1900s there were few trees left on the Roxbury mountainsides. Some farms were abandoned because of the lack of trees for firewood.

Life on the farm kept Fred and his two younger sisters Frieda and Eda busy. Summers at the boarding house were successful, often with a dozen or two who stayed extended periods. Fred was a good student at Roxbury, graduating in 1922 as salutatorian. John Davidson was valedictorian. Mabel Hammond became a teacher. Theodore (Ted) Howard went to work for General Electric. Willard Van Woert, class president, became a pastor and later a music teacher, also moving to NYC. Madison Speenburgh and Elizabeth Hubbell accounted for the seven RCS grads class of '22. Neither sister graduated from high school. His sister Frieda became a nurse, Eda graduated Albany Business School (then Albany Business College, ABC).

The Gould family sponsored several Roxbury students to attend NYU. With Gould financial assistance, Fred entered the College of Engineering, which had just introduced an aeronautical engineering program. It was during his undergraduate years that the School of Engineering and Science, known then as the College of Engineering, had introduced the cooperative plan whereby a student alternated periods in industry with periods in college, and on completion would receive the degree in aeronautical engineering, and civil engineering. The School of Engineering and Science at NYU is located at the University Heights Center. Buildings include the Gould Hall of Technology.

Even with the Gould "grant" Fred needed to take advantage of the opportunity to work. In the summer of 1925 he worked for the US Post Office. His main task was setting up signal towers for the mail planes to follow. The post office was then completing a transcontinental route for flying air mail by night as well as by day. Those folk who worked for the post office between May 15, 1918 and August 31, 1927, formed an informal organization known as Air Mail Pioneers, and in the summer of 1968, the Post Office, on the fiftieth anniversary, awarded Fred an honorary plaque to now "Dean" Teichmann, as a representative of those pioneers still alive and living in the metropolitan area.

While still under the "work study" program, Fred worked for the Brewster Company, which was attempting to build seaplane floats. The engineering staff consisted of only two people. When the chief engineer left, Fred found himself in charge. Working night and day, Fred needed to take the summer off for a brief, but much needed vacation. That vacation delayed his degree by six months.

As a pioneer in airplane design, his next job was with Chance Bought, designing a seaplane. In the 1920s there was a leisurely atmosphere prevailing in the aircraft industry. Many companies were still located in vacant warehouses or factories. Fred wasn't sure what he wanted to do but teaching was NOT the field he wished to enter. He had started his college work in mechanical engineering on the advice of Dr. Charles H. Snow, then dean of the College of Engineering, who spent his summers in Roxbury and knew Fred as a child. The connection between small town Roxbury and NYU with the Gould family was already intact. Having a college dean from NYU routinely in Roxbury only increased the connection.

Dr. Snow was a cousin of Mrs. Shepard. Soon after Fritz's father arrived on the mountain, he took a wagonload of vegetables to the village to sell. One of the first houses he stopped at was Dr. Snow's. Fritz's father still spoke little English and Dr. Snow insisted on joining him on the wagon, and then introduced him to his friends in Roxbury telling them to buy their vegetables from Fritz's father. The elder Teichmann continued to deliver vegetables to several Roxbury houses into the late 1930s.

Dr. Snow's secretary, also a Gould cousin, and her son Ollie Talbot spent some summers in Roxbury. When Fritz went to NYU, he and Ollie roomed together. Eventually Fritz and Ollie married sisters.

In 1921-1922 aeronautical engineering programs in American universities were still in their infancy. Dr. Alexander Klemin, a pioneer in the field, presented a series of lectures. Those lectures led to an aeronautical engineering option at NYU. Subsequently, the Daniel Guggenheim School of Aeronautics was established. Since it was a new field, and the industry was also in its infancy, Fred Teichmann recognized an opportunity when he saw it. The Roxbury Boy was in the right place at the right time with the right training. He was very much in on the "ground floor."

Even as an undergraduate, Fred with others had started a project to build a small plane for use by class members. Students and faculty donated money. Detailed drawings were made for it construction and a wind tunnel model was built and tested in a four-foot wind tunnel. Air passed through the tunnel up to thirty miles per hour. With Roxbury farm boy versatility, Fred had gained full access to the only piece of research equipment NYU owned. The Curtiss Aeroplane and Motor Company, then located in Garden City, New York had donated it.

A toy by today's standards, the wind tunnel during the 1920s and 1930s was an extremely useful new tool. Located in the Sage Building, Jerone Lederer, a graduate assistant, resigned. Once again the timing was perfect. In September 1927, while still a graduate assistant, the "wind tunnel job" was his. His earlier airplane designs, building a "class" plane, now with wind tunnel developing expertise, put Fred in a key position with implications far beyond NYU.

In 1928, graduates in aeronautical engineering at NYU were encouraged to learn to fly. During the summer of 1928 Fred undertook flying lessons, that the university paid for. The biplane was a Pitcairn Orowing with a World War I surplus engine stationed at Hadley Field, New Jersey. On a landing, one of the wires of the wire-braced gear gave way and Fred "thumped" to the ground spinning a rapid complete circle. Other than that particular experience, Fred thought flying was boring. Moreover, to keep a pilot's license, it was necessary to fly at least one hour per week at a cost of twenty-five dollars an hour and he found that his income of $17.50 a week was woefully inadequate to cover expenses.

In the summer of 1929, Fred went to Germany for a short stint with Junkers Flugzeugwerke, A. G. in Dessau, Germany. He became acquainted with chief engineer, Herman Pohlmann who had been a prisoner of war of the British. Pohlmann later designed the famous STUKA, the German dive bomber used at the beginning of WWII.

During the 1920s, the Daniel Guggenheim Fund for the Promotion of Aeronautics was established. One of the activities of this fund was to promote safe private aircraft flying. To further those objectives, an international aircraft competition was established. Part of the specifications for the airplane to be designed included a landing speed of thirty miles an hour and a minimum speed of 110 miles an hour.

Teichmann was an observer in the course of testing the numerous entrants. It was an interesting competition with the first prize going to an American entrant, a monoplane known as the Curtiss Robin, and second prize to Sir Frederick Handley-Page's entrant, a biplane. These airplanes were a far cry from today's sophisticated aircraft, yet they brought the attention of the industry to the efficacy of slots, flaps, spoiler, wing-tip differential ailerons, variable-incidence wings, and a host of other aeronautical technologies. These were the things Teichmann was teaching, working, and writing about!

The year 1929 was the first in a series of great years and dazzling successes for the Roxbury farm boy. In 1929, the instructor in aeronautical engineering Otto Lunde resigned. Dr. Klemin again persuaded Teichmann to stay to become the instructor, and the ascent up the academic ladder began. Fred was instructor for two years, 1928-1930. In September 1930, he became the youngest assistant professor that NYU had ever had.

During 1934-1935 Fred completed a master's degree in mechanical engineering at the Brooklyn Polytechnic Institute. During the summers of 1938 and 1939, Fred worked with the Materiel Division, United States Army at Wright Field, Ohio. The US Air Force had not yet been formed. During the academic year of 1938 and 1939, Fred was an exchange lecturer at the University of Minnesota. During the summer of 1945, Dean Teichmann received a short-term appointment as a technical representative with the assimilated rank of colonel with the United States Air Force in Europe, *where his duties were to evaluate captured research material.*

In 1940, he became an associate professor and then became "full" professor in 1943. The Roxbury Boy who hadn't wanted to teach in the first place had already assembled a brilliant career. More was to come.

Fred served as acting chairman of the Department of Aeronautical Engineering during 1940 to 1942, he was chairman from 1942 to1955. In 1952, he was appointed assistant dean of the Undergraduate Day Division as well as assistant dean of the Graduate Division in 1959, holding both positions until 1969, when he was promoted to associate dean of both divisions.

Dean Teichmann was a member of the American Society of Mechanical Engineers and a founding member of the Institute of Aeronautical Sciences. He was a member of the American Institute of Aeronautics and Astronautics and served on dozens of panels, workshops, projects and committees. Fred was editor (1942 - 1945) of a technical magazine called Aviation Equipment. He served as consulting editor for a series in aeronautical technology published by the Hayden Book Company, Rochelle Park, New Jersey. He was a member of the American Society of Mechanical Engineers. He was a founding member of the Institute of Aeronautical Sciences. Fred was a member of the American Society for Engineering Education.

NYU founded Iota Alpha, an engineering honorary society, he was a member. He became a member of Tau Beta Pi and Sigma Chi. He was a founding member of Sigma Gamma Tau. He's listed in *Who's Who in the East; American Men of Science, and Who's Who in America.*

Dean Teichmann has served on dozens of panels, societies, committees, works shops, and surveys for NYU, the government, numerous corporations, and other academic institutions. High on the list of so many achievements is his pioneering work on avionics and to American civilian and military leadership and development. His first publication, on Airplane Design (1938) was revised four times and was a major contribution to avionics and to American civilian and military leadership. Fundamentals of Aircraft Structural Analysis (1968), Basic Aerodynamics (1972) added to his spectacular career.

He retired in 1972 after spending fifty years at NYU as student, professor, and administrator. He lived at 22 Mount Joy Avenue, in Scarsdale, New York, and spent most of his summers at the house he built on land adjoining his parents' farm on Teichmann Road (Mountain). At age ninety-four Fred fell at home breaking his hip. He died Thursday February tenth, 2000, in St. Agnes Hospital, White Plains, New York

His wife Margaret K. Wessell from Plainfield, New York whom he married in 1941, died in 1991. Frederick's first cousin Eva Teichmann (Williams) is the only other Teichmann who graduated from Roxbury Schools from 1901 - 2000. Eva graduated in 1942, became a teacher, and married Lemuel Evans who taught at RCS before WWII. After Lemuel's death, Eva married Jim Williams and resides in Lewes, Delaware (2000). His only daughter, Karna Teichmann (Castillo) has a son Eduardo and a daughter Anet, also living in Scarsdale (2000). Frederick's son Kurt and wife Mary have a son Matthew and, daughter Rebecca of Lafayette, California (2000).

In October 1974, Frederick K. Teichmann donated a copy of Fundamentals of Aircraft Flight to the Roxbury Public Library. The inscription read:

"I am contributing this book to the Roxbury Public Library in memory of my parents, Lilli and Albin Teichmann, who were always proud of any achievements, however small, of their children."

This author as a child often heard of Teichmann Mountain. It was only a couple of miles across the valley toward Grand Gorge from Roxbury. For reasons author Ploutz could not explain, he had never been there. His very first visit was on a beautiful day with the fall leaves in spectacular color. Ploutz finally made it, the fall of 2002, at age seventy-one. Driving what seemed straight up with childhood and local Roxbury Boy and friend Phil Caswell, they finally reached the near summit where Frederick Teichmann the farm boy, college dean, and avionics pioneer maintained a summer home until 1997. Teichmann had several mentors, the Helen Gould Shepard family in particular helped finance his college training.

The view from Frederick's home was even superior to the view from another famous Roxbury Boy, naturalist John Burrough's home, and is now a New York State historical site. Frederick's home was near the top of one of Burrough's beloved Catskill Mountains. The awesome mountain view to the west of Roxbury and beyond was inspirational. The setting and view are so magnificent *it can put a lump in your throat and tears in your eyes but you're not sure why. It is the beauty of brilliant fall color with a steady but warm breeze.* Teichmann loved Roxbury and the Catskills.

Teichmann grew up there. Teichmann had looked at clouds from both sides. He was a truly inspired mentor who literally "had his head in the clouds" before he trained his country how to fly through them.

Acknowledgement of information provided by: Teichmann's daughter Mrs. Karma Castillo, Scarsdale, N.Y.; Nephew, Joseph E. Ludewig, Cortland, N.Y.; Catskill Mountain News (March 13, 1953; March 20, 1953; Feb 16, 2000); Engineering at NYU News Letter Vol 8, No 2 Winter 1971-1972; Roxbury Schools Yearbook 1922; Roxbury town folk and authors childhood memory.

Locals and some of the Teichmanns still refer to the mountain as Schumann Mountain and Teichmann Road. The twelve Schumans who have graduated RCS from Evelyn (1927) to Elizabeth (2000) all spell their name with one n.

Much has been said in Roxbury Boys about mentoring, the Gould family and the NYU connection. In addition to the Montgomery Hollow grade school in Roxbury, Dr. Charles H. Snow was perhaps Teichmann's most important *mentor.* Snow's wife Alice (Northrop) co-authored a book, *The Story of Helen Gould* (the Gould connection). Charles was a Roxbury resident for over forty years and also the dean of NYU's College of Engineering (retired in 1930).

#

Bruce Caswell, Naturalist, Scout Master Troop 41

Francis Marion Caswell was born in 1904, the youngest with one sister and six brothers, the son of Frank and Ethyl Lynn Caswell. They owned and operated a large prosperous dairy farm on the east side of Old Clump Mountain. He was named for his great-grandfather, Francis Hardenbergh. In his first years, he was very chubby, reminding his family of Frank's portly brother, Bruce. The nicknames Stubby and Bruce stuck for a lifetime, even though Stub became six feet three inches tall and developed an athletic physique. Apparently he never regained his "rightful" name, even graduating in 1924 as Bruce.

John Burroughs thought it was okay to collect bird nests, not birds, dead or alive. Burroughs gave young Stub change to find old nests. The Caswell farm bordered the Burroughs' farm on the south and the Dales' farm on the east. Stub often hung out at Woodchuck Lodge at an early age. Once John paid twenty-five cents for a meadow lark nest. Stub gradually became Burroughs' "gopher" and served as his gopher during many of the visits by Ford, Firestone, Edison, and others.

Marshall and Flora Dales operated a recreational area, a small lake where they rented rowboats and sold homemade ice cream on the porch of their cottage (later Shepard Lake). They apparently contributed to Stub's portly appearance as a youth. Their young niece, Mildred Preston, was frequently there. "Millie" graduated Roxbury in 1919 and was off to Vassar thanks in part to the generosity of Helen Gould Shepard.

When Stub was a teenager, his parents Frank and Ethyl retired and converted Young's furniture factory in Roxbury into a residence. Stub liked it in Roxbury as Mildred Preston and her mother lived next door to the village library. *Unlike* the then elderly Burroughs, Stub was a good athlete. He loved basketball and cross country and *like* the earlier Burroughs loved nature and was happy to be off the farm. We have no record of his attending college.

No longer "Chubby Stubby" Stub excelled as an athlete. In his junior year at Roxbury School, he contracted scarlet fever. Near death, he missed several years of school before significant recovery. Stub's close encounter gave him a burning desire to regain physical health by hiking (the Burroughs influence) skiing, canoeing and tennis. When he finally recovered at age twenty, he returned to high school graduating in 1924 as salutatorian. Classmate Helen Ennist became valedictorian, beating recovered Stubby "a point or two."

His other seven 1924 classmates all amounted to something. Mildred Faulkner was class president. Mary and Walter Griffin and Cornelia Rollins all became teachers. Stub's friend Bernard "BB" Bartley became a NYS trooper and served in the Roxbury area for many years. Robert Lewis moved to New York City and worked in the hotel business. After graduating, Roxbury, Stub went to work for one of his older brothers painting houses and hanging paper.

While still on the farm, Stub had five older brothers who did the heavy lifting. As the youngest, he more often helped his mother with dozens of household chores. An earlier neighbor Jay Gould, and friend and neighbor John Burroughs had also been close to their mothers. Jay's mother and John's mother died early. The early death of Stub's mother from cancer had a profound effect on him. He had managed to deal with the likelihood of his own death but could not reconcile the loss of his mother. Rather than depression or aggression toward others, Stub started to take risks. Serious risks. It would not bring back his wonderful mother but he had clearly lost his compass.

For a time Stub hauled booze from Great Barrington, Vermont. He hauled booze (prohibition) in his red Chevrolet convertible. Several of "Legs Diamond's" associates *persuaded* him that bootlegging was *not* really in his best interest. Legs was later murdered near Albany, New York

Stub left the bootlegging business to save the life he had regained from scarlet fever. At this point, morality probably played only a minor role. He pushed skiing, canoeing, motorcycling, and driving beyond sane limits. By the end of the 1920s Stub:

> Demolished several sets of skis and poles.
>
> Wrecked his red Chevrolet convertible in a crash in Montgomery Hollow.
>
> Destroyed his canoe, nearly drowning in the Esopus River rapids.
>
> Wrapped his motorcycle around an elm tree directly in front of Roxbury School.

The motorcycle accident also left him prostrate with a broken back. Like the scarlet fever experience apparently the recovery time allowed Stub to reevaluate his priorities. He took up the less dangerous activities of, *hunting and fishing.*

Hunting: His *mentor* the elderly John Burroughs had taught him much about nature and of the outdoors. Stub could distinguish the sounds of nature. A blue jay's call could be interpreted as an alarm call. He could interpret the difference between a single leaf out of place in a path as to a squirrel, a deer, or merely the wind. The direction of the wind, the smell of a campfire, or burning leaves in the village could be determined. An acorn on the ground or a leaf missing from a branch suggested an animal feeding. Daylight or dusk seemed to tell him what animals would be doing, even *thinking!* Venison was a frequent meal at the Caswell house.

Fishing: If you go "upstream" and push mud into the water, the fish "downstream" think it's raining. They are far more apt to bite. Never let fish see you, or let your shadow fall on the water. Walk gently, slowly as the big fish (trout) will feel the vibration of the land and will not bite. You can actually train the fish. Throw worms or grasshoppers into your favorite pool for several days at 7:00 P.M. Later throw your bait and hook in at 7:00 P.M. They expect to be fed!

His athletic nature, good looks and daredevil attitude in today's jargon made him *cool.*

In 1932, Stub married Mildred Preston, the "little girl next door" whom he had admired years before. She had gone to Vassar and was now back ready to teach school. Stub and Millie bought ten acres east of Roxbury Village. Stub worked as a house painter and augmented his income with a nursery business growing vegetable and flowers. He handcrafted bows (archery). Poker games at the village firehouse regularly added to the family treasury. Stub could read the faces and body language of players as he had learned the habits of his beloved animals in the woods.

In the 1940s, Stub worked at the Daitch creamery but returned to house painting after a few years. He also served as fire chief and as village water commissioner. In 1945, Stub became a scout master. He enjoyed scouting and was a *mentor* for Troop 41 Roxbury and a long list of scouts. He was recognized in Delaware County and throughout the Catskills, eventually earning the coveted Silver Beaver award, scouting's highest honor.

He guided eagle scouts through the scouting movement and proved to be one of the most successful *mentors* of youth in the Catskills, teaching young men what Burroughs had taught him and what he had learned of nature on his own. Stub was a trusted friend of local game protectors Brian Burgin and Robert Van Benschoten of the New York State Conservation Department, Stub also served on the Forest Practice Board and the Interstate Commission for Control of the Delaware River.

Stub and Millie wanted to perpetuate the earlier lifestyles of neighbor Burroughs and the Dales. They bought the farm between their existing garden in town and the hundred acres on White Man Mountain. Hiking trails were built throughout the property, and they proclaimed it a **wildlife sanctuary**.

They built a large open shed overlooking Roxbury, where they served hamburgers and ice cream. Well-fed raccoons proved an evening show, while a tame woodchuck, and bottle fed orphaned fawns attracted visitors during the day. Few hiked the trails, but hamburgers, ice cream, and the view from the shed towards Woodchuck Lodge and Burrough's grave (now NYS historical site) in the distance attracted a steady flow of admirers. Stub did not write like his now silent idol Burroughs had. Stub likely lived the life John dreamed of living. Stub operated the wildlife sanctuary for thirteen summers.

He spent his old age with a herd of pet deer, which he kept on the property by addicting them to nicotine, thirty raccoons for whom he cooked breakfast each morning, his *tame* turkey, and a bottle of *Wild* Turkey. He died in 1984, a few days after Mildred died of cancer. His son Phil is thought to have buried Stub on his property on White Man Mountain. Stub and John Burroughs, his earlier neighbor, both in life and now in death share much the same but opposite view of the Roxbury Valley below.

\#

1926

Rudolph Blythe, Pharmaceutical Researcher

(Information to be added in next edition)

\#

1928

Charles K. Ives, MD, Roxbury Physician

"Charley" was a local legend by the time he graduated from high school. During graduation exercises it has been customary to sing the RCS alma mater. Perhaps routine to some, when he sang "RCS let us *always* be loyal. Let us all to thy dear name be true," everyone knew he really meant it! The expression "larger than life" fit him well. Standing well over six feet tall, he was a very impressive figure. He was also athletic.

In a small school of Roxbury and with only three males in the class, there were ample opportunities to participate in the sports program. Charlie *excelled* at both basketball and baseball. He also *excelled* at golf, track, swimming, well you get the idea.

Childhood experiences in Roxbury and at school seem to be centered around his athletic performances both on and off the "field." That was true both at Roxbury and his undergraduate college years. One report did include Charlie driving around in a Model-T Ford with no windshield and the June bugs hitting him in the face. At thirty miles an hour a June bug or two with a hard shell, hitting you in the forehead could produce *stars*!

Lest one think he was all sports, he also played the clarinet in the RCS orchestra, was in the Glee club, Record Board, Sportsmanship Brotherhood, and the Chem-Fi club. His RCS class of 1928 with three males, and six females was unique. **All** nine continued on to noteworthy careers, (see **Part III**, Class of 1928).

Charles Keator Ives entered the Cornell University pre-med program in 1928. For Charley, his academic and athletic successes at RCS were to continue. He became an intercollegiate athlete achieving varsity letters as a member of the crew and swim teams.

His childhood goal was to become either a physical education teacher or a doctor of medicine, but a "career" in swimming was also possible, as he set numerous college records. At one point, he casually tried out for the United States Olympic Swimming Team. He probably should have taken the "try outs" more seriously, as he lost by a fraction of a second to a young athlete named Johnny Weismueller.

His Roxbury loyalty continued. Each summer he returned to lifeguard at the Mount Helena Lake and Golf Course with his lifelong friend and future medical colleague, Gilbert "Gil" Palen. Dr. Ives and Dr. Palen would begin their medical careers together and be united in later years to end those careers as well.

In 1932, Charles, an intercollegiate athlete, with a positive, even, cheerful disposition graduated from Cornell and entered Hahnemann Medical College in Philadelphia, Pennsylvania. He completed his studies for a medical degree and graduated from Hahnemann as president of the class of 1938.

Charlie married Ruth Allaben November 24, 1937. She was an aspiring professional musician and daughter of a prominent physician from Binghamton, New York They proved to be a winning team.

Upon graduation from Hahnemann as a new M.D., he had *many* professional opportunities from which to choose. Charlie and Ruth chose Roxbury to establish a family medical practice. Family practice yes, but he also provided obstetric and anesthesia services for both the Margaretville and the Stamford Hospitals and served as coroner.

His career was interrupted by WWII where he served as a captain/physician in the Army Medical Corp in the Philippines. He was discharged in 1947, and his growing family back at the Pikatinni Arsenal in New Jersey was eager to return to Roxbury.

During the thirty years Charlie Ives practiced in Roxbury, his influence was everywhere and it was welcomed. He was school physician who alone provided physicals for the entire school population.

He provided required inoculations, and emergency medical care. He attended *most* of the soccer, basketball, and baseball games between RCS and her rivals during all those years.

At home many meals were missed, the nights shortened or dates cancelled due to emergencies and office visits any time of the day or night. When an expecting mother-to-be would go into labor, Charlie refused to leave the hospital until he had held that precious young life in his hands and was assured everyone was healthy.

During those thirty years, he shared his life and hobbies such as archery, ceramics, fishing, swimming, and fly tying with the Boy Scouts, senior groups, Rotary, VFW, and any group or person needing encouragement or help. He also did that with a casual happy disposition, which was sometimes as important as the medicine they received. There is no record available of receiving a substantial complaint or ever being sued or "dismissed" as family physician. There is evidence, however, of his "neglect" *in collecting a fee from a poor family or an elderly person.* Yes, he made house calls, night or day.

Ruth became ill early in 1961, and died in October. Charlie continued his practice and raised his family of eight children, all but one graduated from RCS (see **Part IV**, alphabet). In 1964, he married Frances (Casey) Jones, a registered nurse and mother of three. "Doc" and Casey continued providing medical services to Roxbury. When the Margaretville and Stamford hospitals reorganized, a change was necessary.

Charlie accepted a position in the Student Health Department at the State University College at Oneonta. (STC then SUNY). It was here that he was reunited with his friend and colleague, Dr. Palen. He and Casey moved to Westville, New York to be closer to work. He remained at the college for fifteen more years until his retirement.

Charlie was born on October 13, 1909, the eldest child of Ralph S. and Ruth Keator Ives. He died in June 1983, leaving eight intelligent, happy, healthy children all of whom went on to successful professional careers. They were Julie Ives (Moberg), Charles K. Ives Jr., Richard S. Ives, Ralph A, James M, Betty Ives (Adams), and Timothy, who graduated from Milford Central, Milford, New York

Acknowledgment for information provided: Susan (Ives) Gorsch (1958), Ralph Ives (son 1962), Roxbury *Yearbook 1928*, author's recollection.

Author Ploutz (RCS 49) recalls personal examples of: 1) community generosity 2) medical treatment 3) athletic ability.

1) Paul recalls receiving *free swimming lessons* from "Doc," as did other members of Stub Caswell's Boy Scout Troop 41, Roxbury.

2) Later in the fall of 1948 Ploutz's right wrist was badly broken in a RCS home soccer game. His wrist was hanging nearly straight down near a ninety degree angle, both radius and ulna badly fractured, but the skin not punctured. As usual "Doc" was at the game, ran onto the field, put Ploutz in his car, and drove rapidly to Margaretville Hospital. The wrist was quickly X-rayed. Charlie

carefully examined the film, then pulled on the wrist from the elbow to separate and align the bones and let them come back together. A plaster cast was applied. A bad break, took ten weeks to mend. *It is straight, has never ached, full and complete use restored.*

3) The following summer (1949) Ploutz was pitching in the Roxbury softball league. As a fast pitch left hander he had experienced some success striking out many players. "Doc" was often the umpire (free of course) but had decided to play and was now at bat. Doc had a huge "strike zone" and Ploutz managed to throw a hot "sizzler" low but still in the strike zone. The forty-year old intercollegiate athlete hit Paul's *best pitch so hard it flew over the fence in right-center field, bounced a time or two and rolled into the east branch of the Delaware River* (literally).

Daughter Susan, and son Ralph with much-appreciated input from many others, have indeed been *modest* in describing their father who had a brilliant mind, great physical ability and great personality. He would have been proud. The people of Roxbury are grateful that "Doc" lost the swimming contest to Johnny Weismueller. They got to have their very own "Tarzan," who inspired others by the consistent example he set with total devotion to his family, medicine, and to the Village of Roxbury.

#

1931

George Brandow, Professor

(Information to be added in next edition)

#

J. Frances Allen <u>AND</u> Lochie J. Allen

(J. Frances first letter)

600 Mount View Street, Apt. 213

Front Royal, Virginia 22630

December 31, 2002

Dr. James Proper

Roxbury Central School

Roxbury, New York 12474

Dear Dr. Proper:

This letter is in response to yours that appeared in the *Catskill Mountain News* of November 27, 2002, and to your personal communication of December 9, 2002, which was forwarded to me here.

I am J. Frances Allen, NOT Frances J. Allen as appeared in the *News*, nor Francis J. Allen in your letter. I am not of the masculine gender.

I graduated from RCS in 1934 with my sister, Lochie Jo Allen. We went through public school together. We both received a College Entrance Regents Diploma. She had the highest four-year average in the senior class, and I was second, averages based on Regents grades only. Because we had been in Roxbury only one year, Walter Meade, who was several points below both of us, was valedictorian and Olive MacLaury was salutatorian. This was a local regulation, not a state regulation.

Limiting the submission to 750 words does not cover one's life nor outstanding contributions. Who or what group is qualified to select the honorees? This only shows its inability to recognize the numerous outstanding graduates of RCS. What do the descendants of some of the graduates of RCS have to do with the selection of those that have been chosen?

The enclosure and the list that follows are compatible---rather laughable. The names of too many who would be a credit to RCS have been omitted.

Under the circumstances, I do not want to have my name

included in any way among the so-called honorees of RCS.

Remove my name from the list. You do not have my permission to include it. There are already sufficient errors in the three publications on Roxbury history. *

Sincerely yours,
J. Frances Allen

J. FRANCES ALLEN, Ph.D.

*

(author invited J. Frances to "reconsider," she generously replied)

J. Frances Allen was born in Arkville, New York, on April 14, 1916, the daughter of J. W. Allen and Mattie Jo Linkous Allen. At her father's retirement in 1923, the family moved to Owego, New York, where J. Frances at seven, with her sister, Lochie Jo, at five, entered the second grade that September in Owego Central School. They continued through the Junior year at Owego Free Academy (OFA), moving to Roxbury for the twelfth grade for 1933 - 1934 because of Lochie Jo's health.

At OFA, J. Frances played flute and piccolo in the band for five years and the flute in the orchestra for four years. She was a member of the Girls' League for three years, in both the Latin Club Play and the Dramatic Club Play, on the Stage Dinner Committee, and on the honor and high honor rolls.

In Roxbury, she played flute in the orchestra, was in the senior play, was on the honor and high honor rolls. She had the second highest average in the senior class. Although the decision toe valedictorian and salutatorian was based on the New York State Regents Exams only, she enrolled in Roxbury Central School for a minimum of two years before having the honor.

J. Frances received a BS degree in 1938 from the State Teachers College, Radford, Virginia, now Radford University, and her MS and Ph.D degrees in Zoology in 1948 and 1952 from the University of Maryland. During the summer of 1937 she attended the Chesapeake Biological Laboratory, Solomons Island, Maryland, and the summer 1938 the Mountain Lake Biological Station, of the University of Virginia, on a DuPont scholarship. Before graduate school, she taught secondary school science in Virginia, West Virginia, and New York State, and an assistant professor of science at Radford College during the summers of 1942, 1944, and 1945.

She was Biological Examiner for the New York State Department of Education in the summer of 1946.

While teaching in Virginia, Dr. Allen was one of the founders of the Virginia Junior Academy of Science, becoming the first secretary of the Virginia Junior Academy of Science Committee.

She was a graduate assistant at the University of Maryland from 1947-1948, instructor (1948-1952), and then became assistant professor of zoology and member of the graduate faculty of the University of Maryland, where she taught, among other courses, fisheries biology and management, shell-fisheries, animal ecology, and marine biology, often taking graduate students on the university's vessel for research on Chesapeake Bay.

During her career, she published twenty-five scientific research papers among her other publications. (Miss Griffin's write-up listed incorrectly J. Frances's first publication.)

Dr. Allen's speeches in Hawaii, Alaska, Puerto Rico, Jamaica, and throughout the continental United States are too numerous to mention.

In 1958, she joined the Systematic Biology Program of the National Science Foundation (NSF) in Washington, DC. In 1967, she left her position there as associate program director to become chief of the Water Quality Requirements Branch, Office of Research and Development, Federal Water Quality Administration, later named the Federal Water Quality Administration, and subsequently the US Environmental Protection Agency (EPA). At the time of her retirement in 1982, she was staff scientist-ecology for the Science Advisory Board, Office of Administrator, EPA.

Dr. Allen was the United States representative to the OECD World Conference on Water Quality in Paris, France, in 1973. In 1974, she was a delegate to the first International Congress on Ecology at The Hague, in the Netherlands. Among awards she received included the Sustained Superior Performance Award from NSF and a bronze medal from EPA.

In addition to other scientific organizations, Dr. Allen is a fellow of the American Association for Advancement of Science, fellow of the Washington Academy of Sciences, co-sponsor emerita of the Institute of Malacology, former trustee and member of the Executive Committee of the Sport Fishery Research Foundation, and one of the first certified fisheries scientists.

She was elected to several national honor societies: including Kappa Delta Pi, Pi Gamma Mu, Chi Beta Phi, Sigma Xi, and Sigma Delta Epsilon.

In 1987, the American Fisheries Society honored Dr. Allen by establishing the J. Frances Allen Scholarship. This scholarship for $2,500 is awarded annually to a female doctoral candidate whose emphasis is in the field of fisheries science. The intent of the scholarship is to encourage other women to become fisheries professionals.

James Peterson and Carl Eklund took a graduate course in ecology from Dr. Allen at the University of Maryland. Both were engaged in research in Antarctica. A station there is named for Carl Eklund. Also, Captain Charles Thomas of the US Coast Guard, later Admiral Thomas, took the same course in ecology from her. He was commander of the ice breaker *Northwind*, and was chief of staff for Admiral Richard E. Byrd, and for Admiral Duchek in their expeditions to Antarctica. Because of Admiral Thomas's experience in the Arctic as well, his book, *Ice Is Where You Find It*, is most interesting.

Dr. Allen has also known three secretaries of the Smithsonian Institution, Dr. Alexander Wetmore, Dr. Carl Schmidt, Dr. F. Dillon Ripley.

Among Dr. Allen's high school students were three who became well known: Dr. Alec Haller, Dr. William Huntly Saunders, both of Pulaski, Virginia, and Dr. Robert Lewis Ketter, of West Virginia. Dr. Alec Haller was in charge of the children's part of Johns Hopkins University Hospital and at the time successfully separated Siamese twins at the head. A television documentary was made of that operation, his other achievements, and his life.

Bill Saunders, while in high school, won first prize, ten silver dollars, in a radio quiz show in 1942 at the Virginia Junior Academy of Science. It was in chemistry. He asked Dr. Allen if she minded his competing in chemistry rather than biology. As a physical organic chemist, Dr. Saunders became chairman of the Department of Chemistry at the University of Rochester, carried out research in London and in Germany, and also has received many honors.

From West Virginia, Dr. Robert Lewis Ketter received his Ph.D in physics and became chairman of the Department of Civil Engineering at the University of Buffalo. Then he became the university's president for twelve years, during which time he supervised the great expansion of the campus. After that he became director of the university's National Earthquake Center. The building for the center was named for him and dedicated to him.

While working on water pollution and water quality criteria, a part of Dr. Allen's program at the U.S. Environmental Protection Agency included the four national laboratories and their field stations: Corvallis, Oregon, and its field station at Newport, Oregon; Duluth, Minnesota, and its field station at Monticello, Minnesota; Narragansett, Rhode Island, and the field station at Bear's Bluff, South Carolina, and the laboratory at Gulf Breeze, Florida.

Dr. Allen retired from the USEPA in 1982 as staff scientist-ecology, Science Advisory Board, Office of the Administrator. Dr. Allen resides now in Front Royal, Virginia.

The Southerlands, Apt. 213
600 Mount View Street
Front Royal, VA 22630
May 4, 2003

(as received from Lochie Jo Allen)

Dear Dr. Ploutz:

I noticed that your comment in my sister's last paragraph about removing her name from the list is public information is questionable, for the list in the paper and one of your lists and "selective." Further, the book incorrectly says she was in the Owego orchestra three years. She was in the orchestra the same four years I was. Since she has agreed to send you more material, the question is moot.

I also read your note to her speaking of Dr. Proper's relationship to you and the title of the proposed book. I assume you will have to change the title, for it seems that the book is to include just the "good ole boys." And although you are using also the girls, the title implies that each one is a product of Roxbury. The teachers we had during the year we were there were very good, and the principal was a fine educator and gentleman. In no way was either J. Frances or I a product of Roxbury, nor can anyone in

Roxbury ever claim to be a "mentor" for us. My father, who had died four years before, and my mother were our "mentors." We gave Roxbury a lot more than it ever gave us. At 15/16, I was organist at the Methodist Church. J. Frances was soloist and we two together began a junior choir—and mother and Mrs. Edith Schuster made the robes for them, the white surplices, and black skirts. The Easter Service of 1934 was magnificent, for mother brought the canaries and from their place in the balcony, they were silent until there was music. J. Frances sang "The Holy City" and the junior choir joined in singing the choruses. No Easter music before or since can match this.. We had a fine Epworth League at church. We made money for the church by presenting a three-act play in nine different towns, including Woodstock (in the days it was just starting its fame). We gave concerts with local talent, including a men's quartet.

I read your note concerning your relationship with Dr. Proper. You mention that he will be co-author. Is he helping you from time to time or is he really going to be a co-author? Since my last nine years of career I was editor for an international society, started their magazine, and was also responsible for many of its other publications, I know the difference between someone's being a co-author and his being acknowledged otherwise as a helper.

Have you been in touch with a printer and his prices? Or perhaps you are contemplating putting the book on the computer and printing it as orders come in---to me a new way of putting out a book. The two science books I edited were printed from my typed copy, so I received copies to go over and copy edit the material from my copies to check for mistakes of the printer and mistakes of mine. I sent the proofs back to the printer before any books were printed. For the two books of my own I had published, I sent my word processor's copies in the exact form I wanted and the printing was done by photographing. If you have decided to for the printing to be done by photographing your copy, have you asked the printer whether he prints by folios that are multiples of 12 or 16 so the copy you send will agree with the amount of paper he will use, thereby saving the cost of possibly extra sheets? Will you then be using justified right?

One of the problems of new books is the type of cover material. It can be quite expensive, but the less expensive kinds are likely to break apart easily if the book is handled very much. The folios may pull out, and often separate pages fall out. The copies of the second and third "histories" of Roxbury are good examples of the failure to order a decent cover that prevails with much handling. I have to use rubber bands around mine!

You may have already published books of your own and need none of this from me, for you will have experienced much of what I have mentioned here. Your job is a big one!

Sincerely,

Lochie Jo Allen

1934

LOCHIE JO ALLEN

(information as received from Lochie Jo Allen)

Lochie Jo Allen was born in Arkville, New York, and at age five moved with her family to Owego, New York. She and her sister, J. Frances, entered the second grade together and continued school through their junior year at Owego Free Academy (OFA). Because of Lochie Jo's health, the family moved back to the Catskills, and the girls finished at Roxbury Central School with College Entrance Regents Diplomas. Lochie Jo had the highest regents four-year average but was denied the honor of valedictorian because of a Roxbury Board of Education rule demanding two years of residence.

In 1938, she graduated from Radford State Teachers College (now Radford University) with both a BS and an AB in Latin. Although she had the highest scholastic average, she was denied Summa Cum Laude, for it was decided for the first time to base the honor not on averages alone but one-third on averages, one-third on faculty vote, and one-third on student body vote. In addition to the degrees, she took two Virginia State exams and thereby was awarded state certificates to teach band and orchestra and public school music. In 1956, she received a MA in English from the University of Georgia, and later took further graduate courses. In 1972 and 1973, she took all courses needed for a Ph.D. at the University of Maryland, but decided not to continue there.

For employment, Lochie Jo taught in high schools thirty years of classes of English, Latin, French, and German. In the first few years, she taught public school music as well. For twelve years, she taught two-thirds of a full load of English classes in the evening and at night for Augusta College, American University, and University of Georgia, these including not only grammar and composition but English, American, European, Asiatic, and world literatures. From May 1961 to September 1964, she was an education specialist for the army at Fort Gordon, just outside of Augusta, Georgia, but returned to teaching. She had continued teaching college and university at night.

If someone wants to know how she spent her "spare?" time, she taught piano lessons, worked at Sears Credit Department on weekends, and was an organist for church. And that was at the time that churches still had morning and evening services. For several years, she directed and accompanied a group of young people called the Holiday Singers, four boys and six girls. This group prepared music for the holidays throughout the year, four-part harmony, and sang for hospitals, nursing homes, retirement homes, jails, the prison, and four of the largest civic clubs. For the Exchange Club Week Fair she managed the talent show, singing between acts when scenes needed changing. She and took home a trophy and best of compliments. For each holiday, costumes were changed, made by Lochie Jo's mother and a couple of other ladies who helped. The boys dressed in black pants, white shirts (sometimes lace), and vests and black bowties. The experiences meant a lot to the young people, for all of them continued with their music, some for their entire careers. She gave all of them their choral music. When she moved to Roxbury, she bought eighteen copies of six Christmas songs in four-part harmony, thinking she could have another group, to learn and to serve, but the idea was dead on arrival.

In 1972, Lochie Jo moved from Augusta to Hyattsville, Maryland, to live with her sister, Dr. J. Frances Allen, who was well-known scientist in the federal government and throughout this country and several others. After Lochie Jo's time at the University of Maryland, she became editor for the American Fisheries Society, an international science organization. She began its magazine *Fisheries*, which circulates worldwide, and other work such as newsletters, brochures, pamphlets, and booklets. On here own time, she edited two science books for sections of the AFS. All of this included working with advertisers, printers, and scientists who submitted papers. She also worked with photographers concerning color, as well as having photos made from slides, and she made decisions on sizing.

When Lochie Jo and her sister retired, they bought a home in Front Royal, Virginia, 1981 through 1985. They were members of the South River Garden Club, the Women's section of the Izaak Walton League, and the Presbyterian Church and its Women's Circle 1. Lochie Jo was organist/choir director at the Rockland Church. In 1985, they moved to Roxbury, New York. From 1986 through the spring of 1997, she played piano for the Red Carpet restaurant on Sundays. For around three years she played piano on the Friday night dinner hour at a resort inn near Margaretville.

Lochie Jo has lectured in several states for women's clubs, men's clubs, libraries on extra-sensory perception and associated areas, poetry writing (all types and its construction throughout history) and the poetry of Tennyson and Browning, also on butterflies and societies promoting such knowledge. She published two books: a poetry book, *A Later Appointment, Please*, and *Seven Decades + of "How Come?"*

After seventeen years in Roxbury, Lochie Jo and her sister returned to Front Royal, Virginia, where they were welcomed with open arms. A family Lochie Jo knew during her first three years of teaching, and also three of her students from Augusta, Georgia, whom she had not seen since 1957, have visited her. and promises from others that they will come this summer. Lochie Jo's sister has had visits from many of her co-workers and friends from the Washington, DC area, and several scientists who still travel back and forth from many states east to Washington. For now the Allens are just off Route 66, which runs from Route 81 into Washington through "Northern Virginia" only about sixty miles to the big metropolis. Lochie Jo says she feels she has come back to the world and is now only a block from the entrance to the Skyline Drive!

The authors research on the Allen sisters was gathered <u>prior</u> to gaining information directly from them. Research from Roxbury Yearbooks as well as their more recent letters, have been "left in" out of respect for their amazing record and for the evidence that they <u>did</u> have the highest class average, even though it went to others. The 1934 Roxbury yearbook lists Walter Mead as valedictorian, Olive MacLaury salutatorian (Mead and MacLaury are included in this text).

Sisters J. Frances and Lochie Allen graduated RCS in 1934. With a class of sixteen there were only five males, eleven females. The year 1934 was great for RCS. Class president Robert Brandow became a Lt. colonel in the army, there were five teachers/professors, a nurse, a naturalist, and two successful farmers!

#

1934

Walter F. Mead, Author, Photographer, Naturalist

Walt Meade was born June 7, 1915, son of Smith and Katherine DePew Meade. Walter profited from a series of local *mentors* who took an interest in his love of nature. He graduated Roxbury Schools in 1934 as valedictorian (see Olive Mac Laury, salutatorian also 1934). Classmate Olive taught Walt to be a bird watcher. Walt was impressed that Olive could identify birds by their songs and, both were admirers of Roxbury boy John Burroughs.
They took frequent bird walks together. Walt played baseball all four years in high school. He was on the student council and vice president of the student association and record board.

Other 1934 graduates included sisters J. Frances and Lochie J. Allen.. There were five males and eleven females in the class of 1934. Robert Brandow was class president and rose to the rank of Lt. Colonel in the Army. Wilma Whitney became a teacher, Betty Ames a nurse. Information on other class members is in **Part III**, year 1934.

Walt's father Smith taught him to hunt, fish, and trap. Even though Walt was growing up in the village, he spent a great deal of time outdoors with his father. They hunted ginseng together and Walt enjoyed his relationship with his father. But, according to Walt, it was his mother who taught him the values by which he lived his life. Walt respected all women as he did his wonderful mother. He saw them as equals, looking up to them years before society accepted their full and obvious value. Walt was "liberated" and having a daughter Donna Meade (Zuidema) only confirmed his enlightened attitude toward women.

Kay Delaney (Orban) was Walt's high school English teacher. Kay sensed Walt's desire to be a writer and encouraged him. Kay also gave Walt his first camera never realizing it would put him on a career path in both writing and photography. Kay encouraged Walt to attend Middlebury College in Vermont. Walt had hoped to attend but when his mother became ill he decided he was needed at home. Kay and husband John Orban had a summer place in Roxbury and stayed in touch with Walt throughout his career.

Bob Smith owned and ran the feed mill in Roxbury. Since Smith Meade worked at the mill Walt got a summer job there during high school and after he graduated. Bob Smith turned out to be a *mentor*, keeping Walt close to him at work. Even when the regular feed mill work was done, Bob would find something for the two of them to do. One hot day, for example, Bob said "Come on Walt, let's go work on Bob Nichol's roof." Bob Nichols was Smith's father-in-law. Walt looked longingly at the other mill employees lounging in the shade, swapping stories, but went along with Bob anyway.

A little later Bob said "I bet you wonder why I made you come do all these things with me." Walt replied with a little adolescent resentment in his voice, "As a matter of fact, I do." "Well," Bob said, "Those guys I leave at the mill, that's about what they are going to achieve in life. But I have an idea that you're going to amount to something and so I want you to learn everything you can from me." Once again a *Roxbury Boy* benefits from a *mentor*.

Walt and his first wife, Letha Hotchkiss, were married February 14, 1937. Walt and Letha agreed to manage the Reynolds farm even though Walt had little farm experience. George Butler was an experienced farm hand who knew what to do on a farm. Walt told George they would run the farm together, even though Ralph Reynolds would continue to think that Walt was running it.

The plan worked as Walt had respect for George's farming ability. They have known each other for years. Walt was to learn how to get bee honey. In the fall the bee hunter "burns for bees," sending up smoke from a burning piece of honey comb. The smoke attracts other bees to the comb that has been previously doused with sugar water.

Visiting bees then make a "bee line" to the trees where they are sorting their own honey. By triangulation, involving possibly three burns, the hunter can figure out where the new bee tree is located, cut it down, and enjoy the honey.

Shortly thereafter, the couple moved to Davenport and farmed for thirty years. In 1972, five years after Letha Meade's death, Walt sold his dairy herd and returned to Roxbury. In 1970, he joined the Manhattan Country School Farm at Meeker Hollow, Roxbury, where he served as farm worker, nature studies teacher, and in 1977, director.

The flora and fauna that occupied his beloved Montgomery Hollow farm was the subject of much of his investigations. Since the mid-1970s, he had shared his life, and his love of the natural world. Virginia (Ginny) Scheer, became his wife in 1979 and succeeded him as director of the Manhattan Country School Farm. Following his retirement there in 1980, he devoted much time to photographing, writing, and speaking about the environment close at hand.

In 1991, Mr. Meade received a Catskill Regional Award from The Catskill Center for Conservation and Development, which has published many of his photos and essays in its quarterly newsletter over the years. 1991 was also when *Purple Mountain Press* published his book, *In the Catskill Mountains: A Personal Approach to Nature.* The book, containing boyhood recollections and seventy-three photographs, has sold about two thousand copies.

Wray Rominger of *Purple Mountain Press* worked closely with Mr. Meade for two years as the book took shape. "Walt was absolutely unique," Mr. Rominger said. "He had a spare, wonderful style of writing and profound patience as a photographer. But it went beyond that, he was first and foremost a teacher. That was his greatest contribution I think--the way he could make people relate to their environment." His love of young people is reflected in the affection with which he is remembered by the alumni of the Manhattan Country School. Many of them were spellbound by his stories of the mountains, told during nature walks, or in the farm's sap house during the long misty days and night of maple syrup season.

"I remember one student asked Walt who was his favorite person in the world. Walt's answer was "The person I'm with," recalled Gus Trowbridge, director of the Manhattan Country School. I've never known a person who could say this with one hundred percent sincerity, but with Walt, it was true.

Roxbury Central for graduating students who show promise in photography, writing, or environmental science.

Books and Exhibits

The self-taught naturalist had been featured in *Three Catskill Storytellers*, a booklet published in 1986 by the Roberson Center for the Arts and Sciences in Binghamton.

Among the area exhibitions that featured his work were "Innovative Traditions" (1991), "Watershed: Land Use and Conflict in the Catskill Mountains," (1992) and a display at Ski Windham co-sponsored by *Kaatsill Life* magazine, to which he was a regular contributor.

Walt died unexpectedly Jan 12, 1993. He had been working with Ginny Scheer and folklorist Mary Zwolinski on a second book, featuring the outdoor records and journals he had kept since the 1930s. Ginny hopes to carry on with that project and publish it posthumously.

Besides his wife, Walt Meade is survived by a daughter, Donna Meade Zuidema, a granddaughter, Judy Zuidema; a grandson and his wife, Jim and Suzanne Zuidema; a brother, Robert Meade of Roxbury; a sister, Grace Todd (valedictorian 1928 spelled <u>Mead</u>) of Subberfield, Florida; and several nieces and nephews.

Funeral services were conducted Saturday at Gould Methodist Reformed Church, with Reverends Richard Dykstra, Herb Haufrecht of Shady who offered reminiscences of Walt Meade at the funeral. Reading a message from noted Catskills authority Alf Evers, who said, "Walt Meade left an eloquent legacy of images and words for the benefit of those interested in nature." Burial was in Roxbury Cemetery. Arrangements were by Miller Funeral. Contributions in his memory may be given to the Walter F. Meade Scholarship Fund, Roxbury Central School, Roxbury, New York, 12474.

Acknowledgement of information on Walt Meade from: Ginny Scheer (Mrs. Walter F. Meade); *Catskill Mountain News* 1/20/1993; Roxbury Schools *Yearbook*, 1934. Author Ploutz had noted that in various sources Mead is often spelled Mead<u>e</u>. His widow Ginny as well as *Purple Mountain Press* refer to Walter as

Meade. His high school Yearbook lists him as Mead and his widow refers to Walt's father as Smith Mead.

#

1934

Olive MacLaury, Professor, Local Ornithologist

The Roxbury Yearbook of '34 lists Olive as valedictorian. Needing additional credits to enter college, she returned for another year. During that time she taught music at the local Brookdale School one day a week while still at the Roxbury School.

At Roxbury, Olive was involved with anything that had to do with music. Musically gifted, she entered the famed Eastman School of Music in Rochester, New York. She majored in voice pedagogy, and minored in piano. Olive was already an accomplished pianist, at least by local standards, but Eastman was *the* place to go. Graduates of Eastman, at least in those days, could usually "write their own ticket" for lucrative positions. Olive returned to Roxbury for the next four years (1939-1942) teaching piano both in Roxbury and Grand Gorge. She was the choir director and soloist at the Gould Reformed Church in Roxbury.

Church attendance improved. The choir in small town Roxbury was reported to be inspiring. Local boys and girls who "couldn't carry a tune in a basket" were eagerly signed up for piano or voice lessons by doting parents expecting miracles. Having taught subnormal inmates at Albion, Olive's patience was legendary. Locals joked that Olive's *mentoring* skills, were so good that she could, in country jargon, "make a silk purse out of a sow's ear."

In 1943, she accepted the position of music teacher at the Albion State Training School. Albion was a facility operated by the New York State Department of Correction. Sweet, young Olive was teaching music to female inmates who were also classified as being subnormal in intelligence. Strong, clear in purpose, Olive enjoyed the challenge and soon became responsible for two church choirs, a chorus, and other musical numbers and special programs at Albion. Women of normal intelligence were finally admitted, and the facility's name was changed to Western Reformatory for Women.

In June 1952, Olive received her master's degree in secondary school administration from the University of Rochester and then passed the New York State Civil Service Examination for the position of education supervisor.

The New York State Narcotics Addiction Control Commission and some of its "population" was transferred to Albion. The director of education for the division was Arthur Layman who had earlier been a teacher at Green Haven Prison. Olive became Mrs. Arthur Layman.

In 1971, New York State closed the entire Albion facility. Olive was only eighteen months from retirement but decided not to seek another position to complete her retirement tenure. Since Arthur had already retired in 1970, the hardworking couple decided to become globe trotters. First the places in the United States they had wanted to see, then the British Isles and its islands. Next, they visited Greece, Hungary, Turkey, Russia, and Yugoslavia often with a second, even third, trip. After Arthur Layman died, Olive managed two trips to Mexico.

A hearty soul, Olive became a soloist at the Christian Science Society of Albion for ten years and organist for the Albion Universalist Church for two years. Olive was also giving vocal lessons as a member of the county chorus for the Presbyterian Church in Albion. Olive was a Daughter of the American Revolution (DAR) for over fifty years, in which she held numerous offices, including state librarian. The ultimate *mentor,* Olive's last two-year teaching gig was for Literacy Volunteers of America.

In 1995, Olive married George Dawson an Albion, New York native. As of 2003 this eighty-year-old couple leads an active, pleasant, healthy life.

Acknowledgements: Information from Roxbury *Yearbook* 1934; notes from Olive E. MacLaury (Layman Dawson); Mrs. Walter Mead; 1934 Classmate J. Frances Allen; Roxbury Village Library.

#

1936

Bruce S. Mead, Valedictorian, WWI, Airline Pilot

(Information to be added in next edition)

#

1939

Otis Van Aken, Boeing Aviation, Engineer

Otis graduated second (salutatorian) in his class of 1924. He, as others had earlier, received a four year Gould scholarship to NYU. The Gould family enjoyed a close relationship with NYU. In 1943, Otis graduated with a BS from the College of Engineering. Lieutenant Van Aken, with the prestigious engineering degree, became a US Navy Reserve Aviation Specialist assigned to Aircraft Carrier Service units at both Seattle (US) and the island of Guam.

After his discharge from WWII and with his experience and engineering degree he was recruited to work with Boeing Aviation. Like the earlier Fritz Teichmann (RCS/NYU), Otis was proficient with mechanical design. From 1946 to 1984 Otis was a mechanical design engineer and engineering manager of the Boeing Airplane Company Commercial Airplane Division in Seattle. The mechanical design engineers convert specifications and requirements for an airplane into actual functioning hardware by producing drawings, documents, and prototypes required to build and maintain the aircraft.

Otis assisted with the development of the flight control systems of most of Boeings, first line aircraft, including the giant C – 47 Stratocruiser, the 707, 747, and 767.

In 1944, he married Virginia Pearson in Seattle. They have a daughter, Diane Snider, and a son, Douglas.

In 1984, he retired from Boeing and now resides in Redmond, Washington, enjoying golf, gardening, travel, reading, and operating his computer.

Acknowledgment for information from RCS *Yearbook 1939* and wife Virginia Pearson.

The class of 1939 included eleven men and thirteen females. Seven of the eleven men served in WWII (see **Part III** for detail). Ellis Shultis was valedictorian.

#

1940

Marvin Russell Blythe, Author and Mathematician

(Information to be added in next edition)

#

1945

Richard Lutz, Carpenter, Contractor, Feed Stores

Richard, the third child of Lena and Fred Lutz was born March 8, 1927. Richard (Dick) was class president and was described in the *Roxbury Yearbook* as independent, self –reliant, and dependable. His mother, Lena Ruteshouser Lutz, and Fred Lutz were industrious. They taught Dick, his older brother Herbert "Deak," and older sister Edna a strong work ethic. Dick seemed to have learned the lesson the earliest. His first teacher said that:

Even in grade school he made creative things of wood (not ashtrays like the rest of us). He made lamps, chairs, tables, bowls, bats, kitchenware, toys, wagons, you get the idea.

By junior high, he was willing to give advice on how to repair the old printing press used to print the *Roxbury Times*, the only local newspaper that his father owned and managed. Lena, his mother, was a seamstress so skilled that she provided gowns for the local elite (what few Roxbury had) and frequently made clothes for the family. Lena was a sister to both Ida Ruteshouser Cronk and Anna Ruteshouser Ploutz, both who lived nearby, and often made clothes for them as well.

With two creative *mentoring* parents, he continued to achieve. In high school, he excelled, demonstrating still more skill and capabilities, taking "orders" from neighbors willing to pay for creative, carefully designed handcrafted items.

It was often said he earned money "the old fashioned way," he *earned* it. Dick built bird houses or whatever you needed at a fair price, often from leftover scraps from the nearby Robert Smith, then Briggs, lumber yard. In the fall, he often sold apple cider by the gallon, partnering with his younger cousin Paul Ploutz (author) or other boys around town. Several gallons of cider were hauled in a wagon behind his bicycle (yes he built the wagon and hitch).

Dick did not become an eagle scout or go to college. At RCS he was active in intramural sports, the senior play, Victory Corps (1944), Red Cross, and other events. He wasn't into booze, drugs, or smoking. Dick was the kind of boy mothers hoped to have.

Dick Lutz (humor us and read this) was trustworthy, loyal, helpful, friendly, courteous, kind, thrifty, brave, clean, and reverent. As a carpenter, and later feed store operator, he may have been a bit light in the clean and reverent part of the scout oath but had a record that *very* few could emulate.

Dick Enlisted in the Navy upon Graduation

When he returned to Roxbury, his pent up carpentry skills and ambition became legend. He started with Ray Cronk (uncle) then formed a partnership with local builder Sanford Hinkley. Having mastered the "management skills" from Cronk and Hinkley, Dick went into his own carpentry business, hiring those he judged to be competent. During his carpentry *era* in small town Roxbury, Dick was responsible for the construction of seventy-five houses, more than any other builder before or since.

Dick married RCS music teacher Margie Webster October 26, 1952. Steven Richard Lutz was born May 5, 1955 (5/5/55). Robert Charles was born March 30, 1957 (3/30/57).

In 1959, Dick bought the well-established local Andrew Lutz feed store. Shortly after that, he also purchased the Robert Smith feed store. If you wanted feed for you cows, horses, chickens, goats, sheep, or dogs you bought it from the Dick Lutz feed store. Not surprising he became a director of the Roxbury Bank, joined Rotary and became a director of the Baltimore and Ohio (B&O) Railroad. By 1976, Roxbury and surrounding communities in the Catskills were gradually getting out of the dairy business. Farms were being sold to "city folks." The railroad into Roxbury was also being eliminated. In Roxbury vernacular, he moved his feed business "lock stock and barrel" to Oneonta, New York.

The Lutz Feed business in Oneonta has been successful for twenty-seven years (2003). Dick and his two eagle scout sons, Steve and Robert provide quality feed products for Otsego, Schoharie, and Delaware Counties, and throughout the Eastern United States.

Dick Lutz is author Paul Ploutz's first cousin and is frequently referred to in **Part I** of *Mentoring Roxbury Boys*. As a child, Paul sat on uncle Fred's lap as he punched out copies of the *Roxbury Times* with all of its spelling errors and type glitches. Over the years Aunt Lena became his favorite aunt. Paul supplied her with dozens of trout, she supplied him with lots of "hand-me-down apparel" which was always too big. Sister Anna, Paul's mother, shared the habit of playing pinochle at the Lutzes over many years during his teenage years and into adulthood. Paul's wife Geri recalls being at Aunt Lena's in the early 1960s. That is a lot of pinochle.

The Lutz family (clan) has made a profound contribution to the school and to the village of Roxbury. Twenty-three Lutzes graduated RCS from 1926 (Pauline M., Roxbury art teacher) to Samuel F.(1980). Teachers, valedictorian, salutatorian, eagle scouts, class presidents, nurses, see **Part IV** of *Mentoring...*

1946

Robert Preston, Class President, WWII, Teacher, Principal

(Information to be added in next edition)

#

1949

Guy Numann, CEO, Manufacturing Corporation

Guy was born in New York City in 1932. Father Frederick was also from New York City while mother Helen was a Nebraska girl. Helen met Fred when he went to work in Nebraska during the depression. The oldest and only son Guy lived in four different homes while attending five different public schools in the Bronx before attending DeWitt Clinton High School for half a year.

Picture Guy in the Bronx learning to dribble a basketball in a poor, crowded neighborhood in a small blacktop playground and it will form a picture of his early "melting pot" environment and his later disdain for bigotry. He did get out of the neighborhood (now called the ghetto) on occasion when his mother took him back to Nebraska a time or two. He seemed to profit considerably from experiencing both rural life and his city blacktop/concrete origin.

Guy was thrilled when one of his father's co-workers in the city bought an unworked farm in Denver, New York Guy spent some summers there. That experience, and the love of rural life by his parents, resulted in them purchasing a store in Denver, New York, partnering with John Snipas, still another co-worker. His father became Postmaster at Denver before trying numerous ways to make a living, finally settling as an insurance agent in Margaretville, New York.

Helen took a job as a waitress in the Kass Inn to supplement family income. Sister Marion and Patricia were in the eight and ninth grades when the whole family settled in at Denver and all enrolled at RCS.

As a boy, Guy was more interested in dribbling and "hanging out" shooting baskets than academic pursuits. Younger sister Marion, on the other hand, was already a superior student. When both Guy and Marion landed at RCS, they were halfway through grades eight and nine respectfully, Marion was advanced to the ninth grade. In the fall of 1946, Guy suffered the *humiliation* of being in the same class as his *younger* sister.

Guy's response was "No way was my younger sister going to get better grades than I was."

As a result, although retaining his desire for sports participation, he put in the effort to get better grades and ultimately became valedictorian of his class (1949).

Guy was the "big gun" on the RCS basketball team. Author Ploutz (also 1949) remembers well being on the "bench" while Numann was consistently racking up points, gaining re-bounds and setting up others to score as a superb team player. Guy had the unique ability to look one way then dribble a different direction. Teammate Ploutz had to <u>look</u> at the ball to dribble, Guy could dribble with either hand while looking at the clock, audience, basket, whatever. He was a Delaware County all star player in basketball. He wasn't *all that tall* but no one could ever tell what direction he would be going, passing, or shooting.

Guy flatters the numerous *mentors* (teachers) he had at RCS. Truth be told, all three of the Numann kids were gifted. When guy "hunkered" down in the ninth grade he was quickly promoted a full year and graduated in only three years. The class of 1949 had twelve students, Guy was valedictorian, Ploutz was seventh. Classmate Marie Griffin set her sights on Guy and he later described her as the "ultimate wife." It took a while. At RCS his classmates thought he treated her like dirt, it seemed to work for them.

Guy experienced "culture shock" going from the Bronx to Nebraska. Going from a New York City high school with thousands of students to one with about one hundred students was very telling on him. He became particularly understanding and experienced working with small and large groups. He excelled at motivation and credits three "small town" RCS teachers in particular.

Susan Root, English, showed him it was important to excel in learning things other than math, science, and physical things, which came easily to him. Teacher "Willie" Crawford showed him that anyone can improve themselves by dedication and individual attention and teaching. Roland F. "Doc" Ross showed him that integrity was very important and was a personal *choice* and did not come from heredity. Overall, his athletic and academic achievements caused him to be the recipient of two college scholarships offers. RCS, through the Jay Gould family donations offered him a scholarship to NYU. The second was to Rensselaer Polytechnic Institute (RPI) from their alumni of section four in New York State. Guy chose RPI.

Now recognized as brilliant, Guy was interviewed at IBM in their board room sitting in the very chair that Charles Watson usually occupied. He competed with candidates from a major part of New York State. Gifted or not, it turned out he did *not* have all the course requirements to enter RPI and had to go to Fordham University in the summer of 1949. As is so often the case, being the best student from a small rural school going to RPI, culture shock was now "academic shock." He found his first few courses *very demanding.*

Guy *did* make the freshman basketball team, but soon relented on his desire to participate in big time sports and joined less time consuming activities. He did still have time for <u>intramural</u> teams in basketball and volleyball. Guy credits his high school *mentors* with giving him the wisdom to select the academic route over becoming a "professional" athlete (jock).

Being inducted into Eta Kappa Nu and/or Tau Beta Pi societies are the highest honors available to engineering students. Of course Guy was in both.

Just prior to gaining his bachelor's degree in electrical engineering in 1953, he interviewed with several companies on the Troy, New York, campus. He choose Stromberg Carlson from Rochester, New York. This choice resulted from him feeling more comfortable with a smaller company in a smaller city as well as their reputation for innovation He started as a production engineer for television production and then worked on production parts for a military radio. This latter activity proved to cause his focus on the field of communication equipment. Then he became involved in engineering design activities with video receivers. As a result of this successful activity he became one of only five people to advise the United States in cooperation with the United Kingdom and Canada in the field of antisubmarine warfare electronic equipment. Then, in 1962, an opportunity arose to join a newly formed startup company, RF Communications, in Rochester, New York

Guy worked on the design and management of numerous types of communication systems and equipment.

One project was with Eastman Kodak, which was used to record images from the moon coming from a satellite called Lunar Orbiter. He progressed up the managerial chain of the company until he became the head of the entire corporation just after the Harris Intgertype Company, later to be named Harris Corporation. The work at Harris gained him experience with military and commercial equipment in both the domestic and international markets.

In 1984, Guy was promoted to other Harris businesses with combined annual sales of over three-hundred million dollars, and, he was relocated to headquarters in Melbourne, Florida.

Key to obtaining this position was what he learned from the four founders of the RF Comm and a course he took from the **Dale Carnegie Institute**. From the founder, Bill Stolze he learned the importance of deep thought and marketing. From *mentor* Elmer Schwitteh he learned the significance of discipline and preparation. *Mentor* Roger Betlin taught him the value of innovation. Herb Van Deu Brul taught Guy the significance of money in business. The course *How to Win Friends and Influence People* also helped him in public speaking and his "People Are Everything" speeches and writings.

The fields of radio and satellite communications, and radio and television broadcast were "hot fields," and the equipment needed worldwide marketing. Guy Numann was there and ready for it.

When Guy retired as president of Harris Communications Sector in 1997 the business had grown to nearly one billion dollars annually with five-thousand employees. Harris Communications had plants in five of the United States, England, Canada, France, and China. As corporate president with overseas factories, he traveled *extensively*.

His inspired leadership included active participation in the Rochester Chamber of Commerce, Rochester Industrial Management Council, Electronic Industries Association, the Telecommunications Industry Association, and several other leadership roles.

Roxbury didn't hear much about Guy in those years but as a moral captain of industry, RPI awarded him an honorary doctor of engineering degree.

Guy and 1949 classmate and teacher Marie Griffin Numann retired to Vero Beach, Florida, to a harbor gated community on the

Indian River. The Numanns maintain a summer home in Rochester but needed to be in a harbor to accommodate Guy's fifty-two-foot yacht. (much shorter than Jay's!)

The Numanns have three children, William, Susan, and Nancy, and as of 2003, five grandchildren. Sister Marian (RCS 1950) who had *gotten better grades* than Guy was salutatorian at RCS, also married her RCS (1950) classmate Keith R. Meade. The Meades have three children. Marian died after a long illness with multiple sclerosis.

Youngest sister Patricia (RCS 1958), as Guy, was valedictorian, pilots her own plane and is an MD with an international reputation. Pat's most recent recognition deals with breast cancer and, as of 2003 she is affiliated with the Upstate Medical Center located on the campus of Syracuse University. Ironically author Ploutz's oldest daughter Lori L. Ploutz- Snyder is a research scientist at Syracuse University with a joint appointment with the College of Medicine. Lori's husband Robert Ploutz-Snyder is a biological research analysis at the Syracuse Upstate Medical Center. Both received Ph.D's from Ohio University where author Ploutz, who retired in 1982, was a professor of science education.

#

Part III

Chronological Listing of RCS Graduates

From 1901 until the year 2000, 1,851 students have graduated from Roxbury Schools. Since no exact, accurate, list of graduates exists in either the school or the community, the following list represents the collective list that parents, grandparents, townspeople, local historians, and Ploutz have compiled over a five-year period. There were periods when neither valedictorians nor salutatorians were announced.

It was necessary to print yearbooks and graduation programs in advance. More confusing still, there were numerous times when boys and girls never quite made it across the stage. Although some may have moved, married, died, never graduated, their name and picture were in the yearbook and/or commencement program. Alvin Van Aken (1944), Elsie Ploutz (Proper) 41, Ester Finch Snyder (1941 valedictorian) and others examined recent and/or moldy yearbooks as Ploutz gradually constructed the one-hundred-year sequence.

We apologize in advance to RCS graduates who may not be listed. If by chance we "graduated you" but you never did, probably no apology is necessary. As of this date, this is the *only* complete one-hundred-year list ever assembled. Information from yearbooks wasn't always accurate or complete. Much of the information as to college attended, and occupation was from volunteer's *memory*. Ploutz, mindful of the abuse, even ridicule, Erma Griffin experienced for her abundance of errors in both editions of *The History of the Town of Roxbury* wishes to "protect" *all the fine people who gave him incorrect information* and accepts their guilt as his own. "We *know* there are omissions, mistakes, we just don't know where they are."

Readers are encouraged to identify omissions and to identify information about those RCS graduates from 1950 to the end of the century. We request your input for accuracy and updates to put Roxbury in the earned position of being friendly to neighbors, tourists, ecologists, (John & Paul), historians (Jay) and to those who think that *mentoring* can make the Catskills, and the world a better place to live.

Please mail information which you know to be accurate to: Roxbury Educational Foundation. Their current address is @ RCS, 53729, State Highway, Rt 30, Roxbury, N. Y. 12474.

Chronological Listing of RCS Graduates 1901-2000

Roxbury Enrollment 1901 – 2000					
1898*	1	1924	8	1950	14	1976	29

Roxbury Enrollment 1901 – 2000

Year		Year		Year		Year	
1898*	1	1924	8	1950	14	1976	29
1899*	5	1925	13	1951	17	1977	36
1900*	2	1926	9	1952	15	1978	23
1901	2	1927	19	1953	16	1979	27
1902	4	1928	9	1954	21	1980	28
1903	3	1929	14	1955	15	1981	30
1904	2	1930	15	1956	14	1982	39
1905	3	1931	16	1957	23	1983	34
1906	2	1932	14	1958	16	1984	27
1907	3	1933	10	1959	22	1985	33
1908	4	1934	16	1960	12	1986	24
1909	5	1935	18	1961	15	1987	27
1910	6	1936	12	1962	20	1988	28
1911	3	1937	23	1963	21	1989	39
1912	7	1938	24	1964	18	1990	37
1913	5	1939	24	1965	22	1991	38
1914	4	1940	22	1966	29	1992	38
1915	14	1941	16	1967	25	1993	26
1916	7	1942	18	1968	24	1994	25
1917	5	1943	22	1969	30	1995	16
1918	9	1944	17	1970	28	1996	24
1919	15	1945	16	1971	24	1997	28
1920	11	1946	16	1972	24	1998	23
1921	8	1947	15	1973	30	1999	29
1922	7	1948	17	1974	30	2000	33
<u>1923</u>	<u>12</u>	1949	12	<u>1975</u>	<u>29</u>		....
141		-415-		554		741	

*Years 1898, 1899, and 1900 are not part of totals or 100 year report.

	141
	415
	554
	<u>741</u>
TOTAL (100 yr.)	1,851

Total number of male graduate	923
Total number of female graduates	<u>928</u>
Total number of graduates	1,851

Class of 1898		-1-	M 1	F 0
Scudder, George	1898	Civil engineer, Erie R.R.		

Class of 1899		-4-	M 2	F 2
Keator, Myron	1899	Lawyer, N. Mexico		
O'Neil, Michael	1899	Engineer, Ashokan Reservoir		
Scudder, Catherine	1899	Teacher, Cushing Academy, Mass.		
Simmone, Rose	1899	Teacher, Mt. Vernon, N.Y.		

Class of 1900		-2-	M 1	F 1
Clark, Harry	1900	Teacher, Cal.		
Demarest, May	1900	Missionary, Japan		

....
......

Class of 1901		-2-	M 0	F 2
Enderlin, Mabel	1901			
Pingree,Beulah Keator	1901			

Class of 1902		-4-	M 1	F 3
Baker, Lena	1902	Teacher		
Cartwright, Anna	1902			
Endress, Mary Scudder	1902			
O'Hara, Michael	1902			

Class of 1903		-3-	M 1	F 2
Kelly, Marian	1903	Club House Mgr. Florida		
Hobson, Helen	1903			
Thomas, Claude	1903	Civil Eng' NYC water(tunnel& shaft)		

Class of 1904		-2-	M 2	F 0
Booth, Frank	1904	WWI;Rot'y;Cut'ryMfg;coll/exp/RCS		
Humphrey, Harold	1904	Inn Manager		

Class of 1905		-3-	M 3	F 0
Hamilton, Andrew	1905	WW I, engineer, incandescent lamps		
Hubbell, George	1905	Mechanical engineer		
Sanford, John K.	1905	Insurance agent		

Class of 1906   -2-   M 2   F 0

Baum, Edward   1906
Smith, William   1906   Civil engineer

Class of 1907   -3-   M 2   F 1

Ballard, Hazel M.   1907   Val'dtn;classpres.;HStch;Baldwin,NY
Clark, Harry M.   1907   Sal'tn,auth,eng'r;TheF'stStory/Whale
Humphey, Robert F.   1907   Veteran W.W. I

Class of 1908   -4-   M 4   F 0

Baum, Leland M.   1908   Valedictorian, school principal
Bookout, Tallman C.   1908   Sal'tn;ClassPres;Prin.Rox1918-20
Hyman, Samuel   1908
Silver, Bruce R.   1908   Mgr. Zinc Co, N. J.

Class of 1909   -5-   M 2   F 3

Andrus, Olive E.   1909   Piano;sing' lessons, Russell SageColl.
Enderlin, Fred W.   1909   Valedictorian, Class Pres; Grocer
Gorsch, Helen   1909   Teacher, Oneonta Normal
Travis, Zena R.   1909   Sal'tn; Oneonta Normal, Supt. RCS
Weyl, Blanche E.   1909   H. S. Teacher, Amsterdam, NY.

Class of 1910   -6-   M 1   F 5

Barrett, D. Belle   1910   Insurance
Chase, Alice   1910
Edsall, Laura   1910   Teacher, Margaretville, NY.
McIntosh, Anna   1910
Parsons, Edith   1910
Smith, Robert L.   1910   Feed business

Class of 1911   -3-   M 2   F 1

Hubbell, Ida   1911   Salutatorian
Thompson, Milton   1911
Vermilya, James   1911   Valedictorian; Chemical Engineer

Class of 1912	-7-	M 2 F 5
Ballard, Violet E.	1912	
Bookhout, C. May	1912	Lay preacher; teacher
Bouton, Charles W.	1912	Farmer, wagon shop business
Cronk, Mabel F.	1912	Salutatorian, teacher, N.J.
Morse, David S.	1912	Valedictorian, teacher
Powell, Edith N.	1912	Teacher
Reed, Lillian E.	1912	Teacher

Class of 1913	-5-	M 3 F 2
Cronk, James	1913	Class President; Veteran W.W. I
Dudley, William M.	1913	Val'dtn; Vet.W.W.I; Rox.1st pilot
Enderlin, Florence	1913	Salutatorian
Muller, August	1913	Teacher, Phonicia, N.Y.
Powell, Ruth	1913	

Class of 1914	-4-	M 1 F 3
Cronk, Lillian	1914	Organist, Gould Church
Easley, Hazel	1914	Teacher, Oneonta
Lewis, M. Leland	1914	Class pres; salutatorian; merchant
Morse, Edna F.	1914	Valedictorian

Class of 1915	-14-	M 4 F 10
Brennan, Agnes M.	1915	
Cole, Eleanor	1915	Teacher, Oneonta
Creamer, Ruth	1915	Teacher
O'Hara, Anna	1915	
Hanbury, Elsie	1915	Teacher
Harris, Janet	1915	
Minnerly, Francis	1915	Class President; dentist
Morse, Grant	1915	WWI;tch/prin;auth.3vol/poetry;Supt.
Parsons, Eva	1915	
Preston, Grace	1915	Teacher, Oneonta Normal
Robinson, Martha	1915	
Ruteshouser, Anna	1915	Valedictorian,(Ploutz)author'smother
Van Aken, Roy	1915	Veteran WW I, Salutatorian; teacher
Weyl, Robert C.	1915	Banker

Class of 1916		-7-	M 3 F 4
Bellows, Mary	1916	Teacher, Syracuse	
Draffen, Harold	1916	Veteran WW I, proprietor, gen. store	
Jaquish, Nellie	1916	Salutatorian, tch; Syracuse Univ.	
Keator, Richard	1916		
Morse, Edith	1916	(Harris)	
Muller, George	1916	Class Pres. Vet. WW 1 Valedictorian	
Richtmyer, Francis	1916		

Class of 1917		-5-	M 1 F 4
Bouchey, Eva K.	1917		
Griffin, Clara L.	1917		
Mac Kenzie, Leroy	1917		
Osche, Minnie	1917	Valedictorian	
Raeder, Francis E.	1917	Salutatorian	

Class of 1918		-9-	M 4 F 5
Bartley, Dorcas	1918	Language teacher	
Bellows, Anna M.	1918		
Blythe, Pauline M.	1918	Teacher, Oneonta Normal	
Murray, Frank	1918	Forestry	
Rose, Florence A.	1918	Teacher, Oneonta Normal	
Rowe, Augusta M.	1918		
Shultis, Cecil M.	1918	Vet. WWI, Major Eng'r; NYC tunnels	
Spencer, Louis C.	1918	Class pres; Sal'tn; Vet WW I; engineer	
Vermilya, Fannie	1918		

Class of 1919   -15-   M 9   F 6

Alberti, Paul R.	1919	
Chase, George D.	1919	Civil Engineer
Cronk, Herbert R.	1919	Civil Engineer
Dixon, Marion E.	1919	Teacher
<u>Edsall, Preston W.</u>	1919	Val'dtn; Prof. PhD.PrinU/sci/UNC.
Eignor, Gladys M.	1919	
Gorsch, Irene	1919	Teacher, Oneonta Normal
Joslyn, Florence E.	1919	
Kelly, Nelson G.	1919	Farmer
Morse, Mary E.	1919	AlbanyBus;100yr./2000,farm/auto
Powell, Grace I.	1919	Bookkeeper
Preston, Kenneth B.	1919	ClassPres; PostM'st; Malius/Sch.
Preston, Milred V.	1919	Vassar (by HelenShepard) Tch; Lib'ran
Reynolds, Ralph H.	1919	Veteran W.W. I, Insurance
Southard, Harold G.	1919	Salesman

Class of 1920   -11-   M 6   F 5

Berry, Lillian	1920	
Bouton, Burrett B.	1920	Class president; Indiana Boys School
Corbin, Lena	1920	Teacher, Oneonta Normal
Davidson, Dorothy	1920	Valedictorian; teacher
Griffin, William E.	1920	Postmaster, merchant
Groves, Marion	1920	Secretary
Hinkley, Freda	1920	Oneonta Normal - teacher
Joslyn, Gladys	1920	Salutatorian
Parsons, Waldo	1920	Pharmacist, Albany Coll. Pharmacy
Shatraw, Milton	1920	
Shultis, Leland C.	1920	Teacher

Class of 1921   -8-   M 1   F 7

Aikman, Pauline	1921	
Bellows, Luella	1921	Teacher
Brownell, Orville	1921	Class president; truck driver
Cantwell, Grace	1921	
<u>Griffin, Ima Mae</u>	1921	Author,reporter,Rox. historian
Hinman, Iva	1921	Valedictorian
Mead, Marian	1921	Salutatorian
Morse, Grace	1921	Oneonta Normal - teacher

Class of 1922   -7-   M 5   F 2

Davidson, John	1922	Valedictorian
Hammond, Mabel	1922	Teacher; Oneonta Normal
Howard, Theodore B.	1922	Clerk, G. E.
Hubbell, Elizabeth	1922	
Speenburgh, Madison	1922	
<u>Teichmann, Frederick</u>	1922	Sal'tn;Prof NYU.auth;GouldS'ship
Van Woert, Willard H.	1922	Class pres;Pastor;Music Tch. NYC.

Class of 1923   -12-   M 7   F 5

Barber, Mildred Efie	1923	Telephone Co, Albany, NY.
Cantwell, Thomas E.	1923	Farmer
Clapp, Roger Quay	1923	Prof. Horticulture, Univ of Maine
Cronk, Pearl Anne	1923	Salutatorian
Gousmann, Robert W.	1923	Val'dtn;Class Pres;engineer, NYC.
Harrington, Mildred L.	1923	Nurse
Hinman, Florence A.	1923	
Mead, Stanley Chester	1923	Appliance business
Osche, William Fred	1923	G.E., refrigeration dept.
Shoemaker, Elwin	1923	Teacher, Prattsville, NY.
Simon, Joseph Patrick	1923	Electrical Engineer
Van Hoesen, Ester G.	1923	Teacher

Class of 1924   -8-   M 4   F 4

Bartley, Bernard	1924	NYS State Trooper
<u>Caswell, Bruce</u>	1924	Sal'tn;fire/chief;Scout M'st;Nat'ist
Ennist, Helen	1924	Valedictorian; stenographer
Faulkner, Mildred	1924	Class president
Griffin, Mary	1924	Teacher, RCS
Griffin, Walter	1924	Guidance counselor
Lewis, Robert	1924	Hotel Clerk, NYC.
Rollins, Cornelia	1924	Teacher

Barber, Elizabeth	1925	
Bookhout, Lynn	1925	Farmer, magazine editor
Bouton, Marjorie	1925	College; Phys.Therapist, Wash. DC.
Fredenburgh, Ida	1925	
Jones, George	1925	Machinist, G. E.
Jordan, John	1925	Sal'tn;Cl. Pres;CornellUniv.Employ
Lewis, Mildred	1925	Teacher
McCann, Harold	1925	
More, Donald	1925	Farmer
Page, Virginia	1925	
Pohlmann, Vincent	1925	Standard Oil Co, Troy, NY.
Sanford, Frances M.	1925	Valedictorian
Van Loan, Lewis	1925	Farmer

Aikman, Dorothy E.	1926	
Blythe, Rudolph	1926	Prof:Phrm;Pioneer,time/rels/med.
Buswell, Franklin E.	1926	Telephone operator, NYC.
Clapp, Henry S.	1926	Salutatorian; Horticulture
Cronk, Birdella	1926	Class pres.;tele' oper;Hobart, NY.
Lutz, Pauline M.	1926	(Hopkins) Teacher, art, Roxbury
O'Kelly, Helen	1926	Music teacher, Bainbridge, NY.
Pitkethly, Edith J.	1926	Nurse, NYC.
Schville, Charles E.	1926	Val'tn; teacher, Grand Gorge, NY.

Bellows, Elizabeth R.	1927	
Bookhout, Earl	1927	Oneonta Normal/accident
Cartwright, Howard	1927	Class president; farmer
Enderlin, Leighton	1927	Rotarian, hardware store proprietor
Fuller, Elsie L	1927	
Groves, Maurice	1927	Salutatorian
Ives, Frances A.	1927	(Jenkins)
Johnson, Eva	1927	
Joslyn, Kenneth C.	1927	
Jump, Wilfred W.	1927	Creamery employee
Kelly, John Harold	1927	WW II, Lt. Col.Army;grocery store
Kilpatrick, Margaret C	1927	Veteran W.W. II, R.N.
Lutz, Edward Albert	1927	Valedictorian
Mackey, James Gerald	1927	Coach, Windham, N.Y.
More, Herbert	1927	Paint store
Page, Richard	1927	Dentist
Schuman, Evelyn E.	1927	Teacher
Simon, Mary M.	1927	Died of TB
Sprague, Verlynn L.	1927	College

Cantwell, Dorothy	1928	Banker
Cantwell, Winifred	1928	Nurse
Craft, Arline	1928	Class president
Dugan, Elizabeth	1928	Teacher
<u>Ives, Charles K.</u>	1928	Rotr'y;WWII;MD;Cornell;"Tarzan"
Lutz, Claude	1928	Veteran W.W. II, insurance
Lutz, Dorothy C.	1928	
Mead, Grace (Todd)	1928	Valedictorian
Mondore, Irving	1928	Salutatorian

Bookhout, Marion	1929	Sal'tn; Rotarian,WWII;Hartwick Coll.
Bookhout, Marjorie	1929	
Brady, Kenneth	1929	Veteran W.W. II; General Electric
Cower, Kenneth	1929	Rotarian, electrician, merchant
Cronk, Vivian	1929	
Draffen, Etta	1929	Nurse
Fredenburgh, Harry	1929	Veteran; Helen Shepard scholarship
Ives, Herbert	1929	Class president; mechanic
Mondore, Grace	1929	
Pitkethly, David	1929	Rotarian, VMI; Lt. Col., Army
Ruteshouser, Dorothy	1929	Teacher
Smith, Doris C.	1929	
Townsend, Alnetta	1929	Teacher, RCS
Trede, Louise M.	1929	Valedictorian

Brady, Anna	1930	Medical assistant
Gerome, Hazel	1930	
Kelly, Kathleen	1930	
LaRue, Edna	1930	
Lutz, Louise	1930	
McWilliams, Madeline	1930	
Minnerly, James	1930	WW II,insurance, boatshop owner
Muller, Florence	1930	
Riley, Desmond	1930	Service station
Schmidt, John W.	1930	Valedictorian; Class president
Van Loan, Olive	1930	
Vicevich, Anthony P.	1930	
Vicevich, Caroline	1930	
Wright, Julian	1930	Salutatorian
Yanson, George	1930	Veteran W.W. II

Class of 1931		-16-	M 7	F 9 `

Brandow, George	1931	Val'dtn;WWII;ProfAgr/Econ;Penn.St
Burroughs, Angie	1931	Pres. Burroughs Society
Cantwell, Ralph	1931	Farmer
Cantwell, Russell	1931	College - education
Carter, Fredrick	1931	Doctor
Dugan, Leona	1931	
Keator, Ella	1931	
Kilpatrick, Robert	1931	Insurance
Lutz, Marian	1931	Nurse
Lutz, Sayers	1931	Class president; feed store owner
Lutz, Zada	1931	
Mondore, Beulah	1931	
Raeder, Marian	1931	Salutatorian
Ricker, James	1931	
Sparling, Clara	1931	(Ploutz)Nurse
Whitney, Gladys	1931	Teacher, Oneonta Normal

Class of 1932		-14-	M 8	F 6

Ballard, Inez	1932	Deputy town clerk, Roxbury
Darham, Sidney	1932	
Dugan, George	1932	Veteran WW II
Dugan, Genevieve	1932	Salutatorian
Fredenburgh, Paul	1932	Veteran W.W. II
Lawrence, Doris	1932	Nurse
Lutz, Edna M.	1932	Bookkeeper
Lutz, Herbert	1932	WWII;Carpenter; H.Shepard/S'ship
Morse, Harrison C.	1932	Rotarian, insurance
Ploutz, Helen	1932	
Proskine, Margaret	1932	
Slauson, Marshall	1932	Class president; Rotarian, town clerk
Tyler, Ivan	1932	Valedictorian; Veteran WWII
White, Douglas	1932	WWIIpilot;Rotary;Val'dtn;RCSTch.

Class of   1933   -10-   M 6   F 4

Biruk, Olga	1933	Salutatorian
Brady, Howard	1933	Veteran W.W. II
Haight, Virginia	1933	(Finch) Valedictorian
Keyser, Gerald	1933	
Keyser, Helena	1933	Class president; teacher
Meade, Marjorie	1933	
Meade, Virgil	1933	Farmer
Morse, Lindon	1933	WWII, Rotarian; Scout Master (41), Ins.
Munsell, Henry	1933	Rot'y; carpenter/mech; G. Church solo
Van Valkenburgh, H.	1933	Auto dealership

Class of 1934   -16-   M 5   F 11

Allen, J. Frances	1934	PhD.IchthyologyFedGov't/WaterPoll'
Allen, Lochie J.	1934	Professor (Allen sisters @ Rox 1 yr)
Ames, Betty	1934	Nurse
Ames, Helen	1934	College
Bookhout, Nora	1934	
Brandow, Robert	1934	Class president; Lt. Col. Army
Dugan, John H.	1934	Farmer
Finch, Dorothy	1934	(Cower)
Gockel, Dorothy	1934	Telephone operator
Haight, Kendall	1934	Farmer
Hewitt, Archibal	1934	
Mac Laury, Olive	1934	Salutatorian; Prof., Albion St. School;
Meade Walter F.	1934	Val'dtn;tch,naturalist,auth;photo'phy
Mondore, Galdys	1934	
Reed, Isabelle	1934	
Whitney, Wilma	1934	Teacher, Oneonta Normal

Class of 1935   -18-   M 13   F 5

Ballard, William	1935	
Berryman, Robert	1935	
Bookhout, Elmer	1935	Class president; stone mason
Bouton, James M.	1935	Rotarian;E Scout;Lt.Col Univ./Ala.
Brady, Richard	1935	Veteran W.W. II
Brandow, John	1935	Veteran W.W. II, Eastman Kodak
Brandow, Marian	1935	(Bookhout)
Cartwright, Arnorld	1935	Farmer
Case, Mary J.	1935	(Morse)
Griffin, Douglas	1935	Sal'tn; Vet, Red Socks farm team
Kittle, Lillian	1935	Valedictorian
McCall, Alfred	1935	
Proskine, Jennie	1935	
Roberts, Lloyd	1935	Veteran W.W. II, bookkeeper
Sanford, Gerald	1935	
Shafer, Paul	1935	Veteran
Suter, Jonas	1935	College, Eastman Kodak
Weeks, Marjorie	1935	

Class of 1936   -12-   M 7   F 5

Mackay, Donald	1936	
Malcomson, Ruth	1936	Salutatorian
Mead, Bruce S.	1936	WWII;Valedictorian;airline/pilot,coll.
Mead, Marguerite E.	1936	
Peck, Thelma	1936	(Shafer)
Restchack, Louis A.	1936	Male model
Schuster, Donald P.	1936	
Stewart, Paul	1936	Service station
Thomas, Wilma A.	1936	Legal secretary
Vizzini, Samuel S.	1936	Class president
Weyl, Donald W.	1936	STCOneonta;tchWWII; "JP".Barber
Whitney, Mariam E.	1936	(Triolo)

Bellows, Muriel	1937	Nurse
Biruk, Sophie	1937	
Blodgett, John	1937	Eagle Scout
Blodgett, Marion	1937	Veteran W.W. II, Eagle Scout
Brady, Lillian	1937	Secretary
Fanning, Mary Ruth	1937	Valedictorian
Gelner, Dorothy	1937	(Griffin)Salutatorian; teacher
Griffin, Sheldon	1937	C' Pres;STCOneonta,tch.ScoutM'st
Hammond, Inez	1937	
Herron, Leroy	1937	Veteran II, farmer
Hinkley, Vincent	1937	Veteran II, veterinarian ass't
Jones, Ruth E.	1937	(Maben)
Kimball, Donald	1937	
Lutz, Willis	1937	IBM, data processing; auto sales
Mc Ewan, Hilda	1937	
Morse, Clarabelle	1937	
Munsell, Evelyn	1937	(Griffin)
Restchack, Martha	1937	Manager A & P store
Sanford, Willis	1937	Veteran WW II
Shuster, Donald	1937	
Todd, Ruth	1937	(Roney)
Tupper, Betty	1937	R.N.
Van Valkenbugh, H.	1937	WWII;Auto Sales,Rox.TownSupv.

Bouton, Frank	1938	C' Pres;WWII;E.Scout,coll;Min'st
Cantwell, James	1938	POW;surv'Bataan/death/marchWWII
Constable, Thelma	1938	
Davis, Ruth	1938	
Dugan, Frederick	1938	Veteran W.W. II
Furman, Eleanor	1938	
Gaarn, Edna	1938	(Morse) Valedictorian
Green, Dorothy	1938	
Green, Florence	1938	Veteran W.W. II, nurse
Hait, Elsie	1938	
Hinkley, Doris	1938	(Stahl)
Hinkley, Sanford	1938	WWII;bldr;Own;PlattekillSki/slope
Kimball, Barbara	1938	
Lawrence, Evelyn	1938	
McKay, Donald	1938	
Morse, Genevieve	1938	
Morse, Harold	1938	
Morse, Loyal P.	1938	Veteran W.W. II, teacher
Ruteshouser, Virginia	1938	(Lutz) Postal clerk, Roxbury
Sanford, Evelyn	1938	Salutatorian
Schuman, Donald	1938	
Shafer, Robert	1938	Veteran W.W. II, jeweler
Stoutenburgh, Marshall	1938	POW,Bataan death marchWWII
Woolheater, Shirley	1938	

Name	Year	Notes
Archibald, Forrest E.	1939	Veteran W.W. II
Archibald, Virginia	1939	
Bouton, Margaret E.	1939	Teacher;graduate Univ. of Maryland
Davis, Carl L.	1939	
Eignor, Lloyd	1939	Farmer
Faraci, John C.	1939	Farmer
Finch, Hazel I.	1939	
Griffin, George D.	1939	POWGer'ny;WWII;P/B'ballY'nkes
Hammond, Frances A.	1939	
Hinkley, Edward G.	1939	Veteran W.W. II
Jones, Virginia R.	1939	
Kuhl, Genevive B.	1939	Class president
McIntosh, Marian E.	1939	
McIntosh, Wilma L.	1939	
Mead, Robert J.	1939	Farmer
O'Hara, Beatrice M.	1939	
O'Hara, Elizabeth J.	1939	
Peck, Elna K.	1939	Secretary
Reed, Leonard	1939	Veteran W.W. II
Reed, Richard	1939	Veteran W.W. II
Shafer, Grace	1939	
Shultis, Ellis	1939	Valedictorian, Veteran W.W. II
Van Aken, Otis	1939	Sal'tn;GouldS'ship/WWII/Eng,Boeing
Whitney, Dorothy E.	1939	

Blythe,MarvinRussell 1940   WWII;Sal'tn;EagleS;auth;math'n
Bouton, Ruth   1940   Class Pres; Veteran.; Army Nurse
Brady, George   1940   WW II, author, agriculture issues
Finch, Cleveland   1940   Eagle Scout
German, Bruce   1940   Farmer
Haight, Gwendolyn   1940
Hammond, Helen   1940
Hinkley, Emily   1940   Postmistress
Kelly, Margaret   1940   Valedictorian; college; teacher
Malcomson, Norman   1940   Veteran W.W. II, Eagle Scout
Miller, Jack   1940   Logger
Moldovon, Anna   1940
Mondore, Muriel   1940
More, Jean   1940
Purchell, Evelyn   1940
Purchell, Richard   1940   Tax assessor
Raeder, George   1940   Farmer
Reynolds, William   1940   Veteran W.W. II, Eagle Scout
Roberts, Donald   1940   Bookkeeper, Margaretville Hos'p
Schuster, Harold   1940   Veteran W.W. II; farmer
Shultis, George   1940   Veteran W.W. II, college graduate
Van Valkenburgh, M.   1940

Colonna, Peter   1941
Hadden, Donald   1941   Town council; farmer; cattle dealer
Haight, Edwin   1941
Hait, Basil   1941
Kelly, Jeanette   1941   Class president; teacher
More, Ann   1941   Vet.WW.II, Salutatorian; RN.
Ploutz, Elsie   1941   Vet.Women'sArm Corp(WAC) rest't
Reed, Alice   1941   Beautician
Reed, Harry   1941
Restchack, Walter   1941   Veteran W.W. II
Schuman, Andrew, Jr.   1941   Justice of the Peace
Shultis, Milton   1941   Veteran W.W. II, contractor
Smith, Harriet M.   1941   Val'dtn;health/Adm/St.Law'rUniv.
Townsend, Bernice   1941
Van Aken, Millard   1941   W.W.II, Signal Corp; Eng. W. Elect.
Wiederman, Julian   1941   POW/GermanyWWII;Rotary,bank'

Bellows, Hilton	1942	Eagle Scout, Veteran; Army
Bellows, Janis	1942	Salutatorian
Caswell, Francis	1942	Veteran W.W. II
Caswell, Thelma	1942	
Gaarn, Carol	1942	
Graham, Mona	1942	
Hinkley, Clyde	1942	Contractor
Hinkley, James	1942	Farmer
Meade, Frank	1942	
Morse, Ralph	1942	
O'Hara, Katherine	1942	
Proskine, John	1942	Veteran; Army, township trustee
Santic, Viola	1942	
Sparling, Stella	1942	
Teichmann, Eva	1942	Teacher; college
Tyler, Belva	1942	Class president
Von Heister, Lenemaja	1942	Valtn, college, English teacher
Weeks, Dorothy	1942	Hard'w/store/prop;Margaretville,NY

Name	Year	Notes
Bellows, Nelson	1943	Veteran W.W. II
Biruk, Minnie	1943	Valedictorian
Brady, Virginia	1943	
Fanning, Natalie	1943	Teacher
Ford, Merwin	1943	Gas co.
German, Charles	1943	Class president; Vet. W.W II
Granger, Leroy	1943	
Griffin, Bernice	1943	
LeFebvre, Shirley	1943	College, St. Lukes, R.N.
Mac Kenzie, Jane	1943	
More, Evelyn	1943	St. Lukes, R.N.
Morse, Betty	1943	
Roberts, Janice	1943	
Segnini, Vera	1943	College
Sherwood, Francis	1943	
Sherwood, Nelson	1943	
Sparling, Glenn	1943	Farmer
Stewart, Nelson	1943	Veteran W.W. II
Todd, Edith	1943	Teacher
Tompkins, Betty	1943	R.N.
Van Wormer,Bernice	1943	
Weddleton, Paul	1943	

Class of 1944		-17-	M 6 F 11
Brower, George	1944		Vet.W.W.II;college;G.E.electronics
Finch, Catherine	1944		L.P. Nurse
Griffin, Muriel	1944		Val'dtn;PhD;Ind/Univ/Prof.O'/STC
Hinkley, Caroline	1944		
Hitt, Ivan	1944		
Kulikowski, Pauline	1944		
Nolan, John	1944		Veteran, mechanic
Proskine, Gordon	1944		College
Restchack, Theresa	1944		
Rose, Margaret	1944		
Schuman, Doris	1944		
Schuster, Margaret	1944		Class president; college
Shultis, Bernice	1944		Salutatorian (s), college
Shultis, Emily	1944		Teacher, home economics
Shultis, Jean	1944		
Smith, David	1944		Sal'tan(s) WW II, Univ.Mich;arts
VanAken, Alvin	1944		W.W II; RCS yearbook collector

Class of 1945		-16-	M 6 F 10
Corum, Nellie	1945		
Griffin, Margaret	1945		
Hinkley, Edna	1945		Bookkeeper, G.E.
Hubbell, Glenford	1945		Bakery proprietor, banker
Kimball, Bernice	1945		
Lutz, Richard	1945		Vet/Navy;carpenter/Lutz feed stores
McIntosh, Margaret	1945		Secretary
Moldovan, Mary	1945		
Ploutz, Lorraine	1945		
Richard, Arlene	1945		Nurse
Rossman, Boice	1945		
Shultis, Hanford	1945		Veteran W.W. II, insurance
Smith, Gilbert	1945		Vet. W.W. II, Val'dtn; college
Stahl, Charis	1945		Salutatorian
Travis, Marie	1945		
Underwood, Daniel	1945		Class president

Class of 1946   -16-   M 7   F 9

Bauer, Marion   1946   Nurse
Ciaravino, Lena   1946   Farmer; Kirkside food service
Eisele, Charles   1946   Veteran Korean
Finch, Esther   1946   Val'dtn;RCS sec,acc'nt clerk;reporter
Greene, Beatrice   1946   RCS school aid
Haight, Gloria   1946
Hewitt, John   1946   Sal'tan;S/Trooper,fact'/mgr;Arkville
Hinkley, Francis   1946   Rotary;carp'tr,tch;S.Kortright,farmer
Long, Vincent   1946 Eng'AeroSpaceAdmWWIIMP,Rotary
O'Hara, Rosetta   1946
Ploutz, Floyd   1946   deceased
<u>Preston, Robert</u>   1946   Class P;WWII;STCCortland.tch prin.
Ullmann, Norma   1946
Underwood, Kenneth 1946   WWIIpilot,flight eng.TWA,JFK
Van Aken, Doris   1946 Employee;AudioSears;M'villeD'Store
Van Valkenburgh, A. 1946

Class of 1947   -15-   M 8   F 7

Bouton, Richard   1947   Vet; farmer; RCS Bd. of Education
Brandow, Edmund   1947   Barber
Cleveland, Jessica   1947   College
Davis, Henry   1947
Ellis, Guy   1947   College
Faraci, Charles   1947 Farmer; contractor
German, Bertha   1947
Griffin, Walter   1947   Soc.St/guid',OSTC,Stam'BOCES
Kelly, George   1947   Salutatorian; class president
Pecor, Glenn   1947   Veteran W.W. II
Preston, Margaret   1947
Schineller, Joyce   1947
Shultis, Naom   1947
Voorhees, Norma   1947   Valedictorian
Whitney, Doris   1947   Librarian

Class of 1948   -17-   M 7   F 10

Ballard, Paul	1948	Vet.W.W II; bee/keeper (Apiarist)
Ballard, Ronald	1948	Veteran Korean, local historian
Brower, Phillip	1948	Veteran Korean
Finch, Phillip	1948	Veteran Korean, escavator
Hunter, Ena	1948	Teacher
Kelly, Annette	1948	
Lutz, Jack	1948	Rotarian, oil distributor; pilot.
Mattice, Doris	1948	
Moldovan, Frances	1948	Nurse
Osborn, Ethel	1948	
Ploutz, Raymond G.	1948	C' Pres;VetWWII,Marine/CorpMP
Roberts, Leah	1948	
Tobin, Betty Lou	1948	
Tyler, Phyllis	1948	
Valk, Margaret	1948	(Long) computer specialist; artist
White, William D, III	1948	E.Scout;tch;Ham'ltnU;KualaLampur
Woodworth, Wanda	1948	

Class of 1949   -12-   M 8   F 4

Constable, Paul	1949	Veteran
Eisele, James	1949	Veteran W.W. II
Gerken, Marlene	1949	
Griffin, Marie	1949	(Numann)STC Oneonta; teacher,
Mattice, Pat	1949	
Mead, Wayland	1949	Vet.Korean,Cornell Univ;Ins.
Numann, Guy	1949	RPI; CEO Manufacturing Co.
Ploutz, Paul	1949	E. Scout, author, Prof.Developer
Slauson, Raymond	1949	Class president; Vet. Vietnam
Snipas, John	1949	Rotarian
Van Aken, Eleanor	1949	
Weber, Caroline	1949	

Class of 1950   -14-   M 9   F 5

Brower, Nancy	1950	
Cartwright, Leta	1950	Secretary
Caswell, Phil	1950	CornellUnivLt.ColArmy,Naturalist
Foster, Naomi	1950	
Greene, Gerald	1950	
Mead, Keith N.	1950	Veteran Korean, Air Force
Mead, Keith R.	1950	Class president; Vet. Nurse; Navy
Munro, Marcia	1950	Syracuse Univ.
Numann, Marian	1950	Salutatorian; Wells College, MD.
Schuman, Bob	1950	Veteran Vietnam
Shultis, Bob	1950	M/Sgt. Special Forces
Slauson, Virgil	1950	
Smith, William	1950	Librarian, Fairbanks, AK
Tyler, Gary Lee	1950	Veteran, Syracuse Univ; musician

Class of 1951   -17-   M 10   F 7

Archibald, Andy	1951	Salutatorian
Bouton, Donald	1951	Veteran
Christian, Freda	1951	Employee, So. Kortright School
DeSilva, Ronald	1951	Class president; Veteran
Finch, Glenn	1951	Veteran Vietnam
Hinkley, Roger	1951	Electrician
Mallasch, Edith	1951	
Minnerly, Janet	1951	College
Peck, Mary Ann	1951	
Peck, Virginia	1951	
Raeder, Jerry	1951	Proprietor, bowling alley
Rose, Marvin	1951	Veteran
Russell, John	1951	Veteran, college; draftsmen
Shultis, Catherine	1951	Valedictorian
Snipas, Vincent	1951	Vet.Vietnam;Secret Service;WhiteH.
Weber, Ann	1951	
Weber, Fred, Jr.	1951	

Davis, Idella	1952	
Demonie, Raymond	1952	Changed name to Higgins
DeSilva, Marilyn	1952	
Finch, Alberta	1952	
Hopkins, Ann	1952	Valedictorian, college
Johnston, Barry	1952	Cornell Univ.
Krom, Gladys	1952	
Mattice, Elsie Jean	1952	
Mattice, Marjorie	1952	
O'Dell, Ruby	1952	
Powell, Cecil	1952	HonorGuard;ArlingtonNat.Cemetery
Seligman, Dolores	1952	
Shultis, Lorraine	1952	Class president, college
Slauson, Dorothy	1952	
Van Aken, Robert	1952	Sal'tn;E.Scout/SyrU;US/F'stry/Ser.

Brower, Joan	1953	Employee, Blue Cross/Blue Shield
Cammer, Marie	1953	
Caswell, Adelbert	1953	
Christian, Raymond	1953	Veteran
Hinkley, Shirley	1953	
Hunter, Velda	1953	X-ray tech. Margaretville Hospital
Johannsen, Joe	1953	Veteran; State HighwayDept.employ
Johnston, Joan	1953	R.N
Johnston, Kay	1953	
Kelly, James	1953	Veteran
Mattice, Ronald	1953	Valedictorian; engineer
Morse, Annette	1953	
Morse, Ronald	1953	Electrican
Riedman, Valentine	1953	College, teacher
Ross, Conrad	1953	College
Smith, June	1953	

Bussy, Leon	1954	Veteran
Cammer, Jean	1954	College
Cartwright, Robert	1954	Veteran Vietnam
Eisele, Joseph	1954	Valedictorian
Enderlin, Barbara	1954	Salutatorian, college, teacher
Enderlin, Stephen	1954	R.P.I.; engineer
Gerken, George	1954	
Gorsch, Rudy, Jr.	1954	T'cher; Syracuse Univ., SUCO. MS.
Hammond, James	1954	Construction work
Hammond, Janet	1954	(German)Postal/employee;Marg'ville
Jenkins, Albert	1954	Realtor
Johannsen, Evelyn	1954	Class president
Lepeltak, Alma	1954	Banking
McKenna, Bruce	1954	Vet.Korea;college;dental components
Mead, Gordon	1954	Roxbury Highway Dept.
More, James	1954	College, Executive Black & Decker
Morse, Laurine	1954	
Munsell, Susan	1954	
O'Hara, John	1954	
Pekrul, Harold	1954	Margaretville School Bus Supv.
Tyler, Gilbert	1954	

Class of 1955   -15-   M 7   F 8

Boerem, Jeanne	1955	
Cammer, Helen	1955	Banking
Christian, Elwood	1955	
Collins, Diane	1955	Salutatorian
Decker, William	1955	
DuMond, Gary	1955	
Etts, Kenneth S.	1955	Veteran
Gaines, Virginia	1955	College
Harrington, Joanne	1955	
Hinkley, Gary	1955	Rotary;contractor/ownerPlattekillSki
Johnson, Loretta	1955	
Munsell, David	1955	Rotarian, contractor
Sears, Abagail	1955	
Stahl, Wayne	1955	
White, Nancy	1955	Val'tn; Hope College; published

Class of 1956 -14- M 5 F 9

Avery, Vivian	1956	Photography Business
Cable, James	1956	
Fusscas, Diane	1956	Class president
George, Laura	1956	
Ives, Julie	1956	(Moberg) Valedictorian, nurse
Jaquish, Patricia	1956	
Long, Loisanne	1956	
Mead, Sylvia	1956	
Morse, Patricia	1956	
Nesbitt, Lawrence	1956	Salutatorian
Purchell, Gordy	1956	Veteran
Shafer, Karl	1956	
Smith, Nancy	1956	
Stepanek, Joseph	1956	

Class of 1957 -23- M 14 F 9

Bubach, John	1957	
Cower, Joe	1957	Val'dtn, college, Eagle Scout
Decker, Stanley	1957	Veteran Vietnam
Dugan, Joan	1957	Class president, nurse
Enderlin, Joan	1957	College, secretary
Fusscas, Anita	1957	
German, Judy	1957	Beautician
Griffin, Ruth	1957	Oneonta STC; reading teacher
Hammond, Kenneth	1957	
Harrington, Marjorie	1957	
Hinkley, Glenford	1957	Contractor
Hunter, Clinton	1957	Veteran Vietnam, farmer
Kelly, Larry	1957	
Myers, Frank	1957	
Osborn, Donald	1957	Employee, Town of Roxbury
Purchell, Robert	1957	College (Frank Booth Scholarship)
Reed, William	1957	Veteran
Rettmeier, Alice Joy	1957	
Slauson, Eula	1957	
Slauson, Gary	1957	
Stahl, Ronald	1957	Salutatorian
Van Valkenburgh, Judy	1957	
Wickham, Gary	1957	

Collins, Stephen	1958	College
Demonie, Alice	1958	
Etts, Judy	1958	
Fuller, Dora	1958	Salutatorian; banking
Ives, Susan	1958	College, teacher
Jaquish, Rose	1958	
Johnson, Marietta	1958	
Lutz, Sylvia	1958	College
More, Arthur	1958	Buffalo State, bus/steal company
Morse, Nancy	1958	Nurse
Munsell, Harry	1958	
Numann, Patricia	1958	Valedictorian; M.D., Pilot
Ross, James	1958	
Saxon, Donna	1958	
Sweatman, Una	1958	
Van Dyke, Patricia	1958	

Dorrance, Daniel	1959	Veteran
Dugan, Robert	1959	Vet. Vietnam, IBM, Auburn Univ.
Enderlin, Jean	1959	College, secretary
Fusscas, Peter	1959	Vet, Vietnam;CEO Lock Title Co.
Graham, Veronica	1959	Florist
Hammond, Joan	1959	Banking
Harrington, Betty	1959	Bookkeeper
Hinkley, Sylvia	1959	Health care
Ives, Charles, Jr.	1959	Teacher; coach
Kunzler, Mary	1959	Syr.Univ,Phys.Ed,Aero.PhotoPilot
Lepeltak, Linda	1959	Banking
McDonald, Heather	1959	Salutatorian, college, theater
Mead, Constance	1959	Wal-Mart employee
Meade, Donna	1959	College
Miller, Linda	1959	
Morse, Emery	1959	
Oliver, Carolyn	1959	
Proctor, Lloyd	1959	Teacher
Rettmeier, Jean	1959	Valedictorian; teacher
Shafer, Carol	1959	
Weber, Elizabeth	1959	Florist/landscaping
Wheeler, Rex	1959	Veteran Vietnam

Class of 1960   -12-   M 6   F 6

Ballard, Eleanor	1960	
Cammer, Robert	1960	Veteran Vietnam
Cronk, James	1960	Vet. Vietnam, Valedictorian; Marine
Edlam, Lorraine	1960	
Meade, Emily	1960	
Meade, Stanley	1960	
Munsell, Antha	1960	Salutatorian; music teacher
Naccarato, Maria	1960	
Raeder, Bruce	1960	College, Corning Executive
Shultis, Charles	1960	
Townsend, John	1960	Grumman Aviation
Voorhees, Bonnie	1960	

Class of 1961   -15-   M 7   F 8

Biruk, John	1961	
Gaines, Nancy	1961	Craft shop propriator
Greene, Phyllis	1961	
Hinkley, Larry	1961	
Hunter, Ruth	1961	
Ives, Richard	1961	Class president, teacher, principal
Kramer, William	1961	Veteran Vietnam
LaRue, Wanda	1961	
Mc Caskill, Nancy	1961	
Purdy, Beatrice	1961	
Reed, David	1961	VetViet'm;tele/Co,Margaretville,NY.
Schreiber, Earl	1961	Valedtn,Head libran,Louisana State
Slauson, Joan	1961	
Stahl, Gordon	1961	Power Co. employee
Weyl, Jane	1961	Salutatorian, college

Ballard, Ethel   1962
Cartwright, Barbara   1962
Eignor, Christie   1962   Salutatorian
George, Evon   1962   Valedictorian
Hinkley, Robert   1962
Ives, Ralph   1962   SUNY Plattsburg, N. Y.
Johnson, Suzann   1962
Mead, Iris   1962
Morse, Joyce   1962
Ogborn, Sandra   1962
Pebler, George   1962 Navy, Veteran Vietnam
Proctor, Cynthia   1962   Teacher
Rettmeier, Charles   1962   Veteran Vietnam
Rossman, Rose   1962
Ruff, Gary   1962   Teacher
Slauson, Linda   1962
Spielman, George   1962   Veteran Vietnam
Van Valkenburgh,Ella 1962
Van Valkenburgh, R. 1962   Blenhiem power plant; IBM
Wheeler, Patricia   1962

Andre, Sandra	1963	Salutatorian, college
Cammer, Larry	1963	
Cartwright, Carol	1963	Valedictorian
Dorrance, Deanna	1963	Wal-Mart supervisor
Furman, Noreen Hait	1963	
Gordon, Donna	1963	
Hadden, Donald, Jr.	1963	Veteran Vietnam
Hinkley, Karen Kay	1963	
Kierdorf, Maureen	1963	Bookkeeper
Mead, Dorothy Ann	1963	
Munsell, Elizabeth	1963	
Paul, Rhonda	1963	
Phipps, Allen	1963	
Purdy, Michael	1963	
Seeley, Evelyn	1963	
Smith, Cheryl	1963	
Sweatman, Viola	1963	Teacher
Taylor, Gary	1963	Veteran Vietnam
Townsend, Robert	1963	Rot'y/contr'or,SuptRox/WaterDept
Wright, Patricia	1963	RCS payroll clerk
Young, Richard	1963	

Andre, Carole	1964	College
Ballard, Marilyn	1964	
Bradley, Timothy P.	1964	
Cammer, Elaine	1964	
Eignor, Nancy	1964	Valedictorian, teacher
Finch, Sandra	1964	
Gerken, Helen Ann	1964	
Haggerty, Robert, Jr.	1964	
Higgins, April	1964	
Johnson, Brenda Lee	1964	
Johnston, Russell D.	1964	Parsons College, Iowa
Lutz, Marian R.	1964	Salutatorian, teacher, Buffalo State
Morse, Gilford	1964	
Rossman, Barent V, Jr	1964	
Sanford, Donna	1964	
Stewart, David, Jr.	1964	Veteran
Townsend, Judith E.	1964	College; R.N.
Walpole, Elizabeth	1964	College

Ballard, Joyce N.	1965	
Bookhout, Jane Arna	1965	Valed'tn; SUNY;Postdam,tch, music
Bussy, Jerry I	1965	
Carr, Joseph	1965	Veteran; Joe's Backhoe Service
Day, Sharon Ellen	1965	
Eignor, Merry Lee	1965	
George, Floyd Arthur	1965	Veteran Vietnam
George, Marshall W.	1965	
Gregory, Linda Ann	1965	Teacher
Gregory, Linden Allen	1965	Veteran Vietnam, Rotarian, teacher
Haight, Francis Sue	1965	Nurse
Hinkley, Linda Ann	1965	
Ives, James Moore	1965	Purple Heart,Vietnam; Bingh'ton
Jones, Perry Durwin	1965	
Martin, Stanley Allen	1965	Teacher
Moore, Anne M.	1965	
Schuman, Thomas A.	1965	Veteran Vietnam
Snegoski, Eileen	1965	Salutatorian, Special Ed. teacher
Spielman, Dennis	1965	Veteran Vietnam
Stevens, Peter John	1965	Exchange student – Australia
Wheeler, Joan L.	1965	
Zuidema, Mary	1965	

Andre, Suzanne	1966	College
Baker, Lola	1966	Music teacher
Ballard, Susan	1966	
Cammer, Jane	1966	(Schuman) Teacher
Cartwright, Steve	1966	Veteran Vietnam
Cole, Lynn	1966	
Dugan, Patricia	1966	
Frevert, Christine	1966	
Gibbs, Richard	1966	Veteran Vietnam
Haggerty, Sharon	1966	
Hartman, Linda	1966	
Hinkley, Donald	1966	Veteran Vietnam, I.R.S. employee
Ives, Betty	1966	(Adams)
Johnston, Beverly	1966	
Kelly, Michael	1966	Valedictorian
Mazzone, Roger	1966	
Meade, Richard	1966	Teacher
Morse, Carol	1966	Insurance
Morse, Thomas	1966	Mer/Mar/ACD/KingPt/ARCO/Capt.
Nesbitt, Ted	1966	
Osborn, James	1966	
Pebler, Wayne	1966	Farmer, Justice of the Peace
Rose, Georgia	1966	
Rutulante, Gloria	1966	
Slater, Flo Jean	1966	
Slauson, Alan	1966	
Stewart, Robert	1966	Salutatorian, Veteran Vietnam
Van Buren, Mike	1966	Veteran Vietnam
Wiedemann, Richard	1966	

Brown, William	1967	deceased
Cattanco, Martha	1967	Exchange Student
Erway, Sandra	1967	
Frevert, Gail	1967	Nurse
George, Mary	1967	
German, Lorraine	1967	P O employee
Giacomo, James	1967	deceased
Gile, Margie	1967	Sal'tn;tch;SUNY,Oswego;Phys/Ther.
Gilham, Sharo	1967	Wildlife rehababilator
Gordon, Scott	1967	Maintenance, M'ville Hospital
Hudler, Jill	1967	
Kelly, Joe	1967	Valedictorian
Kierdorf, Gregg	1967	
Miller, Lynne	1967	
Poole, Cynthia	1967	Teacher;airline host't; sec.NYSEG.
Porter, Michael	1967	SUNY,Oneonta;sci/ tch/Margaretville
Rose, Linda	1967	
Rossman, Dorothy	1967	
Rossman, Mary Ann	1967	
Rowe, Linda	1967	
Shultis, Edward	1967	Veteran; B & B Construction
Spencer, Nancy	1967	
Taylor, Sherry	1967	
Thompson, Barbara	1967	Teacher; postmistress
Weyl, Mary	1967	School Administration/TA @ RCS

Buel, Elaine Fae   1968   (Burroughs)
Bussy, Dennis Ernest 1968
Flaherty, Joseph   1968   Veteran Vietnam
Furman, Noreen   1968
Gregory, Walter Burr 1968
Hewitt, Elizabeth S.   1968   Teacher
Hinkley, Richard Dale 1968   Veteran Vietnam
Jaquish, Georgia Anna 1968
Jaquish, John Henry   1968   Veteran Vietnam
Kelly, Randall C.   1968   Forester
Lutz, Frederick Willis 1968   Albany Coll.Pharmacy;Pharmacist
Martin, George W.   1968   Vet; Vietnam; Val'dtn; Eagle Scout
Moore, Richard Allen 1968   Contractor, Colorado
Millar, Jean Catherine 1968
Purchell, Alan Douglas 1968   Salutatorian
Rutulante, Donna Mae 1968
Sherwood, Thomas F. 1968
Spielman, Bonnie Mae 1968
Stewart, Larry James 1968
Thompson, Richard B 1968   Caprenter
Tischmacher, Vicki   1968   Albany Coll.Phar/Pharmacist,Alaska
Van Buren, Sandra A. 1968
Weyl, Nancy Ann   1968   Secretary/BOCES
Wright, Bonnie Jean   1968

Ballard, Eva M.	1969	
Ballard, Charles J.	1969	
Biruk, Susanna	1969	
Bookhout, Gregg D.	1969	Valedictorian; deceased
Finch, Daniel J.	1969	Pastor
Finch, Eric	1969	Veteran Vietnam
Frevert, Theresa A.	1969	Nurse, hospital administration
German, Charles R.	1969	Teacher, RCS
Greenburg, Kim L.	1969	
Hewitt, Michael J.	1969	Valedictorian, Doctor, radiology
Kelly, Joyce A.	1969	
Millar, Andrew	1969	
Morse, Stanley P.	1969	
Pebler, Barbara J.	1969	
Peck, Marilyn L.	1969	
Poole, Mark W.	1969	Eagle Scout, college; post office clerk
Porter, Richard M.	1969	Water Dept. NYC, Margaretville,NY
Purchell, Linda S.	1969	deceased
Rose, Charles	1969	
Rowe, Bruce C	1969	Farmer
Schuman, James R.	1969	
Sherwood, Gary E.	1969	Pres., RCS Board of Ed., farmer
Slater, Darrell G.	1969	Trailer park owner
Slater, Dennis G.	1969	E. Scout,tch,technology;Inspect'/Rox.
Slauson, Barbara J.	1969	
Stewart, Diane E.	1969	
Tobin, Jacqueline L.	1969	Secretary
Tobin, Jerome W.	1969	Rotarian; electrician
Wiedemann, Karen A.	1969	
White, Perry Lynden	1969	Rotarian, college; writer

Baer, Wayne Howarth	1970	Vet. Vietnam; Golf Course Maint.
Ballard, Kathy	1970	
Bergmann, Thomas	1970	
Brown, George E.	1970	
Bussy, Clyde E.	1970	
Davies, Daniel J.	1970	
Davis, Harold S.	1970	Veteran; Contractor/Nuclear
Finch, Martin P.	1970	Veteran Vietnam
George, Margaret R.	1970	Lawyer
Gile, Steven E.	1970	E.Scout;SUNYCobl's,AlbSt;syst/anal
Higgins, Lewis C, Jr.	1970	Veteran Vietnam (deceased)
Iacovelli, Joseph T.	1970	Veteran
Kasmer, Ann C.	1970	Beautician
Malpleton, David C.	1970	Rotary Exchange Student, Australia
Mc Kertie, Mary D.	1970	
Miller, Gregg R.	1970	Val'dtn,Univ.N.Carolina;Math Prof.
Moore, Janis E.	1970	Farmer
Moscato, Jerry	1970	Veteran Vietnam
Needham, Ralph T.	1970	Vet. Vietnam;Mobile HomeSales/Ser.
Osborn, Joseph	1970	Veteran
Parnell, Carol E.	1970	Government Employee
Rowe, Donald J.	1970	
Ruscio, Paul N.	1970	Vet. Vietnam;Restaurant Manager.
Segnini, Maria Vera	1970	
Shultis, Lela A.	1970	
Slauson, George C.	1970	Veteran; Campground Owner
Taylor, Lori E.	1970	
Thompson, Kathryn	1970	Salutatorian; Home Bureau Dept.

Ballard, Daniel J.	1971	Veteran Vietnam
Ballard, James R.	1971	Valedictorian, Vet;RCS custodian
Carol, David	1971	
Cole, Karen	1971	
Condliffe, David	1971	Woodworker
Eignor, Sally C.	1971	
Finch, Douglas C.	1971	Veteran Vietnam
Ford, Ellen	1971	
German, Cynthia L.	1971	
Griffin, Terrance	1971	
Hewitt, Sarah	1971	
Hinkley, Tonya	1971	Salutatorian, SUNY,New Pultz; tch.
Jones, Mark	1971	Veteran Vietnam
Lutz, Jeffrey	1971	Eagle Scout
Mc Kenzie, Judith	1971	
Millar, Edmund	1971	Horticulturist
Munro, William	1971	Teacher, Physical Ed. Sidney, N.Y.
Munsell, Mary Louis	1971	
Porter, David	1971	
Ruff, Gail	1971	Teacher; Florida
Seals, Barbara	1971	
Shultis, Loren	1971	RCS, bus driver
Shultis, Susan	1971	
Underwood, David A.	1971	Vet.Viet.NYCWaterDept/GG,NY

Ballard, Ernest	1972	
Bergmann, Timothy	1972	
Bergmann, William	1972	
Bolger, Anne	1972	
Clark, Richard	1972	
Clark, Roxanne	1972	
George, Leslie J.	1972	
Gilham, William R.	1972	B. G. Construction, NC.
Gregory, Jan M.	1972	Teacher
Hartman, Maureen D.	1972	
Higgins, William C.	1972	
Hinkley, Thomas M.	1972	Eagle Scout, hospital purser
Jonson, Ulla A. C.	1972	Rotary Exchange Student
Kelly, Ellen M.	1972	Veteran
Lutz, Thomas J.	1972	Eagle Scout
Morse, Frederick	1972	Eagle Scout, insurance
Prout, Cathy L.	1972	
Rossman, Eugene F.	1972	
Savold, Mary Jo T.	1972	Roxbury Dairy Princess
Sherwood, Rande	1972	
Spielman, Connie L.	1972	Medicine P.A.
Sprague, Victor	1972	
Van Valkenburgh, N.	1972	Pediatric nurse
Warner, John A.	1972	

Balcom, Debra E.	1973	
Davies, Kris	1973	
Dwyer, Thomas J.	1973	
Finch, Kristen L.	1973	Salutatorian
Ford, John W.	1973	
George, Neva	1973	
Gilham, Edith A.	1973	Mountainside Res. Ctr/cook
Higgins, Pamela R.	1973	OSHA, secretary/BOCES
Hinkley, Jeffrey B.	1973	Veteran
Jones, Stephen P.	1973	
Kasmer, Alicia	1973	
Kelly, Allison	1973	
Lutz, Fran L.	1973	College graduate
Lutz, Steven R.	1973	Valedtn;E.Scout/LutzFeed,Oneonta
Martin, Donald J.	1973	
Munro, Denise K.	1973	
Porter, Robert B.	1973	
Prout, Robin L.	1973	
Raeder, George E.	1973	
Roberts, Thomas C.	1973	
Rolland, Mary	1973	Pottery business
Rolland, Richard, Jr	1973	Insurance
Rossman, James	1973	
Taylor, Randy D.	1973	Veteran Vietnam
Taylor, Ricky D.	1973	
Thomas, Michael F.	1973	
Tobin, Sandra L.	1973	
Underwood, John D.	1973	
Warner, Diana L.	1973	
Wright, Susan	1973	Cert.EMT;bus/dvr.So/K'right Sch.

Balcom, Julie	1974	
Ballard, Jon	1974	
Echeverra, Juan C.	1974	
Eignor, Robert K.	1974	
Everett, Bruce, Jr.	1974	Veteran, Rotarian, refrigeration
Finch, Betsy	1974	
Finch, William R.	1974	Rotarian
Flachs, Regina	1974	Co-Owner, Cole & Griffin Const.
Ford, Sally A.	1974	
Hait, Sherry	1974	(Albano)
Heylers, Annette	1974	
Hewitt, David A.	1974	
Hinkley, Michael R.	1974	Electrician
Hinkley, Toni A.	1974	Oneonta STC;Tch,Margaretville,NY
Iacovelli, Anthony R.	1974	
Ingram, Debra	1974	
Kelly, Kathleen	1974	Valedictorian
Kohler, Mark L.	1974	
Kohler, Michelle	1974	
Millar, Maureen	1974	
Pearsall, Mercedes	1974	
Ploutz, Raymond E.	1974	
Purchell, Wayne	1974	
Savold, James	1974	Veteran
Schuman, Stephen A.	1974	Employee, Town of Roxbury, NY
Shultis, Ernest	1974	
Van Voorhees, Cheryl	1974	
Van Voorhees, Ron M.	1974	
Wayman, Joyce	1974	
Wiedemann, Judith	1974	

Balcom, Michael F.	1975	
Bergmann, Christine A.	1975	
Bergmann, James C.	1975	
Carmeli, Margaret	1975	SUNYOn'ta;Rutger'sUniv/hosp/adm.
Dwyer, Donna M.	1975	Salutatorian
Elflein, Charles E.	1975	
Everett, Barbara A.	1975	
Flachs, Frank A.	1975	Business man
Gile, James D.	1975	Eagle Scout
Grant, Kathy	1975	
Gray, Joanne L.	1975	
Greene, Susan R.	1975	
Gregory, Dawn L.	1975	Valedictorian; music teacher
Hall, Douglas B.	1975	Construction
Kelly, John	1975	Veteran, Rotarian, Eagle Scout
Little, Nancy	1975	
Lutz, Robert	1975	E.Scout;FamilyFeedBus,OneontaNY
MacDonald, Lynette	1975	
Osborn, Melinda	1975	
Pietrantoni, Steve	1975	
Porter, Mary J.	1975	
Purchell, David	1975	
Purchell, Marcy	1975	
Rossman. Walter	1975	
Samuelsen, Donna	1975	
Sherwood, Dorothy	1975	
Shultis, Anne	1975	
Shultis, Greg	1975	
Slauson, Robert	1975	

Ballard, Joseph P.   1976
Ballard, Kevin R.   1976   Self Emp'Painting, Landscaping
Blakeslee, Dawn M.   1976
Brainerd, Wayne M.   1976   Lt. Col. Army CMOC
Cole, Robert B.   1976   Vet; Owner Cole & Griffin Const.
Elflein, Ruth A.   1976
Destefianis, Mario T.   1976
Finch, Duane   1976   Oswego SUNY graduate, teacher
Finch, Sheryl A.   1976
Flachs, Susan A.   1976   (Cole) LTA, RCS
Ford, Susan J.   1976
Hall, Stephen H.   1976
Hartman, Maryellen C 1976   Food/Shep'd/Hill Golf ;RCS b'driver
Haskin, Jeffrey   1976   Employee, Town of Roxbury
Hinkley, Allen R.   1976   Construction; ski mgr.
Kelly, Claire M.   1976   Valedictorian
Kohler, Melissa L.   1976
Kruger, Susan M.   1976
Mager, Brenda L.   1976
Millar, Anne C.   1976
Miranda, Ilce P.   1976
Munro, Karen S.   1976
Perazone, Brian E.   1976   Army Reserve; Gunsmith
Prior, Eileen   1976
Roberts, Aleta M.   1976
Siska, Michael J.   1976
Snyder, Vincent H.   1976   Floor Sanding business
Wiedemann, Susan A. 1976   Day Care Center business
Yeager, Joanne M   1976

Balcom, Rosemary F. 1977
Barton, Karen M.   1977
Bolger, John T.   1977   Contractor, B & B Construction.
Bubach, John L.   1977   Own excavation co; Trl Park
Carr, David C.   1977
Chambers, William T 1977
Deluca, Anthony E.   1977
Dilello, Ricky M.   1977   deceased
Finch, Laurel E.   1977
Flachs, Kurt J.   1977   Plumbing business
German Anthony P.   1977   Lt. Col.NYAir National Guard Res.
German, Christine M. 1977
Giacci, David V.   1977
Giacci, Gary D.   1977
Gordon, Bruce R. K. 1977
Gray, Steven R.   1977   Veteran
Hall, Lillabet   1977
Higgins, Melanie F.   1977
Hinkley, Steve   1977
Hinkley, Tyrone   1977   Engineer
Hughes, Sharon   1977
Kelly, Nora M.   1977   Valedictorian
Key, Francis S.   1977
Little, Robert   1977
Lutz, John   1977   Eagle Scout; Hospital Adm.
Mead, Michael R.   1977
Oliveiria, Walner A   1977   Rotary Exchange Student
Purchell, Susan A.   1977
Raeder, Nancy L.   1977   (Vosbrink)
Savold, Patricia A.   1977   West Point; Veteran
Schneider, Helene M. 1977
Sherwood, Donald J. 1977
Tischmacher, Roin G. 1977   Banker
Underwood, Mary E.   1977   Hotel Manager
Vosbrink, Walter H, Jr1977   Heavy Equip. Salesman; Caterpillar
Yeager, Kevin H.   1977   Eagle Scout, lawyer

Acampa, Gerard	1978	
Bergmann, Keith	1978	
Bubach, Susan	1978	Teacher
Bussy, Donna	1978	
Cooper, Gary	1978	Roxbury business man
Finch, Stephen	1978	Business man
Flachs, Lisa	1978	Valdtn;MS,Soc.Wk;WorldT.Ct.9/11
Hammond, Perry	1978	Salutatorian
Hanson, Kevin	1978	
Haynes, Tom	1978	
Hinkley, Kenny	1978	Excavator
Hinkley, Sonya	1978	Architect
King, Linda	1978	Veteran
Lindner, Joseph	1978	
Myers, Andrew	1978	
Oi, Hiroho	1978	Exchange student, Japan
Prout, William	1978	
Savold, David, II	1978	Graduate West Point; U. S. Army
Schneider, Lois	1978	Corrections Officer
Thomas, Louise	1978	
Wadsworth, Denise	1978	
Wadsworth, Joseph	1978	
Warner, Cheryl	1978	

Bubach, Eugene W.   1979   Carpenter
Burroughs, Debora M 1979
Carr, Robert P.   1979
Carr, Rosemarie P.   1979
Clark, Monica   1979
De Maroney, James A 1979   Veteran
Dent, Robin L.   1979
Dorrance, Daniel A,II 1979 Veteran, Marine Corp
DuMond, Donna D.   1979
Etts, Ricky A.   1979   Veteran
Faraci, Sue A.   1979   Salutat'n;RCS preschool employee
German, Chris   1979   Vet; Cert. Orthotist & Prosthetist.
German, Timothy R.   1979   Veteran
Grant, Robert H.   1979
Hinkley, Yvonne L.   1979   Post Mistress
Kellar, Mary A.   1979
Kelly, Margaret R.   1979   Valedictorian
Lindner, Heidi G.   1979
Migdol, Leiann S.   1979
Munsell, Diane B.   1979   Nurse
Nader, Katheryne M.   1979
Perkins, Daniel W.   1979   Owns Const. Company, Michigan
Schimmel, Anne M.   1979
Slauson, Dianne Lynn 1979   Greenhouse operator
Slauson, Keith   1979   Veteran
Snyder, Shirley L.   1979   Asso/DegreeUlsterC.Com/Coll.farm
Van Valkenburgh, R.   1979   Teacher; coach, S. Kortright Schools

Aulino, Rosanne   1980
Balcom, Mary F.E.   1980
Balcom, William E.   1980
Bubach, Patricia A.   1980   Dr. of Chiropractic
Carmeli, Anthony J.   1980   SUNYOneonta,Syr.Coll.Forestry
Cartwright, Kennie C. 1980   Owner, Cartwright Construction Co.
Chambers, Patricia A. 1980
Cooper, Susan J.   1980
Cox, William A, III   1980   Vet;Owner,DeliverySys.(Caltabiano)
Farleigh, Joseph C.   1980   Rotarian
Finch, Bonnie   1980
Finch, Wayne G.   1980   Veteran
Gray, Edward R.   1980
Greene, Steven A.   1980   Equip. Operator/Town of Roxbury
Hughes, Randolph C.   1980   Vet;Tractor/Trailor operator/owner
Hynes, Gerald D.   1980   Communications
Kohler, Matthew L.   1980   Veteran
Long, Robert C.   1980   Salutatorian
Lutz, Samuel F.   1980   Rotarian, oil distributor
Migdol, Judith A.   1980
Pietrantoni, Richard   1980   Veteran; Navy
Rossman, Timothy G. 1980
Schwander, Stephen S1980   Valedictorian; Minister
Slauson, Carol L.   1980   Bookeeper, Daitch Creamery
Temple, Sherry A.   1980
Vigna, Alfred J.   1980   Veteran; Technology teacher, RCS
Whitney, Lawrence   1980   Refuse Disposal, Town of Roxbury
Yeager, Timothy   1980

Class of 1981   -30-   M 17   F13

Banks, Dorothy Jean 1981
Brainerd, Todd   1981   deceasesd
Bullock, Sherry Lynn 1981
Campone, James A, Jr1981
Cartwright, Charles   1981
Condliffe, Sharon   1981   Veteran
Cone, Tammy L.   1981
Dorrance, Dawn Marie1981   Veteran
Dorrance, Michael A. 1981   Veteran
Dunham, Bret C.   1981
Eignor, Laurie   1981
Faraci, Gary C.   1981   Siding business
Furman, Kevin J.   1981
German, Neil D.   1981   Employee, Town of Roxbury
Grant, Kelly Anne   1981
Greene, Scott E.   1981   Woodstock Chimes
Haskin, Kenneth R.   1981
Hinkley, Dee M.   1981
Hynes, Timothy P.   1981   Veteran; Verizon lineman
Lang, Karen   1981
Lawrence, Jeffrey   1981   Veteran
McDonald, Rich   1981
Mager, Charles E.   1981   Veteran
Menne, Dianna M.   1981   Graduate program
Parizo, Glen   1981
Roberts, Shari   1981   Graduate program
Sanford, Donald G.   1981   Teach, Margaretville Schools
Slauson, Jeffrey J.   1981
Tietjen, Lauriel L.   1981   Graduate program
Van Aken, Susan   1981   (Dorrance)

Bergmann, George	1982	
Burroughs, John	1982	Well driller, PA.
Cammer, Mark L.	1982	Carpenter
Cammer, Steve R.	1982	Carpenter
Cerullo, Darlene H.	1982	Valedictorian
Cowan, David D.	1982	Contractor
Dunham, Rik	1982	Surveyor; Utah
Farnum, Christopher C	1982	N.Y. State Edu Department
Farnum, Shawn M.	1982	Painter, decorator
Finch, Cindy L.	1982	Veteran
Gardner Christopher	1982	Newspaper photographer
George, Dennis	1982	
Giacci, Steve C	1982	
Gockel, Holly J.	1982	R. N. Prattsville Health Ctr
Gray, Douglas A.	1982	
Hall, Jack	1982	Construction (D. Munsell)
Hanrahan, Beth Ann	1982	
Haynes, Roger	1982	
Hinkley, Lynette Carla	1982	Catskill Railroad
Johnson, Rodger P.	1982	
Johnston, Douglas B.	1982	
King, Thomas A.	1982	
Long, Scott T.	1982	Mgr Foot Locker, Colorado
Madero, Mark	1982	
Manon, Asher J.	1982	Emp. Town of Middletown
Mattice, Melony D.	1982	Recep., Roxbury Health Ctr.
Parizo, Sue Ellen	1982	
Regan, Sharon L.	1982	
Reuter, Johanna M.	1982	
Schuman, David A.	1982	Electrician
Sherman, Dale F	1982	Minister Indians,Fairford, CA
Sherwood, James D.	1982	
Sprague, Kathleen	1982	Owner, beauty salon
Temple, Sharon M.	1982	
Van Valkenburgh, Ed	1982	
Van Valkenburgh, J.	1982	
Vigna, Diana M.	1982	Home schooling 4 children
Whitney, James L.	1982	Landscape business
Wiedemann, Lauria A	1982	

Aulino, Joseph	1983	Real Estate, Rotarian
Brower, Steve A.	1983	
Bullock, Shelly L.	1983	
Cartier, Michael	1983	
Ciaravino, Bryan M.	1983	
Davis, Arnold C, Jr.	1983	Veteran
Davis, Judy	1983	
Davis, Veronica J.	1983	
Ely, Keith W.	1983	
Etts, Terry L.	1983	
Finch, Joy L.	1983	
Finch, Nicholas L.	1983	Excavator
Furman, Kenneth	1983	
Gordon, Bryon	1983	Val'd;MS/PhD; G.Mas;GAO
Goth, Matthew	1983	
Griffin, Steve Paul	1983	
Grocholl, Deidre D.	1983	
Harlow, Robert T.	1983	
Johnson, Julie A.	1983	
Johnston, James G.	1983	
Keegan, Richard W.	1983	
Lang, Lorraine A.	1983	(Bolger)
Mahoney, Beth	1983	
Munsell, Andrea S.	1983	(Cammer) Postal Employee
Purchell, Leah	1983	Nurse
Reuter, Michael J.	1983	Salutatorian
Samuelson, Karen M.	1983	
Sanford, Rex E.	1983	
Sauveur, Timothy S	1983	Veteran; NYC police officer.
Shultis, Leighton K.	1983	
Snyder, Charlie T.	1983	Veteran
Snyder, Fawn	1983	Secretary/BOCES
Stratton, Kathryn L.	1983	
Whittaker, Mark D.	1983	

Bianco, Mary E.   1984
Brainard, Lisa M.   1984   (Faraci) SUNY, Teacher
Brainerd, Kelly L.   1984
Bruen, Deidre A.   1984
Catabiano, Anthony P.1984
Coss, Donna   1984
Davis, Michael A.   1984   Veteran, Desert Storm
Farnum, Kathleen A.   1984   Salutatorian; Teacher
Gockel, Dawn M.   1984
Hall, Larry A.   1984
Harrison, Sheri   1984
Hinkley, Teresa S.   1984
Jaeger, Steve C.   1984   Veteran
Lawrence, Cynthia A.   1984
McCall, Dana A.   1984
Mead, Lori L.   1984
Mead, Helen Ruth   1984
Nilsen, Donna M.   1984   Teacher
Pickett, David F.   1984
Sherman, Merile L.   1984
Squires, Tamara L.   1984
Stratton, Lynda R.   1984
Thorington, Ernest J.   1984
Townsend, Wendy S.   1984   (Greene) SUNY; sec. RCS
Van Aken, Gary   1984
Vigna, John A   1984   Val'dt;West Point;Vet;Dst St.
Washburn, Raymond   1984   Veteran, Desert Storm

Ballard, DavidWilliam1985
Biruk, John W.   1985
Boyle, John T   1985   Teacher
Brannen, Steve   1985   Own business/Florida
Cartwright, Russell   1985   Own business, Colorado
Chow, Alane   1985   Hair Dresser
Curtin, Theresa   1985
Donnelly, KimberlyA1985   Nurse
Fane, William J.   1985
Faraci, Thomas   1985   SUNY Cortland; teacher
Grant, Marilynn J.   1985   Registered Nurse
Harlow, Barbara J.   1985
Johannsen, Barbara J. 1985   Teacher, RCS
Keevan, Russell   1985
Kelkowski, Scott P.   1985
Lawrence, William   1985   Sports Field Mgr/Clark cos.
Lindner, Jo Ann L.   1985   Verizon/Margaretville,NY
McMahon, MarianneE1985
Meskill, Jeffrey J.   1985   Val'dtn ; Vet. Desert Storm,
Mika, Carol   1985
Moseman, Amy C.   1985   Teacher, music; Florida
Nilsen, Sandi   1985
Novak, Cindy L   1985
O'Neil, Daniel J.   1985
Pedersen, Lena   1985   Exchange Student
Pucci, Dominic, III   1985   Oneonta, NY Pol. Dept/Rec
Purchell, Helene   1985   Legal secretary
Roberts, Ellen R.   1985
Rogacevitch, E. P.   1985   RCS employee
Rose, Howard, III   1985
Van Aken, Wendy L. 1985   Clerk, Agway
Van Valkenburgh, D. 1985
Wilson, Pamela L.   1985   Administrative secretary

Bennett, Charles S.	1986	
Biruk, Thomas M.	1986	SUNY,Morris.;El.Eng;comp.
Bresee, Erika Sue	1986	(Thetford)Nurse Fox Hosp.
Buccheri, Dean	1986	
Bullock, Stanley	1986	
Bussy, Kimberly Ann	1986	Salut.; bus. school; ex. Sec.
Buss, Tina	1986	
Cox, David T.	1986	Vet.Mar/tech/own/cons/Co
Ferris, Kevin S.	1986	
Gockel, Joanne M.	1986	
Grant, Carolyn	1986	(Faraci) Gardner&Buhl Acct.
Greene, Tom III	1986	Owner, auto shop; Ashland
Hanrahan, Joe	1986	
Hinkley, Matthew D.	1986	Corrections Officer
Hoyt, Lori	1986	
Jones, Richard F.	1986	
Madore, Michelle Ann	1986	
Mc Nerney, MichaelA	1986	Val'dtn; Air Force Acd. grad.
Miner, Tom	1986	
Myers, Christopher J.	1986	
O'Beirne, Ellen	1986	
Reed, Jeffrey W.	1986	
Reuter, Christopher J.	1986	
Roberts, Charlene	1986	

Albano, Frank V.   1987   Mrg. Albano Farms Stamford
Beaver, Allison M.   1987
Bennett, Diane Lynn 1987
Bussiere, George   1987
Cronk, Doug   1987   Carpenter
Eignor, Amy   1987
Etts, Jodi L.   1987   deceasesd
Faoro, Jill Marie   1987   Rotary Exchange Stdt; Japan
Gardner, Page C.   1987
Gebhard, Michelle   1987   (Pucsci)

Gordon, Julie Anne   1987   STC, Oneonta; 3rd gr. teacher
Goth, Shannon L.   1987
Hadden, David R.   1987
Hamil, Dawn M.   1987   Gardner & Buhl Accountants
Hinkley, Melissa A.   1987   (Shultis); Brookside Hardwar
Holland, Edward   1987
Hulbert, Melissa   1987
Hynes, Michael T.   1987   Vet.; Grand Gorge Disp Pl.
Mc Mahon, Mike   1987   Graduate program
Moore, Denise Lynn   1987   Syracuse;ROTC;math RCS
Reed, Karna Yvonne   1987
Slater, Daniel   1987
Spielman, George L.   1987
Spielman, Wendy E.   1987   (Morrison)Nurse/Fam.Health
Sprague, Vickie Ann   1987
Stahl, Dwayne D.   1987   Eagle Scout
Van Valkenburgh, Dan 1987   Veteran

Bianco, Joann K.	1988	
Bussiere, Josie	1988	Account Clerk, RCS
Cammer, Catherine	1988	B. A, Albany State
Davis, Alan C.	1988	RCS custodian
Diserens, Alain	1988	Ex. Student, Switzerland
Donnelly, Robert	1988	
Ely, Dennis I.	1988	Zaack Clark Painting
Ferris, Penny J.	1988	Veteran, Desert Storm
German, Jennifer L.	1988	U. S. Postal worker
Green, Dawn M.	1988	Nurse's Aid
Grounds, Debra	1988	Nurse, physical therapist
Hinkley, Tracy L.	1988	(Peters)
Laureanti, Ann	1988	
Leibowitz, Tracy	1988	Teacher
MacDonald, Neil	1988	
Marengo, Michael	1988	
Meskill, Janene A.	1988	
Miner, Valerie G.	1988	
Morse, Tracy L.	1988	Veteran Desert Storm
Nikula, Anssi	1988	Rotary Exchange Student
Novak, Dawn	1988	
Origoni, Marcelo	1988	Restaurant Mgr, Oneonta
Pucci, Kristi A.	1988	
Rudolph, John W.	1988	Sal'tn;RotaryBS.RPI;Mgr.
Sherman, Asa J.	1988	Valedictorian; Minister, P.A.
Suess, Christopher	1988	
Washburn, Wendy S.	1988	
Wright, Shawn B.	1988	

Axelsen, Krista Anne 1989
Ballard, Karen Sue   1989
Brittain, Dale   1989
Bruen, Kristen A.   1989
Buccheri, Michael.   1989   College
Bussy, Jerry   1989   Veteran; golf course mgr.
Cox, Jim   1989   (Caltabiano)Sec/Best Buy
Cumming, Aimee L   1989   Soc.Work, Cobleskill, N. Y.
Darling, Jeffrey   1989   College; farming
Ford, Lisa Marie   1989
Fuessle, Brian   1989
Gebhard, Cindy   1989   R. N.
Grant, Jason Wayne   1989
Gray, Juanita M.   1989   Employe, Hidden Inn
Hait, Christy A.   1989   (O'Donnell) College; R. N.
Hamil, Jerry W.   1989   Bee business employee
Heiseler, Nancy V.   1989   College
Heiseler, Peggy S.   1989   College
Hinkley, Lisa S.   1989
Hopkins, Jennifer R.   1989   College
Hynes, Chris J.   1989   Phone Co.
Jamrozy, Valerie J   1989
Johannsen, Beth A.   1989
Laureanti, Alfred   1989
Liddle, Nancy J.   1989
Mattice, Christopher,   1989   College
Mc Connville, Richard1989
Moscato, Edward C.   1989
Needham, Jamie   1989
O'Neil, Dave   1989
Ormsbee, Brian   1989
Sherwood ChristopherJ1989
Snyder, Barbara J.   1989   Nurse (LPN)
Stahl, Dean,   1989   Eagle Scout
Thorington, Yvonne F.1989   Cook, Hidden Inn
Townsend, James   1989   College
Townsend, Kimberly A1989   College; attorney USD.
Van Aken, Dawn Mary1989
Weidman, Eileen E.   1989

Ballard, Thomas	1990	
Bresee, David	1990	
Cooper, Ernest	1990	B. S, SUNY, Potsdam, N.Y.
Cronk, Robert	1990	Rotarian;Becker's Tire
Davis, Hiram	1990	Minister
Davis, Richard	1990	
Faoro, Kimberly	1990	Rotary Ex. Student to Japan
Faraci, Vincent	1990	
Ferris, Koby	1990	
Ferris, Melinda	1990	(Peters)
Gabborin,Giangiacomo	1990	Exchange Student
Gilham, Geraldine	1990	Loan Advisor/Stamford Bank
Gilham, Janine	1990	EMT St. Peter's Hosp/Cardiac
Greene, Joseph	1990	House manager ARC
Hughes, Janet	1990	
Irwin, William	1990	deceased
Jamrozy, James	1990	Corrections Officer
Kellerhouse, Amy	1990	(Cronk)
Kellerhouse, Rebecca	1990	Bus. Owner, Albany, N. Y.
Kirk, Dennis	1990	College;Morrisville; mech.
Long, William	1990	B.S. Clarkson;MS Civil Eng.
Mc Laughlin, Tina	1990	English Teacher, RCS
Mc Mahon, Timothy	1990	Veteran, Desert Storm
Motic, Esther	1990	
Nealson, Robert	1990	Marine Corp
O'Donnell, James	1990	Rotary; Allen Residential
Proctor, George	1990	Painter
Quackenbush, MaryB	1990	
Reed, William	1990	deceased
Roberts, Billie Jo	1990	
Rowe, Matthew	1990	
Rudolph, Christine	1990	B.A. Education; math teacher
Sauveur, Tami	1990	Delhi Tech. Graduate
Spielman, Keri	1990	(Mazzuca) book kpr,Albany
Stock, Gregory	1990	Store Mgr., Hobart, N.Y.
Stretch, Jennifer	1990	
Suess, Matthew	1990	Landscaping

Adams, Steve	1991	
Baum, Jon	1991	US Air Force
Bussiere, Joseph	1991	
Colliton, Tricia	1991	
Condliffe, John	1991	Veteran
Cumming, Toni	1991	
Darling, Laurie	1991	College; soccer coach
Davis, Cathy	1991	
Dee, Anthony	1991	
Dorosky, Cynthia	1991	SUNY Oneonta; teacher
Farleigh, Steve	1991	
Gebhard, Ann	1991	Grad.DelhiTech;sec. BOCES
Green, Shawn	1991	
Grocholl, Peter	1991	Surveyor; Texas; Veteran
Grocholl, Phillip	1991	Truck Driver
Hamil, John	1991	
Hults, Leonard	1991	Hults Plumbing & Heating
Iacovelli, Joel	1991	Carpenter; Cole & Griffin
Jones, Timothy	1991	Veterinary college
Kuhn, Fredrick	1991	Farmer
Lalosh, Alanna	1991	
Lebowitz, Sharon	1991	
Maduri, Frank	1991	Mechanic
Meade, Joanna	1991	SUNY; guidance counselor
Moore, Courtney	1991	Works @ NY stock exchange
Porter, Damian	1991	Employed NYSEG
Riggi, John	1991	Emp., Big Tree Co. Durham
Robertson, Gary	1991	Owner, cleaning service
Rose, Charles	1991	West Point '95, US Army
Sherwood, David	1991	Morrisville Tech. College
Smith, Elaine	1991	
Snyder, Tricia	1991	(Davis)
Spielman, Michelle	1991	Nurse's Aid, PA
Stafford, Melissa	1991	
Thorington, April	1991	
Tubiolo, Tara Jai	1991	
Wright, Dwayne	1991	Delhi Technical College
Wright, Shannon	1991	Emp Wissahikon Sp. Water

Albano, Rose	1992	
Ballard, Jennifer	1992	
Braly, Amanda	1992	
Brannen, Elizabeth	1992	(Bussiere)
Braunsdorf, Kristine	1992	
Bresee, Christy	1992	Emp., Margaretville Hospital
Clark, Zac	1992	Employee, Z-Man Painting
Cross, Rosanne	1992	
Dalto, Viva	1992	
Doroski, Christopher	1992	
Ely, Duane	1992	Fire Fighter, Florida
Faulkner, Melissa	1992	
Georgakopoulos, A.	1992	
Haroldson, Jesse	1992	Emp.'Kurt Flacks H/Plumb.
Hinkley, Daniel	1992	
Hinkley, Winfield	1992	Air Force; Ford Dealership
Irwin, Edward	1992	Co-Salutatorian
Keith, Alan	1992	
Kirk, Denise	1992	HerkimerColl, Criminal just.
Kuhn, Mary	1992	Valedictorian
Lalosh, Richard	1992	Vol. F'man; Carpenter's/Un.
Laureanti, Cheryl	1992	
Mattice, Daniel	1992	
O'Beirne, Terence	1992	Co-Salutatorian
O'Donnell, Michael	1992	
O'Donnell, Patrick	1992	
Porter, Rebecca	1992	(O'Donnell)SUNY; business
Quackenbush, Sarah	1992	
Riggi, Susan	1992	
Robertson, Brian	1992	
Rose, Sharlein	1992	College graduate
Rowe, Dana	1992	Nurse
Slater, Jennifer	1992	Employee DSS
Sprague, William	1992	Employed, Town of Roxbury
Steenland, Brian	1992	
Weidman, Kristine	1992	
Weidman, Shannon	1992	
Wright, Gregory	1992	

Basile, Eric	1993	Veteran
Baum, Ryan David	1993	Eagle S.; West Point, Army
Carr, Joseph John	1993	Construction
Cooper, Jennifer L	1993	
De Maio, Lawrence	1993	Carpenter's Union
Eignor, Daniel L	1993	
German,Jessica L.	1993	Val'dtn;Wells/Trinity Coll.
Iacovelli, Jason C.	1993	
Jackson, Heather D.	1993	
Jones, James K.	1993	Co-Salutatorian; Veteran
Liberatore, Jerome L.	1993	College, physical therapy
Madero, Gary	1993	
Maxim, Patricia J.	1993	(Madero)
McCracken, James R.	1993	Eagle S;B.SF'kln Pierce U
Needham, Tara N.	1993	
Pebler, Wayne R, II	1993	SUNY, Postdam
Petry, William A, III	1993	
Proctor, James E.	1993	B. S. S . Rose
Robillard, Teresa Kay	1993	
Rudolph, Kevin M.	1993	Co-Sal'tn;M.S.PhysicalTher.
Sandler, Scott J.	1993	RCS bus driver
Snow, Eric L.	1993	
Trahan, Jason J.	1993	Golf Pro. (Florida, Windham)
Tucker, Carl A.	1993	Surveyor
Zeiset, Andru C.	1993	

Albano, Eric	1994	Golf course manager
Brannen, Emily	1994	
Dunnigan, Charles	1994	
Fairbairn, Christopher	1994	
Faoro, Andrea	1994	Valedictorian
Faulkner, Kim	1994	Accounting co. employee
Fox, Thomas	1994	College graduate
Georgakapoulos, A.	1994	
Kellerhouse, James	1994	Alb. Acd'my/Boys; Dir/Fund.
Lalosh, Michael, III	1994	
Lettieri, David	1994	
Long, Julie	1994	Sal'tn;BS.SHampt'MS; m/sci.
McMahon, Erin	1994	
Meade, Jessica	1994	SUNY,Cortland; tch. Bronx
Morse, Wendy Sue	1994	
Pearsall, Jennifer	1994	
Proctor, Stacey	1994	(Walker); Concordia College
Rashap, Raven	1994	
Sanford, Robyn	1994	
Schaefer, Sandra	1994	
Schwarz, Kurt	1994	Veteran
Steenland, Heather	1994	
Tobin, Daryl	1994	
Treski, Desire'	1994	
Walker, Matthew	1994	Carpenter(early Ploutz res)

Albano, Jody	1995	Teacher, BOCES
Barraclough, Daniel	1995	Val'dtn;BS/MSEd.Cornell
Basile, Karyn	1995	(Lalosh)
Boyle, Steve	1995	Emp, Village Square Takeout
Glorieux, Jean-Baptise	1995	
Grounds, Richard, Jr.	1995	Sal'tn; B.S. St. Rose; teacher
Kellerhouse,Benjamin	1995	Employee, Daitch Creamery
Maduri, Johanna	1995	
Mattice, Mark	1995	A.S. Alfred Univ.
McCracken, Joseph	1995	E.Scout;B.S.F.PierceU;DEC
Morales, Lisa	1995	
Osborn, Deanna	1995	Employee; Tysco Mallinckrodt
Pebler, Charlie	1995	SUNYMorrisville/Delhi, NY
Rohacevich, Joseph	1995	
Spielman, Heather	1995	

Ballard, Michelle	1996	SUNY Oneonta
Bevins, Nathan	1996	
Brannen, Carol	1996	
Braunsdorf, B.J.	1996	Veteran
Bush, Melissa	1996	
Ciaravino, Michael	1996	Mechanic
Fox, Maureen	1996	B.S. Sienna College, English
Gordon, Bobbi-Jo	1996	R.N. B.A.Syracuse; hospital
Haroldson, Alice	1996	Sal'tn/Hartwick Coll/tch
Krom, Melissa	1996	
Lalosh, Jacqueline	1996	B.S.SUNY Oneonta, H.Ecol.
Lupian, Rafael	1996	
Mc Ginnis, Amy	1996	B.S. Franklin Pierce; teacher
Needham, Tanya	1996	Val'dtn;Skidmore;Pre-med
Proctor, Mary	1996	B.S. St. Rose; advertising
Robertson, Lisa	1996	(George)
Rudolph, Laurie	1996	M.S. Physical Therapist
Slater, Amy	1996	Beautician, Grand Gorge, NY
Snyder, Evette	1996	BS/SUNY;MS RPI;Sci.Tch
Stafford, Michael, II	1996	N.Y. Police Dept.
Tucker, Michael	1996	
Wilson, Robert	1996	
Zorda, Brian	1996	B.S. Siena College
Zorda, Joseph	1996	B.S. Syracuse University

Albano, Marc	1997	Farming
Biruk, David	1997	Salutatorian
Briggs, Jason	1997	
Burroughs, Joshua	1997	Teacher assistant NCOC
Carr, David	1997	
Carr, Michael	1997	Lift Operator, Drogen's
Cook, Christopher	1997	Eagle Scout; Wakeforest
Donnelly, Joe	1997	
Hoskins, Don	1997	
Irwin, Sarah	1997	
Kellerhouse, Gino	1997	EagleS.Val'dtn;Cl'son; GE
Krom, Earl, Jr.	1997	B.S. Cornell, Wildlife Mgt.
Lupian, Jesus	1997	
Lyke, Jediah	1997	
McLaughlin, Erick	1997	NYS PD Acad/Fire & Safety
Myers, Aaron	1997	
Oakley, Bob	1997	Veteran, Marines
Pebler, Elizabeth	1997	B.S. SUNY, Plattsburg
Sass, Heidi	1997	
Shultis, Chris	1997	RCS, custodian
Siedzieniewski, Diana	1997	to Arizona
Slater, Steve	1997	
Slauson, Robert, Jr.	1997	Locally employed
Walsh, Jason	1997	
Wayman, Ellie	1997	
Winnie, Kelli	1997	BS SUNY, Oneonta;H. Ecol.
Zambri, Brad	1997	Heavy Equip/Op;F/Safety
Zeiset, Matthew	1997	Salutatorian; Hartwick Coll.

Braunsdorf, Thomas	1998	Chef;
Di Giovanna, Elena	1998	La Salle University
Di Giovanna, Josephina	1998	College of St. Rose; Teacher
Finch, Kyle	1998	
Kellerhouse, Kyle	1998	Eagle S. SUNY Fredonia;tch.
Mahnken, Jessica	1998	Employee T. Bar Saloon
Major, Tanya	1998	SUNY Oneonta, N.Y.
Morse, Cynthia	1998	
Mudge, Jason	1998	Veteran
O'Brien, Kristopher	1998	
Orr, Joseph	1998	
Perazone, Lisa	1998	Val'dtn;Flbr't;Oxford /StJos
Roberts, Jeremiah	1998	Electricians Ass't.
Roe, Kimberly	1998	
Rossman, Jason	1998	Sal'tn;EagleS.CantonU ShipB
Sass, Richard, Jr.	1998	Culinary school
Schuman, Andrew	1998	
Serrie, Joseph	1998	Drexel Univ; Army ROTC
Stone, Gideon	1998	
Trahan, Stephani	1998	Suny Oneonta 98-99 to NYC
Wojciechowski, Kelly	1998	
Zafra, Marie	1998	
Zeiset, Krysta	1998	Val'dtn; Emerson C; Acting

Ballard, Joshua	1999	Electricians assistant
Barraclough, Brian	1999	Syracuse U; pol. science.
Berrio, Jessica	1999	Major/Marine Biology
Biruk, Archie	1999	Auto mechanic
Blaufox, Margaret R.	1999	
Carrol, Christine	1999	Sal'tn; Syracuse/Cortland
Davis, Julie	1999	Bank teller, Stamford, N. Y.
Howell, Kimberly	1999	
Kirk, Clifton Jr.	1999	
Lalosh, Gregory	1999	OnonadagaComm.Coll;const
Lupian, Guadalupe	1999	(O'Brien)
Major, Tricia L.	1999	Penn View Coll; Elem. Ed.
Martell, Nicholette	1999	
Miccio, Karina	1999	Art Major; Binghamton
Mudge, Rebecca	1999	to Arizona
Oakley, Melissa	1999	Hartwick Coll, Oneonta, NY
Raeder, Nichola	1999	Eagle Scout (20)
Regan, Melissa	1999	
Sanford, Tracy	1999	SUNY Oneonta
Sass, Robert	1999	Employed locally
Schuman, Catherie	1999	
Schwartz, Kyle	1999	
Serrie, Jennifer	1999	Valedictorian; Elmira Coll.
Sherwood, Rachel	1999	Niagara University
Stock, Travis	1999	
Todd, John	1999	Marines
Walker, Alec	1999	Graphic Design;Manhattan
Walker, Andrew	1999	BinghamtonU/Eng/ Phil'phy
Zorda, Christopher	1999	Marist College

Albanese, Gabriel J,II	2000	Fulton Montgomery Comm.C
Ballard, Brianne	2000	Niagara Univ.
Cuttita, Elizabeth	2000	Marist College
De Maio, Jason	2000	
DuMond, Jason	2000	U. S. Army
Fersch, Gabriel	2000	Salutatorian; Alfred Univ.
Gruosso, Joseph	2000	Hunter Mountain
Hinkley, Danielle	2000	Physical Therapy NYC
Holloway, Korey	2000	
Hults, Jenny	2000	
Hults, William	2000	Substitute teacher
Kellerhouse, Katrina	2000	SUNY Oswego
Liberatore, Alana	2000	SUNY, Oneonta, N.Y.
Mc Ginnis, Jennifer	2000	
Mead, Michelle	2000	
Morse, Adam	2000	
Murray, Sabrina	2000	(Todd)
Myers, Jolene	2000	
Palmer, Robert	2000	WeldingSch; Schenectady
Parks, Helen	2000	
Perazone, Tracy	2000	Val'dtn; Colgate Pre-Med.
Perry, Melissa	2000	
Pierce, Ren	2000	
Pinto, Adriana	2000	Exchange Student; Mexico
Porter, Whitney	2000	Canisius College
Roe, Ashley	2000	
Rohacevich,Jonathan	2000	Employed Hunter Mountain
Rose, Samuel	2000	SUNY, Cortland
Schuman, Elizabeth	2000	SUNY, Oneonta, El. Ed.
Snyder, Tamara	2000	Mercyhurst Coll, PA; music
Tucker, John	2000	Employed Hunter Mountain
Williams, Melanie	2000	Cedar Crest College
Zafra, Luis	2000	

PART IV

Alphabetized Listing RCS Graduates 1901-2000

ROXBURY CENTRAL SCHOOL
GRADUATES 1901 - 2000   (alphabetized)

Acampa, Gerard	1978	
Adams, Steve	1991	
Aikman, Dorothy E.	1926	
Aikman, Pauline	1921	
Albanese, Gabriel J,II	2000	Fulton Montgomery Comm.C
Albano, Eric	1994	Golf course manager
Albano, Frank V.	1987	Mrg. Albano Farms Stamford
Albano, Jody	1995	Teacher, BOCES
Albano, Marc	1997	Farming
Albano, Rose	1992	
Alberti, Paul R.	1919	
Allen, J. Frances	1934	PhD.IchthyologyFedGov./WaterPoll'
Allen, Lochie J.	1934	Professor (Allen sisters @ Rox 1 yr)
Ames, Betty	1934	Nurse
Ames, Helen	1934	College
Andre, Carole	1964	College
Andre, Sandra	1963	Salutatorian, college
Andre, Suzanne	1966	College
Andrus, Olive E.	1909	Piano;sing' lessons, Russell SageColl.
Archibald, Andy	1951	Salutatorian
Archibald, Forrest E.	1939	Veteran W.W. II
Archibald, Virginia	1939	
Aulino, Joseph	1983	Real Estate, Rotarian
Aulino, Rosanne	1980	
Avery, Vivian	1956	Photography Business
Axelsen, Krista Anne	1989	
Baer, Wayne Howarth	1970	Vet. Vietnam; Golf Course Maint.
Baker, Lena	1902	Teacher
Baker, Lola	1966	Music teacher
Balcom, Debra E.	1973	
Balcom, Julie	1974	
Balcom, Mary F.E.	1980	
Balcom, Michael F.	1975	

Balcom, Rosemary F. 1977
Balcom, William E   1980
Ballard, Brianne   2000   Niagara Univ.
Ballard, Charles J.   1969
Ballard, Daniel J.   1971   Veteran Vietnam
Ballard, David William 1985
Ballard, Eleanor   1960
Ballard, Ernest   1972
Ballard, Ethel   1962
Ballard, Eva M.   1969

Ballard, Hazel M.   1907   Val'dtn;classpres.;HStch;Baldwin,NY
Ballard, Inez   1932   Deputy town clerk, Roxbury
Ballard, James R.   1971   Valedictorian, Vet. RCS custodian
Ballard, Jennifer   1992
Ballard, Jon   1974
Ballard, Joseph P.   1976
Ballard, Joshua   1999   Electricians assistant
Ballard, Joyce N.   1965
Ballard, Karen Sue   1989
Ballard, Kathy   1970
Ballard, Kevin R.   1976   Self Emp'Painting, Landscaping
Ballard, Marilyn   1964
Ballard, Michelle   1996   SUNY Oneonta
Ballard, Paul   1948   Vet.W.W II; bee/keeper (Apiarist)
Ballard, Ronald   1948   Veteran Korean, local historian
Ballard, Susan   1966
Ballard, Thomas   1990
Ballard, Violet E.   1912
Ballard, William   1935
Banks, Dorothy G   1981
Barber, Elizabeth   1925
Barber, Mildred Efie   1923   Telephone Co, Albany, NY.
Barraclough, Brian   1999   Syracuse U; pol. science.
Barraclough, Daniel   1995   Val'dtn;BS/MSEd.Cornell
Barrett, D. Belle   1910   Insurance
Bartley, Bernard   1924   NYS State Trooper
Bartley, Dorcas   1918   Language teacher
Barton, Karen M.   1977

Basile, Eric   1993   Veteran

Basile, Karyn   1995   (Lalosh)
Bauer, Marion   1946   Nurse

Baum, Edward	1906	
Baum, Jon	1991	US Air Force
Baum, Leland M.	1908	Valedictorian, school principal
Baum, Ryan David	1993	Eagle S.; West Point, Army
Beaver, Allison M.	1987	
Bellows, Anna M.	1918	
Bellows, Elizabeth R.	1927	
Bellows, Hilto	1942	Eagle Scout, Veteran; Army
Bellows, Janis	1942	Salutatorian
Bellows, Luella	1921	Teacher
Bellows, Mary	1916	Teacher, Syracuse
Bellows, Muriel	1937	Nurse
Bellows, Nelson	1943	Veteran W.W. II
Bennett, Diane Lynn	1987	
Bennett, Charles S.	1986	
Bergmann, Christine	1975	
Bergmann, George	1982	
Bergmann, James C.	1975	
Bergmann, Keith	1978	
Bergmann, Thomas	1970	
Bergmann, Timothy	1972	
Bergmann, William	1972	
Berrio, Jessica	1999	Major/Marine Biology
Berry, Lillian	1920	
Berryman, Robert	1935	
Bevins, Nathan	1996	
Bianco, Joann K.	1988	
Bianco, Mary E.	1984	
Biruk, Archie	1999	Auto mechanic
Biruk, David	1997	Salutatorian
Biruk, John	1961	
Biruk, John W.	1985	
Biruk, Minnie	1943	Valedictorian
Biruk, Olga	1933	Salutatorian
Biruk, Sophie	1937	
Biruk, Susanna	1969	
Biruk, Thomas M.	1986	SUNY,Morris.;El.Eng;comp.
Blakeslee, Dawn M.	1976	
Blaufox, Margaret R.	1999	
Blodgett, John	1937	Eagle Scout
Blodgett, Marion	1937	Veteran W.W. II, Eagle Scout
Blythe, Marvin Russell	1940	WWII;Sal'tn;EagleS.;auth;math'n

Name	Year	Notes
Blythe, Pauline M.	1918	Teacher, Oneonta Normal
Blythe, Rudolph	1926	Prof:Phar'cy;Pioneer;time/rels/med.
Boerem, Jeanne	1955	
Bolger, Anne	1972	
Bolger, John T.	1977	Contractor, B & B Construction.
Bookhout, C. May	1912	Lay preacher; teacher
Bookhout, Earl	1927	Oneonta Normal/accident
Bookhout, Elmer	1935	Class president; stone mason
Bookhout, Gregg D.	1969	Valedictorian; deceased
Bookhout, Jane Arna	1965	Valed'tn; SUNY;Postdam,tch,music
Bookhout, Lynn	1925	Farmer, magazine editor
Bookhout, Marion	1929	Sal'tn; Rotarian,WWII;HartwickColl.
Bookhout, Marjorie	1929	
Bookhout, Nora	1934	
Bookout, Tallman C.	1908	Sal'tn;ClassPres;Prin.Rox1918-20
Booth, Frank	1904	WWI;Rot';Cut'ryMfg;coll/exp/RCS.
Bouchey, Eva K.	1917	
Bouton, Burrett B.	1920	Class pres; Indiana Boys School
Bouton, Charles W.	1912	Farmer, wagon shop business
Bouton, Donald	1951	Veteran
Bouton, Frank	1938	Class Pres;WWII,E.Scout,coll;Min'st
Bouton, James M.	1935	Rotarian, E. Scout;Lt.Col Univ./Ala.
Bouton, Margaret E.	1939	Teacher;grad. Univ. of Maryland
Bouton, Marjorie	1925	College;PhysicalTherapist,Wash.DC.
Bouton, Richard	1947	Vet; farmer; RCS Bd. of Education
Bouton, Ruth	1940	Class Pres; Veteran.; Army Nurse
Boyle, John T	1985	Teacher
Boyle, Steve	1995	Emp, Village Square Takeout
Bradley, Timothy P.	1964	
Brady, Anna	1930	Medical assistant
Brady, George	1940	WW II, author, agriculture issues
Brady, Howard	1933	Veteran W.W. II
Brady, Kenneth	1929	Veteran W.W. II; General Electric
Brady, Lillian	1937	Secretary
Brady, Richard	1935	Veteran W.W. II
Brady, Virginia	1943	
Brainard, Lisa M.	1984	(Faraci) SUNY, Teacher
Brainerd, Kelly L.	1984	
Brainerd, Todd	1981	deceasesd
Brainerd, Wayne M.	1976	Lt. Col. Army CMOC
Braly, Amanda	1992	
Brandow, Edmund	1947	Barber

<u>Brandow, George</u>	1931	Val'dtn;WWII;Prof.Agr/Econ;Penn.St
Brandow, Joh	1935	Veteran W.W. II, Eastman Kodak
Brandow, Marian	1935	(Bookhout)
Brandow, Robert	1934	Class president; Lt. Col. Army
Brannen, Carol	1996	
Brannen, Elizabeth	1992	(Bussiere)
Brannen, Emily	1994	
Brannen, Steve	1985	Own business/Florida
Braunsdorf, B.J.	1996	Veteran
Braunsdorf, Kristine	1992	
Braunsdorf, Thomas	1998	Chef;
Brennan, Agnes M.	1915	
Bresee, Christy	1992	Emp., Margaretville Hospital
Bresee, David	1990	
Bresee, Erika Sue	1986	(Thetford)Nurse Fox Hosp.
Briggs, Jason	1997	
Brittain, Dale	1989	
Brower, George	1944	Vet.W.W.II, college; G.E.electronics
Brower, Joan	1953	Employee, Blue Cross/Blue Shield
Brower, Nancy	1950	
Brower, Phillip	1948	Veteran Korean
Brower, Steve A.	1983	
Brown, George E.	1970	
Brown, William	1967	deceased
Brownell, Orville	1921	Class president; truck driver
Bruen, Deidre A.	1984	
Bruen, Kristen A.	1989	
Bubach, Eugene W.	1979	Carpenter
Bubach, John	1957	
Bubach, John L.	1977	Own excavation co; Trl Park
Bubach, Patricia A.	1980	Dr. of Chiropractic
Bubach, Susan	1978	Teacher
Buccheri, Dean	1986	
Buccheri, Michael.	1989	College
Buel, Elaine Fae	1968	(Burroughs)
Bullock, Shelly L.	1983	
Bullock, Sherry Lynn	1981	
Bullock, Stanley	1986	
Burroughs, Angie	1931	Pres. Burroughs Society
Burroughs, Debora M.	1979	
Burroughs, John	1982	Well driller, PA.
Burroughs, Joshua	1997	Teacher assistant NCOC

Name	Year	Notes
Bush, Melissa	1996	
Buss, Tina	1986	
Bussiere, George	1987	
Bussiere, Joseph	1991	
Bussiere, Josie	1988	Account Clerk, RCS
Bussy, Clyde E.	1970	
Bussy, Dennis Ernest	1968	
Bussy, Donna	1978	
Bussy, Jerry	1989	Veteran; golf course mgr.
Bussy, Jerry I.	1965	
Bussy, Kimberly Ann	1986	Salut.; bus. school; ex. Sec.
Bussy, Leon	1954	Veteran
Buswell, Franklin E.	1926	Telephone operator, NYC.
Cable, James	1956	
Cammer, Catherine	1988	B. A, Albany State
Cammer, Elaine	1964	
Cammer, Helen	1955	Banking
Cammer, Jane	1966	(Schuman) Teacher
Cammer, Jean	1954	College
Cammer, Larry	1963	
Cammer, Marie	1953	
Cammer, Mark L.	1982	Carpenter
Cammer, Robert	1960	Veteran Vietnam
Cammer, Steve R.	1982	Carpenter
Campone, James A, Jr.	1981	
Cantwell, Dorothy	1928	Banker
Cantwell, Grace	1921	
Cantwell, James	1938	POW;surv' Bataan/death/m'chWWII
Cantwell, Ralph	1931	Farmer
Cantwell, Russell	1931	College - education
Cantwell, Thomas E.	1923	Farmer
Cantwell, Winifred	1928	Nurse
Carmeli, Anthony J.	1980	SUNY Oneonta,Syr.Coll.Forestry
Carmeli, Margaret	1975	SUNYOne'ta;Rutger'sUniv/hsp/adm.
Carol, David	1971	
Carr, David	1997	
Carr, David C.	1977	
Carr, Joseph	1965	Veteran; Joe's Backhoe Service
Carr, Joseph John	1993	Construction
Carr, Michael	1997	Lift Operator, Drogen's
Carr, Robert P.	1979	
Carr, Rosemarie P.	1979	

Carrol, Christine	1999	Sal'tn; Syracuse/Cortland
Carter, Fredrick	1931	Doctor
Cartier, Michael	1983	
Cartwright, Anna	1902	
Cartwright, Arnorld	1935	Farmer
Cartwright, Barbara	1962	
Cartwright, Carol	1963	Valedictorian
Cartwright, Charles	1981	
Cartwright, Howard	1927	Class president; farmer
Cartwright, Kennie C.	1980	Owner, Cartwright Construction Co.
Cartwright, Leta	1950	Secretary
Cartwright, Robert	1954	Veteran Vietnam
Cartwright, Russell	1985	Own business, Colorado
Cartwright, Steve	1966	Veteran Vietnam
Case, Mary J.	1935	(Morse)
Caswell, Adelbert	1953	
Caswell, Bruce	1924	Sal'tn;fire/chief;Scout M'st;Nat'ist
Caswell, Francis	1942	Veteran W.W. II
Caswell, Phil	1950	CornellUnivLt.ColArmy, Naturalist
Caswell, Thelma	1942	
Catabiano, Anthony P.	1984	
Cattanco, Martha	1967	Exchange Student
Cerullo, Darlene H.	1982	Valedictorian
Chambers, Patricia A.	1980	
Chambers, William T	1977	
Chase, Alice	1910	
Chase, George D.	1919	Civil Engineer
Chow, Alane	1985	Hair Dresser
Christian, Elwood	1955	
Christian, Freda	1951	Employee, So. Kortright School
Christian, Raymond	1953	Veteran
Ciaravino, Bryan M.	1983	
Ciaravino, Lena	1946	Farmer; Kirkside food service
Ciaravino, Michael	1996	Mechanic
Clapp, Henry S.	1926	Salutatorian; Horticulture
Clapp, Roger Quay	1923	Prof. Horticulture, Univ of Maine
Clark, Harry M	1907	Sal'tn,auth,eng'r;F'st Story/Whale
Clark, Monica	1979	
Clark, Richard	1972	
Clark, Roxanne	1972	
Clark, Zac	1992	Employee, Z-Man Painting
Cleveland, Jessica	1947	College

Cole, Eleanor	1915	Teacher, Oneonta
Cole, Karen	1971	
Cole, Lynn	1966	
Cole, Robert B.	1976	Vet; Owner Cole & Griffin Const.
Collins, Diane	1955	Salutatorian
Collins, Stephen	1958	College
Colliton, Tricia	1991	
Colonna, Peter	1941	
Condliffe, David	1971	Woodworker
Condliffe, John	1991	Veteran
Condliffe, Sharon	1981	Veteran
Cone, Tammy L.	1981	
Constable, Paul	1949	Veteran
Constable, Thelma	1938	
Cook, Christopher	1997	Eagle Scout; Wakeforest
Cooper, Ernest	1990	B. S, SUNY, Potsdam, N.Y.
Cooper, Gary	1978	Roxbury business man
Cooper, Jennifer L	1993	
Cooper, Susan J.	1980	
Corbin, Lena	1920	Teacher, Oneonta Normal
Corum, Nellie	1945	
Coss, Donna	1984	
Cowan, David D.	1982	Contractor
Cower, Joe	1957	Val'dtn, college, Eagle Scout
Cower, Kenneth	1929	Rotarian, electrician, merchant
Cox, David T.	1986	Vet.Mar/tech/own/cons/Co
Cox, Jim	1989	(Caltabiano)Sec/Best Buy
Cox, William A, III	1980	Vet;Owner,DeliverySys.(Caltabiano)
Craft, Arline	1928	Class president
Creamer, Ruth	1915	Teacher
Cronk, Birdella	1926	Class pres.;tele' oper;Hobart, NY.
Cronk, Doug	1987	Carpenter
Cronk, Herbert R.	1919	Civil Engineer
Cronk, James	1913	Class President; Veteran W.W.I
Cronk, James	1960	Vet. Vietnam,Valedictorian;Marine
Cronk, Lillian	1914	Organist, Gould Church
Cronk, Mabel F.	1912	Salutatorian, teacher, N.J.
Cronk, Pearl Anne	1923	Salutatorian
Cronk, Robert	1990	Rotarian;Becker's Tire
Cronk, Vivian	1929	
Cross, Rosanne	1992	
Cumming, Aimee Lyn	1989	Soc.Work, Cobleskill, N. Y.

Cumming, Toni	1991	
Curtin, Theresa	1985	
Cuttita, Elizabeth	2000	Marist College
Dalto, Viva	1992	
Darham, Sidney	1932	
Darling, Jeffrey	1989	College; farming
Darling, Laurie	1991	College; soccer coach
Davidson, Dorothy	1920	Valedictorian; teacher
Davidson, John	1922	Valedictorian
Davies, Daniel J.	1970	
Davies, Kris	1973	
Davis, Alan C.	1988	RCS custodian
Davis, Arnold C, Jr.	1983	Veteran
Davis, Carl L.	1939	
Davis, Cathy	1991	
Davis, Harold S.	1970	Veteran; Contractor/Nuclear
Davis, Henry	1947	
Davis, Hiram	1990	Minister
Davis, Idella	1952	
Davis, Judy	1983	
Davis, Julie	1999	Bank teller, Stamford, N. Y.
Davis, Michael A.	1984	Veteran, Desert Storm
Davis, Richard	1990	
Davis, Ruth	1938	
Davis, Veronica J.	1983	
Day, Sharon Ellen	1965	
De Maio, Jason	2000	
De Maio, Lawrence	1993	Carpenter's Union
De Maroney, James A	1979	Veteran
Decker, Stanley	1957	Veteran Vietnam
Decker, William	1955	
Dee, Anthony	1991	
Deluca, Anthony E.	1977	
Demonie, Alice	1958	
Demonie, Raymond	1952	Changed name to Higgins
Dent, Robin L	1979	
DeSilva, Marilyn	1952	
DeSilva, Ronald	1951	Class president; Veteran
Destefianis, Mario T.	1976	
Di Giovanna, Elena	1998	La Salle University
Di GiovannaJosephina	1998	College of St. Rose; Teacher
Dilello, Ricky M.	1977	deceased

Diserens, Alain	1988	Ex. Student, Switzerland
Dixon, Marion E.	1919	Teacher
Donnelly, Joe	1997	
Donnelly, Kimberly A	1985	Nurse
Donnelly, Robert	1988	
Doroski, Christopher	1992	
Dorosky, Cynthia	1991	SUNY Oneonta; teacher
Dorrance, Daniel	1959	Veteran
Dorrance, Daniel A.II	1979	Veteran, Marine Corp
Dorrance, Dawn Marie	1981	Veteran
Dorrance, Deanna	1963	Wal-Mart supervisor
Dorrance, Michael A.	1981	Veteran
Draffen, Etta	1929	Nurse
Draffen, Harold	1916	Vet. WW I, proprietor, gen. store
Dudley, William M.	1913	Val'dtn; Vet.W.W.I; Rox.1st pilot
Dugan, Elizabeth	1928	Teacher
Dugan, Frederick	1938	Veteran W.W. II
Dugan, Genevieve	1932	Salutatorian
Dugan, George	1932	Veteran W.W. II
Dugan, Joan	1957	Class president, nurse
Dugan, John H.	1934	Farmer
Dugan, Leona	1931	
Dugan, Patricia	1966	
Dugan, Robert	1959	Vet.Vietnam, IBM, Auburn Univ.
DuMond, Donna D.	1979	
DuMond, Gary	1955	
DuMond, Jason	2000	U. S. Army
Dunham, Bret C.	1981	
Dunham, Rik	1982	Surveyor; Utah
Dunnigan, Charles	1994	
Dwyer, Donna M.	1975	Salutatorian
Dwyer, Thomas J.	1973	
Easley, Hazel	1914	Teacher, Oneonta
Echeverra, Juan C.	1974	
Edlam, Lorraine	1960	
Edsall, Laura	1910	Teacher, Margaretville, NY.
Edsall, Preston W.	1919	Val'dtn;PhD.PrinU;Pol.sci/UNC
Eignor, Amy	1987	
Eignor, Christie	1962	Salutatorian
Eignor, Daniel L	1993	
Eignor, Gladys M.	1919	
Eignor, Laurie	1981	

Eignor, Lloyd	1939	Farmer
Eignor, Merry Lee	1965	
Eignor, Nancy	1964	Valedictorian, teacher
Eignor, Robert K.	1974	
Eignor, Sally C.	1971	
Eisele, Charles	1946	Veteran Korean
Eisele, James	1949	Veteran W.W. II
Eisele, Joseph	1954	Valedictorian
Elflein, Charles E.	1975	
Elflein, Ruth A.	1976	
Ellis, Guy	1947	College
Ely, Dennis I.	1988	Zaack Clark Painting
Ely, Duane	1992	Fire Fighter, Florida
Ely, Keith W.	1983	
Enderlin, Barbara	1954	Salutatorian, college, teacher
Enderlin, Florence	1913	Salutatorian
Enderlin, Fred W.	1909	Valedictorian, Class Pres; Grocer
Enderlin, Jean	1959	College, secretary
Enderlin, Joan	1957	College, secretary
Enderlin, Leighton	1927	Rotarian, hardware store proprietor
Enderlin, Mabel	1901	
Enderlin, Stephen	1954	R.P.I.; engineer
Endress, MaryScudder	1902	
Ennist, Helen	1924	Valedictorian; stenographer
Erway, Sandra	1967	
Etts, Jodi L.	1987	deceasesd
Etts, Judy	1958	
Etts, Kenneth S.	1955	Veteran
Etts, Ricky A.	1979	Veteran
Etts, Terry L.	1983	
Everett, Barbara A.	1975	
Everett, Bruce, Jr.	1974	Veteran, Rotarian, refrigeration
Fairbairn, Christopher	1994	
Fane, William J.	1985	
Fanning, Mary Ruth	1937	Valedictorian
Fanning, Natalie	1943	Teacher
Faoro, Andrea	1994	Valedictorian
Faoro, Jill Marie	1987	Rotary Exchange Stdt; Japan
Faoro, Kimberly	1990	Rotary Ex. Student to Japan
Faraci, Charles	1947	Farmer; contractor
Faraci, Gary C.	1981	Siding business
Faraci, John C.	1939	Farmer

Faraci, Sue A.	1979	Salut'tan;RCS preschool tch
Faraci, Thomas	1985	SUNY Cortland; teacher
Faraci, Vincent	1990	
Farleigh, Joseph C.	1980	Rotarian
Farleigh, Steve	1991	
Farnum, Christopher	1982	N.Y. State Edu Department
Farnum, Kathleen A.	1984	Salutatorian; Teacher
Farnum, Shawn M.	1982	Painter, decorator
Faulkner, Kim	1994	Accounting Co. employee
Faulkner, Melissa	1992	
Faulkner, Mildred	1924	Class president
Ferris, Kevin S.	1986	
Ferris, Koby	1990	
Ferris, Melinda	1990	(Peters)
Ferris, Penny J.	1988	Veteran, Desert Storm
Fersch, Gabriel	2000	Salutatorian; Alfred Univ.
Finch, Alberta	1952	
Finch, Betsy	1974	
Finch, Bonnie	1980	
Finch, Catherine	1944	L.P. Nurse
Finch, Cindy L.	1982	Veteran
Finch, Cleveland	1940	Eagle Scout
Finch, Daniel J	1969	Pastor
Finch, Dorothy	1934	(Cower)
Finch, Douglas C.	1971	Veteran Vietnam
Finch, Duane	1976	Oswego SUNY graduate, teacher
Finch, Eric	1969	Veteran Vietnam
Finch, Esther	1946	Val'dtn;RCS sec,acc'nt clerk;reporter
Finch, Glenn	1951	Veteran Vietnam
Finch, Hazel I.	1939	
Finch, Joy L.	1983	
Finch, Kristen L.	1973	Salutatorian
Finch, Kyle	1998	
Finch, Laurel E	1977	
Finch, Martin P.	1970	Veteran Vietnam
Finch, Nicholas L.	1983	Excavator
Finch, Phillip	1948	Veteran Korean, escavator
Finch, Sandra	1964	
Finch, Sheryl A.	1976	
Finch, Stephen	1978	Business man
Finch, Wayne G.	1980	Veteran
Finch, William R.	1974	Rotarian

Flachs, Frank A.	1975	Business man
Flachs, Kurt J.	1977	Plumbing business
Flachs, Lisa	1978	Valdtn;MS,Soc.Work;WorldT.Ct.9/11
Flachs, Regina	1974	Co-Owner, Cole & Griffin Const.
Flachs, Susan A.	1976	(Cole) LTA, RCS
Flaherty, Joseph	1968	Veteran Vietnam
Ford, Ellen	1971	
Ford, John W.	1973	
Ford, Lisa Marie	1989	
Ford, Merwin	1943	Gas Co.
Ford, Sally A.	1974	
Ford, Susan J.	1976	
Foster, Naomi	1950	
Fox, Maureen	1996	B.S. Sienna College, English
Fox, Thomas	1994	College graduate
Fredenburgh, Harry	1929	Veteran;Helen Shepard s'ship
Fredenburgh, Ida	1925	
Fredenburgh, Paul	1932	Veteran W.W. II
Frevert, Christine	1966	
Frevert, Gail	1967	Nurse
Frevert, Theresa A.	1969	Nurse, hospital administration
Fuessle, Brian	1989	
Fuller, Dora	1958	Salutatorian; banking
Fuller, Elsie L	1927	
Furman, Eleanor	1938	
Furman, Kenneth	1983	
Furman, Kevin J.	1981	
Furman, Noreen	1968	
Furman, Noreen Hait	1963	
Fusscas, Anita	1957	
Fusscas, Diane	1956	Class president
Fusscas, Peter	1959	Vet, Vietnam;CEO/LockTitleCo.
Gaarn, Carol	1942	
Gaarn, Edna	1938	(Morse) Valedictorian
Gabborin,Giangiacomo	1990	Exchange Student
Gaines, Nancy	1961	Craft shop propriator
Gaines, Virginia	1955	College
Gardner Christopher	1982	Newspaper photographer
Gardner, Page C.	1987	
Gebhard, Ann	1991	Grad.DelhiTech;sec.BOCES
Gebhard, Cindy	1989	R. N.
Gebhard, Michelle	1987	(Pucsci)

Gelner, Dorothy	1937	(Griffin)Salutatorian;teacher
Georgakapoulos, A.	1994	
Georgakopoulos,Anasta	1992	
George, Dennis	1982	
George, Evon	1962	Valedictorian
George, Floyd Arthur	1965	Veteran Vietnam
George, Laura	1956	
George, Leslie J.	1972	
George, Margaret R.	1970	Lawyer
George, Marshall W.	1965	
George, Mary	1967	
George, Neva	1973	
Gerken, George	1954	
Gerken, Helen Ann	1964	
Gerken, Marlene	1949	
German Anthony P.	1977	Lt. Col.NYAir Nat'al Guard Res.
German, Bertha	1947	
German, Bruce	1940	Farmer
German, Charles	1943	Class president; Vet. W.W II
German, Charles R.	1969	Teacher, RCS
German, Chris	1979	Vet. Certified Orthotist/Prosthetist.
German, Christine M.	1977	
German, Cynthia L.	1971	
German, Jennifer L.	1988	U. S. Postal worker
German, Jessica L.	1993	Val'dtn;Wells/Trinity Coll.
German, Judy	1957	Beautician
German, Lorraine	1967	P O employee
German, Neil D.	1981	Employee, Town of Roxbury
German, Timothy R.	1979	Veteran
Gerome, Hazel	1930	
Giacci, David V.	1977	
Giacci, Gary D.	1977	
Giacci, Steve C.	1982	
Giacomo, James	1967	deceased
Gibbs, Richard	1966	Veteran Vietnam
Gile, James D.	1975	Eagle Scout
Gile, Margie	1967	Sal'tn;tch;SUNY,Oswego;Phys/Ther.
Gile, Steven E.	1970	E.Scout;SUNYCobl'sklAlbSt;syst/anal
Gilham, Edith A.	1973	Mountainside Res. Ctr/cook
Gilham, Geraldine	1990	Loan Advisor/Stamford Bank
Gilham, Janine	1990	EMT St. Peter's Hosp/Cardiac
Gilham, Sharon	1967	Wildlife rehababilator

Gilham, William R.	1972	B. G. Construction, NC.
Glorieux, Jean-Baptise	1995	
Gockel, Dawn M.	1984	
Gockel, Dorothy	1934	Telephone operator
Gockel, Holly J.	1982	R. N. Prattsville Health Ctr
Gockel, Joanne M.	1986	
Gordon, Bobbi-Jo	1996	R.N. B.A.Syracuse; hospital
Gordon, Bruce R. K.	1977	
Gordon, Bryon	1983	Val'd;MS/PhD; G.Mas;GAO
Gordon, Donna	1963	
Gordon, Julie Anne	1987	STC, Oneonta; 3rd gr. teacher
Gordon, Scott	1967	Maintenance, Margaretville Hospital
Gorsch, Helen	1909	Teacher, Oneonta Normal
Gorsch, Irene	1919	Teacher, Oneonta Normal
Gorsch, Rudy, Jr.	1954	Teacher, Syr. Univ., SUCO. MS.
Goth, Shannon L.	1987	
Goth, Matthew	1983	
Gousmann, Robert W.	1923	Val'dtn;Class Pres;engineer, NYC.
Graham, Mona	1942	
Graham, Veronica	1959	Florist
Granger, Leroy	1943	
Grant, Carolyn	1986	(Faraci) Gardner&Buhl Acct.
Grant, Jason Wayne	1989	
Grant, Kathy	1975	
Grant, Kelly Anne	1981	
Grant, Marilynn J.	1985	Registered Nurse
Grant, Robert H.	1979	
Gray, Douglas A.	1982	
Gray, Edward R.	1980	
Gray, Joanne L.	1975	
Gray, Juanita M.	1989	Employe, Hidden Inn
Gray, Steven R.	1977	Veteran
Green, Dawn M.	1988	Nurse's Aid
Green, Dorothy	1938	
Green, Florence	1938	Veteran W.W. II, nurse
Green, Shawn	1991	
Greenburg, Kim L.	1969	
Greene, Beatrice	1946	RCS school aid
Greene, Gerald	1950	
Greene, Joseph	1990	House manager ARC
Greene, Phyllis	1961	
Greene, Scott E.	1981	Woodstock Chimes

Greene, Steven A.	1980	Equip. Operator/Town of Roxbury
Greene, Susan R.	1975	
Greene, Tom III	1986	Owner, auto shop; Ashland
Gregory, Dawn L.	1975	Valedictorian; music teacher
Gregory, Jan M.	1972	Teacher
Gregory, Linda Ann	1965	Teacher
Gregory, LindenAllen	1965	Veteran Vietnam, Rotarian, teacher
Gregory, Walter Burr	1968	
Griffin, Bernice	1943	
Griffin, Clara L.	1917	
Griffin, Douglas	1935	Sal'tn; Vet, Red Socks farm team
Griffin, George D.	1939	POWGer'ny;WWII;P/B'ballY'nkes
<u>Griffin, Ima Mae</u>	1921	Author,reporter,Rox. historian
Griffin, Margaret	1945	
Griffin, Marie	1949	(Numann)STC Oneonta; teacher,
Griffin, Mary	1924	Teacher, RCS
Griffin, Muriel	1944	Val'dtn;PhD;Ind/Univ/Prof.OSTC
Griffin, Ruth	1957	Oneonta STC; reading teacher
Griffin, Sheldon	1937	Classpres;STCOneonta,tch.ScoutM'st
Griffin, Steve Paul	1983	
Griffin, Terrance	1971	
Griffin, Walter	1947	Soc.St/guid',OSTC,Stam'BOCES
Griffin, Walter	1924	Guidance counselor
Griffin, William E.	1920	Postmaster, merchant
Grocholl, Deidre D.	1983	
Grocholl, Peter	1991	Surveyor; Texas; Veteran
Grocholl, Phillip	1991	Truck Driver
Grounds, Debra	1988	Nurse, physical therapist
Grounds, Richard, Jr.	1995	Sal'tn; B.S. St. Rose; teacher
Groves, Marion	1920	Secretary
Groves, Maurice	1927	Salutatorian
Gruosso, Joseph	2000	Employed Hunter Mountain
Hadden, David R.	1987	
Hadden, Donald	1941	Town council;farmer;cattle dealer
Hadden, Donald, Jr.	1963	Veteran Vietnam
Haggerty, Robert, Jr.	1964	
Haggerty, Sharon	1966	
Haight, Edwin	1941	
Haight, Francis Sue	1965	Nurse
Haight, Gloria	1946	
Haight, Gwendolyn	1940	
Haight, Kendall	1934	Farmer

Haight, Virginia	1933	(Finch) Valedictorian
Hait, Basil	1941	
Hait, Christy A.	1989	(O'Donnell) College; R. N.
Hait, Elsie	1938	
Hait, Sherry	1974	(Albano)
Hall, Douglas B.	1975	Construction
Hall, Jack	1982	Construction (D. Munsell)
Hall, Larry A.	1984	
Hall, Lillabet	1977	
Hall, Stephen H.	1976	
Hamil, Dawn M.	1987	Gardner & Buhl Accountants
Hamil, Jerry W.	1989	Bee business employee
Hamil, John	1991	
Hamilton, Andrew	1905	WW I, engineer, incandescent lamps
Hammond, Frances A	1939	
Hammond, Helen	1940	
Hammond, Inez	1937	
Hammond, James	1954	Construction work
Hammond, Janet	1954	(German)Postal/employee;Marg'ville
Hammond, Joan	1959	Banking
Hammond, Kenneth	1957	
Hammond, Mabel	1922	Teacher; Oneonta Normal
Hammond, Perry	1978	Salutatorian
Hanbury, Elsie	1915	Teacher
Hanrahan, Beth Ann	1982	
Hanrahan, Joe	1986	
Hanson, Kevin	1978	
Harlow, Barbara J.	1985	
Harlow, Robert T.	1983	
Haroldson, Alice	1996	Sal'tn/Hartwick Coll/tch
Haroldson, Jesse	1992	Emp.'Kurt Flacks H/Plumb.
Harrington, Betty	1959	Bookkeeper
Harrington, Joanne	1955	
Harrington, Marjorie	1957	
Harrington, Mildred L	1923	Nurse
Harris, Janet	1915	
Harrison, Sheri	1984	
Hartman, Linda	1966	
Hartman, MaryellenC	1976	Food/Shep'd/Golf C;RCS b'driver
Hartman, Maureen D.	1972	
Haskin, Jeffrey	1976	Employee, Town of Roxbury
Haskin, Kenneth R.	1981	

Haynes, Roger	1982	
Haynes, Tom	1978	
Heiseler, Nancy V.	1989	College
Heiseler, Peggy S.	1989	College
Herron, Leroy	1937	Veteran II, farmer
Hewitt, Archibal	1934	
Hewitt, David A.	1974	
Hewitt, Elizabeth S.	1968	Teacher
Hewitt, John	1946	Sal'tan;S/Trooper,fact'/mgr;Arkville
Hewitt, Michael J.	1969	Valedictorian, Doctor, radiology
Hewitt, Sarah	1971	
Heylers, Annette	1974	
Higgins, April	1964	
Higgins, Lewis C, Jr.	1970	Veteran Vietnam (deceased)
Higgins, Melanie F.	1977	
Higgins, Pamela R.	1973	OSHA, secretary/BOCES
Higgins, William C.	1972	
Hinkley, Allen R.	1976	Construction; ski mgr.
Hinkley, Caroline	1944	
Hinkley, Clyde	1942	Contractor
Hinkley, Daniel	1992	
Hinkley, Danielle	2000	Physical Therapy NYC
Hinkley, Dee M.	1981	
Hinkley, Donald	1966	Veteran Vietnam, I.R.S. employee
Hinkley, Doris	1938	(Stahl)
Hinkley, Edna	1945	Bookkeeper, G.E.
Hinkley, Edward G.	1939	Veteran W.W. II
Hinkley, Emily	1940	Postmistress
Hinkley, Francis	1946	Rot';carpenter,tch;S.Kortright,farmer
Hinkley, Freda	1920	Oneonta Normal - teacher
Hinkley, Gary	1955	Rotary;contractor/own Plattekill Ski
Hinkley, Glenford	1957	Contractor
Hinkley, James	1942	Farmer
Hinkley, Jeffrey B.	1973	Veteran
Hinkley, Karen Kay	1963	
Hinkley, Kenny	1978	Excavator
Hinkley, Larry	1961	
Hinkley, Linda Ann	1965	
Hinkley, Lisa S	1989	
Hinkley, LynetteCarla	1982	Catskill Railroad
Hinkley, Matthew D.	1986	Corrections Officer
Hinkley, Melissa A.	1987	(Shultis); Brookside Hardware

Name	Year	Occupation
Hinkley, Michael R.	1974	Electrician
Hinkley, Richard Dale	1968	Veteran Vietnam
Hinkley, Robert	1962	
Hinkley, Roger	1951	Electrician
Hinkley, Sanford	1938	WW II;builder;Own;Plattekill Ski
Hinkley, Shirley	1953	
Hinkley, Sonya	1978	Architect
Hinkley, Steve	1977	
Hinkley, Sylvia	1959	Health care
Hinkley, Teresa S.	1984	
Hinkley, Thomas M.	1972	Eagle Scout, hospital purser
Hinkley, Toni A	1974	Oneonta STC;Tch,Margaretville,NY
Hinkley, Tonya	1971	Salutatorian, SUNY;New Pultz;tch.
Hinkley, Tracy L.	1988	(Peters)
Hinkley, Tyrone	1977	Engineer
Hinkley, Vincent	1937	Veteran II, veterinarian ass't
Hinkley, Winfield	1992	Air Force; Ford Dealership
Hinkley, Yvonne L.	1979	Post Mistress
Hinman, Florence A.	1923	
Hinman, Iva	1921	Valedictorian
Hitt, Ivan	1944	
Hobson, Helen	1903	
Holland, Edward	1987	
Holloway, Korey	2000	
Hopkins, Ann	1952	Valedictorian, college
Hopkins, Jennifer R.	1989	College
Hoskins, Don	1997	
Howard, Theodore B.	1922	Clerk, G. E.
Howell, Kimberly	1999	
Hoyt, Lori	1986	
Hubbell, Elizabeth	1922	
Hubbell, George	1905	Mechanical engineer
Hubbell, Glenford	1945	Bakery proprietor, banker
Hubbell, Ida	1911	Salutatorian
Hudler, Jill	1967	
Hughes, Janet	1990	
Hughes, Randolph C.	1980	Vet;Tractor/Trailor operator/owner
Hughes, Sharon	1977	
Hulbert, Melissa	1987	
Hults, Jenny	2000	
Hults, Leonard	1991	Hults Plumbing & Heating
Hults, William	2000	Substitute teacher

Humphey, Robert F.	1907	Veteran W.W. I
Humphrey, Harold	1904	Inn Manager
Hunter, Clinton	1957	Veteran Vietnam, farmer
Hunter, Ena	1948	Teacher
Hunter, Ruth	1961	
Hunter, Velda	1953	X-ray tech. Margaretville Hospital
Hyman, Samuel	1908	
Hynes, Chris J.	1989	Phone Co.
Hynes, Gerald D.	1980	Communications
Hynes, Michael T.	1987	Vet.; Grand Gorge Disp Pl.
Hynes, Timothy P.	1981	Veteran; Verizon lineman
Iacovelli, Anthony R.	1974	
Iacovelli, Jason C.	1993	
Iacovelli, Joel	1991	Carpenter; Cole & Griffin
Iacovelli, Joseph T.	1970	Veteran
Ingram, Debra	1974	
Irwin, Edward	1992	Co-Salutatorian
Irwin, Sarah	1997	
Irwin, William	1990	deceased
Ives, Betty	1966	(Adams)
Ives, Charles K.	1928	Rot';WWII;MD;Cornell;"Tarzan"
Ives, Charles, Jr.	1959	Teacher; coach
Ives, Frances A.	1927	(Jenkins)
Ives, Herbert	1929	Class president; mechanic
Ives, James Moore	1965	Purple Heart,Vietnam; Bingh'ton
Ives, Julie	1956	(Moberg) Valedictorian, nurse
Ives, Ralph	1962	SUNY Plattsburg, N. Y.
Ives, Richard	1961	Class president, teacher, principal
Ives, Susan	1958	College, teacher
Jackson, Heather D.	1993	
Jaeger, Steve C	1984	Veteran
Jamrozy, James	1990	Corrections Officer
Jamrozy, Valerie J	1989	
Jaquish, Georgia Anna	1968	
Jaquish, John Henry	1968	Veteran Vietnam
Jaquish, Nellie	1916	Salutatorian, tch; Syracuse Univ.
Jaquish, Patricia	1956	
Jaquish, Rose	1958	
Jenkins, Albert	1954	Realtor
Johannsen, Barbara J.	1985	Teacher, RCS
Johannsen, Beth A.	1989	
Johannsen, Evelyn	1954	Class president

Johannsen, Joe	1953	Veteran; State High'yDept.employ
Johnson, Brenda Lee	1964	
Johnson, Eva	1927	
Johnson, Julie A.	1983	
Johnson, Loretta	1955	
Johnson, Marietta	1958	
Johnson, Rodger P.	1982	
Johnson, Suzann	1962	
Johnston, Barry	1952	Cornell Univ.
Johnston, Beverly	1966	
Johnston, Douglas B	1982	
Johnston, James G.	1983	
Johnston, Joan	1953	R.N
Johnston, Kay	1953	
Johnston, Russell D.	1964	Parsons College, Iowa
Jones, George	1925	Machinist, G. E.
Jones, James K.	1993	Co-Salutatorian; Veteran
Jones, Mark	1971	Veteran Vietnam
Jones, Perry Durwin	1965	
Jones, Richard F.	1986	
Jones, Ruth E	1937	(Maben)
Jones, Stephen P.	1973	
Jones, Timothy	1991	Veterinary college
Jones, Virginia R.	1939	
Jonson, Ulla A. C.	1972	Rotary Exchange Student
Jordan, John	1925	Sal'tn;ClassPres;CornellUniv.Employ
Joslyn, Florence E.	1919	
Joslyn, Gladys	1920	Salutatorian
Joslyn, Kenneth C.	1927	
Jump, Wilfred W.	1927	Creamery employee
Kasmer, Alicia	1973	
Kasmer, Ann C.	1931	
Keator, Richard	1916	
Keegan, Richard W.	1983	
Keevan, Russell	1985	
Keith, Alan	1992	
Kelkowski, Scott P.	1985	
Kellar, Mary A.	1979	
Kellerhouse, Amy	1990	(Cronk)
Kellerhouse, Benjamin	1995	Employee, Daitch Creamery
Kellerhouse, Gino	1997	EagleS.Val'dtn;Cl'son; GE
Kellerhouse, James	1994	Alb. Acd'my/Boys; Dir/Fund.

Kellerhouse, Katrina	2000	SUNY Oswego
Kellerhouse, Kyle	1998	Eagle S. SUNY Fredonia;tch.
Kellerhouse, Rebecca	1990	Bus. Owner, Albany, N. Y.
Kelly, Allison	1973	
Kelly, Annette	1948	
Kelly, Claire M.	1976	Valedictorian
Kelly, Ellen M.	1972	Veteran
Kelly, George	1947	Salutatorian; class president
Kelly, James	1953	Veteran
Kelly, Jeanette	1941	Class president; teacher
Kelly, Joe	1967	Valedictorian
Kelly, John	1975	Veteran, Rotarian, Eagle Scout
Kelly, John Harold	1927	WW II Lt. Col.Army;grocery store
Kelly, Joyce A.	1969	
Kelly, Kathleen	1930	
Kelly, Kathleen	1974	Valedictorian
Kelly, Larry	1957	
Kelly, Margaret	1940	Valedictorian; college; teacher
Kelly, Margaret R.	1979	Valedictorian
Kelly, Marian	1903	Club House Mgr. Florida
Kelly, Michael	1966	Valedictorian
Kelly, Nelson G.	1919	Farmer
Kelly, Nora M.	1977	Valedictorian
Kelly, Randall C.	1968	Forester
Key, Francis S.	1977	
Keyser, Gerald	1933	
Keyser, Helena	1933	Class president; teacher
Kierdorf, Gregg	1967	
Kierdorf, Maureen	1963	Bookkeeper
Kilpatrick, Margaret	C1927	Veteran W.W. II, R.N.
Kilpatrick, Robert	1931	Insurance
Kimball, Barbara	1938	
Kimball, Bernice	1945	
Kimball, Donald	1937	
King, Linda	1978	Veteran
King, Thomas A.	1982	
Kirk, Clifton Jr.	1999	
Kirk, Denise	1992	HerkimerColl, Criminal just.
Kirk, Dennis	1990	College;Morrisville; mech.
Kittle, Lillian	1935	Valedictorian
Kohler, Mark L.	1974	
Kohler, Matthew L.	1980	Veteran

Kohler, Melissa L.	1976	
Kohler, Michelle	1974	
Kramer, William	1961	Veteran Vietnam
Krom, Earl, Jr.	1997	B.S. Cornell, Wildlife Mgt.
Krom, Gladys	1952	
Krom, Melissa	1996	
Kruger, Susan M.	1976	
Kuhl, Genevive B.	1939	Class president
Kuhn, Fredrick	1991	Farmer
Kuhn, Mary	1992	Valedictorian
Kulikowski, Pauline	1944	
Kunzler, Mary	1959	Syr.Univ,Phys.Ed,AeroPilot
Lalosh, Alanna	1991	
Lalosh, Gregory	1999	OnonadagaComm.Coll;const
Lalosh, Jacqueline	1996	B.S.SUNY Oneonta, H.Ecol.
Lalosh, Michael, III	1994	
Lalosh, Richard	1992	Vol. F'man; Carpenter's/Un.
Lang, Karen	1981	
Lang, Lorraine A.	1983	(Bolger)
LaRue, Edna	1930	
LaRue, Wanda	1961	
Laureanti, Alfred	1989	
Laureanti, Ann	1988	
Laureanti, Cheryl	1992	
Lawrence, Cynthia A.	1984	
Lawrence, Doris	1932	Nurse
Lawrence, Evelyn	1938	
Lawrence, Jeffrey	1981	Veteran
Lawrence, William	1985	Sports Field Mgr/Clark cos.
Lebowitz, Sharon	1991	
LeFebvre, Shirley	1943	College, St. Lukes, R.N.
Leibowitz, Tracy	1988	Teacher
Lepeltak, Alma	1954	Banking
Lepeltak, Linda	1959	Banking
Lettieri, David	1994	
Lewis, M. Leland	1914	Class pres; salutatorian; merchant
Lewis, Mildred	1925	Teacher
Lewis, Robert	1924	Hotel Clerk, NYC.
Liberatore, Alana	2000	SUNY, Oneonta, N.Y.
Liberatore, Jerome L.	1993	College, physical therapy
Liddle, Nancy J.	1989	
Lindner, Heidi G.	1979	

Lindner, Jo Ann L.	1985	Verizon/Margaretville,NY
Lindner, Josep	1978	
Little, Nancy	1975	
Little, Robert	1977	
Long, Julie	1994	Sal'tn;BS.SHampt'MS; m/sci.
Long, Loisanne	1956	
Long, Robert C.	1980	Salutatorian
Long, Scott T.	1982	Mgr Foot Locker, Colorado
Long, Vincent	1946	Eng'AeroSpaceAdmWWIIMP,Rotary
Long, William	1990	B.S. Clarkson;MS Civil Eng.
Lupian, Guadalupe	1999	(O'Brien)
Lupian, Jesus	1997	
Lupian, Rafael	1996	
Lutz, Claude	1928	Veteran W.W. II, insurance
Lutz, Dorothy C.	1928	
Lutz, Edna M.	1932	Bookkeeper
Lutz, Edward Albert	1927	Valedictorian
Lutz, Fran L.	1973	College graduate
Lutz, Frederick Willis	1968	Albany Coll.Pharmacy;Pharmacist
Lutz, Herb ert	1932	WWII;Carpenter;H.Shepard/S'ship
Lutz, Jack	1948	Rotarian, oil distributor; pilot.
Lutz, Jeffrey	1971	Eagle Scout
Lutz, John	1977	Eagle Scout; Hospital Adm.
Lutz, Louise	1930	
Lutz, Marian	1931	Nurse
Lutz, Marian R.	1964	Salutatorian, teacher, Buffalo State
Lutz, Pauline M.	1926	(Hopkins) Teacher, art, Roxbury
Lutz, Richard	1945	Vet/Navy;carpenter/Lutz feed stores
Lutz, Robert	1975	E.Scout;FamilyFeedBus,Oneonta NY
Lutz, Samuel F.	1980	Rotarian, oil distributor
Lutz, Sayers	1931	Class president; feed store owner
Lutz, Steven R.	1973	Valedtn;E.Scout/LutzFeed,Oneonta
Lutz, Sylvia	1958	College
Lutz, Thomas J.	1972	Eagle Scout
Lutz, Willis	1937	IBM, data processing; auto sales
Lutz, Zada	1931	
Lyke, Jediah	1997	
Mac Kenzie, Jane	1943	
Mac Kenzie, Leroy B	1917	
Mac Laury, Olive	1934	Salutatorian; Prof., Albion St. School;
MacDonald, Lynette	1975	
MacDonald, Neil	1988	

Mackay, Donald	1936	
Mackey, James Gerald	1927	Coach, Windham, N.Y.
Madero, Gary	1993	
Madero, Mark	1982	
Madore, MichelleAnn	1986	
Maduri, Frank	1991	Mechanic
Maduri, Johanna	1995	
Mager, Brenda L.	1976	
Mager, Charles E.	1981	Veteran
Mahnken, Jessica	1998	Employee T. Bar Saloon
Mahoney, Beth	1983	
Major, Tanya	1998	SUNY Oneonta, N.Y.
Major, Tricia L.	1999	Penn View Coll; Elem. Ed..
Malcomson, Norman	1940	Veteran W.W. II, Eagle Scout
Malcomson, Ruth	1936	Salutatorian
Mallasch, Edith	1951	
Malpleton, David C.	1970	Rotary Exchange Student, Australia
Manon, Asher J.	1982	Emp. Town of Middletown
Marengo, Michael	1988	
Martell, Nicholette	1999	
Martin, Donald J.	1973	
Martin, George W.	1968	Vet; Vietnam; Val'dtn; Eagle Scout
Martin, Stanley Allen	1965	Teacher
Mattice, Christopher,	1989	College
Mattice, Daniel	1992	
Mattice, Doris	1948	
Mattice, Elsie Jean	1952	
Mattice, Marjorie	1952	
Mattice, Mark	1995	A.S. Alfred Univ.
Mattice, Melony D.	1982	Recep., Roxbury Health Ctr.
Mattice, Pat	1949	
Mattice, Ronald	1953	Valedictorian; engineer
Maxim, Patricia J.	1993	(Madero)
Mazzone, Roger	1966	
Mc Caskill, Nancy	1961	
Mc Connville, Richard	1989	
Mc Ewan, Hilda	1937	
Mc Ginnis, Amy	1996	B.S. Franklin Pierce; teacher
Mc Ginnis, Jennifer	2000	
Mc Kenzie, Judith	1971	
Mc Kertie, Mary D.	1970	
Mc Laughlin, Tina	1990	English Teacher, RCS

Mc Mahon, Mike	1987	Graduate program
Mc Mahon, Timothy	1990	Veteran, Desert Storm
Mc Nerney, Michael A	1986	Val'dtn; Air Force Acd. grad.
McCall, Alfred	1935	
McCall, Dana A.	1984	
McCann, Harold	1925	
McCracken, James R.	1993	Eagle S;B.SF'kln Pierce U
McCracken, Joseph	1995	E.Scout;B.S.F.PierceU;DEC
McDonald, Heather	1959	Salutatorian, college, theater
McDonald, Rich	1981	
McIntosh, Anna	1910	
McIntosh, Margaret	1945	Secretary
McIntosh, Marian E.	1939	
McIntosh, Wilma L.	1939	
McKay, Donald	1938	
McKenna, Bruce	1954	Vet.Korea;college;dental components
McLaughlin, Erick	1997	NYS PD Acad/Fire & Safety
McMahon, Erin	1994	
McMahon, Marianne	1985	
McWilliams, Madeline	1930	
Mead, Bruce S.	1936	WWII, Valedictorian;airline pilot,coll.
Mead, Constance	1959	Wal-Mart employee
Mead, Dorothy Ann	1963	
Mead, Gordon	1954	Roxbury Highway Dept.
Mead, Grace (Todd)	1928	Valedictorian
Mead, Helen Ruth	1984	
Mead, Iris	1962	
Mead, Keith N.	1950	Veteran Korean, Air Force
Mead, Keith R.	1950	Class pres.; Veteran Nurse; Navy
Mead, Lori L.	1984	
Mead, Marguerite E.	1936	
Mead, Marian	1921	Salutatorian
Mead, Michael R.	1977	
Mead, Michelle	2000	
Mead, Robert J.	1939	Farmer
Mead, Stanley Chester	1923	Appliance business
Mead, Sylvia	1956	
Mead, Wayland	1949	Vet.Korean,Cornell Univ;Ins.
Meade Walter F.	1934	Val'dtn;tch,naturalist,auth;photo'phy
Meade, Donna	1959	College
Meade, Emily	1960	
Meade, Frank	1942	

Meade, Jessica	1994	SUNY,Cortland; tch. Bronx
Meade, Joanna	1991	SUNY; guidance counselor
Meade, Marjorie	1933	
Meade, Richard	1966	Teacher
Meade, Stanley	1960	
Meade, Virgil	1933	Farmer
Menne, Dianna M.	1981	Graduate program
Meskill, Janene A.	1988	
Meskill, Jeffrey J.	1985	Val'dtn ; Vet. Desert Storm,
Miccio, Karina	1999	Art Major; Binghamton
Migdol, Judith A.	1980	
Migdol, Leiann S.	1979	
Mika, Carol	1985	
Millar, Andrew	1969	
Millar, Anne C.	1976	
Millar, Edmund	1971	Horticulturist
Millar, Jean Catherine	1968	
Millar, Maureen	1974	
Miller, Gregg R.	1970	Val'dtn,Univ.N.Carolina;Math Prof.
Miller, Jack	1940	Logger
Miller, Linda	1959	
Miller, Lynne	1967	
Miner, Tom	1986	
Miner, Valerie G.	1988	
Minnerly, Francis	1915	Class President; dentist
Minnerly, James	1930	WW II,insurance, boatshop owner
Minnerly, Janet	1951	College
Miranda, Ilce P.	1976	
Moldovan, Frances	1948	Nurse
Moldovan, Mary	1945	
Moldovon, Anna	1940	
Mondore, Beulah	1931	
Mondore, Galdys	1934	
Mondore, Grace	1929	
Mondore, Irving	1928	Salutatorian
Mondore, Muriel	1940	
Moore, Anne M.	1965	
Moore, Courtney	1991	Works @ NY stock exchange
Moore, Denise Lynn	1987	Syracuse;ROTC;math RCS
Moore, Janis E.	1970	Farmer
Moore, Richard Allen	1968	Contractor, Colorado
Morales, Lisa	1995	

More, Ann	1941	Veteran WW.II, Salutatorian; RN
More, Arthur	1958	Buffalo State, bus/steal company
More, Donald	1925	Farmer
More, Evelyn	1943	St. Lukes, R.N.
More, Herbert	1927	Paint store
More, James	1954	College, Executive Black & Decker
More, Jean	1940	
Morse, Adam	2000	
Morse, Annett	1953	
Morse, Betty	1943	
Morse, Carol	1966	Insurance
Morse, Clarabelle	1937	
Morse, Cynthia	1998	
Morse, David S.	1912	Valedictorian, teacher
Morse, Edith	1916	(Harris)
Morse, Edna F.	1914	Valedictorian
Morse, Emery	1959	
Morse, Frederick	1972	Eagle Scout, insurance
Morse, Genevieve	1938	
Morse, Gilford	1964	
Morse, Grace	1921	Oneonta Normal - teacher
<u>Morse, Grant</u>	1915	WWI;tch/prin;auth.3vol/poetry;Supt.
Morse, Harold	1938	
Morse, Harrison C.	1932	Rotarian, insurance
Morse, Joyce	1962	
Morse, Laurine	1954	
Morse, Lindon	1933	WWII,Rot'ry;ScoutMaster(41),ins.
Morse, Loyal P.	1938	Veteran W.W. II, teacher
Morse, Mary E.	1919	AlbanyBus;100yr.@/2000,farm/auto
Morse, Nancy	1958	Nurse
Morse, Patrici	1956	
Morse, Ralph	1942	
Morse, Ronald	1953	Electrician
Morse, Stanley P.	1969	
Morse, Thomas	1966	Mer/Mar/ACD/KingPt/ARCO/Capt.
Morse, Tracy L.	1988	Veteran Desert Storm
Morse, Wendy Sue	1994	
Moscato, Edward C.	1989	
Moscato, Jerry	1970	Veteran Vietnam
Moseman, Amy C.	1985	Teacher, music; Florida
Motic, Esther	1990	
Mudge, Jason	1998	Veteran

Mudge, Rebecca	1999	to Arizona
Muller, August	1913	Teacher, Phonicia, N.Y.
Muller, Florence	1930	
Muller, George	1916	Class Pres.Vet.WW I, Valedictorian
Munro, Denise K.	1973	
Munro, Karen S.	1976	
Munro, Marcia	1950	Syracuse Univ.
Munro, William	1971	Teacher, Physical Ed. Sidney, N.Y.
Munsell, Andrea S.	1983	(Cammer) Postal Employee
Munsell, Antha	1960	Salutatorian; music teacher
Munsell, David	1955	Rotarian, contractor
Munsell, Diane B.	1979	Nurse
Munsell, Elizabeth	1963	
Munsell, Evelyn	1937	(Griffin)
Munsell, Harry	1958	
Munsell, Henry	1933	Rotary;carpenter/mech;G.Church/solo
Munsell, Mary Louise	1971	
Munsell, Susan	1954	
Murray, Frank	1918	Forestry
Murray, Sabrina	2000	(Todd)
Myers, Aaron	1997	
Myers, Andrew	1978	
Myers, Christopher J	1986	
Myers, Frank	1957	
Myers, Jolene	2000	
Naccarato, Maria	1960	
Nader, Katheryne M.	1979	
Nealson, Robert	1990	Marine Corp
Needham, Jamie	1989	
Needham, Ralph T.	1970	Vet.Vietnam;Mobile Home Sales/Ser.
Needham, Tanya	1996	Val'dtn;Skidmore;Pre-med
Needham, Tara N.	1993	
Nesbitt, Lawrence	1956	Salutatorian
Nesbitt, Ted	1966	
Nikula, Anssi	1988	Rotary Exchange Student
Nilsen, Donna M.	1984	Teacher
Nilsen, Sandi	1985	
Nolan, John	1944	Veteran, mechanic
Novak, Cindy L	1985	
Novak, Dawn	1988	
Numann, Guy	1949	RPI; CEO Manufacturing Co.
Numann, Marian	1950	Salutatorian; Wells College, MD.

Numann, Patricia	1958	Valedictorian; M.D., Pilot
O'Beirne, Ellen	1986	
O'Beirne, Terence	1992	Co-Salutatorian
O'Brien, Kristopher	1998	
O'Dell, Ruby	1952	
O'Donnell, James	1990	Rotary; Allen Residential
O'Donnell, Michael	1992	
O'Donnell, Patrick	1992	
O'Hara, Anna	1915	
O'Hara, Beatrice M.	1939	
O'Hara, Elizabeth J.	1939	
O'Hara, John	1954	
O'Hara, Katherine	1942	
O'Hara, Michael	1902	
O'Hara, Rosetta	1946	
O'Kelly, Helen	1926	Music teacher, Bainbridge, NY.
O'Neil, Daniel J.	1985	
O'Neil, Dave	1989	
Oakley, Bob	1997	Veteran, Marines
Oakley, Melissa	1999	Hartwick Coll, Oneonta, NY
Ogborn, Sandra	1962	
Oi, Hiroho	1978	Exchange student, Japan
Oliveiria, Walner A	1977	Rotary Exchange Student
Oliver, Carolyn	1959	
Origoni, Marcelo	1988	Restaurant Mgr, Oneonta
Ormsbee, Brian	1989	
Orr, Joseph	1998	
Osborn, Deanna	1995	Employlee; Tysco Mallinckrodt
Osborn, Donald	1957	Employee, Town of Roxbury
Osborn, Ethel	1948	
Osborn, James	1966	
Osborn, Joseph	1970	Veteran
Osborn, Melinda	1975	
Osche, Minnie	1917	Valedictorian
Osche, William Fred	1923	G.E., refrigeration dept.
Page, Richard	1927	Dentist
Page, Virginia	1925	
Palmer, Robert	2000	WeldingSch; Schenectady
Parizo, Glen	1981	
Parizo, Sue Ellen	1982	
Parks, Helen	2000	
Parnell, Carol E.	1970	Government Employee

Parsons, Edith	1910	
Parsons, Eva	1915	
Parsons, Waldo	1920	Pharmacist, Albany Coll. Pharmacy
Paul, Rhonda	1963	
Pearsall, Jennifer	1994	
Pearsall, Mercedes	1974	
Pebler, Barbara J.	1969	
Pebler, Charlie	1995	SUNYMorrisville/Delhi, NY
Pebler, Elizabeth	1997	B.S. SUNY, Plattsburg
Pebler, George	1962	Navy, Veteran Vietnam
Pebler, Wayne	1966	Farmer, Justice of the Peace
Pebler, Wayne R, II	1993	SUNY, Postdam
Peck, Elna K.	1939	Secretary
Peck, Marilyn L.	1969	
Peck, Mary Ann	1951	
Peck, Thelma	1936	(Shafer)
Peck, Virginia	1951	
Pecor, Glenn	1947	Veteran W.W. II
Pedersen, Lena	1985	Exchange Student
Pekrul, Harold	1954	Margaretville School Bus Supv.
Perazone, Brian E.	1976	Army Reserve; Gunsmith
Perazone, Lisa	1998	Val'dtn;Flbr't;Oxford /StJos
Perazone, Tracy	2000	Val'dtn; Colgate Pre-Med.
Perkins, Daniel W.	1979	Owns Const. Company, Michigan
Perry, Melissa	2000	
Petry, William A, III	1993	
Phipps, Allen	1963	
Pickett, David F.	1984	
Pierce, Ren	2000	
Pietrantoni, Richard	1980	Veteran; Navy
Pietrantoni, Steve	1975	
Pingree, BeulahKeator	1901	
Pinto, Adriana	2000	Exchange Student; Mexico
Pitkethly, David	1929	Rotarian, VMI; Lt. Col., Army
Pitkethly, Edith J.	1926	Nurse, NYC.
Ploutz, Elsie	1941	Vet.Women'sArm Corp(WAC) rest't
Ploutz, Floyd	1946	
Ploutz, Helen	1932	
Ploutz, Lorraine	1945	
Ploutz, Paul	1949	E. Scout, author, Prof.Developer
Ploutz, Raymond E.	1974	
Ploutz, Raymond G.	1948	Classpres;WWII,MarineCorpMP

Pohlmann, Vincent	1925	Standard Oil Co, Troy, NY.
Poole, Cynthia	1967	Tch;airline hostess/sec.NYSEG.
Poole, Mark W.	1969	Eagle Scout, college; post office clerk
Porter, Damian	1991	Employed NYSEG
Porter, David	1971	
Porter, Mary J.	1975	
Porter, Michael	1967	SUNY,Oneonta;sci/ tch/Margaretville
Porter, Rebecca	1992	(O'Donnell)SUNY; business
Porter, Richard M.	1969	Water Dept. NYC, Mar'ville, NY
Porter, Robert B.	1973	
Porter, Whitney	2000	Canisius College
Powell, Cecil	1952	HonorGuard;ArlingtonNat.Cemetery
Powell, Edith N.	1912	Teacher
Powell, Grace I.	1919	Bookkeeper
Powell, Ruth	1913	
Preston, Grace	1915	Teacher, Oneonta Normal
Preston, Kenneth B.	1919	ClassPresPostM'stManlius/Sch/Boy
Preston, Margaret	1947	
Preston, Mildred V.	1919	Vassar(byHelenShepard)Tch;Lib'ry
<u>Preston, Robert</u>	1946	Classpres;WWII;STCCort'd.tchprin.
Prior, Eileen	1976	
Proctor, Cynthia	1962	Teacher
Proctor, George	1990	Painter
Proctor, James E.	1993	B. S. St. Rose
Proctor, Lloyd	1959	Teacher
Proctor, Mary	1996	B.S. St. Rose; advertising
Proctor, Stacey	1994	(Walker); Concordia College
Proskine, Gordon	1944	College
Proskine, Jennie	1935	
Proskine, John	1942	Veteran; Army, township trustee
Proskine, Margaret	1932	
Prout, Cathy L.	1972	
Prout, Robin L.	1973	
Prout, William	1978	
Pucci, Dominic, III	1985	Oneonta, NY Pol. Dept/Rec
Pucci, Kristi A.	1988	
Purchell, AlanDouglas	1968	Salutatorian
Purchell, David	1975	
Purchell, Evelyn	1940	
Purchell, Gordy	1956	Veteran
Purchell, Helene	1985	Legal secretary
Purchell, Leah	1983	Nurse

Purchell, Linda S.	1969	deceased
Purchell, Marcy	1975	
Purchell, Richard	1940	Tax assessor
Purchell, Robert	1957	College (Frank Booth Scholarship)
Purchell, Susan A.	1977	
Purchell, Wayne	1974	
Purdy, Beatrice	1961	
Purdy, Michael	1963	
Quackenbush, Mary B	1990	
Quackenbush, Sarah	1992	
Raeder, Bruce	1960	College, Corning Executive
Raeder, Francis E.	1917	Salutatorian
Raeder, George	1940	Farmer
Raeder, George E.	1973	
Raeder, Jerry	1951	
Raeder, Marian	1931	Salutatorian
Raeder, Nancy L.	1977	(Vosbrink)
Raeder, Nichola	1999	Eagle Scout (20)
Rashap, Raven	1994	
Reed, Alice	1941	Beautician
Reed, David	1961	Vet.Vietnam;tele/Co,M'ville,NY.
Reed, Harry	1941	
Reed, Isabelle	1934	
Reed, Jeffrey W.	1986	
Reed, Karna Yvonne	1987	
Reed, Leonard	1939	Veteran W.W. II
Reed, Lillian E.	1912	Teacher
Reed, Richard	1939	Veteran W.W. II
Reed, William	1957	Veteran
Reed, William	1990	deceased
Regan, Meliss	1999	
Regan, Sharon L.	1982	
Restchack, Louis A.	1936	Male model
Restchack, Martha	1937	Manager A & P store
Restchack, Theresa	1944	
Restchack, Walter	1941	Veteran W.W. II
Rettmeier, Alice Joy	1957	
Rettmeier, Charles	1962	Veteran Vietnam
Rettmeier, Jean	1959	Valedictorian; teacher
Reuter, Christopher J.	1986	
Reuter, Johanna M.	1982	
Reuter, Michael J.	1983	Salutatorian

Reynolds, Ralph H.	1919	Veteran W.W. I, insurance
Reynolds, William	1940	Veteran W.W.II, Eagle Scout
Richard, Arlene	1945	Nurse
Richtmyer, Francis	1916	
Ricker, James	1931	
Riedman, Valentine	1953	College, teacher
Riggi, John	1991	Emp., Big Tree Co. Durham
Riggi, Susan	1992	
Riley, Desmond	1930	Service station
Roberts, Aleta M.	1976	
Roberts, Billie Jo	1990	
Roberts, Charlene	1986	
Roberts, Donald	1940	Bookkeeper, M'ville Hospital
Roberts, Ellen R.	1985	
Roberts, Janice	1943	
Roberts, Jeremiah	1998	Electricians Ass't.
Roberts, Leah	1948	
Roberts, Lloyd	1935	Veteran W.W. II, bookkeeper
Roberts, Shari	1981	Graduate program
Roberts, Thomas C.	1973	
Robertson, Brian	1992	
Robertson, Gary	1991	Owner, cleaning service
Robertson, Lisa	1996	(George)
Robillard, Teresa Kay	1993	
Robinson, Matha	1915	
Roe, Ashley	2000	
Roe, Kimberly	1998	
Rogacevitch, E. P.	1985	RCS employee
Rohacevich, Jonathan	2000	Employed Hunter Mountain
Rohacevich, Joseph	1995	
Rolland, Mary	1973	Pottery business
Rolland, Richard, Jr.	1973	Insurance
Rollins, Cornelia	1924	Teacher
Rose, Charles	1969	
Rose, Charles	1991	West Point '95, US Army
Rose, Florence A.	1918	Teacher, Oneonta Normal
Rose, Georgia	1966	
Rose, Howard, III	1985	
Rose, Linda	1967	
Rose, Margaret	1944	
Rose, Marvin	1951	Veteran
Rose, Samuel	2000	SUNY, Cortland

Rose, Sharlein	1992	College graduate
Ross, Conrad	1953	College
Ross, James	1958	
Rossman, Barent V,Jr	1964	
Rossman, Boice	1945	
Rossman, Dorothy	1967	
Rossman, Eugene F.	1972	
Rossman, James	1973	
Rossman, Jason	1998	Sal'tn;EagleS.CantonU ShipB
Rossman, Mary Ann	1967	
Rossman, Rose	1962	
Rossman, Timothy G	1980	
Rossman. Walter	1975	
Rowe, Augusta M.	1918	
Rowe, Bruce C.	1969	Farmer
Rowe, Dana	1992	Nurse
Rowe, Donald J.	1970	
Rowe, Linda	1967	
Rowe, Matthew	1990	
Rudolph, Christine	1990	B.A. Education; math teacher
Rudolph, John W.	1988	Sal'tn;RotaryBS.RPI;Mgr.
Rudolph, Kevin M.	1993	Co-Sal'tn;M.S.PhysicalTher.
Rudolph, Laurie	1996	M.S. Physical Therapist
Ruff, Gail	1971	Teacher; Florida
Ruff, Gary	1962	Teacher
Ruscio, Paul N.	1970	Vet. Vietnam;Restaurant Manager.
Russell, John	1951	Veteran, college; draftsmen
Ruteshouser, Anna	1915	Valedictorian,(Ploutz)author'smother
Ruteshouser, Dorothy	1929	Teacher
Ruteshouser, Virginia	1938	(Lutz) Postal clerk, Roxbury
Rutulante, Donna Mae	1968	
Rutulante, Gloria	1966	
Samuelsen, Donna	1975	
Samuelson, Karen M.	1983	
Sandler, Scott J.	1993	
Sanford, Donald G.	1981	Teach, M'ville.
Sanford, Donna	1938	
Sanford,l Evelyn	1938	Salutatorian
Sanford, Frances M.	1925	Valedictorian
Sanford, Gerald	1935	
Sanford, John K.	1905	Insurance agent
Sanford, Rex E.	1983	

Sanford, Robyn	1994	
Sanford, Tracy	1999	SUNY Oneonta
Sanford, Willis	1937	Veteran W.W. II
Santic, Viola	1942	
Sass, Heidi	1997	
Sass, Richard, Jr.	1998	Culinary school
Sass, Robert	1999	Employed locally
Sauveur, Tami	1990	Delhi Tech. Graduate
Sauveur, Timothy S	1983	Veteran; NYC police officer.
Savold, David, II	1978	Graduate West Point; U. S. Army
Savold, James	1974	Veteran
Savold, Mary Jo T.	1972	Roxbury Dairy Princess
Savold, Patricia A.	1977	West Point; Veteran
Saxon, Donna	1958	
Schaefer, Sandra	1994	
Schimmel, Anne M.	1979	
Schineller, Joyce	1947	
Schmidt, John W.	1930	Valedictorian; Class president
Schneider, Helene M.	1977	
Schneider, Lois	1978	Corrections Officer
Schreiber, Earl	1961	Valedtn,Head Libr'an,Louisana St.
Schuman, Andrew	1998	
Schuman, Andrew,Jr.	1941	Justice of the Peace
Schuman, Bob	1950	Veteran Vietnam
Schuman, Catherine	1999	
Schuman, David A.	1982	Electrician
Schuman, Donald	1938	
Schuman, Doris	1944	
Schuman, Elizabeth	2000	SUNY, Oneonta, El. Ed.
Schuman, Evelyn E.	1927	Teacher
Schuman, James R.	1969	
Schuman, Stephen A.	1974	Employee, Town of Roxbury, NY
Schuman, Thomas A.	1965	Veteran Vietnam
Schuster, Donald P.	1936	
Schuster, Harold	1940	Veteran W.W. II; farmer
Schuster, Margaret	1944	Class president; college
Schville, Charles E.	1926	Val'tn; teacher, Grand Gorge, NY.
Schwander, Stephen S.	1980	Valedictorian; Minister
Schwartz, Kyle	1999	
Schwarz, Kurt	1994	Veteran
Seals, Barbara	1971	
Sears, Abagail	1955	

Seeley, Evelyn	1963	
Segnini, Maria Vera	1970	
Segnini, Vera	1943	College
Seligman, Dolores	1952	
Serrie, Jennifer	1999	Valedictorian; Elmira Coll.
Serrie, Joseph	1998	Drexel Univ; Army ROTC
Shafer, Carol	1959	
Shafer, Grace	1939	
Shafer, Karl	1956	
Shafer, Paul	1935	Veteran
Shafer, Robert	1938	Veteran W.W. II, jeweler
Shatraw, Milton	1920	
Sherman, Asa J.	1988	Valedictorian; Minister, P.A.
Sherman, Dale F	1982	Minister Indians,Fairford, CA
Sherman, Merile L.	1984	
Sherwood C. J.	1989	
Sherwood, David	1991	Morrisville Tech. College
Sherwood, Donald J.	1977	
Sherwood, Dorothy	1975	
Sherwood, Francis	1943	
Sherwood, Gary E.	1969	Pres., RCS Board of Ed., farmer
Sherwood, James D.	1982	
Sherwood, Nelson	1943	
Sherwood, Rachel	1999	Niagara University
Sherwood, Rande	1972	
Sherwood, Thomas F.	1968	
Shoemaker, Elwin	1923	Teacher, Prattsville, NY.
Shultis, Anne	1975	
Shultis, Bernice	1944	Salutatorian (s), college
Shultis, Bob	1950	M/Sgt. Special Forces
Shultis, Catherine	1951	Valedictorian
Shultis, Cecil M.	1918	Vet.WWI,MajorEng'r;NYCtunnels
Shultis, Charles	1960	
Shultis, Chris	1997	RCS, custodian
Shultis, Edward	1967	Veteran; B & B Construction
Shultis, Ellis	1939	Valedictorian, Veteran WW.II
Shultis, Emily	1944	Teacher, home economics
Shultis, Ernest	1974	
Shultis, George	1940	Veteran W.W. II, college graduate
Shultis, Greg	1975	
Shultis, Hanford	1945	Veteran W.W. II, insurance
Shultis, Jean	1944	

Shultis, Leighton K.	1983	
Shultis, Lela A.	1970	
Shultis, Leland C.	1920	Teacher
Shultis, Loren	1971	RCS, bus driver
Shultis, Lorraine	1952	Class president, college
Shultis, Milton	1941	Veteran W.W. II, contractor
Shultis, Naomi	1947	
Shultis, Paul	1993	RCS bus driver
Shultis, Susan	1971	
Shuster, Donald	1937	
Siedzieniewski,Diana	1997	to Arizona
Silver, Bruce R	1908	Mgr. Zinc Co, N. J.
Simon, Joseph Patrick	1923	Electrical Engineer
Simon, Mary M.	1927	Died of TB
Siska, Michael J.	1976	
Slater, Amy	1996	Beautician, Grand Gorge, NY
Slater, Daniel	1987	
Slater, Darrell G.	1969	Trailer park owner
Slater, Dennis G.	1969	E. Scout,tch,technology;Inspect'/Rox.
Slater, Flo Jean	1966	
Slater, Jennifer	1992	Employee DSS
Slater, Steve	1997	
Slauson, Alan	1966	
Slauson, Barbara J.	1969	
Slauson, Carol L.	1980	Bookeeper, Daitch Creamery
Slauson, Dianne Lynn	1979	Greenhouse operator
Slauson, Dorothy	1952	
Slauson, Eula	1957	
Slauson, Gary	1957	
Slauson, George C.	1970	Veteran; Campground Owner
Slauson, Jeffrey J.	1981	
Slauson, Joan	1961	
Slauson, Keith	1979	Veteran
Slauson, Linda	1962	
Slauson, Marshall	1932	Class president; Rotarian, town clerk
Slauson, Raymond	1949	Class president; Vet. Vietnam
Slauson, Robert	1975	
Slauson, Robert, Jr.	1997	Locally employed
Slauson, Virgil	1950	
Smith, Cheryl	1963	
Smith, David	1944	Sal'tan(s) WW II, Univ.Mich; arts
Smith, Doris C.	1929	

Smith, Elaine	1991	
Smith, Gilbert	1945	Vet. WW.II, Val'dtn; college
Smith, Harriet M.	1941	Val'dtn;health/Adm/St.Lawr'Univ.
Smith, June	1953	
Smith, Nancy	1956	
Smith, Robert L.	1910	Feed business
Smith, William	1906	Civil engineer
Smith, William	1950	Librarian, Fairbanks, AK.
Snegoski, Eileen	1965	Salutatorian, Special Ed. teacher
Snipas, John	1949	Rotarian
Snipas, Vincent	1951	Vet.Vietnam;Secret Serv.;White H.
Snow, Eric L.	1993	
Snyder, Barbara J.	1989	Nurse (LPN)
Snyder, Charlie T.	1983	Veteran
Snyder, Evette	1996	BS/SUNY;MS RPI;Sci.Tch
Snyder, Fawn	1983	Secretary/BOCES
Snyder, Shirley L.	1979	Asso/DegreeUlsterCoCom/Coll.farm.
Snyder, Tamara	2000	Mercyhurst Coll, PA; music
Snyder, Tricia	1991	(Davis)
Snyder, Vincent H.	1976	Floor Sanding business
Southard, Harold G.	1919	Salesman
Sparling, Clara	1931	(Ploutz)Nurse
Sparling, Glen	1943	Farmer
Sparling, Stella	1942	
Speenburgh,Madison	1922	
Spencer, Louis C.	1918	Class pres; Sal'tn;Vet WWI;eng'er
Spencer, Nancy	1967	
Spielman, Bonnie Mae	1968	
Spielman, Connie L.	1972	Medicine P.A.
Spielman, Dennis	1965	Veteran Vietnam
Spielman, George	1962	Veteran Vietnam
Spielman, George L.	1987	
Spielman, Heather	1995	
Spielman, Keri	1990	(Mazzuca) book kpr, Albany
Spielman, Michelle	1991	Nurse's Aid, PA
Spielman, Wendy E.	1987	(Morrison)Nurse/Fam.Health
Sprague, Kathleen	1982	Owner, beauty salon
Sprague, Verlynn L.	1927	College
Sprague, Vickie Ann	1987	
Sprague, Vict	1972	
Sprague, William	1992	Employed, Town of Roxbury
Squires, Tamara L.	1984	

Stafford, Melissa	1991	
Stafford, Michael, II	1996	N.Y. Police Dept.
Stahl, Charis	1945	Salutatorian
Stahl, Dean,	1989	Eagle Scout
Stahl, Dwayne D.	1987	Eagle Scout
Stahl, Gordon	1961	Power Co. employee
Stahl, Ronald	1957	Salutatorian
Stahl, Wayne	1955	
Steenland, Brian	1992	
Steenland, Heather	1994	
Stepanek, Joseph	1956	
Stevens, Peter John	1965	Exchange student – Australia
Stewart, David, Jr.	1964	Veteran
Stewart, Diane E.	1969	
Stewart, Larry James	1968	
Stewart, Nelson	1943	Veteran W.W. II
Stewart, Paul	1936	Service station
Stewart, Robert	1966	Salutatorian, Veteran Vietnam
Stock, Gregory	1990	Store Mgr., Hobart, N.Y.
Stock, Travis	1999	
Stone, Gideon	1998	
Stoutenburgh, Marshall	1938	POW,surv'Bataan deathmarchWWII
Stratton, Kathryn L.	1983	
Stratton, Lynda R.	1984	
Stretch, Jennifer	1990	
Suess, Christopher	1988	
Suess, Matthew	1990	Landscaping
Suter, Jonas	1935	College, Eastman Kodak
Sweatman, Una	1958	
Sweatman, Viola	1963	Teacher
Taylor, Gary	1963	Veteran Vietnam
Taylor, Lori E.	1970	
Taylor, Randy D.	1973	Veteran Vietnam
Taylor, Ricky D.	1973	
Taylor, Sherry	1967	
Teichmann, Eva	1942	Teacher; college
Teichmann, Frederick	1922	Sal'tn;Prof NYU.auth;GouldS'ship
Temple, Sharon M.	1982	
Temple, Sherry A.	1980	
Thomas, Claude	1903	Civil Eng'NYCwater(tunnel& shaft)
Thomas, Louise	1978	
Thomas, Michael F.	1973	

Thomas, Wilma A.	1936	Legal secretary
Thompson, Barbara	1967	Teacher; postmistress
Thompson, Kathryn	1970	Salutatorian; Home Bureau Dept.
Thompson, Milton	1911	
Thompson, Richard B	1968	Caprenter
Thorington, April	1991	
Thorington, Ernest J.	1984	
Thorington, Yvonne F.	1989	Cook, Hidden Inn
Tietjen, Lauriel L.	1981	Graduate program
Tischmacher, Roin G.	1977	Banker
Tischmacher, Vicki	1968	Albany Coll.Phar/Pharmacist,Alaska
Tobin, Betty Lou	1948	
Tobin, Daryl	1994	
Tobin, Jacqueline L.	1969	Secretary
Tobin, Jerome W.	1969	Rotarian; electrician
Tobin, Sandra L.	1973	
Todd, Edith	1943	Teacher
Todd, John	1999	Marines
Todd, Ruth	1937	(Roney)
Tompkins, Betty	1943	R.N.
Townsend, Alnetta	1929	Teacher, RCS
Townsend, Bernice	1941	
Townsend, James	1989	College
Townsend, John	1960	Grumman Aviation
Townsend, Judith E.	1964	College; R.N.
Townsend, KimberlyA	1989	College; attorney USD.
Townsend, Robert	1963	Rot'y/contractor,SuptRox/WaterD.
Townsend, Wendy S.	1984	(Greene) SUNY; sec.RCS.
Trahan, Jason J.	1993	Golf Pro. (Florida, Windham)
Trahan, Stephani	1998	Suny Oneonta 98-99 to NYC
Travis, Marie	1945	
Travis, Zena R.	1909	Sal'tn; Oneonta Normal, Supt. RCS
Trede, Louise M.	1929	Valedictorian
Treski, Bianca	1995	
Treski, Desire'	1994	
Tubiolo, Tara Jai	1991	
Tucker, Carl A.	1993	Surveyor
Tucker, John	2000	Employed Hunter Mountain
Tucker, Michael	1996	
Tupper, Betty	1937	R.N.
Tyler, Belva	1942	Class president
Tyler, Gary Lee	1950	Veteran, Syracuse Univ; musician

Frank Booth
1904

Zena R. Travis
1909

Grant D. Morse
1915

Erma Mae Griffin top right. 1921

Ima Griffin
390-E

Erma (Ima) Griffin

Colonel Charles Lindberg, Colonel Fredrick Teichmann
and other unnamed avionic pioneers.

Fredrick Kurt Teichmann at NYU.

390-G

"Fred" Teichmann, Dean NYU, professor, author, engineer, pilot, colonel, editor, Roxbury farm boy.

Bruce "stub" Caswell and friend at Wake Robin, approximately 1960, Roxbury, New York.

1924

390-H

Charley's Band, Roxbury
top right

Charles Ives, M.D.
1928
390-1

J. FRANCES ALLEN

Owego Free Academy
Band '29, '30, '31, '32, '33.
Orchestra '31, '32. '33.
Dramatic Club Play '32.
Stage Dinner Committee, Chr. '33
Latin Club Play '33.
Girl's League '31, '32, '33.
Honor and High Honor Roll.
Roxbury
Orchestra '34.
Senior Play.
Honor and High Honor Roll.
Second highest honors of class.

LOCHIE JO ALLEN

Owego Free Academy
Band '29, '30, '31, '32, '33.
Orchestra 30, '31, '32, '33.
Latin Club Play '33.
Girl's League '31. '32. '33.
Stage Dinner Committee '33.
Dramatic Club Play Heroine '33.
Junior Cabinet '33.
8th gade English Prize.
Two year Math Prize.
Honor and High Honor Rolls.
Roxbury
Orchestra '34.
Vice Pres. Senior Class.
Highest class average.

Both 1934

Walter F. Mead
1934

Walt, Ginny Scheer (Mrs. Walter F. Meade) and friend
390-K

RICHARD LUTZ

Class President 1; Senior Play 4; Intramural Sports 1, 2, 3, 4; League Winner 4; School R Award 4; Junior Red Cross 3, 4; Victory Corps 2, 3.

Independent, self-reliant, dependable

1945

Richard Lutz 2002

ROBERT PRESTON

Baseball 1, 2, 3, 4; Basketball 2, 3, 4; President of Class 4; Senior Play 4; Intramural Sports 1, 2, 3, 4; Outstanding Athlete Award 3; Junior Prom King 3.

Good looking, bothersome, easy going

RCS graduation picture, class president, 1946.

Guy Numann

Baseball 1,2,4; Basketball 1,2,4; Boys' State 2; Class officer 2; Intramural Winner 1,2,4; Magazine Campaign 1,2,4; Manager 4; Press Club 4; Record Board 4; Senior Play 4; Student Council 4; Soccer 4; Varsity "R" Award 1,4

RCS graduation picture, 1949.

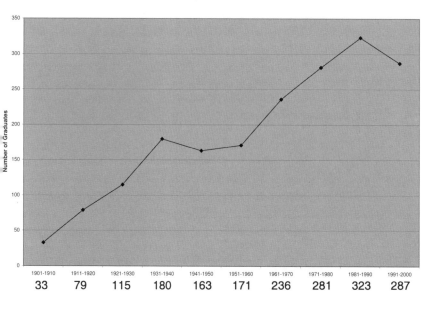

Total Number of RCS Graduates Per 10 Year Periods

1901-1910	1911-1920	1921-1930	1931-1940	1941-1950	1951-1960	1961-1970	1971-1980	1981-1990	1991-2000
33	79	115	180	163	171	236	281	323	287

Most Prominent Families, Number RCS Graduates, 1901-2000

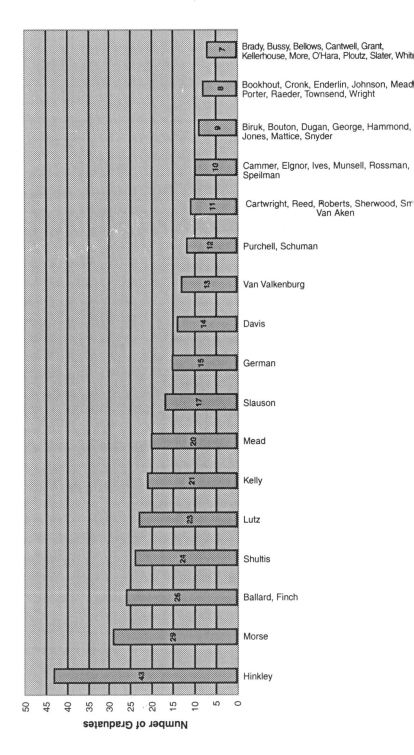

Number of Graduates

Family	Graduates
Brady, Bussy, Bellows, Cantwell, Grant, Kellerhouse, More, O'Hara, Ploutz, Slater, White	7
Bookhout, Cronk, Enderlin, Johnson, Mead, Porter, Raeder, Townsend, Wright	8
Biruk, Bouton, Dugan, George, Hammond, Jones, Mattice, Snyder	9
Cammer, Elgnor, Ives, Munsell, Rossman, Speilman	10
Cartwright, Reed, Roberts, Sherwood, Sm, Van Aken	11
Purchell, Schuman	12
Van Valkenburg	13
Davis	14
German	15
Slauson	17
Mead	20
Kelly	21
Lutz	23
Shultis	24
Ballard, Finch	26
Morse	29
Hinkley	43

Tyler, Gilbert	1954	
Tyler, Ivan	1932	Valedictorian; Veteran WWII
Tyler, Phyllis	1948	
Ullmann, Norma	1946	
Underwood, Daniel	1945	Class president
Underwood, David A.	1971	Vet.Viet;NYCWaterDept/GG,NY
Underwood, John D.	1973	
Underwood, Kenneth	1946	WWIIpilot,flight eng.TWA,JFK
Underwood, Mary E.	1977	Hotel Manager
Valk, Margaret	1948	(Long) computer specialist; artist
Van Aken, Alvin	1944	W.W II; RCS yearbook collector
Van Aken,DawnMary	1989	
Van Aken, Doris	1946	Employ;AudioSears;M'villeD'Store
Van Aken, Eleanor	1949	
Van Aken, Gary	1984	
Van Aken, Millard	1941	W.W.II, Signal Corp; Eng. W. Elect.
<u>Van Aken, Otis</u>	1939	Sal'tn;GouldS'ship/WWII Eng,Boeing
Van Aken, Robert	1952	Sal'tn;E.Scout/Syr.U;US/F'stry/Ser.
Van Aken, Roy	1915	Veteran WW I, Salutatorian; teacher
Van Aken, Susan	1981	(Dorrance)
Van Aken, Wendy L.	1985	Clerk, Agway
Van Buren, Mike	1966	Veteran Vietnam
Van Buren, Sandra A.	1968	
Van Dyke, Patricia	1958	
Van Hoesen, Ester G.	1923	Teacher
Van Loan, Lewis	1925	Farmer
Van Loan, Olive	1930	
Van Valkenbugh, H.	1937	WWII; Auto Sales,Rox.TownSupv.
Van Valkenburgh, A.	1946	
Van Valkenburgh, D.	1985	
Van Valkenburgh, Dan	1987	Veteran
Van Valkenburgh, Ed	1982	
Van Valkenburgh,Ella	1962	
Van Valkenburgh, H.	1933	Auto dealership
Van Valkenburgh, J.	1982	
Van Valkenburgh,Judy	1957	
Van Valkenburgh, M.	1940	
Van Valkenburgh, N.	1972	Pediatric nurse
Van Valkenburgh, R.	1962	Emp'Blenhiem power plant IBM
Van Valkenburgh, R.	1979	Tch; coach, S. Kortright Schools
Van Voorhees,Cheryl	1974	
Van Voorhees,Ron M	1974	

Van Woert, Willard H. 1922 Class pres;Pastor;Music Tch. NYC.

Van Wormer, Bernice 1943

Vermilya, Fannie 1918

Vermilya, James 1911 Valedictorian; Chemical Engineer

Vicevich, Anthony P 1930

Vicevich, Caroline 1930

Vigna, Alfred J. 1980 Veteran; Technology teacher, RCS

Vigna, Diana M. 1982 Home schooling 4 children

Vigna, John A. 1984 Val'dt;West Point;Vet;Dst St.

Vizzini, Samuel S. 1936 Class president

Von Heister,Lenemaja 1942 Valtn, college, English teacher

Voorhees, Bonnie 1960

Voorhees, Norma 1947 Valedictorian

Vosbrink, WalterH,Jr 1977 Heavy Equip. Salesman; Caterpillar

Wadsworth, Denise 1978

Wadsworth, Joseph 1978

Walker, Alec 1999 Graphic Design;Manhattan

Walker, Andrew 1999 BinghamtonU/Eng/ Phil'phy

Walker, Matthew 1994 Carpenter(early Ploutz res)

Walpole, Elizabeth 1964 College

Walsh, Jason 1997

Warner, Cheryl 1978

Warner, Diana L. 1973

Warner, John A. 1972

Washburn, Raymond 1984 Veteran, Desert Storm

Washburn, Wendy S. 1988

Wayman, Ellie 1997

Wayman, Joyce 1974

Weber, Ann 1951

Weber, Caroline 1949

Weber, Elizabeth 1959 Florist/landscaping

Weber, Fred, Jr. 1951

Weddleton, Paul 1943

Weeks, Dorothy 1942 H'ware/store/prop;M'ville,NY

Weeks, Marjorie 1935

Weidman, Eileen E 1989

Weidman, Kristine 1992

Weidman, Shannon 1992

Weyl, Blanche E. 1909 H. S. Teacher, Amsterdam, NY.

Weyl, Donald W. 1936 STCOn'ta;tchWWII;Just'Pce.Barber

Weyl, Jane 1961 Salutatorian, college

Weyl, Mary 1967 School Adm./TA @ RCS

Weyl, Nancy Ann	1968	Secretary/BOCES
Weyl, Robert C.	1915	Banker
Wheeler, Joan L.	1965	
Wheeler, Patricia	1962	
Wheeler, Rex	1959	Veteran Vietnam
White, Douglas	1932	WWIIpilot;Rotary;Val'dtn;RCSTch.
White, Nancy	1955	Val'tn; Hope College; published
White, Perry Lynden	1969	Rotarian, college; writer
White, William D, III	1948	E.Scout;tch;Ham'tnU;KualaLampur
Whitney, Doris	1947	Librarian
Whitney, Dorothy E.	1939	
Whitney, Gladys	1931	Teacher, Oneonta Normal
Whitney, James L.	1982	Landscape business
Whitney, Lawrence	1980	Refuse Disposal, Town of Roxbury
Whitney, Mariam E.	1936	(Triolo)
Whitney, Wilma	1934	Teacher, Oneonta Normal
Whittaker, Mark D.	1983	
Wickham, Gary	1957	
Wiedemann, Judith	1974	
Wiedemann, Karen A	1969	
Wiedemann, Lauria A	1982	
Wiedemann, Richard	1966	
Wiedemann, Susan A.	1976	Day Care Center business
Wiederman, Julian	1941	POW/GermanyWWII;Rotary,bank'
Williams, Melanie	2000	Cedar Crest College
Wilson, Pamela L.	1985	Administrative secretary
Wilson, Robert	1996	
Winnie, Kelli	1997	BS SUNY, Oneonta;H. Ecol.
Wojciechowski, Kelly	1998	
Woodworth, Wanda	1948	
Woolheater, Shirley	1938	
Wright, Bonnie Jean	1968	
Wright, Dwayne	1991	Delhi Technical College
Wright, Gregory	1992	
Wright, Julian	1930	Salutatorian
Wright, Patricia	1963	RCS payroll clerk
Wright, Shannon	1991	Emp Wissahikon Sp. Water
Wright, Shawn B.	1988	
Wright, Susan	1973	Cert.EMT;bus/dvr.So/K'right Sch.
Yanson, George	1930	Veteran W.W. II
Yeager, Joanne M	1976	
Yeager, Kevin H.	1977	Eagle Scout, lawyer

Yeager, Timothy	1980	
Young, Richard	1963	
Zafra, Luis	2000	
Zafra, Marie	1998	
Zambri, Brad	1997	Heavy Equip/Op;F/Safety
Zeiset, Andru C.	1993	
Zeiset, Krysta	1998	Val'dtn; Emerson C; Acting
Zeiset, Matthew	1997	Salutatorian; Hartwick Coll.
Zorda, Brian	1996	B.S. Siena College
Zorda, Christopher	1999	Marist College
Zorda, Joseph	1996	B.S. Syracuse University
Zuidema, Mary	1965	
Zeiset, Matthew	1997	Salutatorian; Hartwick Coll,
Zorda, Brian	1996	B.S. Siena College
Zorda, Christopher	1999	Marist College
Zorda, Joseph	1996	B.S. Syracuse University
Zuidema, Mary G.	1965	

Numerical Ranking

Family Names; graduating 5 or more from RCS 1901-2000.

Albano (5)	Grant (6)	Preston (5)
Balcom (6)	Gray (5)	Proctor (6)
Ballard (27)	Greene (8)	Purchell (12)
Bellows (8)	Gregory (5)	Raeder (8)
Biruk (9)	Griffin (16)	Reed (11)
Bookhout (8)	Haight (6)	Roberts (11)
Bouton (9)	Hall (5)	Rose (10)
Brady (7)	Hammond (9)	Rossman (10)
Brandow (5)	Hewitt (6)	Rowe (6)
Brower (5)	Hinkley (43)	Sanford (10)
Bubach (5)	Ives (10)	Schuman (12)
Bussy (7)	Johnson (7)	Sherwood (11)
Cammer (10)	Johnston (7)	Shultis (24)
Cantwell (7)	Jones (9)	Slater (7)
Carr (7)	Kellerhouse (7)	Slauson (17)
Cartwright (11)	Kelly (21)	Smith (11)
Caswell (5)	Lalosh (5)	Snyder (8)
Clark (6)	Lawrence (5)	Spielman (9)
Cronk (10)	Long (6)	Sprague (5)
Davis (14)	Lutz (23)	Stahl (6)
Dorrance (5)	Mattice (9)	Stewart (6)
Dugan (9)	Mead (19)	Taylor (5)
Eignor (10)	Meade (9)	Tobin (5)
Enderlin (8)	Mondore (5)	Townsend (8)
Etts (5)	Moore (5)	Tyler (5)
Faraci (6)	More (7)	Underwood (5)
Finch (26)	Morse (30)	Van Aken (11)
Flachs (5)	Munsell (10)	Van Valkenburgh (13)
Ford (6)	O'Hara (7)	Weyl (6)
Furman (5)	Osborn (6)	Whitney (7)
George (9)	Pebler (6)	Wiedemannn (5)
German (14)	Peck (5)	Wright (8)
Gilham (5)	Ploutz (7)	
Gordon (6)	Porter (8)	

From 1901-2000 there were a total of 634 "family names" identified. These 100 families account for 917 students or 49% of the total 1851 graduates of RCS for the hundred year period.

RCS 1901-2000 Family Rankings By Number Graduating

Fifty six families graduate 660 or 35 % of all 1,851 students.

Family Rank by Number Graduating:

1.	Hinkley	(43)	Dugan	(9)
2.	Morse	(30)	George	(9)
3.	Ballard	(27)	Hammond	(9)
	Finch	(26)	Jones	(9)
4.	Schultis	(24)	Mattice	(9)
5.	Lutz	(23)	Meade	(9)
6.	Kelly	(21)	16. Bookhout	(8)
7.	Mead	(19)	Enderlin	(8)
8.	Slauson	(17)	Porter	(8)
9.	German	(16)	Reader	(8)
10.	Davis	(14)	Snyder	(8)
11.	Van Valkenburg	(13)	Townsend	(8)
12.	Purchall	(12)	Wright	(8)
	Schuman	(12)	Bellows	(8)
13.	Cartwright	(11)	Greene	(8)
	Van Aken	(11)	17. Brady	(7)
	Reed	(11)	Bussy	(7)
	Roberts	(11)	Cantwell	(7)
	Sherwood	(11)	Grant	(7)
	Smith	(11)	Kellerhouse	(7)
14.	Cammer	(10)	Johnson	(7)
	Cronk	(10)	Johnston	(7)
	Eignor	(10)	More	(7)
	Ives	(10)	O'Hara	(7)
	Munsell	(10)	Ploutz	(7)
	Rossman	(10)	Slater	(7)
15.	Speilman	(9)	Whitney	(7)
	Biruk	(9)		
	Bouton	(9)		

PART V

PROUD TO BE A COUNTRY BOY

I've never seen the subway
Never had to walk my dog
Like myself happy and gay
And I believe a ferry is a boat.
I'm proud to be country.

Never had to double park
Flag a taxi or wait in the dark
Like myself clean and straight
Believe needles are to sew
Proud to be country.

I believe drugs are for colds
And grass is for cows
I'm willing to hug a tree
Like maple syrup and honey from the bee
Proud to be country.

I've never shot a beaver
If I were ever in Spain
I'd cheer for the Bull
Politically correct gives me a pain
Proud to be a country boy.

Never told my parents off
Or ever bullied another kid
Believe in God, salute the flag
How many are there like me?
I'm proud to be a country boy.

FISH SHOULD BE IN SCHOOLS

Your name could be Rob, Sue, Lori or Mac
Your school locker has your coat and back pack
Pencil and note pad ready for 1st period science
Good attitude, ready to learn, no defiance.

Both jocks and nerds now eager to be serious
But listen up, its easy to be delirious
Rats, dogs and books also travel in packs
What about your locker, your lunch and snacks?

Learn about a pride of lions, that's cool. Get's my nod.
But know the difference between pea pickers and a pod?
But seeing a pod of whales, I wish.
But shouldn't school be just for fish?

Whales and dolphins aren't even fish
You'll never see then served in a dish
They're intelligent mammals like jocks and nerds.
Like elephant families that travel in herds.

Learn every day, its never too late
You and nature could just be great.
No such thing as too much knowledge
You'll be an intelligent reader, busy as a beaver.
You'll be losing the scowl, become wise as an owl.
You can be a social spark, and happy as a lark.

Through it all Jim, Ann, Scott, Amy or Mo
Giggle over a gaggle of geese, or kangaroo called Joe
When class is over be happy to see you
Loving nature, you've turned out like me
Take time to smell the flowers, and hug a tree.

GLOBAL WARMING ME & THE TREE

Not afraid of beetles or bees
Love to smell flowers and pretty leaves
Like to see the butterflies
Even feel pain when an animal cries
But what's that have to with roadside litter at all time highs?

Not afraid of spiders, worms or bugs
Think dogs & cats deserve extra hugs
I even like lizards, frogs and snakes
Learn which ones to avoid and reckless mistakes.
But can you protect me from toxic waste?

Not afraid of Grizzly Bears
Even the hawks love the hares
Love the mist from the waterfalls
I'm still learning about nature's laws
Do endangered species result from flaws?

Not afraid of vultures or bats
I'm been known to swing at gnats.
Vultures aren't cute but they have a resolution
Fly gracefully then land with a solution.
But what should I do to reduce pollution?

Never been afraid to be in the dark
Would never kill a bird, or even a shark
I've never been mean or bitter, only mild
I'm absolutely thrilled to be a flower child,
Global warming seems beyond someone like me.

Lost species, urban sprawl, radio active pollution
Toxic waste, litter, global warming, any solution?
Urban sprawl seems necessary to me
But join a cause, save a bird or bee for you see
Its time for us all to hug a tree.

GIVE ME A BREAK

Being young has its draw backs
Mom tells me not to babble
But everyone likes a brook that does
In school teachers say I can't hum
But everyone likes the bird that does.

The raccoon is thought to be a rascal
But dad tells me not be to be
I can't float like a cork
Or fly like an eagle
Or swim like a shark
Give me a break.

A pig is supposed to squeal
But I'm not supposed to
Others sing like a canary
I'm not supposed to tell a secret.
What am I supposed to do?

I'd like to keep my parents happy
Baby sit my sister, clean my room, make it snappy.
At times I'm to be as quiet as a mouse
Everyone knows what they do to a mouse.
Give me a break

Forget to feed the dog, I'm indifferent or cold
Very next day I'm supposed to chill out.
Some times friends will blow you off
Need your glove or bike and they suck you in.
Give me a break!

May not be the brightest bee in the hive.
But you can get down off an elephant
Others say you get down off a duck.
Big brother told me a kid was a goat
Give Me A Break!

YOU'RE HURTING MY EARS

Please be careful what you say
My silence to your rage does not mean approval
I'm just too scared to disagree.

When you shout obscenities, dufus, dork or geek
Skinhead, faggot shows a mean streak
What's your problem and attention you seek?

Klutz, dyke, nerd, queer or straight
What is the source of your perversion and hate?
Clown, nerd, narc or jock maybe OK.

But you need to be aware
That perhaps you protest too much
You may be trying to find someone lower than yourself.

You need to be aware
You're increasing the possibility you're what you describe?
What you say tells more about you than you can hide.

You need to be aware
You degrade others in a hopeless effort to build yourself up
But most of all you're hurting my ears.

TOXIC WASTE

My bike is broken, my skate board is down
Need a new glove my face has a frown
Need braces for my teeth, friends treat me like a clown
You think you've got problems, they're wearing me down.

The land under my school is on toxic waste
The water I drink has a funny taste
I'm only twelve, don't quite understand
If you spray the lawn what's that do to the land?

I'm no longer allowed to play in the park
If I play on the grass guess I'll glow in the dark?
It's enough being afraid of being hugged or mugged
And you think you've got problems?

I've been warned about speaking to strangers
Each place I turn I learn new dangers
Can you help me with all the problems I see?
What kind of future are you planning for me?

Thought that stuff floating in the air was fog
Now that I'm older, I've learned its smog
If it spoils the paint on the car, or kills a tree
What's it do to the lungs of my brother and me?

My allowance goes for pure water for my tooth brush and to drink
I'm only a kid, tell me of my future, I'm afraid to think
Can't ride my bike, talk to strangers, play in the park, breath the air
Can't swim in the lake, eat the fish, please tell me that you care.
Please tell me that you care.

#

Recognition of Gorbechev and Green Cross

Chapter 11 deals with the Viking Scientific Company and <u>one</u> of Paul's several business *failures* even while accepting the concept that "multiple projects produce multiple successes." His "Russian" poem was *not* successful in the usual sense but somehow Ploutz saw a <u>Burroughs</u> quality in the former Soviet leader?

When questioned, he reminded his university classroom audience that John Burroughs seldom seemed concerned about his own image, appearance or reputation. The only time the gentle Burroughs became even remotely aggressive was defending Whitman, Emerson, Muir, birds and ecological issues. As a global politician Gorbechev was *done*. Like Burroughs (though much later) and on a much grander scale, Mikhail understood "the big picture" and the <u>ecological needs of the planet.</u>

The *Ode to Mikhail* was written after the fall of the Berlin Wall and the dissolution of the USSR. Mikhail Gorbechev turned out to be a visionary forming **Green Cross** devoted to solving world wide ecology problems. Ploutz, seeing a *political figure* recognized world wide, put some his own ecological credibility on the line for global issues, wanted to demonstrate his admiration. He wrote **Ode To Mikhail**.

After the Berlin Wall fell and Mikhail Gorbechev allowed Communist Russia to separate without nuclear war or conflict, Gorbachev for a period at least, was considered somewhat of an international hero... The Soviet (USSR) establishment was so hated and feared that Mikhail who had led the separation was viewed both with admiration and fear.

The Soviet Union had enough nuclear bombs to assure mutual destruction of the United States if not the entire world. Now the country was dramatically reduced in size, influence, capability. The World wondered what would become of Russia, Mikhail, the nuclear capability. Boris Yelsin had stood atop a tank in his valiant effort to defend the Russian capital. Lives were lost, hero's were made, Mikhail Gorbechev helped to convert the mighty Russia from a dictatorship (Stalin) to a "reasonable democracy."

Mikhail was finally given a small pension by the Russian government and unlike Napolean was not exiled to the Island of Crete, or in Russia's case, Siberia.

Mikhail founded "GREEN CROSS." Everyone had heard of the **Red Cross**, you know, blood, blankets, medicine, shelter, world wide, a truly wonderful international organization!

Mikhail assumed the responsibility of global concerns for ECOLOGY. Paul felt it to be one of the most forward and inspirational concepts of the Century. Mikhail's initial approach was concern for water, as most of the worldwide and aggressive viral and bacterial problems are water borne.

With his oversized ego Paul thought **Green Cross** should surely *be introduced in America* as it had been throughout Europe. His efforts with U.S. Senators, the Russian Embassy were fruitless. Letters to the Russian Embassy were never acknowledged. E-mails to several of the *Green Cross* addresses in Europe went unanswered. American legislatures, politicians simply weren't interested. They simply couldn't think of a reason to "Deal with it."

Paul felt that Gorbechev was one of the most profound leaders of the Twentieth Century and was entitled to the following poem.

You are allowed by the author to reproduce this poem (with acknowledgement) hoping that in time it will reach the Russian Embassy and "tree huggers" around the world... **Green Cross** with it's clever name, origin and need could, should become the premier ecological organization on the Planet. The Sierra Club, The Nature Conservatory, Audubon Society and more. Read the poem, then see what you can do to make it happen.

Ode To Mikhail

Dear Mikhail, nations are saying thanks!
You've helped us past fears of missiles and tanks.
Past Chernobyl's radio active curse.
We're past three mile island at its worst.

With peace in the former Soviet Union, no fear
Olympic Games again and friendly competition, lets cheer.
Some born great, others greatness thrust upon them, like you.
Mikhail, the world knows you're not through.

Swords hammered into plow shares, for peace.
A new beginning in Sidney, Athens, Rome and Greece.
From the ruins of Berlin and Bonn, to the very last tank
A united Germany, says "donka shank."
Millions more don't know who to thank.

Spain says "mochas gracias" with pinata and glee.
France, finds if difficult to thank anyone, "merci"
Poland, with solidarity, says "jen KOO yen" we're free.
Auswitch, Crackow, the shipyards at Gdansk, all free.
Those who speak English, say "thank you," like me.

One idea did change the world, old friend.
By forming Green Cross, you can do it again!
New problems of great magnitude require haste.
Countries are being polluted with toxic waste.

Air, soil, rivers, oceans, in environmental pain.
It's about agent orange, Amazon forests, acid rain.
Ebola, AIDS, mad cow virus, even killer bees swarming
Diverting attention from the ozone layer, and global warming.

And so Mikhail, its good to hear, you're back in the race.
It's right to return to the moon and space.
But we need to fix things back here on earth and soon.
Six billion people, can't make it to Mars or the Moon.

Good luck, Mikhail, organize Green Cross from Moscow and
Rome.
Organize Green *Cross* in Paris, Nashville, Oxford and Nome.
Green Cross in Chicago, Oslo, Sidney and Home.
London, Lisbon, Lima and Tenenenmin Square.

Green Cross in Denver, Dallas, Beijing and Bon Aire.
From Timbuktu, Hong Kong, the Holy City, for those who care
Billions of people, have had a scare.
Millions of people are now aware.
Humans everywhere, join *Green Cross* and do your share.

#